NATIONALISM IN EASTERN EUROPE

Nationalism in Eastern Europe

Edited by PETER F. SUGAR *and* IVO J. LEDERER

University of Washington Press   *Seattle & London*

Copyright © 1969 by the University of Washington Press
Second printing, 1971
First paperback edition, 1971
Second printing, 1973
Library of Congress Catalog Card Number 74-93026
ISBN 0-295-95008-0 (cloth)
ISBN 0-295-95147-8 (paper)
Printed in the United States of America

Nationalism in Eastern Europe is Number 1 of the Publications on Russia and Eastern Europe of the Institute for Comparative and Foreign Area Studies, formerly Far Eastern and Russian Institute Publications on Russia and Eastern Europe.

Introduction

In the eighteenth century, a new force evolved slowly in western Europe, until by the century's end, that force emerged as one of the strongest of the influences that determined both the domestic and international behavior of nations and states. This new force, nationalism, which still plays a very important role today in states both old and established and newly emerging, has its own history and has produced many variants. Numerous books and articles have covered the emergence, nature, and history of nationalism; historians, political scientists, economists, sociologists, and scholars of many other disciplines have devoted much time and effort to the production of the very impressive literature.

In several of these works eastern Europe is mentioned, in some cases only in an occasional sentence or paragraph, in others, more extensively, to the extent of a separate chapter. Yet the conclusion that eastern Europe has not received adequate attention becomes unavoidable. Several reasons account for this neglect. Nationalism was originally a western movement, and access to western materials was much easier than access to sources in eastern Europe. The variety of languages spoken east of Germany and Italy posed a difficult linguistic problem and the general knowledge that western scholars (including those in this country) had of eastern Europe was minimal when compared to that which they had of their own countries. Furthermore, eastern Europe was "not really important" when scholars were interested either in more than the national scene or in the development of ideas surveyed by their fields. Until fairly recently, even eastern European scholars paid relatively little attention to the history and nature of nationalism in their respective countries. With notable exceptions they did one of two things: they either used nationalism to explain developments in their countries or the part these countries played on the international, specifically the eastern European, scene or they equated their nationalism with that of western Europe in an effort to demonstrate that their nations did not live on the fringe of but were an integral part of the "European scene."

During the years since the first World War, but especially since the second, when anticolonial movements, the emergence of new states, "modernization," and many other developments directed the scholars' attention to the nationalism that played an important role in these events and trends, eastern Europe no longer fell into that group of nations and states that were considered new, emerging, modernizing, and so on. They were far ahead, not only of most Asian and African states, but even of most Latin American ones. Yet in the nineteenth century the eastern European states underwent a development not too dissimilar from the events that concern us so much today. It is much easier to find models or even parallels in last century's eastern Europe for today's events outside Europe and North America than it is to equate them—as is so often done—with those that occurred in western Europe or the United States in the eighteenth century and even earlier.

These are the reasons why a study devoted exclusively to the history of nationalism in eastern Europe seemed necessary. From a purely scholarly point of view, the gap in the literature on nationalism needed to be filled; from a practical angle the models that could help the student of the contemporary scene and, even more important, help the men who work in various capacities to advance those nations that are trying to catch up had to be presented. Overriding all is the fact that the "West" has finally realized that eastern Europe is important in its own right. During the last twenty-five years, serious efforts have been made by governments, scholars, and even the general public to understand eastern Europe, but this effort cannot be successful without an understanding of the history and especially the history of nationalism in and of eastern Europe.

The authors and editors of the present volume had these and several other considerations in mind when they decided to cooperate. While one volume cannot satisfy the various needs or supply the answers to the many questions that have been raised concerning eastern Europe during the last quarter century, they hope that their effort represents a useful first step to be followed, hopefully soon, by others. The editors, besides thanking the contributors, take full responsibility for the organization and format of this volume, but the credit for the information it contains belongs fully to the authors of the various chapters.

The editors are also responsible for the spelling of names of both people and places. They decided to spell names exactly as those individuals spelled them or, in the case of people who lived in the early centuries, as their compatriots spell them today. In the case of geographic names, mainly those of cities, it was decided to use the spelling or variant that was "official" at the time that is discussed by the various authors when these places are mentioned. Whenever a given place is appearing in this volume for the first time all other spellings or versions are added in parentheses. For example when the capital of Transylvania is first mentioned it appears as Kolozsvár (Cluj, Klausenburg), but when the city is discussed in the period after 1918 it is referred to as Cluj. The editors have also decided to use names in native languages and not their English versions (i.e., Beograd, not Belgrade) except in a few cases, for example, Vienna, where the English version is so fully accepted that using the German version would appear pedantic.

PETER F. SUGAR
IVO J. LEDERER

Seattle, Washington
1969

Contents

ix

NATIONALISM IN EASTERN EUROPE

PETER F. SUGAR

External and Domestic Roots of Eastern European Nationalism

I

Most writers concerned with nationalism, national minorities, national self determination, and other related problems have tried their hand at defining the meaning of the numerous terms and concepts that must be clearly understood if the discussion of these complex issues is to result in their clarification and not in additional confusion. That they are seldom understood, let alone clearly, is proved both by the ever recurring need to define the same terms and by the fact that these definitions have not been universally accepted. In spite of the past experiences of so many, a chapter introducing a volume dealing with nationalism must begin with definitions, if for no other reason than to clarify the sense in which the relevant terms will be used in this chapter.

To begin with, it is useful to distinguish between terms that might be called "natural" (in the sense of historic or tribal) and terms that relate to more recently "acquired characteristics" of man in society. The former category pertains to such expressions as *people, nationality, patriotism,* and *country*. All others belong in the latter.

By *people* is understood simply human beings, apart from their ethnic, linguistic, religious, political, or other affiliations. This word stands for the totality of men and is used as a synonym for humanity.

Nationality denotes a group of people of all classes, religious persuasions, professions, and educational levels who are distinguishable from all others by speaking the same language, sharing in some of those cultural values that are tied to the use of a particular language and springing from a certain undefinable yet real feeling of kinship. In this sense nationality differs from clan or tribe only in degree and by carrying no connotation of institutional unity or formalized loyalty. The German speaking inhabitants of Germany, Austria, and Switzerland belong, according to this usage, to the same nationality irrespective of other factors that divide them.

Country is used as a linguistic-geographic concept only, denoting regions inhabited by members of one nationality and disregarding political boundaries and other considerations. Using this definition, the Walloon districts of Belgium and the French cantons of Switzerland are part of the French *country*.

Finally, in the group of "natural" distinctions, we use *patriotism* to denote a basic loyalty to one's patrimony, one's home. We find something of this distinction in French where *pays* always refers to France, but *patrie* might denote either all of France, or the region in which the speaker was born, or both. Patriotism might be narrow, local patriotism, or might embrace a larger segment of the territory inhabited by members of a nationality, or even the entire country, but for the purpose of this chapter it is considered patriotism only as long as it demonstrates merely a basic, human preference for the well-known and the familiar.[1]

If they want to survive, people must live in groups. This gathering together is a precondition for the development of nationality. They unite because they already share some values in common and additional common traditions develop after their union. These newly formed nationality groups need a country in which they will feel at home, sharing it with others who "belong." Sociological, economic, psychological, and geographic necessities make nationality, country, and patriotism the heritage of everybody. Individuals might change even these basic affiliations and adjust to others. Some are able to change completely once they migrate from one country to another; others might be able to share in two traditions in the way

[1] For a good discussion of man's selective loyalty see the opening pages of Carlton J. H. Hayes, *The Historical Evolution of Modern Nationalism* (2d ed.; New York, Macmillan, 1949).

that Joseph Conrad did in English literature and Heinrich Heine did in French; but in most cases the transition is painful. Witness the many emigrants who, although adjusted to their new environment, continue to be concerned sentimentally or actively with the "old country." All these variations involve only feelings and attributes that have been listed as "natural," stemming exclusively from living in society.

These "natural" characteristics form the basis for the "acquired" traits. Within a given nationality, individuals of the same faith, cultural level, or profession will prefer each other's compay. Depending on where the emphasis is placed, these choices produce demands for institutionalized groupings representing the preferences of those who joined them. The various associations will ask for numerous privileges: religious freedom, free use of a language, internal self-government, the right to set professional standards, and many others. These demands are not political, even less are they nationalistic in character.

Political and nationalistic traits emerged only when this kind of demand was formulated by a group whose membership included all those who had given their primary loyalty to a specific group. Yet this new group was not necessarily of its original nationality. Before political and national traits can emerge, two new developments had to occur: the state and the nation had to come into being. Their creation was the work of the monarchs from the time of the late Middle Ages and in early modern times. The *state* is a political-administrative unit, an institution created by the successful princes. It describes the geographic area over which a given ruler is able to extend first his nominal and later his effective dominion. It goes without saying that the *state* defined in this manner is not synonymous with *country*. The state can include people of different nationalities, while members of the same nationality may live in several states.

Because states seldom coincided with countries and often contained members of several nationalities, they evoked no basic loyalties. Rulers soon realized that without such loyalties their artificial creations, the states, could not last, and the search for unifying ideologies began. Religious unity, national churches, the submission of of church to state, dynastic loyalty, and the equating of the ruler with the state are among the devices that were tried as the basis for state-directed loyalties. This centralizing, state-creating activity of kings and princes slowly succeeded in pushing regional, class, or professional loyalties to a secondary position in the thinking of the people over whom they ruled. When this effort succeeded, not without heavy fighting, to put state-centered thinking in the place of the more subjective loyalties, and even in the place of nationality consciousness, the nation was born.

Nation, like *state*, is a political concept. It pays relatively little attention to nationality (it can even be hostile to nationality), but treats all people living within the state as a unit, a nation. Only in the British Isles do we find a recognition of original multinationality in the name *United Kingdom of Great Britain*. Some other states, notably Switzerland and Belgium, honor the fact of multinationality in the recognition of more than one official language. The U.S.S.R. does not go that far, but has named some of the federal republics after their non-Russian inhabitants. In most cases the creation of nations went hand in hand with an attack on nationalities and produced Spaniardization, Frenchification, Germanization, Russification, Magyarization, Polonization, and so on, in the name of unity and centralization, creating, meanwhile, the modern minority problem. When state and nation became dominant social units, *country* and *state*, *nationality* and *nation* became synonyms in the minds of members of the majority. The minorities clung to their nationality, and in the nineteenth and twentieth centuries tried to create their own states. By the end of the eighteenth century, people were state-, nationality-, and even nation-conscious, but in most places were not yet nationalists.

The changes just sketched evolved over centuries and were paralleled by other developments. They are all well known. During the same period that saw the gradual centralization produce the state and superimpose "acquired" social characteristics on those we called "natural," there also occurred the decline of feudalism, the rise of towns and commerce, the growth of the bourgeoisie, the gradual urbanization of the economy, the reurbanization of the church, the beginnings of modern capitalism, and several other changes. These various changes influenced each other, occurred over a long period of time (permitting mutual accommodation), and were always closely supervised by the princes who had the power to enforce their will. The entire process was not revolutionary but evolutionary. In this sense even the transformation of "natural" into "acquired" manifestations of loyalty seems to fit into a rather long-range pattern of change.

The scientific revolution of the seventeenth and the enlightenment of the eighteenth centuries introduced forces into society that were not controlled by princes nor the nobility nor the bourgeoisie. Not being tied to estates or classes, the ideas of the scientist and the philosopher were revolutionary, and nobles, priests, or even rulers who accepted these new notions became "class enemies." Others who retained their old loyalties did so with less conviction and often in spite of many doubts. The new, basic, "scientific" dogmas of this new secular religion were natural law, reason, progress, and humanitarianism. They were interconnected: natural law ruled the universe; human reason was capable of discovering, understanding, and describing these laws and once known, these laws served as norms for the transformation of society, ensuring progress for all of humanity, which in this sense, became the goal of all endeavors.

Within this framework, numerous interpretations of the meaning of the terms of science and the enlightenment, their relationship, and the goals of human action appeared. Almost all philosophes had their own ideals and ideas including those covering human relationships, the organization of society, and the ideal form of the state. Humanitarians and idealists as they were, not a single one among them rejected the state as the optimum social unit. We have to think only of Bolingbroke, Locke, Voltaire, Montesquieu, and Rousseau to realize how different the proposed ideals were. In spite of their disagreements the various philosophes were unanimous in advocating drastic change. Fighting the established order and each other, claiming to be scientific, and offering infallible solutions based on natural law, they felt compelled to present their views not in the form of specific proposals dealing with one or a few manifestations of organized communal living, but as closed philosophical systems designed to answer all objections in advance. They succeeded in creating the ideological justification, the catalyst around which the growing need and demand for change could crystallize to produce the years of general upheaval, 1776–1815, which ushered in the contemporary period of history. The clashing views of these years, the changes they produced, and the unresolved questions they left behind were expressed once again as philosophical systems, introducing the age of *isms*.[2]

The great transformations wrought by the Revolutionary and Napoleonic Wars, the very intensity of the long struggle, and the propaganda campaigns that accompanied them transformed the absolute monarchies of western Europe into nation states. The *ism* that justified this transformation and the loyalty demanded by the nation state is nationalism. It can, therefore, be defined as an artificially fostered group feeling demanding that the primary and overriding loyalty of each individual, irrespective of his other attachments and obligations, be reserved to both the nation state in which he lives and the theory on which this request rested.

When we differentiated between the "natural" and "acquired" social characteristics of man, we admitted that the latter can be regarded almost as the result of "a rather long-range pattern of change" originating in the former. Nationalism, based on a set of organized and systematized beliefs and assumptions, mainly sociopolitical in nature, cannot be tied in so easily with our first two groups of concepts. It is not a characteristic that either the individual or the group has acquired. It is a revolutionary dogma that has to be inculcated by education and propaganda into each member of each generation. Just as religious dogma before or Marxist after it, nationalism underwent numerous changes and suffered from heresies and deviations with each change producing its own textbooks, propaganda slogans, and saints. In every case nationalism could not have existed and could not now exist without its theoretical justification and its educational-propaganda apparatus.

Those who are interested in the changes of this new faith that developed roughly between 1750 and 1815 can turn to numerous excellent volumes tracing the history of nationalism.[3] They will find

[2] For an explanation of the expression "the age of isms," see Robert R. Palmer, *A History of the Modern World* (2d ed.; New York: Alfred A. Knopf, 1956), p. 430. See also the most useful essay by Frederick M. Watkins, *The Age of Ideology—Political Thought, 1750 to the Present* (Englewood Cliffs, N.J.: Prentice-Hall, 1964).

[3] The most useful studies on nationalism are: Carlton J. H. Hayes, *Essays on Nationalism* (New York: Macmillan, 1926) and *The Historical Evolution of Modern Nationalism;* Hans Kohn, *The Idea of Nationalism: A Study in its Origins and Background* (2d ed.; New York: Macmillan, 1961) and *Prophets and People: Studies in Nineteenth Century Nationalism* (New York: Macmillan, 1947); Eugen Lemberg, *Geschichte des Nationalismus in Europa* (Stuttgart: Curt E. Schwab, 1950); Boyd C. Shafer, *Nationalism: Myth and Reality* (New York: Harcourt, Brace & World, 1955);

that the changes originated mainly in western Europe, just as the preceding sketch devoted to the definition of our terms, followed events that occurred in that part of our earth. Nationalism in its various forms penetrated into eastern Europe from the West, but in this migration it underwent important changes. We will explore the reasons and nature of these changes in the remaining pages of this chapter.

II

Professor Hans Kohn recognized the basic problem of eastern European nationalism when he stated that

so strong was the influence of ideas that, while the new nationalism in Western Europe corresponded to changing social, economic, and political realities, it spread to Central and Eastern Europe long before a corresponding social and economic transformation . . . . The new ideas encountered in the different countries a great diversity of institutional and social conditions, bequeathed by the past, and were shaped and modified by them. Their different interpretations produced different types of nationalism—one based upon liberal middle-class concepts and pointing to a consummation in a democratic world society, the other based upon irrational and pre-enlightened concepts tending towards exclusiveness . . . .[4]

Some of the implications of this analysis are clarified further by Kohn.

Nationalism in the West arose in an effort to build a nation in the political reality and struggle of the present without too much sentimental regard for the past; nationalists in Central and Eastern Europe created, often out of myths of the past and the dreams of the future, an ideal

Leonard W. Doob, *Patriotism and Nationalism: Their Psychological Foundation* (New Haven: Yale University Press, 1964); Karl W. Deutsch, *Nationalism and Social Communications; An Inquiry into the Foundations of Nationality* (Cambridge, Mass.: M.I.T. Press and New York: Wiley, 1953); Hubertus C. J. Duijker and N. H. Frijda, *National Characteristics and National Stereotypes* (Amsterdam: North Holland Publishing Co., 1960); Leonard Krieger, "Nationalism and the Nation-State System," *Chapters in Western Civilization,* ed. Contemporary Civilization Staff of Columbia College (3rd ed.: New York: Columbia University Press, 1962); Karl W. Deutsch and William J. Foltz (eds.), *Nation Building* (New York: Atherton, 1963); Louis L. Snyder, *The Meaning of Nationalism* (New Brunswick, N.H.: Rutgers Press, 1954).

[4] Kohn, *The Idea of Nationalism,* p. 457.

fatherland, closely linked with the past, devoid of any immediate connection with the present, and expected to become sometime a political reality. Thus they were at liberty to adorn it with traits for the realization of which they had no immediate responsibility, but which influenced the nascent nation's wishful image of itself and its mission . . . .[5]

Western nationalism, Kohn suggests, was based on reality, eastern nationalism on myths and dreams. Nationalism makes sense, at least according to the explanation offered in the preceding pages, only in a centralized nation-state. In the nature of the state we might find the first clue why eastern and western European nationalism were so different.

In the Western world, in England and in France, in the Netherlands and in Switzerland, in the United States and the British dominions, the rise of nationalism was a predominantly political occurrence; it was preceded by the formation of the future nation state, or, as in the case of the United States, coincided with it. Outside the Western world, in Central and Eastern Europe and in Asia, nationalism arose not only later, but also generally at a more backward stage of social and political development: the frontiers of an existing state and of a rising nationality rarely coincided; nationalism there grew in protest against and in conflict with the existing state pattern—not primarily to transform it into a people's state, but to redraw the political boundaries in conformity with ethnographic demands.[6]

This difference between the situation in western and eastern Europe is not difficult to understand when one considers that

unlike western Europe, where relative national homogeneity was achieved before the nineteenth century . . . eastern and east-central Europe has nurtured differences to the present day. The reasons are manifold. Whereas migrations had ceased in the West at an early date, in the East they continued far into modern times, often in the form of deliberate colonization . . . . The borders of the eastern states, too, remained fluid . . . and each acquisition of territory . . . brought masses of people differing nationally and culturally from the dominant statebuilding group. Moreover, the influence of Rome, particularly that of the Roman Catholic Church, operated during the Middle Ages to slough off dis-

[5] *Ibid.*, p. 330.
[6] *Ibid.*, p. 329.

similarities in the West, while in the East it only accentuated distinctive differences as it met and clashed with Byzantine culture and the Greek Church. The unifying effect of royal power was potent in the West partly because the linguistic and cultural consciousness of the masses was as yet in a rudimentary stage in early modern times. Therefore effective resistance to the process of assimilation failed to develop. In the East, on the other hand, feudal and local particularism did not yield to political and administrative centralization until the nineteenth century, when nationalism was becoming a conscious force. What had been the privileges and prerogatives of local satraps in previous centuries was presumed to be in the nineteenth the birthright of the people, sanctioned by the national ideal . . . .[7]

No wonder that eastern European nationalism did not tend towards "a consummation in a democratic world society," but was "tending towards exclusiveness," seeking to find a justification, a specific *mission* for a given group that quite often did not even include all members of the nation or nationality. When such a group, the Polish or Hungarian nobility for example, was willing to include all members of their nationality in their nationalism, eastern European nationalism became *messianic*. Messianism cannot be egalitarian; it claims rights for a chosen people, the *Volk*, not for the individual or the citizen. This *Volk* concept is practically totalitarian. It stands for a group that has its history, national characteristics, culture, rights, and mission. It has to achieve this mission because some vaguely conceived laws (God-given, historical, natural) demand it. The individual, as a member of this *Volk*-community, has no history, no characteristics, rights, or so on, on his own. He is a *Volks-genosse* ruled by the will of the *Volk*, and if he opposes it he is considered by the majority as only slightly better than a traitor.

This will, *Volkswille*, should not be confused with Rousseau's general will. Rousseau's will was the result of a social contract, a freely performed human action excluding even majority rule. A member of a *Volk* was subject to the *Volkswille* from birth. This confusion of nationality and nation, of cultural, political, and linguistic characteristics was further extended to justify the *Volk's* mission. This mission could be accomplished only if it had free play

[7] Oscar J. Janowsky, *Nationalities and National Minorities (With Special Reference to East-Central Europe)* (New York: Macmillan, 1945), pp. 19–20.

in a *Volksstaat,* nation-state. Once again one must be careful. The nation state of western Europe developed along lines discussed in the first section of this chapter. It was simply the result of the process of democratization, the transference of sovereignty from the ruler to the subjects, now transformed into citizens, the members of the nation. The *Volksstaat* was a similar political unit, but it existed to fulfill the mission of the *Volk,* and sovereignty rested with those few who supposedly expressed the *Volkswille*, the members of the political nation. Consequently the specific groups that originally accepted nationalism from the West could broaden the basis of their operation by nominating themselves as the depositories of the *Volkswille* by using the arguments developed in the West to justify the existence of their continued hegemony in their states.

This was, roughly speaking, the *Volk* concept in eastern Europe. It differs as sharply from the humanistic-romantic concept first developed in Germany as the western nation-state differed from the eastern European *Volksstaat*. Germany was the main transmitter of most western ideas, including nationalism, to eastern Europe although direct influences were by no means negligible. Western ideas were not only modified by the German thinkers, they were often used to produce new interpretations of old beliefs. This was inevitable. Human experience is not uniform, and ideas cannot be separated from the other aspects of reality. At least since the days of Charlemagne, Germany was in close contact with the West, was part of the cultural world of western Christianity, and in the eighteenth century had numerous towns and cities, a bourgeoisie, a common literary language, and was ruled by native princes. On the other hand, Germany was not a state in the modern sense of the word, suffered from great internal tensions that became acute after the outbreak of the Austrian War of Succession that was fought when the ideas of nationalism were germinating. Germany, furthermore, was behind England, France, and the Netherlands in terms of economic development and sociopolitical progress. If shadings and degrees are left aside it might be said that Germany had as much in common with eastern as with western Europe. As westerners, Germans were fascinated by the enlightenment and were influenced by modern nationalism, but they were easterners enough, to feel a need to adjust the various new ideas to the realities of their quasi-feudal economy and political structure. The German variants of basically western European ideas were more easily adaptable to eastern European needs than the originals. By the time they became operating forces east of Germany they were at least twice removed from their western models.

Liberty to the French and British meant the absence from oppressive government. The same word in Germany stood for the absence of too many oppressive governments and thus carried a connotation of the creation of a German nation and state. In eastern Europe liberty represented the absence of oppressive foreign rule, religious freedom, and the creation of states, but not yet nations because those educated enough to understand (or misunderstand) the new ideas—the Polish szlachta, the Romanian boyars, the Hungarian and Croatian nobility, the leading churchmen, and the bureaucrats—were unwilling, at least in the eighteenth century, to give up their privileges. Moving from west to east the same word acquired at least three meanings.

The same adaptive transformation can be observed in the concept of the *Volk*. Although he did not invent the *Volk* concept, Johann Gottfried von Herder's name is associated with it as closely as Rousseau's is with the social contract. Herder's *Volk* comes close to our definition of *nationality*. He never confused it with *nation*. When he wrote about the latter he always used the German word *Nation*. He contrasted the interests of nationality with the effects of national policy sharply in his letter No. 121 written in 1797 in which he asked: what are the rules of justice in history? He observed that

> . . . cold history judges in accordance with the goals of states in conformity with a supposedly positive right, and even it [history] becomes often very hot in following this approach. The good of the fatherland, the honor of the nation becomes its [history's] battle cry and, in the case of underhanded action, the motto of the state.[8]

Herder pointed out that this approach, going back to ancient Athens, made humanity unhappy and finally culminated in the spirit of the Spanish-French state polity that "blackened the most brilliant with the shadow of vanity. . . . Humanity . . . is forgotten because

[8] Bernhard Suphan (ed.), *Herders Sämmtliche Werke*, XXXIII (Berlin: Weidmannsche Buchhandlung, 1877–1913), XVIII, *Briefe zur Beförderung der Humanität*, 282.

according to [this polity] it exists only for the state, namely for kings and ministers."[9] Herder went on to point out that his contemporaries, who had rejected this approach, were pursuing a similarly dangerous "phantom of light"[10] when they tried to find an ideal state structure applicable to the needs of all nationalities. Herder justified his criticism of the state and its actions by pointing out that "the happiness of one nationality cannot be forced upon, trusted upon, or loaded on another or all others. The roses in the wreath of liberty must be gathered by everybody's own hands and must spring with pleasure from one's own needs and own desire."[11] On the one hand we have the state and the nation, on the other nationality [*Volk*] and liberty that must correspond not to polity or an ideal state form, but to the need of each nationality.

In another letter written during the same year, (No. 123), Herder tried to explain that for each nationality liberty is essential because

we cannot be either happy, nor dignified or morally good until, for example, a single slave is unhappy because of the guilt of men . . . . The essence of human nature encloses a universe whose motto is: "Nobody for himself alone, all for one. Therefore let us all be happy and valuable for each other. An endless variety tending towards unity is in all and advances all."[12]

This is a romantic and, even more, a humanitarian concept. It condemns those who place the state, even the ideal state, ahead of people. People are, admittedly, of an endless variety; nationalities are the units in which people gather in accordance with their different desires. Each nationality must be free because, in spite of all differences, humanity tends toward unity that profits all and that can be achieved only by the cooperation of all nationalities. "By its own efforts not a single nationality of Europe was raised to the level of culture,"[13] wrote Herder elsewhere.

Herder's nationalities had but one common mission: to add their

[9] *Ibid.*
[10] *Ibid.*, p. 283.
[11] *Ibid.*,
[12] *Ibid.*, pp. 299–300.
[13] Eugen Kühnemann (ed.), *Herders Werke*, Part IV, Section III, *Ideen zur Philosophie der Geschichte der Menschheit*, p. 677 in Joseph Kürschner (ed.), *Deutsche National-Litteratur*, LXXVII (Stuttgart: Union Deutsche Verlagsgesellschaft, n.d.).

bit to the total of human culture and happiness. They had to find themselves first by rediscovering their languages and history. But, warned Herder,

. . . the historian of humanity should be careful in this [the rediscovery of the past] not to make one nationality into his exclusive favorite and thus slight all others whom circumstances had deprived of happiness and fame. The German learned even from the Slav; the Kymr and the Lett might have been Greeks if their situation among people would have been different.[14]

We can see, without difficulty, how different Herder's concept of the *Volk* and its mission was from those of his eastern European followers. His goal was a happy humanity composed of free nationalities cooperating with each other peacefully as equals. He was a humanitarian and a champion of nationality. Those who later used his words and ideas in eastern Europe were statists and nationalists.

III

Herder was very influential in introducing nationalism into eastern Europe. We have just discussed what happened to his *Volk* concept and its mission when it migrated eastward into non-German regions. His influence on the Slav revival is an even better known and equally important subject. The Slav movement began among the Czechs and Slovaks. With the exception of Josef Dobrowský (1753–1829) all Czechs and Slovaks from Jan Kollár (1793–1852) and Pavel Josef Safarik (1795–1861) to František Palacký (1798–1876) acknowledged, to a greater or lesser degree, their and their fellow nationals' debt to Herder. Yet their reading of Herder was entirely their own and certainly not in their master's spirit. Examination of a short passage from Herder's *Ideen zur Philosophie der Geschichte der Menschheit* will illustrate: On only three printed pages did Herder discuss "Slavische Völker."[15] Half of this short section is devoted to a description of the region inhabited by Slavs and to praising their pacific nature, their concentration on agriculture, commerce, and mining, their cultural activity and military passivity. These paragraphs end with the lines:

[14] *Ibid.*, p. 676.
[15] *Ibid.*, pp. 667–70.

All this did not help them to face oppression; on the contrary it fostered it. Because they never competed for the mastery of the universe, because they never had war-like hereditary princes among them and rather paid taxes if they were permitted to inhabit their lands in peace, several other nations, but mainly those of the German group committed crimes against them.[16]

Herder continued with a short summary of the various German attacks on the Slavs from Charlemagne's time to his own and found it quite natural that under the German and Tartar yokes, the latter attacking the Slavs from the East, the Slavs became "guileful and developed the indolence of servants."[17] Yet Herder still perceived remnants of the old Slav virtues surviving in his days. This made him optimistic because he believed that times were changing, that more and more rule by military might was being replaced by the rule of law, favoring peaceful diligence and friendly intercourse among nationalities. For this reason, wrote Herder, addressing the Slavs:

you too, people who have sunk to such depths from your once happy state, will finally awake from your long and lazy sleep and will, freed from your chains of slavery, enjoy as your property your lovely regions from the Adriatic Sea to the Carpathian Mountains, from the Don to the Mulda [sic] able to celebrate there your old feasts devoted to the glorification of peaceful diligence.[18]

The passage ends with a plea for a history of Slavdom as a unit to complete the panorama of humanity.

In these few pages of Herder we might detect the germs of future Pan-Slavism. Herder always thought of the Slavs as members of one nationality. We can also see why the Slavs increasingly came to see the Germans as their archenemies. But beyond that we find little except a preference for peaceful and fruitful pursuits, sympathy for a pacific, industrious, exploited group of people, and the expression of the hope that the wrongs of the past will be righted and the Slavs permitted to profit from the yield of the lands that they inhabit and cultivate. The oppression of the Slavs is clearly con-

[16] *Ibid.*, pp. 668–69.
[17] *Ibid.*, p. 669.
[18] *Ibid.*, p. 670.

demned, but nowhere did Herder single out the Slavs as a chosen people with a mission. Yet Kollár already believed in such a mission when he wrote that

. . . everywhere the Slavs, like a mighty flood, will extend their limits; the language which the Germans wrongly consider a mere speech of slaves will resound in all places, even in the mouths of their rivals. The sciences will flow through Slav channels; our people's dress, their manners and their songs will be fashionable on the Seine and on the Elbe. Alas, I was not born in that great age of Slav dominion, nor may I rise from the grave to witness it.[19]

Kollár, among other things, regarded the language of his people as the carrier of science. In this he came near to his master's spirit. Herder was a great defender of linguistic individuality. But even his demand that each nationality's language be respected was often used for other purposes. Eastern Europeans often quoted from a letter written by Herder at the death of the Emperor Joseph II to prove that he was in favor of nationalism, and that he criticized Joseph for attempting to denationalize the peoples he ruled. Herder's acual words give a different impression. In his "Discussion after the Death of the Emperor Joseph"[20] when A asks what preferences of the people the emperor had disregarded, B answers that he will bring up only one example, that of language, and says:

What does a nationality, especially one still lacking in culture, cherish more than the language of its fathers? In it lives its entire wealth of ideas concerning tradition, history, and the fundamental principles of life, all its heart and soul. To deprive such a nationality of its language or to lower it in value means to rob it of its only eternal value which parents leave their children.[21]

A then points out that Joseph knew several of his people well from personal experience, but B continues: "this makes it even more amazing that he did not realize how much he meddled with their most cherished rights . . . . Truly, just as God tolerates the lan-

---

[19] Quoted in Hans Kohn, *Pan-Slavism: Its History and Ideology* (2d rev. ed.; New York: Vintage Russian Library, 1960), p. 9.

[20] Suphan, *Herders Sämmtliche Werke*, XVII, 47–63.

[21] *Ibid.*, p. 58.

guages of the world, so the ruler too should not only tolerate but respect the various languages of his peoples."[22] Herder argued for the need to respect the languages and cultures of each nationality because they were the instruments for the spreading of civilization. He was concerned with civilization, not nationalism. But nationalists, as so many others, read only what they want to read. Taken out of context, "is it not a major idea to base the most far-reaching plans for the welfare of so many nationalities, Hungarians, Slavs, Romanians, etc., entirely on *their* way of thinking in a manner which is *entirely their own* and *dearest* to them?"[23] has nationalistic connotations. But even by itself this sentence contains nothing that could point to a nation's privileges or its mission.

The meaning of Herder's words was twisted to fit the mood of eastern Europe. He was a prolific writer, well-known, much studied, and his stress on language and folk poetry was easily understood. Other Germans, less well-known in eastern Europe, but nevertheless influential, better fitted the needs of those in eastern Europe who thought they were the disciples of Herder. Friedrich Schleiermacher wrote clearly of national missions,[24] and Friedrich Schlegel, pontificating practically in the midst of the eastern Europeans, in Vienna, wrote and said many things—in spite of his conservative bent—that suited the incipient nationalists of that part of the continent. His views, for example, differ sharply from those of Herder when he judges Joseph II. Schlegel stressed the importance of public opinion and pointed to "the great obstacles" that Joseph placed in his own way by ignoring public opinion "in the Netherlands and Hungary"[25] ". . . It would, moreover, have had a beneficial influence on his own mind, had he placed himself in living contact with public opinion, and had he watched and studied it more."[26] Public opinion, which varied so greatly in the Habsburg lands, was considered a valid, legitimate force by Schlegel who believed that Joseph II, and rulers

[22] *Ibid.*, pp. 58–59.

[23] *Ibid.*, p. 59.

[24] "God has pointed out to every people its particular mission on earth and has breathed into it its particular spirit, in order that in this way He may be glorified by each one through its particular mode." Quoted in Carlton J. H. Hayes, *Nationalism: A Religion* (New York: Macmillan, 1960), p. 47.

[25] L. Percell and R. H. Whitelock (trans.), Friedrich Schlegel, *A Course of Lectures of Modern History* (London and New York: G. Bell & Sons, 1894), p. 305.

[26] *Ibid.*, p. 307.

in general, had to follow it. Schlegel was more practical than Herder and thus points to another consideration that we cannot neglect in regard to eastern European nationalism.

Herder was basically a romantic humanitarian. If he was a nationalist at all, he was a cultural nationalist. From the poets of *Sturm und Drang* nearly to Hegel's time this was the dominant philosophy in Germany—notwithstanding the movement that began in Prussia in 1806—the country that we described as the main bridge between western and eastern Europe. We have seen that in western Europe nationalism was deeply concerned with "political reality." Eastern European nationalism, though influenced by the German cultural emphasis, was also political practically from the beginning. Anybody who has tried to retranslate a text into the original language knows that the result will have little in common with the original. The translation that the eastern Europeans made of German cultural nationalism into political ideas had little to do with western European political nationalism. The two were so dissimilar that without the German bridge the ideas of western Europe would have evoked a much fainter echo in the East than they did. This does not mean that western, especially French, influences were lacking in eastern Europe. There are numerous indications that the works of the philosophes were well-known in the Czech lands, Poland, and Hungary by 1780 at the latest, but their readership was largely limited to the nobility, especially to the magnates. Furthermore when we read the works or speeches of the early prophets of eastern European nationalism, irrespective of their social origin, we find that their interpretation of the ideas of the philosophes is influenced partly by the notions of German romanticism, but mainly by the local varieties of political theory.

By about 1780, the term *nation* had acquired in the West the meaning outlined in the first section of this chapter. In eastern Europe the word had only a political value, it meant the *political nation*, those who had specific privileges. In eastern Europe, Rousseau's Social Contract became limited to the relationship between the princes and the members of the political nation, and Montesquieu's division of powers served to justify the claims of special-interest groups who tried to acquire more power. The American, British, and the various French constitutions of the revolutionary years had little in common with the Hungarian, Polish, or Croatian constitutions, with the Bohemian *Staatsrecht,* or the privileges of the accepted nations in Transylvania. Yet Franklin, Sieyès, Bolingbroke, Mirabeau, and many others, were constantly quoted by those who tried to defend or extend the scope of the existing eastern European constitutions. The writings and oratory of those eastern Europeans who were familiar with the expressions of the western movement and who used them constantly are responsible for the erroneous impression that the same issues were debated in the assemblies of Paris, Vienna, or Pozsony (Bratislava, Pressburg). Fatherland, constitution, nation, liberty, social contract, division of powers, religious freedom, natural law, and other expressions of this kind were used both in western and eastern Europe. Even if we assume that their meaning was understood by those who used them on the banks of the Seine, the Danube, the Vistula, or the Vltava (Moldau), we must realize that they meant different things to the western and eastern European writers and orators of that time, and that they often mean different things today than they did in the late eighteenth or early nineteenth centuries. What is accepted to be the true meaning of these words today is nearer to what the men in Paris discussed than to what was understood in Vienna, Pozsony, Zagreb, or Prague. Western nationalism has a history that accounts for the difference we find between our present-day concepts and the various French deputies' of the revolutionary quarter-century.

Nationalism was born in western Europe as part of a general trend and with political meaning. Moving eastward its emphasis became cultural-linguistic in Germany, reverting, once again, to politics when it moved out of Germany into the lands of Slavs, Greeks, Turks, Romanians, and Magyars. If we understand that the western ideas underwent numerous changes during their eastward migration, that in the East they were not only understood in a sense that differed from the original, but also that in eastern Europe they were fused with local concepts, we see how they became the main causes of a historic transformation that was *sui generis* to a large extent. It is this peculiar development that differentiates eastern and western Europe even more sharply in contemporary history than they were in previous periods. Before we turn to the chapters that will describe the peculiar ideas, concepts, and conditions prevalent in the various countries of eastern Europe and their fusion with those coming from the West, we must complete this introduction by pointing to some of those local features that were, more or less, characteristic for all of eastern Europe at the turn of the eighteenth century.

IV

In works dealing with the nationalism of eastern Europe we usually find that much attention is paid to the problem of historic and nonhistoric nations.[27] This division separates those who have been masters of their own destiny in fairly modern times from those who have not or whose independence had been so many centuries earlier that they effectively lost the memory of that independence. While this distinction is roughly the equivalent of our separation of nationality and nation, it goes much further. It implies that nationalities have no history or at least that they played no role in history simply because they were not dominant forces from the political point of view; that they had not established, maintained, or ruled states. While this distinction is valid, judged by the sole criterion of political supremacy, it embodies several fallacies that render it more difficult to evaluate the emergence of modern nationalism in eastern Europe.

Every social group that has retained through its customs, mores, traditions, folkways, religious institutions, language, histories (even though sometimes written by members of other groups) even the vaguest, correct, or false memories of the past or the ability to reconstruct the past, has a history. Western ideas of nationalism could not have produced the great diversities in eastern Europe had they not fused with a great number of local traditions, often cherished by the so-called nonhistoric nationalities. Not all these traditions of the region were based on relatively recent events or tied to existing political structures, but all were either alive or revivable.

This raises a second point connected with the theory of historical versus nonhistoric nations. Even disregarding the fact that this distinction is based on a single criterion—the political role various groups played in their states—its validity can be questioned simply because political overlordship alone was insufficient to assure su-

[27] The differentiation between historical and nonhistoric nations originated with Karl Marx. Its fullest explanation can be found in Otto Bauer, *Die Nationalitäten-frage und die Sozialdemokratie* (Vienna, 1907; 2d ed., 1924, as Vol. II of Max Adler and Rudolf Hilferding [eds.], *Marx-Studien*).

premacy in the days of modern nationalism. Even less was this political—even military—domination ever sufficient to make any nation "historic." By themselves the Normans could not have created and maintained England, the Franks France, the Magyars Hungary, the Bulgars Bulgaria, and so on. Specialists of earlier periods recognize this fact. They study medieval France, England, Poland, and not the feudal classes alone. They realize that the economic, social, and cultural activities that were the private preserves of the ruling groups in earlier times do not constitute the totality of history. Nor can this distinction between rulers and ruled be accepted as valid for eastern Europe simply because there the rulers and ruled often spoke different languages. Those of our colleagues who considered this division of the nationalities of eastern Europe as meaningful created unnecessary difficulties for themselves by not recognizing the equal potential of all groups. All of them had played a part in the region's history, were conscious or potentially aware of their past and identity, and, therefore, were able to assert themselves under favorable circumstances with the help of certain stimuli. Political domination or subservence within the existing East European state structures at any given period is not the best criterion when we try to generalize about the development of nationalism in eastern Europe.

This does not mean that those who ruled or had the relative advantages of wealth or power in eastern Europe in the eighteenth or nineteenth centuries were not better placed to utilize the ideas of the West than were the less fortunate. But we know of instances where the roles were reversed. The Vojvodina Serbs continued to supply their brothers south of the Sava-Danube line with ideas even after 1815, when Serbia gained virtual autonomy. The Romanians in the Principalities were better off, even under Phanariote rule, than were those of Transylvania, yet Romanian nationalism originated west of the Carpathians.

Constitutions were one of the greatest influences in the development of East European nationalism, and we will discuss them at some length. But let us notice first that even this weapon turned out to be double edged. In Poland a constitution contributed directly to the country's decline and finally to its partition by preventing the timely introduction of reforms. Among the Czechs it kept Bohemians and Moravians apart for a long time in the nineteenth century.

In these and other countries, especially Hungary, the veneration of these documents prevented real change when change was badly needed. The constitutions of eastern Europe, which were in reality only generalized feudal contracts, fascinated even those people who had no such documents of their own. While it did not hurt the Vojvodina Serbs to treat the patents of Leopold I[28] almost as their constitution, the Romanians of Transylvania certainly suffered by trying to find one in their distant past. The famous *Supplex libellus Valachorum*, the petition that they submitted to Leopold II in 1791, was based on the assumption that only ancient rights can assure any in the present. For this reason they asked that their rights, taken from them in an unconstitutional manner in 1437,[29] should be restored. By taking this approach they made it impossible for Leopold to help them even if he would have been interested in so doing. In 1437 only the nobility had rights; in 1791 there was no Romanian nobility in Transylvania. Leopold could have restored or granted rights enjoyed by the nobility only to Romanians of the middle class, which he could not do at the very moment he was desperately trying to make peace with the nobility of Hungary and Transylvania. It is questionable whether another approach would have brought better results, but it is certain that the constitutional way had to bring failure.

Even if constitutions were not unmixed blessings, they nevertheless secured great advantages for those who had them in the period that gave birth to modern democracy. In western Europe, emerging nationalism was closely connected with democratic and constitutional tendencies. Of these three interrelated principles, only constitutionalism was well known in eastern Europe, and, therefore, it became the strongest single influence shaping the area's emerging nationalism. It is this influence, not the constitutions themselves, that is of interest to us.

We must discuss constitutions in the broadest possible sense in-

[28] The three documents that the Vojvodina Serbs cherished were the diplomas of Leopold I issued on August 21, 1690, and August 20, 1691, and the confirmatory decree of March 4, 1695.

[29] In 1437, a peasant revolt broke out in Transylvania. After its defeat the Hungarian nobility of this province concluded an alliance with the German cities and the Székely leadership for the protection of their interests. This was the beginning of the Union of the Three Nations depriving everybody else, first of all the Romanians, of practically all rights.

Constitution

stead of dealing with them as legal documents if we want to understand their importance for nationalism. Legally, only Poland, Hungary, Transylvania, and Croatia had basic documents that could
qualify as constitutions; the *Staastrechts* of the Czech lands fall in
this category, but they were inoperative after 1749. In the various
lands and territories, these documents regulated the manner of administration and determined the legal rights and obligations of and
the relationships between the various social strata, from the lowest
to the ruler. In this sense even the special regulations of the Vojvodina and the military borders[30] could be considered as constitutions,
especially since the inhabitants of these districts used them in this
sense during the long decades of change in eastern Europe. If we
disregard the small nationalities (Sorbs, Kashubs, Wends, and so
forth), all of them, except the Ukrainian-Ruthenians and Slovaks,
had some document or collection of documents performing a quasi-
constitutional function.

These documents had several features in common: they all rested
on some mystical theories as well as on specific historical developments. The first of these attributes was symbolized by the various
crowns. "The notion 'Corona Regni Poloniae' appeared first in the
second half of the fourteenth century under Casimir the Great
[1333–70], became a symbol of the indivisibility of the lands of the
Kingdom."[31] The Lublin Union of 1569 was already concluded between the Polish Crown and Lithuania, with Livonia subordinated
to both. As a symbol of indivisibility the Polish Crown played the
role of the English and Hungarian crowns, but the Hungarian
Crown, the Crown of St. Stephen, also represented divine sanction
for the supremacy of the *Regnum Marianum*. Although less pronounced, divine qualities were attributed to the Crown of Wenzes-
las in Bohemia; while the Croats, besides feeling some attachment
to the Crown of St. Stephen, had their own Crown of Zvonimir, the

---

[30] On the Vojvodina see n. 28. The best recent discussion of the position of the
military border regions is Gunther E. Rothenberg, *The Austrian Military Border in
Croatia, 1522–1747* (Urbana, Ill.: University of Illinois Press, 1960) and the same
author's *The Military Border in Croatia, 1740–1881* (Chicago: University of Chicago Press, 1966). The military border was finally abolished in 1881.

[31] P. Skwarczyński, "The Constitution of Poland before the Partition," *The Cambridge History of Poland*, ed. W. F. Reddaway *et al.* (2 vols.; Cambridge, England:
Cambridge University Press, 1951), I, 50.

symbol of their Triune Kingdom, although it was not a constitutional formula like the Hungarian Crown.

The crowns were not only considered the symbols of national sovereignty, just as flags are today, but were supposed to have a mystic personality and inherent rights that included the ownership of all lands over which individuals who once wore them ruled. While only the Hungarians built a legal-constitutional theory around their crown,[32] the other nations were not far behind. If we realize that between the two world wars Hungary still attempted to use the rights of her crown as an argument bolstering her revisionist claims, we can easily imagine how important the theory of the crown was a century or a century and a half earlier.

Symbols are a useful source of strength, but they only represent beliefs that are held by men. These beliefs, held by those whose rights and privileges they justified, were embodied in the various constitutions and other legal documents. These same privileged individuals were those who first came in contact with western ideas and shaped the development of East European nationalism.

All constitutions in our region, irrespective of how they originated, were contracts between the ruler and the estates. These differed somewhat from the estates of western Europe. In the two largest countries, Hungary and Poland, the church was not considered an independent estate,[33] giving the nobility an ever larger role in the "political nation" than they had in the West. Only members of the "political nation" had rights. Although these rights were extensive and included the power to alter the basic constitution, they were not unique. The *ius resistendi* was known in England as well as in Poland and Hungary, while Hungary's *Coronation Diploma* and Poland's *Pacta Coventa,* which rulers had to accept before they

[32] For Hungary's Doctrine of the Holy Crown see Patrick J. Kelleher, *The Holy Crown of Hungary* (Rome: American Academy in Rome, 1951) and Charles d'Eszlary, *Histoire des institutions publiques hongroises* (2 vols.; Paris: M. Rivière & Co., 1963) II, 7–15.

[33] The three estates in Poland were the King, the senators who served in their capacities of ecclesiastic or civil office holders, and the deputies, who represented the gentry of their districts. In Hungary only the upper nobility with hereditary titles and the upper clergy sat in the Upper Chamber of the Diet. The deputies, representing the gentry of the counties, formed the membership of the Lower Chamber in which the third estate, the free royal towns and boroughs, was also represented by one deputy.

26   PETER F. SUGAR

could be crowned, had their equivalents in Venice, Sweden, and the
German Empire. But nowhere was the political nation as narrowly
conceived or with so many rights as in eastern Europe. When the
idea of nationalism gained a foothold in eastern Europe it was first
considered as an additional argument in favor of the established
order. The western concepts of nation and national rights, which
were regarded as natural rights, were equated to mean the political
nation and its rights. Thus western political thinkers and writers
could be quoted verbatim, although those who used these phrases
were defending what their authors were attacking: narrow, often
helplessly outdated principles and privileges. This is the type of
nationalism that Endre Arató has recently called the nationalism of
the nobility in contrast to that of the bourgeoisie.[34] This is an interesting distinction to which we will devote the last part of this chapter.

In the lands ruled by the Ottomans, only Moldavia and Wallachia
could be called constitutionally ruled provinces even if this expression is used in the widest possible sense. In the Principalities the
Porte's rule and influence was limited by the terms of the agreements that placed these lands under Ottoman overlordship.[35] In
these Romanian lands the power of the local rulers, the hospodars,
was also limited both by law and custom, giving the boyar class a
position quite similar to that of the members of the political nations
in Hungary and Poland. The boyars, twice removed from the source
of power, did not have the influence of the nobility in the lands to
the north and west of theirs and played a less-important part in the
development of nationalism. In general, Moldavia and Wallachia
are the transition zone between the non-Ottoman and Ottoman-
dominated regions of eastern Europe.

Yet, even the Balkan peoples were not completely at the mercy

[34] Endre Arató, "A magyar nacionalizmus kettős arculata a feudalizmusból a kapitalizmusba való átmenet és a polgári forradalom időszakában," *A magyar nacionalizmus kialakulása és története,* ed. Erzsébet Andics (Budapest: Kossuth, 1964), pp.
79–142.

[35] In 1417, just a year before his death, Prince Mircea the Old of Wallachia acknowledged the suzerainty of the sultan over his country. After the defeat of Vlad
the Impaler in 1462 the dependence of Wallachia on Istanbul became permanent.
After the death of Stephen the Great in 1502, his son, Bogdan, had to acknowledge
the overlordship of the sultan in Moldavia also. These agreements of vassalage left
most of the domestic problems in the hands of local princes and limited the rights
of the Ottomans in the two principalities.

of Istanbul, although after the deaths of Sultan Suleyman (1566) and the Grand Vizier Mehmed Sokolli (1578) they may have gotten this impression. Yet the misrule of over two hundred years that followed the disappearance of these two men was not the result of governmental policy but of the inability of the government to enforce its will and check local misrule and abuses. More than two centuries later the Serbs were still able to differentiate between Istanbul and the local authorities and revolted, in 1804, to reestablish the influence of the central government in their lands.

Central government in the Ottoman Empire meant indirect rule. Unable to rid their state of its theocratic foundations, the Ottomans faced a dilemma that they never solved: they recognized only religious differences between people, and, as a Muslim state, had laws only for Muslims. In Europe they ruled over numerous people who followed the precepts of other faiths and while the Ottomans had no theories that would have permitted them to regulate the lives of non-Muslims, yet they could not abolish the various religions with which they could not deal because their own religion forbade the forcible conversion of "people of the book." Their inability either to demand conformity from their subjects or to rule nonconformists prevented the establishment of an integrated state structure and brought about the introduction of the millet system, a minority policy based on religious toleration and the internal self-government of the nonconformists.

The failure to either rule or integrate did not relieve the Ottoman overlords from the responsibility and need to maintain law and order in the lands over which they exercised sovereignty. Unable to legislate for their Balkan subjects, they lumped all Christians into one millet and made the Patriarch in Istanbul responsible for their taxes and loyalty. In each region they left local institutions not only unchanged, but gave them legal status by issuing *kanunnâmeler*, law codes, for them. In the beginning these *kanunnâmeler* did little more than recognize as binding the existing customs and conditions, leaving local administration in the hands of those who were responsible for it in the past. While placing numerous burdens on the population, these documents also assured the continuation of existing customs, economic establishments, political command chains, and so on, in short the legalized survival of the identity of nationalities. These *kanunnâmeler* never achieved either the status or the influ-

ence of constitutions, but they assured differentiation among the
various Balkan districts, gave them some, even if minimal, rights,
and maintained the cohesion and assured the survival of certain
institutions (zadruga, parish, and so forth), thus creating the framework within which modern nationalism could develop. If we add
to the *kanunnâmeler* the various documents granting special privileges to certain groups and professions for economic, military, and
political reasons, we find another set of legal papers that played an
important role in assuring that nationalism found, in the Balkans,
also, local institutions and groups that were able to adapt it to their
need. While the *kanunnâmeler* were more and more honored in
their breach only in and after the seventeenth century, the importance of the privileged groups (Phanariotes, Corbadcis, guildsmen,
and so on), grew tremendously during the same period. These
groups carried on their, from the Ottoman point of view, often subversive activities as well protected by the privileged position they
enjoyed as were the members of the political nations by their constitutions.

V

Constitutions, quasi constitutions, and other documents were not
the only local force influencing the development of nationalism in
eastern Europe. In certain regions, notably the Balkans, religion was
even more important. We are interested in religion only as an in-
stitutional-political factor, but even in this limited sense, religion
played an important role in eastern Europe's history from the introduction of Christianity to the present.

The Balkans were not only the battleground between Orthodoxy
and Catholicism, Constantinople and Rome, but also of the two approaches to civilization that these two churches or cities represented. Church Slavonic and the Cyrillic alphabet are as closely
associated with the southern Slavs as with the great apostles Cyril
and Methodius. Religious and theological, as many differences were
in their origin, they soon acquired political implications. From the
days of Boris (852–89) and the introduction of Christianity into
Bulgaria, to the problems raised in our times by the assumption
that a Catholic was by definition a Croat just as a Serb was Orthodox, religion always had political meaning in the Balkans. Most
wars and campaigns had religious connotations, and religion soon

began to figure among the "national characteristics" of the Balkan people. The Greek rite in the Orthodox church was Byzantine or Greek in orientation, the Slavonic rite was Bulgarian or Serb, while Catholicism represented Croat and Slovene, if not German or Hungarian interests. This made Albania, Bosnia, and Macedonia prime regions of conflict some thousand years before the Macedonian question, the Congress of Berlin, or the London Conference of 1913 made the world at large conscious of the existence of these issues.

In 893–94 Clement became the first Bishop of Ohrid (Okhrida). From this moment on, the issues that troubled the relationship between the Patriarch and the Slavonic churches were as much if not more political than theological in nature. It is no coincidence that Ohrid was transformed into a patriarchate by Simeon (893–927) in 926. He had assumed the title Tsar during the previous year. If the emperorship was to be meaningful, the Tsar of Bulgaria had to equal the ruler in Constantinople in all respects; first of all he had to have his own patriarch.

The same development occurred among the Serbs. In 1217 Stevan Nemanja II (1196–1228) accepted a crown and the royal title from Rome, but he turned to the Oecumenical Patriarch, who temporarily lived in Nicaea since the fall of Constantinople in 1204, to obtain an archepiscopal see for his brother, the future St. Sava. When Serbia became the strongest power in the Balkans, her ruler, Dušan (1331–55), acted exactly as the Bulgar Simeon had before him. In 1345 he took the title Tsar and established a Serb patriarchate at Peć (Ipek). For both, Simeon and Dušan, full independence from Byzantium and beyond that imperial power was unthinkable without a church controlled by themselves alone.[36]

The Patriarch of Constantinople considered the establishment of these new patriarchates as detrimental to his dignity and to the unity of the church. It is just as obvious that the development of a Serb metropolitanate (and later patriarchate) displeased, for similar reasons, the various bishops of the Ohrid see. This jurisdictional fight would have ended around 1459 if it had been nothing more than

---

[36] "D'après les principes orthodoxes, l'empereur deveit être assisté d'un patriarche." Konstantin Jireček, *Geschichte der Serben* (Gotha, 1911), p. 387, quoted by Ladislas Hadrovics, *L'église serbe sous la domination turque* (Vol. IV of Coloman Benda [ed.], *Bibliothèque de la revue d'histoire comparée* [Paris: Presses Universitaires, 1947]), p. 40.

that. Ohrid had relinquished the patriarchal title in 1393, and the Patriarch of Constantinople, more powerful than ever before after 1453, attached the Serb bishoprics to the Ohrid metropolitanate after the last remnants of the Serb state and with it the patriarchate of Peć disappeared at the battle of Smederovo in 1459. But more was involved than simply church unity and the problem of ecclesiastic jurisdiction.

Church unity is important for all theologians. When Mehmed II Fatih, after his conquest of the city, installed Gennadius Scholarius as Patriarch of Constantinople and head of the Christian millet, this unity seemed assured. The Greek contention that for both theological and political reasons it was more important than ever to maintain this unity during the centuries of absolute Ottoman rule is well founded. It is, therefore, hard to refute the argument that it was the patriarch's duty to enforce uniformity of rituals, liturgy, organization, and language in the church. Yet the counterarguments of the Slavs make equally good sense. These point out that dogmatic uniformity was sufficient to maintain the unity of the faith, while the replacement of Slavonic by Greek in the churches made the service incomprehensible to most faithful, excluded Slav-speakers from high church offices, and made resistance to the Ottomans more difficult. Slav historians of the nineteenth and twentieth centuries write about the double yoke when they discuss the Ottoman period in the histories of their countries: the political-economic of the Ottomans and the religious-linguistic of the Greeks. The charge against the Greeks is certainly not theological and reflects the thinking of people who wrote under the influence of modern nationalism. But there is truth in what they wrote.

The seemingly ecclesiastic disputes within the rank of the Orthodox church had a second lay dimension. The Slavs objected to Greek domination of their churches, but they were far from united among themselves. The Bishop of Ohrid was caught in the middle. He objected to certain directives from Constantinople, but at the same time resisted demands of his Serb parishioners. His difficulties are best illustrated by the unsuccessful attempt of Bishop Paul of Smederevo (1528–33)[37] to reestablish an independent Serb church. This

[37] For the details of the revolt of Bishop Paul see Hadrovics, *L'église serbe*, pp. 42–44.

minor civil war "shows to what extent church and state organizations were interchangeable."[38] The revolt of Bishop Paul can only be understood if we consider it as a political movement. It was but a minor incident in a long chain of events in which the fortune of religious institutions serves as the best indicator for the rise and decline of the political fortunes of the Balkan Slavs.

Prior to Bishop Paul's action, we had the establishment and dissolution of the patriarchates of Ohrid and Peć. After his attempt we find the following major developments: in 1557 the patriarchate of Peć was reestablished at the insistence of the Grand Vizier Mehmed Sokolli (Sokolović). By the time of its final elimination by the Ottomans in 1766, the see of Peć had served its purpose as a focus for what was left of Serb feeling and had been replaced by the metropolitanate of Sremski Karlovci founded in 1690 by Patriarch Arsenije III Crnojević under the well-known circumstances. Ohrid closed its doors in 1767. It does not matter whether these two old bishoprics were abolished by the Ottomans on their own or on Phanariote initiative. They had been closed as centers of political subversion and dissent. It was too late to stop this worldly activity of the clergy. Sremski Karlovci and numerous monasteries took the place of Peć and Ohrid.

To change cities of residence was not easy for the Serb patriarch. He left Peć to save his life and that of his followers, but not without securing guarantees for the independence of his church. Before moving, he submitted certain requests to the Emperor Leopold I. These were copied from the millet system at its ideal best. The patriarch claimed autonomous jurisdiction over a large territory that included practically all the Balkans, with the exception of what is today Turkish or Greek territory and Croatia and Hungary.[39] But it is not quite clear whether he claimed what he did as a Serb or as an Orthodox. Leopold tried to clarify this point. In his first patent of August 21, 1690, he added even Greece to the lands under the patriarch's authority, but restricted his jurisdiction to Serbs living in all these countries.[40] As most of these were outside the emperor's jurisdiction the question of which Orthodox was a Serb created difficulties only in the Banat of Temesvár over which Serbs and Roma-

[38] *Ibid.*, p. 42.
[39] *Ibid.*, pp. 141–42.
[40] *Ibid.*, p. 143.

nians fought as late as 1919–20 at the Paris Peace Conference.[41]

The question of the nationality of Orthodox people reappeared in a much more drastic and more nationalistic form one hundred and seventy years later with the struggle for the establishment of an autocephalous Bulgarian church. This struggle, although it began earlier in the nineteenth century, took on serious dimensions in 1860 and was first and foremost a national fight. Because church and state were almost identical in the popular mind, those interested in creating an independent Bulgaria believed that the establishment of a national church was a logical first step. Only political considerations can explain the attempt of founding a Bulgarian Uniate church in 1861. It had almost no chance of gaining acceptance, but it was well suited to frighten both the Patriarch at Istanbul and the Russians. The fight ended in 1870 with the establishment of the exarchate. Article X of the Sultan's relevant firman allowed the extension of the exarchate's jurisdiction from its original territory, which lay roughly between the Danube and the Balkan Range, to all those regions in which two thirds of the population declared in favor of the new church. If some western imperialists around 1870 believed that trade follows the flag, the nationalists in Serbia, Bulgaria, and Greece were convinced that the flag follows the church. The fight that began over ecclesiastic jurisdiction became known as the Macedonian Question and is still not fully settled today, almost a hundred years after the establishment of the exarchate. The last chapter of the story that began with Simeon and Dušan, if not earlier, has not yet been written.

It is not too difficult to see how the line between religion and nationality, or church and state, became blurred in the Balkans. The southern Slavs and Romanians received their Christianity and culture from Byzantium. The eastern Roman Empire was as much Orthodox as it was Roman or Greek, with the church, the ruler's main support, subordinated to the state. An individual who spoke Greek, belonged to the Orthodox church, and was a subject of the Emperor was a Byzantine in the eyes of the southern Slavs and Romanians. This was the model they tried to duplicate, and when they

[41] The question of the Banat in 1919–20 is discussed in detail by Ivo J. Lederer, *Yugoslavia at the Paris Peace Conference. A Study in Frontier-making* (New Haven, Conn.–London: Yale University Press, 1963), pp. 98–99, 125, 126, 130, 181, 224, 310, 312.

became powerful enough to think in terms of empire their churches had to be patriarchal. Church and state appeared as the two sides of the same coin. When the Ottoman occupation obliterated one side of the coin, the Greeks, Slavs, and Albanians transferred whatever attachment they felt for the state to the church, the most important surviving institution with which they could identify their past, present, and hopes for the future. This is why Bishop Paul opposed both Istanbul and Ohrid, and why in the formative days of modern nationalism it proved to be difficult to separate religion from nationality. The history of "Yugoslavism" and the troubles the Russian Pan-Slavs had in finding a place in their schemes for Czechs (and more especially, Poles) are good nineteenth-century illustrations of this difficulty. Yet without this equating of church with nationality the rebirth of the Balkan states, even with the help of foreign ideas and the intervention of the Great Powers, would have been much more difficult than it was. In this sense at least religion in the Balkans played the role that constitutions had in the lands north of the Danube.

But religion was also influential in the Habsburg domains or in the Polish lands. "The Catholic Germans of the Habsburg lands felt [around 1780] a much greater kinship with the Hungarians, Croats, and Italians than with the Protestant Prussians . . . ."[42] These Germans could have felt this way only towards a limited segment of their non-German fellow subjects. The nationalistic aspects of the Hussite and Taborite movements were never fully forgotten in Bohemia.

One of the crucial aspects of the nationalist ideology of the anti-Habsburg government in Hungary was the desire to secure freedom of religious practices. The majority of the insurrectionists were Protestants. Even in the foreign policy aspects of the revolutions—in the cases of Bethlen and George Rákóczi—the religious question played an important role. The principle of faith does not join the nobility's national ideology for theological reasons, but as a condition of personal freedom demanding the right for everybody to choose his religion according to his own conviction.[43]

[42] Kohn, The Idea of Nationalism, p. 348, n. 43 quoting from Emil Horner (ed.), Vor dem Untergang des alten Reichs, 1756–1795 in the series Sammlung . . . in Entwicklungsreihen; Reihe Politische Dichtung (Leipzig: Reclam, 1930), I, p. 13.

[43] R. Ágnes Várkonyi, "A nemzet, a haza fogalma a török harcok és a Habsburg-ellenes küzdelmek idején (1526–1711)," A magyar nacionalizmus, ed. Andics, p. 54.

The event of later years confirms this judgment. Eastern Hungary, with its large number of Protestants, was much more revolutionary during the critical years of 1790–92 than was the rest of the country, while the so-called conservatives who collaborated with Vienna in the period between 1820 and 1848 were Catholics. Both groups belonged to the nobility, but their brand of Magyar patriotism was influenced by their religious convictions. The problem of accepted or only tolerated religions was an important *de facto* distinction everywhere although it existed *de jure* only in Transylvania. By the eighteenth century one did not have to belong to a specific church in the Habsburg lands to be accepted as a Magyar, Croat, Czech, or German by those following another kind of worship.

In Poland the situation was different. Here Catholicism continued to be the hallmark of Polishness. One of the major problems after the first partition was the question of the dissenters, and the inability of the Poles to solve it contributed mightily to the subsequent partitions. Here the identity of church and nationality was possibly even closer than in the Balkans. Orthodoxy alone was insufficient to establish belonging among the southern Slavs. Among the Poles, Catholicism (or adherence to the Uniate church) was a must for those who wished to be regarded as Poles. This problem continued to plague Poland even after the third partition and later after the rebirth of the state. It made it almost impossible for a large segment of the population, especially in the eastern provinces, to develop any feeling of loyalty for Poland. Here the two factors discussed so far were of equal importance. For the Poles the constitution was as sacred as the Bible, and the church as much part of the state as was the Diet. This made change even more difficult for the Poles than for other people and accounts for much that happened in their land in the seventeenth and eighteenth centuries—the loss of their state at a time when other nations had begun to fight for the rebirth of theirs.

VI

George Weill makes the point that human rights or historic rights are the two basic approaches to nationalism.[44] The first of these two, rational and concerned with the problems of the present, was the western approach. The latter, prevalent in Germany and eastern

[44] George Weill, *L'Europe du XIXe siècle et l'idée de nationalité* (Paris: A. Michel, 1938), pp. 11–13.

Europe, was romantic and aimed at the revival of the "good old days." Both constitutions and religious institutions had developed slowly in these golden days from modest beginnings into their "perfect" forms proving, to the satisfaction of the early nationalists in eastern Europe, that their "nation" had a special, creative genius that had been stifled either by foreign oppression (Habsburg or Ottoman) or by partisanship and corruption introduced and abetted by foreigners (Russians, Germans, Phanariotes, Greek prelates, and so on). To give this genius free play once more several things had to be done. First of all, every foreign influence from the linguistic to the political had to be eliminated. Then the people had to be convinced of their talents and gifts by being made aware of their identity and past greatness. While these tasks were accomplished the remains of the past—institutions, economic and social structure, and so on—had to be protected to serve as the link with the past and as the starting point for the future that the revived nations were to construct. A lag of centuries was to be bridged in this manner. As a result of this approach to nationalism, xenophobia, historicism, and a forced feeling of superiority emerged as decisive forces in eastern Europe. Although these three concepts do not carry connotations that differentiate their eastern European variants from those in other parts of the world, they, nevertheless, deserve to be discussed.

For the peoples of eastern Europe external pressures (German, Russian, Byzantine, Ottoman) never ceased, and often they put pressure on each other. Masters or subjects, they never knew peace. Practically all historians agree that this absence of peace and the endless pressures produced a certain feeling of interdependence among groups who had numerous differences of their own (landlord vs. peasant; nobility vs. bourgeoisie; members of different estates; ruler and ruled, and so on). Hayes points out that it was the *Drang nach Osten* of the Teutonic Knights and the Hansa that "eventually aroused the national feeling of Czechs and Poles."[45] Lemberg expands this idea and states that it is his "theory that pressure and danger, attacks directed against feelings of self-esteem and pride, the need for self-justification and for proving one's worth were the strongest motivating factors in the development and excesses of nationalism."[46] There can be little doubt about the validity of these

[45] Hayes, *Essays on Nationalism*, pp. 30–31.
[46] Lemberg, *Geschichte des Nationalismus*, p. 182.

and similar statements. But pressure and danger, had not only positive results by creating a feeling of belonging, they also had negative effects. Beginning with the grudge felt toward enemies, a feeling of hatred developed that in most cases finally extended not only to almost everybody and everything alien but even to the slightly unfamiliar. Whatever was connected with the group-self was by definition good and unchangeable; everything else was bad and corrupting.

The justifications for this feeling varied. For the Ottomans everything Christian was bad for theological reasons. To them it was axiomatic that they were superior to the West due to a more perfect religious-moral way of life, and they held to this belief, unwilling to learn from their enemies, even when defeats proved that they were far from invincible. When reform based on western models finally became inevitable, the reformers had to justify their action in traditional Muslim terms to gain even the most limited grudging acceptance.[47] German and everything German was anathema from the Baltic to the Sava. German meant Reformation and military aggression in Poland, while in the Czech lands and Hungary it stood for the Counterreformation and foreign rule. Everywhere it was identified with treachery, economic privileges, and expansionism. The Magyars possessed similar qualities when seen by the other nationalities living in the lands of St. Stephen's Crown. Croats were not only unacceptable to Serbs because they were Catholics, but also because they supposedly lacked military talent, while the Croats despised the Serbs not only because they were Orthodox, but also because they lacked culture. The Greeks saw only barbarians in the other inhabitants of the Balkans, while these people detested the Greeks who were supposedly domineering, mercenary, and the lackeys of the Ottomans.

It is understandable and certainly not anything specifically regional to find the various people of eastern Europe distrusting and even despising each other. Black and white thinking was and is not

---

[47] The oldest study in a western language dealing with the reform movement in Turkey is Edouard P. Engelhardt, *La Turquie et le tanzimat*, II (Paris: A. Cotillon, 1882). Among the recently published works the following two discuss this problem well, but from completely different points of view: Bernard Lewis, *The Emergence of Modern Turkey* (London–New York–Toronto: Oxford University Press, 1961) and Şerif Mardin, *The Genesis of Young Ottoman Thought; A Study in the Modernization of Turkish Political Ideas* (Princeton, N.J.: Princeton University Press, 1962).

limited to these lands. But we find similar and equally strong feelings within each national group in spite of their common negative attitude towards foreigners. Some of these feelings are endemic in all parts of the world: peasants distrust city dwellers and assume that governments exist only to collect taxes and levy soldiers; the growing antagonism of merchant, artisan, and landowner; regional differences; and provincialism—all are among those phenomena that make the emergence of the modern state and nation difficult everywhere. But in eastern Europe additional forces contributed to these centrifugal tendencies. Poland's provincial diets, Hungary's county governments, the institution of the military border in Croatia and Slavonia, the survival of the zadruga and bratsvo among the southern Slavs, tribalism in Albania, and the numerous privileges that in eastern Europe survived long after they had disappeared in the West divided the various nationalities even further. The Slav trader of the Ottoman empire had to overcome not only the advantages that the Greek enjoyed by being in business for a much longer time, but also those that Ottoman practice assured to the latter. In Hungary the prairie towns saw in the free royal towns their most dangerous competitors. Free peasants felt little community with the serfs. Numerous similar differences existed that were either considered worth defending or pernicious depending on the interest of those who came in touch with them. The circumstances that made linguistic demarcations usually coincide with institutional, social, and economic differentiation made the bridging of the many gaps even more difficult. The result of all these divisions produced numerous small segments whose xenophobia extended to everybody who belonged to another group.

The xenophobia both hindered and advanced the development of nationalism in eastern Europe. It divided every nationality into so many antagonistic fragments that it proved difficult to pull them together. But once this was done the distrust of everything foreign became a force in developing the identity and cohesion of the various nationalities. The poet Vörösmarty admonished his countrymen:

> Be faithfully devoted to your fatherland
> Oh Hungarian . . .
> Nowhere in the wide world

> Is there room for you but here
> Blessed or cursed by faith
> Here you must live and die.[48]

All nationalities shared this feeling once nationalism had taken root among them. They were convinced that they had to live and die on the land that they considered to be exclusively theirs. If there was no room for them elsewhere, there was no place left for others in their territories either. It proved very difficult to reach this point. Poland had to suffer and finally had to be partitioned before the search for an answer to the question, "did the disappearance of the state inevitably entail the eventual dissolution of the nation,"[49] broke down old dividing lines. The Hungarian peasant had to experience the bloody civil war of 1848–49 before he saw in the Magyar landlord (whom he continued to hate and to distrust) a closer relative than in the non-Magyar speaking peasantry. The Czechs had to see their moderate aims discredited by the *Ausgleich* to cease to be Bohemians, Moravians, or members of parties, while Czechoslovak nationalism never acquired general acceptance. The mistrust between the Romanians of Transylvania and the Regat plagued the interwar years in Romania, and one can still question the strength of Yugoslav nationalism when faced with particularistic feelings. Although it became somewhat more sophisticated and muted, distrust of one's neighbor, internal or external, is still the greatest difficulty faced by statesmen and politicians in eastern Europe today. It is important to remember that these antagonisms, while reinforced by nationalism, antedate it and have contributed much to its development.

On the eve of the *Ausgleich* František Palacký wrote: "We were in existence before Austria and we will still be here after she is gone."[50] He wrote with the assurance of a man who faced an im-

---

[48] From the poem "Szózat" by Mihály Vörösmarty (my translation—P.F.S.).

[49] Peter Brock, "Polish Nationalism." Paper presented at the Far Western Slavic Conference at Stanford University in April, 1965. The quotation is taken from p. 2 of the mimeographed text of this paper.

[50] This translation of Palacký's well-known sentence can be found in S. Harrison Thomson, *Czechoslovakia in European History* (2d ed.; Princeton, N.J.: Princeton University Press, 1953), p. 214.

pending calamity with the reassurance born from long study of his people's history.[51] The insight gained from his scholarship convinced Palacký that nothing could destroy the genius of his people and his countrymen shared his feelings because the works of this "father of the nation"[52] had rekindled their national consciousness and pride. Palacký's work was unique. He was the only historian whose work can be equated, for all practical purposes, with the beginning of a nationality's nationalism, and he was also the only one to place his people into the stream of the general European development instead of stressing their peculiar mission.

The other nationalities had their historians, too. Their work was also important and widely read, but instead of starting and shaping the new nationalistic trend it simply adjusted to it and reinforced its tendencies. But all historians shared the conviction expressed by Palacký's sentence: historical facts guaranteed the bright future of their nations. It was inevitable, once nationalism began to germinate in eastern Europe, that the thinking of patriots took a historical bend. Not only did the various institutions, traditions, values, and beliefs to which they adjusted the new impulses reaching them from the West make sense only in a historical context, but it was history alone that could uphold their claims and hopes, which a dismal present did not justify. The histories of Poland and Hungary supplied enough examples of ability and power to make it plausible for those who wanted to believe that all that was needed to make their countries great again was the revival of old and still existing talents. The Czechs could point to long centuries of intellectual leadership when they tried to convince themselves that they had a future in an age where cultural-technological progress was valued. The Romanians thinking of independence and unity in the face of overwhelming odds felt encouraged by the deeds of Stephen the Great and Michael the Brave. The Ottoman Empire had been a great power only a few decades ago. There was no reason why it could not regain its position among nations if it rid itself of vice and corruption. History, particularly selective history, was full of lessons, examples, and badly needed encouragement.

[51] By the time of the *Ausgleich* Palacký had finished his monumental work, *Geschichte der Böhmen* (10 vols.; Prague: Kronberger und Weber, 1836–1867).

[52] It was Masaryk who called Palacký "father of the nation."

Religious belief strengthened this feeling. Both Hungary and Poland claimed to be the *Regnum Marianum;* the Greeks were the champions of the only Orthodox Christian tradition; the Islamic outlook of the Ottomans assured them that their greatness was ordered by the Almighty. In dealing with these beliefs, all grounded in history, it is difficult to distinguish between religious conviction, superstition, romanticism, and wishful thinking. But they were, nevertheless, a force. The two Marian kingdoms as well as Moldavia and Croatia claimed to have saved Christianity and the West, serving as the ramparts of civilization against numerous attacks from the East. The West was in their debt, and the time for paying it had arrived. Zygmunt Krasiński wrote, addressing the Poles: "Whatever electric currents flow above the earth, You [God] gathered them all round our shades, that they might light up our returning bodies, when they rise up from the grave—to Europe's shame!"[53] Speaking for the Hungarians, Vörösmarty put the same feeling into one short demand addressed to humanity at large: "A thousand years of suffering demand life or death."[54]

In these and numerous other ways, pleas and hopes for a future justified by past greatness and services were addressed by all, if not always to mankind at large, then at least to the rulers. That the past on which these demands were based was as romantically distorted as were the visions of the future is something the eastern Europeans shared with Germany at least. They too demanded a place in the sun, but unlike the Germans, the eastern Europeans did not think of themselves as simply the men of the future, they were also those of the past, and the place they claimed was theirs by historic right. For this reason, history served not only as the proof of the validity but also as the justification of their claims. Soon it became a weapon. Long before the Austrians Bauer and Renner, the historians of eastern Europe began to differentiate between those capable of establishing and maintaining states and those who could not. Almost every nationality discovered its own "civilizing mission" through historical studies and based certain rights on this activity.

This question of rights and priorities became of paramount im-

---

[53] From the poem "Psalm Dobrej Wali" by Zygmunt Krasiński. For the original and the translation see M. A. Michael (trans.), T. M. Filip, *A Polish Anthology* (London: Duckworth, 1944), pp. 374–75.
[54] Vörösmarty, "Szózat."

portance, but they overlapped. No nationality had an unbroken written historical record with the exception of the Ottomans, and the validities of these contradictory claims were difficult to prove. Who could really solve, with the help of unimpeachable historical evidence, the problems arising from the medieval relations of Hungarians and Croats, or Czechs and Germans? Who could clarify the problems separating the Greek and Slav Orthodox churches? Did the Transylvanians miss the Battle of the White Mountain in 1620 on purpose? Was the Zrini-Zrinski-Zrinyi family Croat or Hungarian? Were the Hunyadis Hungarians or Romanians? These questions should have had little relevance for the difficulties the various people of eastern Europe faced in the late eighteenth and in the nineteenth centuries, but because everybody had to prove his own claims and missions, they grew into issues of the first magnitude. The Romanians, to use only one example, had a legitimate interest in the origins of their nation, but when this question was used both by them and the Hungarians to attack or defend the socioeconomic status quo in nineteenth century Transylvania, serious scholarship was perverted and the ridiculous aspects of the dispute were overshadowed only by its tragic implications. In these, its least scientific aspects, history served to increase everyone's self esteem and to diminish the stature of all others. Herder, as will be remembered, warned the historians not to make this mistake.

Each nationality attempted to produce a history at least as long and glorious as its neighbors, whose claims conflicted with its own. However, even biased and distorted history proved incapable of producing the desired result. What could not be claimed, even by the broadest and most imaginative use of the slightest evidence, was simply invented. Forgers like Kálmán Thaly and Wenzel Hanka became national heroes. Ferenc Kazinczy got so disgusted by the myth-creating activities of his countrymen (although the worst aspects occurred only after his death) that he admitted: "I am not ashamed to confess that I shudder at those who flatter panther wearing Árpád, and I count it a disgrace to be regarded as their companion."[55] Kazinczy was one of the few discriminating

[55] G. F. Cushing, *Hungarian Prose and Verse* (London: Athlone Press, 1956), p. XIV. Cited with a slight change in the translation by George Barany, "The Awakening of Magyar Nationalism," p. 13; this paper was presented to the Pacific Coast Branch of the American Historical Association in August, 1963.

people. The majority read true, exaggerated, and sometimes purely fictitious national histories with equal pleasure as long as they satisfied their growing need for national self-satisfaction.

At the beginning these histories were written in either German or Latin because the local languages, neglected for centuries, proved to be inadequate vehicles of expression. Linguistic reform, based on folk language and poetry, became as necessary as history for the national revivals in eastern Europe. The impetus was, once again, the German example. The romantic-cultural nationalism of Germany emphasized the importance of language as the carrier of national identity. Linguists like Obradović, Karadžić, Bessenyei, Kazinczy, Štur, Dobrowský, Sofroni, Koraes, Rhigas, and many others were as, if not more, important in the early development of eastern European nationalism as were the historians. Their work was consciously undertaken to serve the various nationalities in their efforts to reassert themselves. Most of these linguists were also poets who turned tales and legends into fact in their works. By the middle of the nineteenth century the average reader did not know whether his favorite poet put history into verse or created history with his rhymes. Poet and historian united their talents and imagination. Who cared about the truth when he read about Pan Tadeusz, Toldi, Kraljević Marko, and the other heroes; when he could laugh and cry identifying with these great figures of his nation? Poet and historian created the atmosphere, the enthusiasm, and the pride that transformed the past, the traditional institutions of each region, and the ideas of the West into tools in the hands of their politically minded countrymen.

This atmosphere had to be created artificially. Poland and the Ottoman Empire were rapidly disintegrating in the eighteenth century while by then the other nationalities of eastern Europe had lived under foreign rule for at least two centuries. There was little reason for optimism, let alone enthusiasm. Leadership was either lacking or was separated by language, privilege, or tradition from the masses. The uprising of the Romanian peasantry in Transylvania under Horia (Ion Ursu), Cloşca, and Crişan in 1784 was the most violent expression of dissatisfaction, but the unrest of the lower classes was universal. The Hungarian peasantry was on the brink of a *Jacquerie* in 1790, and the Polish and Romanian peasants had equally little reason to identify themselves with their nobles and boyars. The merchants and artisans, who had practically no political rights,[56] were less than enthusiastic defenders of the sacred constitutions and institutions. This fragmentation, already discussed on these pages, had to be overcome. Because those who enjoyed advantages were unwilling or slow to make sacrifices, unity in feeling was achieved by what we call propaganda today, and which became the work of the historians and poets. As revivers and glorifiers of the past if not inventors, these people could not attack privileges, the only surviving remnants from the days of greatness, until the "nation" was strong enough to withstand the stress of internal reorganization. These early propagandists were prevented from taking an egalitarian approach not only by the internal divisions within the groups to whom they spoke, but also by the subordinated position of their conationals within the existing state structures. Instead of equality the protagonists of nationalism offered superiority, the reversal of the positions occupied by the various nationalities within the various states.

In the development of nationalism anywhere, a moment arrives when a given group begins to believe that it is the "chosen people," and that all individual or class demands and complaints must be subordinated to the "national interest." In the relevant literature this type of nationalism is usually labeled integral. In the West this tendency gained substantial ground only after 1848 and did not become dominant until the last quarter of the nineteenth century when racism, social Darwinism, and imperialism represented a stage in the general development of western social and political thought. In eastern Europe this least tolerant form of nationalism appeared much earlier than in the West because nothing but this self-glorifying doctrine could have welded nationalities together in the face of the numerous external and internal difficulties.

The results were not only intransigance and righteous insistence on claims and rights, but certain specific new approaches to nationalism. Among these the Hungarian theory of right by conquest and the various pan-movements are the most noteworthy. Pan-movements originated among the Slavs, formally among the Czechs, in-

[56] Towns and cities were underrepresented, if represented at all, in the local or central legislatures of the various countries, provinces, or counties. Even municipal government was limited seriously in most parts of eastern Europe.

formally and even earlier among the southern Slavs.[57] While idealism, romanticism, and some superficial linguistic study were among the considerations that produced Illyrism, Austro-Slavism, Pan-Slavism, and Yugoslavism, it was mainly the realization of the particular Slav groups that they were too weak to go it alone that made them expand the limits of brotherhood. As a mere Montenegrin, Vladika Petar could not oppose the powerful Marshal Marmont, but as a son of "the greatest of all nations"[58] he could negotiate with him. Jovan Rajić, a Vojvodina Serb, disregarded religious and linguistic differences and published, in 1794, *A History of the Various Slav People, Especially Bulgars, Croats, and Serbs* showing a new awareness of the potential unity of these people. The same need for additional strength explains the more sophisticated later attempts at Slav unity centered in Prague that the Poles, living under Russian rule, could not join. The Slav example was followed by others. The young Turks developed Pan-Turanism, and the scientific work of Sándor Körösi-Csoma was the result of an attempt to find more Hungarians in central Asia and western Siberia. Nothing illustrates better that the root of all these movements was a search for strength than the fact that Latinism originated not in France or Spain, not even in divided Italy, but among the Romanians of Transylvania. In these pan-movements we see the same forces at work which we have observed in the development of eastern European nationalism. Only in these cases their scope was expanded to give them more weight.

VII

There is only one way in which the pieces of a jigsaw puzzle can be fitted together to produce a flawless, complete picture. Religious and laic institutions, constitutions and other political documents, the aversion to foreign rule, class privileges and economic change, the various forms of xenophobia, belief in a special mission, real or imaginary historical interpretations of the past, and the western

[57] The interesting study by Ante Kadić, "Croatian Renaissance," first presented at the meeting of the Far Western Slavic Conference at San Francisco State College in April, 1963 and dealing with the early manifestations of proto-pan-Slav feelings among the southern Slavs, still awaits publication.

[58] Alfred Fischel, *Der Panslavismus bis zum Weltkrieg; Eingeschichtlicher Ueberlick* (Stuttgart-Berlin: Cotta, 1919), p. 214.

ideas that were adapted to local needs are the pieces of a puzzle with one important difference: although always adding up to eastern European nationalism, they could and were joined together in different ways producing variants of the same basic picture. Some solutions were rejected, others gained general acceptance, but all versions contained the same basic puzzle pieces. The framework into which these pieces were set was determined by the geographic, political, social, and economic circumstances as well as by the power structure of eastern Europe in the eighteenth and nineteenth centuries. The shapes of the various pieces added further limitations to the possible pictures that could be assembled, but the human element with all its idealistic and realistic, selfless and selfish, pedestrian and imaginative impulses had, nevertheless, a wide choice of solutions. People were at least as important in determining the nature of eastern European nationalism as were the forces that moved them or those they set into motion.

Some groups, like the nobles in Poland, Hungary, Croatia, and the Romanian principalities, the tribal leaders in Albania, the knezes in the Serb lands, the merchants and professional people among the Czechs and Greeks, the Ottoman civil servants and soldiers, and the clergy almost everywhere, were in a better position to take the leadership of their peoples than were others. Better education and therefore contact with western ideas, privileges, control of the main political and economic institutions, and a traditionally accepted position of leadership were among the advantages they enjoyed. Certain elements, like the Bohemian nobility that wavered between German and Bohemian loyalties but could not identify itself with the Czech masses, were unable to profit from their privileged position. Others, like the Romanian boyars, proved too weak to retain leadership, while a third group, like the Greek merchants, was too disunited to become a decisive force. But revolutionary groups, willing and able to lead, emerged everywhere and fashioned, as much as possible, events and the emerging nationalistic trends in their own image. These are the people whom Seton-Watson has recently called the *intelligentsia* to distinguish them from the learned and educated.[59] The contribution of these

[59] Hugh Seton-Watson, *Nationalism and Communism, Essays 1946–63* (London: Methuen and Co., 1964). The most relevant is the first essay, "Nationalism and Multinational Empires," pp. 3–35.

people to the emergence of nationalism in eastern Europe will now be surveyed.

Just as in western Europe and Germany, nationalism in eastern Europe was a revolutionary force aiming at transferring sovereignty from the rulers to the people (irrespective of who "the people" were). Eastern European nationalism shared with all others the basically anticlerical, constitutional, and egalitarian orientation that gave it its revolutionary character. In spite of these similarities eastern European nationalism differed substantially from that of Germany and western Europe for reasons we have discussed on the preceding pages. Keeping in mind the features that eastern European nationalism shared with the West, as well as those which differentiated it, we can divide it further into four main groups. For convenience's sake we will call them bourgeois, aristocratic, popular, and bureaucratic eastern European nationalisms. Manifestations of almost all varieties can be detected in every region of eastern Europe. Yet at least in the early periods of nationalism, one of them dominated, and put its imprint on subsequent developments.

Of these four varieties, bourgeois nationalism most resembled that of the West. The aristocratic version, basically a contradiction in terms, produced the least constructive results. Popular nationalism vaguely resembles Jacksonian democracy, while the bureaucratic variety has much in common with the nationalism of the newly emerging countries of Africa and Asia in our days. Bourgeois nationalism triumphed only among the Czechs, Poland and Hungary are the best examples of the second, or aristocratic; Serbia and Bulgaria of the third; Turkey, Greece, and Romania of the fourth. There are good explanations for this development. Details will become clear from the material presented in the chapters devoted to individual countries even if the authors do not use the same expressions, but the basic characteristics of each variety and some indications of the circumstances under which they emerged must be surveyed now.

In the Czech provinces of the Habsburg Empire the aristocracy was powerful but foreign. Unable to share the aspirations of a population to which they did not belong, the nobles in these lands could not take effective advantage of their power. When their interest coincided with that of the rest of the population, as in the case of the struggle for more local and less centralized government, aristocrats and commoners collaborated. But this occasional partnership was insufficient to assure a leading role to the aristocracy in the shaping of Czech nationalism. At the same time these provinces, which had been closely associated with Germany and western Europe all through their history, shared the intellectual and economic progress of the West and were, therefore, able to approach nationalism in an almost western manner. This tendency was not only reinforced but to a large extent determined by the economic development of Bohemia and Silesia in the eighteenth century. Moravia, more backward in this respect, always tended to be more conservative than were the other two provinces whom it followed only because alone it could achieve nothing. In the two industrially most advanced provinces, a real third estate and within it a strong and viable bourgeoisie had developed and was ready to assume leadership by the time nationalism began to be a force. The various interests of the middle class were already strong enough by the time of the death of Maria Theresa to bridge, at least temporarily, the gap between Czech and German and to hold their own against both aristocracy and the lower classes. When, in the second half of the nineteenth century, Germans and Czechs ceased to cooperate, and most of the nobles and class-conscious workers were placed into the "enemy camp" as far as the Czechs were concerned, their nationalism became even more western or bourgeois in its outlook. From the beginning, in its advocacy of constitutional monarchy, parliamentarianism, federalism, paternalistic democracy, and economic emphasis, Czech nationalism closely resembled that of the classical liberals in the West. But there were also significant differences between Czech and western bourgeois nationalism, placing the Czech variant, according to our definition, in the eastern European family of nationalism.

As the Czechs had no state of their own, they were forced to include linguistic equality among the goals they tried to achieve within the framework of the Habsburg Empire. This lack of a state also made it imperative for Czechs to champion outdated rights and institutions (Staatsrecht, and so on) to justify their other demands. Consequently their outlook became less realistic and more historical-traditional than the bourgeois nationalism of western Europe. They looked to the West, sharing its traditions and development, but geography and political realities forced their nationalism into an eastern mold.

In Poland and Hungary, the situation was quite different from that in the Czech lands, although both countries had had close relations with the West for centuries. First of all, hostility to practically everything German was not as late in developing in these countries as it was among the Czechs, but was of long standing. Second, both countries lacked a real middle class, and a large percentage of those who could be called bourgeois were Germans. Finally, the aristocracies that controlled both the agrarian economy and the local and central legislatures were the most numerous in Europe. Within the ranks of the nobility there were great divisions—magnates and gentry were separated not only by the relative importance of their titles, but also by wealth, political influence, and levels of education. The interests of aristocracy and bourgeois often clashed, but facing rulers and commoners they managed to present a united front. Together they had an economic, political, and ecclesiastic power monopoly buttressed and protected by social status that produced enough strength to challenge even royal power. Charles VI (Charles III in Hungary) and Maria Theresa were forced and able to manage and manipulate the Hungarian nobility fairly successfully; Joseph II, the Saxon kings, and Stanislas Augustus in Poland were less successful. All of them, even Joseph II, realized sooner or later that they could not rule without the cooperation of the nobility.

The nobles looked at nationalism as a new, additional argument that could be used by them in their battle against their rulers, foreign or native, and it made relatively little difference to them under what flag they fought this battle. As long as they were able to equate *natio* with the "political nation," the *una eademque nobilitas* (to use the phrase of the Hungarians), and by doing this expand the circle of their supporters without giving up any or only secondary privileges, they were ready to become nationalists and to use their arguments. Nationalism was, as far as they were concerned, only a new proof of the correctness of their belief that the only legitimate source of power was the nation that they identified with their class. When pressed or in need of help, the nobles were willing to share some of their privileges with certain people, but they never admitted that others were entitled to what they enjoyed. They reserved for themselves the right to decide when, and who should be admitted, and to what degree, into membership in the political nation. They considered participation in the political life of their countries not a right but a privilege based on historic-feudal documents and tradition. Consequently their nationalism, although honestly patriotic and often revolutionary, remained exclusive, tradition bound, and estate conscious. This tendency was only reinforced by the policies of their adversaries, the emperors of Austria and Russia and the kings of Prussia.

Although commoners rose to positions of prominence in the nineteenth century in partitioned Poland and Hungary, the prestige of the nobility remained strong enough to induce those members of the middle class who achieved economic or political eminence to adopt the values and the way of life of the aristocracy. The nationalism of Poland and Hungary remained aristocratic until the end of the second World War. The spirit animating it did not change even if the personalities promoting it were non-nobles. This is why we cannot agree with the arguments presented by Endre Arató.[60] In regard to Hungary alone, he differentiates between the manifestations of aristocratic and bourgeois nationalism and his views of aristocratic nationalism do not differ substantially from that presented in these pages. Arató recognizes that aristocratic nationalism was dominant in Hungary in the developing years of modern nationalism, but he claims that it was superseded by bourgeois nationalism in the the two decades following 1830. The main difference between the two, in Arató's opinion, was that while aristocratic nationalism was mainly political in a narrow class sense, bourgeois nationalism placed the main emphasis on economic reform and in general paralleled the dominant trends of western nationalism in its demands. While Arató is correct in pointing to certain desiderata voiced by the leaders of the Lower House of the Hungarian Parliament in the 1840's, he forgets to mention the importance of economic issues in the unsuccessful negotiations that took place during

---

[60] The position taken by Arató in his chapter "A magyar nacionalizmus . . ." (see n. 32) is not unique, but reflects the approach of eastern European historians since the second World War to the problem of nationalism. It it with this approach and not specifically with Arató that this author disagrees.

the previous decades between the aristocratic nationalists and Vienna. Julius Miskolczy's study[61] shows quite clearly the importance of economic considerations in the program of those whom Arató considers aristocratic nationalists. Even if we admit that in the 1840's economic issues were stressed more than they had been previously, we must remember that

> . . . men like Kossuth tried to connect the claims of supremacy of the estate-conscious nobility with the demands of newly emerging nationalism. They opposed the crown as champions of the nation state concept, but denied to their non-Magyar fellow citizens the right to develop their nationalities in the name of the old Hungarian estate-state.[62]

In this quotation we find not only the reason for the tragic civil war that raged in Hungary in 1848–49 when national unity was so badly needed, but an additional explanation of why and how Hungarian nationalism retained its aristocratic character. It might have been the large number of minorities living within the boundaries of what the Magyars and Poles considered to be their countries that made them believe that they had to protect historical rights. The result is still the same.

The Romanian boyars were in the same advantageous position that the Hungarian and Polish nobles enjoyed. In spite of men of the stamp of Constantin Golescu, they stuck to their reactionary views consistently, in 1821, 1831–32, and 1848, until any solution under their leadership became impossible. The liberal group that emerged and was defeated in 1848 was too small and too powerless after that date to assert itself in the difficult political situation that prevailed in Moldavia and Wallachia prior to the Crimean War. Finally the various views expounded by the different nationalistic groups in the Principalities found little or no echo among the Romanians living in Transylvania, the Bukovina, or Bessarabia. The only point on which all Romanians agreed was the desire for national unity. The only form of nationalism that could count on the

[61] Julius Moskolczy, *Ungarn in der Habsburger-Monarchie,* of Karl Eder, Hugo Hantsch, and Hans Kramer (eds.), *Wiener Historische Studien* (Vienna–Munich: Herold, 1959), V, 57–62.

[62] Emil Franzel, *Der Donauraum im Zeitalter des Nationalitätenprinzips* (Bern: Dalp Taschenbücher, A. Francke; Munich: Leo Lehnen, 1958), p. 69.

Bureaucratic Nationalism.

irredentist

support of all Romanians was irredentist. This form of nationalism could offer hope for final success after 1859 when a united Romania made it an official state policy, and by so doing, the government became the leader of the national movement. Irredentist nationalism became the slogan with which the bureaucracy justified its actions and omissions and its condemnation of all opposition as unpatriotic. Nationalism became identified not only with nation and state, but also with the policy of the government.

Bureaucratic nationalism also developed in Greece and Turkey. While the Greek movement started among the merchants and other middle-class elements, this group lacked leadership, was dispersed all over Europe, and was unable to shape events during Greece's war of independence. The civil war that paralleled this event also proved that no other element of the population was able to impose its views on the rest. Greek factionalism remained a serious problem, making united action difficult even after Greece had gained her independence following the intervention of the Great Powers. Under these circumstances only the government and the bureaucracy could make their voices heard effectively everywhere in the country. The foreign dynasties and their military and civil servants, both foreign and domestic, were anything but popular and were in need of an issue that could unite the factions of the population and reconcile it with the government. Irredentist nationalism offered the solution for these needs and developed into the main domestic and foreign propaganda weapon that was entirely in the hands of the government. For reasons somewhat different from those in Romania, the same type of nationalism developed in Greece also. When one thinks of the Venizelist invasion of Asia Minor after the first World War and the Cyprus controversy in our days, it becomes quite evident how little the nature of Greek nationalism has changed since its inception.

Turkey presents the clearest case of bureaucratic nationalism. In this country the possibilities for the development of various kinds of nationalism were the most limited in all of eastern Europe. There was neither an aristocracy nor a middle class in the Ottoman Empire, and the clergy could not espouse nationalism, an ideal that clashed with Muslim theology and political theory. The intellectual and political life of the Turks in the Ottoman Empire was limited almost entirely to the military and civil servants, including students of the schools that trained people for jobs in the bureaucracy. Ideas of change and reform were limited to this circle and always had the improvement of the state's administrative organs and international position as its goals. Nationalism developed slowly under these circumstances. At first it was not an independent philosophy or movement, but simply an additional tool in the hand of those who tried to reorganize the bureaucratic machinery and strengthen the state. The first Turk who separated nationalism from bureaucratic reform and treated it as an issue by itself was Ziya Gökalp (1875–76–1924) whose first writings appeared in 1911,[63] but his ideas failed to influence the Turkish masses, although they shaped the thinking of many of his politically minded contemporaries, including Mustafa Kemal. It was the latter who tried to make nationalists of the Turks, but even he insisted on a special kind of nationalism that suited his plans and his vision of his country's future. His government promulgated the official nationalism of the Kemalist movement and opposed all its other manifestations. Not until the second half of the 1930's do we find significant nationalistic manifestations in Turkey that are free from bureaucratic sponsorship.

Popular nationalism, which could also be called populist or egalitarian nationalism, emerged in Serbia and Bulgaria. In these lands the long years of Ottoman rule had a leveling effect. The nobility had disappeared except in Bosnia and Macedonia where conversion to Islam had saved the estates of certain families. Not too numerous, these Muslim Slavs did not appear to differ from the feudatory and later hereditary Turkish landlords until the linguistic issue became important in the eyes of the Serb and Bulgarian nationalists. But because the lands that these people inhabited were not incorporated into Serbia or Bulgaria until the twentieth century, when nationalism was firmly enough established to be able to handle the seeming contradiction presented by the speech and faith of these people, their existence had little influence on the nationalism of Serbs and Bulgarians during its formative period. During these years the growing Slav merchant class was still too small to offer leadership. When it did, as in Bulgaria in the middle decades of the

---

[63] The best study in a western language dealing with Ziya Gökalp is Uriel Heyd, *Foundations of Turkish Nationalism. The Life and Teachings of Ziya Gökalp* (London: Luzac & Co. and The Harvill Press, 1950).

nineteenth century, it was both idealistic and realistic enough to develop an egalitarian policy. The views of the great peasant masses were, as those of this class usually are, basically democratic and directed mainly against landlordism. The facts that the landlords were mostly foreigners and that the traditional institutions and language of the peasantry had survived centuries of foreign rule thanks to the millet system furnished the ingredients for the development of popular nationalism.

This type of nationalism was developed by the native lower clergy and the Serbs and Bulgarians, mainly merchants, who lived outside the borders of the Ottoman Empire. The clergy's grievances and goals were similar to those of the peasantry, from which most of them sprang. In their case, *diocese* took the place of land and *foreign bishops* that of the foreign landlords. The Serbs of the Vojvodina and the Military Border, the Bulgars in Istanbul, Russia, Wallachia, and later Serbia furnished the required sophistication and the theoretical nationalist justification that shaped the native ingredients into popular nationalism. Under the existing social and economic conditions this was the only form of nationalism that could go beyond theory in Serbia and Bulgaria. As in the aristocratic nationalism of Hungary and Poland, the popular nationalism of Serbia and Bulgaria was subsequently diluted by princes, bureaucrats, and the advocates of the middle class, but it never lost its basic approach and character. Bulgaria was called "the peasant state" with good reason.[64] It takes little imagination to find one of the reasons for the grave difficulties Yugoslavia had to face between the two great wars of this century in the conflicting approaches to nationalism that the major nationalities of this country favored. Serbia's basic popular approach was weakened and became partly aristocratic when Beograd (Belgrade) tried to dominate Zagreb and Ljubljana. Neither approach suited the Croats whose approach was a mixture of the aristocratic and bureaucratic, nor the Slovenes, whose nationalism was bourgeois. Three different approaches to nationalism produced three different views of the state that their union had created. The tendency of the broad approach represented

[64] Edward Dicey, *The Peasant State. An Account of Bulgaria in 1894* (London: J. Murray, 1894), coined the excellent phrase "the peasant state," although his work leaves much to be desired.

by the pan-movements, in this case Yugoslavism, was replaced and reversed when the varying nationalisms of three disparate people had to be reconciled within one state structure. Nationalism, which originally justified the demands for independence and union, revealed itself as a force that found its goal in itself.

T. ZAVALANI

Albanian Nationalism

I

The debate concerning the origin of the Albanians is still unresolved, though no one questions the fact that they are the oldest inhabitants of the Balkan Peninsula. Their language, customs, social organizations, and traditions have very little if anything in common with those of their Slav and Greek neighbors. Although a small country, Albania's geography is sufficiently diverse to have made communication difficult prior to modern times and to favor small local units and their autonomous development. With their villages consisting of scattered *kulas* ("towers") on the mountain slopes, high plateaus, and deep narrow valleys the Albanian clans have maintained their local patriotism and customs practically to the present. This diversity was further enhanced by the religious differences that have developed in Albania. The north, contiguous to the lands of Latin Christianity, favored Catholicism; the south, in close contact with the Greek world, turned to Orthodoxy. The Christian faiths suffered a serious setback when about two thirds of the population inhabiting the central regions of the country accepted Islam at the time of the Ottoman conquest of the country following the death of Skanderbeg (Gjergj Kastrioti) in 1468. The important part played by Albanian Muslims in the history of the Ottoman Empire is well known. Numerous grand viziers, viziers, paşas, and military commanders of Albanian origin contributed substantially to the exploits of the Ottomans. What is not so well known is the part these Muslim Albanians played in their own country. Just as the converts of Bosnia and Macedonia, the Albanian Muslims too developed a landowning-administrative aristocracy that practically ruled Albanian lands at will and was able to defend its position and privileges whenever some overzealous Ottoman governor tried to challenge its authority. The clans, Muslim as well as Christian, defended their regions and self-governing communities in the highlands against the local Muslim lords with the same determination with which they opposed the actions of the Ottoman bureaucracy. When, in the eighteenth and nineteenth centuries, the central government of the Ottoman Empire declined and became less and less able to enforce its will, local Albanian governors asserted themselves more and more.

The eighteenth century is generally accepted as the century in which modern nationalism developed. Among the preconditions for its growth the following appear to have been the most important: advanced centralization, religious unity, leadership by a self-conscious class (aristocracy, bourgeoisie, intelligentsia), foreign intellectual stimulus, discontent with foreign rule, and linguistic unity. Albania enjoyed none of these preconditions for the development of modern nationalism. There was an aristocracy, but it was far from united. The traditional leaders of the clans based their claims to leadership and eminence on quite different arguments than did the Muslim landlord-administrators with their Ottoman titles. The views of the central government held by these people differed sharply, and they were as ready to fight each other as they were to fight Ottomans or other non-Albanians.

The existence of two main dialects, Gheg in the north and Tosk in the south, created some difficulties in achieving national unity but these were clearly overcome at the first national gathering in Prizren in 1878. In the end it was on this linguistic unity and the feeling of oneness, as opposed to the Slav and Ottoman newcomers, that Albanian national unity was founded.

II

The decline of the control that the Ottoman government was able to exercise over its numerous provinces reached castastrophic proportions in Anatolia during the second half of the eighteenth century. In the Balkans

the central government was able to maintain some measure of direct control. But there too the *ayan,* the new aristocracy of "notables," were steadily taking over the functions of government, and by the end of the eighteenth century the notables of Rumelia, with their private armies, treasuries, and courts of law, had rivalled the independence of the Anatolian valley-lords.[1]

Few if any of these *ayan* have become as well known universally as the Albanian Ali of Tepelen, better known either as Ali Paşa of Janina (Iõánnina) or Ali the Lion. Ali, who was courageous, reckless, and unscrupulous, rose rapidly in the Ottoman service and was finally appointed Governor of Janina. Once he gained this position he decided to carve a state for himself in southern Albania without formally breaking ties with Istanbul. During the years 1798–1820, so crucial a juncture in European and Balkan history, he was not only able to repulse the various armies sent against him by the sultan, but was also strong enough to play a minor role on the stage of world history. This aspect of his activities is well enough known. Less known and more important for our purpose is his rule over the people under his jurisdiction.

Ali of Tepelen, himself illiterate, was in many ways a "modern" ruler. He recognized the importance of strong central government, of sound finances, and of a mercenary army fully dependent on its master. In building his "state" he showed equal tolerance for all creeds and was equally harsh on all those, like the Muslim Tchameria or the Christian Suli and Himara clans, that resisted his centralizing tendencies. He was a harsh ruler, collected heavy taxes mercilessly, but "he . . . established the most perfect tranquility, and security of Persons and Property throughout his dominions whose Inhabitants, Greeks, and Turks, are richer, happier, more contented than in any other part of European Turkey."[2] According to another contemporary observer speaking of the people living under his rule,

. . . there is a spirit of independence and a love of the country in the whole people which, in a great measure, does away with the vast distinction observed in the other parts of Turkey between the followers of the two religions; for when the natives of other provinces . . . being asked

[1] Bernard Lewis, *The Emergence of Modern Turkey* (London–New York–Toronto: Oxford University Press, 1961), p. 38.

[2] Letter of W. Hamilton to Lord Hawkesbury, May 6, 1803, in J. W. Baggally, *Ali Pasha and Great Britain* (Oxford: Blackwell, 1938), pp. 87–88, quoted by Leften S. Stavrianos, *The Balkans Since 1453* (New York: Rinehart, 1958), p. 219.

what they are will say "we are Turks" or "we are Christians," a man of this country answers "I am Albanian."[3]

Ali Paşa of Janina was not the only one to establish a personal state within the state in Albania. In northern Albania Mehmet Bushati rose through the ranks of the Ottoman service to the governorship of Shkodër (Skutari). He established something like a dynasty, being followed by his son, Kara Mahmut, and then by the latter's nephew, Kara Mustafa. The latter became an ally of the Paşa of Janina whose niece he married, but his rule lasted longer, until 1831. At the peak of their power the Bushatis ruled over the entire northern part of Albania, extending their domain southward to Tirana and Elbasan.

The attitude of the Bushatis towards the central government was the same as Ali the Lion's; nominal submission, but *de facto* independence and, if necessary, even armed resistance. But their policy towards their fellow Albanians was totally different. Northern and eastern Albania's high mountains harbor the "eagles' nests" of the most independent-minded mountaineer clans. These had been able to keep their self-governing communities and traditional law codes through the centuries of Ottoman rule, and their only contact with official authorities, represented by the governor of Shkodër, was their own chief, the standard-bearer. The Bushatis did not attempt to break down this system to establish a centralized administration, but concluded alliances with these proud mountain people irrespective of their religion. The success of this policy is best attested to by the following facts: for the first time in history the mountain clans agreed to pay a tax of one ducat yearly for each household; Muslim and Catholic fought side by side in the Bushati armies; peace and with it economic prosperity came to northern Albania.

The sultans Selim III and Mahmud II, both of whom had ideas of reform, could not agree to Bushati rule any more than they could accept the independence of Ali of Tepelen. Kara Mahmut died fighting the armies of his nominal overlord in 1796 and his successor lost his domain, though not his life, while defending the fortress of

[3] J. C. Hobhouse, *A Journey Through Albania and Other Provinces of Turkey in Europe and Asia to Constantinople During the Years 1809–1810* (London: J. Cawthorn, 1813), p. 139.

Rosofat in 1831. Sultan Selim III pardoned Kara Mustafa and even used him once more in his bureaucracy.

The masters of Janina and Shkodër were not nationalists. Even their patriotism can be questioned, although they professed to be Albanians when it suited their purpose. Doubtless their main motive for action was lust for power and wealth. Nevertheless a study of Albanian nationalism in modern times must begin with them. They were able to unite for several decades considerable parts of the country under common administrations, to curb the particularism of numerous local lords, to make clans of differing religions collaborate in peace as in war. Although using different methods both Ali and the Bushatis taught their countrymen lessons in the advantages of centralized government, and by leading Muslims in battle against the Sultan-Caliph they successfully destroyed the belief that every Muslim was a Turk with interests best represented by the Porte. Local solidarity beyond the clan level made its appearance in Albania under their leadership. The precedent, while of transient significance at the time, became important half a century later when Ali Paşa and the Bushatis became heroes in the eyes of Albanian nationalists who viewed their exploits as early manifestations of nationalism.

But prior to the appearance of bona fide nationalists, decades of seeming inactivity followed the turbulent days of the Bushatis and Ali Paşa. The period between 1826 and 1876 is known in Ottoman history as the *Tanzimat*. The man who commanded the imperial forces to which Kara Mustafa surrendered in 1831, the Grand Vizier Mehmet Reşid Paşa, was the first outstanding leader of the reform movement centered in Istanbul. The movement aimed at rejuvenating the Ottoman Empire by eliminating corruption, and by introducing numerous reforms, particularly in administration and fiscal management, usually along French lines. While it is not our purpose to survey and assess the *Tanzimat* as such it is useful to note the influence it had in Albanian lands.

In moving against Kara Mustafa, Reşid Paşa seemed as much interested in eliminating all centers of resistance to the central government as in introducing reforms into regions that his armies were reconquering. For this reason he not only had to defeat the last Bushati, but he also had to make certain that no one take his place.

This accounts for his order that resulted in the wholesale massacre of Albanian landlords who came to his headquarters at Bitolj (Monastir), protected by safe-conducts, to offer their submission to the sultan. The reforms introduced into Albania after 1831 included: new taxes that had to be paid regularly by everyone, without regard to past privileges and immunities; the demand of service in the Ottoman army coupled with an interdict on the possession of arms by the civilian population; the introduction of a new administrative division and a new fiscal system patterned on that of France. While these reforms made sense from the point of view of the central government, and while the interdict against arms in civilian hands conformed to universal standards, they were deeply resented by the Albanians. The new administrative units disregarded local conditions and traditional units and placed people accustomed to obeying the same authorities under different jurisdictions; new taxes are always unpopular; service in the Ottoman army, far away from home, was considered a burden and with good reason; and for an Albanian to give up his arms, whose possession he considered his right as well as evidence of independence and virility, was an utmost indignity. In the northern mountains the *Tanzimat* reforms remained a dead letter. No one paid taxes, arms were not handed in, the administration was ignored, and the several clans continued to rule themselves according to traditional law, the *Kanun of Lek Dukagin,* called after the man who first codified it in the fifteenth century. Fighting the sultan's battles was a tradition that remained honored, but Albanians continued to fight as professionals in their own units under the leadership of their own standard bearers.

Elsewhere the reforms were carried out, more or less, with the help of local dignitaries. Without them the civil servants sent to Albania from Istanbul could not perform their functions. The reforms appeared to be taking effect and the new bureaucracy functioned, but the old established holders of power continued to enjoy their privileges, prestige, estates, and influence.

Everywhere, especially in the highlands, reforms were resented without reference to their utility and value. They represented change imposed from the outside and seemed to jeopardize long-cherished local habits and traditions. Moreover, they entailed new obligations. Resistance, often taking the form of armed uprisings, became the order of the day. The names of leaders who fought and were defeated joined the list of the other "national heroes," and locally conceived resistance to Istanbul, inconceivable in Muslim theory, continued as in the days of Ali Paşa and the Bushatis. These movements protected old and often outdated local customs against attempts at modernization and might reasonably be labeled reactionary. But just as tradition promoted resistance in other parts of eastern Europe, the actions of Albanians stemmed from a defensive, even blind love of their own way of life, tradition, right, and privilege. They thus kept alive, nurtured, and strengthened the tendencies already evident in the previous period. They also made possible the forging of genuine nationalists, and set the stage for Albanian action during the turbulent years of 1875–78.

III

It was only during the Balkan crisis of 1875–78 that the Great Powers became fully conscious of the Albanians. At the time of the Bushatis and Ali Paşa, Europe was deeply involved in the crises of the French Revolution and the Napoleonic wars. Ali Paşa became known in the cabinets of the west. The British and French briefly regarded him as a useful but not too important or reliable potential ally in their struggle for the mastery of the Mediterranean. Yet no one thought of him as an Albanian leader. He was simply seen as a Muslim paşa, an appointee of the sultan, seeking his own personal advantage. After 1815, when nationalism began to intrude into the calculations of European statesmen, Ali, in his capacity of Ottoman paşa and a Muslim, appeared to the British as a nuisance. But by then they had become masters of the Mediterranean and, indeed, sponsors of Mahmud II's reforms. The resistance of Albanians against the *Tanzimat* reforms was of no real concern to the Great Powers. Public opinion, that rather novel and often nationalistic phenomenon in Europe, was almost totally oblivious of the Albanians. Greece, with its glorious heritage and merchant colonies all over Europe, had captured the continent's imagination as soon as it rose against its Ottoman masters. And while the Slavs found a protector in Russia, for ideological and politico-diplomatic reasons, Albania remained unimportant to those powers, large and small, interested in the future of the European provinces of the Ottoman Empire.

The Albanians started the movement for national emancipation much later than their neighbors because they had to overcome serious linguistic, religious, and regional differences. The Bushatis, Ali Paşa, and other local leaders never did make up their minds as to what they really were: local leaders, petty dynasts, or Muslim dignitaries of the Ottoman Empire. Thus they fought for the sultans as often as they fought against them. In the name of the sultan they opposed the independence drives of their Greek or Slav neighbors who began to look at the Albanians as Muslims-Ottomans-Turks, in short, enemies and allies of Istanbul. They had done nothing to disabuse the Great Powers who thought of Albanian lands as a "Turkish" province of the Ottoman Empire. No one seemed interested, therefore, in liberating the Albanians, whose actions in 1875–78 came as a general surprise.

This surprise came in the form of a memorandum containing the resolutions of the Albanian or Prizren League submitted to the Congress of Berlin on June 15, 1878. The main problems faced by and the decisions taken at the Congress of Berlin require no review here. But it is worthy of note that Albanian affairs, seldom mentioned in studies of the Berlin Congress, did raise significant problems for the statesmen and diplomats assembled in the German capital. Although the western powers and Austria-Hungary were determined to nullify the advantages secured by Russia at San Stefano, they were willing to award prizes to the victors. Among these was Montenegro to whom the statesmen at Berlin assigned the districts of Gusinje and Plava. These territories had an Albanian population and for the first time a great majority if not all Albanians, and not only the people living in these regions, felt menaced as well as slighted. Political committees suddenly sprang up everywhere, and in June, 1878, their leaders gathered at Prizren to establish an Albanian League for the Defense of the Rights of the Albanian Nation. Their association is known either as the Albanian or the Prizren League. Among its prominent members were Ilyaz Paşa of Dibra, the hereditary chief of the Catholic Mirdita, Prenh Bid Doba, Hodo Paşa of Shkodër, and Ali Paşa of Gusinje. Although refusing any official position, the leading figure of the meeting was Abdul Frashëri, the first member of a leading southern Albanian family to play an important role in Albania's history. It was he who united all those present and instilled in them the will to fight for more than just Gusinje and Plava. "The fatherland has invited us to place ourselves at its service. We make no distinction between creeds. We are all Albanians."[4] This became the tenet of the Prizren League, and they so informed the Congress of Berlin. Bismarck dismissed the League's appeal and denied that something called the Albanian nation existed. He was soon to learn otherwise.

The Albanians did more than send memoranda to Berlin. When the Montenegrins tried to occupy the regions alloted to them, they found Albanians under Ali Paşa of Gusinje waiting for them. After heavy fighting the Montenegrins retired. Ali Paşa became a hero to whom the great Albanian poet, the Franciscan father, Gjergj Fishta, dedicated the most moving cantos of his epic *Lahuta e Malcis*. Montenegro turned to the powers again, and in April, 1880, a special border commission accepted the so-called Corti Compromise. This awarded the Hoti and Gruda districts to Montenegro in place of those for which the Albanians fought two years earlier. While the Sublime Porte accepted this solution, the Albanian League not only rejected it, but once more prevented the Montenegrins from taking the territory awarded to them. The powers had to revise their decision for a second time. This time they assigned the port of Dulcingo to Montenegro, and while the Albanians rejected this solution, too, the powers determined to enforce their will by force if necessary. Pressure was put on the Ottoman Government; ships of the great powers appeared before Dulcingo and threatened Izmir. Dulcingo finally surrendered when an Ottoman army joined the naval forces blockading it. The action of the Prizren League was not in vain. In the final settlement Montenegro received only about half the territory she had been first granted,[5] and the Great Powers became clearly aware of the Albanians.

The question presented by Montenegrin claims was not the only one to which the League paid close attention. The southern borders of Albania were also in danger. Although they did not participate in the wars of 1875–78, the Greeks were determined to participate in the division of the spoils. For the first time in modern history Epirus appeared as a Greek claim in documents submitted to the

[4] Stavro Skendi, "Beginnings of Albanian Nationalist and Autonomous Trends; The Albanian League, 1878–1881," *The American Slavic and East European Review*, XII, No. 2 (April, 1953), p. 220.

[5] See map in J. Swire, *Albania; The Rise of a Kingdom* (London: Williams and Ungate, 1929), p. 48.

delegates at Berlin. According to the definition of the government in Athens, the border of this province was the Kalamas River with Janina falling into Greece. Great Britain was strongly opposed to any discussion of the Greek claims at Berlin, and Disraeli informed the delegates "that Her Majesty's government 'has given Athens' the advice not to count on territorial gains."[6] But on the insistence of France, Greek claims were nevertheless considered. It was decided that Greece and Turkey should discuss the problem, submitting their findings to the powers.

At Berlin the British suggested that Greek claims be modified before they were discussed. According to the British, the lower valley of the Kalamas, the northern limit of classical Greece, should represent the maximum demand of Greece, leaving Janina in Ottoman territory. The French insisted that this city be handed over to the Greeks. To this the Ottomans objected pointing out that the Albanians would never accept the cession of Janina. In Albania the Prizren League made preparations for armed resistence. After long negotiations, during which several solutions were suggested and rejected, the Ottomans offered to accept the Arta River, approximately seventy miles south of the Kalamas, as the dividing line between their country and Greece. The ambassadors of the powers at Berlin, sitting as a commission, gladly accepted this solution. Lord Granville, foreseeing Greek objections, flattered and warned the Greek minister at London, Coumoundouros, to show "that the Greek people possess that self-control, that judgement, and that statesmanship which alone consolidate the lasting welfare of nations."[7] Greece accepted the decision of the powers, and the final settlement of the Ottoman-Greek border was signed on May 24, 1881. In this case the Albanians obtained success without recourse to arms.

In defending borders that were both theirs and the Ottoman Empire's the members of the Albanian League could and did work hand in hand with Istanbul. Hence outsiders often regarded the League as simply an instrument created by the Ottoman government. In reality, the League grew from local committees into a national organization that was quite willing to fight the Ottomans.

[6] Édouard Driault et Michel Lhéritier, *Histoire Diplomatique de la Grèce de 1821 à nos jours* (5 vols.; Paris: Presses Universitaires, 1925–26), III, 505.

[7] *Ibid.*, IV, 136.

Differences between Ottoman authorities and the League are even more clearly discernible in the sphere of internal affairs.

One of the League's most important activities was its attempt to secure national autonomy for the Albanians. Like the Czechs, the Albanians realized that given the weakness and relative backwardness of their country they would face grave dangers should they achieve independence at once, and their aim was autonomy and self-government within the Ottoman Empire with goals not too different from those of the Czech Austro-Slavs. They demanded that their lands form a single administrative district, that in this district Albanians should be admitted to high positions, that taxes be used to improve their lands, that schools be opened with Albanians teaching in Albanian, and that complete religious freedom and equality be introduced. These demands were included in a charter, and the League organized extended exchanges between the north and the south to popularize the charter and to bring the various parts of the country into closer union. Lord Goschen, the British Ambassador at Istanbul, favored the Albanian demands. On July 26, 1880, he wrote to Lord Granville: "Whatever the history of the movement may be, I venture to submit to your Lordship, as I have done before, that *the Albanian excitement cannot be passed over as a mere manoeuvre conducted by the Turks in order to mislead Europe and evade its will.* Nor can it be denied that the Albanian movement is perfectly natural . . . ."[8] In the same letter Goschen expressed the opinion that "if a strong Albania should be formed the excuse for the occupation by a Foreign Power in case of the dissolution of the Ottoman Empire would be greatly weakened . . . I consider that, in proportion as the Albanian nationality could be established, the probability of European intervention in the Balkan Peninsula would be diminished."[9] In other words, Goschen considered the Albanian demands both justified and advantageous for the future peace of the Balkans. The Ottomans thought otherwise. In April, 1881, they sent an army to Albania, broke the resistance of

[8] Goschen to Granville, July 26, 1880, in *Accounts and Papers*, 1880, Vol. 81, Turkey No. 15 (1880), No. 81 quoted by Skendi, "Beginnings of Albanian National-ist . . . ," pp. 228–29 and Swire, *Albania; The Rise of a Kingdom*, p. 54 (Goschen's italics).

[9] *Ibid.*, quoted by Skendi, "Beginnings of Albanian Nationalist . . . ," p. 228 and Swire, *Albania*, p. 1.

the local forces and arrested the leaders of the Albanian League. Abdul Frashëri was first condemned to death, a sentence then commuted to life imprisonment. Several others, including Prenk Bib Doba, were deported to Anatolia. The recommendation of Lord Fitzmaurice, British representative on the International Commission for Eastern Rumelia, stressing that "the Commission ought not separate without having given . . . tangible proof to the Albanians that the powers were concerned for their welfare,"[10] were completely disregarded.

Although its aims were seemingly defeated by 1886, the work of the Albanian League had lasting effects. Its action contributed substantially to the maintenance of the territorial integrity of the country, it brought the existence of the Albanian nation to the attention of the Great Powers, it produced for the first time united Albanian action, and brought to the forefront leaders capable of assessing the national condition, articulating Albanian aspirations and relating these to contemporary European developments. The struggles of the League, moreover, gave its leadership invaluable experience in the face of complex problems. The background was, after all, disheartening; it was aptly described by Swire as follows:

The preservation by the Turks of the authority of the feudal Beys, and the fostering of jealousy between them to the extent that on occasions we even find one supporting the suzerain power against another, in pursuit of some local advantage; the discord between the tribes of the north; the feuds and civil strife; the opportunities offered to Albanians in the Turkish service; the conversion of many Albanians to Mohammedanism; and the security provided by the Porte against the Slav and other foes; all these factors had combined to submerge the spirit of nationalism. They had not, however, drowned it.[11]

The Albanian League rekindled the feeling of national identity at the time of mounting nationalism throughout the Balkans and a crescendo in the rivalries of the Great Powers.

Beginning with 1878 we thus find signs of burgeoning nationalism in Albania. Great efforts were made to create a unified language,

---

[10] Sir Edward Hertslet, *The Map of Europe by Treaty* (London: Butterworths, 1875–1901), IV, 3006.

[11] Swire, *Albania,* p. 42.

to minimize religious differences and stress ethnic unity, and to instill national pride in the population. Just as the early nationalists did elsewhere in eastern Europe, the Albanians, too, turned to history for arguments that would substantiate their tenets. The pre-Ottoman, even the pre-Christian past became important, and something like Albanian Illyrianism developed. A search for national heroes and heroic episodes began. Fragmentary, contradictory, and often even flimsy accounts of the past were coupled with the discoveries of modern archeology, ethnography, and linguistics and were used by writers and poets to create a history of which every Albanian could be proud. In their zeal they sometimes drew far-fetched conclusions from flimsy evidence. The Albanians succeeded in involving their conationals in such endeavors better than did the early nationalists of the other eastern European countries. Consequently, too, many Albanians formed too exalted an opinion of themselves and their past and expected Europe to grant them what belonged to them by hereditary right. They had to learn at great expense that freedom had to be conquered by each people for itself, and then had to be defended.

Among these early nationalists one can easily discern two schools. The first—enthusiastic, romantic, popular, and often fanciful—was constituted, as elsewhere, by a veritable phalanx of poets and writers of genuine talent. The greatest among them was Gjergj Fishta. Born in a northern mountain village, he became a Franciscan, and was trained for the priesthood in Rome. His long epic poem, *Lahuta e Malcis* (The Saga of the Mountain), written in the Gheg dialect of the north became the bible of Albanian nationalists. Using the verse form of Albanian folklore, it is a long story depicting the age-old struggle of Albanians and Slavs. It concentrates mainly on the heavy fighting that took place during the period of the Berlin Congress and mixes historical fact with legend in several of its most famous cantos. The poem also deals with the political actions of the same period, including those of the Albanian League and the Great Powers. All these events are discussed from the point of view of the free Albanian mountaineer who did not pay his taxes and refused to serve in the sultan's army. Love of freedom and religion, both Christian and Muslim, are exalted, but the ancient superstitions and pagan spirits are treated with understanding and sympathy. The fairies Ora and Zana guide the dragons, who in Albanian tradition represent courage, and the brave warriors in a titanic struggle against the apocalyptic beast Kulshedra and the Montenegrins. At the end the dragons destroy Kulshedra. Reaching this ending, Father Fishta gave free vent to his powerful imagination, creating the most beautiful and impressive passages of his work. He is rightly revered by the Albanians as their greatest poet; he was equally skilled in writing lyric, epic, or satirical poetry. His poems were recited by highland bards and inspired the mountaineers with an ardent patriotism while teaching them respect for each other's religion. "We are brothers, nobody can separate us," was the slogan that became popular under the influence of his writings.

The *Lahuta e Malcis,* written in a special form of the Gheg dialect of the north, was practically incomprehensible to the Tosk speakers of the south. This region produced its own poets—among whom Naim Frashëri, the brother of the leader of the Prizren League, is the best known. Although he was not as talented as Father Fishta, and lacked the fiery imagination of his northern compatriot, he shared his sincere patriotism and love of the country. His soft-spoken, bucolic poems exalt the beauty of the land, the simple life of the peasants and shepherds, the charm of women carrying water or washing clothes in the rivers. The warmth, sincerity, and nostalgia of these poems, expressed by a poet who, ironically, had to leave Albania at an early age, has inspired two generations of Albanians with love of country.

Most of the poets and writers had to work in exile. Their works were printed abroad and distributed clandestinely in Albania where, after 1786, the Albanian language was banned. The only exceptions to this ban were the Jesuit and Franciscan schools in Shkodër, which enjoyed the protection of Italy and Austria-Hungary. In theory these were seminaries for training priests, but lay students also attended and several national leaders of the second generation were trained in these schools.

In spite of these difficulties, Albanian nationalism began to take shape under the influence of poets and the schools. The danger that religious differences would hopelessly split the nation was averted, and Muslims and Christians alike came to think of themselves as Albanians. Yet, this process was slowed down by the sporadic local conflicts rising from religious differences, which continued to plague Albania.

The poets and writers concentrated on the revival or creation of a national spirit, and both by avocation and in their aim they were enthusiastic and ambitious. The political leaders of the nationalist movement were less sanguine: they strongly believed that the international situation and especially the conditions in the Balkans during the last quarter of the nineteenth century were not favorable for achieving full Albanian independence. They feared that a weak, poor, and defenseless Albania would easily become the prey to the nationalistic-imperialistic proclivities of her stronger neighbors and expected no help from the Great Powers. For all too long, Albanian politicians hoped to obtain from Ottoman authorities administrative and cultural autonomy of the Albanian provinces of Shkodër, Kossovo, Bitolj, and Janina, all within the framework of the Ottoman Empire. Their views and tactics were put to a test by the Revolution of the Young Turks in 1908.

IV

In July, 1908, the Young Turks forced Sultan Abdul Hamid II to restore the Constitution of 1876, which he had suspended in 1877. The victorious revolutionaries proposed and attempted to transform the Ottoman Empire into a liberal constitutional monarchy, into a commonwealth where each nationality would enjoy full political and religious equality and the right of self-government. In part, at least, they sought to eliminate the causes for continued intervention into internal Turkish affairs by the Great Powers and to counter the hostile propaganda of the Balkan states.

The political wing of the Albanian nationalists, who organized a mass demonstration in favor of the revolution in the Kossovo district, hailed this program because it promised them, by peaceful means, the type of self-government within the Ottoman Empire that they had been demanding for thirty years. Their approach and program seemed to be vindicated; all over Albania political clubs were opened, and an impressive nationalistic propaganda campaign was developed through pamphlets, lectures, and mass meetings. In November, a National Congress assembled at Monastir. Among the delegates were Father Fishta and Midhat Frashëri, son of Abdul Frashëri, the leader of the Prizren League. The Congress placed great emphasis on education, gave a tremendous impetus to the printing activities in the country, especially in Bitolj, Korcha, Shkodër, and Salonika (Thessaloniki), and established numerous schools all over the country. The two schools of Shkodër were enlarged to provide secondary education for lay pupils, while a teacher-training institute was established in Elbasan. The Congress elected a Committee of National Unity to take over the management of Albania and sent its most prominent leaders as deputies to the Ottoman Parliament in Istanbul.

The action of the Albanians, and other minority groups, went much further than the limit the Young Turks had in mind. The political party of the Young Turks, the Committee of Union and Progress, countered these activities by a program of Ottomanism, which aimed to assure a large measure of central control in the Ottoman Empire and, while maintaining the principle of self-government for the nationalities, demanded that they be Ottoman patriots primarily. In practice, Ottomanism signaled the return to the old oppressive measures of the previous Ottoman regime. The new persecutions appeared even more intolerable than the old ones because the new regime was more efficient and because its reversal of policy dashed the hopes and enthusiasm generated by the revolution.

The Albanian leaders in Istanbul, far distant from home, were somewhat out of touch, did not see what went on in their country, and could not judge the reaction of their conationals. They could not give leadership to the growing popular movement from afar. Furthermore, they continued to believe that their policy was correct and persisted in efforts to persuade the Ottoman government to grant self-government to Albania within the empire. The leaders of the Turkish Committee of Union and Progress did not realize the advantages they might gain by granting the Albanians' demands at the very time they faced a growing hostility among the Balkan states and refused to change their policy.

While the Albanian deputies tried to negotiate at Istanbul a revolt broke out in Albania, on the Kossovo Plains. The most prominent leaders of this insurrection were the landlord Hassan Prishtina and Isa Buletin, a self-made man of peasant origin, a born leader of fearless courage and unbending character. The revolt, engulfing all the northern and central sections of the country, lasted for three years (1909–12). In the south the movement gathered only few followers and the struggle there was limited to the action of guerrilla bands.

By the middle of June, 1912, Hassan Prishtina and an army of some 50,000 men established headquarters in his home town, Prishtina. The situation seemed favorable and victory possible, but operations were suspended when news arrived that the Ottoman government had resigned and that the new Grand Vizier, Mukhtar Paşa, was willing to negotiate with the revolutionaries. Two hundred and fifty delegates from every corner of the country arrived at Prishtina, studied and rejected the government's proposals as unsatisfactory. The Albanians demanded the dissolution of Parliament and the appointment of Qamil Paşa to the position of Grand Vizier. Qamil was the popular choice of the Ottoman Empire for this position, and under the growing pressure of international events he was appointed Grand Vizier in early August, 1912. It was to his government that the Albanians submitted their requests. The twelve points of the Albanians[12] included, in addition to the usual demands of administrative unity, political self-government, and educational, linguistic, and cultural freedom, the demand that all Albanians be allowed to bear arms at all times and the request that two former grand viziers, Hakki and Said paşas, be impeached.

Ibrahim Paşa, heading a delegation appointed by the Turkish government, arrived from Istanbul and began to negotiate. He refused to consider only three of the Albanian demands. He argued that if Albanians were to serve as soldiers only in their homeland the unity of the national army would be destroyed, because the other nationalities would be justified in demanding the same consideration. He pointed out that achievement of other demands would give Albanians mastery over their own country and that it would be to the advantage of the Albanian authorities to administer unarmed citizens, who would no longer need arms to defend themselves against foreigners. He also refused the impeachment of the two paşas, arguing reasonably that only the chamber can impeach cabinet members, but Parliament had been dissolved.

The Albanians insisted that all their demands be accepted and resumed fighting. Isa Buletin, with 20,000 men, occupied Skopje where his men behaved in exemplary fashion. His action induced the Ottoman government to make one further concession and to

[12] For the twelve points see Swire, *Albania*, pp. 122–23 and Edith P. Stickney, *Southern Albania or Northern Epirus in European International Affairs, 1912–1923* (Palo Alto, Calif.: Stanford University Press, 1926), p. 191 ff.

grant Albanians the right to be armed at all times; satisfied, the Albanians returned to their homes.

The Ottomans kept their word and at the end of August granted virtual autonomy to Albania. Mehmed Derralla Paşa was appointed *mütasarrif* of Prizren and Hassan Tahsin Paşa vali of Janina. Although not by peaceful means and *not* as a result of the action of its leading Albanian advocates, Albanian autonomy within the Ottoman Empire became a reality. Unfortunately for Albania, her wish was granted at an inauspicious moment. The international situation, combined with their own three-year long struggle, forced the Ottoman government to accept their demands just when a larger conflict was rapidly coming to a head. The Balkan powers were on the point of completing arrangements for joint action against the Ottoman Empire. Their aim was the dismemberment of European Turkey, and the emergence of an autonomous Albania threatened to upset the division of the hoped-for spoils over which they wrangled so hard and for so long. No wonder that they were enraged. Their feelings were well expressed by a Greek newspaper that wrote "that a spirit of solidarity would ultimately develop among the Balkan States whose interests were equally threatened by the action of the Albanians."[13] Yet a new fact had to be considered now: the Albanian revolution was successful in producing meaningful autonomy, albeit within the framework of the Ottoman Empire. The first Balkan War demonstrated the error of judgment committed by those Albanians who relied on the power of the Ottoman Empire for the protection of their national interests. The Turkish armies collapsed with amazing rapidity and in less than two months the war was over. Albanian armed civilians could hardly oppose the well-trained armies of the Balkan states, and although Janina held out against the Greeks for three additional months, most of the country was soon occupied by the Montenegrin, Serb, and Greek armies.

In these critical days Ismail Kemal Vlora, a prominent nationalist and deputy in the Ottoman Parliament, emerged as the new Albanian leader. He had left Istanbul for France at the height of the Albanian revolt, expecting to be arrested. Now he moved to Bucureşti and from there called on all nationalist organizations to send delegates to Vlorë (Valona), his native (and unoccupied) city, to

---

[13] Swire, *Albania,* p. 124.

form a new National Congress. On his way home Vlora stopped in Vienna and was assured of Austro-Hungarian help. Although Vlorë was blockaded by the Greek navy, eighty-three delegates assembled and, on November 28, 1912, proclaimed the independence of Albania. Ismail Kemal Vlora, "father of the nation," formed the first Albanian national government and so informed the governments of Europe. An independent Albania, however, did not correspond to the plans of the Balkan victors. Since they had the blessings of Russia, they were opposed by Austria-Hungary and Italy. The situation was not much different from that of 1878, except that in 1913 the powers assembled in London rather than in Berlin. The Austro-Hungarians were mainly interested in preventing Montenegro and Serbia from joining borders and the Serbs from obtaining access to the Adriatic. The Italians did not want to see the Greeks on the Straits of Otranto and for this reason became champions of Albanian independence. Before long it became clear that under Italian and Austro-Hungarian pressure the powers would sanction the creation of an independent Albania, notwithstanding the opposition of the Balkan states. And that is indeed what finally happened.

While the decision to create the Albanian state was relatively easy, the matter of its precise frontiers and administrative structure were not. The conference of ambassadors entrusted with finding a solution finally agreed on certain essentials, contained in the eleven-point agreement published on July 29, 1913.[14] While it created an independent state, this decision stipulated that Albania must be ruled by a foreign prince, her civil and financial administration be handled by a commission appointed by the Great Powers, and that her gendarmerie, the only armed force foreseen, be under the jurisdiction of the same commission and officered by the Dutch.

The ambassadors did not mention the question of Albania's borders. The northern and eastern borders had been fixed earlier, on March 13, 1913, but the question of the southern border proved more difficult to settle and was not drawn until August 11, while the second Balkan War was in progress. The next day Sir Edward Grey admitted that "in making the agreement the primary essential was to preserve the agreement between the Great Powers themselves . . . ."[15] Nothing shows better than this statement why the

[14] For full text see *ibid.*, pp. 173–74.
[15] *Parliamentary Debates, House of Commons* (1908–1928) 51:817.

powers approved the establishment of an independent Albania and what considerations were taken into account. Actually, the settlement left the Balkan states as well as Albania dissatisfied, because some 800,000 Albanians were left beyond the country's borders. When Prince Wilhelm von Wied, chosen by the powers as Prince of Albania, finally landed on March 7, 1914, he found his new country practically in anarchy.

The Serbs and Montenegrin were more or less willing to accept the decision of the powers and, after attempting to reverse the verdict by local action, finally withdrew. The Greeks, however, were not so easily reconciled to the new status quo. They accepted it reluctantly only in February, 1914, and agreed to abide by the Protocol of Florence that was signed two months earlier. They also agreed to evacuate Albanian territory, but before doing so numerous Greek units shed their uniforms and on February 28 appeared on the scene as the local Greek population of what, by Greek definition, was northern Epirus. Then they mounted a *coup d'état,* and established the Provisional Government of Northern Epirus in Gjirokastër (Argyrocastron). Christaki Zographos, a former Minister of Foreign Affairs of Greece, became head of this government and warned that "if Europe wished to avoid the misfortune of leaving to Albanian invaders only smoking ruins, 'she should intervene in time to take measures which, without modifying the bases of the decision of the Powers, would save a people and safeguard the principles of humanity.' "[16] The Powers could hardly uphold their own decisions while permitting the Greeks to upset them. The appeal to humanity by Zographos was at best curious in light of the Greek governmental action that resulted in a bloody civil war and made over 100,000 people homeless. Albanian guerrilla bands under Sali Butka and units of the new gendarmerie under Dutch officers promptly took the field. To help the "Epirots," a regular Greek regiment was dispatched to the region. The powers tried to do what Zographos asked them to do: to uphold their decision in form while upsetting it in substance. They left the district to Albania in the Corfu Agreement of May 17 granting autonomy to the Orthodox minority.

While these events took place in the south and while the Great

---

[16] Stickney, *Southern Albania* . . . , p. 43.

Powers were still searching for a prince, Turhan Paşa of Përmeti, a former Ottoman diplomat, established a National Government in Durrës (Durazzo). It replaced that of Ismail Kemal Vlora who was in Europe pleading for justice for his country. This new government was opposed by the Muslim majority of central Albania which, largely under the influence of foreign propaganda, demanded a Muslim ruler for Albania. The opposition movement degenerated into a sort of *jacquerie* and caused anarchy in the country.

Taking advantage of this rebellion, the Greeks launched a new attempt to gain southern Albania, disregarding the decision reached at Corfu. What followed was wholesale butchery, and the Albanian atrocities were repeatedly discussed in the British Parliament. While the Greeks were holding the south and the heart of the country was in the throes of anarchy, Wilhelm von Wied reached Albania.

The European powers promptly recognized him as official ruler and sent diplomats to his court in Durrës. The International Control Commission handed over to him its powers and retained only advisory functions. It had achieved one task, the organization of the gendarmerie. The efficiency of this organization was promptly put to the test. Well armed by the Turks, Greeks, and Serbs, rebels set out from Tirana to attack Durrës. The city was well defended by the new force and its Dutch officers, but Prince Wied, trying to avoid bloodshed, failed to take his officers' advice and missed the opportunity to crush the rebellion.

The rebels, having failed at Durrës, first moved southward, but later returned and made a second attempt on the city. On this occasion, in July, 1914, Colonel Thomson, the Dutch commander of the garrison lost his life. This created consternation and panic from which the Italians tried to profit. They induced the prince to take refuge on one of their ships, the "Pisani," and announced the fall of the city. But the city held and the International Control Commission continued to function. During the critical days of July, 1914, the Italians tried to press for concessions. They appeared to enjoy a considerable advantage, being the only power that still maintained a fleet before Durrës. They refused to authorize the payment of a £250,000 due from a loan guaranteed by themselves and Austria-Hungary unless Albania agreed to give Italy important concessions in regard to forests, fisheries, and other industries. Prince Wied refused to accept these demands. With the outbreak of World War I,

Vienna stepped into the picture and tried to manipulate Italy. After first refusing to support the Prince, it then promised support in exchange for a declaration of war on Serbia. The Prince refused, pointing out that Albania had been declared a neutral state by the Eleven Points of London of July 29, 1913. With the start of European hostilities the Austro-Hungarian and German members of Durrës's garrison left for home and the Dutch were recalled when their position became hopeless. The fall of the city could no longer be averted. Prince Wied blamed the Powers for the situation and for failing to back him in fulfilling the duties they had entrusted to him, and left the country.

Thus Albania faced the war with foreign troops on her soil, with rebellion and disunity everywhere, and without a government recognized either at home or abroad. During the war the country faced the severest trials, and in 1918–19 Albania's independence was once again discussed by the Powers, this time assembled at Paris.

V

The secret Treaty of London (April 26, 1915), granted Italy, among other advantages, the city of Vlorë with a sufficient hinterland of Albanian territory to insure the city's defenses. Italy also acquired a protectorship over those parts of Albania not assigned to her and her allies. Foreign claims included the renewed demand of Greece for southern Albania and those of Serbia and Montenegro for an extension of their borders to the Drin River. The Treaty of London satisfied all these demands, and, consequently, Albania, whose neutrality had been guaranteed in 1912, became a battleground. When the war ended, the greater part of her territory was in the hands of the Italians, the Korçë district was administered by the French, and an international force held Shkodër.

On January 14, 1920, David Lloyd George, Francesco Nitti, and Georges Clemenceau reached agreement and awarded the Vlorë district to Italy in accordance with the Treaty of London. At the same time they gave the districts of Korçë and Gjirokastër to Greece and northern Albania to Yugoslavia. What the Yugoslav portion was to be remained vague as the wording that "in particular, the part attributed to Yugoslavia must be given her access to the sea to make possible the construction of a railway line along the Drin valley up to the mouth of the Boyana"[17] allowed various interpretations. Concerning the rest of the country the three statesmen agreed "that the whole [sic] of Albania be placed under mandate, believing that this will give full satisfaction to the Albanians in their aspirations towards unity and self-government."[18] This decision followed the Venizelos-Tittoni agreement of July 29, 1919, which made Italy the champion of Greek claims at the meetings of the Big Four.[19]

As far as the powers involved in these negotiations and agreements were concerned the Albanian question was part of a much larger one, the Adriatic question. In the eyes of the Americans they belonged to that group of agreements, the secret treaties concluded without their knowledge, which they refused to recognize as the basis for negotiations or settlements. It is, therefore, not surprising that in connection with Albania, Wilson's opinion was:

The President notes with satisfaction that the British and French governments have not lost sight of the interests and future well-being of the Albanian people. The American government can well understand that the division of Albania into three parts, as it is stipulated in the Anglo-French agreement, would be acceptable to the Yugoslav government, but it is as strongly opposed to anything that would harm the Albanians in order to please the Yugoslavs, as it is opposed to injuring the Yugoslavs to the advantage of the Italians. He is of the opinion that the difficulties between Christians and Moslems would be aggravated if the two parts of the country were placed under the control of nations which have neither the same language nor the same government and economic power.[20]

When the Adriatic question proved too difficult to settle and the peacemakers agreed to allow direct negotiations between Italy and Yugoslavia, the Americans, on March 6, 1920, made the following reservation:

Albanian questions should not be included in the proposed joint discussions of Italy and Yugoslavia, and the President must reaffirm that he

[17] Justin Godart, *L'Albanie en 1921* (Paris: Presses Universitaires, 1922), p. 205.
[18] *Ibid.*, p. 206.
[19] The text of the Venizelos-Tittoni agreement can be found in Stickney, *Southern Albania . . .* , p. 114. Paragraphs two and three of this agreement concern the Greek and Italian claims on Albanian territory.
[20] Godart, *L'Albanie . . .* , p. 207.

cannot possibly approve of any plan which assigns to Yugoslavia in the northern districs of Albania erritorial compensation for what she is deprived of elsewhere.[21]

As Swire has aptly remarked, "the destiny of Albania was thus at last disentangled from other issues; it was not, however, settled."[22] While the Rapallo Treaty of November 12, 1920, did not even mention Albania, the question of her future remained unresolved and was left to the Conference of Ambassadors together with many other problems when the formal peace negotiations were ended.

The future of Albania was determined by a combination of international and domestic developments. While interallied discussions were unfolding at Paris, various events took place in Albania. Until the Tittoni-Venizelos agreement of January 14, 1920, the Albanians were ready to believe that the victors would honor their wartime promises of freedom and liberty for all victims of foreign domination. This agreement destroyed their faith not only in the sincerity of the victors in general, but especially in the sincerity of the Italians. Prior to the events in Paris, General Ferrero, commander of the Italian forces in Albania, solemnly declared before an assembly of Albanian notables gathered at Gjirokastër that his country stood for an independent Albania, which Italy would protect. As a token of his good faith he hoisted the Albanian flag over the town. Foreign Minister Baron Sidney Sonnino confirmed the general's statement with the reservation that Vlorë would remain Italian.

The Italians went even further. They called delegates from the territories under their occupation to Durrës, formed an assembly, and established a provisional government under the premiership of Turhan Përmeti, who had served under Prince William von Wied. Midhat Frashëri and the Catholic bishop Louis Bumchi were members of the government, together with the Orthodox Dr. Mihal Turtulli, who, as Albanian delegate at Paris, made a convincing presentation of proof that Korçë and Gjirokastër were ethnically Albanian. Unfortunately, he was allowed to speak only before a fact-finding commission that had no real authority. Furthermore, he had no official status because Italy refrained from giving official notice of the formation of an Albanian government. On the contrary, the Italian

[21] Swire, *Albania,* p. 309.
[22] *Ibid.,* p. 310.

government claimed the right to represent Albania abroad. When the military administration was replaced by civilians, the Durrës government soon degenerated into a tool of its Italian masters. Just as earlier in the same decade, the Albanians found that the powers were disposing of their future without Albanian concurrence or even representation. Once again the time for direct action had come.

A group of patriots began to prepare for a national congress. In view of foreign armies on Albania's soil, they took military precautions, entrusting Ahmed Bey Zogu, the young hereditary leader of the Mati district and the future King Zog, with the protection of the congress. On January 28, 1920, the assembly opened in the small town of Lushnjë (Lussino) not far from Vlorë. The first act of the fifty-six delegates was to replace the Durrës government by one of their own, under the presidency of Suleyman Delvina, a former bey in the Ottoman civil service. They refrained from making important decisions concerning the form of government reserving that issue for a Constituent Assembly that was to meet at a more propitious time. The state was provisionally entrusted to a regency of four men representing the four major religious denominations of the country: Muslim, Catholic, Orthodox, and Bektashi. The delegates used the power given to them by the local assemblies that had dispatched them to Lushnjë to nominate the members of the first Albanian Parliament and to select Tirana as their temporary capital. The Italians attempted to prevent the implementation of these decisions. Some shooting took place on the outskirts of Tirana, but the strong stand taken by the provisional government selected at Lushnjë, together with the resignation of the Durrës government, left the Tirana group in power. On March 27, 1920, the Parliament held its first meeting at Tirana. The inaugural message of the Regency Council expressed the hope that Italy would change its policy in favor of Albania and added that "at this historic hour we believe that we satisfy a duty of honor by expressing our heartfelt thanks to President Wilson for his defense of our rights. We are convinced that the great American Republic will continue to support our rightful national claims."[23]

A few days before Parliament assembled the international contingent under General de Fourtou withdrew from Shkodër. The Albanian government appointed Ahmed Zogu (Zogolli) as governor

---

[23] Quoted from a document in the author's possession.

of the city. But the Mount Tarabaş region had previously been handed over to the Yugoslavs by the French. The Tirana government thus exercised power only in the Italian-held regions and Shkodër. In the north the Yugoslavs held, in addition to the Mount Tarabaş region, the strategic line in eastern Albania established by General Franchet d'Esperey at the time of the armistice. Korçë was still held by the French. In the south, the critical moment came in May. Rumor had it that the French withdrawal was imminent, and that the French army would be replaced by the Greek. The Supreme Council sitting in Paris found it necessary to warn the Greeks against creating a *fait accompli* while the question of Albania's borders remained undecided. The Greeks themselves did not wish to create trouble because the negotiations leading to the Treaty of Sèvres, from which they expected great advantages, were in progress. Consequently they agreed to the Protocol of Kapeştitza (May 15, 1920), which would leave only twenty-six villages in their hands following the French withdrawal on June 21, but the question of the permanent border remained unsolved.

Nevertheless, the Tirana government still faced serious problems. The presence of Italians, Greeks, and Yugoslavs on Albanian territory could not be solved at once, nor by the Albanians alone, yet domestic difficulties had to be settled at once and by them. The most serious challenge to the government came from Essad Toptani, the man who had organized the Muslim revolt against Prince William Wied. He did not dare to leave Paris, where he cooperated with the Greeks and Yugoslavs, but managed to organize an uprising. His supporters, backed by the Italian commander at Vlorë, were defeated at Breza by Bayram Tsuri. Avni Bustem, a young Albanian student, murdered Essad on the steps of the Hotel Continental in the Rue de Rivoli. Rustem's trial ending in his acquittal, the subsequent fact-finding mission of the French senator, Justin Godart, and the events in Albania changed the French attitude, which now became more favorable to Albania.

Albania certainly needed all possible backing since the next crisis occurred in Italian-occupied Vlorë. Here a revolutionary committee determined to engineer the departure of the occupying forces and the reincorporation of the city into Albania. Before acting the members of "The Committee of National Defense appointed by the people of Vlorë" addressed, on May 29, 1920, a memorandum to the commander of the town, General Piacentini. After recalling the events since the arrival of the Italians in 1914, the note ended by stating:

To-day the Albanian people, like others, are not minded to submit to being sold like cattle in the European markets as the spoil of Italy, Serbia, and Greece. They prefer to take up arms, and demand of Italy the administration of Valona, Tepeleni, and Tchamouria, and to place them under the administration of the Tirana Government. The Committee of National Defense assembled here request that your Excellency will give your answer to this demand of the people of Valona and of all Albania by tomorrow at 7 P.M. The Committee will not be responsible for what may happen in the event of failure to give a favorable answer.[24]

Gunfire was the answer. The ensuing struggle lasted until September 2, when the last Italian troops left Vlorë. Patriotism had defeated a superior force equipped with the most modern weapons. The Albanians were aided by the social unrest in Italy that preoccupied the government in Rome and prompted Italian soldiers to resist being shipped to Vlorë and dockers to resist in the loading of ships. In general, indeed, there was little Italian popular support for the government's Albanian policy. Consequently, the new Giolitti-Sforza cabinet in Rome decided to hand over all of Italian-held Albania, except the island of Saseno opposite Vlorë, to the Tirana government. The agreement of August 2, 1920, was thus the first concluded by a great power with Albania on the basis of equality. It greatly contributed to the consolidation of the Tirana government's power, to internal security, and to the restoration of the 1913 borders.

But these borders were still far from secure. Yugoslavia and Greece still maintained their claims, and the Conference of Ambassadors in Paris delayed its decision. To strengthen its position, Albania applied for membership in the League of Nations and was admitted on December 17, 1920, largely owing to the support of the British delegate, Sir Robert Cecil (later Lord Cecil of Chelwood). At Geneva the Orthodox bishop, Fan Noli, a Harvard-educated politician and capable orator, made a good impression at a time when

[24] For the full text see Swire, *Albania,* pp. 318–19, from which these passages were taken.

Albania's integrity was again threatened by the Mirditë revolt. The Yugoslav army backed this revolt explaining that it was aiding Christians persecuted for their faith. Albania appealed to the League for help. Lloyd George demanded that the Council of the League discuss the issue pointing out that "the Conference of Ambassadors has established the frontiers of Albania and the parties concerned will be immediately notified." Mr. H. A. L. Fisher of Great Britain acted as *rapporteur* during the ensuing debate. In his report he stressed that ample evidence was at hand to show that the revolt was organized and the arms were supplied by the Yugoslavs, that

... all this evidence gives ground . . . to conclude that there must exist a plan to detach Northern Albania from the Tirana Government . . . [while] on the other hand evidence . . . shows that the great masses of the population, including the leaders of the Christian Church, are in favour of a united Albania and that Albanian nationalism is proving to be stronger than religious affinities.[25]

On November 19, the League finally passed a resolution referring to the fact that Albania's borders had been fixed ten days earlier by the Conference of Ambassadors and that the Kingdom of the Serbs, Croats, and Slovenes accepted this decision and promised to withdraw its troops from Albania.[26] In the words of Lord Balfour, "No statesman, no nation, organisation, or machinery in the world could have done what the League of Nations has done in this matter."[27]

The League action was legally based on the decision of the ambassadors of November 9, 1921. This decision reestablished, with slight rectifications to her neighbors' advantage, Albania's borders of 1913.[28] More detrimental to Albania than these losses of territory were the resolutions embodied in an agreement signed by the ambassadors on the same day. The preamble stated that " . . . the integrity and inalienability of her [Albania's] frontiers . . . is a ques-

---

[25] Godart, *L'Albanie* . . . , p. 258.

[26] The text of this resolution is in Swire, *Albania*, pp. 375–76.

[27] Lord Cecil of Chelwood, *Great Experiment: An Autobiography* (London: Jonathan Cape, 1941), p. 129.

[28] For full text see *Official Journal of the League of Nations*, No. 1195, December, 1921.

tion of international importance" and recognized "that the violation of these frontiers or the independence of Albania might constitute a danger for the strategic safety of Italy."[29] The first point of the agreement encouraged Albania to turn to the League should she feel menaced. Point two contained the germ of future troubles by stating (in reference to point one) " . . . that, in the above-mentioned event they [Great Britain, France, Italy, and Japan] will instruct their representatives on the Council of the League of Nations to recommend that the restoration of the territorial frontiers of Albania should be entrusted to Italy."[30]

While the ambassadors and the League took decisions that assured Albania's existence, the agreement placed her clearly in the Italian zone of influence and, thus, jeopardized the results of the other two resolutions. It took three long years before an international border commission fixed the exact borders of Albania, marking them actually with rows of concrete pyramids. Albania, aided by the general pressure for peace and the internal troubles of Italy, achieved the borders of 1913 and independence. Thus by 1924 the country was able to establish an effective government, to unite the nation, and to be effectively represented before the councils of nations. This was possible because, in spite of diversity and some unrest, the Albanians felt and acted, for the first time in modern history, as one nation clearly conscious of its unity.

VI

Once the country's independence seemed to be assured, the long-delayed decision concerning a form of government had to be taken. National feeling had made enough progress to eliminate from the possible alternatives all foreign princes, even a Muslim. The main division was between a handful of young, mostly foreign-educated intellectuals who favored a democratic, parliamentary republic and farreaching economic, social, and cultural reforms and a coalition of civil servants, landlords, and clan elders who argued against sweeping changes—pointing out that these would jeopardize the state's stability. Ahmed Zogu, already suspected of dictatorial tendencies, was leading the conservatives during the 1924 electoral campaign that selected delegates for the Constituent Assembly. To prevent his

[29] Full text in Swire, *Albania,* pp. 369–70.
[30] *Ibid.,* p. 369.

victory, the left-wing nationalists under the leadership of Fan Noli
and backed by military commanders in northern and southern Albania staged a coup in June, forcing Ahmed Zogu to flee to Yugoslavia. The new government under Fan Noli lasted only six months.
It was ineffective, torn by dissension, and it failed to carry out reforms and to legalize its position by plebiscite. Ahmed Zogu organized his followers from Beograd with Yugoslav help, staged a
counter coup and returned to power in December. Acclaimed as
the "savior of the Fatherland" he held absolute power as President
of the Republic until 1928, and from that year until 1939 as King
Zog I. The years of his rule, 1925–39, are the only period in modern
history during which Albania enjoyed independence and a reason-
able degree of internal stability.

Zog's reign was undemocratic and dictatorial, but perhaps for
cogent reasons: A born autocrat, he ruled a country surrounded by
hostile neighbors; furthermore, Albania was poor and dependent on
foreign help. In accordance with the Ambassadors' Agreement of
1921 this help had to come from Italy. By the time Ahmed Zogu
became president, Italy was in Fascist hands and Mussolini's political philosophy was not too far removed from that of Albania's president and future king. It was, therefore, almost "natural" that Ahmed
Zogu abandoned the Yugoslavs with whose help he returned to Albania and turned to Italy, signing with them, on November 27, 1926,
a Pact of Friendship and Security, the Tirana Pact. Even some of
Ahmed Zogu's supporters were afraid that this pact allowed Italy
to intervene in Albania at will, but a letter of Baron Aloisi[31] reassured them that Italy had no right to land troops in Albania unless
asked to do so by the Albanian government.

The situation was contradictory. It was clear that the pact made
Italy the supreme foreign force in Albania, and there could be little
doubt that Italy wanted to take over the country. On the other
hand Rome made it clear that it would not send troops to Albania—
and without an occupation Albania could not be taken over. At the
same time it was obvious that the ambitious Ahmed Zogu would
not give up power voluntarily. Thus the events of 1939 were already
being foreshadowed in 1926.

King Zog had swept aside all attempts at a parliamentary democ-

---

[31] For text see *ibid.*, pp. 379–80.

racy and imposed his personal rule. On the other hand his policy of relying too exclusively on Italy's support resulted in the Italian invasion of Good Friday, 1939. Yet some constructive initiatives that had been taken in the first years of independence were carried out under the monarchy. The autocephalous Orthodox church of Albania was recognized by the Patriarchate under King Zog's reign after the first step towards its creation had been taken by Bishop Fan Noli before Zog came to power. In 1922, he established the autocephalous Albanian Orthodox church. He had previously translated the liturgy into Albanian. This made it possible for the church to do away with priests who served the interests of Greek propaganda. The last of these priests, Bishop Yakopos of Korçë, was expelled from Albania, in spite of Greek protests, in 1922. Coupled with this church reform was the decision of the Albanian government to close all Greek schools. These two measures cut off the two main avenues of Greek influence in southern Albania. The new generation of Albanian Orthodox knew no Greek and showed little desire to accept Greek rule.

Even more important was the second positive achievement of the years of independence. The government introduced an excellent system of public education. The time was too short to start a university; the emphasis had to be first of all on elementary and then on secondary schools. Schools had to be built, textbooks prepared, teachers trained. In 1921, a French *lycée* with French professors opened at Korçë; the teacher-training establishment in Elbasan and the Franciscan and Jesuit institutions in Shkodër were expanded; a gymnasium was opened at Tirana where all instruction was in Albanian. The Shkolla Teknike, established by the American Junior Red Cross in Tirana in 1921, trained mechanics, agricultural experts, and offered some engineering courses. The name of its director, Mr. Fultz, became a synonym for competence, devotion to duty, and sincere love for the country he had come to serve. His students worshipped him, and they were made to feel proud of the workmanship which they produced. The Near East Foundation operated an agricultural school at Kavajë, and a girls school that had been established in Ottoman times by the Kyrias family in Korçë was transferred to Tirana, giving courses in Albanian and English. It was with great regret that the students saw their foreign teachers leave when all schools were nationalized in 1934. The reason given for this measure was fear of too many Italian schools, but in fact the government was afraid of the liberal ideas of the foreign teachers. Every year more and more scholarships were granted to graduates of the secondary schools for university study in western Europe. Most of them went to Italy, France, Austria, or Germany; a few to Great Britain. Most of them studied law, agronomy, medicine, and the various sciences. By the early thirties a number of them had returned and were appointed to various administrative positions. A certain degree of struggle developed within the various governmental services—the newly trained worked for reform, while older officials opposed all change. Most difficult was the task of the young judges who tried to apply newly promulgated codes of law impartially. They were faced constantly with the intervention of influential men who tried to keep criminals out of the hands of justice. Time worked in favor of the new generation, and Albania would probably have undergone a peaceful social revolution had her independence not been destroyed by Italy in 1939.

This rising young intelligentsia, the hope of the country, had a difficult life not only because its efforts were often obstructed by their senior colleagues, but because the autocratic government objected to all opposition, even to criticism or unsolicited advice. A constitutional monarchy on paper, Albania was ruled in actuality by a clique of court favorites whose wishes were carried out in a parliament peopled with deputies chosen by the palace and subsequently approved by a severely restricted electorate. Fortunately for the intelligentsia the police regime had no ideological commitment, was not the monopoly of a party, and was using inefficient methods. Consequently there was a certain freedom of thought expressed in the press and books and censorship was exercised only in the case of openly Communistic publications. The leniency of the censorship can be explained by the lack of sophistication of the old school ruling clique who failed to understand the problems of political censorship, and the young men who served as censors were in secret sympathy with the ideas expressed by the writers. Nevertheless autocracy and conservatism opposed to reform alienated the intelligentsia from the government. The ruthless repression of any organization suspected of opposition and the harsh punishments imposed on its members were particularly resented.

This intelligentsia was very small in comparison to the large, mainly agricultural masses of the population who needed reform, especially economic reform, even more than did their better educated countrymen. Albania had no industries, not even a bank. In 1925, a group of Italian banks received a concession to establish the National Bank of Albania with the right to issue currency. When one realizes that this bank had its headquarters in Rome it becomes obvious how dependent the country's fiscal policy was on the goodwill of Italy. During the same year a group of Italian financial institutions established the *Societá per lo Sviluppo Economico d'Albania* (SVEA) under the sponsorship of the government. This group extended a loan of fifty million gold francs to Albania for the purpose of developing utilities, roads, bridges, and industries. The interest rate of 14 percent was guaranteed by Albania's customs revenues. These were never high enough to assure the yearly payments, and Albania, in a constant state of bankruptcy, was at the mercy of its Italian creditors. Mussolini took advantage of this situation to extort more and more political and economic concessions from Albania.

Unfortunately the money received was not used for productive purposes, though a few roads and bridges were built and public buildings erected. The peasant-landlord relationship remained what it had been for centuries. Land reform and the introduction of modern agricultural methods and implements were neglected. Consumer goods, which had to be imported, were expensive and added to the steadily worsening trend of Albania's balance of trade. The hope that oil deposits would be found to reverse this situation remained an unfulfilled dream. The mineral deposits, with the exception of bitumen that helped to build Mussolini's *auto-strade,* were not exploited although the country had rich deposits of copper, chromium, iron, nickel, and so on.

Economic stagnation brought general poverty, misery, and in the northern mountain districts even periodic famine. Apart from a few rich people, the population's living standard was very low indeed. Frustration was widespread among peasants, small craftsmen, and traders. They were at best uncommitted, felt no loyalty to the government, and most of them were both socially and politically quite ready to believe the lavish promises of Communist propaganda.

While, from the economic view, there is some validity in the Communists' assertion that Albania was an Italian colony as early as 1925, this is certainly not true in the political sphere. Zog was not prepared to share his power with any one. While willing to grant economic concessions to Italy, he exploited every chance to affirm the political independence of Albania. He had to permit the Italians to organize and train his army, but placed his gendarmery in the hands of British officers. Albanian delegates attended the meetings of the Balkan states and always worked for regional unity to prevent encroachments by the Great Powers. When, in 1934, Mussolini's demands reached a stage where their acceptance would have meant the end of Albanian independence, King Zog's refusal was unequivocal. Mussolini withdrew his military mission, stopped economic aid, and staged a naval demonstration. The Albanian government remained firm. From that point on it was only a question of time before Mussolini would attempt to obtain by force what he could not achieve by economic penetration—mastery over Albania.

VII

The mastermind behind the Italian invasion of Albania that took place on Good Friday, 1939, was Count Galeazzo Ciano, Mussolini's son-in-law and Foreign Minister. Knowing that King Zog, who had married a year earlier and was now awaiting the birth of his first child, was deeply devoted to his family, he speculated

that King Zog will give in. There is, above all, a fact on which I am counting: the coming birth of Zog's child. Zog loves his wife very much as well as his whole family. I believe that he will prefer to insure to his dear ones a quiet future. And frankly I cannot imagine [Queen] Geraldine running around fighting through the mountains . . . .[32]

Whether for this reason or because he realized that in the atmosphere of appeasement and defeatism of the spring of 1939 all resistance would be in vain, King Zog went into exile when an Italian force landed with 100,000 men after he had rejected Mussolini's ultimatum. But the Albanians fought on for days. Thanks to the daring initiative of local commanders, armed resistance was opposed to invaders who had postponed their landing by twenty-four hours. The invasion and occupation could not be prevented, but the Al-

[32] *The Ciano Diaries, 1939–1943* (ed., High Gibson), (Garden City, N.Y.: Doubleday & Co., 1946), p. 52.

banians had the satisfaction of going down fighting with honor unblemished.

The Italians installed a puppet Albanian government, but power was in the hands of Italians on all levels of the administration. Victor Emmanuel III became King of Albania and was represented in Tirana by a viceroy. Fascism became the country's official political creed. The exploitation of the country's mineral resources began in earnest. Italy spent great amounts of money, particularly on construction projects, making the war years into boom years for Albania.

In spite of this economic upswing the Italian occupation had one very damaging result: it involved Albania in the second World War. Potentially even greater damage might have resulted from an extended, peaceful Italian occupation. Italian citizens were given the right to settle and acquire land in Albania. These settlers, bringing modern techniques and machinery with them, could have raised the yield of the Albanian lands to about three times what it had been in 1939. Given the Italian policy, this would have meant two million Italian settlers in an Albania with only about one million inhabitants of its own. Within two generations the Albanians would have been reduced to a minority in an Italian province.

The outcome of the war prevented this development, but brought others that remain unsolved. To the present, the Greek government considers itself at war with Albania and has revived its claim to "northern Epirus." Greek agents, presenting themselves as northern Epirots, work all over the world with some success. Even more detrimental were the developments in the country itself that culminated in the Communist take-over.

Resistance and guerrilla warfare began as soon as the shock of the sudden Italian invasion wore off. Soldiers, gendarmes, and civilians who had taken to the mountains organized themselves into bands under the leadership of well-trained officers, mountain chieftains, and even civilians turned into fighters. They harassed the army of occupation, attacked convoys, and surprised smaller garrisons. Prior to and during the first years of the second World War, two main underground organizations developed. The smaller of these was the Legality Movement under the leadership of Abaz Kupi, which favored the restoration of King Zog. Much more important was the movement of the Nationalist Party, which in 1942

took the name Balli Kombëtar (National Front). Led by Midhat
Frashëri, scion of a famous family and a man of long service and
scholarly accomplishments, it counted among its followers most of
the intelligentsia that had objected to King Zog's autocracy. The
program of this party, published in October, 1942,

. . . was progressive and highly nationalistic in character; it sought the
restoration of a free, ethnic and democratic Albania on a modern social
basis, with freedom of speech and thought; it promised to fight for an
Albania regulated economically and socially, and for the elimination of
"exploiters and exploited"; it required land for the landless peasants and
a good living for all workers; it promised free education and justice for
all, irrespective of age, region, and religion; it called for all to fight to the
finish against all who collaborated with foreign occupiers and all unpatriotic elements.[33]

Despite this far-reaching program, outstanding leadership, and
genuine support, the Balli Kombëtar failed to gain the upper hand
because its organization was weak, its contact with the peasants was
not sufficiently stressed, and its measures against the Communists
were not stringent enough.

Until 1941, the scattered Albanian Communist groups had not
been able to form a party. During the war they held back until the
Nazi attack on the Soviet Union, at which time they executed the
political somersault that characterized Communists everywhere at
that time. Overnight they discovered in themselves a hidden vein of
patriotism and a hatred for the foreign invader. They were ready
to organize and fight.

This organization was carried out on Tito's orders by two prominent members of the Yugoslav Communist Party's regional committee for the Kossovo and Metohia district, Dušan Mugoša and
Miladin Popović. After long discussions and several clandestine
meetings, Tito's emissaries succeeded in persuading the various
Communist groups to send representatives to a secret conference in
Tirana where, in November, 1941, the Albanian Communist Party,
calling itself Party of Labor, was established. The lack of support
was overcome when the Communists succeeded in organizing the

---

[33] Stavro Skendi (ed.), *Albania.* ("East-Central Europe under the Communists
Series," Robert F. Byrnes [ed.], [New York: Praeger, 1956]), p. 79.

National Liberation Movement in September, 1942, which created, in turn, a General Council of National Liberation. Less than a year later this council created, under Communist leadership, the Army of National Liberation of Albania that spent the remaining years of the war eliminating the adherents of Abaz Kupi and Midhat Frashëri. These activities were carried out in spite of the fact that the National Liberation Movement and the Balli Kombëtar had agreed in the village of Mukaj, in August, 1943, to fight together. The action of the Communists plunged Albania into the nightmare of civil war. The Communists managed to convince the British that they were the only ones ready to fight the Germans occupying Albania after Italy's collapse; they received the bulk of the war material sent to Albania by the Allies and with it were able to defeat the nationalists in a sudden attack. The nationalists, unable to recover from the damages suffered during this initial blow, waged a losing battle and in November, 1944, most of their leaders were forced into exile. After that time the task of the Communists was easy. They speedily liquidated some of the remaining nationalist leaders and established their regime firmly in Albania.

Albanian nationalism prior to the Italian invasion in 1939 sprang in the main from individuals, small leadership groups, a handful of intellectuals and others who voiced the hopes and demands of the Albanian people. Much of what they said and did was patriotic, but could not be connected easily with the various intellectual movements that produced the numerous nationalist schools in Europe. Given the social structure and isolation of Albania this is not too surprising. Albanian nationalism was, to a large extent, a mixture of local pride, honest patriotism, and instinct. This the masses shared with their vocal leaders who could always count on the people to follow them when they appealed to it to defend freedom and independence.

In the spontaneous resistance to the Italian landings in 1939, when Albania's government had disintegrated, we see the first manifestations of a real nationalism that reaches beyond local patriotism. The resistance movements and their programs, including that of the Communists who used patriotic and not ideological slogans during the war years, are further proof that nationalism had penetrated into the masses. While it is tragic that this should have occurred at a time when the country's independence was first destroyed by an imperialistic neighbor and then submerged into and subordinated to an alien doctrine, it is also proof that the hope of those who do not despair about the future of Albania has a solid foundation. Even the behavior of Albania's Communist masters seems to support this assertion.

The years of greatest danger for Albania's independence were those of 1944–48. Yugoslavia, the creator of the Albanian Communist Party and the country's old enemy, was still an ambitious neighbor. Beograd continued to master the party that it had created, while Yugoslav aspirations, under the cover of ideological unity, were extended from northern Albania to the entire country. Albania was considered as the potential seventh member of the Yugoslav Federation. The Stalin-Tito break gave the Albanian Communists the chance to separate themselves from their much too powerful and ambitious confrères and mentors and to seek the friendship of a great power that was ideologically acceptable. Their actions were clearly designed to solidify Albanian Communist power at home and to thwart their neighbors' plans. In this sense Communist politics followed an established historical pattern, and in resisting the claims of Yugoslavia it sought not only the independence of the party but also that of the country. In this light the switch from Moscow to Peking was the logical product of an overexposed national position. Khrushchev's reconciliation with Tito eliminated Moscow as the guarantor of Albania's national and party independence. Peking was not only ready to assume Moscow's former role but was also conveniently far enough not to represent a danger by itself. Albania is independent today, although she is not free. When and under what conditions she will be able to regain freedom is impossible to foretell. That day will ensue from fundamental changes in the general international power structure. These changes are hardly imminent, but the Albanian people, having withstood numerous vicissitudes over the centuries, and occupations from Roman to Ottoman times will be there, fortified in its recently found unity and nationalism, when the moment finally arrives.

MARIN V. PUNDEFF

Bulgarian Nationalism

Roots of National Consciousness (before 1762)

In the imagery of Bulgarian history, few tableaux have been as graphically painted and as effective as that of a pall of utter darkness enveloping the Bulgarian lands in the eighteenth century and a crushed and dazed population, victimized by Ottoman overlords and Greek clergy, groping through it without the lights of education and national consciousness. In this deep gloom, in 1762, a patriotic monk from one of the Mount Athos monasteries, Father Paisii, lit the flame of passionate nationalism with his *Slavianobulgarska istoriia,* dispelled the darkness, awakened his fellow Bulgarians to a sense of national identity and purpose, and inspired them to conquer the obstacles to national reassertion and emancipation. It was a Biblical theme in local variation: over boundless chaos, the Word was voiced, and chaos yielded to purpose and order. It was also a local echo of the western European notion of the long night of the Middle Ages from the twilight of classical antiquity to the dawn of the Renaissance. The image was first conjured up by Marin Drinov who, in a study of Paisii and his impact published in 1871, painted the Dantesque picture of an "oppressed, suffocated, and shattered multitude" that had lost its identity and had abandoned all hope until Paisii resurrected its national history and stirred it "to take shape once again as one people."[1]

Drinov's great authority as the first Bulgarian academic historian and professor at the University of Kharkov assured this vivid interpretation of general acceptance. In the years preceding and following the liberation of the country in 1878, publicists, poets, teachers,

[1] M. Drinov, "Otets Paisii, negovoto vreme, negovata istoriia i uchenitsite mu," *Periodichesko Spisanie na Bulgarskoto knizhovno druzhestvo,* No. 4 (1871), pp. 3–26.

painters, and politicians made such wide use of it that it could be counted upon to rouse the imagination and patriotic emotions of every Bulgarian. It became an indispensable part of Liberation Day (March 3) oratory and held a central place among the themes of public education and citizenship training. Historians, native and foreign, took it over and enlarged upon it without realizing the degree to which Drinov had succumbed to the imagery and propaganda employed by Paisii himself.

As Bulgarian historical scholarship reached higher levels of factual knowledge and sophistication, the validity of this view began to be questioned. One of the first to voice skepticism about Drinov's interpretation and to suggest corrections was Ivan D. Shishmanov, professor of comparative history of literature at the University of Sofia from its establishment in 1889 to 1928 and inspirer of a remarkable following of disciples. Shishmanov's work in the literary history of the Italian Renaissance gave him perspectives and basis for comparisons in the "Bulgarian Renaissance," which no one had yet explored. In a study published in 1914, he called attention to the necessity of investigating the socioeconomic and cultural conditions existing before Paisii and emphasized that, while "personalities played a significant role in the process of our Renaissance as heralds or accelerators of the mass movement, their part in the process should not be exaggerated nor the part of the people as a whole belittled."[2] Shishmanov pointed to the rebellious activity of the *khaiduti*, ("bandits," *Turk.*) to the great body of folk epos inspired by these Robin Hoods, to the sporadic uprisings, and to the literature in colloquial Bulgarian during the two centuries before 1762 as indications of the state of mind of Bulgarians before Paisii spoke out and of the existence of a common identity and a quite general framework of thought in the Bulgarian lands.

In the succeeding three decades, the host of historians educated or influenced by Shishmanov and his colleagues Boian Penev, Vasil N. Zlatarski, and others, penetrated deeply into unexplored aspects of the Bulgarian Renaissance in the eighteenth and nineteenth centuries and brought to light much detail from its prehistory. Particularly fruitful were the studies of Professor Ivan Duj-

---

[2] I. D. Shishmanov, "Paisii i negovata epokha. Misli vurkhu genezisa na novobulgarskoto vuzrazhdanie," *Spisanie na Bulgarskata akademiia na naukite,* VIII (1914), 1–18.

čev in the field of Catholic activity in parts of Bulgaria in the seventeenth century. A product of the universities of Sofia and Rome, Dujčev searched the Vatican archives for the records of the information-gathering investigations that preceded the appointments of Roman Catholic bishops to Bulgarian dioceses, and contributed much information on Bulgarian conditions at the time.[3]

In the development of a Bulgarian national consciousness and Europe's awareness of a Bulgarian "nation" and its aspirations, the importance of the work of Bulgarian Catholics in the seventeenth century is thus beyond controversy. Their detailed knowledge of the history and territorial extent of their fatherland (*patria*, in the sources), the emphasis on the use of the native language and the Cyrillic script in sharp contrast to the policy of the Greek clergy, and the concentration upon the political goal of liberation testify to an overriding concern with national identity and interests rather than to efforts to cultivate an isolated religious implantation. Contemplating the response that Catholic work found among Bulgarians in the seventeenth century, it is difficult to accept the traditional picture of utter darkness and torpor as realistically portraying the state of affairs in the preceding sixteenth century. The consciousness expressed, for example, in the appreciation of Bulgarian Catholics for having been given a "bishop of our own race and language" (*pastira ot nashega plemena i iezika*) undoubtedly had deep roots.

Education using the native language and the Cyrillic alphabet was available in many localities in schools organized at Orthodox monasteries and churches or by lay teachers. These monastic "cell schools" were, of course, intended to prepare young men for a calling in the church, but some of them went into lay pursuits as copyists, drafters of documents, clerks in the employ of merchants, and teachers, and became the lay intelligentsia of the time. A monastery library often contained not only religious texts and the monastery's charters from kings and local magnates, but also copies of medieval chronicles, lives of Bulgarian saints, royal charters, and so on, made by monastery brethren during visits to Mount Athos, the Rila Mon-

---

[3] I. Dujčev, *Il Cattolicesimo in Bulgaria nel sec. XVII secondo i processi informativi sulla nomina dei vescovi Cattolici* (Rome, 1937), and "Proiavi na narodnostno samosuznanie u nas prez XVII vek," *Makedonski Pregled*, XIII, No. 2 (1942), 26–51; M. Pundeff, "Les Racines du Nationalisme Bulgare," *Revue des Études Slaves*, XLVI (1967), 127–38.

astery, and other great monastic communities. In the centuries following the Turkish conquest, the centers where national historical
sources, education in the national tongue and alphabet, and national consciousness were preserved were thus the numerous monasteries, estimated at about 120 and serving a people of 1,500,000
in the seventeenth century.[4] This was due particularly to the fact
that after the conquest the sultans recognized the monasteries'
charters and honored their established freedoms and privileges.

The many foreigners who passed through Bulgarian lands also
observed the widespread rebellious mood and desire of the Bulgarians to rid themselves of the Ottoman rule.[5] The continuous expression of this mood were the guerrilla bands of *khaiduti,* who first appeared in the fifteenth century and represented the reactions of the
common people to injustices and oppression. Usually operating in
the mountains in small groups under a proven leader (*voivoda*) and
a standard bearer (*bairaktar*), the *khaiduti* filled both the need for
some defense against the oppressors and for a symbol of resistance,
and therefore enjoyed wide support and admiration, judging from
the great body of folklore that glorified their exploits. Heroic legends sprang up around the famous *voivodi* like Chavdar of Rila,
Strakhil of Pirin, and many others, and were added to the existing
historical epos to form a rich folk tradition from which the people
of all Bulgarian lands drew their sense of common history, identity,
and hope for freedom. The earliest figures in the recorded historical
epos are kings of the second Bulgarian kingdom, as well as local
magnates. Especially rich was the folklore around the exploits of
Krali Marko, who took part in the battle on Kossovo Polje in 1389
and became a hero of Serbian folklore as well. This historical epos
reflected the popular memories of the obliterated Bulgarian state
and the longings for seeing it restored. It can be said that the creative popular mind never abandoned the idea of the re-establishment
of the Bulgarian state.[6]

While recorded Bulgarian epos does not reach as far back as

---

[4] Khristo Gandev, *Faktori na bulgarskoto vuzrazhdane, 1600–1830* (Sofia, 1943),
pp. 20–46.

[5] On the rebellions, see I. Kinov and others, *Vuoruzhenata borba na bulgarskiia
narod sreshtu osmanskoto gospodstvo* (Sofia, 1961), pp. 11–24.

[6] I. Snegarov, *Kulturni i politicheski vruzki mezhdu Bulgariia i Rusiia prez XVI–
XVIII v.* (Sofia, 1953), p. 12.

Chanson de Roland or *Nibelungenlied,* it fulfilled the same function of creating national heroic legends that helped to develop and nurture a sense of national identity among the popular masses. As Dujčev concluded, this identity developed in the Middle Ages and was particularly strengthened by the confrontation with the Turks.[7] The decapitation of the nation in the course of the conquest deprived it of leaders, but it also democratized the struggle against the conquerors by moving the popular masses into the foreground. As any conflict does, the confrontation with the Turks compelled the Bulgarian people to search for its inner resources, define its identity, and seek allies in kindred peoples and sympathetic quarters. In the face of so alien a conqueror as the Turk, the definition and maintenance of identity was not difficult; the striking differences of language, religion, and alphabet, and the pride in their own civilization and heritage set conquerors and conquered, the *ghazi* and the *raya,* sharply apart and reinforced the cohesion of each of the antagonistic nationalities.

The process of the formation of the Bulgarian nation in the Middle Ages is a complex one and is beyond the scope of this study. It should suffice to point out here that it began with the amalgamation of the Slavs and the proto-Bulgars after the creation of a state on lands in the Byzantine Empire in 679 A.D. and, especially, after the adoption of Christianity in 865 and the rise of a common culture based on a state religion, a distinctive way of writing set apart from the Greek alphabet of the empire, and the Slavic vernacular. The continuous struggle with the empire, for survival or gain, and the confrontation with the Greeks—the best defined nationality in Europe at that time—mobilized all resources the Bulgarians had and stimulated them to acquire similar features of identity. In this process of identity-building, the role of the Cyrillic alphabet cannot be overstated. It made possible the use of the Bulgarian language, the creation of a native culture, and the establishment of an independent national church. At a time when these things were inconceivable in western Europe, the Bulgarians had—through the work of Cyril and Methodius and their disciples Kliment of Ohrid, Naum

---

[7] Dujčev, "Proiavi . . . ," p. 51. For similar views in regard to western Europe, see H. Koht, "The Dawn of Nationalism in Europe," *American Historical Review,* LII, No. 2 (January, 1947), 265–80, and Royal Institute of International Affairs, *Nationalism* (London, 1939), pp. 8–17.

of Pliska, and others in Bulgaria—a distinctive national alphabet, religious and secular literature, and a national church whose status as an independent patriarchate was recognized by Constantinople in 927. Combined with military power and a large realm, these accomplishments led the Bulgarian Tsar Simeon even to try to seize the imperial title and hegemony.

The creation of a "Slavic" culture in Bulgaria challenged the medieval doctrine of the three holy languages of Christianity (Hebrew, Greek, and Latin) and led to the first break in the monopoly that Greek and Latin had as vehicles of Christian religion and culture. From Bulgaria, the "Slavic" alphabet, liturgy, literature, and law spread to Serbian, Russian, and other lands and played a vital role in such momentous developments as the Christianization of Russia in the tenth century.[8] Old Bulgarian thus became the base of the international language of Slavic civilization that carried cultural accomplishments and influences throughout the Balkans and northward to Russia. These historical developments gave the Bulgarian intelligentsia of the Middle Ages a consciousness of the role of Bulgaria in the world, which found expression in the idea of Tŭrnovo as the Third Rome (more than a century before the Russian doctrine of Moscow the Third Rome was enunciated under influences from Bulgaria)[9] and in the idea of Bulgaria as the seedbed of Slavic civilization. Exaggerated or justified, such notions of the national achievements and importance fed national pride and provided inspiration for the passionate patriotism of Paisii in the eighteenth century.

Paisii and the Rise of Nationalism (1762–1870)

For western and central Europe, the eighteenth century was a time of emergence of new forces, awakening, and enlightenment. For the Balkans, closed off and weighed down by the declining Ottoman Empire, the eighteenth century was also, though less rapidly and noticeably, a time of economic change and awakening.

[8] V. A. Istrin, *1100 let slavianskoi asbuki* (Moscow, 1963); *Khiliada i sto godini slavianska pismenost, 863–1963. Sbornik v chest na Kiril i Metodii* (Sofia, 1963). For details of the rise of a national ideology in the ninth and tenth centuries, see M. Pundeff, "National Consciousness in Medieval Bulgaria," *Südost-Forschungen,* XXVII (1968), 1–27.

[9] R. L. Wolff, "The Three Romes: The Migration of an Ideology and the Making of an Autocrat," *Daedalus* (Spring, 1959), pp. 291–311.

Amidst decaying Turkish feudalism, the expanding commerce and manufacture—as a rule carried on by members of the subject populations—were swelling the old urban centers, causing the growth of new ones, and producing a moneyed class that, for the most part, saw in the Ottoman system various obstacles to its progress. Gradually this class became the carrier of ideas concerning the interests of the various ethnic groups from which it had sprung.

Located in the European core of the empire and still quite isolated, Bulgarian society in the first half of the eighteenth century remained largely untouched by the changes that were beginning to generate a national revival among the Greeks and the Serbs. Although the ethnic complexion of many towns was beginning to change again in favor of the Bulgarian element and numerous mountain settlements of craftsmen and livestock traders were becoming towns, a national bourgeoisie was still lacking.[10] In fact, the few Bulgarians who attained wealth and status in the main towns tended, for advantage or convenience, to become Hellenized and merge into the Greek bourgeoisie. National consciousness continued to be fostered mainly by churchmen in the monasteries and the cell schools. It was the church intelligentsia and the monastic communities that were first reached by the excitement of the national resurgence among the Serbs and the Greeks; they felt the need of a patriotic history with which to inculcate pride in the national past, confidence in the national future, and resistance to Hellenization.

The task of filling this need was undertaken by Father Paisii. Born in 1722 at Bansko, in the diocese where the Rila Monastery was located, Paisii apparently spent his early youth at this great seat of learning and in 1745 joined his older brother at the Khilendar Monastery on Mount Athos. At that time Mount Athos was a confederation of some twenty self-governing monasteries whose singular prestige in the Eastern Orthodox world for piety and learning and rich libraries attracted monks and pilgrims from all Balkan lands and Russia. Although tolerance and mutual help were the rule and some monasteries were ethnically mixed, there was a strong sense of national identity among the monks—not unlike the students in medieval universities—which drove them to disputes and

---

[10] On economic conditions in this period see I. Sakazov, *Bulgarische Wirtschaftsgeschichte* (Berlin, 1929) and Z. Natan, *Istoriia ekonomicheskogo razvitiia Bolgarii* (Moscow, 1961).

squabbles, often quite violent, over the historical merits and de-merits of the nationalities they represented. In the Bulgarian-Ser-bian Khilendar Monastery and in the Mount Athos community in general, Paisii became exposed to the waves of the Serbian and Greek national revivals and was often stung, according to his own testimony, by the ridicule Greek and Serbian monks heaped on Bulgarians for being backward, ignorant, and lacking a great na-tional past. He resolved to show that they were wrong.

For some years he collected historical material on Mount Athos and in Bulgarian centers. In 1761, traveling on monasterial business, he visited the great center of the Serbian revival, Karlowitz (Srem-ski Karlovci), where he consulted the Russian translations of Mauro Orbini's *Il Regno degli Slavi* and *Annales Ecclesiastici* of Cardinal Caesar Baronius.[11] On his return, he moved, because of monkish squabbles, to the predominately Bulgarian Zograf Monastery where, in 1762, he completed his compilation and made a clean copy of the manuscript. The title he wrote on it, *Slavic-Bulgarian History of the Bulgarian People, Kings, and Saints and of All Bulgarian Deeds and Events . . . for the Benefit of the Bulgarian Nation,* mirrors well its content and intent.[12] It was an effort in Church Slavic mixed with spoken Bulgarian, to show the place of Bulgari-ans among the Slavs and in history in general; it was a story of the people and their great men written for the people. Its striking char-acteristics were impassioned and dynamic patriotism, rationality, and appeal to reason. Writing in the year of Rousseau's *Social Con-tract,* which became the bible of French revolutionaries, Paisii used a vocabulary that in western Europe was the hallmark of deism and rationalism. In his two prefaces "The Benefit from History" (based on the Russian preface of *Annales Ecclesiastici*) and "To Those Who Wish to Read and Hear What Is Written in This History," Paisii addressed himself to the "wisdom-loving reader" and ex-plained the great benefits history bestows in "enriching the mind" and "giving sense" to man to manage himself and his home and to

[11] On the domestic and foreign sources Paisii used see *Paisii Khilendarski i nego-vata epokha (1762–1962)* (Sofia, 1962), especially the exhaustive survey of Paisii studies by V. Traikov and Dujčev, pp. 605–44, and A. N. Robinson, *Istoriografiia slavianskogo vozrozhdeniia i Paisii Khilendarskii* (Moscow, 1963).

[12] There is no English translation of Paisii's history. The only study in English is by J. F. Clarke, "Father Paisii and Bulgarian History," in *Teachers of History,* ed., H. S. Hughes (Cornell University Press, 1954), pp. 258–83.

great rulers to govern well. The judgments of God and "the intelligence with which he governs the kingdoms of this world" were not easy to comprehend, and at times it "seemed as if he did not care for us and had relegated us to endless oblivion." However, it only seemed so because from the history of the Jews, Paisii reassured his readers, one could see that God had often committed them to captivity and desolation only to reassemble them again and restore their kingdom. And so it was with the eastern kingdom of the Greeks and the kingdom of the Bulgarians.[13] "We think," Paisii concluded in his first preface, "the Bulgarian kingdom . . . has not been irrevocably abandoned by God and forgotten. But who will rise to God's intelligence and follow his counsel to lift up and reassemble those who have been scattered and heal those who have been crushed; this only God knows in his divine judgments."[14]

Turning to the task of patriotic education and awakening of national pride, Paisii called on those "who love and hold dear your nation and your Bulgarian fatherland"

to know what is known of the deeds of your fathers as all other peoples and nations know about their own nationality and language, have their own history, and are proud of their nationality and language.

Read and know so that you will not be ridiculed and abused by other peoples and nationalities. I grew very fond of the Bulgarian nation and fatherland and applied much effort to collect from various books and histories until I assembled and put together the history of the Bulgarian nation. I have written it for your benefit and pride, for you who like to know about your nation and language. Copy this little history and pay to have it copied by those who can write and keep it so that it will not perish.

There are those who do not care to know about their own Bulgarian nation and turn to foreign ways and foreign tongue; they do not care for their own Bulgarian language but try to read and speak Greek and are ashamed to call themselves Bulgarians. O, you senseless and stupid people! Why are you ashamed to call yourselves Bulgarians and do not read and speak your own language? Or had the Bulgarians no kingdom and

---

[13] The influence of the Christian succession or Third Rome idea may be detected here. Further in the text Paisii uses the concept of the Latin-Greek-Bulgarian seniority in Christendom. Cf. *Slavianobulgarska istoriia,* rendered in modern Bulgarian by P. Dinekov (Sofia, 1960), pp. 62–63, 70–74, 85, and 90–94.

[14] Translated from the original (that is, Nikifor's copy, made by the Rila Monastery monk in 1772 and used by Drinov) *Istoriia Slavenobolgarskaia,* as edited by B. S. Angelov (Sofia, 1961). The quotations that follow are from this version.

state? They have ruled for many years and their glory and renown have been known in the whole world and many times they have exacted tribute from powerful Romans and wise Greeks. Emperors and kings have given them their royal daughters as wives in order to have peace and amity with the Bulgarian tsars. In the entire Slavic race the Bulgarians have had the greatest glory, they first called their rulers tsars, they first had a patriarch, they first were converted, and they conquered the largest territory.

Their present plight, Paisii urged his compatriots, must not make them feel inferior to the Greeks and their intelligence and culture, and seek to become Greeks; there were many nations wiser and more glorious that the Greek, but Greeks did not abandon their language, education, and nation to join others. In fact, "Bulgarian simplicity and kindness" as well as hospitality and charity were superior to "Greek wisdom and sophistication" that led the Greeks to be callous to the needy and to cheat the guileless. The Bulgarians were indeed "mostly simple peasants and craftsmen," but the Bible showed from Adam to David and Joseph that none of these men was a merchant nor a wily or haughty man and that God preferred the simple and kind plowmen and herdsmen and raised them first to glory on earth. Into the historical Bulgarian-Greek confrontation, Paisii introduced the romantic theme of rural virtue versus urban evil, of natural man's superiority over refined products of civilization, which in the eighteenth century one associates with Rousseau and Herder. Independently of his contemporaries in the West, he voiced a Biblical and classical theme—other notions and foreign influences were later added to it—which gave rise to a strong native tradition of ruralism, populism, and democratism.

Paisii presented a brief history of the Bulgarian nation, starting with the Deluge and ending with the fall of Bulgaria under the Turks. Its accuracy and execution leave much to be desired, but so do historical writings in much of Europe and America of that time. Judged by its purpose, it was excellent. It was spirited, sincere, unpretentiously written, keyed to its audience, effective. Coming from a Mount Athos bookman, it had authority. Paisii probably exaggerated for effect the dangers and inroads of Hellenization. If there was indeed a powerful tide of denationalization, the limited number of copies made of his manuscript could not have stemmed it. Extant business records show rather that the nascent Bulgarian bourgeoisie used its native language and, at least at home, remained for the most part as Bulgarian as the rural population. Nor can it be said that Paisii preached fierce chauvinism.[15] His purpose and tone were not aggressive, they were defensive; he denied any intention to defame the Greeks and even expressed regret that Bulgarians and Greeks had not been able to join hands against the Turks. By painting a contrast between Greek national cohesion and pride and Bulgarian apathy and laxity and invoking the Greek danger, Paisii employed the most effective challenge—the challenge of Hellenism—which had worked throughout Bulgarian history to develop the sense of identity and national worth; he hoped the challenge would work again. By using very effective means and focusing on the rising Bulgarian bourgeoisie, Paisii reveals himself as a skillful propagandist and perspicacious cleric who realized that the middle classes, rather than the ecclesiastical intelligentsia, could carry the national cause to the goal of emancipation.

The immediate effect of Paisii's history is difficult to gauge. If he had any hopes to have it published, they did not materialize, and the manuscript remained unprinted for more than eighty years, until 1844. However, as a friar often on the road as a pilgrim or traveling to solicit donations for his monastery, he had opportunity to take his manuscript throughout the Bulgarian lands and let it be copied by those whom he fired with his patriotic message. Some sixty copies have been found scattered from Macedonia to the Bulgarian colonies in Bessarabia. His earliest known and most ardent follower was the priest at Kotel, Stoiko Vladislavov, later Bishop Sofroni Vrachanski, who made a copy during Paisii's visit to Kotel in 1765 and placed it in the local church, adding the curse that "whoever might take it or steal it be anathematized by God." These copies, and others that must have been lost in the troubled conditions prevailing in the Bulgarian lands, were undoubtedly read by many and used in patriotic sermons and for education.

Just because Paisii's impact in his own time was limited, he cannot be regarded, as traditional accounts have depicted him, as an

---

[15] Clarke, "Father Paisi," p. 270. For a critique of Clarke's understanding of Paisii, see G. Schischkoff, "Otec Paisij von Chilendar und seine 'Istorija Slavjanobolgarskaja,'" *Südost-Forschungen* (Supplement), XXI (1962), 19–20.

isolated and well-nigh miraculous phenomenon. There were others active in similar ways.[16] The second half of the eighteenth century was a time of stirring, of quickening change. External impulses from revolutionary France and expansive Russia were felt throughout the Balkan peninsula as both countries increasingly sought to use nationalism and the yearnings for freedom for their own purposes. As the prospects for liberation brightened for the Balkan nations, interest in national history grew. In 1792, another monk, Spiridon of Gabrovo, compiled a *Brief History of the Bulgarian Slavic People*. Other histories, not in the international Church Slavic language, also appeared. Knowledge about the national past no longer remained buried in monasterial libraries.

As the eighteenth century closed and the nineteenth opened, the repercussions of Napoleon's victories over Austria reached the Balkan peoples. His destruction of the Venetian empire and occupation of the Ionian Islands in 1797 and of the Dalmatian coast and Croatia after 1805 brought French power and influence to the peninsula and shook the old order to its foundations. The Serbs rose in revolt in 1804, and the Greeks, stirred by French propaganda flattering their classical past, began to prepare for one. In the western Bulgarian lands seething with unrest under the decaying Ottoman system, Osman Pazvantoğlu, a Muslimized Slav who rose in the Ottoman administration, used the chaotic conditions to declare his authority, based at Vidin, independent from the central government. Issuing manifestoes in the phraseology of the French Revolution to win popular support, Pazvantoğlu helped to spread the message of liberty, equality, and fraternity.

In turn, the eastern Bulgarian lands were stirred by the Russo-Turkish war of 1806–12, fought in large part south of the Danube. As in other wars, the Russians were anxious to enlist Balkan Christians, and many Bulgarians were eager to help in a war that they hoped would lead to national liberation. Bishop Sofroni Vrachanski, who had just published with the assistance of Bulgarian merchants in Romania the first book in modern Bulgarian, became their principal spokesman. Writing memoranda to the Russian government, advising the high command on Bulgarian affairs, and issuing manifestoes, he articulated the national hopes and aspirations. The peace

---

[16] B. S. Angelov, *Suvremennitsi na Paisii* (2 vols.; Sofia, 1963–64) discusses fifteen bookmen contemporaries of Paisii.

that the Russians signed in order to concentrate on the impending French invasion did not bring freedom for Bulgaria, but it made it possible for thousands of Bulgarians to settle in southern Russia, especially in Bessarabia, which Russia now acquired, where their colonies grew rapidly in wealth and importance.[17]

It was at this time, it seems, that the image of Russia as "Diado Ivan" (Grandfather Ivan) planning to liberate Bulgaria gained currency among the people, especially in eastern Bulgaria where the Russo-Turkish wars were usually fought. The image and its propagation were the work of the bookmen and clerics; it had no grounding in the popular epos.[18] Playing upon two potent notions —mighty help from the outside and the solicitude of kinsmen—the image grew into a major component of the ideology of the nascent liberation movement. However, it cannot be understood as reflecting, in this period, an exclusive or special Bulgarian-Russian relationship. In the opening decades of the nineteenth century, this reliance and hope were shared by all Balkan Christians; Bulgarians, Serbs, Greeks, Romanians. Balkan nationalisms had not yet entered the phase of mutually exclusive and antagonistic movements. The common plight and the common aspiration often produced significant examples of mutual assistance and cooperation. This was strikingly so in the Greek revolt of 1821, which, launched from the Greek colonies in Russia and Romania with expectation of Russian help, was intended to liberate all Balkan nationalities and was wholeheartedly aided by Bulgarians there and in Bulgaria proper.[19]

All these events quickened the process of awakening in the Bulgarian lands. Demand for secular and patriotic education grew apace. Beginning with Svishtov in 1815, a number of communities supported so-called Hellenic-Bulgarian schools that introduced the Bell-Lancaster "mutual" method of instruction then practiced in England. The impulse to establish purely Bulgarian secular schools came from the publication in 1824 of an encyclopedic textbook by Dr. Petur Beron. Known as the "Fish Primer" because it had pictures of a dolphin and a whale, it provided instructional material "for the Bulgarian schools," as its author stated on the title page. Through the solicitude of Vasil Aprilov, a wealthy Bulgarian mer-

[17] V. Diakovich, *Bulgarite v Besarabiia* (Sofia, 1930).

[18] Snegarov, *Kulturni i politicheski vruzki*, pp. 16–25.

[19] N. Todorov, *Filiki eteriia i bulgarite* (Sofia, 1965), pp. 9–10.

chant, the first secular school was opened in his native town of Gabrovo in 1835 to serve, as Aprilov stipulated, "all of Bulgaria." By 1878, most towns and larger villages had schools of the new type. Many communities also had "reading rooms" that served as the local library, theater, and community center, and served to spread enlightenment and patriotism.

Aprilov belonged to that part of the rising bourgeoisie that Paisii had berated for turning Greek, and which he sought to redeem for the task of building national consciousness and leading the nation to independence. He exemplified the process of change that took place from Paisii's time to the middle of the nineteenth century. Born in 1789 in the rising manufacturing town on the northern slopes of the Balkan Mountains, Aprilov belonged to a well-to-do merchant family that had branches abroad. In 1800, he was sent to Moscow, where his brother was a prosperous merchant, to obtain a good education. There he attended a Greek school and lived with a Greek family to learn the language well. He pursued his education at the German high school in Braşov (Brasso, Kronstadt) and in Vienna, where he studied medicine, but eventually turned to commerce and manufacture and established himself in Odessa. As a successful businessman, he moved in Greek circles, supported the Greek revolutionary effort, and had a reputation as a Hellenophile. A stronger influence in his life, however, was the rising tide of romantic Slavophilism and Pan-Slavism among the Russian intelligentsia. A young scholar, Iurii Venelin (1802–39), produced in 1829 the first major investigation of medieval influences of Balkan Slavs (especially Bulgarians) on Russia entitled *The ancient and contemporary Bulgarians in their political, ethnographic, historical, and religious relations to the Russians* and written with a contagious Slavophile enthusiasm for Bulgaria as the "classical land" of Slavic antiquity.[20] Venelin's writings, published by the University of Moscow or sponsored by the Imperial Academy of Sciences, rather than Paisii's manuscript history, had a traceable effect on the Bulgarians in Russia, including Aprilov. The Odessa Bulgarians, in fact, erected

[20] A Slav born in Austria, Venelin was at first a teacher in Bessarabia where he evidently developed his interest in the Bulgarians. He published several other works, generally of minor scholarly value but of great influence on the growth of Bulgarian national consciousness. Cf. V. Zlatarski, "Iurii Ivanovich Venelin i znachenieto mu za bulgarite," *Letopis na Bulgarskoto knizhovno druzhestvo v Sofia*, III (1901–1902), 90–160.

a monument in 1841 on Venelin's grave in Moscow as an expression of gratitude. Both Venelin and Aprilov pressed the view, later supported by Marin Drinov, that Cyril and Methodius were Bulgarians by origin and thus gave impetus to the religious and public celebration of the two saints as the "Bulgarian Apostles" in Bulgarian communities every year on May 24. The annual celebration grew before 1878 into the national holiday of Bulgarians everywhere.[21]

Venelin's widespread searches for historical, ethnographic, and linguistic materials, including travel in Bulgarian lands, set an example for Slavists in Russia and elsewhere, who began to collect systemically the materials on national identity and to publish them in grammars, dictionaries, folklore collections, source publications, and historical studies. Even Americans contributed to this process of "rediscovery of a lost nationality," as Bulgarians were perceived in the West. Under the auspices of the American Board of Commissioners for Foreign Missions in Boston, American missionaries were particularly successful among the Armenians who turned to Protestantism as a means of casting off the Greek ecclesiastical domination and achieving the status of a separate religious community. Similar conditions drew American missionaries to the Bulgarian lands, and in 1844 one of them, Elias Riggs, composed a Bulgarian grammar for the use of English-speaking persons. With his encouragement and the use of the mission press, Konstantin Fotinov began in 1842 the publication of the first Bulgarian periodical. Riggs was also instrumental in the making of the first complete translation of the Bible into modern Bulgarian, published in 1871 and widely known as the "American Bible."[22] American schools, including Roberts College in Istanbul, helped to educate many of the leaders of modern Bulgaria and created an avenue of vital contacts with the English-speaking countries.[23] American educators and Bulgarian graduates from these schools played an essential part in the

---

[21] V. Kiselkov (*Khiliada i sto godini slavianska pismenost*, p. 343) believes that the celebration was initiated in the thirteenth century.

[22] W. W. Hall, *Puritans in the Balkans: The American Board Mission in Bulgaria, 1878–1918* (Sofia, 1938), pp. 1–47.

[23] In its first forty years (1863–1903) Roberts College educated 195 Bulgarians, the largest national group. Cf. R. H. Davison "Westernized Education in Ottoman Turkey," *The Middle East Journal* (Summer, 1961), pp. 289–301; C. E. Black, "The Influence of Westen Political Thought in Bulgaria, 1850–1885," *American Historical Review*, XLVIII, No. 3 (April, 1943), 507–20.

events of the 1870's that led to the national liberation. This record prompted a Bulgarian nationalist scholar in 1918, writing with an eye on the coming peace conference, to suggest that Bulgaria owed her "revival and independence no less to America than to Russia."[24]

Throughout the Bulgarian lands this process was expanded and accelerated by a "whole Pleiad of awakeners and enlighteners" and "apostles of the Bulgarian liberty," to use the language of Bulgarian nationalism.[25] Teachers, writers, poets, publicists, all committed to the cause of national uplifting, spread their message in a rising flow of journals, books, and newspapers published for the most part, because of Turkish censorship, in the Bulgarian colonies abroad and other outlying centers.[26] Under the influence of German romantic nationalism and scholarship, reaching Bulgarians directly or through the Austrian Slavs and the Russians, a considerable effort was made to discover such elements of national identity as folklore, grammar and vocabulary, and historical sources. The most significant of these early efforts were the collection of folk songs from the various Bulgarian lands published in Zagreb in 1861 by two brothers from Struga, Macedonia, named Dimitur and Konstantin Miladinov, with the aid of the celebrated Bishop Iosif Strossmayer, to whom they dedicated their *Bulgarski Narodni Pesni*; the folklore collection of Liuben Karavelov, *Pamiatniki narodnogo byta bolgar* (Moscow, 1861); and the fundamental dictionary, *Rechnik na blugarskii iazyk*, which Naiden Gerov began in 1845 and which eventually incorporated in six volumes the literary and spoken language. The main focal point of such efforts became the Bulgarian Literary Society, founded in 1869 in Braîla, Romania, with Marin Drinov as president.[27]

---

[24] D. Mishew, *America and Bulgaria and Their Moral Bonds* (Bern, 1918), p. 12. A more significant generalization is made by Hall that "Bulgaria, alone of all the Balkan states, has been receptive to the message of American Protestant missionaries."

[25] N. Nikitov, *Apostoli na bulgarskata svoboda* (Sofia: Bulgarsko Delo, 1943). "Bulgarsko Delo" (Bulgarian Cause) was a government foundation set up during World War II to serve purposes of internal and external nationalist propaganda.

[26] On publishing in the Bulgarian language before 1878 see P. Atanasov, *Nachalo na bulgarskoto knigopechatane* (Sofia, 1959); B. M. Andreev, *Nachalo, razvoi i vuzkhod na bulgarskiia pechat*, Vol. I (Sofia, 1946); and V. Pundev, *Periodicheski pechat predi osvobozhdenieto* (2 vols.; Sofia, 1927–1930).

[27] The Society became, in 1911, the Bulgarian Academy of Sciences, and from its inception sought to publish—in the manner of such societies and academies in other countries—the *monumenta* of Bulgarian history, language, and folklore. On the

The problem of the national language—always crucial in the processes of nation-building—had become particularly difficult in the first half of the nineteenth century. The language of education and literature, Church Slavic, was a hindrance rather than an effective vehicle although it had been invaded by the spoken language, because it remained stilted, bore a Russian imprint, and was removed from the people. The spoken language, on the other hand, was split into several dialects, had become heavily mixed with Turkisms, and had failed to develop native terms for the civilization of the nineteenth century. Its total vocabulary was unknown, its grammar and spelling undefined. As the founder of the first Bulgarian newspaper, Dr. Ivan Bogorov, pointed out, "at the present time, it is the easiest and the most difficult thing to write in Bulgarian."[28]

As the need to develop an effective tool of communication grew acute, the controversy—should the national language be based on the Church Slavic or on the living language—became sharp. By 1870, the controversy was resolved in favor of the living language due mainly to the flood of writings of the new secular intelligentsia. The prevalence of writers and publicists from eastern Bulgaria among the new intelligentsia, furthermore, assured their dialect of dominance and eventually it became the criterion of correct usage. Due to the Russian education of many of these writers and publicists and their translations from Russian, the vocabulary and grammar of the emerging national language became heavily invaded by Russisms. Efforts to establish a distinctive and practical spelling were initiated by Drinov, who called for the creation of a common literary language—"our principal national mainstay"—through the adoption of a uniform orthography "according to the spirit and peculiarities of our language" and uniform vocabulary and rules of grammar.[29] Alarm at the invasion of Russisms was also beginning to be voiced, but the demand for purity of the national language did

---

Academy as the center of nationalist scholarship, see my article, "The Bulgarian Academy of Sciences," in *The Far Eastern Quarterly* (September, 1969).

[28] Andreev, . . . *Bulgarskiia pechat*, I, 37. Bogorov's newspaper in 1846 and the ventures of many others at the time failed largely because they were at a loss finding a language of communication with their readers.

[29] M. Drinov, "Za novobulgarskoto asbuke," *Periodichesko Spisanie*, No. 2 (1870), pp. 9–29.

not develop into a major nationalistic issue until after the liberation of the country.

Nationalist Triumphs and Defeat (1870–1878)

The nationalist success of the Serbs and the Greeks, disappointment with Russian policies, and a growing realization that Russia pursued only her own interests convinced the Bulgarians that they must rely chiefly on themselves and mount their own liberation effort. This feeling was strengthened by the course of the Crimean War and the defeat of Russia by France and England. The new ideas were articulated and personified mainly by Georgi S. Rakovski, a restless spirit and fiery romantic revolutionary, who had roamed in many lands and become conversant with European politics. In his own activities, Rakovski, particularly influenced by the Italian *Risorgimento* and Mazzini's ideology of "Young Italy" and "Young Europe," sought to fuse the activities of *khaiduti* bands and the sporadic local flare-ups of rebellion into a national revolutionary movement and to link it with the revolutionary movements in Europe. Hailed by contemporaries as the Bulgarian Garibaldi, he saw in the Italian struggle for liberation from Austrian domination and for unification the pattern to be followed. Rakovski became acutely aware of the divergence of the interests of conservative Russia and revolutionary Bulgaria and wrote, among other things, a pamphlet *Migration to Russia, or the Deadly Russian Policy Toward the Bulgarians* to warn against the depopulation of Bulgarian lands.[30]

Rakovski's views heralded most of the essential elements of the ideology of the revolutionary movement that took shape between the end of the Crimean War and the Bulgarian revolt in 1876. His own plan for action gave direction to all subsequent revolutionary activities. It called for the creation of a network of secret revolutionary committees in the Bulgarian lands to prepare for a general uprising, which was to be directed by a headquarters in Beograd and aided by an invading force—or legion, as Rakovski called it—assembled and trained there. At times Rakovski also sought to make common cause with Serbia, Romania, and Greece, and toyed with the idea of a Balkan federation, but came to realize that the Balkan

[30] I. Ormandzhiev, *Nova i nai-nova istoriia na bulgarskiia narod* (Sofia, 1945), p. 241. Rakovski was also passionately interested in national history and was the first to write about Paisii, having used the copy of his history that Aprilov saw in Odessa.

nations were more apt to pursue their own interests and ambitions than to help each other.[31] Serbian-Bulgarian cooperation, in particular, held promise until, under the impact of the Italian unification, Serbia was attracted by the role of a southern Slav Piedmont and appeared to covet a position of supremacy.

The ideology of Bulgarian revolutionary nationalism was truly developed by Liuben Karavelov. Spending nearly ten years in Moscow, he came to know official and revolutionary Russia well. Official Slavophiles and Pan-Slavists like I. S. Aksakov frightened him with their program of bringing the "brother Slavs" in Turkey and Austria "under the mighty wing of the Russian eagle," while discouraging the independent liberation movement of the Slavs as undesirable and impossible, frowning upon the rising demand for a Bulgarian national church as disrupting the unity of Bulgarians and Greeks within Orthodoxy, and advising the Bulgarians to end their resistance to the Turks and migrate to Russia. He found himself ideologically close to Herzen, Bakunin, Dobroliubov, and Chernyshevskii, especially to the latter who urged Bulgarians and Serbs to rely upon themselves and beware of the "perfidious friendship" of Slavophiles like Aksakov.[32] Moving to Bucureşti and cast by circumstances in the role of a Bulgarian Mazzini, Karavelov joined the growing struggle between the "young" and the "old," between the hotheads and the conservatives in the Bulgarian nationalist movement, by preaching his basic conviction that "liberty is not received, it is taken" and that, like Italy, Bulgaria *fara da se.* He rejected the idea of the "old" for a Turkish-Bulgarian dualism on the model of the Austro-Hungarian Compromise and declared that "only those nations can say that they are human beings, who have civil, religious, scientific, social, national, and personal freedom." The supreme deity in his creed was the "Goddess of Liberty"; the ultimate goal was a free, enlightened, self-reliant nation unified in its own national state. After attaining their freedom and ordering their own state "according to the best institutions among the enlightened nations, that is, the Americans, Belgians, and the Swiss," Bulgarians were to join other Balkan nations in a federation on the American

[31] L. S. Stavrianos, *Balkan Federation. A History of the Movement Toward Balkan Unity in Modern Times* (Northampton, Mass.: Smith College, 1944), pp. 84–89.
[32] L. Vorob'ev, *Liuben Karavelov: Mirovozzrenie i tvorchestvo* (Moscow, 1963). pp. 38–71.

or Swiss model to withstand the encroachments of the Great Powers.[33]

Karavelov was particularly apprehensive about Russian aims. Speaking out boldly, he warned that "the well-being of the Bulgarians will not come from the North" and that to rely on Russia was "to suffer for another century." Russia, he was convinced, pursued only her own interests: she was responsible for the exodus of thousands of Bulgarians from the Bulgarian lands and the settlement of thousands of Tartars and Circassians there; she had not mentioned a word about Bulgaria at the Paris Congress in 1856; she sided with the Greek patriarchate against the Bulgarians' desire to restore their religious independence; she was even willing to guarantee the existence of the Ottoman Empire. The little help given for the education of some Bulgarians was hardly of any use to the Bulgarian people, since most of the students settled down in Russia or were recruited for police work in Moscow. Russian influence in language and literature was baneful. The liberation of the Turkish and Austrian Slavs and their unification under the aegis of the Russian autocrat, as the Russian Pan-Slavists urged, would mean the liberty and unity Prussia brought to Germany rather than a truly "human brotherhood." Striking a prophetic note, Karavelov said:

> If Russia comes to the Balkan peninsula as a liberator and savior, Slavic brotherhood will be an accomplished fact; however, if she comes as a conqueror and a brutally despotic power, requiring all to fall on their knees, then her successes will crumble at once. If the Slavic nations in Austria and Turkey are struggling with such energy to take the foreign yoke off their necks, they will never voluntarily put their backs under the brotherly saddles of the Russian Slavs. In brief, Slavic brotherhood will be realized only when each Slavic nation is free and independent, when every Slav affirms his own national characteristics . . . .[34]

While Karavelov preached political nationalism from Bucureşti, Bulgarians within the Ottoman Empire were agitated by a surge of religious nationalism. In the theocratic order of the empire, people were legally grouped in semiautonomous bodies (millets) accord-

[33] M. Arnaudov, *Liuben Karavelov: Zhivot, Delo, Epokha, 1834–1879* (Sofia, 1964), pp. 376–78.
[34] *Ibid.*, pp. 491–98.

ing to religious allegiance, religion rather than domicile or political allegiance determined the law under which a person lived. When reforms were introduced and rights granted, as under the *hatti-sherif* of 1839, their enforcement fell to the millets. In order to enjoy directly whatever benefits the Ottoman system conferred, a nationality needed the status of a separate millet; this in turn was a matter of religious identity and autonomy. Since the loss of their religious independence with the collapse of the Patriarchate of Tŭrnovo in 1393, Bulgarians belonged to the general Christian millet, whose spokesmen before the Ottoman authorities were the Greek Patriarch in Istanbul and the Greek bishops and priests in the provinces. Subordination to this Greek "Phanariote" hierarchy was intensely resented, for nationalistic or economic reasons, by Christians throughout the empire. One by one, the subordinate nations broke away from the ecumenical patriarchate and declared themselves autocephalous, or self-governing. By 1870, it was the Bulgarians' turn to do so.

The Crimean War made conditions ripe for the move. Anti-Greek feeling among the Bulgarians had risen sharply since the 1830's as the conflicts of economic interests and the effects of nationalist education and propaganda made themselves felt. The interests of the rising Bulgarian middle class clashed with those of the entrenched Phanariote Greeks in Istanbul itself, where there was a sizeable and vocal Bulgarian colony, as well as in the Bulgarian provinces. Patriotic education reminded Bulgarians of the religious independence they had wrested from the Greeks in the past. Nationalist propaganda alleged that the Phanariotes, merchants, and clergy, were bent on denationalizing the Bulgarians in order to keep them subordinated forever and dwelled on the abuses and corrupt practices of the Greek prelates in Bulgarian dioceses. At first agitation was limited to demands for Bulgarian bishops and priests and abolition of the sale of offices and other corrupt practices, but the Crimean War and the pressure of the European Powers on the Ottoman Empire to reform itself encouraged the Bulgarians to seek more. The legal basis for their new demands was the *hatti-humayun* of 1856, which provided for a reorganization of the millets. At the request of the Ottoman government, the patriarchate held a church council in 1858–60 to consider changes, but of the bishops attending only three were Bulgarians and the modest Bulgarian demands for elective bishops, who were to know the local language and receive a fixed salary, went unheeded.

The Bulgarians in Istanbul and, through their newspapers, those in the provinces finally realized that the only solution was complete separation from the patriarchate. The first step was taken on Easter Day, 1860, when the Bulgarian bishop officiating in the Bulgarian church in Istanbul omitted, at the demand of the congregation, the name of the Patriarch from the service. With this act the Bulgarian-Greek religious conflict entered its final phase, which ended in 1870 with the issuance of a firman by the Ottoman government that recognized the Bulgarians as a separate religious community and provided for the organization of a Bulgarian exarchate.[35]

The Bulgarian-Greek conflict embroiled not only the Ottoman government, but the Great Powers as well. Turkey saw in it an opportunity to split further the Orthodox world that Russia had sought to lead as a bloc against her. A similar view was held by France and Austria, while Russia was generally baffled by the dilemma of pursuing a Pan-Slavist policy and supporting the Bulgarians or upholding the unity of the Orthodox world. Many Bulgarian nationalists felt that the Ottoman government, France, and Austria aided the Bulgarian cause whereas Russia hindered it. The Crimean War and the consequent assumption of responsibility by the Concert of Europe for the affairs of Turkey drove home the realization that to associate the national cause exclusively with Russia was to rely on a power that France, England, and others in the West held suspect and at bay. As a consequence, an increasing number of Bulgarian nationalists sought to fathom the complexities of interests and policies in the European Concert and to enlist support in the West for their objectives. In her years of triumph after 1856, France presented a particular promise because she played the role of nation maker in Italy, Romania, and elsewhere and sponsor of Catholicism everywhere. The first move to use France was made in the bishopric of Kukush in Macedonia, where the population requested, in 1859, a union with the Catholic church as a way of getting rid of the Greek bishop sent from Istanbul. In the following year a union

---

[35] Text in G. Noradounghian, *Recueil d'actes internationaux de l'Empire Ottoman* (Paris, 1902), III, 293–95. The Bulgarian-Greek enmity was further deepened when, in 1872, the patriarchate declared the Bulgarian church schismatic. The schism was not healed until 1945.

with Rome was formalized, and in April, 1861, Pope Pius IX installed Iosif Sokolski as the Uniate Archbishop of Bulgaria. Strictly an expedient against the Greek prelates, the union with Rome proved short-lived; few Bulgarians were inclined to see the religious unity of the nation violated.[36] The encounter of Protestantism with Bulgarian nationalism had a similar history.[37]

The re-establishment of a self-governing Bulgarian church in 1870 and the delimitation of its territory had a significance for Bulgarian nationalism comparable only to that of Paisii's message in the preceding century. In the conceptual framework of the surrounding theocratic society, it was the supreme recognition of the Bulgarian nation and its identity and the first step toward the restoration of national independence in religion as well as in politics and economics. Because a religious community had charge of its own schools under the millet system, the exarchate also signified the liquidation of the Greek cultural and educational penetration of the Bulgarian lands under its jurisdiction. The territorial jurisdiction of the exarchate was defined in the firman, which specified the purely Bulgarian bishoprics and allowed for the addition of others by plebiscite if two thirds of the population of disputed bishoprics should opt to join it. The result was a territory stretching from the delta of the Danube to the Aegean coast and to Ohrid in Macedonia and Niş (Nish) in the Morava region.[38] Although it left some areas in dispute between Bulgarians and Greeks, the exarchate's domain provided the essential ethnic boundary that Bulgarians hoped would soon be the political frontier of the re-established national state.[39]

[36] It was also an issue of Russophobes versus Russophiles among the Bulgarian nationalists. The Russophiles succeeded in persuading Archbishop Sokolski to go to Russia and renounce the union; the Russophobes charged that the archbishop had been kidnapped and held captive. Cf. I. Sofranov, *Histoire du mouvement bulgare vers l'église catholique au XIX-e Siècle*, Vol. I (Rome, 1960).

[37] J. F. Clarke, "Protestantism and the Bulgarian Church Question in 1861," *Essays in the History of Modern Europe*, ed. D. C. McKay (New York, 1936), pp. 79–97.

[38] Cf. map in H. R. Wilkinson, *Maps and Politics: A Review of the Ethnographic Cartography of Macedonia* (Liverpool: University Press, 1951), p. 60.

[39] In subsequent decades, Serbian nationalists claimed that Serbs in "South Serbia" (Macedonia) had opted for the Bulgarian exarchate because there was no other choice. An attempt to draw a satisfactory political line between Bulgarians and Serbs in Macedonia was made in 1912; see below.

Liberation from what Bulgarians had come to view as the "Greek spiritual subjugation" sharpened the desire for liberation from its twin incubus, the Turkish political domination. Although conservatives and moderates among the well-to-do Bulgarians and the new church hierarchy sought to brake the revolutionary movement and advocated an evolutionary approach to liberty through the autonomy and educational machinery of the exarchate, liberal and radical nationalists in the colonies abroad as well as throughout the lands of the exarchate gained a growing audience for their programs of political action. The central figure among them was Karavelov, who held all clergymen suspect and called in his newspapers (*Liberty*, later *Independence*) for the achievement of freedom through a national revolution; as he put it, "Freedom needs not the Exarch but Karadzhata" (meaning Dimitur Karadzha, the renowned leader of *khaiduti* bands who fell fighting the Turks in 1868).

Karavelov and other revolutionaries set up a "Central Committee" in Bucureşti to direct all revolutionary activities and to establish an internal revolutionary organization with a network of secret committees preparing the ground for a general uprising. Chief organizer of the secret committees was a young deacon, Vasil Levski, a proven fighter in *khaiduti* bands and member of Rakovski's legion in Beograd, who had been taught by experience that *khaiduti* raids could accomplish nothing without a simultaneous massive revolt. In the pantheon of Bulgarian nationalism Levski is endowed with almost all virtues and impulses of the ideal Bulgarian: he was simple of manner and speech, self-effacing, dedicated, lion-hearted.[40] Combining idealism with realism, he had embraced the cause of liberty with a quiet passion that made him say once that after Bulgaria was liberated he would serve some other nation's quest for freedom. His ideal of the future Bulgarian state was a democratic republic, in which all nationalities (Bulgarians, Turks, Jews) would enjoy absolute equality before the law, and which would lead to a Balkan federation. One of the first native populists, he believed in the virtues of the peasant masses and blamed the vices of the Ottoman

[40] Levski, meaning lionlike, was the nickname given to him while he served in Rakovski's legion. The lion rampant was already established as a national symbol and was used on *khaiduti* uniforms. After 1878, it also provided the name of the Bulgarian unit of currency, the lev.

system for the antagonism between Bulgarians and Turks.[41] A veritable "Apostle of Liberty," Levski traveled clandestinely through Bulgarian lands north and south of the Balkan range and succeeded in organizing a widespread network of committees. In 1873, however, he was betrayed, caught, and executed by the Turkish authorities. The work of organizing for revolution suffered a severe setback.

With Levski dead and Karavelov disillusioned, the leadership of the revolutionaries passed to Khristo Botev, Stefan Stambolov, and other young men, all in their twenties. A poet as well as national and social revolutionary, Botev combined Byronic qualities with a Garibaldian flair for spectacular action and pre-Marxian socialism. He was one of the first Bulgarian leaders with an intellectual background; his father, a schoolteacher, was a product of the Hellenic-Bulgarian schools and had translated one of Venelin's works into Bulgarian. Botev spent some time studying in Odessa on a Russian government scholarship but became imbued with the ideas of Herzen, Chernyshevskii, and other Russian revolutionaries. He settled in Bucureşti where he talked revolution with Karavelov and Levski, published newspapers, and wrote poetry and articles marked by fiery patriotism and a keen social conscience.[42] The uprising in Hercegovina in 1875 finally provided an opportunity to pass from words to deeds.

The spread of the revolt to Bosnia and the prospect of intervention by Serbia and Montenegro on behalf of the insurgents spurred the Bulgarian revolutionaries to plan a general insurrection. Inadequately organized, the so-called "April" uprising broke out in the spring of 1876 mainly in the villages and hamlets on the southern slopes of the Balkan mountains and in the Rhodope region, but sympathetic revolutionary action flared up in other regions. In a Garibaldian move, Botev crossed the Danube at the head of a detachment of two hundred guerrillas after capturing an Austrian ship and announcing to the European press the Bulgarians' resolve to fulfill their vow of "Liberty or Death." Uncoordinated with the activities of the insurgents, the movements of Botev's detachment ended on Mt. Vola above Vratsa where Botev died in an engage-

[41] On Levski's ideology see I. Undzhiev, *Vasil Levski: Biografiia* (Sofia, 1967).

[42] Cf. Botev's biographies cited in G. Konstantinov and others, *Bulgarski pisateli: Biografii, Bibliografiia* (Sofia, 1961), pp. 147–54.

ment with Turkish forces. In the insurgent regions the Turkish government, frightened by the spread of rebellion among the *raya* near the capital and the threat to the main imperial route in Europe, Istanbul—Edirne (Adrianople)—Plovdiv (Philippopolis)—Sofia —Niš, gave free rein to the troops, augmented by Circassians and irregulars armed for the purpose, to overpower the insurgent population in bloodbaths and massacres. In a swirling climax of racial and religious fanaticism whole villages were destroyed, and people of all ages, who had taken refuge in their churches, were burned alive or slaughtered.

Information on the horrors in Bulgaria first reached western Europe through the reports of Edwin Pears, J. MacGahan, an American newspaperman, and the American consul Eugene Schuyler. Schuyler's official report "which found its way into print" and MacGahan's accounts "startled England like a peal of thunder." While the Conservative government of Disraeli sought to belittle them and save its policy of sustaining Turkey against Russia, liberal opinion swept England in a storm of moral indignation. Its principal spokesman, William Gladstone, called, in his pamphlet *Bulgarian Horrors and the Question of the East* (which sold in 200,000 copies) and in numerous speeches, for compelling the Turks "one and all, bag and baggage" to clear out of "the province they have desolated and profaned." Similar public reaction in France, Russia, and elsewhere in Europe set the stage for an intervention by the Concert of Europe. The Eastern Question became now essentially "the Bulgarian Question."[43]

As Russia prepared to intervene, the Powers agreed to hold a conference of their ambassadors in Istanbul and press Turkey to institute reforms in the ravaged provinces. In the preparations for it, the Russian ambassador, N. P. Ignatiev, invited Schuyler to collaborate with a member of his staff, A. N. Tseretelev, in drafting proposals for establishing autonomy in the Bulgarian lands within the Ottoman Empire. The main problem was whether to propose the creation of a large autonomous entity embracing all the lands of the Bul-

---

[43] For details of the wave of indignation at the atrocities and sympathy for the Bulgarians, which exceeded in intensity the Philhellenic agitation in the 1820's, see D. Harris, *Britain and the Bulgarian Horrors of 1876* (Chicago: University of Chicago Press, 1939) and R. W. Seton-Watson, *Disraeli, Gladstone and the Eastern Question* (London, 1935; F. Cass reprint, 1962).

garian exarchate or to divide them into two autonomous units in order to assuage the fears of Austria and overcome the objections of England to favoring the Slavic element in the Balkan peninsula at the expense of the Greek. As the conference convened, the Russians had a "maximum" proposal reflecting Schuyler's views in favor of a united Bulgarian province and a "minimum" proposal splitting the Bulgarian lands in two to appease Austria, England, and the Greeks.

The ambassadorial conference took the Russian proposals as the basis for discussion and, as it was expected, adopted the "minimum" proposal. Presented in January, 1877, the project for reforms was rejected by Turkey on the ground that the constitution, adopted the previous December, took care of things. From the point of view of the Bulgarian nationalists, however, both proposals and the discussions of the European diplomats provided a validation, with some divergencies, of the ethnic frontiers drawn in the establishment of the Bulgarian exarchate in 1870.

The failure of the diplomats to obtain results from Turkey led to a revival of the idea of Russian military intervention. With all European powers, even England, accepting it, the war began in April, 1877. To Bulgarians everywhere it was the climax of the struggle that was to result in national liberation. Bulgarian volunteers from the colonies in Russia and Romania as well as from Bulgaria proper flocked to the headquarters of the invading Russian army in Bessarabia and formed the nucleus of a "Bulgarian Territorial Army." The Bulgarian corps received its flag from the citizens of the Russian town of Samara and fought well in several battles, especially that of Shipka Pass. Despite its weaknesses, the Russian army took the major Turkish strongholds in its path, including Edirne, and threatened to enter Istanbul. As Turkey sued for peace, the stage was set for drawing up a settlement in the Istanbul suburb of San Stefano.

The peace of San Stefano (March 3, 1878), termed preliminary because the Concert of Europe was entitled to pass on it, was Russia's chance to crown her decisive but costly intervention with gains that would avenge the Crimean defeat, place her in a dominant position in the Balkans, and resolve her Straits problem. Since seizing Istanbul and the Straits was out of the question because of British opposition, they were to be bypassed on a land bridge to the Mediterranean in the form of a large Bulgarian state tied to Russia by gratitude, kinship, and political and cultural dependence. The blueprint for this construction was in the proposals of the Istanbul conference.

With Ignatiev as its architect, the essence of the San Stefano settlement was the establishment of a large Bulgarian state. Bulgaria was to be an autonomous principality, under the nominal suzerainty of Turkey, embracing nearly all the lands identified as Bulgarian in the proposals of the Istanbul conference and in the creation of the exarchate.[44] Russian forces and administrators were to remain in Bulgaria for two years to help in the creation of a Bulgarian machinery of government.

Despite the technicality of Turkish suzerainty and the loss of northern Dobrudja and other small areas of the exarchate's territory, the San Stefano settlement was the supreme fulfillment of the program of Bulgarian nationalism as it had developed in the century since Paisii. To the religious emancipation and ethnic unity attained in 1870, San Stefano added political liberation and the formation of the nation-state, the ultimate goal of nationalists everywhere. Unlike other nations that had to achieve political unity gradually, the vast majority of the Bulgarians attained it at once. The three main provinces of the Bulgarian exarchate, Moesia (between the Danube and the Balkan Mountains), Thrace, and Macedonia, with a segment of the Aegean coast,[45] were now one body stirring to begin a full national life. Under its own church and state, the nation felt free, united, on the threshold of a great future. Throughout the Bulgarian lands jubilation was understandably ecstatic. An address to the Russian Emperor, Alexander II, carrying 230,000 signatures (among them those of Marin Drinov, Stefan Stambolov, Exarch Iosif, and other national leaders) expressed well the sentiments of "eternal gratitude" to the "Tsar-Liberator" and the brotherly Russian people for removing the stone from the grave where Bulgaria had been entombed for centuries by Ottoman rule and making possible her resurrection. Rising to a new life, Bulgarians hoped to

[44] The major exception was northern Dobrudja that Russia gave now to Romania to compensate for retaking southern Bessarabia that she had yielded to the Romanian Principalities in 1856. For a map of the San Stefano boundaries, see Wilkinson, *Maps and Politics*, p. 86.

[45] Extending to but not including Salonika, which Ignatiev at one point felt should be included in Bulgaria as the birthplace of Cyril and Methodius.

join the ranks of the civilized nations and, like others, become useful to mankind.[46]

Bulgarian nationalism's hour of triumph, however, was brief. The flaw of the San Stefano settlement was that it was an exclusively Russian creation, to which a number of powers, large and small, were set to take exception. England viewed negatively the arrival of Russia on the shores of the Mediterranean via a large Russian-oriented Bulgarian state, while Austria had declared her opposition to a large Slavic state in the Balkans and felt entitled to Bosnia and Hercegovina. Opposed to an Austrian annexation of Bosnia and Hercegovina, Serbia felt that, if it came, she should be able to expand to the south, that is, into Macedonia. Greece, receiving nothing while Bulgaria became the largest state in the peninsula, was bitter. The undoing of the San Stefano settlement came quickly. Meeting in Berlin in June and July, 1878, the powers of the concert of Europe redrew the Balkan map to satisfy England and Austria. Bulgaria was dismembered: of its three main provinces, Moesia and an area to the southwest including Sofia were constituted as the Bulgarian principality under Turkish suzerainty and Russian administration for nine months; Thrace without the Aegean coast was returned to the Ottoman Empire as a distinct province (Eastern Rumelia) with a Christian governor and Turkish garrisons; Macedonia and the Aegean coast were also returned to the Ottoman Empire, but without privileged status or protection. England and Austria thus attained their joint and individual objectives: the large Slavic state in the heart of the Balkans, through which Russia hoped to reach the Mediterranean, was dismantled, and Russia was confined to a sphere of influence north of the Balkan Mountains. Once again, as in the Crimean war, Russia was isolated and defeated in her abiding aims.

For Bulgarians the Berlin settlement was a sudden and traumatic experience. In the span of only four months, the national cause had moved from jubilant triumph to stunning defeat. The Bulgarians

---

[46] Text of the address in *Osvobozhdenie Bolgarii ot turetskogo iga: Dokumenty,* II, (Moscow, 1964), 564–68. Alexander II was already known as the tsar-liberator for his emancipation of the Russian serfs in 1861. In foreign policy Pan-Slavist propaganda depicted him as the liberator of the Slavs oppressed by the Ottoman and Habsburg empires.

felt, that the body of the nation had been carved up on a table in Berlin by callous men to satisfy their own interests, without letting the victim be heard. The outcry of anguish, bitterness, and consternation was as general as the joy had been four months earlier. Even Russia was not spared in the protest; as Stambolov expressed it, if Russia was not prepared to defend the integrity of the Bulgarian nation, she should not have undertaken to liberate it.[47] Popular resentment and indignation flared up in Eastern Rumelia and Macedonia to protest and resist the reintroduction of Turkish rule. In many towns "Unity" committees were formed that, under the guise of charitable activities, were to prepare for armed action against the dictates of the Congress of Berlin. In Eastern Rumelia numerous gymnastic societies sprang up to train, with Russian instructors and weapons, for the same purpose. In Tŭrnovo, where a constituent assembly convened to consider a constitution for the principality, national leaders and spokesmen for the rising number of refugees from the territories reoccupied by Turkey pressed for disbanding the assembly until the Great Powers allowed the reunification of the nation. Only pressure from Russia, then unable to afford complications on account of Bulgaria, forestalled drastic action.[48]

The Problems of National Unification (1878–1912)

After the Congress of Berlin the program of Bulgarian nationalism could only be the unification of the nation's lands dismembered by Great Power rivalries and "through no fault of the Bulgarian people."[49] Its simple but enormously appealing formulation was "Reestablishment of San Stefano Bulgaria." The principality, free from direct Turkish control and under favorable Russian tutelage, was to provide the nucleus of the unification process. One of the first moves in this direction was to transfer the capital, at Drinov's suggestion, from Tŭrnovo to Sofia as the natural center of the Bulgarian lands, which symbolized the primacy of none and from where develop-

---

[47] Ormandzhiev, Nova i nai-nova istoriia na bulgarskiia narod, p. 410. An irrepressible nationalist, Stambolov later greeted the newly elected prince, Alexander of Battenberg, with a placard "Remember Integral Bulgaria!"

[48] Kiril, Patriarch of Bulgaria, Suprotivata sreshtu Berlinskiia dogovor. Kresnenskoto vustanie (Sofia, 1955).

[49] Ormandzhiev, Nova i nai-nova istoriia na bulgarskiia narod, p. 406.

ments in Thrace and Macedonia could be more effectively influenced.

Ideas on how to liberate Thrace and Macedonia and unite them with the principality became polarized by the issue of force. The "young" elements joined by spokesmen of the refugees advocated the preparation of uprisings aided, directed, and assured of success by the intervention of the principality. The conservative and moderate "old" elements, mindful of the internal and external problems of the new state and of Russia's unwillingness to be embroiled in complications, pointed to the risks and consequences of defeat and counseled maintaining and strengthening the Bulgarian hold on the lands still under Turkey and persuading the Great Powers to abide by what they had endorsed at the Istanbul conference. Instead of jeopardizing the entire national cause by precipitous action, the "old" argued, the existing religious and spiritual unity of the nation achieved through the exarchate should be carefully protected and strengthened as the foundation on which some day the political unity of San Stefano Bulgaria would be restored. In recognition of this argument, the seat of the exarchate remained in Istanbul where it continued to represent the Bulgarian millet in the Ottoman Empire and to minister to its religious and educational needs.[50]

The return of large Christian areas to Ottoman rule, everyone agreed, could only be temporary. Alarmed by the appearance of "Big Bulgaria" at San Stefano, Greece became determined to obtain as much of these areas as possible. Similarly, Serbia saw possibilities for expansion only in the direction of Macedonia and Salonika (Thessaloniki). Irked by the Austrian acquisition of Bosnia and Hercegovina but unable to do anything about it, Serbia, under King Milan Obrenović, turned to a policy of subservience to Austria in exchange for Austrian support of expansion into Macedonia. With Bulgarian, Greek, and Serbian interests converging upon Macedonia, the Eastern Question after 1878 became essentially the "Macedonian Question." Each of the three Balkan nations turned to history, ethnography, and education to justify its claims. While Bulgarians regarded their rights as proven by the role of Macedonia in the

---

[50] Religious unity through the exarchate was also stressed in the Turnovo Constitution that provided (Art. 39) that the principality was "an integral part of the Bulgarian ecclesiastical territory" and was subordinated to the supreme authority of the Bulgarian church "wherever this authority may be located."

national revival, by the exarchate, and by the decisions of the Istanbul conference, Greeks cited ancient history to prove that the Macedonians were simply "Slavic-speaking" or "Bulgarian-speaking" Greeks. Entering the Greek-Bulgarian controversy after 1878, the Serbs in turn cited medieval history to show that on the eve of the Turkish conquest Serbia encompassed Macedonia. In 1886, Serbian nationalists organized in Beograd a "Society of St. Sava" dedicated to the "purpose of educating the 'Serbs' in Turkey in the spirit of nationalism."[51] Fearful of a recreation of San Stefano Bulgaria, Turkey impeded the functioning of the Bulgarian exarchate by procrastinating with the appointment of bishops and acknowledging Serbian demands for schools in Macedonia. Encouraging the rivalries of their Christian enemies, the Turks tried to prevent the formation of a Balkan coalition that might oust them from the peninsula.

In the principality, the issues arising from framing and applying the constitution created two political parties, Liberals and Conservatives. The Liberals, also called the "young," regarded themselves as the heirs of the two great traditions of the national revival, nationalism and democracy, and plunged headlong into struggles to uphold them. One of their leaders, Petko R. Slaveikov, published a newspaper *Tselokupna Bulgariia* (Integral Bulgaria) dedicated "first and foremost" to "maintaining and publicizing the aspirations of our nation toward unification."[52] Providing effective and passionate expression of the national sentiments, Slaveikov declared that "as long as we Bulgarians live in the lands of our forefathers, we shall forever be opposed to the artificial and forcible dismemberment which befell us at a time when more than ever we believed that we were near our goal. We shall not retreat or abandon our goal until we are fused and united as one nation in one state." In pressing the program of impassioned democracy and nationalism, the Liberals increasingly clashed with the Russian representatives in Bulgaria who regarded many of them, especially after the assassination of Alexander II, as nihilists and anarchists.

Fundamentally, Russian policy in Bulgaria aimed at preserving and consolidating the position of influence and control obtained in 1878. Frustrated by the Berlin Congress in its larger objectives, the

[51] W. S. Vucinich, *Serbia between East and West* (Palo Alto, Calif.: Stanford University Press, 1954), p. 25.
[52] As quoted in Andreev, . . . *Bulgarskiia pechat,* II pp. 18–19.

Russian government was determined to keep at least the Bulgarian principality tied to itself. To many Bulgarians this policy, coupled with the highhanded behavior of Russian administrators and generals in the country, seemed to lead to the transformation of Bulgaria into a "trans-Danubian *guberniia*" of the Russian Empire. Bulgarian-Russian relations were further exacerbated by the Russian opposition, for fear of complications, to the nationalist drive to engineer the addition of Eastern Rumelia to the principality. The first prince, Alexander of Battenberg, who—youthful and ambitious—identified himself with Bulgarian nationalism, also contributed substantially to the process of estrangement.[53]

It was in the nature of things that the program of unification would concentrate first on joining Eastern Rumelia to the principality and, after this was accomplished, on regaining the Aegean coast and liberating Macedonia. In 1885 the nationalists organized a widespread agitation that culminated in the ousting of the governor in Plovdiv and the proclamation of unity with the principality. Three days later Prince Alexander and Stambolov, then Speaker of the National Assembly, arrived in Plovdiv to accept the act of union.

Acceptance of the act by Turkey, the Great Powers, and the Balkan states was, of course, another matter. Russia, feeling challenged in her authority by the independent Bulgarian action and fearful that the union would make the refractory prince and the Bulgarian nationalists even more unmanageable, declared herself opposed to the unification and recalled her officers serving as instructors and advisers to the Bulgarian army. England, on the other hand, declared herself in favor of it, recognizing that Bulgarians were no mere tools in Russian hands and that Bulgarian nationalism was useful against Russia. While Russia and England thus reversed their positions of 1878 to take account of assertive Bulgarian nationalism, Austria vacillated between support of Bulgarian Russophobia and protection of her imperial interests, as well as those of Serbia, against the threat of recreation of San Stefano Bulgaria.

Encouraged by Austria, Serbia declared war on Bulgaria to stop this first move of Bulgarian nationalism and to restore the "equilib-

[53] For the complex details see the best recent study of the subject by Charles Jelavich, *Tsarist Russia and Balkan Nationalism: Russian Influence in the Internal Affairs of Bulgaria and Serbia, 1879–1886* (Berkeley: University of California Press, 1958).

rium" in the Balkans. To Serbian nationalists as represented by King Milan, the war was a necessity in order to prevent the eventual addition of Macedonia to Bulgaria. To Bulgarian nationalists, it was the ultimate proof of Serbian jealousy and treachery. The two Slavic nations thus became locked in a combat, the stakes of which, their nationalist leaders told them, were Macedonia and hegemony in the peninsula.

Contrary to Serbian and Austrian expectations that the war would be no more than "a promenade to Sofia," it brought a quick Serbian defeat. Rushing from the Turkish frontier to meet the Serbian invasion, the Bulgarian forces prevailed in a battle at Slivnitsa. To prevent a rout, Austria confronted Prince Alexander with a demand to halt the advance or face Austrian troops. In these circumstances, the peace that was negotiated and signed at Bucureşti returned matters between Bulgaria and Serbia to the status quo before the war.

Feelings, however, could not be as easily repaired. By its timing and purpose the Serbian attack was plainly intended to deal a mortal blow to the Bulgarian nationalist program, and Bulgarian nationalists never forgot or forgave. Instead of shattering the nation, the attack galvanized it by the reaction of outrage, patriotism, and self-preservation that it universally evoked. Even Dimitur Blagoev, then beginning his career as "the father of Bulgarian Marxism," felt that "The sudden attack of Serbia and the recall of the Russian officers from the Bulgarian army raised a storm of indignation in the whole country and caused the national energy to rise to the highest level. All able to bear arms hurried to rally under the banner of fighting for the unification and the integrity of the fatherland."[54] Proud and joyous over the victory, the nation felt that it had passed its first test on the battlefield with flying colors and proven its mettle, and was so told by its friends and well-wishers abroad. Although brief and, as the European press described it, miniature in size, the war provided the necessary psychological experience to create in the nation a spirit of self-reliance and confidence in itself, its purposes, and its future. It was very important for subsequent events that the war also created in Bulgaria the image of the treacherous and cowardly Serb fleeing before the righteous wrath of courageous and selfless patriots. Poets, politicians, historians, and

[54] As quoted in *Istoriia na Bulgariia*, II (Sofia, 1962), 74.

teachers took it over and embedded it in the consciousness of every Bulgarian. Ivan Vazov, then thirty-five and rising toward his position of national poet, wrote stirring stanzas in contemplation of the sacrifices and cemeteries at Slivnitsa.[55] Military leaders welcomed it as the stuff of which legends and traditions could be built for the young Bulgarian army.

The successes of Bulgarian nationalism, however, made Bulgarian-Russian relations worse. The victory in the war and the unification were great personal triumphs for Prince Alexander, who became the symbol for many Bulgarians of what youth, resolution, and independence could achieve. In Russia, Alexander III, who still lived in the shadow of his father's assassination, saw the behavior of the Bulgarians only in the light of dangerous radicalism, insubordination, ingratitude, and injury to Russian prestige. The emperor's wrath focused on the prince. Using disaffected Bulgarian officers and Russophile politicians and clergy, Russian efforts succeeded in spreading the idea that the prince had to be sacrificed for Bulgaria. A military coup was carried out on August 21, 1886, and the prince was forced to abdicate and leave the country.

Flouting Bulgarian nationalism, Russian policy backfired again. Popular sentiment, expressed and channeled mainly by Stambolov, surged in support of the symbol of Bulgarian independence. Within a week Stambolov, Slaveikov, and other nationalist leaders reversed the coup and asked the prince to return. A brusque personal intervention of Alexander III, however, convinced the prince that he could not remain in Bulgaria against the emperor's wishes and that civil war would be fomented by Russia as a pretext for occupying the country. He bowed to the emperor's will and left Bulgaria for good. As he left, he appointed a regency headed by Stambolov.

Instead of crumbling under the tremendous Russian pressure, which included the dispatch of naval vessels to Varna, the Russophobe nationalists held together and began to search for allies. Austria and England, concerned over the prospect of a Russian occupation of Bulgaria, were ready to act on behalf of their interests and, indirectly, on behalf of Bulgarian independence. Even Turkey was viewed as a possible ally against Russia: Stambolov favored a per-

[55] For a penetrating discussion of Vazov as the leading nationalist writer, see P. Christophorov, *Ivan Vazov: La formation d'un écrivain bulgare* (1850–1921) (Paris, 1938).

sonal union with Turkey whereby the sultan would become tsar of Bulgaria and a dual Turkish-Bulgarian empire would be formed to resist the Russian encroachments; a similar idea was also explored in regard to Romania.[56] With Austria and England ranged against Russia and, in Bulgaria, Russophobes ("Austrophiles," "Anglophiles," "Turkophiles") ranged massively against Russophiles, Russian policy faced a new fiasco. In a dramatic move to head it off, on November 18, 1886, Russia declared all relations with Bulgaria severed and withdrew to what she hoped would be a more successful policy of boycott and isolation.

Seeking to break Bulgarian nationalism, Russian policy broke on it. Having prevailed, the Russophobes turned in July, 1887, to a German prince and officer in the Austrian army, Ferdinand of Coburg-Gotha, to fill the vacant throne. Young, ambitious, and crafty, Ferdinand decided to brave the Russian hostility and build his position in Bulgaria by playing up to the forces and ideals of Bulgarian nationalism. With Stambolov as Prime Minister until 1894, the new regime dealt firmly with the Russophile elements and recalcitrant members of the clergy who had refused to recognize Ferdinand because of his Catholic faith.[57] Expanded through the union with Eastern Rumelia and relatively stabilized, the country began to make rapid economic and cultural strides. Under a nascent policy of industrial protectionism and economic nationalism, industry expanded, employment opportunities for educated persons were diversified, and new outlets for the surplus labor in the villages were created. Uniform compulsory education, at first to the fourth grade and later to the seventh, was introduced in 1878. In 1889, a Higher School was founded in Sofia, which became, in 1904, the state university and the home of nationalist scholarship in history, language, literature, folklore, ethnography, and so on, as well as the nursery of the nation's intelligentsia. Thousands of Bulgarians from the colo-

[56] *Istoriia na Bulgariia*, II, 103–6. The idea of a dual Bulgarian-Turkish empire, with Bulgarians controlling the European territories and Turks controlling those in Asia, had its origins before 1878. Now it had the added virtue of solving the problem of the liberation of Macedonia and other areas still under Turkish rule.

[57] This was a complex issue of religious nationalism, loyalty to Orthodox Russia, and constitutional provisions. The constitution stipulated that the "dominant" religion in Bulgaria was Christianity of the Eastern Rite and that the prince must be of that religion; exception was made only for the first elected prince. Given the absolute papal rule of baptizing all children of Catholic parents in the Catholic faith, Bulgaria seemed destined to be ruled by a Catholic dynasty.

nies in Bessarabia and from Macedonia and other areas still under Turkey flocked to the free part of the fatherland to help in the process of building the new state and to take advantage of the opportunities for advancement; hundreds made notable careers in politics, education, scholarship, civil service, and other spheres of life in Bulgaria.[58] In the span of a quarter of a century, Bulgarians did so well that they convinced foreigners, and of course themselves, that they were "the leading race in the Balkans."[59]

In the seven years of Stambolov's tenure of office, the nationalist program was pushed cautiously and prudently. Considering his earlier record, this may appear odd. In office Stambolov developed into a responsible statesman wary of adventurism. His principal concerns were to obtain from Turkey the recognition of Ferdinand as the lawful prince of Bulgaria and to withstand the Russian boycott and hostility. In Macedonia, therefore, he preferred to strengthen the religious and educational work of the exarchate rather than to support the schemes of revolutionaries, and in 1890 he succeeded in obtaining Turkish consent under the firman of 1870 to the appointment of Bulgarian bishops to the still vacant sees of Ohrid and Skopje. His Macedonian policy won him the enmity of the Macedonian revolutionaries and refugees in Bulgaria who asserted that with his anti-Russian and pro-Turkish policy, he stood in the way of Macedonia's liberty, and that it could not be achieved without Russian backing.[60] Macedonian extremists and Russophiles began to combine forces for action, including assassination plots, to overthrow "the regime of Stambolov."

[58] For some of the Macedonians and Bessarabians who achieved prominence see *Les Macédoniens dans la vie culturo-politique de la Bulgarie* (Sofia, 1919) and V. Diakovich, *Bulgarska Besarabiia* (Sofia, 1918). This writer's grandfather, Marin Pundev, was one of those who returned from Bessarabia after 1878.

[59] Hall, *Puritans in the Balkans,* p. 267.

[60] In fact, Russia had switched to support of Serbian interest and propaganda in Macedonia to retaliate for the Bulgarian intransigence. Cf. *Istoriia na Bulgariia,* II, 117, and C. Jelavich, "Russo-Bulgarian Relations, 1892–1896: With Particular Reference to the Problem of the Bulgarian Succession," *Journal of Modern History,* XXIV, No. 4 (December, 1952), 341–51. Jelavich notes that "owing to the deterioration of Russo-Bulgarian relations, Russia threw her weight behind Serbian aspirations to the same territory. Russia hoped by this policy to attack the Bulgarian government at its most sensitive point—Macedonia. Russia believed that in this manner she could force the Bulgarian government to succumb to Russian pressure. If this failed, Russia expected the Bulgars to overthrow their government when they saw Macedonia slipping from their grasp."

By 1894, Stambolov's enemies found an ally in Ferdinand. Increasingly jealous of the strong prime minister, Ferdinand was also anxious to solidify his position in Bulgaria by appeasing Russia and pleasing the nationalists. Stambolov was dismissed from office in May, 1894, and when a few months later the unyielding Emperor Alexander III died, the way was opened to a reconciliation with Russia. Sacrificing religion for power, Ferdinand even decided to have his first-born son, Boris, rebaptized in the Orthodox Church and invited Emperor Nicholas II to be the godfather. Resumption of relations with Russia followed, and the general recognition of Ferdinand as the lawful prince of Bulgaria opened a new era, which lasted until 1918 and in which he fostered an alliance of court and army on the basis of the nationalist program and emerged as the only important maker of decisions.

In Macedonia, Stambolov's cautious policy and the inroads of Serbian and Greek propaganda led the revolutionary elements to decide on an independent course of action. Following the traditions of the Bulgarian revolutionaries before 1877, they established in Salonika in 1893 a "Central Macedonian Revolutionary Committee" to set up an internal organization and to prepare for a general uprising. The purpose of the internal organization, better known by its initials IMRO, was to attain autonomy for Macedonia that, as in the case of Eastern Rumelia, was to serve as the prelude to unification with Bulgaria. The moving spirits of the Internal Macedonian Revolutionary Organization were Damian Gruev and Gotse Delchev, two schoolteachers in the employ of the exarchate.

In 1895, nationalists and refugees from Macedonia in Sofia set up an external "Supreme Macedonian Committee" that soon developed frictions with IMRO over aims and methods. While the "internals" in Macedonia favored autonomy—which to some of them meant the prelude to unification with Bulgaria and to others, the prelude to a Balkan federation—the "supremists" in Sofia, linked with the court and the army, were for a "maximalist" program and Bulgarian annexation of Macedonia. In the *khaiduti* tradition of the past, both organizations fostered incursions of armed bands of *komitadjii* (or committeemen, as the Turks called them) into Macedonia and other Turkish areas to keep the spirit of resistance and revolution inflamed. However, as Serbia and Greece began to draw together in opposition to the aims of Bulgarian nationalism in Macedonia, it was increasingly realized that a struggle against so many enemies could not succeed and that the solution of the Macedonian question might lie in the creation of a Balkan federation that Macedonia would join as a full-fledged member. Within IMRO, a federalist segment became increasingly vocal, and its views found support in two social movements, the Marxist and the Agrarian, which were rising in Bulgaria to challenge the middle-class parties and all their values, including the ideals of Bulgarian nationalism.

Like many other products of Europe, Marxism reached Bulgaria through Russia. Its early development was mainly the work of two individuals, Dimitur Blagoev and Ianko Sakuzov, who first encountered radicalism while studying in Russia. A Macedonian, Blagoev had won a Russian scholarship on the recommendation of Petko Slaveikov to study for the priesthood, but his interests lay elsewhere. In 1883, he organized fellow students at the University of St. Petersburg into the first Marxist (Social Democratic) group in Russia and was deported for these activities. In Bulgaria, he propagated Marxism and organized a Marxist movement. His brand of Marxism remained thoroughly Russian. Sakuzov, on the other hand, had spent only a brief period in the Russian environment, and pursuing his studies in western Europe, became oriented toward western European, especially German, Marxism. In the division of moderates and extremists that affected the Marxist movement throughout Europe, Blagoev emerged as the spokesman of the "narrow" or revolutionary Bulgarian Marxists who, eventually, became the Bulgarian Communist Party, while Sakuzov became the leader of the "broad" or evolutionary Social Democratic wing in the Bulgarian Marxist movement. Adamantly committed to class struggle and proletarian internationalism, the "Narrows" saw all nationalist programs as an expression of "bourgeois" mentality and a device for pitting peoples against one another for the benefit of the ruling classes, while the "Broads" were less adamant in opposing the cause of Bulgarian nationalism and in fact often supported it.[61] Both wings, however, were in favor of solving Balkan conflicts through a Balkan federation of socialist states.

Under the pressure of serious economic problems, the Bulgarian peasantry itself began to seek organizational and political ways to

---

[61] I. Sakuzov, *Bulgarite v svoiata istoriia* (Sofia, 1922), pp. 327–29.

defend its interests and to make its weight felt in the determination of national policies. In 1899, an Agrarian Union was formed that soon came to be dominated by a fiery peasant ideologist and reformer, Alexander Stamboliiski. Under his leadership, the peasantry demanded that attention be focused on the internal economic and social problems and developed a considerable skepticism about liberating "the brethren under foreign rule." An effective speaker, Stamboliiski spread widely the ideas of peasant internationalism, cooperation rather than conflict with Bulgaria's neighbors, and creation of a Balkan federation.[62]

In Macedonia, however, the revolutionaries—many of them teachers and priests on the payroll of the exarchate—remained intent on preparing a general uprising. Coordinating their activities with revolutionaries in the Edirne region (eastern Thrace) and the Aegean coast (western Thrace), they set off an uprising in the summer of 1903 that inflamed wide areas and for some three months challenged the Turkish authority in numerous places. Uncoordinated with the Bulgarian government, however, the uprising was doomed to a bloody suppression. In the course of overpowering the insurgents, the Turkish forces destroyed some two hundred villages, killed thousands, and forced thirty thousand people to flee to Bulgaria. Settling down mainly in Sofia, the refugees joined the earlier arrivals from Macedonia and Turkish Thrace in pressing for policies to assure their return to families and homesteads. By shattering many Bulgarian communities, denuding some areas of their Bulgarian element, and making the work of the exarchate suspect and difficult, the uprising was a severe blow to the Bulgarian population in Turkey. Its failure started a process of weakening the Bulgarian hold on these areas. This process was accelerated by the defeats in the second Balkan War and World War I and ended in the drastic reduction and, in many localities, eradication of the Bulgarian element in Macedonia and eastern and western Thrace.

The fiasco of insurrectionary action brought to the fore ideas of a coalition of Balkan states to oust Turkey from Europe. Such a

---

[62] G. M. Dimitrov, "Agrarianism," *European Ideologies,* ed. F. Gross (New York: Philosophical Library, 1948), pp. 416–25. An ideological heir of Stamboliiski, Dimitrov has lived in the United States since 1945 when the Agrarian-Communist conflict forced him to leave Bulgaria; see below.

coalition could, of course, operate only on the basis of a partition of Macedonia and other areas of European Turkey according to the interests of the members of the coalition. After the elimination of the Obrenović dynasty in 1903, Serbian interest in Macedonia was greatly intensified. In the same year, Turkey agreed to recognize the existence of a Serbian nationality in the empire, a move designed to play Serbs and Bulgarians against each other. Traditionally loyal to Russia, the Karageorgević dynasty now in power set on a course to prevent, with Russian assistance, the "one-sided settlement of the Macedonian Question on the lines of the Bulgarian nationalist claims."[63]

In Sofia, the defeat of the Internal Macedonian Organization in 1903 strengthened the hand of the Supremists who pressed the view, often at the instigation of army and court circles, that "the cause of Macedonia" could be served best by relying on Bulgaria and her diplomatic and military powers. Bulgarian policy turned increasingly to exploring the possibilities for a Bulgarian-Serbian military alliance against Turkey. An element of urgency entered into these efforts in 1908 when the Young Turks seized power and, with their plans to rejuvenate the Ottoman Empire and to "Ottomanize" its populations, threatened the aspirations of Bulgarian, Serbian, and Greek nationalists. In Bulgaria, Prince Ferdinand took advantage of the turmoil in Turkey to proclaim Bulgaria's independence and to assume royal status by calling himself "Tsar of the Bulgarians."[64] In Austria, the Turkish events were used to announce the annexation of Bosnia and Hercegovina and thus bar—permanently, it was hoped—the Serbian aspirations to these Slavic provinces. By 1911, when Italy began a war with Turkey over Tripolitania and reached for some of the Turkish possessions in the eastern Mediterranean, the conviction had been formed in Sofia, Beograd, and Athens that the time had come to act in defense and furtherance of the national interests lest the great powers make all the gains.

[63] Vucinich, *Serbia Between East and West,* pp. 122–26.

[64] In assuming the title of *tsar* used by the Bulgarian medieval rulers, Ferdinand sought once again, as in naming his son after Boris I, to tap the deepest sources of Bulgarian historical traditions and nationalism. Greatly stimulated by proclamation of independence and the revival of the medieval tradition, the nationalists explained that "Tsar of the Bulgarians," rather than "of Bulgaria," signified the unity of Bulgarians everywhere under the scepter of Ferdinand.

New Triumphs and Defeats (1912–1918)

The formation of a Balkan League against Turkey began with the signing of a Bulgarian-Serbian treaty in March, 1912, a secret annex of which provided for partition of Macedonia along stipulated lines and arbitration by the Russian emperor if disagreement arose. Two months later, a Bulgarian-Greek alliance followed, but it failed to stipulate a line between Bulgarian and Greek interests in the territories to be liberated from Turkey.[65]

As war preparations began, powerful emotions of patriotism and nationalism swept over the country. Stamboliiski was convinced that Ferdinand was deluding the people and pursuing, with militarists and chauvinists, adventurist policies for his own and Austria's interests, but the peasant masses did not remain immune and were ready to take up arms to solve, once and for all, the national problems that Turkey symbolized. When Stamboliiski commented in despair that the whole nation seemed to have lost its mind, another Agrarian leader explained that "the nation has not lost its mind, it it only giving vent to what has piled up in its soul for centuries."[66] The war on Turkey was to be the first real chance for Bulgarians to avenge the five centuries of enslavement and to prove to the world that, although they had received their freedom through foreign intervention, they deserved it. It was to be the noble charge of the young, strong, and righteous nation on the crumbling citadels of a decaying empire to free "the still enslaved brethren" from its clutches, unify itself, and fulfill its historic destiny. With Istanbul standing as the ultimate citadel of the enemy, the medieval history of the nation seemed about to repeat itself.

Conscious that they had a rendezvous with destiny and that, as the "hub" of the alliance, the eyes of the world were upon them, the Bulgarian troops hurled themselves against the fortresses in eastern Thrace, where the main Turkish army was concentrated, and took them one by one. Within two weeks, the capture of Istanbul appeared imminent.[67] To a world watching with admiration and

[65] The details are in E. C. Helmreich, *The Diplomacy of the Balkan Wars, 1912–1913* (Cambridge, Mass.: Harvard University Press, 1938). The alliance included Montenegro, whose war expenses Bulgaria agreed to meet.

[66] V. A. Zhebokritskii, *Bolgariia nakanune balkanskikh voin 1912–1913 gg.* (Kiev, 1960), p. 205.

[67] Mindful of the sensitivities of Russia and other Great Powers, the Bulgarian cabinet was against entering Istanbul, but Ferdinand and the military leaders were

to Bulgarians, it seemed that the hour of triumph of Bulgarian nationalism had struck.

The spectacular victories and the lure of Istanbul, however, deflected attention from developments which, in a short time, led to one of the worst defeats suffered by Bulgarian nationalism. The principal political objective for which Bulgaria had undertaken the war was Macedonia with its main city and seaport, Salonika. However, the logic of geography, reinforced by the Bulgarians' supreme confidence and sense of *noblesse oblige,* drew the Bulgarian forces into eastern Thrace, while it was left to Serbian and Greek forces to clear Macedonia of Turkish garrisons. When Bulgarian units advanced to Salonika, they found the Greeks already there, and frictions developed. Similarly, Serbian troops advanced beyond the lines stipulated in the Bulgarian-Serbian treaty, and the Serbs began to demand a revision of the treaty on the principle of "effective occupation." When Turkey sued for peace and, by the treaty of London (May 30, 1913), ceded all territories in Europe (except Albania, which was to become an independent state) west of the Enos-Midia line in eastern Thrace, the Balkan allies found themselves in a maelstrom of problems arising from the division of the gains. The explosive situation was further aggravated by Romania's demand to have a voice in the territorial settlement and compensations. A Romanian spokesman declared, "just as Austria could not tolerate a great Serbia, so Romania could not tolerate a great Bulgaria."

In Bulgaria, extreme and moderate nationalists—with the cabinet in the middle—debated what to do. When it was learned that Serbia and Greece had concluded an alliance against Bulgaria, a war party of "all-or-nothing" maximalists and Macedonians, supported and at times inspired by Ferdinand, began to press for cutting "the Gordian knot" by the sword. The fatal decision to attack the Serbian and Greek positions in Macedonia on June 29 was made by Ferdinand himself as commander-in-chief, presumably for the purpose of forcing Russia to intervene diplomatically and rule in Bulgaria's favor. The folly of this thinking became obvious within two weeks, as the attack not only failed to produce the desired results but gave Ro-

---

bent on celebrating victory in the ancient imperial city. Cf. H. R. Madol, *Ferdinand of Bulgaria: The Dream of Byzantium* (London: Hunt & Blackett, 1933), pp. 170–77.

mania and Turkey an opportunity to invade Bulgaria. Embattled on all sides, Bulgaria had no alternative but to sue for peace. Within the span of only a few months, Bulgarian nationalism had descended from supreme triumph to utter defeat.

The peace that Bulgaria made with her Christian neighbors in Bucureşti (August 10, 1913) carved up Macedonia in three pieces, the smallest of which—the so-called Pirin region—was given to Bulgaria, while Serbia took the Vardar River valley with Skopje, Bitola, and Ohrid, and Greece kept southern (Aegean) Macedonia with Salonika and other ports. The Bulgarian rights to western (Aegean) Thrace were not disputed, and Bulgaria received the coastline between the estuaries of the Maritsa and Mesta rivers. Romania took southern Dobrudja from Bulgaria.[68] A separate Bulgarian-Turkish peace returned most of eastern Thrace and Edirne to Turkey.

For Bulgarians, stunned by the course of events moving from universally acclaimed victory to a "national catastrophe," the territorial settlement presented a baffling mixture of losses and gains. The feeling that Bulgaria had been robbed of Macedonia by her allies was general, yet a part of Macedonia was incorporated into the country. Aegean Thrace was an important gain, yet the loss of eastern Thrace and the great human costs and sacrifices in storming Edirne and the rest of the Turkish fortresses overshadowed it. Only the seizure of southern Dobrudja by Romania stood out clearly as an absolute wrong, but even with the loss of this ancient Bulgarian region, Bulgaria came out of the Bucureşti settlement considerably enlarged. Sober calculation of gains and losses, however, did not fit the mood of the nation. Sullen and indignant, its *élan* stopped, it seemed to "furl the flags for better times," as Ferdinand's proclamation to the army put it, and resolve to await the opportunity to right the wrongs.

[68] Various efforts were made to safeguard Bulgarian rights in regard to Macedonia, but they were rebuffed. The Bulgarian delegation asked for a clause in the treaty to guarantee autonomy to the religious communities and freedom to the schools in the annexed territories. Absence of such a guarantee was to make the work of the exarchate impossible. In a noteworthy attempt to secure justice for Bulgaria, leading American missionaries presented a memorandum affirming that "the great bulk of the population of the region which we have indicated as the Macedonian field of our work is Bulgarian in origin, language and customs, and forms an integral part of the Bulgarian nation." Quoted in Hall, *Puritans in the Balkans,* pp. 253.

Yet a profound crisis of Bulgarian nationalism was in the making. Confidence in the established national leadership was shaken, and the consensus on the national goals was replaced by doubts. Much was said about victories won by brave peasants only to be squandered by inept and reckless leaders. Voices were raised by Socialists, Agrarians, and others, holding Ferdinand accountable for the national disaster. Events, however, continued to move with great speed and before the new thinking could take shape and assert itself, World War I began with the act of Serbian nationalists in Sarajevo. It took another national catastrophe in 1918 to bring the crisis to a head.

Unlike some of her neighbors, Bulgaria had no treaty commitments when the general conflict broke out. The Central Powers and the Entente scrambled for allies, and by the summer of 1915 the bidding for Bulgaria's participation became high. Since Macedonia was the central objective of Bulgarian irredentism, the only question the nationalists asked was: which side was willing, and would ultimately be able, to deliver Macedonia? Ferdinand, whose ties were with Austria and Germany, and the Macedonians, including the refugees of 1913, saw only one possible course: to join Austria and Germany, who were willing to outbid the Entente and had scored better than the Entente in the first year of the war. Despite vigorous opposition, best expressed by Stamboliiski, Ferdinand concluded a secret alliance with the Central Powers, who guaranteed to Bulgaria the annexation of not only Serbian Macedonia but of the Morava region as well (a part of the original domain of the exarchate acquired by Serbia in 1878) and even persuaded their ally, Turkey, to yield small parts of eastern Thrace.[69] In a joint campaign Serbia was over-powered and, occupying the promised territories, the Bulgarian troops dug in on the Serbian-Greek border to face the Entente forces arriving through Salonika.

The opportunity to recover Dobrudja came in 1916 when Romania, after being an ally of Austria, declared war on her in the hope of obtaining Transylvania. The Bulgarian forces occupied

---

[69] The texts of the agreements are in B. D. Kesiakov (ed.), *Prinos kum diplomaticheskata istoriia na Bulgariia, 1878–1925*, (3 vols.; Sofia, 1925–26), I, 71–76. In a stormy encounter, Stamboliiski warned Ferdinand that if he intervened in the war he would lose his throne. Ferdinand had him tried for lese majesty and sent to prison where he spent the war years.

Dobrudja against Romanian and Russian opposition and took part in the capture of Bucureşti. By the short-lived peace settlement of Bucureşti (May 7, 1918), nullified a few months later by the Allied victory, Bulgaria recovered southern Dobrudja while northern Dobrudja (also a part of the original domain of the exarchate) became the "condominium" of the four Central Powers. When Romania reacquired Bessarabia in the wake of the Russian collapse in 1917, voices were raised in Bulgaria to secure autonomy for the 300,000 Bulgarians who assertedly still lived in this Danubian province.[70]

Despite military victories and conquests that earned the Bulgarians the "Prussians of the Balkans" label in war propaganda, it became evident, after the American intervention, that Bulgarian national aspirations faced another catastrophic defeat. The American intervention, however, held out a promise as well. The Americans were likely to use their weight to secure the just and equitable solutions favored by the American missionaries and the International Commission to Inquire into the Causes and Conduct of the Balkan Wars which the Carnegie Endowment for International Peace had sponsored. President Wilson's Fourteen Points included the principle of self-determination of nations that, if applied by the peacemakers, meant redrawing the boundaries along ethnic lines and thus in favor of Bulgaria. Very importantly, Bulgarian-American relations remained normal despite the fact that the two countries stood in opposing camps.[71] As the war moved toward its denouement, the Bulgarians made a serious effort in preparing their case for the peace conference by compiling the evidence upon which the Wilsonian program of national self-determination was expected to be implemented. Nationalist scholars from the University of Sofia, publicists, and spokesmen of the refugees labored hard to collect a large body of mainly ethnographic material. They published most of it in western languages in neutral Switzerland, feeling that it proved beyond the shadow of a doubt Bulgaria's rights to the territories contested with Serbia, Greece, and Romania.[72]

[70] J. Ancel, *L'unité de la politique bulgare, 1870–1919* (Paris: Éditions Bossard, 1919), p. 52.

[71] V. S. Mamatey, "The United States and Bulgaria in World War I," *American Slavic and East European Review*, XII, No. 2 (April, 1953), 233–57. On the American side, the preservation of diplomatic relations was due largely to the strong advocacy of such a policy by the missionaries.

[72] After the Fourteen Points were announced, the Bulgarian war aims were defined by the Prime Minister, Vasil Radoslavov, as being the unification of Bulgaria in her

A grave blow to the self-image of Bulgarian nationalism, the denouement of World War I began with the defeat of Bulgarian forces on the Salonika front, destroying the nationalist myth of the invincibility of the Bulgarian soldier. Weary of unrelieved service, demoralized by privations and reports of bad conditions in the rear, the Bulgarian soldiers yielded to the superior power of the Entente army, and in a general retreat began to leave the Macedonian front and head for home. The release of Stamboliiski from prison to influence the soldiers' mood proved of no avail, and when mutineers declared the establishment of a peasant republic in Radomir, Stamboliiski and other Agrarian leaders assumed the leadership of the powerful popular wave of bitterness and revolt that ended the rule of Ferdinand. Preparing to flee to Germany, on October 3, 1918, Ferdinand abdicated in favor of his son Boris. The era of great nationalist and military ambitions that he fostered and exploited for his own purposes came to a disastrous end.

The Crisis of Nationalism (1918–1934)

As the second national catastrophe in five years, the defeat in 1918 plunged the country into a moral crisis of unprecedented dimensions. All factors for disintegration were at hand. The nation had been strained to the breaking point by relentless effort that had been pressed, with slight respite, since 1912 and in which one fifth of the population served under arms. The toll in casualties was paid by nearly every family, and the meager resources of the land were utterly spent. An agricultural country normally having a surplus of food, Bulgaria faced a famine as the economic machinery broke down and the heavy influx of new refugees and others into the cities created additional demands. Demoralized soldiers believed the propaganda of Socialists and Agrarians that the wars had been instigated for the interests and ambitions of the monarchy and the bourgeoisie and that a class war or a rural-urban showdown was needed to rid the country of the crust of monarchists, chauvinists, militarists, and profiteers. As social hatreds and antagonisms, long

ethnographic frontiers encompassing Macedonia, the Morava region, and Dobrudja. Cf. Ancel, *L'unité de la politique bulgare*, pp. 63–64. For samples of the literature prepared for the defense of these claims, see M. Pundeff, *Bulgaria: A Bibliographic Guide* (Washington, D.C.: U.S. Government Printing Office, 1965), pp. 16–18.

in the making but held under the surface, erupted, the fabric of society and established values broke repeatedly in spasms of bitter violence.

First blood was spilled when army mutineers from the Radomir republic marched on Sofia to take the capital and overthrow the government. After bloody fighting, the attempt was repulsed by a hastily assembled force under the command of Alexander Protogerov, an IMRO leader who had risen to general's rank in the Bulgarian army, and the Radomir republic was suppressed, but the specter of social revolution remained in the country. Frightened by it, the old proponents of the nationalist program—the upper urban strata, monarchists, regular and reserve army officers, members of IMRO and other irredentist organizations, and refugees—began to pull together against the "rabble" and the "defeatists" who, they felt, were responsible for the disintegration of order and values. Challenged in their beliefs and thrown out of jobs and careers by the limitations on Bulgaria's army, regular officers formed a "Military League" to serve as the bulwark of nationalism and advance the interests of the army. No longer an effective internal organization in Macedonia, IMRO shifted its base of operations to the Pirin region and, drawing upon the refugees as an ample supply of manpower for terrorist activities, set itself up as the ominous arbiter as to whom and what in Bulgaria served or injured "the interests of Macedonia." Young, timid, and burdened by his father's sins, Boris left things to take care of themselves.

Despite the turmoil in the country, the delegation at the Paris peace conference worked strenuously to present the evidence for Bulgaria's territorial rights and to secure a verdict based on national self-determination and ethnic boundaries. These efforts, supported by the vigorous and eloquent pleas of American missionaries, made the American and Italian delegations receptive to some of the arguments and claims.[73] The American view was that Bulgaria should keep western (Aegean) Thrace, which Greece wished to take; should receive back southern Dobrudja, which Romania had annexed in 1913; and should receive eastern (Turkish) Thrace as close

[73] Hall, *Puritans in the Balkans*, p. 263. Although not at war with Bulgaria, the United States, it was agreed, was to take part in the formulation and enforcement of the Bulgarian treaty as guarantor of the peace settlement and the international organization incorporated in it.

as possible to the Enos-Midia line drawn in 1913.[74] Concentrating on the newly created kingdom of Serbs, Croats, and Slovenes, the Italian delegation argued that "the military balance between Bulgaria and Serbia had been severely altered in the latter's favor through the creation of the large Yugoslav state," and felt that in Balkan geopolitics Bulgaria should "serve as a counterweight to the new Yugoslave union." The peace treaty, signed at Neuilly on November 27, 1919, however, let Romania keep southern Dobrudja and gave Serbia additional pieces—the western border areas—of Bulgarian territory. Western Thrace was assigned to the Allied Powers for final disposition. Bulgaria was pledged to accept their decision while the powers promised to "ensure the economic outlets of Bulgaria to the Aegean Sea."[75]

Bulgarian nationalists saw the Neuilly treaty as part of a settlement in which punitive and annexationist considerations had prevailed over the Wilsonian program and as a supreme injustice. New parts of the body of the nation, they felt, were severed and, while Serbian, Greek, and Romanian nationalisms triumphed with greatly enlarged territories, Bulgaria had been reduced to the status of a minor Balkan state, truncated and surrounded by neighbors determined to keep her down. The treaty had been handed to Bulgaria and burdened her with reparations beyond her capacity to bear. To the nationalists and the refugees, the only possible reaction to the Neuilly *Diktat* was to seek to overthrow it.

However, according to Stamboliiski, who had meanwhile become Prime Minister as a result of national elections, the only sensible course was to seek to fulfill the treaty's obligations and to implement the Agrarian program of social reform at home and reconcilia-

---

[74] *Papers Relating to the Foreign Relations of the United States, 1919, The Paris Peace Conference*, VII (Washington, D.C.: U.S. Government Printing Office, 1946), 243–46 and 436–38; G. P. Genov, *Bulgaria and the Treaty of Neuilly* (Sofia, 1935), pp. 17–59. Professor Genov's book is the best statement of the Bulgarian nationalist view of the peace settlement in a western language.

[75] Article 48 of the Treaty of Neuilly. After the Senate's refusal to ratify the Treaty of Versailles, the United States withdrew from its place in the peace settlement. By the treaties of Sèvres and Lausanne the remaining Allied Powers gave western Thrace to Greece. At the Lausanne conference Bulgaria was offered an outlet at Dedeagatch, but she turned it down as inadequate in meeting the obligation of the Allied Powers under Article 48 of the Treaty of Neuilly. Subsequently, Greece reopened the question, but Bulgaria took the position that the matter was between her and the powers who had signed the Treaty of Neuilly.

tion and unity in intra-Balkan relations. He strove to organize a "Green" International of the peasant parties in eastern Europe as a bulwark against the "Red" International of Lenin. He was particularly anxious to end Bulgaria's isolation in the Balkans through an understanding with Yugoslavia, which he saw as a step toward south Slav unity and the ultimate goal of a Balkan federation.[76] The Macedonian problem was not to be allowed to stand in the way and was to find its solution in a new framework of Balkan unity.

This was, of course, not a policy calculated to endear the Agrarians to the nationalists and the refugees. In the postwar period, the latter became particularly powerful in the affairs of the country. Five wars, transfers of territories, unsettled conditions, and policies by its neighbors of uprooting the Bulgarian element had sent into Bulgaria repeated waves of people from Macedonia, Thrace, and Dobrudja, who longed to return to their homelands and demanded policies to that end. As part of the settlement in 1919, Bulgaria also signed a convention with Greece for reciprocal emigration of Bulgarians from areas held by Greece and Greeks from Bulgaria, and although the emigration was to be voluntary, the Bulgarian population in Aegean Macedonia and Thrace was quite thoroughly uprooted to make room for Greeks resettled from Asia Minor under a similar Greek-Turkish convention.[77] Furthermore, harsh policies of Serbianization in Macedonia and Romanianization in Dobrudja kept borders alive with illegal crossings of refugees and guerrilla bands on punitive expeditions. All in all, some 500,000 refugees burdened a poor agricultural country of less than 6,000,000, which had little ability to cope with their needs and agitation.[78] Their vari-

---

[76] Upon the outbreak of hostilities between Serbia and Austria in 1914, Stamboliiski stated in the National Assembly that he hoped "our brothers, the Serbs, will be victorious over the Austrians." When some deputies shouted "Traitor! You are a Serb," he replied that he was "neither a Serb nor a Bulgarian [but] a South Slav." Cf. Stavrianos, *Balkan Federation*, p. 209.

[77] S. P. Ladas, *The Exchange of Minorities: Bulgaria, Greece and Turkey* (New York: Macmillan, 1932). For a sample of Bulgarian writings on the de-Bulgarianization process, see L. Miletich, *Razorenieto na trakiiskite bulgari prez 1913 godina* (Sofia, 1918).

[78] T. I. Geshkoff, *Balkan Union: A Road to Peace in Southeastern Europe* (New York: Columbia University Press, 1940), pp. 66–67. Geshkoff, it may be noted, was an associate of Stamboliiski. At the Genoa Economic Conference in 1922, Stamboliiski pointed out that many of these refugees had taken to brigandage because of their desperate plight and had created border incidents. He proposed that the Balkan states should declare amnesty, allowing them to return to their homes, that the property

ous organizations included survivals of the old revolutionary networks, pressure groups, and "scientific" institutes for documenting and defending their rights.[79]

The most powerful of these irredentist organizations, as it was already noted, was IMRO. A state within the state in the Pirin region, it had the allegiance of some of its population and of Macedonian refugees elsewhere in Bulgaria. With its considerable forces, resources, and immunity, it effectively menaced its enemies in Yugoslavia and Greece as well as in Bulgaria. Its armed bands frequently crossed into Serbian and Greek Macedonia to wreak terror and keep those areas inflamed. It conducted its own foreign relations and maintained contacts with such disparate enemies of the postwar status quo as the Italian Fascists, Austrian and Hungarian revisionists, Croat nationalists, Russian Bolsheviks, and the Comintern. Yet, IMRO was facing a period of crisis that ended in its disintegration. Its objective of liberating Macedonia from foreign rule no longer meant fighting against a decayed Ottoman Empire condemned by the civilized world; now it meant fighting against two young Balkan states determined to keep the fruits of their own nationalist drives backed by the international system of the victorious powers. Moreover, "the cause of Macedonia" had lost its appeal to the peasant masses of Bulgaria. While another effort on behalf of Macedonia's freedom was unthinkable without the support of Bulgaria, the broad mass of the Bulgarian people in villages and towns had become alienated from this cause and was even hostile to the restless refugees and the risks and burdens that they put on the country. Some within IMRO understood the new realities and sought to adjust to them, but many others continued to live by the tenets and methods of the earlier era. Conflicts arising from these divisions were soon to take a heavy toll.

---

they had left behind should be restored to them, and that the terms of the peace settlement safeguarding the rights of minorities should be observed. His proposals were represented by his enemies in Bulgaria as intended to deliver the refugees to the enslavers of their homelands.

[79] Especially active and productive among them was the "Macedonian Scientific Institute," which published the quarterly *Makedonski Pregled* and numerous studies. Bulgarians from Thrace organized a "Thracian Scientific Institute," which engaged in similar publishing activity. Irredentism was also a strong motivation among the sizeable number of Macedonian immigrants in the United States and Canada who had their own organizations and maintained contact with those in Bulgaria.

In 1923, however, IMRO still held together thanks to the momentum left from the past and the fear of the aims of Stamboliiski's government. In effect an undeclared war was fought between it and the Agrarian regime. Several attempts on the lives of Agrarian ministers were made, and on December 4 and 5, 1922, IMRO seized the town of Kiustendil in a show of strength. When the Agrarian government concluded an agreement with Yugoslavia, on March 23, 1923, to curb the activities of the armed bands, IMRO declared it an act of treason and sentenced Stamboliiski to death. Joining the Military League and the Agrarian regime's many other enemies, it took part in the bloody events of June 9–14, 1923, which resulted in the overthrow of the Agrarian government and the assassination of Stamboliiski.

The new regime under Professor Alexander Tsankov ended the brief postwar era of repudiation of the "San Stefano Bulgaria" program, but contrary to hopes in IMRO and other circles, it did not reverse the actual foreign policy pursued by Stamboliiski. Tsankov, who began his career in politics as a "broad" Socialist, had been one of the earliest advocates of Bulgarian-Serbian political and economic cooperation. Mindful of Bulgaria's prostrate position, he affirmed the policy of fulfilling the obligations under the peace settlement and specifically declared that the agreement concerning the activities of the armed bands would be observed. His main concession to the pressures of the nationalists was to intensify the demands for the observance of the rights of the Bulgarian minorities in Yugoslavia, Greece, and Romania guaranteed by the minorities treaties these countries had signed.

Stymied and divided, IMRO faltered in search of a new road. Some of the federalists in it had turned to the Communist solution and advocated tying the Macedonian cause to the chariot of world revolution. For a brief moment in 1924, the two principal leaders of IMRO, Todor Alexandrov and Alexander Protogerov, subscribed to this idea by signing the so-called Vienna Manifesto but later repudiated their signatures. The dissensions, which this move sharpened, turned into internal warfare, and the first to die was Alexandrov himself. He was replaced on the IMRO three-man Central Committee by Ioan Mikhailov, a young man backed by Bulgarian military circles and Italian Fascists and fired by ambition. He considered Protogerov an obstacle and had him killed in 1928. By 1934, when a new government of the "nineteenth of May" finally suppressed IMRO in Bulgaria, the casualty list of this gangsterism had reached several hundred.[80]

In the years between the end of the war and the new era which Hitler's regime in Germany opened in European affairs, Bulgarian nationalism went through its most confused period. Defeated on the battlefield, discredited by two national debacles, and abandoned by the bulk of the people, it survived in numerically small pockets such as the officers' corps, segments of the intelligentsia and the bourgeoisie, and, of course, the refugees' organizations. Even there, however, it lost its noble and romantic aspects and took divergent, often antagonistic, forms which began to pit moderate nationalists against virulent extremists and those who sought a career, adventure, and gain through nationalism. After 1923, the officers' corps became divided along these lines between followers of Damian Velchev, one of the planners of the coup against the Agrarian regime who recognized the need for reconciliation with the peasant masses and evolved toward republicanism, and officers close to King Boris. Moderate nationalists among the intelligentsia formed the so-called "Father Paisii All-Bulgarian Union" and the "Union of Bulgarian Scholars, Writers, and Artists" to propagate mild nationalism and revisionism, while radical rightists began to echo the ideologies of Italian Fascism and German National Socialism and formed several ambitious and militant organizations. The most important among these small groups were the "National and Social Movement" of Professor Tsankov (who gave way as Prime Minister in 1926 to Andrei Liapchev, a Macedonian), the *Ratnitsi* (meaning promoters, defenders) led by Professor Asen Kantardzhiev, and the "Bulgarian Legion" led by Ivan Dochev. Closely paralleling his father's pattern of ruling, Boris increasingly sought to manipulate the political life of the country and to stabilize the monarchy through an alliance with the forces of nationalism, irredentism, and militarism.

The severe nationalist and social malaise after the war also produced a literature of national introspection that purported to analyze the causes of the debacles in the political leadership as well as in the national character and psychology, the meaning of Bulgarian history, the true origins and heritage of the Bulgarian nation, and

[80] E. Barker, *Macedonia: Its Place in Balkan Power Politics* (London: Royal Institute of International Affairs, 1950), pp. 43–63.

so on. National psychoanalysis, which became a favorite pastime of the intellectuals, discovered in Bulgarians every conceivable human flaw, from stubbornness to submissiveness and from base egotism to senseless selflessness. More noteworthy were some of the efforts to interpret the meaning of the nation's history. Colonel Petur Durvingov, a Macedonian whose military thought and personality influenced generations of officers and drew attention abroad, turned in the postwar years to philosophical and moral questions. In a book on the "spirit of the history of the Bulgarian nation,"[81] he propounded a thesis of geographic determinism: The history of Europe in the early Middle Ages, when the Bulgarians appeared on the historical stage, had been in essence a struggle for a better life of the primitive peoples of the hinterlands against the advanced peoples living on the shores of the Mediterranean. Bulgarian history had begun as part of this struggle, and it became the lot of the Bulgarian nation to hurl itself through the centuries against the bastions of the Greek in order to gain access to the Mediterranean. The essence of Bulgarian history was thus a drive to reach the Aegean Sea. Quoting the English Queen Mary who had said that "When I die, you will find the word Calais written on my heart," Durvingov felt that "the generations which fought the wars of 1912–18 would be right in saying that when we die these words will be found written on our hearts: we fought for the shores of the Aegean Sea, however dimly we understood this." The struggle with Serbia over Macedonia was caused, according to him by the failure of the Serbs to understand the spirit of their own history, which was to reach the stores of the Adriatic Sea.

There was also renewed interest, stimulated by a sense of the futility of nationalist wars and by the effects of the depression, in the old visions of the advocates of Balkan unity and federation. Efforts to "de-Balkanize the Balkans," which found expression in the four Balkan conferences of 1930–33 and various agreements of economic and cultural cooperation, had wide support in Bulgaria, as did the policy, initiated by King Boris in 1933, to create a special

---

[81] *Dukhut na istoriiata na bulgarskiia narod* (Sofia, 1932). Durvingov's many writings include treatises on Bulgarian military strategy (translated into Turkish and Serbian) and tracts on patriotic regeneration. In 1932, he was signally honored by election to the Bulgarian Academy of Sciences.

relationship with Yugoslavia in order to end Bulgaria's isolation in Balkan affairs.[82]

The trend toward Balkan unity ended, so far as Bulgaria was concerned, in 1934 when Bulgaria's four neighbors concluded the so-called Balkan Entente to maintain the territorial status quo. In its annex, their pact adopted the definition of aggression from the London Conventions of 1933, whereby failure of a state to suppress armed bands invading the territory of another state constituted an act of aggression. The new encirclement and the threat of punitive action if IMRO activities continued, caused general concern in Bulgaria where a Greek invasion on similar grounds in 1925 was well remembered.[83] International developments were thus added to internal unrest and disillusionment with democratic processes to produce the circumstances in which a combination of civilians identified as the Political Circle *Zveno* (link) and members of the Military League led by Damian Velchev carried out a bloodless *coup d'état* on May 19, 1934, and installed a government of "national regeneration" under Kimon Georgiev, a former leader of the league identified with the *Zveno* circle. While the motives of Velchev, Georgiev, and other participants in the coup are difficult to isolate and identify, there is merit in the view that they felt "unless they did so, the king might introduce a dictatorial regime, in the interests of the extreme nationalists and in the interests of Italy and Germany" and that Velchev "was not anxious to institute Army rule, which was in his opinion the chief evil from which Bulgaria had been suffering since 1923."[84]

An authoritarian regime, the new government disbanded the political parties, dissolved the National Assembly, and instituted a rule by decree. Press and publications were placed under censorship

[82] The rapprochement with Yugoslavia, intended to win support for a revision of the Balkan status quo, was misunderstood, nationalists felt, as a "Slavic brotherhood" movement and brought much harm to "the Bugarian soul and the Bulgarian national consciousness." Cf. B. Primov, *Makedoniia v istoriiata na bulgarskiia narod* (Sofia, 1943), pp. 132–33.

[83] On the invasion, the League of Nations investigation, and the indemnity Greece was required to pay, see G. V. Sarailiev, *Le Conflit gréco-bulgare d'octobre 1925 et son réglement par la Société des Nations* (Amsterdam, 1927).

[84] Great Britain, Foreign Office, *Bulgaria: Basic Handbook* (London, 1943), p. 6. Boris, it should be noted, married one of the daughters of the Italian king in 1930.

and an agency of "social renovation" was established to combat skepticism and apathy and popularize the new regime's ideas of civic responsibility, community of interests of labor and capital, class cooperation, and social peace. In foreign policy, despite its authoritarianism, the new regime was oriented toward the western democracies and the League of Nations. In regard to IMRO, it moved swiftly to suppress the gangster and terrorist elements and restore the full authority of the central government in the Pirin district, an operation that proved surprisingly easy and disproved the alleged strength of these elements.[85] The new regime also moved to re-establish diplomatic relations with the Soviet Union.

Revisionism and the "Third Catastrophe" (1935–1944)

Velchev and his friends had long felt that the role King Boris, with his ties in Italy and Germany, played was unhealthy and often talked of establishing a republic. Maneuvering to save his throne, Boris succeeded, in 1935, in removing them from power and creating his own authoritarian regime based on loyal bureaucrats and army officers. Velchev, who attempted another coup, was imprisoned for life, the Military League was dissolved, and the army was put under a loyal and strong-willed officer, General Khristo Lukov, whose task was to rebuild it with younger officers and reorganize it in line with a rearmament program made possible by Germany's repudiation of the restrictions of the peace settlement and by a soaring Bulgarian-German trade. In 1937, Boris sought to consecrate this alliance of crown and army, which his father had fostered and which he had renewed, by making "the patriarch of the Bulgarian army," General Danail Nikolaev of 1885 fame, the godfather of his son Simeon.

The emergence of Boris as the supreme leader of the army and the nation (in the terminology of his own propaganda) stimulated a great deal of writing on nationalistic themes, old and new. The theme Boris found especially useful was that Bulgarians were originally Huns and were at their best when they were true to the Hun-

---

[85] Their leader, Ioan Mikhailov, however, managed to escape to Turkey, which refused a request for his extradition. Others also made their way to Italy and Hungary where they trained with Croat nationalists for acts of terrorism. One of them, Vlado Chernozemski, carried out the assassination of the Yugoslav King Alexander at Marseilles in 1934. In Bulgaria, the surviving friends of Protogerov dissolved their ties on their own accord.

nic heritage of state organization based, as in military units, on one will, unconditional subordination, absolute loyalty to the head of the state, and strict responsibility. This Hunnic theory of the origin and essence of the nation served his purposes well, not only by glorifying the authoritarian state controlled by one will, but also by curbing the sense of Slavic kinship to Russia and Yugoslavia and combating the influence of Russian bolshevism in the country.[86] Linguistic nationalism and purism, rooted in the nineteenth-century issues of national linguistic identity, became quite vigorous and addressed itself to the task of purging the language of the Russian influences and imports as well as of foreignisms in general.[87] Cultural nationalism, which also became assertive in this period, reminded Bulgarians that in the ninth century when "great rulers in Western Europe were utterly illiterate," Bulgaria was the cradle of Slavic civilization ruled by one of the best educated men of his time; that the literary language of Russia was nothing but an outgrowth of the language of the Bulgarian religious literature in the Middle Ages; that civilization from Bulgaria saved the Serbs from the Latinization to which the Croats succumbed; that Bulgarian Bogomilism was the first reform movement in the Christian Church, which through the Hussite movement, matured into Protestantism, the Enlightenment, and the French Revolution; that the Russian Princess Olga, who spread Christianity in Russia before Vladimir's conversion in 988, was a granddaughter of Boris I; that the greatest medieval jurist teaching at Bologna, Bulgarus, was a Bulgarian; that Napoleon had Bulgarian blood in his veins; that the maker of Yugoslavia, Nikola Pašić, was born of Bulgarian parents.[88] The propaganda of cultural nationalism was intended to combat the "spirit of negativism," the feelings of inferiority, and skepticism and synicism, which were also a part of the story of Bulgarian nationalism in the interwar period. Contemptuous and cynical phrases like

[86] For an elaborate statement of this theory and its nationalist implications, see D. D. Susulov, *Putia na Bulgariia* (Sofia, 1936). Here, as elsewhere, no attempt is made to indicate the validity of views and theories; they are introduced only as components of the ideology of Bulgarian nationalism.

[87] M. Moskov, *Borbata protiv chuzhdite dumi v bulgarskiia knizhoven ezik* (Sofia, 1958), pp. 89–137.

[88] These and other evidences of "what the Bulgarian has given to other nations" are assembled in S. Chilingirov, *Kakvo e dal bulgarinut na drugite narodi* (Sofia, 1941).

bulgarska rabota ("Bulgarian business") and *balamite gi izbikha v balkanskata voina* ("the suckers died in the Balkan war"), which had wide currency in the postwar generations, filled nationalists with rage but the attitude they expressed proved difficult to fight.

While he built strength at home, Boris steered a course of cautious revisionism in foreign affairs, the first objective of which he declared to be the recovery of southern Dobrudja from Romania. With Axis encouragement he concluded in 1937 a pact of "eternal friendship" with Yugoslavia, but the enthusiasm and sincerity of the earlier rapprochement were gone. In recognition of realities, the Balkan Entente granted Bulgaria, in July, 1938, the right to rearm in exchange for a pledge to abstain "from all recourse to force." Much more important was the development of Bulgarian-German relations. In September, 1937, Boris personally initiated, through his trusted envoy, Purvan Draganov, and Hermann Göring, negotiations with the German government for delivery of armament amounting to 100,000,000 German marks payable over ten to fifteen years. When German economic agencies objected to the size and terms of the proposed transaction, the German foreign ministry took "the stand that a solution must at least be found which takes account of our political friendship with Bulgaria and the fact that economically Bulgaria has oriented herself completely toward Germany." Agreement was reached on March 12, 1938, in the form of a secret protocol, whereby a credit of 30,000,000 marks was extended.[89]

On the domestic scene the king's personal rule was encountering challenges and opposition from all segments of the political spectrum. Nationalist extremists and rightists, expecting to be supported by their counterparts in Germany and Italy, had no patience with his ways of a fox rather than a lion and made constant bids to share power with him. In the National Assembly, which the king allowed to reconvene in 1938, leaders of the political parties (which continued to be outlawed) who managed to get elected, spoke in vigorous opposition to his domestic and foreign policies. When seeking to carry their views to the people, six deputies identified with the left wing of the Agrarian Union (Nikola Petkov, Dimitur Matsankiev, and others) were charged with illicit activities and

[89] *Documents on German Foreign Policy, 1918–1945*, Series D, V (Washington, D.C.: U.S. Government Printing Office, 1953), pp. 232–35, 254–55.

maintaining contact with the Agrarian leaders Kosta Todorov and Dr. G. M. Dimitrov and were expelled from the assembly by a vote of the government majority. During the debates, they and other opposition deputies (Petko Stainov, Dimitur Gichev, Grigor Vasilev, and others) charged that foreign policy commitments were again, as in 1915, being made behind the back of the people.[90] Having a pliant majority of new men in the assembly, Boris was able to hold his opponents on the left in check, and through his personal contacts in Germany and Italy he was also able to checkmate the drives of his opponents on the right. By 1939, Boris possessed, more effectively than his father in 1914, all the necessary power to be regarded by every interested government as the only director of Bulgarian policy who mattered.

Contrary to everybody's suspicions, however, Boris had as yet made no formal commitments to the Axis powers and had gotten nothing beyond the arms credit agreement with Germany. This became evident during the months after the Munich conference that had, southeastern European leaders believed, given Germany a free hand to change the status quo in the area. When the question of what was to become of Romania was brought into focus, the nationalists began to clamor that Bulgaria was the only vanquished country that had not gained from the spreading revision of the territorial settlement. Boris, then, brought the Bulgarian claims to Dobrudja "for the first time to the attention of the Führer" on the eve of Hitler's meeting with the Romanian king (November 20, 1938), but found the Germans anxious to preserve the tranquillity of southeast Europe as a vital supply area and unwilling to become embroiled in the territorial disputes of the minor states.[91] This in essence remained Germany's position until the summer of 1940.

Adhering to formal neutrality, Bulgaria kept her revisionism quiescent during the first year of the war until the Russian demand for Romania's cession of Bessarabia in June, 1940, provided the first

---

[90] Bulgaria, Narodno Subranie, *Stenografski dnevnitsi* (Sofia, 1938), pp. 295–330.

[91] *Documents on German Foreign Policy*, V, 335, 351–52, and 360. Draganov also presented on December 8, 1938, Bulgaria's claims to Aegean Thrace, stressing that "even if only a few Bulgarians were living there now" as a result of the shifts of populations, the region should be "regarded as age-old Bulgarian territory" and that "if this question should at some time be resolved in Bulgaria's favor, it would also be to the interest of Germany, who would thereby also receive an outlet to the Aegean Sea."

chance to score a gain. On Hitler's advice, Romania yielded to the Russian demand and agreed to satisfy Bulgaria's claims (and, through German-Italian mediation, those of Hungary). In a transfer carried out in September, 1940, southern Dobrudja was returned to Bulgaria amidst general jubilation. The government propaganda and the extremist nationalists lost no time attributing the recovery of the region to "the benefactors of Bulgaria," Mussolini and Hitler, although it was generally known that the British and Soviet governments were also in favor of it.

The opportunity to pursue the next nationalist objective—the recovery of Aegean Thrace—followed swiftly. Preparing to attack Greece from Albania Mussolini wrote, on October 15, to Boris that "if Bulgaria wished to have an outlet to the Aegean, this was a favorable moment to obtain it" by invading Greece from the northeast. Assessing the dangers, Boris invoked "adverse public opinion in the country" and declined.[92]

As Italy bogged down and a danger of Greek-based British air raids against the Romanian oilfields developed, Hitler decided on a swift campaign to clean up the situation in Greece. For this action the army to be amassed in Romania needed operational freedom in Bulgaria. In a meeting with Boris on November 17, Hitler obtained his consent to the deployment of German forces in Bulgaria provided that, for security reasons, it was done immediately before the attack (scheduled for the spring of 1941) was to begin.[93] Bulgaria's adherence to the Tripartite Pact, it was agreed, was also to come later. Hitler informed Boris that, in the talks he had had with Soviet Foreign Minister Molotov four days earlier, the Soviet Union had asked for the same kind of political and military position in Bulgaria that Germany held in Romania, in order to improve its security vis-à-vis the Straits.

Pursuing interests reminiscent of 1878 and the ensuing years, Russia sought now, as then, to join forces with Bulgarian nationalism in order to reach her objectives at the Straits. On November 25,

[92] P. Badoglio, *Italy in the Second World War* (London: Oxford University Press, 1948), pp. 26–28. After the Italian attack, the lack of respect for the Italian martial spirit in Bulgaria turned into sympathy for the Greeks despite the Bulgarian-Greek grievances and the queen's Italian origin. Cf. D. Patmore, *Balkan Correspondent* (New York: Harper and Bros., 1941), pp. 237–73.

[93] H. Greiner, *Die oberste Wehrmachtführung, 1939–1943* (Wiesbaden: Limes Verlag, 1951), p. 240.

the Soviet government made a twelve-point proposal directly to Bulgaria to conclude a mutual assistance pact based on "the community of interests" of the two countries. It recalled the Soviet support in the recovery of southern Dobrudja and stressed the Soviet Union's "full understanding for the interests of Bulgaria in Western Thrace" and its readiness to help in their realization. There were, however, "authentic reports that Turkey will oppose by military means the advance of Bulgaria toward the south," and since the Soviet Union also found Turkey antagonistic to its interest in the Straits, common interests dictated the conclusion of a mutual assistance treaty "which would be helpful to Bulgaria in realizing her national aspirations not only in Western but also in Eastern Thrace." The pact would not "in any circumstances affect the internal regime, the sovereignty or the independence of Bulgaria" and if a threat of attack or actual attack by Turkey developed, "the Soviet Union will assist Bulgaria with all available means and support her in the realization of Bulgaria's well-known claims in the European part of Turkey." The Soviet Union would render all necessary military and economic assistance to Bulgaria and was prepared to drop its objections to her accession to the Tripartite Pact "on condition that the mutual assistance pact between the Soviet Union and Bulgaria be concluded. It is entirely possible that in that case the Soviet Union will join the Tripartite Pact."[94]

As in the second year of World War I, at the end of 1940 Bulgaria had thus become the focus of the interests of the major contending powers, and, just as in 1915, Germany held the advantage. Although she was not prepared to offer Bulgaria as much territory as Russia did, her power to bring about Bulgaria's acquisition of Aegean Thrace was at hand and, most important of all, her nazism was a lesser menace to the internal stability of the country than Russia's communism. England, with her commitment to Greece and power remote from the area, offered no alternative although she, too, had on occasion urged the peaceful revision of the question

[94] Text of the Soviet proposal in M. Pundeff, "Two Documents on Soviet-Bulgarian Relations in November, 1940," *Journal of Central European Affairs* (January, 1956), pp. 367–78. The text has also been published in *Documents on German Foreign Policy, 1918–1945*, Series D, XI (Washington, D.C.: U.S. Government Printing Office, 1960), 772–73, from which the quotations are taken. Leaflets distributed by Bulgarian Communists indicated that Russia would support Bulgaria in taking Turkish Thrace to the Enos-Midia line (p. 726).

of western Thrace. The choice of Boris, therefore, had long been predetermined. In its reply to the Soviet proposal, the Bulgarian government disclaimed any interest in the Straits question and stated its resolve to "avoid anything which could involve [Bulgaria] in problems of grand international politics." The Bulgarian people did "have their national ideals, but precisely [the settlement of the southern Dobrudja question] shows that these can be realized in a peaceful manner. As long as Bulgaria tries to achieve peacefully her revisionist claim to the western part of Thrace, there exists no Turkish danger."[95]

With the German army ready to cross the Danube, the Bulgarian government formalized its relationship with the Germans by signing the Tripartite Pact on March 1, 1941; Bulgarian participation in the impending operation against Greece was specifically ruled out, and Bulgaria was to receive only western Thrace between the estuaries of Maritsa and Struma rivers after the military operations there had ended.[96] However, an unexpected development—Yugoslavia's repudiation of the Tripartite Pact—opened much wider vistas for the realization of the nationalist program. Enraged by it, Hitler resolved to destroy Yugoslavia and, summoning Draganov, he declared that "this had settled the question of Macedonia."[97] In subsequent negotiations Boris again succeeded in dodging military participation in the operation against Yugoslavia and, as Yugoslavia began to collapse, he received Hitler's ruling that Bulgaria should obtain Yugoslav Macedonia "in accordance with the ethnic boundary."[98] As a result Bulgarian administration was established, pending final disposition at the peace settlement, in western Thrace, Yugoslav Macedonia (with the exception of several towns near Albania that

[95] *Ibid.*, pp. 756–57.

[96] *Ibid.*, XII (Washington, D.C., 1962), 68, 203. A protocol between German and Bulgarian General Staff representatives on the problems of the stay of German forces in Bulgaria provided that "the Bulgarian Army will, by agreement of the two Governments, not be employed offensively against" Greece and that it "will be reinforced in order to secure the new order in the Balkans" (*ibid.*, pp. 67–71). It may be noted that earlier the Germans entertained the idea of keeping western Thrace for a deal with Turkey and were inclined to give Salonika to Yugoslavia rather than to Bulgaria; Ribbentrop promised as much when Yugoslavia joined the Tripartite Pact on March 25, 1941 (cf. *ibid.*, XI, 1084; XII, 353).

[97] *Ibid.*, XII, 372.

[98] Greiner, *Die oberste Wehrmachtführung*, p. 278; *Trial of the Major War Criminals* (Nuremberg, 1947–49), XXVII, 60–62.

Italy took despite the strong objections of Bulgaria), and the Morava region.[99]

The dream of national unification nurtured since San Stefano appeared attained. Some areas (Greek Macedonia, Turkish Thrace) still remained beyond Bulgaria's reach, but for the most part the "lost territories" had been recovered and, as Boris liked to stress, without sacrificing Bulgarian lives or declaring war on anyone. Enthusiasm for what had been accomplished without cost, fanned by nationalists and propagandists, was at first considerable. A new image of Boris as "the tsar-unifier" was fostered and much was said about his grandiose and permanent achievements to cover up the facts of the difficulties with Italy and the provisional nature of Bulgaria's control of Yugoslav Macedonia and western Thrace. When Germany attacked Russia and the war entered a new phase, however, Bulgarians realized that just as in 1915–18 the gains depended on a German victory over Russia and England and that the gamble might again lead to national disaster. When Germany declared war on the United States in the wake of the Pearl Harbor attack and requested her associates in the Tripartite Pact to do likewise, for many Bulgarians the prospect of disaster turned into a certainty.[100] Others who believed that Boris was a master maneuverer and would bring things to a successful outcome were smitten into despair by his sudden and mysterious death in 1943.

In the deteriorating situation the Germans considered giving Alexander Tsankov and other rightists and nationalists a large role, but finally settled on a regency under the king's brother, Kiril, to maintain continuity and stability in Bulgaria. Prompted by Allied bombings, successive cabinets made clandestine attempts to obtain from the United States and England terms for an armistice, but

[99] *Documents on German Foreign Policy*, XII, 577. Ohrid, regarded by Bulgarian nationalists as the cradle of Bulgarian culture in the western domains of the nation, was occupied by Italian troops and was not yielded to Bulgaria until May. The Germans, it should be noted, kept Greek Macedonia and Salonika in their own hands. CF. map in R. Busch-Zantner, *Bulgarien* (Leipzig, 1943), and E. Kofos, *Nationalism and Communism in Macedonia* (Salonika, 1964), pp. 99–107.

[100] On the German request see Hugh Gibson (ed.), *The Ciano Diaries, 1939–1943* (Garden City, N.Y.: Doubleday & Co., 1946), p. 417. Realizing the grave public effect of its step (war was also declared on England as America's ally), the Bulgarian government explained that the war was to be only "symbolic" since Bulgaria had no points of contact with the United States and England and that Bulgaria remained at peace with Russia.

nothing resulted because the Bulgarians insisted on keeping the territories gained with German help, whereas the Western Powers were committed to having Russia deal with Bulgaria.[101] The Germans, however, were aware of these attempts and as they prepared to leave the Balkans in August, 1944, they considered three operations to seize Skopje from the Bulgarians, disarm their forces in Macedonia and Thrace, and intervene in Sofia against the defecting government. According to these plans Macedonia was to be set up as an autonomous unit under Ivan Mikhailov, who was to be flown in from Zagreb where he had spent the war years as a guest of the Croat nationalists. Mikhailov was also to take part with his "well-developed apparatus of terrorists" in the strike against the government in Sofia.[102] The rapidly deteriorating military situation, however, forced the Germans to relinquish these plans and to concentrate on withdrawing from Greece and Yugoslavia.

For the third time in thirty-one years, Bulgaria was facing a national debacle. When the Soviet Union declared war on September 5, 1944, and the Red Army moved into the country, there was little doubt that the social revolution, which "bourgeois" nationalists abhorred and which they had escaped after the second debacle in 1918, was at hand. What remained to be seen was whether Soviet Russia would make Bulgarian nationalism its ally, as it had sought to do in 1940 and as tsarist Russia had done on occasion before 1917, and to what extent it might pursue the old Russo-Bulgarian dream of San Stefano Bulgaria, or if she would act in a different manner.

Nationalism under Communism (1944–   )

Soviet policy became the controlling factor in Bulgaria after the entry of the Red Army into the country. As far as Bulgarian nationalist aspirations were concerned, the evolution of the Soviet

[101] The Anglo-Soviet agreement, sanctioned by the United States, was made in June, 1944, but was not publicized. A broad hint of it appeared in Churchill's House of Commons speech of August 2, 1944, in which he said that Bulgaria, like Romania, must make her terms primarily with Russia. Cf. H. Feis, *Churchill–Roosevelt–Stalin: The War They Waged and the Peace They Sought* (Princeton, N.J.: Princeton University Press, 1957), pp. 338–43. For details on the Bulgarian side, see V. Bozhinov, *Politicheskata kriza v Bulgariia prez 1943–1944* (Sofia, 1957), pp. 26–114.

[102] Ribbentrop to the German Minister in Sofia, August 31, 1944; *Nuremberg Trial Document* NG3912 (unpublished).

position was reflected by the statements of Bulgarian Communists. In theory, they were committed to the eradication of "bourgeois" nationalism and chauvinism, the implantation of proletarian internationalism and patriotism, and the creation of a Balkan federation of Communist states. In practice, however, the Soviet Union was not averse to enlisting, for its own purposes, the nationalism of one Balkan country against another, as its bid to Bulgarian nationalism in 1940 shows. The development of the Macedonian question in 1941 left Moscow confused, and, in the absence of a Soviet ruling on the matter, Bulgarian Communists claimed jurisdiction over revolutionary activities in Yugoslav Macedonia on the basis that it was a part of Bulgaria. It was not until 1943 that Tito prevailed in this jurisdictional dispute between Bulgarian and Yugoslav Communists due to a superior organization and a program to recognize the "Macedonian nation" within the proposed Yugoslav federal union and reestablish the Macedonian unity that had disappeared in 1913.[103]

Thus, by the time the Red Army occupied Romania and Bulgaria, the Soviet Union was committed to supporting Tito's program for Macedonia as well as Yugoslavia's territorial integrity. Now an internal matter within the Soviet domain, Bulgaria's recovery of southern Dobrudja in 1940 was likely to be ratified since the Soviet Union had been in favor of it. Turkey, an associate of the Western Powers, could not be pressed at this time for concessions to Russia in the Straits question nor, consequently, for cession of her part of Thrace to Bulgaria. What remained, therefore, was the question of western (Aegean) Thrace, which the Soviet government, like the tsarist governments before it, felt should be in Bulgarian hands, especially when Bulgaria herself was in Russian hands. With Soviet approval, Bulgarian troops and administrators remained in western Thrace more than a month after they had withdrawn from other occupied areas.[104] However, when Churchill flew to see Stalin on October 9, 1944, with this in mind,[105] Stalin conceded that Bulgaria

---

[103] Barker, *Macedonia*, pp. 83–98.

[104] S. S. Biriuzov, then commanding Soviet troops in Bulgaria, asserts that Bulgarian troops had to stay in western Thrace because the British had failed to clear the Aegean islands of Germans. Cf. his memoirs *Sovetskii soldat na Balkanakh* (Moscow, 1963), p. 193.

[105] W. H. McNeill, author of the volume of *Survey of International Affairs* entitled *America, Britain, and Russia: Their Cooperation and Conflict, 1941–1946* (London:

must evacuate western Thrace as a precondition for signing an armistice agreement.[106] The territorial issues were deferred to the negotiation of the peace treaties and to another chance for Russia to play the champion of Bulgarian nationalist claims. In the interval the Russians became increasingly involved in a conflict with Bulgarian national sensitivities that seemed headed for a repetition of their blunders of the 1878–86 era.

Ever since Stamboliiski put his imprint on Bulgarian political life, the Bulgarian peasants had become keenly conscious of the idea that the country rested, economically and politically, on their shoulders and that, being the great majority of the nation, they needed only a democratic system to be "masters in their own house." The bourgeois parties, they felt, had led the nation into two disasters and they had to take over in 1919 to save it. The cost of this ideology was the hostility of both the bourgeoisie and the Communists to the Agrarian regime in 1919–23 as well as sharp divisions in the Agrarian leadership itself, but the ideology survived nonetheless. As World War II evolved toward another defeat of the nationalist program of the bourgeoisie, the peasantry, especially that portion that followed left-wing leaders, prepared to recover the role from which it had been bloodily removed in 1923 and to save the nation once again. It was willing to share this task with others (Communists, Socialists, *Zveno* and Military League members, and Independents who formed with it the so-called Fartherland Front coalition), but the domination of Bulgarian political life by anyone else was out of the question.

The Soviet government, however, was intent on making the Bulgarian Communists the dominant force in Bulgaria. It had employed them in making its proposal known to Bulgaria in 1940, and in the war years it fostered a Communist-led underground movement and Communist propaganda to revive the notion of "Grand-

Oxford University Press, 1953), believes (p. 494) that western Thrace was "one of the first issues, and perhaps the one which brought Churchill in such haste to Moscow."

[106] This was undoubtedly due to the Anglo-Soviet agreement that recognized Greece as a British area of control. Churchill and Stalin renewed it by stipulating in percentages their influence in the countries involved. In Bulgaria, Russia was to have 75 per cent of the influence while England and the United States were to share the remaining 25 per cent. Cf. Winston S. Churchill, *The Second World War*, VI (Boston: Houghton Mifflin, 1953), pp. 227–28.

father Ivan" solicitous of the future of the Bulgarian people and to depict as "national treason" any move to exclude Russia from a leading role in Bulgarian affairs. Its concept for the reshaping of the political life and social structure of the country was the dictatorship of the proletariat, that is to say, of the Communist Party. Agrarian leaders and others in the Fatherland Front coalition were held suspect either of compromises with the bourgeoisie or, as relations within the Grand Alliance worsened, of ties with England and the United States.

Thus, by the beginning of 1945, a rift opened between peasant expectations and Soviet policies. Much else contributed to it as it widened to become once again a chasm between Bulgarians and Russians: ruthlessness in executions and "liquidations" of thousands of nationalists and "Fascists," dispossession of the propertied segments, Russification and sovietization of the country, primitiveness and criminality among the Russian soldiery. The first open sign of conflict was the removal of Dr. G. M. Dimitrov from the leadership of the Agrarian Union and his departure into a second exile (he had spent the war years in exile in Cairo) in the United States. As the conflict deepened, several major trials of army officers and others were staged to head off the powerful trend toward anti-Russian nationalism.[107] Their climax was the execution of the Agrarian leader, Nikola Petkov, in 1947, on charges of plotting to create a pretext for the armed intervention of the Western Powers in Bulgaria or, in short, of "national treason."[108]

While nationalist opposition to Russian dictation and its agents was being beheaded, the Soviet government attempted to win over some nationalist sentiment by assuming the role of sponsor of Bulgaria's national interests and protector of her national independence against real and alleged foreign designs and encroachments. At the Paris Peace Conference, Molotov publicly assured the Bulgarian delegates that the Greek demands for portions of southern Bulgaria would be blocked and the integrity of Bulgaria's territory, including

[107] Another measure was the removal of the monarchy through a plebiscite in 1946 and the establishment of a republic. For an account of these developments, see U.S. Senate Foreign Relations Committee Document No. 70–1, *Tensions within the Soviet Captive Countries: Bulgaria* (Washington, D.C.: U.S. Government Printing Office, 1954).

[108] *The Trial of Nikola D. Petrov* (Sofia, 1947), pp. 39–41.

southern Dobrudja, would be preserved; he also assumed the posture of champion of Bulgaria's cause in the formulation of the reparations and other clauses of the peace treaty signed in 1947.[109]

However, while this Soviet posture was unequivocal and constant in relation to Greece and the western Powers, in Bulgarian-Yugoslav affairs Soviet policy changed sides to harness first Yugoslav and then Bulgarian nationalism to changing Soviet interests. In 1944, as the Balkans north of Greece became communized, the main Soviet ally in the peninsula was Tito, whose program of recognizing a Macedonian nation within a federated Yugoslavia and seeking to unify it within an initial Balkan federation of Yugoslavia and Bulgaria was in principle backed by the Soviet leaders. For Tito, who was emerging as a Yugoslav nationalist with large visions, this program meant developing national consciousness among the population of Bulgarian Macedonia (the Pirin region), along the same line as this was done in Yugoslav Macedonia,[110] and with the participation of Yugoslav Macedonians, and eventually joining the two parts under a Yugoslav roof. This process of instilling national consciousness within a Communist framework was to extend to Greek Macedonia, also aiming to detach it, at an opportune moment, from Greece. Surrendering her part of Macedonia, Bulgaria was to join the Yugoslav six-member federation as its seventh unit.

For Georgi Dimitrov and other Bulgarian leaders, this program had acceptable and unacceptable aspects. Committed to a policy of "Macedonia for the Macedonians" and turning Macedonia from an "apple of discord" into a "healthy unifying link," they were willing to allow the development of a common national consciousness in Bulgarian and Yugoslav Macedonia as the Yugoslav leaders envisioned it. The joining of Bulgarian Macedonia to Yugoslavia's part and the addition of Bulgaria to the Yugoslav federation on terms

[109] V. Bozhinov, *Zashtitata na natsionalnata nezavisimost na Bulgariia, 1944–1947* (Sofia, 1962), pp. 151–227. Soviet delegates also lent some support to Bulgarian counterdemands for the "return of western Thrace" to Bulgaria.

[110] The principal tool in this process of nation building was to be the language. The language of the Macedonian Slav, as recorded in folklore and writings in the nineteenth century, was either Bulgarian, if he was educated, or a dialect that had the characteristics of Bulgarian, if he was not. The effort after 1945 was, therefore, to create a distinct Macedonian language. For the results see H. G. Lunt, *A Grammar of the Macedonian Literary Language* (Skopje, 1952). For a Bulgarian nationalist view of the language of the Macedonians see K. Mirchev, *Srubskata nauka za ezika na makedonskite bulgari* (Sofia, 1943).

other than absolute Bulgarian-Yugoslav parity was quite another matter. As differences on the question of parity hardened and Bulgarian and Yugoslav nationalisms clashed for the second time since 1941 within the framework of communism, the plans for federating were shelved with explanations that England and the United States were opposed to them.[111]

However, the old ideological commitments of the Bulgarian leaders lingered on. By 1947, the federation plans were revived and when Dimitrov and Tito conferred at Bled, Yugoslavia (August, 1947), an agreement was reached to begin the process of uniting the two countries by establishing a customs union and eliminating frontier restrictions and formalities. The Macedonian problem was to be solved within the framework of the federation by joining Bulgarian Macedonia to the Macedonian republic in Yugoslavia. Until the federation became possible, the groundwork was to be laid through the cultural rapprochement of the populations of the two Macedonian regions. As a result of the agreement, ninety-three teachers arrived in the Pirin district from Yugoslav Macedonia to assist in the teaching of the correct Macedonian language and Macedonian history.[112] Bookshops were established in a number of towns, filled with books, journals, and newspapers from Yugoslav Macedonia, and a Macedonian National Theater began to present plays in the new language.

At the height of these activities, larger events erupted and put an end to them. Visiting Bucureşti in January, 1948, Dimitrov discussed the idea of a customs union with Romania and, in reply to questions from the press, elaborated on the prospects of a federation embracing all Balkan countries, including Greece. He was immediately rebuffed in *Pravda* and, using the incident to halt the trend toward local initiative and independence, Stalin summoned

---

[111] Barker, *Macedonia*, p. 101.

[112] The basic themes of the new Macedonian history were that the Macedonians had their own distinct historical development, that their national revival was wrongly represented by Bulgarian nationalists as part of the Bulgarian revival, that they had fought against the "tyranny" of the Bulgarian exarchate just as hard as against that of the Greek patriarchate, that the IMRO of Gotse Delchev was a truly Macedonian organization for national liberation while the IMRO of Todor Alexandrov was an instrument of Bulgarian expansionism, and that the Macedonian republic in Yugoslavia was the first national state of Macedonians everywhere. Cf. D. Mitrev, *BKP i Pirinska Makedonija* (Skopje, 1960).

the Bulgarian and Yugoslav leaders for a meeting in Moscow. There, he and Molotov lectured them on the absolute necessity of checking with the Soviet government before they made any plans, arrangements, or statements, but while Dimitrov bowed to abuse and dictation, the Yugoslav leaders became even more defiant toward Soviet "big-power chauvinism" and control. As the Stalin-Tito feud broke out into the open in June, 1948, Dimitrov dutifully, if perhaps regretfully, took his place behind Stalin in the concerted Cominform effort to isolate Yugoslavia and bring the Yugoslav leaders down. The propagandists from Yugoslav Macedonia were thrown out of the Pirin region, the border was sealed, and a propaganda barrage was opened to depict Tito's Macedonian policy as a smokescreen for imperialist and chauvinist designs. Yugoslav propaganda responded with charges that the Bulgarian leaders never intended to apply the principle of self-determination in their part of Macedonia or to allow the development of national identity and a measure of autonomy there.[113]

So began the latest phase of the recurrent conflict between Bulgarian and Yugoslav nationalisms in the context of the common ideology of communism. In the years since 1948 it has evolved from violent hostility verging on the use of force in the Stalin era, through fluctuating policies in the Khrushchev era, to the present restraint from vituperation. In its beginning in the Stalin era, it was dramatized by the hunt of so-called Titoists that focused on Traicho Kostov, a local Communist, then secretary of the party and Dimitrov's likely successor. Although he was accused of conspiring with Tito (and American diplomats) and executed as a Titoist shortly

---

[113] For the tenor of Bulgarian propaganda in the Stalin era, see D. K'osev, *Titovata banda—orudie na imperialistite* (Sofia, 1951); *Documents sur la politique hostile et agressive du Gouvernement yougoslave contre la Republique Populaire de Bulgarie* (Sofia, 1952); and P. Traikov, *Natsionalizmut na skopskite rukovoditeli* (Sofia, 1949). The line of Yugoslav policy is evident in D. Mitrev, *Pirinska Makedonija vo borba za natsionalno osloboduvanje* (Skopje, 1950); D. I. Vlahov, *Makedonija: Momenti od istorijata na makedonskiot narod* (Skopje, 1950); L. Mojsov, *Bugarska radnicka partija (komunista) i makedonsko natsionalno pitanje* (Beograd, 1948); and Mitrev, *BKP i Pirinska Makedonija*. In this context the postwar writings of Ivan Mikhailov may be noted: *Stalin and the Macedonian Question* (St. Louis: Pearlstone Publishing Co., 1948) and *Macedonia: A Switzerland of the Balkans* (St. Louis: Pearlstone Publishing Co., 1950), both translated by Christ Anastasoff. (The latter is an IMRO propagandist connected with the Central Committee of the Macedonian Political Organizations of the United States and Canada in Indianapolis.)

after Dimitrov's death in 1949, Kostov was in fact guilty of anything but the crimes with which he was charged. He had been cool to the idea of surrendering Bulgarian Macedonia to Yugoslavia and federating on any basis other than Bulgarian-Yugoslav parity, and was for this reason regarded in Yugoslavia as a Bulgarian nationalist. His nationalism had manifested itself more clearly and sharply in relations with the Soviet Union when, in Stalin's presence, he took exception to injustices in Soviet-Bulgarian economic agreements.[114] In the context of the Soviet-Yugoslav conflict, Stalin simply equated Kostov's nationalism with that of Tito, and, suspecting an existing or a possible future connection between the two, provided the opportunity to Vulko Chervenkov, a Moscow-trained Stalinist and Kostov's main rival, to be his accuser, liquidator, and successor.[115]

In the years since Stalin died and Chervenkov was replaced by Todor Zhivkov, Kostov has been exonerated, rehabilitated, and posthumously declared a "Hero of Socialist Labor."[116] Although not explicitly vindicated for his stand against Soviet policies of economic exploitation in Stalin's time and Tito's designs, he remains the principal symbol to fellow Communists and the people at large in Bulgaria of the fact that a Communist can and must be guided in dealing with other Communist countries by his own country's concrete interests rather than by abstract formulae of international proletarian solidarity.

Stalin's demise and the Soviet recognition of many national roads to socialism brought the earlier phase of drab sameness in the Soviet bloc to an end and opened the way for the reassertion of national individuality. Bulgarian national institutions, traditions, and sources of strength are increasingly revived in the obvious hope that they can be harnessed to the purposes of the regime. For example, the Patriarchate, which perished in the Turkish conquest in the fourteenth century, has been reestablished in order to end, it would seem, Bulgaria's ecclesiastical inferiority vis-à-vis the Ecumenical Patriarchate and the Balkan national churches; the National Li-

---

[114] M. Djilas, *Conversations with Stalin* (New York: Harcourt, 1962), pp. 183–85.

[115] Cf. V. Chervenkov, *Leçons fondamentales de la découverte de la bande trait-chokostoviste et la lutte pour son anéantissement* (Sofia, 1950). The record of Kostov's trial is in *The Trial of Traicho Kostov and His Group* (Sofia, 1949).

[116] *Traicho Kostov: Izbrani statii, dokladi, rechi* (Sofia, 1964), p. 6.

brary, long named after the Communist leader Vasil Kolarov, has been renamed the Cyril and Methodius National Library; and the official gazette, *Durzhaven Vestnik,* recovered its traditional name and appearance after more than a decade of denationalized title and format. Examples of a rising national tone can be readily found in current writings on history, folklore, and literature.

It is, of course, the hope of the regime that the new nationalism it fosters can be channeled in the desired directions and will not affect Bulgarian-Soviet relations. On the Soviet side, Stalin's economic exploitation policies have been modified, as the abolition of joint companies and the creation of a thoroughgoing system of economic cooperation and mutual assistance in the COMECON indicate, but areas of conflict of national political and economic interests, which gave rise to Nikola Petkov's and Traicho Kostov's nationalism, remain. One such area of conflict is COMECON's international division of labor that has allocated to the participating countries fields of economic specialization in accordance with their present state of development and which has already set off a powerful wave of nationalism in Romania. Whether the COMECON division of labor will survive the conflict with Romanian nationalism or will be abandoned and whether the kind of nationalism Romania has developed will infect Bulgaria, which also has a disadvantageous economic role, remains to be seen.[117]

In the two decades since World War II, Bulgarian nationalism has thus been mainly stimulated by conflicts in which Bulgarians have been on the defensive. This defensive nationalism is principally a reaction to the policies of intervention, dictation, and exploitation that Russia has pursued in Bulgaria since 1944, and, in another direction, a reaction to the designs of Yugoslavia concerning Macedonia and Yugoslav-Bulgarian relations. Aggressive nationalism, discredited by three military fiascoes, has receded and its romantic, irrational, mystical, and virulent aspects seem to be buried. There is even a kind of sobriety and sophistication that is born out of debacles and disappointments. It would be a mistake to conclude, however, that expansionist nationalism could not rise again. If Russia should move toward an armed conflict with any of Bulgaria's

[117] For further details and a discussion of recent developments, see my forthcoming article, "Nationalism and Communism in Bulgaria," in *Südost-Forschungen,* XXIX (1970).

neighbors, she undoubtedly will seek to rekindle Bulgarian nationalist aspirations and use Bulgarian nationalism in the same ways as she did in 1940 in relation to Romania, Turkey, and Greece and in 1948–53 in relation to Yugoslavia. In Bulgaria as elsewhere, so long as conflicts of interests, which groups of individuals consider national, occur or are created, nationalism—defensive or aggressive—will surge as a powerful response.

JOSEPH F. ZACEK

Nationalism in Czechoslovakia

I

It is unhappily apparent that a "Czechoslovak nation," a single community composed of the majority of Czechs and Slovaks, sharing
a "Czechoslovak national consciousness," and asserting a "Czechoslovak nationalism," has never really existed. Unlike many of their
spokesmen, the popular masses of the Czechs and Slovaks have
seldom exhibited an awareness of ethnic unity and a supreme devotion to over-all "Czechoslovak" interests, even after the establishment of the First Czechoslovak Republic in 1918. In dealing with
nationalism in Czechoslovakia, therefore, it is necessary to deal
with separate "Czech," "Slovak," and "Czechoslovak" nationalisms
in their age-old competition with German and Magyar nationalisms.
The Moravians, the other major Slavic component of Czechoslovakia, have at times manifested a distinct territorial patriotism but
generally have not considered themselves ethnically different from
the Czechs. The peoples of other territories that have been joined
for significant periods of time to the Czech and Slovak lands, such
as Silesia, the Lusatias, and sub-Carpathian Ruthenia, have had
comparatively little influence upon the development of Czech and
Slovak nationalisms. As for the influence of foreign nations other
than the German and Magyar, only Poland, France, and Russia are
of real significance. In the earlier periods of history, the Czechs had
very close relations with the Poles, and the latter may justly claim
an important part in the beginning of the Czech "National Revival"
in the late eighteenth and early nineteenth centuries. The French
have contributed the stirring example of their revolutionary period,

the molding influence of their admired "western" culture, and the stability of their military-political alliances. Russia, as the most powerful of the Slavic nations and the potential deliverer of its smaller brothers from their oppression, has been the logical focus for the Pan-Slavic sentiments with which the Czechs and Slovaks have in difficult times bolstered their own national consciousness.[1]

[1] Within its prescribed limits, this study is confined to the presentation of the basic issues involved in the historical development of Czech, Slovak, and Czechoslovak nationalism, the major points of view on them, including the important Marxist revisionary ones, and a selection from their extensive bibliography. In addition to the specialized studies listed in subsequent footnotes, the following nation-oriented histories and source collections and surveys of nationalism are of basic value.

Histories: Ernest Denis, *La Fin de l'indépendance bohême* (2 vols.; Paris, 1890) and *La Bohême depuis la Montagne Blanche* (2 vols.; Paris, 1901–3); Kamil Krofta, *Nesmrtelný národ* (Prague, 1940); Hermann Münch, *Böhmische Tragödie* (Braunschweig, 1949); S. Harrison Thomson, *Czechoslovakia in European History* (2d ed.; Princeton, N.J.: Princeton University Press, 1953); F. Hrušovský, *Slovenské dejiny* (6th ed.; Turč. Sv. Martin, 1940); Joseph A. Mikuš, *La Slovaquie dans le drame de l'Europe* (Paris, 1955); abridged English trans., Kathryn D. Wyatt (Milwaukee, Wisc.: Marquette University Press, 1963); Jozef Lettrich, *A History of Modern Slovakia* (New York: Praeger, 1955); and Joseph M. Kirschbaum, *Slovakia: Nation at the Crossroads of Central Europe* (New York: Robert Speller, 1960).

Collections: V. Mathesius (ed.), *Co daly naše země Evropě a lidstvu* (2 vols.; Prague, 1939–40); František Heřmanský (ed.), *Duchem a mečem: Čtení o slávě, velikosti a utrpení našeho lidu* (Prague, 1958); Zdenka and Jan Munzer (eds.), *We Were and We Shall Be: The Czechoslovak Spirit through the Centuries* (New York: Frederick Ungar, 1941); Albert Pražák, *Národ se bránil: Obrany národa a jazyka českého od nejstarších dob po přítomnost* (Prague, 1946); František Bokes (ed.), *Dokumenty k slovenskému národnému hnutiu v rokoch 1848–1914* (2 vols. to date); Bratislava, 1962–65; and J. Tibenský, *Chvály a obrany slovenského národa* (Bratislava, 1965).

For broad studies of the Czechs and Slovaks as "nationality problems" within the Habsburg monarchy, see the following in the *Austrian History Yearbook*, Vol. III, Part 2 (1967): Jan Havránek, "The Development of Czech Nationalism," pp. 223–60; Václav L. Beneš, "The Slovaks in the Habsburg Empire: A Struggle for Existence," pp. 335–64; and L'udovít Holotík, "The Slovaks: An Integrating or a Disintegrating Force?", pp. 365–93.

Surveys of nationalism: Kamil Krofta, *Národnostní vývoj zemí československých* (Prague, 1934); Krofta, *Vývin národného povedomia u Čechov a Slovákov* (Prague, 1935); J. Kapras, *Jazykové a národnostní dějiny v české koruně* (Prague, 1931); Kapras, *Národnostní vývoj v českém státě* (Prague, 1931); F. Roubík, *Národnostní vývoj českých zemí* (Prague, 1946); H. Hassinger, *Die Entwicklung des tschechischen Nationalbewusstseins und die Gründung des heutigen Staates der Tschechoslowakei* (Kassel, 1927); Julius Botto, *Slováci: Vývin ich národného povedomia* (2 vols.; Turč. Sv. Martin, 1906–10); *Slováci a ich národný vývin* (Brat, 1966); B. S. Buc, *Slovak Nationalism* (Middletown, Pa.: Slovak League of America, 1960); and pertinent sections of these three works: Hans Kohn, *The Idea of Nationalism* (New York: Macmillan, 1944); Stephen Borsody, *The Tragedy of Central Europe* (New York:

II

Czech nationalism has had a much longer and more extensive development than Slovak nationalism, and until 1918 was much stronger and possessed a much more definite character than its Slovak counterpart. The roots of modern Czech nationalism can be identified quite clearly in the late Middle Ages, certainly not later than in the early fifteenth century. In its long evolution it has, of course, varied in intensity and nature during different historical periods. During the Hussite Revolution of the fifteenth century, the National Revival of the nineteenth, the twenty years of independence in the twentieth, and the brief period immediately following the second World War, the Czechs were actively nationalistic, successfully asserting their national identity against that of other peoples. In the interim periods, especially under Habsburg absolutism in the seventeenth and eighteenth centuries and the recent Nazi Protectorate, they were hard pressed to maintain a sense of national consciousness and, in the latter case, even their physical existence. The character of Czech nationalism has also varied in time. To use the classifications of Carlton J. H. Hayes, it has at different times been "Jacobin," "traditional," and "liberal."[2] During the Hussite period, it was of the "Jacobin" variety, broadly based on the popular masses, fanatical and rigorous at home, and spreading abroad with missionary zeal. In the late eighteenth century, it was the conservative "traditional" nationalism of the historic Bohemian aristocracy. From the early nineteenth century, Czech nationalism has been "liberal": bourgeois-dominated, generally evolutionary in theory and practice, coupling demands for national autonomy and basic individual liberties, and seeking the welfare of the Czech nation within a family of nations. While it would be difficult to prove the claim of a recent student of the subject that "the national movement of the Czechs is probably the most important and most representative example of East-Central European nationalism,"[3] it

---

Macmillan, 1960); and Walter Kolarz, *Myths and Realities in Eastern Europe* (London: Lindsay Drummond, 1946).

[2] Carlton J. H. Hayes, *The Historical Evolution of Modern Nationalism* (New York: Macmillan, 1931).

[3] Stanley Buchholz Kimball, *Czech Nationalism: A Study of the National Theatre Movement, 1845–83* (Urbana, Ill.: University of Illinois Press, 1964), p. vi.

has been a well-rounded and comprehensive phenomenon. Most of the classic factors associated with nationalism are well represented in the Czech experience. Geography, "race," and language have been crucial from the very beginning. Religion was of cardinal importance in the medieval period, romantic messianism and political self-determination in the modern one. Almost always absent, however, have been symptoms of "integral" nationalism: cultural arrogance and intolerance, illiberal government at home, and militarism and imperialism abroad. Well mirrored in Czech culture as a whole, the Czech national movement has had an especially strong influence upon the national historiography from the earliest monastic chroniclers to the present-day Marxists.[4]

Geography has been the ultimate determinant of Czech nationalism. From their first historical appearance in Bohemia-Moravia in the sixth century, in an area apparently already abandoned by the migrating German tribes, the Czechs have been the western vanguard of the Slavs, doomed forever to face the aggressive expansion of their German neighbor and the more subtle threat of his advanced culture. František Palacký, the famous Czech historian of the nineteenth century, expressed this in classic form in his *History of the Czech Nation:*

The chief content and basic feature of the whole history of Bohemia-Moravia is . . . the continual association and conflict of Slavdom with Romandom and Germandom. . . . And because Romandom had no direct contacts with the Czechs themselves but almost entirely through Germandom, we may also say that Czech history as a whole is based chiefly on conflict with Germandom, or on the acceptance and rejection of German customs and laws by the Czechs. . . . [It is] a struggle waged not only on the borders but in the interior of Bohemia, not only against foreigners but among native inhabitants, not only with sword and shield but with spirit and word, laws and customs, openly and covertly, with

[4] On the influence of nationalism upon the writing and philosophy of Czech history, see especially: Francis Lützow, *Lectures on the Historians of Bohemia* (London and New York, 1905); Richard Georg Plaschka, *Von Palacký bis Pekař: Geschichtswissenschaft und Nationalbewusstsein bei den Tschechen* (Graz and Cologne, 1955), with rich Czech and German bibliography; J. Werstadt, *Odkazy dějin a dějepisců* (Prague, 1948); and Eugen Lemberg, "Voraussetzungen und Probleme der tschechischen Geschichtsbewusstseins," in Lemberg and Ernst Birke (eds.), *Geschichtsbewusstsein in Ostmitteleuropa* (Marburg/Lahn, 1961), pp. 94–127.

enlightened zeal and blind passion, leading not only to victory or subjection but also to reconciliation.[5]

As Palacký indicated, the Czechs have met the German threat not only with forcible opposition but also with voluntary assimilation. This "partial Germanization" has helped them to preserve much of their Slavic character, but it has also perpetuated the bitter Czech-German rivalry in the area to the present day. The history of Czech nationalism, then, is the history of this long rivalry-association and the influence it has had upon the conception the Czechs have formed of their own national character and mission. The following pages will sketch the major phases of this relationship.

It was already the pressure of the Germanic Franks that impelled the Czech settlers in Bohemia-Moravia into the loose empires of Samo in the seventh century and of Great Moravia in the ninth. The Christianization of the Czechs in the ninth century removed the pretext for the German "crusades" against them, especially after they had decided upon the Roman rather than the Byzantine liturgy (and thus fatefully chose a western rather than an eastern cultural orientation, as well). However, German influences now threatened the Czechs through the German church hierarchy: the Czechs did not receive their own bishopric until 973, their own archbishopric until 1344. From the tenth century onward, and especially from the beginning of the thirteenth, the Přemyslid princes of Bohemia deliberately increased this danger by contracting military and marital alliances with their German counterparts and encouraging large-scale German immigration of monks, farmers,

---

[5] František Palacký, *Dějiny národu českého v Čechách a v Moravě* (3rd ed.; 5 vols. in 11; Prague, 1876–78), I, Part I, 12–13. More recent surveys of the historic Czech-German rivalry, from partisans of both sides, are E. Wiskemann, *Czechs and Germans: A Study of the Struggles in the Historic Provinces of Bohemia and Moravia* (London: Oxford University Press, 1938); S. Harrison Thomson, "The Conflict of Slav and German," *A Handbook of Slavic Studies*, ed. L. I. Strakhovsky (Cambridge, Mass.: Harvard University Press, 1949), pp. 140–76; S. Harrison Thomson, "Czech and German: Action, Reaction, and Interaction," *Journal of Central European Affairs*, I (Oct., 1941), 306–24; E. Rádl, *Válka Čechů s Němci* (Prague, 1928); K. Bittner, *Deutsche und Tschechen: Zur Geistesgeschichte des böhmischen Raumes* (Brno and Leipzig, 1936); Rudolf Jung, *Die Tschechen: Tausend Jahre deutsch-tschechischer Kampf* (Berlin, 1937); Eduard Winter, *Tausend Jahre Geisteskampf im Sudetenraum* (Salzburg and Leipzig, 1938); and Hermann Aubin, "Deutsche und Tschechen: Die geschichtliche Grundlagen ihrer gegenseitigen Beziehungen," *Historische Zeitschrift*, CLXV (1939), 457–79.

miners, merchants, and skilled townsmen of all varieties into their underpopulated lands, especially into the border areas. Apparently even the rulers of Great Moravia had sworn a vague, personal allegiance to German sovereigns, and with the Přemyslids began the fateful, much-disputed feudal relationship between the princes (later kings) of Bohemia and the German (later Holy Roman) emperors. Přemysl Otakar II (d. 1278) sought to wear both crowns, and Charles of Luxembourg, Bohemia's Czechophile king (d. 1378) actually succeeded, thus binding these two political entities even more closely together. The German language and German culture made significant inroads among the Czechs, especially through the appeal that German chivalry had for the Bohemian nobility. In opposition, Czech culture also developed rapidly, together with a Czech national consciousness and a native Czech resentment of the "foreign intruder." Criticism of the German's cultural arrogance and apprehension at his special civic and economic privileges and his overbearing influence at the Bohemian court and in most Bohemian towns is registered in the earliest Czech chronicles, such as those of Cosmas Pragensis (eleventh century) and of "So-Called Dalimil" (fourteenth century). Such feelings also provided an important stimulus for the Hussite Revolution.

The traditional non-Marxist view of the Hussite Revolution is that, although the complex result of many causes, it was primarily a religious reformation, an especially strong and broadly-based Bohemian variant of the European reaction to the general moral crisis of western Christendom in the fourteenth century. Czech Marxists look upon it as "the most powerful anti-feudal struggle of the mass of people in the medieval period" and lay primary emphasis upon its social and economic aspects—the chiliasm and Christian communism of the Taborites, the popular character of the movement, and its international revolutionary appeal.[6] Although both interpre-

---

[6] Pre-Hussite Czech national consciousness is discussed in F. Graus, "Die Bildung eines Nationalbewusstseins im mittelalterlichen Böhmen (Die vorhussitische Zeit)," *Historica*, XII (1966). Josef Macek is the leading Czech Marxist authority on the Hussite Revolt. See his *Husitské revoluční hnutí* (Prague, 1952), abridged in *The Hussite Movement in Bohemia* (Prague, 1958); also his "Národnostní otázka v husitském revolučním hnutí," *Československý časopis historický* (hereafter cited as *ČSČH*), III (1955), 4–30. Macek's views are critically summarized by Stanley Z. Pech, "A Marxist Interpretation of the Hussite Movement," *Canadian Slavonic Papers*, IV (1959), 199–212. See also: M. Machovec, *Husovo učení a význam v tradici českého národa* (Prague, 1953); and *Mezinárodní ohlas husitství*, ed. J. Macek (Prague, 1958).

tations undervalue the national character of the Hussite revolt, and despite the fact that Hus's own Czech nationalism was quite moderate, the nationalistic features of the movement were strong and closely intertwined with the others.[7]

At Prague University, an early center of the reform movement, Czech realists opposed German nominalists, and in 1409 the native "Czech nation" successfully contested the hitherto superior voting rights of the three "German nations" (Bavarians, Poles, and Saxons). In the towns, the artisans, mostly of Czech extraction, demanded greater rights from the German patricians. With the mass exodus of German-Catholic townsmen the Bohemian towns as a whole were radically Czechized and became the domain of a new and important Czech bourgeoisie. The Czech vernacular, polished by Hus himself and animated and enriched by religious controversy, now underwent great development. With its increased subtlety of literary expression, it was introduced into the Hussite church services and increasingly into the royal and municipal chancelleries. The entire Hussite experience had a profound, galvanizing effect upon the growth of Czech national consciousness. The reaction to Hus's martyrdom in 1415 was shared by the majority of the Czech population and the entire range of social classes. The striking military successes of the Hussite "Warriors of God" in turning back five great Catholic-German "crusades" as well as their own campaigns to aid coreligionists abroad (but never, as Czech historians are fond of pointing out, for purposes of territorial aggrandizement)

---

[7] On the national aspects of Hussitism, see Kamil Krofta, "Hnutí husitské po stránce sociální a národní," in his *Duchovní odkaz husitství* (Prague, 1946), pp. 86–117, in French translation as "L'aspect national et social du mouvement hussite," *Le Monde Slave*, V (1928), 321–51; and his *Žižka a husitská revoluce* (2d ed.; Prague, 1937), pp. 127–84. The following studies cumulatively describe nationality conditions in the Czech lands from the eve of the Hussite Wars through the Thirty Years' War: J. Kapras, *Národnostní poměry v české koruně před válkami husitskými* (Prague, 1911); V. Vojtíšek, *Národní stav v zemích českých za doby Žižkovy: Praha doby Žižkovy* (Prague, 1924); J. Klik, *Národnostní poměry v Čechách od válek husitských do bitvy bělohorské* (Prague, 1922); J. Kapras, *Národnostní poměry v české koruně od válek husitských do bitvy bělohorské* (Prague, 1912); Wilhelm Weizsäcker, "Über die Nationalitätenverhältnisse in Böhmen von den Hussitenkriegen bis zur Schlacht am Weissen Berge," *Mitteilungen des Vereins für Geschichte der Deutschen in Böhmen*, XLI (1924), 117 ff.; V. Líva, "Národnostní poměry v Praze za třicetileté války," *Český časopis historický* (hereafter cited as *ČČH*), XLIII (1937), 301–22, 487–519.

stirred national pride. Catholic Europe's characterization of the Czechs as "a nation of heretics" provoked a feeling of defensive solidarity permeated with a national religious messianism, a mystical conviction that the Czech nation was the most Christian of all and had been elected by God to revive the fallen church.[8] To be sure, the greatest significance of the Hussite reformation for Czech national feeling would not be evident until four centuries later, when the romantic "Awakeners" would rediscover the period and make it the core of Czech history.

The religious question remained the prime mover of the historical development of Bohemia to the battle of White Mountain. But beginning with the battle of Lipany (1434), where the conservative Utraquist faction clashed with and defeated the radical Taborites, Hussitism progressively ceased to act as a force for national unity. It is true that for some time longer, under the wise rule of the last native king, the Utraquist George of Poděbrady (1458–71), the Czechs managed to preserve the position of their creed and their language. Indeed, the development of the latter was even stimulated by the flowering of Czech humanism and the introduction of printing in Bohemia (1468). But the death of George was crucial for the destiny of the Czech nation. With him died the last opportunity to establish a native dynasty on the Bohemian throne and the last hope for the Czech nation to go the way of Spain, France, and England, to undergo a flourishing national development under a strong, centralized monarchy.[9] After his death, he was followed by foreign dynasties that did not identify themselves with the Czech nation. Under the weak Jagellonians (1471–1526), the nation began to fragment along class lines into a *Ständestaat*, with the uncontrolled nobility systematically subverting the townsmen and degrading the peasantry into serfdom. German influences rapidly reentered the land in a now familiar pattern, and German immigrants were soon joined by the influx of German Lutheranism with its strong appeal for Protestant Bohemia. After 1526, the new Habs-

[8] On the origins of Czech messianism in this period, see the two studies of Rudolf Urbánek: "Počátky českého mesianismu," *Sborník V. Novotného* (Prague, 1930), pp. 124–45; and "Český mesianismus ve své době hrdinské," *Pekařův Sborník* (2 vols.; Prague, 1930), I, 262–84.

[9] On the significance of George's reign, see Frederick G. Heymann, *George of Bohemia: King of Heretics* (Princeton, N. J.: Princeton University Press, 1965), pp. 586–611.

burg sovereigns actively fostered the use of the German tongue in the public administration and among the upper nobility of Bohemia. Warning voices were raised (e.g., Viktorin Kornel ze Všehrd, Mikuláš Dačický z Heslova), and in 1615 the Bohemian Estates were belatedly moved to pass a stringent language law. All officials of the kingdom and all members of the Estates and of the urban patriciate were required to know and use the Czech language; all immigrants were required to have it taught to their children. The Germans in the land were forbidden, on pain of expulsion, to regard themselves as a separate and independent community. But this measure came too late, just five years before the battle of White Mountain, which was to throw open the door to massive German influences in the Czech lands.

White Mountain (November 8, 1620) was not a national conflict, but a feudal one. The mercenary forces of a rebellious Protestant Bohemian oligarchy (including both Czech and German nobles), supporting a foreign (German) claimant to the throne, fought those of the Catholic Habsburg monarch. The degraded masses of the nation remained passive. Nevertheless, the Czech nation shared fully in the drastic consequences of the nobles' defeat.[10] For the next century and a half its development stopped. It had lost a large part of its native leadership, its chosen religion, the widespread use of its language, and its historic right of self-rule. A quarter of the nobility, a quarter of the bourgeoisie, and the cream of the Czech intelligentsia (including the Unity of Czech Brethren)—about thirty-six thousand families, it has been estimated—were exiled or emigrated voluntarily. The estates of the nobles were confiscated and given to foreigners —Germans, Walloons, Frenchmen, Spaniards, Irishmen, Italians— whose ties were primarily with the Viennese court and who felt little empathy with their Czech subjects. As a result of the war, the population of Bohemia-Moravia had fallen from about three million to about nine hundred thousand. To repair these losses, Germans were settled not only in the borderlands but also in numerous "islands" in the interior. The towns also resumed their German caste; Prague would remain a "German" city until the middle of the nineteenth century. Catholicism became the single permissible religion, and the Jesuits were entrusted with the eradication of every trace of the

---

[10] See J. Polišenský, *Třicetiletá válka a český národ* (Prague, 1960).

proud Hussite epoch. In the process they destroyed much of the Czech cultural heritage, save for the remnants which were carefully hidden in the outlying regions, on the fringes of Moravia and in Slovakia. The German language was granted equal status with the Czech, but favored in official and polite circles, it soon became the exclusive language of the nobility and the bourgeoisie. Czech, taught only in the lowest parish schools, became the mutilated language of servants and peasants. The Crown of St. Václav was declared to be hereditary in the Habsburg dynasty, and the powers and privileges of the Bohemian Estates were limited and assumed by imperial offices staffed by imperial bureaucrats. During this period, the few protests that were raised against these national depredations came from exiles abroad (such as Jan Amos Komenský, Pavel Stránský, Pavel Skála ze Zhoře) and occasionally from patriotic Czech members of the Catholic priesthood (Bohuslav Balbín, Tomáš Pešina z Čechorodu). If by the late eighteenth century the complete extermination of Czech national consciousness had not yet occurred, it was only because the Habsburg "absolute monarchs" had not pursued their ends with deliberate system and efficiency.

Paradoxically, it was the belated attempt of the "Enlightened Despots," Maria Theresa and especially Joseph II, to adopt such a course, to completely unify, centralize, and standardize the public life of all of the Habsburg lands, that was partially responsible for the Czech "National Revival" (*Národní obrození*) in the last decades of the eighteenth century. The origins and early nature of this phenomenon are a major historiographical problem.[11] The Czech "rebirth" appears to have been both a part of the general continental emancipation that stemmed from the Enlightenment and the French Revolution as well as a specifically Bohemian and Czech reaction to the rationalistic and romantic stimuli from abroad. Certainly foreign nationalisms were contagious—not simply French nationalism, proclaiming the "rights of man," but the Polish nationalism expressed during the Partitions; the nationalism of the great Slav brother, the

---

[11] Viewpoints and literature are exhaustively reviewed by Albert Pražák, "Názory na české obrození," in his valuable collection of studies entitled *České obrození* (Prague, 1948), pp. 63–110. There exist only a few other basic works on the Revival. See: Jakub Malý, *Naše znovuzrození* (6 vols. in 4; Prague, 1880–84); Louis Leger, *La renaissance tchèque au dix-neuvième siècle* (Paris, 1911); and the new Marxist interpretations by J. Kočí, *Národní obrození: Nový nástup lidových sil* (Prague, 1952), and *Naše národní obrození* (Prague, 1960).

Russian, aroused by his triumph over Napoleon; and the fiery, romantic love of one's fatherland preached at German universities such as Jena, which many young Slavs (especially Slovaks) were now able to attend. Friendly encouragement came to the Slavs from such figures as Goethe and Schlözer, and Herder prophesied a splendid future for them.[12]

Some Czech historians see the Czech revival as primarily a domestic phenomenon, or rather a domestic reaction to certain "enlightened" policies introduced by Joseph II. The "religious school," best represented by Tomáš G. Masaryk and Albert Pražák, claims that it was a renewed contact with the religious-national ethos of the Hussite period, made possible by the broad tolerance of Joseph's regime. His Patent of Toleration (1781) released the Czech Protestant spirit, and his removal of the function of censorship from clerical hands permitted once again the study of the glorious Hussite past. The "politico-literary" school holds that the measures taken by Joseph to centralize completely the administration of the imperial lands at Vienna provoked the Bohemian nobility into a belated local territorial patriotism. To find support for their defense of the historic political rights of the Bohemian kingdom and the privileges of the Bohemian Estates, they began to support the study of Bohemian history and even the use of the old Czech language in opposition to German, the language of centralization. The scholars whom they patronized were mostly enlightened Catholic priests and monks, themselves alienated by the anticlericalism of the regime. Still another group of scholars (including the Marxists) fasten upon social-economic factors, especially Joseph's encouragement of industrialization and economic competition and his easing of the burdens of serfdom in 1781. By granting the peasants (still the most nationally conscious Czech stratum) mobility and the right

---

[12] For varying opinions on foreign influences upon the National Revival, see: E. Lemberg, *Grundlagen des nationalen Erwachens in Böhmen* (Liberec, 1932); Hans Raupach, *Der tschechische Frühnationalismus: Ein Beitrag zur Gesellschafts- und Ideengeschichte des Vormärz in Böhmen* (Essen, 1939); Matthias Murko, *Deutsche Einflüsse auf die Anfänge der böhmischen Romantik* (Graz, 1897); K. Bittner, *Herders Geschichtsphilosophie und die Slawen* (Liberec, 1929); Herbert Peukert, *Die Slawen der Donaumonarchie und die Universität Jena, 1700–1848* (Berlin, 1958); Marjan Szyjkowski, *Polská účast v českém národním obrození* (3 vols.; Prague, 1931–46); Richard Pražák, *Maďarská reformovaná inteligence v českém obrození* (Prague, 1962); and Květa Mejdřická, *Čechy a francouzská revoluce* (Prague, 1959).

to send their sons for training as artisans or for higher study, he released a vast reservoir of national spirit and created a force that would stubbornly resist his plan to Germanize completely the lives of all of his subjects.

Whatever the priority of causes, it is clear that the first phase of the National Revival was a Bohemian *Landespatriotismus*, the product of the efforts of a coalition of the Bohemian nobility and a group of scholars, mostly historians of clerical calling (Gelasius Dobner, Mikuláš Adaukt Voigt, František Martin Pelcl, František Pubička, Josef Dobrovský). The second phase was a Czech cultural resurgence, the work of a second generation of "Awakeners." These were a handful of romantic young enthusiasts (Josef Jungmann, František Palacký, Ján Kollár, Pavel Šafařík), mostly sons of the lower middle class or the more prosperous peasantry, of Moravian and Slovak extraction, and Lutheran in religion. More optimistic than the first generation, they intended to do nothing less than to prod the moribund Czech nation back into life. This was to be done through a linguistic and literary revival, through the transformation of the mangled Czech vernacular into a sophisticated vehicle of a nationally oriented literature. They compiled grammars and dictionaries, wrote works of belles-lettres and scholarship, published periodicals and newspapers, and Czechized old Bohemian cultural institutions or founded new ones. The career of František Palacký, titled "Father of the Nation" because of his intimate involvement with almost every important event, institution, issue, and program of the Revival, provides a cross section of their efforts.[13]

Palacký was born in 1798 in northeastern Moravia, into a prosperous peasant family that had secretly preserved the traditions of the Czech Brethren. While studying for the ministry at the Evan-

[13] Studies of the ideological and class makeup of the National Revival are the following: Albert Pražák, *Duch naší obrozenské literatury* (Prague, 1938); and his *Obrozenské tradice* (Prague, 1928); J. M. Lochman, *Náboženské myšlení českého obrození* (Prague, 1952); F. Vodička, "České obrození jako problém literární," *Slovo a slovesnost*, X (1947–48), 30–42; and his collection of studies, *Cesty a cíle obrozenské literatury* (Prague, 1958); Jan Muk, *Po stopách národního vědomí české šlechty pobělohorské* (Prague, 1931); F. Kutnar, *Obrozenský nacionalismus* (Prague, 1940); and his *Sociálně myšlenková tvářnost obrozenského lidu* (Prague, 1948); M. Hroch and A. Veverka, "K otázce sociální skladby české obrozenské společnosti," *Dějepis ve škole*, IV (1957), 153–59; and Jan Novotný, "Příspěvek k otázce úlohy některých lidových buditelů v počátcích českého národního obrození," *ČSČH*, II (1954), 600–629.

gelical Lyceum in Pressburg (Bratislava, Pozsony), he was "converted" to a fervent Czech nationalism. He determined to devote himself to the writing of Czech history, especially that of the Hussite period, and went to Prague for that purpose in 1823. There he was taught by Dobrovský and befriended by the counts Franz and Kaspar Sternberg, who made him their archivist and ultimately obtained for him the post of Royal Bohemian Historiographer with a commission to compose a new "pragmatic" history of Bohemia. This task consumed the major part of his lifetime. Nevertheless, he still found time for numerous other patriotic activities: he was a member and official of the Royal Bohemian Society of Sciences and the Bohemian National Museum and editor of the latter's two learned journals; he tried to publish a Czech encyclopedia; he helped to found a major publishing foundation, the *Matice česká;* he was a member of the committee to build a national theatre; and he was one of the principal Czech political spokesmen from 1848 until his death in 1876.

Palacký's numerous writings both expressed and shaped the Czech national sentiment of the time. This is especially true of his *Dějiny národu českého v Čechách a v Moravě* (History of the Czech Nation in Bohemia and Moravia),[14] the most significant single product of the literary efforts of the "Awakeners." It was at once the foundation stone of modern Czech historiography and a stirring national manifesto, written "to show the Czechs what they had been and what they should be." The work clearly qualifies Palacký as a "national prophet," and the philosophy of Czech history embodied in it is an excellent example of "nationalist messianism," to use the apt labels of Hans Kohn.[15]

[14] The work had actually begun publication in German—*Die Geschichte von Böhmen grösstentheils nach Urkunden und Handschriften*—as Palacký's agreement with the Estates specified. After his participation in the events of 1848–49, which provoked the German press violently against him, he "left the ranks of German historians forever" and continued his writing exclusively in Czech. The change in the work's title is also indicative of Palacký's reorientation.

[15] Hans Kohn, *Prophets and Peoples: Studies in Nineteenth Century Nationalism* (New York: Macmillan, 1947). The "national prophets" developed "a philosophy of history and society in the center of which stood their own nation and the principle which was to sum up its idea and faith," *Prophets,* p. 11. Their philosophy is characterized by "nationalist pride, often cloaked in humility and grounded in real or imaginary sufferings and offenses, [and] claims to serve the cause of universal peace

In his *History*, Palacký described the age-old Czech-German conflict (to 1526), but interpreted it in terms that gave it universal significance. In his philosophy of history, nations, as carriers of ideas and principles, are the chief historical agents.[16] Through them mankind progresses gradually and eternally toward "deiformity" (likeness to God), chiefly through the "natural law of polarity," the unending conflict between spiritual and material forces. A nation's worth lies in the worth of the ideas it advances, in its contribution to human progress, not in its size or strength. The Czech nation, Palacký believed, had been assigned a great humanitarian, often tragic role. It was

small, indeed, but richly gifted, unusually progressive, enlightened, devoted to productive and useful work; not aggressive but heroic, fighting gloriously not only for its own life and its own independence and freedom but for the highest treasures of human society; meriting much from mankind, but through the disfavor of fate, the malice of its neighbors, and the lack of inner concord, sentenced to cruel suffering.[17]

In the history of Bohemia, the "law of polarity" manifests itself, of course, in the struggle between Slavdom and Germandom. It is a competition between two disparate national characters, between the authoritarian, predatory German and the peaceful, democratic Czech. In the long course of this struggle, the Czech nation reached its "deiform period" (i.e., came closest to fulfilling its historical mission) in the Hussite reformation, which Palacký thus identified as the core of Czech history. In it the Czechs had placed themselves among the earliest champions of the rights of the individual against the absolute authority of church and state. The Hussite was the first attempt at a Christian reformation, the first in a chain of pro-

and justice." Hans Kohn, *Reflections on Modern History* (Princeton, N.J.: Princeton University Press, 1963), p. 134.

[16] In English, Palacký's philosophy has been sketched several times by Hans Kohn: in his *Not by Arms Alone: Essays on Our Time* (Cambridge, Mass.: Harvard University Press, 1940), pp. 65–83, and in "The Historical Roots of Czech Democracy," in Robert J. Kerner (ed.), *Czechoslovakia* (Berkeley and Los Angeles: University of California Press, 1949), pp. 91–105. See also Joseph F. Zacek, "Palacký and His History of the Czech Nation," *Journal of Central European Affairs* (hereafter cited as *JCEA*), XXIII (1964), 412–23, and the sources listed there.

[17] Václav Vlček, "Dějepisecké dílo Františka Palackého," *Osvěta*, VI (1876), 402.

gressive movements and democratic revolutions in Europe that had shaped the character of western man. As such, it had forever guaranteed the Czech nation a high place in the history of human enlightenment.

Through his philosophy of history, Palacký gave Czech nationalism a new, positive content, and a firm western, liberal, and humanitarian foundation. He had also solved the problem of finding a justification for the continued existence of the small Czech nation. "Through him Czech history became of importance for the history of Europe, the Czech question, a universal question. . . . The Czechs found their place in modern Europe on the side of the great and progressive democratic currents and peoples."[18]

Palacký's definition of Czech national character and mission, the only comprehensive philosophy of Czech history before that of the Marxists, has been the one most widely accepted by the Czechs ever since. Its chief propagator until the eve of World War II was the philosopher-statesman, Tomáš G. Masaryk. Masaryk ignored its anti-German element and laid stress upon its humanitarian aspect, especially in a religious (ethical, not theological) sense. For him, the "Czech Question" was a moral and religious one.[19] Palacký's interpretation was not universally accepted by Czech historians, however, especially by the positivist "Goll School" and its spokesman, Josef Pekař.[20] Pekař denied the existence of any specifically

[18] Kohn, *Not by Arms Alone*, p. 81.

[19] There is no single, comprehensive exposition by Masaryk of his own philosophy. See his *Palackého idea národa českého* (5th ed.; Prague, 1947) for his understanding of Palacký. See also S. Harrison Thomson, "T. G. Masaryk and Czech Historiography," *JCEA*, X (April, 1950), 37–52.

[20] German historians, from Palacký's personal opponent, Constantin Höfler, to the current Sudetens in exile, have—of course—bitterly contested Palacký's view. Their version of the history of Bohemia-Moravia has generally insisted that the Germans did not appear there chiefly at the beginning of the thirteenth century as "immigrants and colonists," but had maintained uninterrupted settlements there from the earliest times; that the German contribution to the civilization of the area, in every aspect and in every period, has been of great, even pre-eminent importance; that the constitutional tie between the Kingdom of Bohemia and the Holy Roman Empire made the former "a German province"; and that, for these reasons, the Germans have rights of habitation in the area equal to those of the Czechs and superior cultural and political ones. The tone of the German "case" has varied, from those willing to grant relationships of mutual benefit (e. g., Luther's debt to Hus) to those who insist that the German mission in Bohemia-Moravia has been to help the Czech nation "to divest itself of its inborn bestial nature" and to "lead it toward humanity." This point of view is developed, in varying degrees, in the histories of Bohemia-Moravia by Adolf

Czech national idea and saw the basic force in Czech history as simply self-preservation against German pressures. He regarded the Hussite period with its fanaticism, chiliasm, and sectarianism as medieval, not modern, and traced its origins to broad European, not indigenous Czech stimuli.[21] The conservative Pekař has suffered heavy criticism from his countrymen to the present day. Popular resentment of his skeptical, "scientific" attack upon the flattering Czech self-image was only increased when, in the period preceding the second World War, German historians began to distort his views subtly for their own purposes. Czech Marxists have also castigated him severely, labeling him "nationally indifferent."

In the hands of so many self-professed disciples and angry critics, Palacký's philosophy has also undergone various distortions. Especially as Czech-German hostility mounted in the late nineteenth century and in the twentieth, both parties frequently ignored Palacký's emphasis upon the beneficial results that had often marked their relationship and his regard for universal human welfare over national welfare. The Czechs came to regard themselves as "a rampart against Pan-Germanism," and the Germans to see them as "the vanguard of Pan-Slavism," later of "Bolshevism."

By the mid-nineteenth century, what the "Awakeners" had sought—a revival of Czech culture and an aroused national consciousness—had been accomplished. At about the same time, the coming of the Revolution of 1848 to Bohemia added a new, political element to Czech nationalism.[22] It forced the "Awakeners" out of

Bachmann and Bertold Bretholz; in the Sudeten German histories by Josef Pfitzner, Alfred Schmidtmayer, and Emil Franzel; and in Kurt Glaser, *Czecho-Slovakia: A Critical History* (Caldwell, Idaho: Caxton, 1961). See also: Alfons Dopsch, *Die historische Stellung der Deutschen in Böhmen* (Vienna, 1919); Helmut Preidel (ed.), *Die Deutschen in Böhmen und Mähren: Ein historische Rückblick* (2d ed.; Gräfeling, 1952); and two Czech replies by Kamil Krofta, *Die Deutschen in Böhmen* (Prague, 1924), and *Das Deutschtum in der tschechoslowakischen Geschichte* (2d. ed.; Prague, 1936).

[21] Pekař's interchange with Masaryk on "the meaning of Czech history" can be followed in his *Masarykova česká filosofie* (2d ed.; Prague, 1927), and in Masaryk's reply, "Ke sporu o smysl českých dějin," *Naše doba,* XX (1912–13), 6 ff. See also their polemics in Vol. XVIII (1912) of the *Český časopis historický,* and Pekař's *Smysl českých dějin* (Prague, 1929).

[22] The Bohemian Revolution is still among the least known of the 1848 uprisings among western scholars. See: Otakar Odložilík, "The Czechs on the Eve of the 1848 Revolution," *Harvard Slavic Studies,* I (1953), 179–217; Arnošt Klíma, "Bohemia," in Francis Fejtö (ed.), *The Opening of an Era: 1848* (London, 1948), pp. 281–97;

their studies and into the arena, and placed the leadership of the Czech national movement henceforth almost exclusively into their middle-class hands. As expressed by Palacký in his letter to the Frankfort Parliament, at the Slavonic Congress in Prague, and at the Imperial Constituent Assembly at Kremsier, their first political program was Austrophile and federalistic. They resolutely rejected absorption into an all-German state: "I am not a German. . . . I am a Czech of Slavic blood," wrote Palacký to Frankfort. Nor did they seek complete independence for the Czechs. (Palacký himself was thoroughly convinced that the mounting trend toward "world centralization" supported by the technological revolution would make the independence of small nations increasingly difficult.) Instead, they wished to preserve the Habsburg Empire as a bulwark against both German and Russian aggression, requiring however that it guarantee all nationalities within it complete equality of rights. At Kremsier, in 1849, Palacký even abandoned the traditional plea of the nobility for the restoration of Bohemia's historic political rights and proposed instead a federation of eight entirely new, autonomous national units, organized on ethnic principles and cutting across old historical frontiers. One of these was to be a "Czechoslovak" national unit.

Palacký's plan, often referred to in subsequent years as a promising solution to the problems of a multinational state, was, of course, rejected.[23] It was the last serious consideration given to demands for

and his *Rok 1848 v Čechách* (Prague, 1949); Karel Kazbunda, *České hnutí roku 1848* (Prague, 1929); F. Roubík, *Český rok 1848* (Prague, 1931); J. Macůrek, *Rok 1848 a Morava* (Brünn, 1948); and Josef Vochala, *Rok 1848 ve Slezsku a na severovýchodní Moravě* (Opava, 1948).

[23] The plan is discussed in Otakar Odložilík, "A Czech Plan for a Danubian Federation—1848," *JCEA*, I (1941), 253–74; and in Robert A. Kann, *The Multinational Empire: Nationalism and National Reform in the Hapburg Monarchy* (New York: Columbia University Press, 1950), II, 26–35. Palacký has received considerable criticism from the Marxists for his political activities and theories, especially those of 1848. Led by the Soviet historian, I. I. Udaltsov, Czech Marxists have charged that he was exclusively the spokesman of his social class, the Czech liberal bourgeoisie. As such he helped to engineer its cooperation with the Bohemian feudal aristocracy and to whip up the "historic rights" and "equality of nationalities" issues, with the sole purpose of deterring a rising social revolutionary movement among the lower classes. By helping to preserve the reactionary Habsburg monarchy in 1848, Palacký and his class "threw a shadow on the name of the Czech nation." See Joseph F. Zacek, "Palacký and the Marxists," *Slavic Review*, XXIV (1965), 297–306; and V. Vomáčková, "K národnostní otázce v buržoazní revoluci 1848 v českých zemích," *ČSČH*, IX (1961), 1–16.

Czech autonomy until the last year of World War I. Palacký and his "Old Czech" party returned to their coalition with the nobility, to the "historic rights" argument, and, especially after the creation of the Dual Monarchy in 1867, to "passive opposition" to parliamentary life. ("We existed before Austria," wrote Palacký. "We shall exist when it is gone.") About 1890, the "Old Czechs" were superseded by the more belligerent "Young Czechs" as leaders in the provincial and imperial diets. These abandoned over-all national goals and chose, through a policy of parliamentary obstructionism and bargaining, to work for piecemeal political and cultural concessions from the vacillating government. They concentrated, with considerable success, on extending the use of Czech in schools and in the public administration and on receiving proportionate Czech representation in the parliamentary bodies. Toward the end of the century and especially after the granting of universal manhood suffrage in 1907, parties representing the Czech proletariat and peasantry also developed and began to agitate for more radical class goals, thus further splintering the national political platform. All Czech demands were violently opposed by the Bohemian German minority, which was terrified of losing its privileged position in the kingdom, and by the Magyars, fearful that any such concessions would encourage similar demands in their half of the Dual Monarchy.

Frustrated politically, Czech national consciousness nevertheless grew mightily in the course of the nineteenth century, helped by the increasing part Czechs were taking in the industrialization of the Habsburg lands not only as a skilled proletariat but as independent entrepreneurs, and by the high Czech birth rate.[24] It ex-

---

[24] Broader studies of the development of Czech nationalism in the nineteenth and early twentieth centuries: Alfred von Skene, *Entstehen und Entwickelung der slavisch-nationalen Bewegung in Böhmen und Mähren im XIX. Jahrhundert* (Vienna, 1893); František Červinka, *Český nacionalismus v XIX. století* (Prague, 1965); J. F. N. Bradley, "Czech Nationalism in the Light of French Diplomatic Reports, 1867–1914," *Slavonic and East European Review* (hereafter cited as *SEER*), XLII, No. 98 (Dec., 1963), 38–53; and his "Czech Nationalism and Socialism in 1905," *American Slavic and East European Review*, XIX (1960), 74–84; K. Kosík, "K některým otázkám národně osvobozeneckého boje českého lidu v XIX. století," *Nová mysl* (1954), 37–52, 162–82; Jiří Kořalka, "K některým problémům národní a národnostní otázky v českých zemích v období kapitalismu," *ČSČH*, X (1962), 376–91, reprinted in German in *Österreichische Osthefte*, V, No. 1 (1963), 1–12; K. Krejčí, "La lutte pour la libération nationale des tchèques et des slovaques au XIXe. et commencement du XXe.

pressed itself in every important field of creative and scholarly endeavor, producing a roster of illustrious names, some of them of European-wide significance. It was enshrined in a growing number of Czech institutions, such as the Sokols (1862), the independent Czech University at Prague (1882), and the Czech National Theatre (1883).[25] It manifested itself in numerous popular demonstrations and on ceremonial public occasions. Sentiments expressed and declarations made on these occasions (for example, at the laying of the foundation stone of the Czech National Theatre in 1868, and at the Ethnographic Congress in Moscow in 1867) were often markedly pan-Slav, rather than exclusively Czech, in nature. By thus stressing their blood ties and ethnic solidarity with millions of fellow Slavs, the Czechs were able to offset their own frustrations with the general prospect of a great Slav future.[26] However,

---

siècle," *Journal of World History*, V, Part 3 (1960), 700–733; J. Kolejka, "České národně politické hnutí na Moravě v letech 1848–1874," in *Brno v minulosti a dnes* (ed.) Jaroslav Dřímal, II (Brno, 1960), 301–71; O. Říha, "O národním hnutí a národnostní otázce, 1848–1918," *ČSČH*, II (1954), 47–68; Oldřiška Kodedová, "Národnostní otázka v letech 1905–7," *ČSČH*, III (1955), 192–222; and Jurij Křížek, "Česká otázka v buržoasní politice na počátku první světové imperialistické války," *ČSČH*, VII (1959), 625–43; and J. Havránek, J. Kořalka, J. Mésároš, and Z. Šolle, "Narodnye massy v cheshkom i slovatskom natsionalnom dvizhenii XIX veka," *Voprosy istorii*, No. 1 (1966), pp. 105–16.

[25] Detailed studies of two institutions in which Czech nationalism was centered throughout the nineteenth century, the National Museum and the National Theatre, are: Josef Hanuš, *Národní museum a naše obrození* (2 vols.; Prague, 1921–23); and Stanley B. Kimball, *Czech Nationalism: A Study of the National Theatre Movement, 1845–1883* (Urbana, Ill.: University of Illinois Press, 1964).

[26] Although the Czechs have traditionally been regarded as Slavophile and even Russophile, and though both pan-Slavism and neo-Slavism originated among them, it should be clear that these sentiments and movements were almost exclusively cultural and literary, seldom political in nature among them. With the exception of Karel Kramář, Czech political leaders before 1918 opposed any political connection or unification with Russia, and such men as Palacký, Karel Havlíček, and Masaryk even opposed a Russian cultural orientation for the Czechs. Among the Slovak leaders, Ľudovít Štúr stands out for his pronounced "Pan-Russianism." See: Hans Kohn, *Pan-Slavism: Its History and Ideology* (Notre Dame, Ind.: University of Notre Dame Press, 1953), pp. 3–26, 231–54; and his "The Impact of Pan-Slavism on Central Europe," *Review of Politics*, XXIII (July, 1961), 321–33; J. F. N. Bradley, "Czech Pan-Slavism before the First World War," *SEER*, XL, No. 94 (Dec., 1961), 184–205; Hugo Hantsch, "Pan-Slavism, Austro-Slavism, Neo-Slavism: The All-Slav Congresses and the Nationality Problems of Austria-Hungary," *Austrian History Yearbook*, I (1965), 23–37; and Michael B. Petrovich, "Ľudovít Štúr and Russian Panslavism," *JCEA*, XII, No. 1 (April, 1952), 1–19. Predictably, the Marxists have been eager to stress the influence of the "Slavonic Idea" upon the Czech and Slovak Revivals. See

they also contributed in this way to the marked "racial" enmity that had begun to develop between the Czech and German inhabitants of Bohemia since 1848. Among the "Sudeten Germans," whose own nationalism began to rise in intensity to match that of the Czechs, such "racial" concepts also appeared, especially from the 1880's on, in the National Socialism and Pan-Germanism of leaders such as Georg von Schönerer.[27]

The outbreak of the first World War caught the Czechs unprepared and without a concerted plan of action. Since 1848, no significant Czech or Slovak political spokesman had demanded an independent state. In 1914, the majority of Czech patriots probably would still have been satisfied with full self-government within the Habsburg Empire. Only gradually during the course of the war did domestic public opinion swing from autonomy to independence. Czech leaders quickly realized that a victory of the Central Powers would be fatal for the Slavs of the Dual Monarchy, but even they were divided in orientation. Karel Kramář, for example, thought in terms of a Russian grand duke sitting on the throne of a Bohemian kingdom, and a close relationship of the latter with Russia. Masaryk, who was willing to accept a western prince if necessary, preferred a republic with a western orientation. Under Masaryk's direction, four years of many-sided national effort by the Czech legions and emigrants living abroad, by the "Mafia" and the domestic population, resulted in the state he had desired, a republic including not only the Czechs but also the neighboring Slovaks. During the war, and especially in their declarations of independence and union in Octo-

especially: "Materiály z konferencie o myšlienke slovanskej vzájomnosti a jej úlohe v národnooslobodzovacom boji našich národov," *Historický časopis slovenský* (hereafter referred to as *HČ*), VIII (1960), 193–467, an important collection of studies; and Anton Popovič, "K problematike slovanskej idey na Slovensku v matičnom období (1863–1875)," in *Príspevky k medzislovanským vzťahom v československých dejinách* (Bratislava, 1960), pp. 165–99. Two broader surveys are J. Macůrek (ed.), *Slovanství v českém národním životě* (Brno, 1947), and J. Mikulka and J. Šťastný (eds.), *Slovanství v národním životě Čechů a Slováků* (Prague, 1968).

[27] See S. Harrison Thomson, "The Germans in Bohemia from Maria Theresa to 1918," *JCEA*, II (July, 1942), 161–80; Andrew G. Whiteside, *Austrian National Socialism before 1918* (The Hague, 1962); and his "Industrial Transformation, Population Movement, and German Nationalism in Bohemia," *Zeitschrift für Ostforschung*, X, No. 2 (1961), 261–71; Jiří Kořalka, "La montée du pangermanisme et l'Autriche Hongrie," *Historica*, X (1965), 213–53; and his *Všeněmecký svaz a česká otázka koncem 19. století* (Prague, 1963).

ber, 1918, in Paris, Prague, and Turčansky Svätý Martin, leaders of both Czechs and Slovaks had spoken of a common "Czechoslovak nation" and of the desire of their peoples to form a "Czechoslovak state." Much of the subsequent record is testimony that the two terms were far from synonymous.

III

Slovak nationalism has had a much shorter history than Czech nationalism, but a more linear development. Created late in the eighteenth century and painfully nurtured throughout the nineteenth by a tiny (chiefly Lutheran) intelligentsia, the Slovak nation was so weak in 1914, so utterly lacking in self-consciousness, that it might easily have disappeared again had it not been for the war. After 1918, however, stimulated by independence, Slovak nationalism steadily increased in strength, reaching full self-assertion in the Slovak Republic of 1939–45. Its character before 1918, insofar as this can be determined from the words and acts of a handful of isolated individuals, was essentially "liberal." From 1918 on, strongly influenced by the militant, clerical Slovak People's Party, it increasingly assumed clear-cut "integral" characteristics, qualities that found full expression after 1939. Factors of race and language were especially important in Slovak nationalism before 1918, especially with the advent of systematic Magyarization. Language also played an important role in frustrating a "Czechoslovak" nationalism. Religion and political self-determination became important components only after 1918. There is no well-developed Slovak "national philosophy." In the nineteenth century, some accepted the idea that the Slovaks, because of their enforced isolation and uninterrupted settlement in the geographic area believed to have been the cradle of Slavic civilization, had best preserved the unspoiled Slavic nature and tongue.[28]

From the fall of the Great Moravian Empire to the Magyars at the end of the ninth century until 1918, the Slovaks had no independent history of their own. Without a "heroic" period to use as a point of reference, scholars have been reduced almost entirely to the use of linguistic and literary criteria in determining the origins

---

[28] There is an interesting attempt to describe clinically Slovak "national character" by Anton Jurovský, "Slovenská národná povaha," in *Slovenská vlastiveda,* II (Bratislava, 1943), 333–98.

of Slovak national consciousness. Extreme Slovak nationalists, and to some degree the Marxists today, recognize a distinct Slovak language and literature in Great Moravia itself.[29] Some recent studies, based upon the science of historical linguistics, have located the formative period of Slovak nationality between the eleventh and thirteenth centuries. Other students of the problem, such as Andrej Mráz and Ernest Denis, place the introduction of the Slovak vernacular as a literary medium (and the beginning of a Slovak "national revival") in the seventeenth century, at the Counter Reformation center of Trnava.[30] Perhaps the majority of the remaining scholars, including those who accept the "Czechoslovak" tradition, postpone a Slovak literary-national emergence to the mid-nineteenth century, possibly to the late eighteenth.[31]

In the Middle Ages, after being conquered, the small Slovak population did not develop strong leaders of its own and was gradually enserfed. In the fifteenth century, Hussite arms and ideas penetrated into Slovakia, especially when it came under the control of the

[29] The national character of Great Moravia, especially in connection with the origins of a distinguishable Slovak nation, is a much-debated topic among the Marxists. They variously describe the population of the empire as being of "Moravian-Slovak nationality," "Great Moravian nationality," and "Moravian nationality." (Many Czechoslovak bourgeois historians have, of course, regarded Great Moravia as the prototype of a joint "Czechoslovak" nation.) Of the growing literature and polemics on this problem, see: J. Dekan, "O vznikaní národností pred X. storočím na území našej vlasti," *Věstník Československé akademie věd,* LXIII (1954), 399–404; and his *Začiatky slovenských dejín a Ríša Veľkomoravská* (Bratislava, 1951); J. Kudláček, "K otázke o vznikaní národností na našom území," *HČ,* IV (1956), 397–410; and his "K novším názorom o vznikaní ranofeudálnych národností na našom území," *HČ,* V (1957), 357–67; Dekan, "Skutočnosť a mýtus v bádaní o vzniku ranofeudálnych národností," *HČ,* VI (1958), 257–68; L. Havlík, "K otázce národnosti na území Velké Moravy," *HČ,* V (1957), 493–503; O. R. Halaga, "K otázce vzniku slovenskej národnosti," *HČ,* X (1962), 238–62; Ján Tibenský, "Problémy výskumu vzniku a vývoja slovenskej feudálnej národnosti," *HČ,* IX (1961), 397–419; R. Krajčovič, "Problém vzniku slovenskej národnosti z jazykového hľadiska," *HČ,* V (1957), 484–92; E. Pauliny, "Poznámky k vzniku slovenskej národnosti zo stanoviska historickej jazykovedy," *HČ,* VII (1959), 104–8; Arvid Grébert, *Slovaks and the Great Moravian Empire* (Middletown, Pa.: Slovak Institute of Cleveland, 1963).

[30] See Ernest Denis, *La question d'Autriche: Les Slovaques* (Paris, 1917); Ján Pöstenyi, *Slovenský národný život v Trnave v rokoch 1488–1820* (Trnava, 1943); Branko Varsik, *Národnostný problém trnavskej univerzity* (Bratislava, 1938); and Ludwig von Gogolák, *Beiträge zur Geschichte des slowakischen Volkes,* Vol I: *Die Nationswerdung der Slowaken und die Anfänge der tschechoslowakischen Frage* (1526–1790) (Munich, 1963).

[31] See J. M. Kirschbaum, "Slovak Literary History in Marxist and Western Interpretations," *Canadian Slavonic Papers,* VI (1964), 117–34.

Czech *condottiere*, Jan Jiskra of Brandýs, and various "military brotherhoods." Although the extent of the influence of Hussitism upon the Slovaks is debated, it did prepare a mild welcome for the subsequent Lutheran Reformation among them and accounted for the fact that the Slovak Protestants used the Czech language in their liturgy until very recent times and that the Slovaks shared a common literary language with the Czechs until the mid-nineteenth century.[32] The first undisputed sign of national stirring occurred in the late eighteenth century, with the attempt to develop a separate Slovak literary language.[33] This was especially desired by the Jesuits, who wanted a language better suited to local proselytizing, and who wished to erect a tactical barrier between the Czechs and Slovaks. In 1787, Anton Bernolák (1762–1813), a Catholic priest, unsuccessfully tried to develop the western Slovak dialect into a literary sub-

[32] M. Mišík, *Husiti na Slovensku* (Banská Bystrica, 1927); Branko Varsik, *Husiti a reformácia na Slovensku do žilinskej synody* (Bratislava, 1932); Varsik, *Husitské revolučné hnutie a Slovensko* (Bratislava, 1965); P. Ratkoš, "Husitské revolučné hnutie a Slovensko," *HČ*, I (1953), 26–41; L. Hoffman, *Ohlas husitského revolučného hnutia na Slovensku* (Turč. Sv. Martin, 1954); J. Macůrek and M. Rejnuš, *České země a Slovensko ve století před Bílou horou* (Prague, 1958). The Marxist studies stress the "antifeudal" character of the movement as its strongest influence upon the Slovaks.

[33] Survey-studies of Slovak nationalism from the late 1700's to 1918: E. Várossová, *Slovenské obrodenecké myslenie: Jeho zdroje a základné idey* (Bratislava, 1963); J. Tibenský, "Počiatky slovenského národného obrodenia," *HČ*, II (1954), 520–38; E. Kovács, "Maďarské a slovenské národné hnutie v prvej polovici minulého storočia," *Naša veda*, III (1956), 52–56; Jozef Butvin, "Slovenské národné obrodenie v dobe predšturovskej," *Dějepis ve škole*, IV (1957), 297–309; and his "Zjednocovacie snahy v slovenskom národnom hnutí v tridsiatych rokoch 19. storočia," *Historické štúdie*, VIII (1963), 7–67; and his *Slovenské národnozjednocovacie hnutie, 1780–1848* (Bratislava, 1965); Ján V. Ormis, "Slovenské národné obrany v rokoch 1832–1848," *HČ*, XI (1963), 552–79; V. Matula, "K niektorým otázkám slovenského národného hnutia štyridsiatých rokov XIX. storočia," *HČ*, II (1954), 375–406; Q. Matejko, "Predrevolučné Slovensko a jeho mentálne základy," *Slovenské pohľady*, LIX (1943), 400–421; Július Mésároš, "Slovanská otázka v politike slovenskej buržoázie v druhej polovici 19. storočia," *HČ*, VIII (1960), 324–59; and his "Die Idee der slawischen Schicksalsgemeinschaft in der slowakischen nationalen Bewegung in der zweiten Hälfte des 19. Jahrhunderts," *Historica*, X (1965), 159–211; and his "Otázka slovenského národného hnutia od revolúcie 1848–1849 do národné oslobodenie," in *Úlohy slovenskej historickej vedy v období socialistickej výstavby* (Bratislava, 1961), pp. 94–120; and his "Kríza dualizmu a slovenské národné hnutie v deväťdesiatych rokoch," *HČ*, XIV (1966), 372–411; and his *Roľnícka a národnostná otázka na slovensku, 1848–1900* (Bratislava, 1959); Jaroslav Dubnický, "Stav a úlohy historického bádania v období slovenského národného obrodenia, *Ibid.*, 79–93; and J. Paučo, "Slovakia's Mid-Nineteenth Century Struggle for National Life," *Slovak Studies*, I (1961), 69–84.

stitute for Czech. The new language was little understood in central and eastern Slovakia, Slovak Protestants rejected it, and Czechophile Slovak scholars such as Kollár and Šafařík denounced such a cultural schism.[34] However, when the next attempt was made in the 1840's, utilizing the more suitable central Slovak dialect, it was successful. The new literary Slovak language was the handiwork of L'udovít Štúr (1815–56).[35] Like his colleagues, Jozef Hurban and Michal Hodža, Štúr was a Lutheran and, though suspicious of Czech designs, no Czechophobe. His motivations were chiefly political: the new language was to unite all Slovaks, both Catholic and Protestant, and to mobilize them against the increasingly fierce campaign of Magyarization to which they were being subjected. Such a visible sign of difference from the Czechs might also placate the Magyars' suspicions of Slovak separatist intentions.

Like their Czech counterparts, the Slovak "Awakeners" also represented their nation in its brief participation in the Revolution of 1848.[36] Through their "Petition" of Liptovský Sv. Mikuláš and at the

[34] Bernolák also established a Slovak Learned Society in 1792, staffed mostly by the Catholic clergy, and libraries. On the man and his period, see the extensive collection of articles, *K počiatkom slovenského národného obrodenia: Sborník štúdií Historického ústavu SAV pri príležitosti 200. ročného jubilea narodenia Antona Bernoláka* (Bratislava, 1964), and J. Tibenský, "Bernolák's influence and the origins of the Slovak awakening," *Studia Historica Slovaca*, II (1964), 140–89. According to the Marxists, the "objective base" for this revival was "the development of capitalist relations" in Slovakia at the end of the eighteenth and the beginning of the nineteenth centuries.

[35] On Štúr and his period, see: Hélène Tourtzer, *Louis Štúr et l'idée de l'indépendance slovaque, 1815–1856* (Paris, 1913); D. Rapant, "Doba Štúrovská," *Historický sborník*, IV (1942), 129–36, on themes and problems; K. Goláň, "L'udovít Štúr a slovenské národné hnutie v štyridsiatych rokoch XIX. storočia," *HČ*, III (1955), 87–103; and his collection of articles, *Štúrovské pokolenie* (Bratislava, 1964); *L'udovít Štúr: Život a dielo, 1815–1856* (Bratislava, 1956), a collection of summary articles; and J. Butvin, "L'udovít Štúr a jeho úloha v slovenskom národnozjednocovacom hnutí," *Historické štúdie*, XII (1967), 5–20.

[36] On Slovak political and cultural affirmations from the late eighteenth century to the late nineteenth: D. Rapant, *K počiatkom Maďarizácie* (2 vols.; Bratislava, 1927–31); Rapant, *Ilegálna Maďarizácia, 1790–1840* (Martin, 1947); Rapant, *Slovenské povstanie roku 1848–49: Dejiny a dokumenty* (5 vols.; Bratislava, 1937–67); Rapant, "Slovak Politics in 1848–1849," *SEER*, XXVII, Nos. 68–69 (1948–49), 67–90, 381–403; Albert Pražák, "The Slavonic Congress of 1848 and the Slovaks," *SEER*, VII, No. 10 (June, 1928), 141–59; K. Rebro, "Attempts at a Rightful Solution of the Slovak National Question in the Revolutionary Years 1848–1849," *Studia Historica Slovaca*, IV (1966); Rapant, *Viedenské memorandum slovenské z roku 1861* (Turč. Sv. Mart., 1943); L'udovít Holotík, "Memorandum slovenského národa z roku 1861," *HČ*, XI (1963), 3–30; Rudo Brtáň, "Ste výročie Martinského Memoranda: Jeho ohlas v slovenskej literatúre," *Vlastivedný sborník Považia*, IV (1961),

Slavonic Congress in Prague, they demanded recognition of Slovak nationhood (in reaction to Magyar claims such as Kossuth's that a Slovak nation had never existed), self-government and official use of the Slovak language in Slovakia, Slovak schools and a university, universal suffrage, and such civil liberties as freedom of assembly, of association, and of the press. Hurban actually called for a general rising against the Magyars, which the latter speedily crushed. In 1861, in a "Memorandum of the Slovak Nation," the Slovaks again affirmed their "national individuality" and voiced their demands. In 1863, they also established the *Slovenská matica,* which until its closing by the government in 1875 was an energetic center for scholarship and education among the Slovaks. Except for these few significant national affirmations, the Slovaks seemed pathetically unable to resist the brutally systematic attempts of their masters to assimilate them forcibly into a Magyar national state. Dispossessed of their schools and institutions, their Catholic hierarchy infiltrated with Magyarones, granted almost no parliamentary representation, and suffering crushing poverty, they had only two feasible alternatives— to accept Magyarization or to emigrate.[37] Isolated from the major currents of European affairs, the feeble Slovak culture and Slovak national consciousness were dying in 1914. In another generation, assimilation by the Magyars would probably have been complete. During the war that saved them, the Slovaks remained inarticulate. Only when the Habsburg state's collapse was imminent did a small number of their spokesmen lead the passive, indifferent masses into a new joint state with the Czechs.

To maintain that Slovak national consciousness was almost nonexistent in 1918 is not to imply that, by default, a "Czechoslovak" national consciousness was strong. It is true that throughout the preceding century, a large number of illustrious Czechs and Slovaks (Palacký, Karel Havlíček, Masaryk, Štúr, Milan Štefánik, and even

---

51–65; F. Bokes (ed.), *Memorandum v slovenskej literatúre* (Bratislava, 1961); the collection of articles, *Matica slovenská v našich dejinách, 1863–1963* (Bratislava, 1963); and Jozef Butvin, "Snahy o založenie Matice slovenskej: K otázke úlohy kultúrnych organizácií v slovenskom národnom hnutí," *HČ,* XI (1963), 169–92.

[37] It is estimated that in the forty years preceding World War I, eighty thousand Slovaks emigrated. More prosperous and aggressive than their countrymen back home, they exerted considerable influence upon the direction of Slovak national aspirations, both during the war and after. See B. S. Buc, "The Role of Emigrants in Slovak Nationalism," *Slovakia,* IX, No. 4 (1959), 32–46.

Andrej Hlinka, to name but a few) had declared their belief in the existence of a single "Czechoslovak nation" in two branches. Štefánik summed up their views with the words: "Who are the Czechs? The Czechs are Slovaks who speak Czech. And who are the Slovaks? The Slovaks are Czechs who speak Slovak." It is also true that many important factors favored the development of a single nationality: ethnic similarity, a millennium of geographic proximity, a common written language until the mid-nineteenth century, and especially close relations in various historic periods, such as the Great Moravian Empire, the period of Hussite-Lutheran friendship in the sixteenth and seventeenth centuries, and especially the Czech National Revival in the late eighteenth and early nineteenth centuries.[38] In the latter, not only had Slovakia yielded up to the Czech "Awakeners" the hoard of old Czech cultural remnants that she had preserved since 1620, but many of the "Awakeners" themselves, such as Kollár and Šafařík, had been Slovaks. Nevertheless, a deep and broadly based "Czechoslovak" sentiment had not resulted due to other, nullifying factors, long-term trends reinforced by events of the nineteenth century. Since Great Moravia, the two peoples had never been united politically, and the failure of Palacký's federative prosal in 1849 and the success of the Compromise of 1867 simply confirmed that they would not be able to draw upon even a half-century of common political experience before being merged in the new Czechoslovakia. The joint literary-cultural experience also had not been a dynamic one. After White Mountain, the Slovaks had become simply caretakers of an antiquated Czech cultural tradition with which the Czechs themselves progressively lost contact. In the nineteenth century, when the Czechs rediscovered their old culture and began to expand it aggressively and to incorporate western intellectual currents into it, the Slovaks, isolated by their new literary lan-

---

[38] On the important Czech-Slovak ties in the Revival period and in 1848, see: J. Hanák, "Slovaks and Czechs in the Early Nineteenth Century," *SEER*, X, No. 30 (April, 1932), 588–601; Albert Pražák, "Czechs and Slovaks in the Revolution of 1848," *Slavonic Review*, V, No. 15 (1927), 565–79; and his "Czechs and Slovaks after 1848," *Slavonic Review*, VI, No. 16 (1927), 119–29; Jan O. Novotný, *O bratrské družbě Čechů a Slováků za národního obrození* (Prague, 1959); and his "Príspevok k otázke bratrských vzťahov Čechov a Slovákov v období národného obrodenia," *Historické štúdie*, III (1957), 7–72; and his "Příspěvek k vzájemným vztahům Čechů a Slováků v první etapě revoluce 1848," *HČ*, XI (1963), 366–88; and his "Otázky obrozeneckých vztahů Čechů a Slováků v dosavadní historiografii," *HČ*, VI (1958), 269–90.

guage and effective Magyarization, ceased to share in it. Finally, the Slovaks did not experience the socioeconomic effects of the heavy industrialization that affected the Czech lands. They remained almost a classless society, peasants and small tradesmen led by their clergy and a tiny intelligentsia. Perhaps the most that can be said is that a feeling of "Czechoslovakism" was growing slowly in Czech and Slovak educated circles before World War I. But it had clearly not matured to the point where it could successfully meet the test set for the two peoples by their unification in 1918.[39]

IV

In a peculiarly nationalistic period and area, the nationalism of interwar Czechoslovakia was not outstanding. Certainly it manifested the same shortsighted "economic nationalism" as did its Danubian neighbors and zealously maintained diplomatic and military alliances against revisionism in East Central Europe. But the generous boundaries granted Czechoslovakia at Paris and the

[39] This is essentially the view of the Slovak historian, Daniel Rapant, in his survey of the problem, "Československé dějiny: Problémy a methody," *Pekařův Sborník,* II (1930), 531–63. Closer relationships are stressed by: Albert Pražák, *Československý národ* (Bratislava, 1925); also in his *Češi a slováci: Literárnědějepisné poznámky k československému poměru* (Prague, 1929); Milan Hodža, *Československý rozkol: Príspevky k dejinám slovenčiny* (Turč. Sv. Martin, 1920); Kamil Krofta, *Češi a Slováci před svým státním sjednocením* (Prague, 1932), reprinted as "Tchèques et Slovaques jusqu'à leur union politique," *Le Monde Slave,* X (1933), 321–47; and V. Chaloupecký, "Československé dějiny," *ČČH,* XXVIII (1922), 1–30. Th. J. G. Locker, *Die nationale Differenzierung und Integrierung der Slovaken und Tschechen in ihrem geschichtlichen Verlauf bis 1848* (Haarlem, 1931), gives the pros and cons, inclines toward separateness. Czech and Slovak Marxist historians accept the view that relations between their peoples were very close at every stage of history, and have set themselves the task of deliberately strengthening such ties through their writings and teaching. See especially these two collections of studies: Ľ. Holotík (ed.), *O vzájomnych vzťahov Čechov a Slovákov* (Bratislava, 1956); and František Janek (ed.), *Upevňovanie vzťahov Čechov a Slovákov pri vyučovaní dejepisu* (Bratislava, 1961). Also: Zd. Urban, "K otázkám československých vztahů od nástupu imperialismu do vzniku Československé republiky," *Dějepis ve škole,* III (1956), 386–94; J. Tkadlečková, "Slovakofilské hnutie v českých krajinách koncom 19. storočia," *HČ,* IV (1956), 469–86; J. Jablonický, "Príspevok k československým vzťahom od konca 19. storočia do roku 1914," *Historické štúdie,* IV (1958), 5–54; Jaroslav Svoboda, "K česko-slovenským kulturním vztahům před první světovou válkou," *Slezský sborník,* LX (1962), 29–46; Vladimír Kulíšek, "Úloha čechoslovakismu ve vztazích Čechů a Slováků (1918 až 1938)," *HČ,* XII (1964), 50–74; Jiří Horák, "Kulturní vztahy česko-slovenské," *Věstník Československé akademie věd,* LXIV (1955), 264–81; and Jan Novotný, *Češi a Slováci za národního obrození a do vzniku československého státu* (Prague, 1968).

wealth of economic resources inherited from the Habsburg monarchy removed any incentive for revisionism and irredentism on
its own part. The Czechoslovak national problem was chiefly a domestic one, that of large national minorities.[40] The borders of the
new state had not been drawn simply on the basis of national self-
determination, but in consideration of historic and "natural" frontiers and of economic and strategic principles as well. As a result,
Czechoslovakia was almost a multinational microcosm of the Habsburg Empire, encompassing, roughly, seven million Czechs, two
million Slovaks, over three million Germans, three-quarter of a
million Magyars, a half-million Ruthenes, and eighty thousand
Poles. Of these, the Germans, Magyars, and Poles had not wished
to become part of the new state, and the Slovaks and Ruthenes had
joined in the expectation of gaining autonomy. The new regime's
approach to this difficult situation was unwise. Czechoslovakia did
not become "a sort of Switzerland," as Eduard Beneš, Masaryk's
colleague, had predicted in Paris in 1919. Buoyed by the psychology
of the victor and distrustful of the loyalty of the Germans and Magyars and of the maturity of the Slovaks and Ruthenes, the Czechs
rejected the idea of a federation of the various nationalities. Instead, they proclaimed a unitary, centralized "Czechoslovak national state," the domain of a "Czechoslovak nation," in which
Czechoslovak would be the official language. In such a state, a
Czechoslovak majority would govern, other national groups would
be "minorities," and Czech influence would predominate.

In comparison with their plight in the other countries of East
Central Europe, the national minorities suffered much less in Czech-

[40] The following sources are a thin cross section through the voluminous literature
on the minorities problem in interwar Czechoslovakia: E. Sobota, *Das tschechoslowak-
ische Nationalitätenrecht* (Prague, 1931); *National Policy in Czechoslovakia*
(Prague, 1938), a collection of parliamentary speeches by various ministers; Vladimír
Slaminka, *Národnostní vývoj Československé republiky* (Prague, 1938); K. Krofta,
The Germans in the Czechoslovak Republic (Prague, 1937); K. Krofta, "Ruthenes,
Czechs, and Slovaks," *SEER*, XIII, Nos. 38–39 (1935), 363–71, 611–26; Konrad
Henlein, "The German Minority in Czechoslovakia," *International Affairs*, XV (1936),
561–72; C. A. Macartney, *Hungary and Her Successors: The Treaty of Trianon and
Its Consequences, 1919–1937* (London and New York: Oxford University Press,
1937); Rudolf Wierer, "Die nationale Frage in der Tschechoslowakei seit 1918," *Der
Donauraum*, VII, Nos. 2–3 (1962), 88–99; K. Gajan, "Nationalismus a české a ně-
mecké strany v Československu v meziválečném období," *Příspěvky k dějinám KSČ*,
VII (1967), 190–200; and J. W. Brügel, *Tschechen und Deutsche, 1918–1938* (Munich, 1967).

oslovakia, a genuine parliamentary democracy permeated with the liberal-humanitarian philosophy of President Masaryk. As "Czechoslovak citizens" they were guaranteed full political, religious, and economic equality with the dominant Czechs and Slovaks, and the regime observed the cultural provisions of the international minorities treaties more scrupulously than any other government in that part of the world. The regime was not flawless in its realization of these principles and policies, however, and serious and legitimate grievances did exist. There is no doubt that discrimination against the Germans and Magyars was practiced in the execution of the land reform and in the awarding of government jobs and contracts. The Ruthenes possessed no linguistic, cultural, or historic ties with either Czechs or Slovaks. Sub-Carpathian Ruthenia had been added to the Czechoslovak state at Paris primarily for its strategic value as a territorial link with Romania, another member of the future Little Entente. Certain Ruthene emigrant spokesmen in the United States had made plans with Masaryk in 1918, whereby their nationally undecided kinsmen at home were to become an autonomous part of the new Czechoslovakia. (The native Ruthenes belatedly agreed to this in 1919.) But the Czech government made no serious attempt to grant autonomy to this hopelessly backward and rural area, exercising a benign "colonial" administration there instead. American Slovaks had made a similar agreement with Masaryk (the "Pittsburgh Agreement" of 1918), in which the native Slovaks were promised their own administrative system, diet, courts, and the official use of the Slovak language in Slovakia. Again the central government, regarding the "Agreement" simply as a desideratum perhaps to be accomplished gradually, made few concessions to Slovak autonomy. To great Slovak resentment, a Czech "ruling complex" was set up to administer their "backward" province until they could be trained to do so themselves. Slovak nationalism, newly unchained and hypersensitive (and thus sharply out of phase with Czech nationalism, now mature and complacent in its triumph), was sharply provoked by the frequently tactless, condescending tutelage of the free-thinking, anticlerical, "Hussite" Czechs, no matter how much it was needed or how well it was intended. The Czech regime, on its part, expected gratitude from the Slovaks and underrated their resentment.

These complaints, aggravated by economic hardship resulting

from the reshaping of old frontiers and trade relationships and the great depression, produced mounting restlessness among the various nationalities in the interwar period. Germans and Magyars, steadfastly refusing to accept minority status in lands where they had previously had a ruling position, denied their allegiance to Czechoslovakia and agitated for union with their contiguous motherlands. Among the Ruthenes a Ukrainian nationalism began to develop. In Slovakia, autonomist sentiment, especially strong among the Catholic clergy, the rural bourgeoisie, and the peasantry, centered around the Slovak People's Party of Father Andrej Hlinka.[41] Together, these forces not only made impossible the desired growth of a Czechoslovak cultural identity but even of a Czechoslovak state patriotism. Yet, despite this grave situation, it is doubtful that the state would have been dismembered in 1938–39 without the interference from without of Germany and Hungary.[42] Both were determined not only to reincorporate their separated nationals but to destroy completely the "synthetic" Czechoslovak state. By systematically encouraging the grievances and supporting—even forcing and escalating—the demands of Hlinka's Populists (for territorial autonomy) and Henlein's Sudeten German Party (for territorial and "personal" autonomy), the Magyar irredentists and German Nazis succeeded. As the result of the Munich Agreement (September, 1938), and the subsequent Žilina Agreement and the First Vienna Award, the Second Czechoslovak Republic lingered on for a few months as a diminished, federalized state before it was forcibly dissolved into an independent Slovak Republic and the Protectorate of Bohemia-Moravia, the one a puppet, the other an exploited subject of the Third Reich.

[41] The Marxist explanation for the growth of the Slovak autonomist movement (which interprets it as an attempt by the Slovak petty bourgeoisie and feudal landlords to achieve an economic hegemony in the region) is given by Juraj Kramer, *Slovenské autonomistické hnutie v rokoch 1918–1929* (Bratislava, 1962), summarized in his "Die slowakische autonomistische Bewegung in den Jahren 1918–1929," *Historica*, VII (1963), 115–43.

[42] Material on the well-known Hitler-Henlein relationship is abundantly available. On external interference in Slovakia, see Juraj Kramer, "Ausländische Einflüsse auf die Entwicklung der slowakischen autonomistischen Bewegung," *Historica*, III (1961), 159–93; and his *Irredenta a separatizmus v slovenskej politike* (Bratislava, 1957); J. Danáš, *L'udácky separatizmus a hitlerovské Nemecko* (Bratislava, 1963); and the numerous thorough studies by Jörg K. Hoensch, especially *Die Slowakei und Hitler's Ostpolitik: Hlinka's Slowakische Volkspartei zwischen Autonomie und Separation, 1938–1939* (Cologne & Graz, 1965) and *Der ungarische Revisionismus und die Zerschlagung der Tschechoslowakei* (Tübingen, 1967).

V

For the Czechs the second World War was in many ways like the first, with Czech diplomats and soldiers fighting abroad and a coerced domestic population patiently waiting for liberation. But during the incorporation of the pseudoautonomous Protectorate into the Reich, the Czech nation was faced with a greater challenge to its existence than it had ever been offered by its Teutonic foe— with the threat of combined cultural and physical destruction, based on a vicious theory of racial inferiority and backed by modern scientific means of mass indoctrination and extermination.[43] For the Czechs were not only to be subjected to the routine economic exploitation and police brutality common to the German-conquered areas; as early as 1940, the Nazis had evolved a plan to settle permanently the Czech-German conflict. The Czech nation was to be completely destroyed through assimilation, deportation, and extermination, and Bohemia-Moravia was to be completely repopulated with Germans. According to Nazi theory, the Czechs were "partially Germanic," strongly permeated with German elements. The half of the population considered closest to the Germans racially (the better educated classes) was to be Germanized and assimilated, chiefly by means of the "Kapaunen System," the gradual redirection of its interests exclusively toward economic endeavor. The half that could not be "racially absorbed" (the diehard intelligentsia and the "Mongoloid" element) was to be deported and exterminated.

The exigencies of the war, particularly their need for the industrial output of the Protectorate, prevented the Nazis from carrying out their diabolical design. The preliminary steps were taken, how-

[43] For Nazi plans and actions during the Protectorate and Czech reactions, see: Gerhard Jacoby, *Racial State: The German Nationalities Policy in the Protectorate of Bohemia-Moravia* (New York, 1944); Radomír Luža, *The Transfer of the Sudeten Germans: A Study of Czech-German Relations, 1933–1962* (New York, 1964), with an excellent bibliography; Ihor Kamenetsky, *Secret Nazi Plans for Eastern Europe: A Study of Lebensraum Policies* (New York: Bookman Press, 1961); Václav Král, "The Policy of Germanization Enforced in Bohemia and Moravia by the Fascist Invaders during the Second World War," *Historica*, II (1960), 273–303; Václav Jaroš (ed.), *Šest let okupace* (Prague, 1946), a collaborative work on all aspects of the occupation; and two documentary collections by Václav Král—*Lesson from History: Documents Concerning Nazi Policies for Germanization and Extermination in Czechoslovakia* (Prague, 1961), and *Die Deutschen in der Tschechoslowakei, 1933–1947* (Prague, 1964).

ever. The German language was given parity with Czech in public life and absolute precedence in official channels. All Czech universities and higher schools were closed and the secondary and lower ones drastically curtailed and refashioned. Czech applicants for entrance into German universities were to undergo a "racial" examination and, if accepted, were to study only scientific-technical fields, not philosophy, history, or law. Czech cultural life was diminished and stringently censored. (For example, Smetana's opera, Libuše, could not be performed because it contained the prophecy that the Czech nation would never perish.) A systematic campaign of destruction was waged against the memories of all exponents of Czech national independence—their monuments, publications, and ideas.[44] "Racial" examinations of Czech school children were begun covertly in 1942. The Czech intellectual elite and middle class were singled out by the Nazi program of terror and supplied a disproportionate number of some 200,000 persons who passed through concentration camps and the 250,000 reported to have died during the occupation.

Czech resistance was crippled but not destroyed. There were few outright collaborators. However, except for spontaneous public demonstrations in 1939, the assassination of the Protector, S. S. General Reinhard Heydrich, in May, 1942, and the final Prague uprising in May, 1945, the Czech resistance movement—perhaps characteristically—was not given to spectacular acts of violence. Rather, it consisted of a steady (and valuable) program of intelligence collection, work delays and sabotage, and strikes.[45] The assassination of Heydrich, itself, was instigated by the London government over the objections of the native underground. After replacing the unsuccessful von Neurath as Protector, Heydrich—employing terror, "belly bribery," and governmental concessions—began rapidly to gain the cooperation and obedience of the Czech populace, espe-

[44] The Nazi attacks on the arch-Czech nationalist, Palacký, are detailed by Jaroslav Werstadt, "František Palacký a náš osvobozenský boj," *ČČH*, XLVII (1946), 75–105.

[45] This view seems tenable despite the many flattering publications on the Czech wartime resistance that have appeared in Czechoslovakia during the last two decades. It is true, of course, that controls were very tight in the Protectorate and that Bohemia and Moravia were ill-suited to partisan warfare. The Heydrich operation is described in Alan Burgess, *Seven Men at Daybreak* (London: Evans Bros., 1960). See also H. G. Skilling, "The Czechoslovak Struggle for National Liberation in W.W.II," *SEER*, XXXIX, No. 92 (Dec., 1960), 174–97.

cially the workers. The London government, suffering a serious loss of prestige in the eyes of the allied governments because of this domestic docility, decided upon the murder as a means of rupturing this growing *rapprochement* and forestalling the apparent possibility of the Germans attempting to recruit Czech divisions to fight at their side. The Czech underground opposed the act in the fear that reprisals would literally decimate the Czech nation. The actual retribution, although it included the obliteration of the villages of Lidice and Ležáky, fell short of this. However, added to the many other brutal experiences that they had suffered under the *Herrenvolk* of the Protectorate, it helped to provoke the Czechs at the war's end into their most violent nationalistic expression since the Hussite Revolt: a demand for the mass expulsion of the German population from liberated Czechoslovakia. The Czech government abroad had been considering this since 1940, and by early 1947 over three million Germans had been transferred, under compulsion and not without significant harshness, especially at local levels.[46] The vacated border areas were rapidly resettled with Czechs and Slovaks. The expulsion did not result merely from a popular demand for retribution or from governmental expediency. It was the consensus of informed Czech opinion that the twenty-year attempt to integrate the German minority into the multinational Czechoslovak state had been a failure, and that based on the record of the Sudeten Germans since 1918, coexistence with them in a common state was politically and psychologically impossible. The Czechs, too, had thus decided to solve the Czech-German conflict "once and for all."

Probably only a small minority of the Slovaks had been outright separatists in 1939. The state they received with Hitler's assistance, the Clerico-Fascist Slovak Republic ruled by Monsignor Tiso, was a petty replica of Nazi Germany in its domestic regimentation, police brutality, and rabid ideology ("Slovak National Socialism"). Its

---

[46] The transfer of Germans and Hungarians from Czechoslovakia is described in Joseph B. Schechtman, *Postwar Population Transfers in Europe, 1945–1955* (Philadelphia: University of Pennsylvania Press, 1962), pp. 43–148. A Czech view is given by Luža, a German one by Theodor Schieder (ed.), *The Expulsion of the German Population from Czechoslovakia: A Selection and Translation from "Dokumentation der Vertreibung der Deutschen aus Ost-Mitteleuropa,"* Vol. IV, Pts. 1–2 (Bonn, 1960). See also Francis S. Wagner, "Hungarians in Czechoslovakia, 1945–1949," in *Hungarians in Czechoslovakia* (New York, 1959), 11–37.

foreign policy, armed forces, and economy were closely integrated with those of the Reich. Nevertheless, it enjoyed considerable domestic support during its first years. The war brought a certain prosperity, and there were many new administrative and commercial careers open to members of the young, self-conscious Slovak intelligentsia. Even as a German vassal the Slovak Republic managed to preserve a precarious national identity. (Indeed, as part of his defense during his trial for treason in 1947, Tiso asserted that had the Slovaks not declared their independence in 1939, they would have been completely partitioned between Germany and Hungary.) Possessing the full trappings of an independent state, it served as a symbol for the Slovak masses of their ability to run their own affairs. Only when threatened with direct German control and the probability of sharing in a German defeat did popular enthusiasm wane. To forestall an imminent Nazi occupation of Slovakia in the face of the advancing Red Army, the Slovak National Council, a broad national front of Communists and right-wing opponents of Tiso established in 1943, together with partisan and regular army elements, organized the Slovak national uprising in late August, 1944. Though crushed in two months, the uprising was of considerable significance for future Czech-Slovak relations. It was declared in the name of the entire Slovak nation, which thereby proclaimed, it was said, its wish for a return to brotherly coexistence with the Czech nation, on condition of absolute equality, in a renewed Czechoslovak state. It is difficult to determine whether the uprising and its declaration were really "a spontaneous expression of the will of the Slovak nation" or simply a coldly realistic calculation on the part of its leaders. The former interpretation was officially accepted by the London government.[47]

[47] Since the post-Stalin "thaw," Czech and Slovak Marxists also tend to accept this view, stressing the national and anti-Fascist (rather than the class) character of the uprising and attempting to tie it to the coup of February, 1948. See M. Hübl, "Slovenské národní povstání—začátek národní a demokratické revoluce," *HČ*, XII (1964), 519–34; the extensive bibliography on the subject by Růžena Machánková, *Geschichte der Slowakischen Nationalaufstandes, 1944* (Bratislava, 1961); the documentary collection, Yveta Šuchová, *Slovenské národné povstanie v dokumentoch* (Bratislava and Prague, 1964); the encyclopedic dictionary, M. Kropilák and J. Jablonický (eds.), *Malý slovník Slovenského národného povstania* (Bratislava, 1964); the collection of articles, *Slovenské národné povstanie roku 1944: Sborník príspevkov z národnooslobodzovacieho boja, 1938–1945* (Bratislava, 1965); and the supplementary bibliography, "Bibliografia publikácií a článkov k 20. výročiu SNP," *HČ*, XIII (1965), 309–28.

One other development during the war is of significance in a consideration of Czechoslovak nationalism, the expressed willingness of the exile government to incorporate the postwar state into an East Central European federation. Together with the Polish government in exile, Czech representatives actually made preliminary steps toward a Czechoslovak-Polish Confederation, itself ultimately to be only the nucleus of a larger East Central European regional federation.[48] When Soviet displeasure halted these negotiations, President Beneš turned instead to a Soviet alliance as the basis for Czechoslovakia's security in the postwar world. Czechoslovakia was to become "a bridge between East and West." Such a political, economic, and cultural reorientation, based upon the lesson of Munich and in harmony with a resurgent popular Czechoslovak Slavophilism and Russophilism, prepared the ground for the initial gains of the Communists in Czechoslovakia immediately following the war.

VI

Since 1948, "national communism" has manifested itself much less in the Czechoslovak Socialist Republic than in most of the other satellites. The country has acquired the title of "the cautious satellite," "the model satellite," and "the loyal satellite" from western Sovietologists. The regime has failed to evolve a "Titoist" figure, and until its recent initiation of the "new model" economic system (emphasizing decentralization of planning and management and the use of the profit motive as an incentive), it was unimaginatively doctrinaire and Stalinist. With the exception of the workers' uprising in Plzeň (Pilsen) in 1953 and occasional manifestations of students and intellectuals since then, the populace has been outwardly docile. Nevertheless good, pragmatic reasons exist for this situation, of which the "Czech national character"—the oft-alleged "Schweikism" with its preference for passive resistance to spectacular or suicidal actions—is one of the least important. More feasible ex-

---

See also the critical review article by Jörg K. Hoensch, "Der slowakische Nationalaufstand in der Geschichtschreibung der ČSSR," *Osteuropa*, XV (1965), 509–15.

[48] See Edward Táborský, "A Polish-Czechoslovak Confederation," *JCEA*, IX, No. 4 (Jan., 1950), 379–95; and P. S. Wandycz, *Czechoslovak-Polish Confederation and the Great Powers, 1940–43* ("Indiana University Graduate School Slavic and East European Series," III [Bloomington, Ind.: Indiana University Press, 1956]).

planations include a comparatively high standard of living; the evolutionary and nonviolent traditions deeply ingrained since the First Republic; disillusionment with the West for its behavior at Munich in 1938, and its failure to liberate Prague in 1945, to forestall the Czechoslovak coup in 1948, and to assist Hungary in 1956; the lack of a historical Russophobia among the Czechs and Slovaks; and the country's need for economic ties with the Soviet Union and Soviet support against a possibly resurgent Germany.[49] It is quite clear that integration into the "Socialist Commonwealth of Nations" has not really effaced nationalism from Czechoslovakia. As we have seen, Czech and Slovak Marxist historians have not even denationalized their nations' past. Although they regard nationalism (i.e., political nationalism, not national cultural differences) as a passing phenomenon in the development of human society and Czech and Slovak history as part of a broad European development, they have reinterpreted and utilized—but have not rejected—the great historical periods and traditions of their nations, and have maintained pride in their peoples' "progressive" achievements of the past.[50] Certainly old national antagonisms remain, notably those involving Czech relations with the Slovaks and Germans.

Postwar Czechoslovak regimes have abandoned the fiction of a single Czechoslovak nation and language. The officially accepted principle is the one proclaimed in the Slovak national uprising (and earlier enunciated by the Slovak autonomists), that the Czechs and Slovaks are two equal nations, closely bound by language and culture and representing a single "Czechoslovak unity." This principle has not found significant political expression in the postwar Czechoslovak state, however.[51] During the war, the Communists had begun

[49] See Ivo. D. Ducháček, in S. D. Kertesz (ed.), *East Central Europe and the World: Developments in the Post-Stalin Era* (Notre Dame, Ind.: Notre Dame University Press, 1962), pp. 112–19. An excellent historical explanation for current Czech and Slovak behavior is given by William E. Griffith, "Myth and Reality in Czechoslovak History," *East Europe*, XI, No. 3 (Mar., 1962), 3–11, 34–36, 40–41.

[50] Czech Marxists, in particular, consider themselves officially as "the inheritors of the great traditions of the Czech nation" and the spiritual descendants of the Hussites. See also the collection of articles entitled *Proti kosmopolitismu ve výkladu našich národních dějin* (Prague, 1953), which combats the assertions of "bourgeois historians" that Czechoslovak national and cultural evolution has lagged behind or has been heavily tutored by that of other nations.

[51] See Pavel Korbel, "Prague and the Slovaks," *East Europe*, XII, No. 3 (March, 1963), 6–12.

to encourage and exploit Slovak visions of autonomy and some had even thought in terms of a Slovak republic within the Soviet Union. The Košice Program of April, 1945, the first political blueprint of the liberated country and labeled "the Magna Charta of the Slovaks," did indeed recognize that "the Slovaks shall be masters in their Slovak land in the same way as the Czechs in their native Czech country." However, since the disappointing Communist showing in the 1946 elections in Slovakia, the Communist leadership has steadily moved away from a federal solution and toward centralism. The Czechoslovak constitutions of 1948 and 1960 provide for a unified state, with the Slovaks granted only the trappings of regional autonomy and legislative and executive organs subject to the ultimate control of Prague. As a result, Slovak nationalism has been increasingly expressed through the Slovak Communist Party, a subordinate but very obstreperous wing of the Czechoslovak Communist Party.[52] As early as 1952, during the Stalin-dictated purges in the country, Vladimír Clementis, the former foreign minister, and a group of Slovak intellectuals were executed for various "crimes," including "Titoism and bourgeois and secessionist nationalism." Since Clementis, no single leader has emerged to personify Slovak national aspirations. In early 1963, as part of a marked upsurge of Slovak nationalism, Slovak writers and journalists demanded full rehabilitation of these persons. Sharp anti-Czech and anticentralist criticism was coupled with calls for more rapid de-Stalinization by the regime. The result has been a progressive rehabilitation of the Clementis group and renewed promises by Prague of expanded self-government for the Slovaks.[53] Another notable expression of Slovak nationalism appeared recently in connection with the celebration of the twentieth anniversary of the Slovak uprising. Slovak newspapers, revising the accepted interpretation, derogated and criticized the Soviet share in it. It is clear that the Slovaks' national consciousness has not ebbed, and perhaps has even been swelled by their accumulation of industrial and administrative skills under the new regime.

Among the tens of thousands of Czech and Slovak exiles and

[52] See Edward Táborský, "Nationalism vs. Proletarian Internationalism in the Communist Party of Czechoslovakia," *JCEA*, XIX (Jan., 1960), 402–40.

[53] Slovak activities in 1963 are described in Vojtěch N. Duben, *Ledy se hnuly: Československý kulturní a politiký kvas, 1963* (New York, 1964), especially pp. 63–72.

emigrants abroad, national differences are indulged more openly, if less effectually. To a significant extent, the two groups live apart culturally and institutionally. The "Czechoslovak Question" is still seriously debated in their publications (e.g., the newspapers *Naše hlasy* of Toronto, and *Americké listy* of New York), with the full range of possible solutions—unitary, federalist, and separatist— being advocated. The majority of Czech exiles abroad still seem to be loyal to the old Palacký-Masaryk ideals. The most audible Slovak voices are virulently separatist. With each passing year, as the exiles become increasingly assimilated by their new environments and as their knowledge of conditions "at home" and their ability to do anything about them diminishes, their views become increasingly academic and their influence upon the drift of Czech and Slovak nationalism lessens.

Since the cession of Sub-Carpathian Ruthenia to the Soviet Union in 1945, the expulsion of the Sudeten Germans, and a partial exchange of populations with Hungary in 1946–47, Czechoslovakia has sharply reduced her minority populations.[54] Of a total population of 14,333,000, Magyars number about 563,000; Germans 114,-000; Poles 72,000; and Ruthenes 58,000. (Czechs number 9,284,000, and Slovaks 4,196,000.) With the exception of the Germans, the cultural rights of these groups are constitutionally guaranteed. It is doubtful that the inflammatory national minorities issue is completely dead, however. The full exchange of Magyar and Slovak populations was frustrated by the Hungarian government, possibly with an eye to maintaining grounds for future revisionist and irredentist action. Though both countries have had socialist regimes since 1948, nationalist frictions have not entirely disappeared. For example, although the Prague central government has required that in the mixed area of southern Slovakia public announcements and forms and firm names appear both in Slovak and Hungarian, the practice has been increasingly ignored in the last few years. The growth of Sudeten *revanchism*, anxiously followed and genuinely feared in Czechoslovakia, is a greater problem. (To some extent, of course, the Czechoslovak regime has deliberately fostered this fear among its population to facilitate domestic control.) The Sudeten movement, well organized among the rank and file and effec-

[54] See Miloš Hájek and Olga Staňková, *Národnostní otázka v lidovědemokratickém Československu* (Prague, 1956).

tively led by expelled politicians and scholars, has found considerable official support in the Federal Republic of Germany.[55] The Bonn government has stated its wish to "normalize relations" with East Central Europe and has repeatedly stressed that it has no territorial claims against Czechoslovakia and that it repudiates the Munich Agreement of 1938. However, it has also declared that "the German democracy [the Federal Republic] cannot be indifferent to the fate of those ethnic Germans who became tragically entangled in the events caused by the Hitler regime," cannot ignore "conditions detrimental to the vital interests of the German people" such as the expulsion of the Sudetens "from their hereditary homes" and the "inhuman measures" used in connection with it as well as the "cultural disenfranchisement" of the small German group that has remained.[56] The position of the Czechoslovak government is that

[55] Notable spokesmen have been the recently deceased Wenzel Jaksch (SPD) and Hans Christoph Seebohm (CDU), the latter sometime Federal Minister of Transportation who still publicly affirms the validity of the Munich Agreement and demands the German boundaries of 1939. The problem of Czechoslovak-German relations since World War II is treated in Elizabeth Wiskemann, *Germany's Eastern Neighbors: Problems Relating to the Oder-Neisse Line and the Czech Frontier Regions* (New York: Oxford University Press, 1956); A. Šnejdárek, "Československo-německé styky po r. 1945," *Mezinárodní otázky,* I (1956), 84–109; and *Německá otázka a Československvensko, 1938–1961: Sborník statí* (Bratislava, 1962). The pro-Czech view of contemporary Sudeten activities is given by Boris Čelovský, "The Transferred Sudeten-Germans and Their Political Activity," *JCEA,* XVII (July, 1957), 127–49; and A. Šnejdárek, *Revanšisté proti Československsku* (Prague, 1963). On the extensive "scholarly" activities of the Sudetens, German-nationalist and anti-Czech, see the bibliography edited by J. Kořalka, *Protičeskoslovenský revanšismus v historiografii* (Prague, 1961), and the following Sudeten-authored works: H. Raschhofer, *Die Sudetenfrage* (Munich, 1953); Wilhelm K. Turnwald, *Renascence or Decline of Central Europe? The German-Czech Problem* (Munich, 1954); and Göttinger Arbeitskreis, *Deutschlands Ostproblem: Eine Untersuchung der Beziehungen des deutschen Volkes zu seinen östlichen Nachbarn* (Würzburg, 1957). Somewhat more hopeful for the future are the publications of the "Commission of Historians of the ČSR and DDR," stressing past German-Czech rapport, such as Karl Obermann and Josef Polišenský (eds.), *Aus 500 Jahren deutsch-tschechoslowakischer Geschichte* (Berlin, 1958). Even more so was the announcement in late 1967 of the beginning of cooperative efforts of West German and Czechoslovak historians, through the good offices of UNESCO, to mutually revise their historical textbooks.

[56] *Germany and Eastern Europe: Two Documents of the Third German Bundestag, 1961* (reports by Wenzel Jaksch) (2d. ed.; Bonn, Brussells, N.Y., 1963), p. 55. The variety of current German opinion on the continuing validity of the Munich Agreement is given in Otto Kimminich, "Stellungnahmen zum Münchener Abkommen in der deutschen Presse," *Bohemia: Jahrbuch des Collegium Carolinum,* VII (1966), 357–69.

the Sudeten issue is legally closed. Its analysis of the German problem, balanced between Marxist optimism and Czech national pessimism, was well expressed by Václav Husa, the recently deceased
Czech historian. Husa explained that the danger of German aggression was not a permanent "geopolitical reality" but merely part of
the imperialist phase of the capitalist epoch, with which it will ultimately disappear. He goes on:

Today, when our country is a firm member of the huge socialist camp led
by the Soviet Union, when our own government is fully in the hands of
the working people, when there is no longer the danger of betrayal by
domestic classes, and when at our side stand even the working people of
the German Democratic Republic and the peaceful forces of all the
countries of the world, there can never again be a repetition of Munich
and of March 15, 1939. Nevertheless, one cannot fail to see that the
historical threat of aggression still exists and that it gains strength with
the renewal of West German militarism, supported in every possible way
by American imperialism. . . .[57]

In the light of the increasing disintegration of the bipolar world
in recent years, it is quite possible that old national rivalries will
erupt again, on and within the borders of Czechoslovakia. In the
light of history, their reconciliation would seem to require forces
greater than the primeval protagonists—Czechs, Slovaks, Germans,
and Hungarians—themselves. The problem demands immersion in
a much deeper solvent. In the short run, this might well be the often
recommended regional federation in East Central Europe[58] and ultimately Europe-wide political integration. In the long run, the ultimate solution—denationalization—may come as the by-product of
the inexorable evolution of mass technology. By providing mass
literacy, mobility, communications, and material abundance, and
by requiring an ever wider and ever more closely integrated community for its successful development, modern technology may

[57] Václav Husa, "Šmeralovo hodnocení Palackého výkladu českých dějin," *Zápisky
katedry čsl. dějin a archivního studia*, III (1958), 165. Husa continues by affirming
the continued validity of Palacký's old warnings against the Germans.

[58] This was the topic of a symposium entitled "Czechoslovakia and its Neighbors:
Nationalism *vs.* Federalism," held at the Second Congress of the Czechoslovak
Society of Arts and Sciences in America, in New York in 1964. The scholarly con-
tributions representing the positions of Czechoslovakia, Germany, Austria, Hungary,
Poland, Yugoslavia, and Russia are to date available only in abstracted form.

make the old nationalism—not only in Czechoslovakia but throughout the world—impossible. *

* As this chapter was essentially completed in 1965, certain of its conclusions (especially those expressed in Section VI) require revision in the light of more recent
events in Czechoslovakia. Prominent among the latter are the broad program of domestic liberalization effected in 1968 under the popular First Secretary of the Czechoslovak Communist Party, the Slovak Alexander Dubček; the resultant invasion by
Warsaw Pact armies in August, 1968; and the federalization of the country in early
1969. The major effect of these developments upon the character of nationalism in
Czechoslovakia has been the clear manifestation of a new and continuing sense of
Czech-Slovak solidarity among the wide masses of both peoples.

STEPHEN G. XYDIS

Modern Greek Nationalism

Greek nationalism is inextricably bound to the emergence of Greece as a nation-state in the early nineteenth century, but its origins go farther back in history. It is related to the rise of nationalism and of nation-states in seventeenth-century western Europe and was affected by the interaction of European and Ottoman international politics. To a great extent, although it had roots in the protonationalism that appeared in the Byzantine biotope between 1204–1453, it was reflexive and mimetic in character and a symptom of the expansion of a new ideology that spread from western Europe in all direction until, today, it has encompassed the entire globe.

In western Europe the main features of this process were the increasing tribute paid to Caesar at the expense of God, the decline of the spiritual and moral authority of the church and of other traditional values, and the corresponding rise in secularism or materialism. Religious dogmas were questioned; "superstition" was attacked; the physical sciences were stressed more and more. A new sensuality revealed itself at first in neopagan and classicizing forms. Patriotism modeled on the fervent sentiments of Plutarch's heroes[1] tended to replace religious ardor just as the sovereign state came to replace the church as the paramount authority. Politicians, literati, scientists, and merchants philosophized about the need for rational government, for enlightened instead of arbitrary despotism, echoing

[1] E. G. Berry, *Emerson's Plutarch* (Cambridge, Mass.: Harvard University Press, 1961), p. 2, points out how radicals and revolutionaries referred to Phocion and Timoleon as model heroes.

Platonic views about the philosopher king. Appeals were issued, demanding the overthrow of absolutist regimes and their replacement by constitutional monarchies, republics, or democracies based on contractual agreements between ruler and ruled and on natural rights. The search for similar manifestations in the nascent world of modern Greece will help to reveal the complex origins and the substance of Greek nationalism in its early phases.[2]

Preindependence Greek Nationalism

Ethnos is the contemporary Greek word for "nation." When the initial *e* is pridefully capitalized, this word stands for the nation par excellence, the Greek nation. At the time around the outbreak of the Greek War of Independence, however, this word, as literary sources indicate, was seldom used. Another word, *genos*, that sounds archaic if not obsolete today, was, instead, most popular at that time. One of the characters in an anonymous dialogue now attributed to Adamantios Koraes, which was printed in 1821 in Vienna in the *Literary Hermes*, the second modern Greek periodical ever to appear, complained about "the abuse of the word 'genos' which is characteristic of all rabble-rousers."[3] In classical Greek usage that word indeed seems more suitable for expressing the concept of "nation" than does *ethnos*. According to the Classical Greek dictionary, it is equivalent to "race," "stock," "kin"; it also means "offspring" or "generally a race of beings, a clan, a house, a family, an age, or a generation." To the above, the modern Greek dictionary adds only the meaning of "origin."

Was this early preference for *genos* symptomatic of the classicizing tendencies of the times that were common in western Europe and were linked to the rise of nationalism, or was it regarded as the Greek equivalent of the Arab-Ottoman *millet* with its religiopoliti-

---

[2] Several of the substantive criteria about the growth of European nationalism are based on C. J. H. Hayes's studies of nationalism, *The Historical Evolution of Nationalism* (Richard Smith: New York, 1931) and *Nationalism: A Religion* (New York: Macmillan, 1962).

[3] A. Koraes, *Three Dialogues* (in Greek), ed. K. Th. Dimaras (Athens, 1962), pp. 45–46. As one of the characters in this dialogue puts it: "All, in truth, mention the 'genos,' all are doing good for the 'genos,' and pour out their precious sweat for it. All . . . are ready to sacrifice themselves for the 'genos' while their deeds testify either to their complete indifference to it or to their readiness to sacrifice the 'genos' if they are given a choice between the two sacrifices."

cal flavor?[4] Or was it, as it etymologically seems to be, a translation of the word "nation"? Further literary research and careful content analysis of many texts of that period might provide an answer to these questions. A spot check of a text of Koraes, whose contributions to Greek nationalism will be discussed, suggests another explanation, that he reserved *genos*, especially when its initial letter was capitalized, for the nation par excellence, the Greeks, whereas he applied the term *ethnos* to nations already having states of their own.[5] Thus it would be normal for the Greeks, once they had set up a state of their own, to use *ethnos* as they do today, while applying *genos* to all Greeks regardless of their nationality or citizenship.[6]

But whatever the reasons may be for the replacement of *genos* by *ethnos* in modern Greek, the great popularity of *genos* at the beginning of the past century, which Koraes ironically noted, clearly reflects the deepening historical consciousness and pride of the Greeks of those times in their *progonoi*, their ancestors, whom they believed to be the ancient Greeks. This belief in a common descent

[4] Iosif Bryennios (*ca.* 1340–1431) used the term "genos" for the Christian nations, both the Eastern Orthodox and the Roman Catholics. The term "ethnos," on the other hand, he reserved for the non-Christian nations, N. B. Tomadakis, *Iosif Bryennios and Crete toward 1400* (in Greek) (Athens: Vayonakis, 1947), p. 72.

[5] See excerpts from Koraes' "Political Counsels," K. Th. Dimaras, *The Political Theme in Koraes* (in Greek) (Athens, 1963).

[6] The five constitutions of the provisional governments during the revolution until King Otho's arrival in Nauplion in 1833 use the word "ethnos" which suggests not only the secular connotation of the concept but also its connection with emergent statehood. Found in ancient Greek, the word "ethnos" means a number of people living together, a company, a body of men; also a nation, a people, a class of men, a caste, a tribe, even a trading association or a guild. Only six additional entries in Liddell and Scott's ancient Greek dictionary are connected with this noun either as adjectives or as other, composite nouns. If, however, a modern Greek dictionary is consulted, for example Dimitrakos' *Lexicon of the Modern Greek Tongue,* one discovers not only the last three above-mentioned meanings but also the fact that the definition given hews very closely to Max Weber's "Types of Social Organization," *Theories of Society,* ed. T. Parsons, E. Shils, D. Naegele, J. R. Pitts (Glencoe, Ill.: The Free Press, 1965) p. 306. "Ethnos," according to the modern Greek definition, is "the totality of people of the same stock having a common history, an approximately similar culture, and consciousness of a common stock." One also discovers fifteen or so additional entries connected with this noun—nouns such as *ethnismos* or *ethnikismos* (nationalism); *ethnegersia* (national uprising), with the related adjective; *ethnikopoiisis* (nationalization); *ethnikotis* (nationality); *ethnomartys* (national martyr); or adjectives such as *ethnoktonos* (ethnocidal or genocidal); *ethnolatris* (nation-reverer); *ethnoprepis* (nation-worthy); *ethnoprovlitos* (nation-projected). These lexical facts clearly indicate that Greek ethnocentrism is a modern, not an ancient phenomenon.

from the Greeks of antiquity was well in harmony with the classicizing style that had its counterpart in neoclassicism and the Greek revival movement in western Europe and the emergent United States.[7] Both "progonolatry" and neoclassicism are well illustrated in a ceremony that took place in Athens in 1813, eight years before the outbreak of the Greek War of Independence. In this ceremony, a teacher holding branches of olive and laurel in his hands renamed the young students, uttering the following words: "From now on your name will no longer be Ioannes [John] or Pavlos [Paul], etc., but 'Pericles,' 'Themistocles,' or 'Xenophon,' etc. For the rest, fear God, help your fatherland, and also love philosophy."[8] By that time the popularity of classical names had become so great that Patriarch Gregory V (the Ottomans hanged him over the gates of the patriarchal church during the Greek revolution even though he had excommunicated the revolution's leaders) felt obliged to issue a circular prohibiting the use of such pagan, gentile, revolutionary names, an action symptomatic of the growing tension between the new secular spirit and the traditional religious values.

Commenting on the same subject of name changing then popular, Ali Paşa, the Lion of Janina, shrewdly observed: "You Greeks have something big in your minds. You no longer christen your children 'Ioannes' [John], 'Petros' [Peter] or 'Constantinos' but 'Leonidas,' 'Themistocles,' 'Aristides.' What are you cooking up now?"[9]

The gradual adoption of the classical and pagan term "Hellene" by which Greeks call themselves today was another symbolic sign of the growing secularism, nationalism, and ancestor worship occurring at the turn of the eighteenth century. In the Byzantine and post-Byzantine era, a Greek called himself *Rhomios* or *Roman* and under the Ottoman administration he was known as *Rum,* a term

---

[7] For the Greek revival in the United States, S. G. Xydis, "Ancient Greece in Emergent America," *Greek Heritage,* II, No. 5 (1965), 84–87. R. M. Gummere, *The American Colonial Mind and the Classical Tradition* (Cambridge, Mass.: Harvard University Press, 1963), pp. 115–18, on Samuel Adams' references to the tyrannicides Harmodius and Aristogeiton and his attitude toward 1776. K. Lehman, *Thomas Jefferson, American Humanist* (New York: Macmillan, 1947), Berry, *Emerson's Plutarch. The Federalist Papers* abound in classical references.

[8] K. Th. Dimaras, *History of Modern Greek Literature* (in Greek), (2d ed.; Ikaros, Athens, n.d.), p. 163 (cited hereafter as *Modern Greek Literature*).

[9] *Ibid.,* p. 164.

that definitely had a strong religious connotation. "Hellene," on the whole, was synonymous with "pagan." Westernized Greeks such as Koraes used the term *Graikos* for themselves, virtually transliterating into Greek the terms *Graeci, Grecs,* or *Greeks,* under which they were known in the West. In the first decades of the nineteenth century, however, Greeks brought up in the neoclassic ideas of the Enlightenment and especially of the French and American revolutions promoted the classical appellation of "Hellene" for their countrymen. This appellation was willingly accepted by the uneducated classes during the Greek War of Independence because, it seems, popular tradition had preserved the legend of a superhuman race called "Hellenes" who had preceded both the Romans and the Greeks in the Balkan peninsula.[10] Since then, the exogenous, western term *Graikos* with its somewhat pejorative connotation in French became obsolete, while the endogenous, Byzantine term *Rhomios* still lingers on in the vernacular, and in its Turkish form of *Rum* survives in Turkey to denote Turkish nationals of the Greek Orthodox faith in contrast to the Greek nationals, the *Yunanlar* or Ionians.

The soil in which Greek nationalism grew was limited neither to the territories occupied by present-day Greece in the Balkans nor even to the Ottoman territories in eastern Europe, but extended into western Europe itself. It consisted of a complex, loose, and polycentric network of various groups, each led by its own elite, yet tied together not only by a common religion but also by a common language that had no alphabetical problems like those that, for example, beset the Albanians. Because the elite members of these groups had better channels of communication with the West and considerable information about it,[11] they became conscious of the values of western nationalism earlier than did other groups in the Ottoman Empire, the Ottoman Turks themselves included.

A linguistic coincidence facilitated the process of cultural diffusion from the West and Greek receptivity to it. Western elites, es-

[10] J. T. Kakridis, "The Ancient Greeks and the Greeks of the War of Independence," *Balkan Studies,* IV (1963), 265–76.

[11] H. and M. Sprout, *The Foundations of National Power* (Princeton, N.J.: Van Nostrand Co., 1963), p. 417, refer to the concept of "social mass" according to the views advanced by J. Q. Stewart and W. Warntz. Social mass depends, according to these views, not only on the work energy available per capita but also "on the amount of information at hand to be communicated from one person to another, or incorporated into the patterns of mechanical or intellectual tools."

pecially since the Renaissance, were well acquainted with the alphabet and language of ancient Greek through their passionate interest in the Greek classics. Romaic, the native tongue of the new Greek elites, was a linear descendent of ancient Greek and of the New Testament's *Koine,* and in the same alphabet. Thus, from an early stage there was something of a shared language that facilitated a dialogue between western neoclassicism and neo-Hellenism. Contemporary Greeks were less likely than other Balkan peoples to regard the West as an altogether alien environment. Western intellectuals, conversely, may have found it easier to communicate with members of the Romaic elites than with those of other Balkan elites. In the printing of books, the advantages of this linguistic coincidence for the modern Greeks were plain. To print books in Romaic was no problem if one had the type to print the *Iliad* of Homer. But to cast type for characters other than Greek or Latin represented an altogether new venture. The earliest book printed entirely in Greek, the grammar of Constantinos Lascaris, appeared in Milan in 1476. The first printed book in modern Greek followed in 1526.[12] On the other hand, it was two centuries later that the first printed book in Turkish appeared, a lag largely due, it should be acknowledged, to Muslim aversion to nonmanuscript scriptures.[13]

This language-sharing with important elements of the western elites facilitated the diffusion of the printed word, and the translation of western books into modern Greek contributed to the linguistic and cultural diffusion among the recipient elites. Romaic, while preserving Byzantine and post-Byzantine values for those who used this tongue, also helped focus, derived as it was ultimately from ancient Greek, on the values of this earlier culture, which happened at the time to be so much appreciated in the West. As a result, if utopian extremes were avoided, which was not always the case as the desires of some modern Greek literati to revert to the use of ancient Greek prove, Romaic could become a medium of modernization and a bearer of western values while fulfilling its

[12] P. Topping, "La Bibliothèque Gennadeion. Son Histoire et ses Collections," *L'hellénisme contemporaine,* IX (March–June, 1955), 134. This was the celebrated *epitome* of the eight parts of discourse.

[13] B. Lewis, *The Emergence of Modern Turkey* (New York: Oxford University Press, 1961), p. 51. The printing press reached Persia in 1812 (Tabriz) and 1823 (Tehran), G. E. Kirk, *A Short History of the Middle East* (New York: F. A. Praeger, 1963), p. 105.

conservative function of being "the enduring and indestructible reservoir of the thoughts, the sentiments, the values, and the aspirations of a people," and of serving as "a powerful anchor which inevitably keeps a people moored, so to speak, to its past and perpetuates its particular genius."[14]

But Romaic, like any other language, tended to establish a discrete communications "circuit," contributing to the cohesion of the people—both elite and masses—that spoke it, as well as contributing to their corresponding sense of separateness from those who did not. Within the Ottoman Empire, the Greek-speaking element or subpopulation constituted a broad, loose network that extended beyond the empire's confines to the Greeks of the diaspora, who had fled to the West with Constantinople's fall[15] or who settled there later as traders.

A more extensive but less homogeneous bond within the Ottoman Empire lay in common religious values, those of Eastern or Greek orthodoxy. Religion united a greater number of people than the Greek-speaking, Greek Orthodox subpopulation, including a considerable number of Slav- and Romanian-speaking subjects of the sultan. However, this more extensive circuit, though looser than that of the language because of greater numbers and less cohesive because of the language differences, was organized and institutionalized as a millet[16] within the Ottoman system of government. At the head of this organization, with its roles and status, was the Patriarchate of Istanbul, an office that to this day is held by Greek-speaking religious officials. Its hierarchy tended to regard itself as the guardian of the Greek Orthodox flock against encroachments by both Ottoman Turks and Latins. Its Academy, an institution dating from the time of Emperor Heraclius (610–641), had been revivified in the sixteenth century to become, by the middle of the seventeenth, a center of secular learning in the tradition of the University of Padua.[17] Several restrictions on the performance of religious duties as well as the imposition of a head tax contributed

---

[14] K. D. Ushinsky (1824–70), as cited in G. S. Counts, *The Challenge of Soviet Education* (New York: McGraw-Hill, 1957), p. 20.

[15] D. J. Geanakoplos, *Greek Scholars in Venice* (Cambridge, Mass.: Harvard University Press, 1962), pp. 280–81.

[16] See above, chap. i, pp. 27, 30, 31, 53.

[17] P. Sherrard, *The Greek East and the Latin West* (New York: Oxford University Press, 1959), pp. 176, 178.

ward maintaining a sense of separateness of the *Ahali al-Kitab*, the people of the Book (Bible), from the Muslims. Moreover, the Eastern Orthodox had close links with their correligionists outside the Ottoman Empire, especially with Russian Christianity. This fact had important political implications. Pressures from below occasionally converged with pressures from outside upon the Ottoman Empire.

One of the Greek-speaking elite clusters grew up around the patriarchate in the capital of the Ottoman Empire. Its members, the Phanariotes, lived in the Phanar district, the northwest corner of Istanbul where the patriarchate was situated, and developed into a sort of aristocracy that felt frustrated by the limitations imposed on it by Ottoman rule. This frustration solidified its cohesion and in-group feeling, generating an increasing hostility toward the outgroups. Many Phanariotes were merchants on a grand scale with relations with the West. They were also the managers of patriarchal affairs and, in addition to their knowledge of western manners, customs, and language, had a close understanding of Ottoman administration. Gradually, as the tide of Ottoman expansion was halted and the sultan was in need of able negotiators, some members of this post-Byzantine elite "infiltrated" the Ottoman government, becoming officials of the imperial administration either in Istanbul (as Grand Dragomans, for instance) or as Hospodars of the Danubian Principalities of Moldavia and Wallachia, where their rule lasted from the beginning of the eighteenth century until the outbreak of the Greek War of Independence. The Phanariotes constituted links between the Ottoman government and the West, while their exploitation of the people of the Danubian Principalities stimulated the emergence of Romanian nationalism.

Traders comprised most of the other Greek-speaking elite clusters that gradually developed at various points in the Ottoman Empire. By the end of the eighteenth century, for example, Salonika-centered trade, which dominated the Balkans and extended to Venice, Germany, Austria, Poland, Hungary, and to commerce with Russia, was largely in Greek hands. Thus, side by side with the Phanariotes, a commercial bourgeoisie was emerging, becoming not only a factor in the growth of Greek nationalism, but, according to one author a catalyst for the growth of nationalism among other

Balkan peoples as well.[18] Its dissatisfaction with the Ottoman economic system tended to strengthen the sense of separateness that stimulated national consciousness and desires to do away with this system. The cohesiveness of this elite group tended to be increased by the arbitrary levies and requisitions imposed by the government or local paşas. Consequently, mutually negative attitudes and stereotypes emerged.

In the archipelago, on some of the Aegean islands, a shipowner elite with experience in fighting the Barbary pirates was growing. Since the Treaty of Küçük Kainarci (1774) its members availed themselves of the privilege of flying the Russian flag and of the permission to sail back and forth through the Turkish Straits for trading purposes. During the reciprocal blockades imposed by Britain and France during the Napoleonic wars, these captains of Ydra, Spetsai, or Psara shrewdly exploited the risks of blockade running in order to enrich themselves. The members of this elite cluster, some of whom spoke Albanian rather than Greek, indicating that a common language was not the only factor in the emergence of Greek national consciousness, also enjoyed special privileges of self-government within the Ottoman Empire.

The same was true of the landowners in the Morea, the Peloponnese. They, too, enjoyed a considerable measure of autonomy including the privilege of communicating with the Porte, not through the Ottoman governor of the Peloponnese but through two or three of their own representatives whom they sent to Istanbul with regular credentials and full powers. The earnings of the Greek Peloponnese landowners were, however, only on half of their Turkish counterparts in the Morea, and after unequal taxation the per capita earnings were reduced to one quarter, naturally producing Greek discontent at the inequity and injustice of fiscal treatment.[19]

Inequity and injustice also fostered crime and outlawry, which in its turn, threatened public order. To deal with this problem of the outlaws, the Klephts, the Ottomans relaxed the Muslim rule that only the faithful had the right to bear arms. Non-Muslims

---

[18] N. G. Svoronos, *Le commerce de Salonique au XVIII° siècle* (Athens, 1954), pp. 193, 198, 354–56.

[19] M. Sakellariou, *The Peloponnese during the Second Turkish Domination, 1715–1821* (in Greek) (Athens, 1939), pp. 224–25.

were allowed arms to protect themselves and to maintain order in the mountainous and remote regions of Greece and the Balkans. The institution of the Armatoles developed, and its members occasionally were recruited from among the outlaws themselves. The over-all result was that throughout the Ottoman Empire during its declining years certain elements with fighting experience developed that could be valuable for an uprising and eventually for fulfilling the police and defense functions of new states. These elements had a folklore of their own with powerful anti-Turkish strains if for no other reason than because the government was in the hands of the Ottomans, and because, for the klephts especially, government was hateful in itself as a symbol of law and order. It was a klepht, Theodoros Kolokotronis (1770–1843), who became the foremost military leader of the Greeks during their war for independence.

Outside the Ottoman territories, Greeks of the diaspora had settled early in Florence, Rome, and Venice. Some, like Cardinal Bessarion (ca. 1423–72), became members of the Roman Catholic elite. Until 1669, when Crete fell to the Ottoman Empire, a Greek elite had flourished there, and the Greeks in the Ionian islands had reached sufficient strength by the middle of the sixteenth century to induce Venice to permit the opening of Greek schools.[20] In the Most Serene Republic itself, San Giorgio dei Greci was this elite's focus. Greek printers brought out Greek books in Venice, and Greek icon painters, both there and in the Ionian islands, painted Byzantine figures in western perspective abandoning the traditional gold-leaf backgrounds. In Spain, an artistic equivalent of Cardinal Bessarion or of the Phanariotes was the Cretan Domenikos Theotokopoulos, El Greco, who was proud enough of his origin to sign his pictures in Greek. Later on, Greek communities thrived in Trieste, Vienna, Budapest, Paris, Marseilles, London, Moscow, and in certain German cities. By the end of the eighteenth century, a respectable part of the Austrian trade was in Greek hands.[21]

Finally, there was the gossamer web of communication, the increasing throng of mobile idea carriers who formed an intelligentsia: preachers, teachers, educators, civilian administrators, literati. These agents were active not only because the European territories of the Ottoman Empire were drawn to the centers of

[20] Sherrard, *The Greek East and the Latin West*, p. 175.
[21] Svoronos, *Le commerce de Salonique . . .* , p. 352.

other elite clusters, to Istanbul, and the courts of the Phanariote Greek princes in Bucureşti or Jassy but also because they roamed beyond the empire's confines. They studied in the West, settled among the flourishing Greek merchant communities abroad, and were attracted by cultural centers such as Padua, Paris, or Leipzig, or by courts such as St. Petersburg. Sometimes they attained high offices in the host country, as did Ioannes Capodistrias in Russia, acquiring experience in the conduct of affairs of state in the European world.

This complex, sprawling, polycentric Greek world about to become a nation and establish a state was, in the Ottoman Empire at least, held in strict subordination under the millet system, which also offered certain advantages for those to whom it applied. The millet system embodied not only duties but certain rights, especially in family relations, religion, and education. Of these, the emerging Greek leaders, aided by the discreteness of the Greek Orthodox church, took advantage. The authoritarianism of the Ottoman ruling system tended to enhance distinctions and to create much mutual hostility within the society as a whole, including aggression against scapegoats, with the Phanariotes often cast in that role.

International political factors contributed to the maintenance and aggravation of fission evident among the peoples of the Ottoman Empire during the period of its decline. In roughly chronological sequence the most important of these exogenous political factors that had an impact within the Ottoman realm were the policies of the Roman Catholic church followed by those of Russia and France.

In spite of the failure to bring an end to the schism of 1054 between Rome and Constantinople and to mobilize effectively an anti-Ottoman crusade, the Vatican sought to proselytize the Greek Orthodox element of the Ottoman Empire. In proselytizing it undermined the institution of the patriarchate and drove it closer to either the Ottoman administration or to Protestant movements, but Rome's propaganda, nevertheless, poured oil on the flames of hate between Christian and Infidel.[22] Russia, on the other hand, a puis-

---

[22] A poem in Greek concerning the gathering of Christian children for the janissary corps produced in the mid-sixteenth century had been published by G. Zoras, "Alcune nuove testimonianze sull' istituzione del 'pedomazoma,'" *Balkan Studies,* IV (1963), 102–8.

sant member of the Eastern Orthodox world with its own patriarchate in Moscow from 1588 to 1700, often counterbalanced the policies of Rome. Peter the Great and Catherine the Great, in contrast to Ivan IV, whose policies had been directed westward and who had declined to take part in any anti-Ottoman crusade, embarked on expansionist policies at the expense of the Ottoman Empire and sought allies among the empire's subject peoples.

Last came the French influence, first with the philosophes and the Enlightenment, then with the Revolution and the *Directoire* with its Napoleonic aftermath. During the *Directoire*, for instance, the French made a serious effort to create a pro-French party not only among the Phanariotes, but also among the Greek merchants of Macedonia, an area that had acquired some importance during the struggle of France against Britain and Russia.[23] All these exogenous factors—Rome, Russia, and France—served to agitate the Greek members of the *rum-i-millet* in various ways, arousing tension between them and their rulers and thus strengthening solidarity and protonational cohesion.

A selective survey of the records that certain of the idea-carriers left to posterity indicates the extent to which this is true. From these records scholars obtain insights about the way in which that particular sociopolitical attitude that goes under the name of nationalism developed among the members of this millet. Not the least important of these foreign influences was the impetus they gave to the nascent historicism of the educated Greeks during the Ottoman era.

With the Greeks, belief in descent from the ancient Greeks was not a nineteenth-century phenomenon as the Athenian school ceremony of 1813 might suggest. In late Byzantine times, during the proto-Renaissance that was cut short by the Ottoman conquest of Constantinople and the Peloponnese, neoclassic elements similar to those that contributed to the Renaissance in Italy and, thence, to secularism and materialism, became visible in strong contrast to the imperial, universalist, Roman, Christian *Weltanschauung of Byzantium* at its zenith in the tenth and eleventh centuries.[24] George Gemistus (*ca.* 1355–1452), whose adoption of the classicizing sur-

[23] Svoronos, *Le commerce de Salonique* . . . , p. 361.
[24] R. Jenkins, *Byzantium and Byzantinism* (Cincinnati, Ohio: University of Cincinnati, 1963), pp. 6 ff.

name "Pletho" is but one indication of his neopagan inclinations, insisted in a memorial addressed to Emperor Manuel II Palaeologus (1350–1425) that "we, over whom you rule, are Hellenes by race, as evinced by our language and ancestral education."[25] If, as Max Weber pointed out, belief in a common descent, regardless of whether an objective blood relationship exists or not,[26] may be one of the characteristics of an ethnic group, then it is justifiable to discern in the above thought of Gemistus an early sign of Greek nationalism and in his person the first neo-Hellene.[27] It is no coincidence that Gemistus was attacked by the Patriarch for his anti-Aristotelian, classicist, neopagan ideas and that one of his most important books was ordered destroyed. And it was fitting that the remains of this Platonist who had tried to counteract the religious and political domination of the Latin West, on the one hand, while saving the Greek heritage from the Ottoman threat, on the other,[28] should have been buried in the Tempietto Malatestiano at Rimini that was built by another classicist, Leon Battista Alberti.

Imbued with a spirit that recognized the new superiority of the West but found solace in the thought of the "glory that was Greece," Greek writers of the diaspora or those living in territories that had escaped the Ottoman conquest directed their thoughts to the fate

[25] S. Lambros, *Palaeologan and Peloponnesian Matters* (in Greek), III, 246–65. According to S. Runciman, *The Fall of Constantinople*, (Cambridge, England: Cambridge University Press, 1965), p. 15, it was in Thessaloniki that intellectuals such as Nikolaos Cabasilas started the fashion of calling themselves "Hellenes" instead of "Romaioi." However, A. E. Vakalopoulos, in his *History of Modern Hellenism* (in Greek), (Thessaloniki, 1961), I, 67–68, refers to sources indicating that the term "Hellene" emerged in the early thirteenth century at the time of the Emperors of Nicaea and in connection with the conflict of the Byzantine emperors with the Franks and the papacy. The latter, evidently basing itself on the *donatio Constantini* (a forgery), disputed the right of the eastern Emperors to the title of Emperor of the Romans and called them Emperors of the Greeks, *Graeci*, in a somewhat derogatory sense. The Byzantine emperors, on their part, while not abdicating from their viewpoint that they were the rightful heirs of Constantine, expressed pride in being termed *Graeci* or Hellenes and retorted by quoting the ancient Greek saying that "all non-Greeks are barbarians." Thus they adopted a derogatory propaganda term as a badge of pride. As Vakalopoulos notes, this national awakening was fanned from above. See also S. G. Xydis, "The Mediaeval Origins of Greek Nationalism," *Balkan Studies*, IX (1968), 1–20.

[26] See note 6, above.

[27] D. A. Zakythinos, *Le despotat grec de Morée*, II (Athens, 1953), 350–51.

[28] Sherrard, *The Greek East and the Latin West*, p. 120.

of their correligionaries who had come under the rule of Islam. In the process, they produced stereotypes concerning national character. Yet Christian against Muslim rather than Greek against Turk was at this time the tension-maintaining theme that set up a wall of separation between conqueror and conquered and stimulated among the latter a new sense of cohesion. Thus, in 1468, Cardinal Bessarion urged Emperor Frederick to wage a crusade against the Turks, and in 1553 another Greek sought to encourage Charles V and Francis I to launch an expedition against the Osmanlis and "restore liberty to the scattered Greek peoples."[29] Leo Allatius (1586–1669), a Uniate active in Italy, wrote a poem in ancient Greek entitled "Hellas" in which he expressed hopes for the liberation of the *genos*. However, for proselytizing purposes, appealing as he was to the masses, he used the Greek vernacular.[30] Another Greek who lived in Italy during the first half of the seventeenth century, Nikolaos Sofianos, deplored the decline of the Greek *genos*, while envying the western Europeans their flourishing literature and science. He was convinced, however, that the Greeks would regain their place among civilized nations "if they wished to read and listen to the books which the ancients had bequeathed to them."[31] Frankiskos Skoufos, born in 1644 in Crete and, like Allatius, a Roman Catholic propagandist, published a rhetoric in the vernacular in order "to be of benefit to the *genos*." He also composed a prayer calling upon "Christ, liberator of all the world," to liberate eventually the Greek or *genos* from the slavery of the Hagarenes. "Until when," he exclaimed in this prayer, "shall a *genos* as glorious and as noble have to prostrate itself before the godless turban?"[32] Elias Miniatis (1669–1714), who lived in Venice-held Greece, echoed Skoufos' prayer, addressing a similar one to the Virgin Mary. "Until when, oh Immaculate Virgin, shall the thrice-miserable *genos of* the Greeks remain in shackles of incredible slavery?" he wrote.[33] This nurturing of the hope for freedom from Muslim domination went hand in hand with Catholic propaganda and stimulated a sense of continuity between pre-Christian and post-Byzantine Hellenism,

---

[29] Geanakoplos, *Greek Scholars in Venice*, pp. 194–95.
[30] *Modern Greek Literature*, p. 94.
[31] *Ibid.*, pp. 95–96.
[32] *Ibid.*, pp. 100–101.
[33] *Ibid.*, p. 114.

spreading the faith in the descent from the ancient Greeks among
the people of the enslaved *genos*.

In the Danubian Principalities, the Phanariote rulers from 1709
to 1821 were "the eyes of the Ottoman Empire turned toward
Europe." They and their courts were open to western ideas that
were then channeled to Istanbul. One of them, Constantinos Mavrocordatos (1711–69), ten times hospodar of Wallachia or Moldavia,
was an admirer of the French Enlightenment, helped the serfs in
his principality, and introduced a sort of constitutional charter.[34]

By Mavrocordatos' time the influence of Russian propaganda, too,
began to be felt, bringing new stimuli to nascent nationalism and
national pride. Two biographies of Peter the Great written in Greek
vernacular were printed in Venice in 1736. Cosmas the Aetolian
(*ca.* 1714–79), a peripatetic teacher of great fervor who roamed
the Greek mainland for almost twenty years as an agent of Russian
influence, urged the establishment of a Greek educational system
"because our Church is Greek and our *genos* is Greek."[35]

The improvement in living conditions of the Greeks in the Ottoman Empire during the eighteenth century was accompanied by
an increase in the number of Greek schools. While the number of
self-exiled Greek literati dwindled, that of young people going to
Italy and other western European countries for purposes of study
increased. These young men returned full of exciting impressions
that they communicated to others,[36] acting as agents for "the revolution of rising expectations."

For a number of the Greek intellectuals who traveled abroad at
that time, the great attraction was Russia. Since the times of Peter
the Great, Russian propaganda had been organized among Greek-
speaking elements in the Ottoman Empire, and the accession of
Catherine II to the throne in 1762 meant that Greeks would be
welcome to St. Petersburg. Addressing the Empress, a leading Greek
intellectual of the period, Eugenios Voulgaris (1716–1808), referred
to the belief prevalent among his countrymen that the "fair *genos*"
would play an important role in freeing the Greeks and other cor-
religionary *ethni*.[37] These prophesies, it should be noted, were de-

---

[34] *Ibid.*, pp. 108–9. Also *Great Greek Encyclopedia*.
[35] *Modern Greek Literature*, p. 134.
[36] *Ibid.*, p. 135.
[37] *Ibid.*, p. 126.

rived from Russian-inspired leaflets in the Greek vernacular that had been circulating in Greece since the time of Peter the Great. Precursors of modern psychological warfare, these prophesies were to be expunged of their pro-Russian bias at the time of the French Revolution and slanted according to the needs of French propaganda.[38]

. Born in Venice-held Corfu, Voulgaris studied philosophy in Padua, which was dominated by the secularist spirit and constituted a center of attraction for numerous Greek scholars since the fall of Constantinople.[39] After being ordained a deacon (1735 or 1738), he taught the philosophy of Leibnitz and Wolff at Janina but, following a quarrel with a conservative-minded rival there, left in 1750 to become the director of another school in what is today northern Greece, in Kozani. Three years later, he was invited by Patriarch Cyril to the newly founded (1749) Athonian Academy. Though very successful there—students from many parts of the Ottoman Empire flocked to attend his lectures—he was again involved in some dispute, and in 1761, Patriarch Seraphim invited him to Istanbul to teach at the Patriarchal Academy. The somewhat too magnificent celebration of a Russian feast day there, however, seems to have created quite a scandal with the Porte, so Voulgaris had to leave again. After a brief stay in the Danubian Principalities, he went to Halle and Leipzig in 1763. His *Logic* was published in the latter city. In 1766 and 1768 he published two Voltaire works in translation as well as a *Treatise on Religious Toleration,* coining a Greek word for this concept. During his stay in Leipzig, he met Theodore Orlov who recommended him to his empress. Invited to St. Petersburg, Voulgaris arrived there in 1772, at the very time of the first Russian Mediterranean expedition (1769–75) against the Ottoman Empire in which the Orlov brothers played a stellar role. For this Russian expedition Voulgaris prepared various leaflets that circulated in Greece. Catherine entrusted him with the task of translating into Greek a French law code. In a memorandum addressed to the Empress he advocated the liberation of Greece. At the end of this war Voulgaris was appointed Archbishop of Scla-

---

[38] *Ibid.,* pp. 126–27. A cleric, Theoklitos Polyeidis, wrote these "prophesies" in about 1750. Paisios Ligaridis, who died in Russia in 1678, also was an agent of Russian propaganda and wrote an interpretation of the "prophesies," *ibid.,* pp. 136–37.

[39] Sherrard, *The Greek East and the Latin West,* pp. 172–73.

vinia and Cherson, which office he held for two years before resigning and returning to the Russian capital.

Voulgaris' works included a translation of Vergil into Homeric hexameters as well as philosophical and scientific treatises. It is likely that he produced a manuscript translation of Locke's *Essay on Human Understanding*.[40]

His was a purely national attitude, and in maintaining it Voulgaris enjoyed absolute Russian support. Following the deep revulsion that Catherine experienced against the French philosophe she had once welcomed to her court, Voulgaris, in 1790, attacked Voltaire. An indirect proof of how strong the national feeling already was at the end of the eighteenth century is the fact that one of his enemies, Athanasios Psalidas, accused him of having despised his fatherland and the entire *genos* by living abroad.[41] In his old age Voulgaris not only anathematized Voltaire, whose works he had admired and translated in his youth, but also became a strict conservative in religious questions. Yet, on the whole, he was an agent of secularism in the Greek world of the eighteenth century. For him, nationalism served as a sort of substitute faith. His life illustrates admirably the channels through which western ideas were diffused into the Greek realm and how receptive a milieu this was at the time.[42]

By the end of the eighteenth century the secular spirit, including nationalist attitudes, was replacing traditional values at an accelerating rate. A split was clearly developing between the politicoreligious institutions and especially their leadership, on the one hand, and the Greek-speaking *millet*, on the other. The latter was developing secularist, bourgeois, anticlerical, anti-Phanariote (anti-

[40] A. Anghelou, "Comment la pensée grecque a fait la connaissance de l'Essai de John Locke," *L'hellénisme contemporaine*, IX, (July–August, 1955), 230–49. Other works of Voulgaris, who had learned Latin, Italian, German, French, Hebrew, and Russian, included: *Orthodox Confession* (Amsterdam, 1767); *Ode to Catherine* (1774); *Booklet Against the Latins* (Istanbul, 1796); *Genealogical List of the Ottoman Sultans with the History of George Kastriota* (Moscow, 1812).

[41] *Modern Greek Literature*, p. 143.

[42] This life sketch is based on *ibid.*, pp. 137–41, as well as on the article on Voulgaris in the *Great Greek Encyclopedia*. The Voltaire works translated by Voulgaris were *Memnon* (from prose to verse) 1766; *Essai sur les dissensions des églises en Pologne*, 1768. Between 1771–72 he may have translated various signed or unsigned Voltaire pamphlets against the Turks. See also A. Camariano, *Spiritul revoluţionar Francez şi Voltaire in limba greacă şi română* (Bucharest, 1946).

aristocratic) sentiments and was attracted by science and the rationalism of the philosophes. The patriarchate turned more and more conservative, while the Phanariotes weakened and felt ill at ease in this new, materialistic, liberal, antiautocratic climate of the Enlightenment with its scientific interests and its struggle against superstition. The acceptance of the heliocentric Copernican system was, in itself, a revolutionary move, with physics becoming a symbol of freedom against the restraints of age-old ignorance.

In the thought of Ioannes Moisiodakas (*ca.* 1720–1800) one finds reverberations of the battle between the ancients and the moderns that, at an earlier time, had divided western European thinkers. This intellectual, who died an embittered and forgotten man, noted that the Greeks were overpowered either by their reverence for antiquity or by its neglect. The first tendency led to the prevailing conviction that everything the ancients had discovered or cultivated was noble and accurate; the second produced a shortage or almost complete lack of ancient writings. Moisiodakas himself attached great importance to natural science—in his view it made men aware of the fact that they were all brethren,[43] a neo-Stoic approach that foreshadowed the liberal, Mazzinian aspects of nationalism.

A remarkable example of the impact of the Encyclopedists and of French Enlightenment on the Greek intellectual scene, with all its implications for secularism and nationalism, was D. Katartzis (*ca.* 1730–1807), a Phanariote who attained the rank of Grand Logothete in Wallachia. The author of a grammar in the vernacular, he expressed great *pride* in the popular language. The Romaic tongue, to him was "the best of all languages." It should be written in such a way as to be understood by the rest of the *ethnos.* The language of the elite, he felt, should not be separated from that of the people. In his counsels that "we must write easily the language which all of us know since childhood, as do the British, the French, and all other *ethni* of Europe,"[44] are clearly revealed the processes of diffusion through mimesis.

Some of the remarks of Katartzis were intended to refute a statement by Voltaire—that it would be hardly appropriate for Greeks to use the term "fatherland" because they ignored the existence of a Miltiades or an Agesilaos and were but slaves of the Turks. The

[43] *Modern Greek Literature,* pp. 149, 151.
[44] *Ibid.,* p. 153.

remarks reveal that this Phanariote was more than just an exponent of what has been termed cultural nationalism.[45] While admitting that "we are not an *ethnos* that constitutes a state [*politeia*], but are subject to a more powerful *ethnos*," Katartzis went on to say that

. . . although we do not participate in the administration of the state together with those who are fully in power, we are not, nevertheless, entirely nonparticipants. Thus, we form an *ethnos* that at the same time binds our ecclesiastical leaders with the supreme administration and us among ourselves, and in many matters also binds our political leaders. Many of our civil (political) laws, customs, and all our ecclesiastical laws are valid . . . and our nation in many parts of Turkey has minute political systems with privileges. There are, furthermore, many of our *genos* who hold offices, namely patriarchs, high prelates, and administrators with imperial berats. Some of them wear the *kavadhi* [headgear indicative of high rank], the ecumenical patriarch, for instance, or the grand dragoman, and, often, the princes of Moldavia and Wallachia. All these participate in government and, therefore, fall under Aristotle's definition of a citizen.[46]

Katartzis then went on to argue (somewhat along the lines advanced by Montesquieu)[47] that the Greeks were justified in loving their nation more than their family, and their family more than themselves. Indeed, he maintained that they should love their own imperfect and weak state even more than members of independent nations, well ruled and flourishing, did theirs.[48]

A protégé of Katartzis, Rhigas Velestinlis (Pherraios) became an outstanding proponent of nationalism at the time of the French

[45] Hayes, *The Historical Evolution of Nationalism*, pp. 184 ff., *Nationalism as a Religion*, pp. 136 ff. As cited by K. Th. Dimaras, *The Liberalism of D. Katartzis* (in Greek) (Athens, 1964), p. 38, the Voltaire passage reads as follows: "Ce mot de patrie sera-t-il bien convenable dans la bouche d'un grec, qui ignore s'il y eut jamais un Miltiade, un Agésilas, et qui sait seulement qu'il est l'ésclave d'un janissaire, lequel est l'ésclave d'un aga, lequel est l'ésclave d'un vizir, lequel est l'ésclave d'un basha, lequel est l'ésclave d'un padisha que nous appellons à Paris le Grand Turc?"

[46] Dimaras, *The Liberalism of D. Katartzis*, pp. 14–15.

[47] *Ibid.*, p. 38. Dimaras cites the Montesquieu passage as follows: "Si je savois quelque chose qui me fut utile et qui fut préjudiciable à ma famille, je le rejetterois de mon esprit. Si je savois quelque chose qui fut utile à ma famille, et qui ne fut pas à ma patrie, je chercherois à l'oublier. Si je savois quelque chose utile à ma patrie et qui fut préjudiciable à l'Europe et au genre humain, je le regarderois comme un crime."

[48] *Ibid.*, p. 16.

Revolution. Before dealing with his contribution to Greek nationalism, something more must be said about another feature of nationalism, the growth of historic awareness, and about the beginnings of a regular press.

Historical awareness is suggested by the publication in 1773 by Spyridon Papadopoulos of a six-volume translation of *The History of the Present War between Russia and the Ottoman Porte*, to which a translation from certain chapters of Voltaire was added. In the foreword the author observed that his work could be useful for the *genos*.[49] In the same category is a *History of Cyprus* (1788) by Archimandrite Kyprianos, and *A Summary History of the Russian Kingdom* (1787).[50]

The year 1790 witnessed the publication of the first Greek periodical (the *Ephemeris*) in Vienna. It lasted until 1797, when the Austrian authorities closed it down because its publishers, the Poulios brothers, had printed several revolutionary pamphlets by Rhigas, with whom they were closely connected. Other periodicals appeared in Vienna a few years later: the *Greek Telegraph* (1812–29) and the *Literary Hermes* (1811–21),[51] which was to be connected with Koraes and would channel Herder's ideas to the Greeks. Such media serve to strengthen the fabric of nations and states.

Printed books preceded the appearance of Greek newspapers and periodicals, and like them, were first published outside the Ottoman Empire. While the first book printed (1476) entirely in Greek was the grammar of Constantinos Lascaris, the first in modern Greek was a paraphrase of the *Iliad* by Nikolaos Loukanis in Venice in 1526. The following year, a grammar of the Greek vernacular was also published in Venice, and in Milan in 1481 appeared the first scriptures, the *Book of Psalms*.[52]

Within the Ottoman Empire, the first Greek printing press was set up in 1627 by Patriarch Kyrillos Loukaris (1572–1638), but was short-lived. Also under patriarchal auspices, however, others followed in 1662, 1756, and 1797. Outside of Istanbul, printing presses

---

[49] *Modern Greek Literature*, p. 160. Dimaras does not give the name of the author. The translator tries to find points of contact between the ancient and modern Greeks and writes that among the Maniots the "megalopsychia" of their ancestors has not disappeared.

[50] *Ibid.*, p. 160.

[51] *Ibid.*, pp. 167–68.

[52] Topping, "La Bibliothèque Gennadeion . . . ," pp. 134–35.

were functioning by 1706 in Aleppo and in Jerusalem by 1728. There were others in the capitals of the Danubian Principalities, Jassy and Bucureşti by 1628 and 1682. Printing presses were established at Izmir and Moschopolis, trade centers in Asia Minor, and in northwest Macedonia.[53]

In addition to the early presses for classical works established in Venice, presses were set up for Greek publications throughout Europe and in St. Petersburg from 1670 to 1786. Modern Greek titles showed a progressive rise from 1670 on, although printings were small, averaging less than a thousand. Manuscript copies, however, from monastic scriptoria, schools, and other cultural centers vied with printed works, at least from 1670 to 1774.[54]

Rhigas and Koraes

Nationalism and statehood *in esse* or *in posse* are closely linked, as students of nationalism recognize. But Rhigas Velestinlis (or Pherraios) inspired by the example of the French Revolution, not only drafted a constitution for the Greek and other elements of the Ottoman Empire in the Balkans and the Aegean, but was also ready to implement with forceful deeds his patriotic poems and proclamations, and to make use of a military manual he had written. In his "Thoureios," a revolutionary poem sung to the tune of the French "La Carmagnole," the "until when . . ." formula that Skoufos and Miniatis had addressed to Christ and the Virgin Mary acquired an activist, secular, authentically nationalistic ring: "Until when, oh palikars, shall we live in dire straits . . . ." This revolutionary song, it was recognized at the time, was the hymn of the Greeks "to their Virgin Mary, whom they called 'Freedom.' " It was popular at the time of the Greek War of Independence two decades later.[55]

Born in 1757 in the Thessalian village of Velestinon, the ancient Pherae (hence his alternative surnames), Rhigas, the son of well-to-do parents, was first educated by a priest, then sent to a school at neighboring Ambelakia. He became a teacher in another village of the Mount Pelion region. When he was twenty, he killed a Turkish notable in a fit of anger and, escaping to Mount Olympus,

[53] *Modern Greek Literature*, pp. 98, 109–10. Also *Great Greek Encyclopedia*.
[54] *Modern Greek Literature*, pp. 123–24.
[55] *Ibid.*, p. 176. For the "Thoureios," in particular, A. Daskalakis, " 'Thoureios Hymnos.' Le chant de liberté de Rhigas Velestinlis," *Balkan Studies*, IV, 315–46.

joined a band of Armatoles led by one of his uncles. Later, after a brief stay at Mount Athos at the monastery of Vatopedi, Rhigas went to Istanbul with a letter of introduction to the Russian ambassador. There, he became for a while a member of the household of the Phanariote Alexandros Hypsilanti, and learned French and German. When his patron was appointed hospodar of Moldavia, Rhigas accompanied him to Jassy. However, after a quarrel with him in 1787, he left to become secretary of the non-Phanariote hospodar of Wallachia, Nikolaos Mavroyenis. Nine years later, after his patron, held responsible by the Ottoman government for the defeat of the Turkish arms in the war with Russia, had been beheaded, Rhigas left Bucureşti for Vienna.

The French Revolution and the victories of Napoleon had filled him with enthusiasm and transformed him into a pioneer of the Greek Revolution. It was in the Austrian capital that he began preparing a revolt of the Greeks and of the other subjects of the sultan with the aim of setting up a Balkan Federation, an idea he had conceived during his stay in the Danubian Principalities. With the cooperation of two Greek printers, he published several books and secret proclamations in the Greek vernacular for the purpose of inspiring his countrymen with the desire for liberation from the Ottoman yoke. Probably a Freemason, he founded a secret revolutionary society with members in Greek communities both inside and outside the Ottoman Empire. Rhigas tried to enlist the cooperation of discontented Turks, such as the Paşa of Vidin, in his revolutionary plans. Among his publications were translations from French novels, a novel with an anti-Phanariote character, a treatise on military strategy and tactics, and a translation of Abbé Mably's *Fortunes, Progress, and Misfortunes of the Greeks* (a work also known to the authors of the *Federalist Papers*). Rhigas also intended to prepare a translation of Montesquieu's *L'ésprit des lois*.[56] A map of the Balkans and of the coast of Asia Minor that he published was embellished with reproductions of ancient Greek coins and with a portrait of Alexander the Great. This reveals Rhigas' classically clothed revolutionary intentions and suggests his role as the precursor of ideas not only of the Balkan Federation, but also of the *Megali Idea* (the Great Idea), which was to become the guiding

---

[56] *Modern Greek Literature*, p. 173.

star of Greek nationalism until the Greek defeat in Asia Minor by Mustafa Kemal's Turks. Rhigas' publications, incidentally, circulated in Budapest, Trieste, Izmir, Jassy, Bucureşti, Zemlin, Patras, Preveza, and Janina.

The uprising of the Paşa of Vidin against the Sultan in 1797 prompted Rhigas to take action. He left Vienna and arrived in Trieste, where he intended to embark for Mani, then liberate the Peloponnese, invade Epirus, Greek Macedonia, Albania, and the rest of Greece. Betrayed to the Austrian police, he was taken back to Vienna where he was charged with preparing a revolt against a friendly and allied state. Extradited to Turkey, this dynamic, exuberant, liberal nationalist was executed, at the age of forty-one, in the dungeons of Beograd's fortress in June, 1798.[57]

Koraes, another outstanding personality of emerging Greek nationalism, referred to Rhigas and his companions as "gallant martyrs of liberty," showing the extent to which religious terms were by now applied to the secular ideas of the French Revolution in the Greek-speaking, Orthodox world. A pamphlet by Rhigas on "The New Political Administration" had been attacked by the church, which had also issued a patriarchal circular condemning French culture as a symbol of liberalism.[58] Nonetheless, these revolutionary ideas in classicistic form could not be eradicated. At the opening of the nineteenth century two subversive pamphlets were circulating in Greece containing crude attacks in French revolutionary style against the Greek landowners, the Phanariotes, the merchants, and the higher clergy—the elites that had come to exercise influence over Greek and other subject peoples in the Ottoman Empire or played a role in the Ottoman administration.[59]

At this historical juncture, which led to the setting up of an independent Greek state, the first goal and achievement of Greek nationalism, Adamantios Koraes (1748–1833) is, with Rhigas, a principal exponent of Greek liberal nationalism, although he was an

---

[57] This biographical sketch is based on *Modern Greek Literature*, pp. 168–76, also on the biography in *Great Greek Encyclopedia*. For Rhigas' political activities, A. Daskalakis, *Rhigas Velestinlis, La Révolution française et les préludes de l'indépendence hellénique* (Paris, 1937), and, more recently, A. J. Manessis, "L'activité et les projets politiques d'un patriote grec dans les Balkans vers la fin du XVIIIᵉ siécle," *Balkan Studies*, III (1962), 75–118.

[58] *Modern Greek Literature*, 157.

[59] *Ibid.*, p. 158.

intellectual rather than a man of deeds.[60] A classical philologist yet no antiquarian, he studied the materialist Helvétius and the sceptics Hume and Voltaire. He fervently believed in progress and closely identified himself with the ideas of the Enlightenment and of the revolutionary nationalist France of 1789, the *Directoire*, and the early Napoleonic era. Koraes admired Benjamin Franklin and George Washington, met Jefferson and corresponded with him about the future of Greece.[61] The objective of this Greek statesman without a state became the liberation of Greece. When the French seized the Ionian islands from Venice and set up the Septinsular Republic, he proposed direct action for achieving this objective. He did likewise in 1821 when the Greek War of Independence broke out. At other times he favored such indirect means as education, schools, enlightenment and the transferring of contemporary French ideas into the Greek world; in short—renovation rather than revolution.

Koraes, the child of a prosperous merchant of Izmir, acquired at an early age an excellent knowledge of ancient Greek and Latin. Sent to Amsterdam in 1771 on business, he remained there for seven years but was a failure as a businessman. Holland was at that time a haven for free thought, and Koraes enjoyed life there. He returned to Izmir in 1778, but four years later went to Montpellier to study medicine. Finally he settled down in Paris in 1788, and stayed there for the rest of his long life. Falling under the spell of the classicizing and liberal spirit that prevailed in that city and pervaded European nationalism in the early nineteenth century, Koraes dropped the practice of medicine and devoted himself to the study of the Greek language. Language, in his view, was the most inalienable possession of the *ethnos* and was virtually its synonym, for all members of the nation shared in its possession in democratic equality. In 1789 he published the *Characters* of Theophrastus, the first of his

---

[60] This biographical sketch is based on *ibid.*, pp. 195–203, and S. G. Chaconas, *Adamantios Koraes* (New York: Columbia University Press, 1942).

[61] S. A. Larrabee, *Hellas Observed* (New York: New York University Press, 1957), pp. 4, 34–35. Koraes' interest in the U.S. constitution is evident in one of his dialogues, entitled "On Greek Interests." *A. Koraes. Three Dialogues*, K. Th. Dimaras, ed. (Athens, 1960), p. 97. For correspondence with Jefferson, *Bulletin of the Bureau of the Rolls and the Library of the Department of State* (Washington, D.C., 1894–1903), Vols. VI, X.

editions of ancient Greek authors (twenty-six volumes in all) which established him as a classical scholar. Between 1798 and 1805, Koraes also published several pamphlets addressed to the Greeks in the Ottoman Empire, to excite enthusiasm for the French revolutionary cause and to inspire them with faith in the French. The titles, "Fighting Song," "Fighting Bugle-Call," "What the Greeks Must Do in the Present Situation," are illustrative of their spirit. Suggesting his radicalism was another pamphlet entitled "Brotherly Teaching," which was against a patriarchal work called "Fatherly Teaching."[62] To the new Septinsular Republic Koraes dedicated his translation of Beccaria's *Dei Delitti e delle Pene* (1802). In 1803 he wrote a long memorandum in French on the current state of Hellenism. Between 1804 and 1821, as the tide of revolution receded with the Empire and then with the Bourbon restoration, he reverted to his editions of classical Greek authors. In the forewords to these editions, which munificent Greek merchants financed, he presented his political, educational, linguistic, and other theories. Between 1809–14 he published Plutarch's *Parallel Lives,* which served as a strong stimulus to patriotism throughout the western world. His ambition was to publish all ancient Greek works on politics and ethics.

When the Greek War of Independence—or Greek Revolution— broke out in 1821, Koraes, now seventy-three, once again turned his attention to direct political action and became a sort of unofficial representative of revolutionary Greece in Paris. His *Political Counsels,* published in September, 1821, reveal him cognizant of the theories of natural law and of social contract as well as of the concepts of the general will and of collective legislation through elected representatives—all theories that contributed heavily to the development of nationalism and nation-states in the West. The *Political Counsels* also show that Koraes was aware of the problems that lay ahead: of the need to avoid strife and to blend liberty with justice in the new Greek state that was being born. In politics, as in linguistics, he was a middle-of-the-roader. Like Aristotle, he regarded the middle class as "unshakable pillars" of support for the fatherland and the state and advised them to act as mediators between the

[62] *Greek Literature,* pp. 158, 199.

other two classes, teaching both of them how to prosper and be happy.[63] He also gave counsel to the wealthy and the powerful of the *genos* as well as to its youth. It is not surprising that Koraes, whom some of his compatriots accused of being a Jacobin,[64] should have clashed with the first governor of Greece, Ioannes Capodistrias.

While promoting education, Koraes extolled the role of printing. One of its many great benefits in his view was that it had become a "real scourge of hypocrisy" and that it "had dispersed the darkness that covered the life of citizens and taught the peoples that the virtue of the citizen is not one thing and that of the Christian another, that the virtuous citizen is he who directs all his acts to the community rather than to his own interest."[65]

Nationalism and the Greek War for Independence

Transforming the sentiments and normative ideas of nationalism into the institutional reality of a nation-state required, as in the case of other revolutionary movements of an ethnocentric or classicentric character,[66] something more than the expression of the agitational ideas and feelings by outstanding members of various unorganized elites. It called for revolutionary organization, revolutionary deeds, and the creation of an embryonic governmental apparatus. In Greece, the period of 1814–30 witnessed the emergence of these three types of organized activities.

In 1814, among the Greeks in Odessa, the Quaker-sounding *Filiki Etairia* (Friendly Society) was set up by a trio of Greeks—two Epirotes, Nikolaos Skoufas and Athanasios Tsakalof, and one Dodecanesian, Emmanuel Xanthos. Their aim was to organize and to prepare the Greeks for an uprising. In promoting this goal, their organization, which was modeled on lines similar to those of the

[63] K. Th. Dimaras, *The Political Theme in Koraes, with Excerpts from his "Political Counsels"* (Athens, 1963), p. 81.

[64] *Greek Literature*, p. 208.

[65] Dimaras, *The Political Theme in Koraes*, p. 46.

[66] The terms "classicentric" or "taxicentric" have been coined by the author in *Greece and the Great Powers, 1944–1947* (Thessaloniki: Institute for Balkan Studies, 1963), p. 75, to define ideologies centered not around the nation but around a particular class, such as the "proletariat," or the ruling class, for example, in the Holy Alliance.

Carbonari in Italy, sought to enlist the support of eminent Greeks outside the Ottoman Empire while within it tried to get the co-operation of Ali Paşa of Janina and of Alexander Karadjordje of Serbia, being successful only with the latter. Especially after 1818, the organization's membership grew rapidly, and its headquarters were moved to Istanbul. By 1819–20 its membership in the Ottoman capital is believed to have risen to 15,000, and fantastic plans—never carried out—were made to destroy the Ottoman fleet in the Bosporus and seize the sultan in his palace. What accounted largely for the growth of the society's membership was the belief, shrewdly cultivated by some leaders, that the mysterious authority behind the organization was none other than Russia. In 1820 Capodistrias, then the Secretary of State of Tsar Alexander I, was offered (for the second time) the *Etairia's* leadership but again declined the offer. Instead he recommended for this post Alexandros Ypsilanti (1792–1828), who had served as an officer in the Russian army and had lost his right arm during the battle of Dresden in 1813. This scion of a distinguished Phanariote family enthusiastically accepted the offer and promised to devote his life and entire fortune to the cause. On March 6, 1821, with a *Hieros Lochos,* the Sacred Legion (note the classical Theban name), he left Kishinev, crossed the River Prut and invaded the Danubian Principalities. Earlier, during that same year, another member of the *Etairia,* Kolokotronis, coming from Zakynthos (Zante), had secretly landed in the Peloponnese. Then, supposedly on March 25, the day of the Annunciation, occurred the event that is celebrated today in Greece as the equivalent to the American Fourth of July. Germanos, Bishop of Patras, who was also a member of the *Etairia,* raised the standard of revolt in the monastery of Hagia Lavra in the northern Peloponnese. The nationalist Greeks of the diaspora thus converged with those who had grown up within the boundaries of the Ottoman Empire, in order to fulfill the *Etairia's* aims, the establishment of a nation-state.

The *Etairia* very soon lost control of the revolution but its aims were eventually fulfilled. The leaders of the revolt and their rebellious deeds soon became new national symbols and myths of the Greek War of Independence for the relatively small number of Greeks who emerged into statehood in 1830 and for those who did not. These myths and symbols were piled Pelion-on-Ossa-like on the earlier ones, derived mainly from classical Greece. Iconographically they at times provided parallels for them. For Thermopylae there was now the "Hani tis Gravias," and the modern Leonidas was Athanasios Diakos.

The five constitutions, enacted from 1822 until the arrival of King Otho in Nauplion (Nauplia) eleven years later were not only living symbols of the aspirations of the *genos* to become an *ethnos;* they also served as a framework for the government of the nation in revolt. Though partly based on the traditions of autonomy developed during the Ottoman era, all of them, except that of 1832, were republican, like those of revolutionary France, and included bills of rights. One of them, indeed, the Constitution of Troezen of 1827, included the basic juridicopolitical concept of nationalism that sovereignty resides in the people.[67]

The identical preambles of the first two provisional Greek constitutions, of Epidaurus (1822) and of Astros (1823) were, in their turgid prose, the equivalent of declarations of independence. To the sovereigns of post-Napoleonic Europe, they sought to justify the "national struggle" in terms of natural rights as well as in those of a conflict between Christians and Muslims.

The Greek Nation, under the frightful Ottoman oppression . . . declares today . . . before God and man, through its rightful representatives gathered in national assembly, its political existence and independence.

Our war against the Turks, far from being based on demagogic and rebellious principles or on any selfish interests of a part only of the entire Hellenic Nation, is a national war, a sacred war, the only motive of which is the recovery of our rights of personal freedom, of property, and of honor which . . . all well-ruled and neighboring peoples of Europe enjoy, but which the cruel and unprecedented tyranny of the Ottomans sought to deprive us of by force . . . .

Was there any reason why we should enjoy less than other nations these rights, or are we of a lower or baser nature so as to be considered unworthy of these rights and be condemned to eternal slavery under the irrational will of a ruthless tyrant who, like a robber, came from afar without any contract to subjugate us?

Motivated by such principles of natural rights and desirous of becoming similar to the rest of our Christian brothers, we have started a war

[67] G. K. Aspreas, *The Political History of Modern Greece, 1821–1928* (in Greek) (Athens: Sideris, 1930), pp. 63 ff.

against the Turks . . . having decided to succeed in our purpose and to rule ourselves with just laws or to be wholly lost.[68]

During the Greek War of Independence the nationalist spirit was expressed mainly in deeds, not words. In Greece proper, even as a bastion of besieged Missolonghi was named in honor of Koraes,[69] culture came to a standstill. But outside the arena of conflict these deeds inspired the nationalistic fervor that pervades the verse of two Zantiot poets, Andreas Calvos (1792–1869) and Dionysios Solomos (1798–1857). The former, a classicist in form but a romantic in content, wrote mostly in Italian, being a friend and admirer of Ugo Foscolo. But he was so moved by the events of the Greek revolution that he penned, between 1824 and 1830, a number of odes in the Greek vernacular that are ranked among the minor masterpieces of Greek literature.[70] As for Solomos, who also wrote Italian verse at first, it is sufficient to mention the titles of his main poems to show the extent to which his mind was influenced by the Greek War of Independence. In 1823, this outstanding Greek poet wrote his "Hymn to Liberty" that, put to the music of Nikolaos Mantzaros, has become the Greek national anthem. In 1824 and 1825, he wrote "Lord Byron's Death" and "The Destruction of Psara," respectively. In 1826 he started on his poem "Missolonghi" or "The Free Besieged," which he never finished. When he died, he also left unfinished a "Carmen Seculare" in which he intended to depict the state of the Greek nation and to envision its future. An admirer of the language of the people, of folk poetry, of klephtic songs, he was the first to bring unity to modern Greek poetry. His nationalism was liberal and cultural.[71]

Irredentist Greek Nationalism: "The Megali Idea" (1830–1922)

From 1830, when emergent Greek nationalism attained its first objective, the setting up of a state in territory freed from Ottoman rule, until almost a century later, Greek nationalism in a new irredentist, expansionist, state-based guise was symbolized in the "Me-

[68] A. Mamoukas, *Matters Pertaining to the Rebirth of Greece* (in Greek) (Piraeus, Athens, 1839–1852), II, 43 (Epidaurus, 1821) and 127 (Astros, 1822).

[69] *Greek Literature*, p. 201.

[70] *Ibid.*, pp. 220–21.

[71] *Ibid.*, pp. 226–30; 230–42. For an English biography of Solomos, see R. Jenkins, *Dionysios Solomos* (Cambridge, England: Cambridge University Press, 1940).

gali Idea," which the first U.S. Minister to Athens, Charles K. Tuckerman, writing in the seventies, described as follows:

. . . the Great Idea means that the Greek mind is to regenerate the East —that it is the destiny of Hellenism to Hellenize that vast stretch of territory which by natural law the Greeks believe to be theirs, and which is chiefly inhabited by people claiming to be descended from Hellenic stock, professing the Orthodox or Greek faith, or speaking the Greek language.

As Tuckerman pointed out further, these people,

in the aggregate, vastly outnumber the people of Greece proper, and are regarded by the "Free Greece" as brethren held in servitude by an alien and detested power. There are in European Turkey . . . not far from fifteen millions of people, of which number less than four millions are Ottomans. The rest are Slavonians, Greeks, Albanians, Wallachians, etc., who profess the Greek religion or speak the Greek dialect . . . .[72]

Tuckerman continued, in another section of the same chapter which he devoted to the Great Idea as follows:

However divided public opinion in Greece may be as to the proper time and method for attempting the realization of the Hellenic Idea, the Idea itself never leaves the teeming brain of the Greek. He may, in his impatience, disgust or despair, denounce it as chimerical, and join in the laugh of scorn which its mention evokes among foreign nations; but at heart he still cherishes it—if not as a practical possibility, as a tenet of his political and religious faith.[73]

Note the blend of the secular and the religious again that derives from the earlier period of Greek nationalism and is still reflected in the fact that all five post-independence constitutions of Greece refer in Article 1 to the established religion, the Greek Orthodox faith.

While the germs of this missionary, state-based, irredentist, expansionist nationalism are to be found in Rhigas' prestatehood

[72] C. K. Tuckerman, *The Greeks of Today* (New York: G. P. Putnam, 1878), p. 120. A. Pollis-Koslin, in a doctoral dissertation for Johns Hopkins University, 1958, entitled "The Megali Idea: A Study of Greek Nationalism," emphasizes this concept as a superordinate value making for social and political cohesivenes of Greek society and state.

[73] Tuckerman, *Greeks of Today*, pp. 123–24.

statesmanship, the first act of state that clearly suggested this trend as a policy was King Otho's visit to Izmir in 1833.[74] The Great Idea's first, most articulate political spokesman was Ioannes Kolettes, a former doctor of Ali Paşa who during the revolution has served as Secretary of the Interior and then in other posts. Early in 1844, as premier of the first constitutional government of independent Greece, he stated in Parliament:

The Kingdom of Greece is not Greece; it is only a part, the smallest and poorest, of Greece. A Greek is not only he who lives in the kingdom but also he who lives in Yannina, or Thessaloniki, or Serres, or Adrianople, or Constantinople, or Trebizond, or Crete, or Samos, or in whatever country is historically Greek, or whoever is of the Greek race. The soldiers of the revolution are not only those who rebelled in 1821 but all those who fought for liberty since the fall of Constantinople, . . . The heroes of the independence do not belong solely to the kingdom, to the small Kingdom of Greece. They belong to all the provinces of the Greek world from the Haimos to the Tainaron, from Trebizond to Cilicia.

He then added:

There are two great centers of Hellenism: Athens and Constantinople. Athens is only the capital of the kingdom. Constantinople is the great capital, the City, the joy and hope of all Hellenes.[75]

The national and political reasons for the irredentism that the above-quoted passages from Tuckerman and Kolettes reveal appear quite natural if one takes into account that only a fraction of the *genos* had become an *ethnos* in 1830 and that the War of Independence had only been partly successful. While outside the Kingdom of Greece the older factors still inspired action, as indicated by the uprisings in Crete in the forties, sixties, and nineties for *enosis* (union), nationalism in independent Greece itself inevitably appeared in a novel and expansionist guise. Yet, as the passages

---

[74] C. W. Crawley, *The Question of Greek Independence 1821–1833* (Cambridge, England: Cambridge University Press, 1930), p. 220.

[75] E. Driault and M. Lhéritier, *Histoire diplomatique de la Grèce de 1821 à nos jours* (Paris: Presses Universitaires, 1925), II, 253–54. This excerpt is from a speech of Kolettes of January 14, 1844.

from Tuckerman show, beyond irredentism, there was also a sense of cultural mission in the Megali Idea: the Hellenization of peoples living south of the Balkan range and of the Black Sea on both sides of the Aegean. In its most utopian form, the goal of the Megali Idea was the recreation of the Byzantine Empire, with a restored Constantinople as the capital of a multinational, Greek Orthodox, Hellenized state.

This exalted notion of pan-Hellenism, this Greek equivalent of "Manifest Destiny," of *la mission civilizatrice*, of "the white man's burden," of the "Third Rome," or of Pan-Slavism or Pan-Germanism, a nationalistic fancy of a mimetic or reflexive origin, found its expression in the writings of the foremost Greek historian of that era, Constantinos Paparrhigopoulos (1815–91). He wove together the "glory that was Greece" with the somber, splendid greatness of Byzantium into one great majestic historical tapestry as the background for the emergence of modern Greece. Born in Istanbul where his father had been a banker and a representative (*vekil*) of the Morea, Paparrhigopoulos was of Peloponnesian origin. His father, with other Greek notables, was killed by Turks in 1821 when the Greek revolution broke out. Like many other Greeks living in Istanbul at that time, his mother fled to Odessa with the child Constantinos, where he was educated at the Richelieu Lyceum on a scholarship granted by Alexander I. In 1830 he went to Greece and attended a school at Aegina, and later studied at universities in France and Germany. Returning to Athens, he became an official in the Ministry of Justice, but in 1845 had to resign from his post because he was not born in territory now part of independent Greece. After teaching for a few years at a gymnasium in Athens, Paparrhigopoulos was appointed professor of history at the University of Athens in 1851. His first publication, in 1843, *On the Colonization of the Peloponnese by Certain Slavic Tribes*, reveals some of the exogenous stimuli of pan-Hellenism and the Megali Idea. Its purpose was to refute the theories of the German historian Jacob Ph. Fallmerayer who, in a volume published in 1830, had sought to demonstrate on the basis of medieval sources that during the Middle Ages Slav tribes had migrated into Greece from the north and had completely wiped out the Greek population. The result was that modern Greeks, in spite of their pride of descent, were not descendants of the ancient Greeks, but Slavs. This book had stirred up quite a furor in Greece,[76] where philoclassical elements had come greatly to the fore. In his study Paparrhigopoulos, while not denying the fact that Slavs had indeed descended into the Peloponnese in the early Middle Ages, argued that they had arrived there not as conquerors but as peaceful nomads and had been culturally assimilated by the indigenous Greeks.

But the most important contribution of Paparrhigopoulos was his monumental five-volume *History of the Greek Nation* published between 1860 and 1872. This work, together with supplements by Karolidis for the most recent decades, remains the basic history used in Greece even today. "This was the first work in which the entire history of the Greek people was presented as a dynamic and uninterrupted sequence of related periods and interrelated events in a truly epic spirit," writes one of Paparrhigopoulos' biographers. Paparrhigopoulos' account of medieval Hellenism was, for the period, of particular importance and originality for he 'demonstrated the great importance of medieval Hellenism for the Greek *ethnos*' and paved the way for "the Rehabilitation of the Fame of Byzantium."[77] The value of this history, Paparrhigopoulos' biographer adds, resides not only in its scholarly character but also in its effect on the nation.

No other book has been read as widely and no other factor exerted a greater influence and educational power on the soul of the Greek people . . . . He brought to life the Greek past and also inspired faith in the fortunes of the future . . . . His main line was that of the nation's unity through time . . . . He revived the national spirit and inspired the nation with self-confidence.[78]

In philology, Georgios Hadzidakis (1848–1941) was this historian's counterpart. He emphasized the linguistic continuity of the

[76] Tuckerman, *Greeks of Today*, p. 130. The more recent item mentioned in note 26, which presents in a novel way Fallmerayer's ideas, also created a slight stir and triggered refutative efforts by G. G. Arnakis, "Byzantium and Greece," *Balkan Studies*, IV (1963) 379–400.

[77] S. Kougeas, in *Great Greek Encyclopedia*. Dimaras, *Modern Greek Literature*, p. 263, emphasizes that Paparrhigopoulos shaped in an admirable way his account of history without having been the first to give to the modern Greeks the sense of their historical continuity of the background. He acknowledges that the historian wanted to write a biography of the Greek race throughout the centuries.

[78] *Ibid.*

Greek language since Homeric times thus with his elder colleague, the historian, building up Greek national pride in the past, and imbuing the modern Greeks with hope for the future and a sense of mission as well.

Generally, the emergence of an independent state meant a new, more centralized structure of modern Hellenism. Gone was the Phanariote elite based in Istanbul with its subordinate but brilliant centers in Moldavia and Wallachia. Many of its members now settled in the capital of the new little kingdom where, in spite of the jealousy of the autochthonous elite, they distinguished themselves in the political and cultural life developing in Athens.[79] The scope of patriarchial power contracted especially when the Greek autocephalous church and the Bulgarian exarchate were set up in 1850 and 1870, respectively, the latter a symbol of Bulgarian, not Greek nationalism. Greeks from the diaspora likewise tended to converge on Greece, with nationalism in several European countries contributing to this influx. With the *enosis* of the Ionian islands with Greece in 1864, the quite impressive cultural elite that had developed there was swallowed up, as it were, by the kingdom's growing center. Within the kingdom itself, schooling, the press, military service, mails, the telegraph, the building of roads and railroads, symbols (e.g., flags), elections, national holidays and anniversaries, led to a compact communications network that did not exist before when the Peloponnese, mainland Greece, and the islands were part of the Ottoman Empire.

This new nation-state became a base for revolutionary activity among the Greeks who were still under Ottoman rule. Its entire policy tended to be oriented toward the external, superordinate goal of the Megali Idea rather than to any internal goal, to the probable detriment of internal economic growth.[80] Few were the Greek politicians who advocated "nationalism in one country." Most of them were "Trotskyites," in the ethnocentric not the classicentric sense. They favored permanent revolution in the territories of the Ottoman Empire in the belief that the expansion of the Greek state to include at least the irredenta, if not to fulfil the maximum aims of

---

[79] *Modern Greek Literature*, pp. 269 ff. (for literature and ideas). For example, A. Mavrocordatos, a Phanariote, who had distinguished himself during the War for Independence, served as premier of Greece on several occasions.

[80] Pollis-Koslin "The Megali Idea . . . ," pp. 11 (abstract) and 390–92.

the Megali Idea, was an indispensable precondition for the progress of the Greek state that otherwise was too small and poor in resources to prosper on its own. Even on the few occasions when attention was primarily focused on goals of internal progress of the nation, as during the repeated premierships of Charilaos Tricoupis in the eighties, the notion prevailed that this was necessary in order to make external expansion possible. This was a policy of *reculer pour mieux sauter*.

Throughout the hundred-odd years of its life, the nationalist spirit of the Megali Idea naturally underwent several changes in response to the course of the Eastern Question and developments in Balkan history. At the time of the Crimean War it assumed an interesting character of noncommital. At that juncture some Greeks saw themselves belonging neither to the West nor to the East, but participating in both. "Greece," according to an article in the *Spectateur d'Orient in 1853*,

could feel repugnance neither for the Latino-Germanic nor for the Slav civilization. On the contrary, the Greek element is the common denominator of the two races because, on the one hand, Western civilization cannot refuse to call itself Greco-Latin, and Eastern civilization, on the other hand, bears with pride the name of Greco-Slav . . . . A Greek feels equally at home in Paris and in Moscow. It is the Greek who is the most universal man and the only real catholic of Europe.

The article continues:

France and Britain can spend their treasure, sail all over the Archipelago with their fleets, unfurl their flags on the Parthenon and Hagia Sophia. The Greek will never cease being Orthodox and considering Russia as his brother. Russia may cross the Danube with its innumerable armies, the Cossack might tether his steed to the columns of the temple of Olympian Zeus. The Greek, though, will never cease being a friend of freedom and of the science of the West and will look to the West and to its civilization with admiration and love.[81]

Toward the third quarter of the nineteenth century, it should be added, Slavophobic elements in the Megali Idea became far more marked. They were a reaction to the Pan-Slav movement that

[81] "La société grecque," *Le Spéctateur d'Orient*, I (1853), 36–37.

was evolving to the north and was enveloping the Balkans with Russians as its foremost and most dangerous proponents. The Russian government tended to support the Slav and especially the Bulgarian elements in the Balkans, at what the Greeks felt to be their expense; Russia had views of its own as to who should inherit the "Queen of Cities" in case the "sick man of Europe" died.

The aforementioned passages vividly suggest the search for national identity, positive and negative nationalism, that went on in Greece throughout the era of the Megali Idea that also witnessed a tug-of-war between ancients and moderns. At the outset the Megali Idea was marked by a strong revulsion against Koraes' modernism in ancient garb with a corresponding stress on the garb itself. This trend reached its logical and absurd climax in a book of 1853 by a contemporary of Kolettes, the poet Panayotis Soutsos (1806–68), of Phanariote origin, who urged full reversion to the forms of Ancient Greek.[82] From the eighties on, however, a more realistic, more scientific, more modern approach toward the problem of national identity and of language prevailed. From the West came the influence of August Comte and his positivism. The language of the people, the *dimotiki,* not the noble tongue of the ancients, was now studied, appraised, and glorified as the means of expression of modern Greekness, a bearer of modern Greek values. A parallel trend might be observed in the interpretation of the Megali Idea from this time on.

After the first disastrous defeat of Greek arms during the Greek-Turkish war of 1897, which starkly revealed the frailty of the small Greek state, certain signs appeared that indicated an interest in superordinate values of a different sort than those symbolized by the Megali Idea. The long poem entitled "The Gypsy's Dodecalogue" (1907) of Kostis Palamas (1859–1943), who, with Solomos, is often regarded as the outstanding poet of modern Greece, is a good example of this trend. On the other hand, the struggle over the fate of Macedonia at the beginning of the twentieth century and the Balkan Wars of 1912–13 witnessed a vigorous flare-up of the expansionist spirit that the Megali Idea symbolized for the Greeks, although in a more realistic form than had been the case during the romantic thirties and forties of the previous century, when the other Balkan nations had not yet acquired full statehood.

[82] *Modern Greek Literature,* pp. 265–66.

At the conclusion of World War I, the abortive Treaty of Sèvres (August 10, 1920) turned out to be the closest the Greeks would ever come to the goals Kolettes had outlined in 1844. The peace conferences that led to this and other treaties gave such Greek statesmen as Eleftherios Venizelos the opportunity to develop their views on Greek nationality, revealing the rationalizations for Greek nationalism and expansionism at the time. The modern principle of self-determination, which Wilson and Lenin had preached, proved to be a handy and persuasive argument when Greek-speaking populations were clearly involved and statistically in a majority in a particular region in dispute. In other cases, as in that of northern Epirus (southern Albania) where the linguistic criterion was less useful, the concept of Greek "consciousness" was put forward. For certain territories (such as northern Epirus), historical grounds, too, were invoked: the fact that "from times immemorial" the particular area had come within the sphere of Hellenism, "agent and creator of a superior civilization."[83]

However, in a dramatic confrontation with Mustafa Kemal's emerging Turkey, whose nationalism had been greatly stimulated by the nationalism of modern Greece and of other Balkan states that had managed to break away from the Ottoman Empire at various times since the beginning of the nineteenth century, the Megali Idea was completely shattered by the defeat of the Greek Army in Asia Minor in August, 1922.

Interwar Greek Nationalism

The Treaty of Lausanne of 1923, which replaced the abortive Treaty of Sèvres, not only delimited the political boundaries of modern Greece along lines still holding good today except for the addition of the Dodecanese by the Italian Peace Treaty of 1947, but surgically, as it were, removed from the Megali Idea most of its solid irredentist core. Over a million Greeks of Turkey settled in Greek territory in accordance with the Greek-Turkish agreement of 1923 for the compulsory exchange of populations, while almost half a million Turks moved from Greece to Turkey.[84] As a result, the ethnographic structure of the Greek realm became unequivo-

[83] Pollis-Koslin, "The Megali Idea . . . ," pp. 349–52.
[84] S. P. Ladas, *The Exchange of Minorities, Bulgaria, Greece, and Turkey* (New York: Macmillan, 1932).

cally that of a nation-state with diaspora possibilities greatly curtailed after the stringent American immigration laws of 1924. Because of the Lausanne settlement, the ethnic homogeneity of Greece as well as that of neighboring Turkey was greatly strengthened, constituting the basis for the development of new manifestations of nationalism, nationalist pride, and nationalist aspirations.

In Greece the shattering of the Megali Idea after the defeat in Asia Minor and the exchange of populations left quite a spiritual vacuum. Soon, however, new nationalist aspirations started taking shape. The post-World War I weariness with nationalism, the new emphasis on the values of economic development and social justice symbolized by the Weimar Constitution and the Soviet experiments, the very practical need of dealing with the vast problems of settling the refugees from Turkey among a population of five million: all stimulated aspirations toward ideals of national economic development, toward the fulfilment of internal goals that had been largely neglected during the era of the Megali Idea. Externally, on the other hand, there was a revival of the humanistic ideas of liberal nationalism and of the international nationalism symbolized by the League of Nations. This suited the foreign policy of Greece as a *status quo*-ist state after World War I. There was also the appearance of new superordinate goals such as the sponsorship and support of regional cooperation in the Balkans and, among the Communists, support of the Comintern, Balkan Federation, and then Stalinism.[85] At this time, Rhigas was often viewed, not as the forerunner of the Megali Idea, but as the prophet of Balkan cooperation.

The most remarkable feature of the new spirit of Greek nationalism in the interwar period was the conscious effort to close, once and for all, the long chapter of Greek-Turkish hostility by promoting the cause of Greek-Turkish friendship. In 1930, Eleftherios Venizelos, the architect of the Treaty of Sèvres (at least in its Greek aspects), and Kemal Atatürk, the toppler of this paper edifice, established a basis for friendly relations between Greece and Turkey that opened the possibilities for a new sort of interaction between the respective nationalisms of the two Aegean states.

On the other hand, Greek nationalism, after the shattering of

[85] D. G. Kousoulas, *Revolution and Defeat. The Story of the Greek Communist Party* (London: Oxford University Press, 1965), pp. 2 ff., 13–14, 22 ff., 54 ff.; 56–60.

the Megali Idea, was still in need of an adequately inspiring single symbol for its national interests and goals. The strength of the need is suggested by the fact that late in the thirties, under the dictatorship of Ioannes Metaxas, efforts were made to create a new national myth, partly in response to Stalinist internationalism (which for Greece would entail the loss of Macedonia and of Thrace),[86] and to Mussolini's *mare nostrum*-ism with its Imperial Roman overtones. It was also, in part, a mimesis of integral Italian and German nationalism (fascism and nazism). This was the myth of "The Third Greek Civilization," the other two Greek civilizations being those of Byzantium and Ancient Greece. The roots of this ideal went back to Paparrhigopoulos's history, which was anathema to the Communist Party of Greece.[87]

Less remotely, however, Ion Dragoumis (1878–1920), whom Metaxas had known as a comrade in Corsican exile during World War I, appears, in certain respects at least, as the forerunner of the new approach to the nation. His essays indicate that in his search for an understanding of Greekness, he had been influenced by Maurice Barrés and Nietzsche. In 1911, he wrote that the Megali Idea was a fantasy. The Greek race, in his view, was not one of the

---

[86] *Ibid.*, pp. 54 ff.

[87] The Secretary General of the Communist Party of Greece (KKE), Nikolaos Zachariadis, in his opening speech on the occasion of the Seventh Party Congress in October, 1945, defined the "Megali Idea" as the notion that the contemporary Greeks were descendants, inheritors, and continuators of ancient Greece and the Byzantine Empire and, consequently, that they had "a historic even divine mission vouchsafed from above." Their goal: to recreate Greek grandeur and restore the Byzantine Empire. Paparrhigopoulos, he added, had provided the historical "justification" of this thesis. His was an idealist, not a materialist, interpretation. "Our own mission," Zachariadis went on to say, "is to prove that in spite of the fact that we exist in the same spot and that our language is derived from ancient Greek, the Greek nation, ethnologically and socially, has no relation with the regime and the slave society of racial discrimination that prevailed in ancient Greece . . . nor with the barbarism of Asiatic despotism and of serfdom which characterized the empire of the East Roman state. Our own mission is to prove that the nation is a historical category which appeared and developed with the appearance and development of capitalist relations of production; that the neo-Hellenic nation, having roots from the times of the Byzantine Empire, developed and was finally shaped under the conditions of Turkish domination." *Rizospastis*, October 6, 1945. It should be added that Zachariadis, in the above-mentioned speech, stressed the materialistic as against the idealist thinkers of Ancient Greece. Marx's doctoral thesis, it should be recalled, was on Epicurus, a materialist like Democritus. Even the Greek Communists, it would seem, suffer from progonolatry, to a certain extent at least.

conquerors, nor was it outright militaristic. It had neither the capability nor the need to dominate quantitatively, and therefore should distinguish itself qualitatively through its culture. When the Young Turks reintroduced the Midhat Constitution, he had wondered whether the Greek element in the Ottoman Empire might not eventually come to exercise a condominium with the Turks in a great Anatolian empire.[88] The cultural and esthetic aspects of this new approach toward nationalism, which attached importance not only to the many historical events associated with Greece and to the visible records that Greek and Byzantine culture had bequeathed, but also to its landscape—the trees, rocks, mountains, and sea—were accentuated in the poetry of Angelos Sikelianos (1884–1951) and of Odysseus Elytis (1913–   ).

During the thirties the term *phyli* (race) tends to be stressed as against the terms *ethnos* and *genos*. Metaxas wrote in 1935, i.e., before he became paterfamilias dictator: "We are Greeks, a physiological development of one and the same race throughout the centuries." As for high ideals, these, he maintained, were necessary for youth. The aspirations for greater material comfort and ease were not enough. They were for the old, not the young. Greek youth, he observed, after being deprived of the Megali Idea, had turned either to humanitarian ideals that other nations with a different mentality had developed, or to internationalism, pan-Europism, cosmopolitanism, or the mere satisfaction of individual wants. With some, a diffuse leftism had become fashionable and with others, reactionary fascism. The Greek educational system and new educational theories were partly to blame for this situation. The purpose of education in Greece, especially of primary education, should be to educate not human beings but Greeks:

Let us not delude ourselves. "Men" exist only zoologically. Psychically, however, they are "Greeks," "French," "British," "Germans," "Bulgars," etc. Each man sees life, thinks, and acts as a function of his nationality, his race. Raciality is a physiological phenomenon. Greek youth must understand this in order to find its way.

[88] Cited in "Who Killed the Megali Idea?," *Greek Themes*, XI, No. 5 (May, 1966), p. 281 (cited hereafter as *Greek Themes*). Also S. G. Xydis, "Where Greece Stands Today," *Atlantic Monthly*, Supplement (June, 1955), p. 18.

It had been a mistake, he maintained in this article, the seventieth of a series in a grand newspaper debate with Eleftherios Venizelos, to believe that it was possible to include Hellenism in territorial limits when it was "the genius of the race" to have no limits. The unity of Hellenism lay in its culture, which was a manifestation of the "vitality, genius, and power of our race." It was the task of the center of Hellenism, the Greek state, to create this culture "which it should then radiate to the tips of the tentacles of the Greek race thus solidly binding together all the segments of the race in a conscious whole." It was also the task of the "center of Hellenism" to create that state power and dynamism through which it would be able to defend the existence, life, and development of its tentacles outside its boundaries. Metaxas, at the same time, acknowledged that it was in the nature of great ideals to be unattainable and that antagonisms would exist as to specific ideas, methods, and systems for approaching this goal.[89]

Greek Nationalism after World War II

World War II and its immediate aftermath brought not only material disasters but also new elements of national pride and new national symbols. It inaugurated a period of schizoid nationalism that reflected the pattern of international politics in a bipolar world and the conflict between ethnocentrism and classicentrism that is still going on as developments in eastern Europe on both sides of what used to be called the Iron Curtain suggest. To "Thermopylae" and "1821" were now added October 28 (a new national holiday), the "Epic of Albania,"[90] and the "Victory of Grammos," whereas from the viewpoint of Greek national communism there was EAM-ELAS, the National Liberation Front and its Army, and "The Resistance," "The Third Round" or the "Democratic Army."

The internal and external debates over the peace settlement after World War II testified to the strong flare-up of externally directed nationalism that, some of Greece's western friends felt, was detri-

[89] *The Personal Diary of Ioannes Metaxas* (Athens: Ikaros, 1960), IV, Annex I, 611–15.

[90] Georgios Grivas, in many of his EOKA proclamations, referred to the "Albanian Epic," which is a commonplace in political rhetoric today. G. Grivas-Dighenis, *Memoirs of the EOKA Struggle 1955–1959* (Athens, 1961), p. 33.

mental to the urgent national goals of rehabilitation and reconstruction while their foes charged that it indicated a re-emergence of the dynamics of the Megali Idea. While ethnocentric territorial claims, official or unofficial, of the Right or of the Left, extended in all directions, the pro-western Greek government and its supporters promoted only those claims that were directed against states they believed were foes of the West, whereas the Communists and their adherents did exactly the reverse. They raised claims to Turkish Thrace and Cyprus, condemning as chauvinistic the claims advanced by their opponents, which were at the expense of the "People's Democracies" coming into being north of Greece. Loyalties of a different kind thus split and polarized the forces of Greek nationalism.[91]

The leitmotiv of the claims of the Greek government to the Council of Foreign Ministers and the Paris Peace Conference in 1945–46 was national security in contrast to the peace settlement after World War I, when ethnic arguments were prevalent.[92] Evidently, the Greek policy-makers were motivated by the hope that such strategic arguments would also induce Britain and the United States to recognize a fundamental community of interests based on their desire to bolster their own security throughout the world.

The pro-western political world that finally prevailed in Greece, after the struggle from 1946 to 1949 to suppress the Communist-led rebellion, left its imprint on the Greek Constitution of 1950, a revision of the Constitution of 1911, itself a revision of the Constitution of 1864. Several articles in this new organic law referred, for the first time, to the national values of Greek-Christian civilization.[93] Their inclusion proves the extent to which traditional values of na-

---

[91] S. G. Xydis, *Greece and the Great Powers 1944–1947*, p. 522. At the Paris Peace Conference, the Yugoslav representative charged on September 6, 1946, that the Greeks since antiquity had, like the Phoenicians, been colonizers "in the body of other peoples," *ibid.*, p. 330.

[92] *Ibid.*, pp. 524–25.

[93] Article 16, paragraph 2, provides that "in all elementary and intermediate schools teaching shall be aimed at the ethical and intellectual instruction and the development of the national conscience of youths on the basis of the ideological principles of Greek-Christian civilization." Article 100 provides that "the civil servant shall be loyal and devoted to the country and the national ideals; . . . Ideologies seeking to overthrow the existing political or social regime by violent means shall be absolutely contrary to the status of a civil servant." A. J. Peaslee, *Constitutions of Nations* (2d ed.; The Hague: M. Nijhoff, 1956), II, 94, 109.

tionalism were now shaped and given new dignity in response to a bipolar world situation. This response, stimulated by the cold war and the fear of communism, was accompanied by the remnants of the Slavophobia of the late nineteenth century. The values of the Greek heritage were now seen as part of the Greco-Roman-Judaic culture in general, and Greek national pride tended to focus on these cultural values, serving to underpin the loyalty of many Greeks to NATO and the international organizations of western Europe, i.e., to international if not to supranational goals, in spite of the negative attitude of the majority of western allies to Greek desires in the Cyprus question.

In the presentation of the Greek viewpoint in the dispute over Cyprus, which involved the question of *enosis* of the island with Greece if the Cypriots so desired, arguments were based primarily on the principle or the right of self-determination. This had not been the case during the debate of the Greek claims in connection with the Bulgarian and Italian peace settlements in 1945–46. *Enosis*, of course, is one aspect of the Megali Idea. As a slogan, it had been prominently featured in the agitation that had led to the cession of the Ionian islands to Greece by Britain in 1864. The British and Turkish opponents in the Cyprus dispute were quick to point out this analogy and to argue that the claim for self-determination was a disguised demand for *enosis*, hence, for the annexation of the island by Greece,[94] and a symptom of the revival of the Megali Idea.

Arguing against these allegations about the supposed revival of the Megali Idea, the Greek Foreign Minister, Evangelos Averoff-Tossizza, told the Turkish Ambassador in Athens, Settar Iksel, in a private exchange in October, 1956, that if the Turkish charges were put forward in order to create an effect, he fully understood. If, however, Turkish leaders really believed these charges, then their lack of realism astonished him. Greece, a country of eight million people, could not entertain a Megali Idea toward Turkey with its twenty-four million and a territory nearly double that of France, a country so strong that even a Great Power would have trouble occupying it. The Megali Idea, he added, had a *raison*

---

[94] For instance, Selwyn Lloyd, in his speech before the General Committee at the ninth session of the U.N. General Assembly, on September 23, 1954, *Report on the Inscription of the Cyprus Item . . .* , Cmd, 9300 (London: H. M. Stationery Office, 1954), p. 3.

d'être in its time because the existence of Hellenism outside of
Greece gave the concept a certain realistic basis. Hellenism, however, was no longer dispersed, but had been gathered within clearly
defined national boundaries. Anyone who believed that Greece
should or could embark on such a venture would be insane and
criminal. The current "Great Idea" was the improvement and development of Greece's material resources and the promotion of
Greek culture. In both these spheres, the Greeks believed they
could build an absolutely different but very beautiful Megali Idea.
It was enough to speak with any Greek politician or any group of
Greeks to see that this aspiration, in the sense mentioned in Turkey,
was no longer entertained, nor could it be entertained in the future.
The facts of life were stacked against it. Only with bad faith could
it be maintained that Greece had the aspirations she had prior to
1920. It was another matter to maintain, he added, that Hellenism,
"which recently suffered so much for the cause of freedom," should
not believe that an island inhabited 80 per cent by Greeks should
have the right to decide its own future "and to unite with Greece
if it so wished." That was a matter alien to the Megali Idea, and
Greece would be "a country unworthy of its history and would act
as a country on a lower culture would if it did not respond to the
demand of the people of Cyprus."[95] In a conversation in October
of the following year, this time with the Yugoslav Ambassador in
Athens, Averoff-Tossizza again emphasized the culture- and econ-
omy-oriented ideals of contemporary Greece.[96]

During various debates on the Cyprus question in the Greek
Parliament, several political leaders likewise dissociated the demand
of Cypriots for self-determination from the Megali Idea. For example on December 12, 1958, Panayotis Canellopoulos, not only
a former Prime Minister but also a sociologist, declared that Greece
had no right to seek *enosis;* it only had the right to ask for the freedom of the Cypriots. It had no right, he said, to formulate ideals
belonging to the nineteenth and the beginning of the twentieth
centuries. The ideals of any expansion or change of frontiers were
in essence incompatible with contemporary economic and social

---

[95] Personal Papers of Mr. E. Averoff-Tossizza, Athens.
[96] *Ibid.*

reality.[97] In another speech, on February 26, 1959, during the stormy Parliamentary debates on the Zurich and London agreements on Cyprus, he said:

> Of course we desired *enosis* for decades or rather from the very outset, since there was the new kingdom, there was the trend—instinctive in the nineteenth and the beginning of the twentieth century, absolutely justified historically—toward expansion and incorporation of all those parts of territory in which a majority of Greeks lived or even beyond, because the "Megali Idea" reached areas in which the Greeks had no majority, but lived in territories regarded as linked with the name of Greece. But that was until the beginning of the twentieth century, if you wish until 1922, the law which moved the history and not only the heart of Greece. . . . It continued, after the dropping and abrogation of the "Megali Idea" to be a sentimental attachment toward those territories at least in which Greeks were in a majority . . . like the Dodecanese, Cyprus, Northern Epirus, which from the population viewpoint, were regarded as Greek.
>
> That was a sentiment. But we had to overcome it. It is a far greater step when a people, in spite of its feelings, solves a problem than when it maintains its sentiments and does not solve the problem and merely voices its sentiment.[98]

More recently, in a published interview, Canellopoulos expressed similar views that would have been blasphemous, if not inconceivable, in the times of Kolettes or Tuckerman. On this occasion he observed that this aspiration had constituted merely a transient historical need and that its rhetoric had occasioned disasters, such as the Greek-Turkish war of 1897, and had prevented the creation of a good and concrete present. The achievements of 1910 and 1913, he maintained, were not connected with the Megali Idea but had been realistic and linked with specific aims. On the other hand, he proposed that the "Hellenic Idea" had not died and could not die, but was still alive.[99] Another former premier, Panayotis Pipinelis, spontaneously told this writer in the summer of 1964: "I am a nationalist. But nationalism changes in content at various periods of

[97] *Journal of the Debates of Parliament* (in Greek), December 12, 1958, pp. 297–98.

[98] *Ibid.*, February 26, 1959, p. 237.

[99] *Greek Themes*, IX (May, 1966) 285–86.

a nation's history as does its content from nation to nation. As a nationalist today, I believe," he added, "that the nation's goal is to become a highly developed small state with high living standards and a society like Sweden's or Switzerland's." Thus, in the view of this conservative, the goals of Greek national effort and the focus of national pride are economic, social, and cultural development—the ideals of developing nations—not those of external expansion. Center Party leaders have expressed similar sentiments.

While non-Communist and anti-Communist Greek nationalists ("bourgeois" nationalists, in their foes' terminology) seem to emphasize welfare if not Socialist ideals as a content of contemporary Greek nationalism, the Communists and their sympathizers seem to have become quite nationalistic judging from their attitude toward the Cyprus problem, for example. Thus, side by side with the spokesmen of a realistic, sophisticated, western-oriented nationalism of the type already cited, the leaders of EDA, the Union of the Democratic Left, which was a façade party for the outlawed KKE (Communist Party of Greece), sought, like the extreme right wing, to exploit traditional, popular, anti-Turkish stereotypes that linger on among the masses whose mind is still pervaded by primary school histories redolent with the anti-Turkism of the Megali Idea. Ethnocentric attitudes for them are means toward an end. Fanning them is part of the anticolonial struggle that, in their view, is going on not only in Cyprus but in Greece itself. For, according to the Communist line, Greece is suffering under the yoke of Anglo-Saxon imperialism, having supposedly gone through a period of "golden occupation" under the Americans since the "Truman Doctrine" until well into the fifties. Inasmuch as Marx and Engels considered nationalism a feature of capitalism that would disappear with the advent of socialism, there is nothing inherently unorthodox, from the Marxist point of view, in these nationalist manifestations of EDA, in view of the fact that Greece, unlike its northern neighbors, is a "capitalist" and "bourgeois" country.

Exploiting the West's neutral or negative attitude toward the Greek viewpoint on the Cyprus question, EDA leader Ioannes Passalidis, speaking before Parliament on June 11, 1958, emphasized the values of negative rather than of positive nationalism by urging the government to "drop the *slavish policy toward the foreigners* that leads to the abyss of hydrogen (bomb) destruction" and to adopt *"a really Greek foreign policy* of peace and friendship toward all peoples which would serve the interests of Greece only" (emphasis added).[100] Since 1956, it should be noted, EDA has not advocated withdrawal of Greece from NATO and adherence to the eastern bloc, but merely the maintenance of an independent policy along Gaullist lines.[101]

The same emphasis on negative nationalism is revealed in EDA's attitude toward Greece's association with the European Economic Community. EDA opposed such an association. A *fortiori* it rejected any idea of Greece's integration in the political community that might result from the economic cooperation of the Six in the Common Market. Ilias Iliou, leader of EDA, wrote:

> The great monopolies today find national areas too narrow and . . . tend to form broader unitary state entities within which states would be dissolved. The phenomenon thus occurs that those who express tendencies which are supranational and related to the "Megali Idea" appear today as champions of fusions which for the Great Powers may constitute a success . . . and for the Germans the realization of the Hitlerian idea of Lebensraum with other methods, but for small states and especially for Greece with its economic frailty and lack of racial bonds with the Great, will mean annexation, absorption, disappearance as a national entity.[102]

This is remindful of the attitude of certain eastern European states that balk at moves toward integration in the "Socialist Commonwealth of Nations." Needless to say, opponents of Communism in Greece are wont to contrast EDA's solicitude for Greece's sovereign entity with the espousal by the KKE (Communist Party of Greece), at various times since its inception in 1918, of the cause of an autonomous or independent Macedonia at the territorial expense of Greece.

Like his "bourgeois" political opponents, however, the EDA leader saw no possibility of a revival of the Megali Idea in its classical sense. The conditions for selling to the masses an "expansionist-chauvinistic" idea did not exist, he believed. In the past this idea had

---

[100] *Journal of the Debates of Parliament,* June 11, 1958, pp. 15, 17.

[101] *Ibid.,* April 5, 1956, p. 27 (Passalidis). For Greek attitudes toward NATO and the United States, T. A. Couloumbis, *Greek Political Reaction to American and NATO Influences* (New Haven: Yale University Press, 1966).

[102] *Greek Themes,* XI, No. 5 (May, 1966), 289.

been cultivated, he maintained, by the ruling classes of Greece because it served their interests and diverted the attention of the oppressed classes from their internal social struggle. An incorrect educational system that was "ancestor-struck" and directed toward a false linguistic ideal, together with historical titles supposedly derived from the Byzantine and Alexandrian history, had nourished the Megali Idea. The imperialist Great Powers, on their side, had intrigued to incite the Greek ruling class in this direction as they had done with the ruling classes of other Balkan countries. Rhigas' call for a revolt not only of the Greeks but of the Bulgars and Albanians and even of the Turks, of whites and blacks, and his desire for a multinational bourgeois state that would be the successor of the feudalist Ottoman Empire had been logical. It had, however, been Utopian because "there was no precedent for the transition from the feudal to the bourgeois processes of production . . . in countries with mixed ethnic populations . . . without oppression and clashes." As a result the new national states in the Balkans had been formed in a process of a century and a half of struggles, clashes, and wars, with persecutions, exterminations, and exchanges of populations "which created, to a substantial degree, a forced coincidence between ethnic and state boundaries." The peaceful solution of equal treatment of nationalities had prospered only during the last half century in multinational states (e.g., the U.S.S.R. and Yugoslavia) which were proceeding to the stage of socialism.[103]

About the future, Iliou, in spite of his ostensibly strong preference for negative nationalism in the present, was extremely vague. "Social and technological developments," he wrote cautiously, in this post-Khrushchevian era,

were changing from moment to moment the structures of humanity . . . . modernization, the liquidation of serious relics of obscurantism, knowledge, scientific research, the submission of nature to the service of Man, the new humanism that corresponds to the scientific and technical state of our epoch, cultural flowering within a climate of peace, democracy and the abolition of any form of exploitation and oppression would contribute to the substance of really Megali Idea. While mankind crosses the threshold of a really new epoch where unprecedented prosperity and civilization can be assured for all men, the ambition of a small but highly intelli-

[103] *Ibid.*, pp. 287–88.

gent people must be not to ruminate on old ideas . . . or to bite the bait which is offered to it by those who have an interest in diverting it and delaying it, but to be a pioneer in the emulation for a new world.[104]

Such ideas, which must be viewed against the background of Communist attitudes toward a Balkan Federation and suggest that if there were a new drive toward that aim, Turkey this time might be invited to join in such a regional Communist organization, are largely based on the efforts of the Paparrhigopoulos of Greek Marxism, Yannis Kordatos (1891–1961) to interpret Greek history since ancient times in terms of historical materialism.[105] Like Zachariadis attacking the extreme idealist view that the Greek nation was directly derived from the ancient Greeks and that even the Byzantine Empire had been absolutely Greek, he observed that nations were a social phenomenon of modern times and, like Marx, maintained that they would disappear with the disappearance of capitalism. Both the Greek protonationalism that briefly but brightly had flickered in the times of Pletho and the nationalism that had led to the Greek revolution were, he believes, ideological expressions of a particular class, the class of traders, the bourgeoisie. These "forces," as contrasted to the passive nationalism of the growing urban proletariat and the agrarian masses oppressed by the feudalism of the *sipahi* and the *kodjabashi,* had expressed themselves in active nationalism. It had been this trading-class bourgeois nationalism that had activated the Greek "war of national liberation" through the *Filiki Etairia,* the foremost members of which had been Greek traders living abroad. At the time this bourgeoisie had played a progressive role, Kordatos wrote, again quoting Marx, opposing certain Greek Communists such as Zachariadis or Zevgos who maintained that the Greek bourgeoisie had been reactionary from the very outset. If this class had been unable to fulfill all its progressive, liberal

[104] *Ibid.,* p. 289.

[105] Kordatos has written in modern Greek the following works: *History of Ancient Greece* (3 vols.; Athens: Publications of the Twentieth Century, 1955–1956); *History of Modern Greece* (4 vols.; Athens: Publications of the Twentieth Century, 1957–1968); *New Prolegomana to Homer* (Athens: Publications of the Twentieth Century, 1951); *The Social Significance of the Greek Revolution of 1821* (Athens, 1924); *Pages from the History of the Agrarian Movement in Greece* (Athens: Historical Philological Institute Yannis Kordatos, 1964); *History of Province of Volo and Aghia from Ancient Times to the Present* (Athens: Publications of the Twentieth Century, 1960).

aims, it failed because during the revolution the feudal Greek landowning class, the *kodjabashi,* and the higher clergy together with the big shipowners had managed to take over the leadership of the revolution. To this outcome foreign powers had contributed in their own reactionary way. In no way had the Greek "national liberation struggle" of 1821 been the creation of a popular struggle of the lower class, of bankrupt merchants, of clerks of trading concerns, of simple sailors, of small property owners, or of poor peasants. To believe that would be to fall into the error of "spontaneity."[106]

In general, viewing the present in order to divine future trends, it might be said that within the territory of the nation-state itself, ethnic and social homogeneity is increasing because of the breakdown of the peasant economy and the gradual development of a farm economy, the tighter complex of roads, the rise in literacy, and the great increase in broadcasting and the number of radio sets throughout the country. The emergence of a new postwar generation that does not differentiate between native-born and refugees; the higher average age of the population caused by the low birth rate and considerable emigration; educational reforms and economic development, are other endogenous factors that will surely have a bearing on future trends.[107] There are exogenous factors, too, which must be considered: the steady communications bombardments from outside by the Voice of America, the BBC, or Radio Moscow, for example; the foreign language translations encouraged by outside powers, the closer people-to-people communications through the influx of tourists and the outflow of workers to Germany and elsewhere in Europe. What bearing will these factors have on

[106] *History of Modern Greece,* I, 9–10, 17–19, 21–23, 28. Rhigas, he stresses, wanted to transform the Ottoman Empire into a republican confederation and planned not a social but a national revolution, *ibid.,* p. 336. Also II, 7–12, and IV, 8–11. Kordatos' distinction between active and passive nationalism, which he does not develop, and the great importance that he attaches to the *Filiki Etairia* as an activating factor in the Greek revolution suggests that his Marxist historical materialism was not unaffected by Leninism with the *Etairia* constituting a sort of "vanguard of the bourgeoisie" and of the whole nation.

[107] I. T. Sanders, *The Rainbow and the Rock* (Cambridge, Mass.: Harvard University Press, 1962), p. 304. Sanders sees a growth from village parochialism to nationalism, a growing sense of villagers that the central government is concerned with their welfare, and their transformation from subjects into citizens, in other words, greater national cohesiveness. *Ibid.,* pp. 315–16.

Greek nationalism? In the past, reflexively or mimetically, outside factors played a significant role in molding Greek nationalism even in a period when international communications were far less developed than they are today. Just as in the sixteenth century post-Byzantine painters introduced western perspective in their icons, or just as Eastern Orthodox Russia of the tsars embraced Marxism, an ideology of the industrial revolution of western Europe, so is it possible for moccasins and blue jeans to be worn and made even in states that are only in the take-off stage of economic development.

At present, at any rate, Greek nationalism seems to have two faces, one turned West, the other turned East. This resembles the dualistic situation prevailing at the time of the Crimean War, which had marked the end of the British, French, and Russian parties in the politics of the newly established Greek state. Reading the debates of Parliament on foreign policy issues such as Cyprus between 1954–59, one cannot avoid such an impression, especially in view of the nationalistic phenomena of polycentrism observable in states of what used to be called the Soviet bloc. In these debates, both pro-westerners and pro-easterners accused each other of supranational loyalties and sought to monopolize for themselves the assets of nationalism and patriotism.

Further investigation, however, would be required to provide real insight into such problems. In a world that seems to be developing from loose bipolarity to multipolarity, a nationalistic rejection of both East and West, a "plague on both your houses" attitude is not to be excluded. In the Greek Communist Party, or EDA, the pro-Soviet elements appear at present to have the upper hand. Thus a turn toward Peking seems unlikely. Besides, Albania has pre-empted such a position, and the nationalist overtones of Greek communism would preclude such a turn. Uncommittedness would be another possibility. Would this be in the style of Yugoslavia or of the United Arab Republic? General Grivas-Dighenis, during his EOKA period at least (1955–59), strongly advocated a move to- ward both Tito and Nasser,[108] but, as the then Greek Foreign Minister pointed out, this would leave Greece without any countervailing force in the Balkans. Many Greeks feel more western European than just western, even though Greeks going, for example, to Paris,

[108] Grivas-Dighenis, *Memoirs of the EOKA Struggle, 1955–1959,* p. 197.

used to say until quite recently that they were going to Europe. Greece has become an associate member of the European Economic Community. In spite of close political relations with Great Britain and the United States in the postwar period and attitudes of sympathy toward those two nations until the Cyprus problem was raised in the United Nations in 1954, French culture had preserved a powerful hold on the Greek elite. In the United Nations most Greek representatives still deliver their speeches in French, while the Ministry for Foreign Affairs gets the official U.N. records in the French, not English, version. Greek stereotypes about the "Anglo-Saxons" usually derive from French sources. For most Greeks an "Atlantic Community" is a chimerical notion. Thus it is not inconceivable that the westernism in Greek nationalism should pin itself more to the concept of a *Europe des patries*. That concept holds much attraction for the Greeks who, not unlike the French, find solace in their memories of past grandeur and always seek somehow to discover new ways for restoring it. Even before de Gaulle, a sort of Gaullism existed in Greece, nurtured by a deep sense of history and a lively sense of national pride coupled with a realization of political weakness.

The military officers who carried out the "Revolution of April 21, 1967," included admirers of De Gaulle. Their authoritarian regime stresses in its slogans that Greece is—and should be—a country of Greek Christians. This shows how modern Greek nationalism as a secular religion still retains powerful religious overtones, to a great extent as a response now to the challenge of the Marxist-Leninist, even Maoist, opiate of the working classes that prevails in countries to the north of Greece. It shows, too, that this nationalism is regarded as a psychosocial shield for maintaining the national identity of the Greeks as a group against what is felt to be an always potentially threatening and vast sea of Slavdom at the north, somewhat as Israelism and Jewishness fulfill a similar function for a people who feel surrounded by a furiously hostile ocean of Muslim Arabs.

GEORGE BARANY

Hungary: From Aristocratic to Proletarian Nationalism[*]

I

The remarkable thing about Hungarian nationalism is that, as the French say, the more it changes the more it remains the same. Unlike the peasant nationalisms of some East Central European peoples awakened by the clergy and by an educated national intelligentsia, premodern Hungarian nationalism, like its Polish or Croatian counterparts, had deep roots in the class consciousness of the Hungarian nobility. Imbued with the Catholic idea of the unity of the lands belonging to the Crown of St. Stephen,[1] and jealous of its economic and legal privileges, this Hungarian "feudal" nationalism became at times (in the sixteenth and seventeenth centuries) violently Protestant and anti-Habsburg[2] without questioning, how-

[*] Part of the material used in this study was gathered on a research trip to Austria in the summer of 1964. The trip was made possible by an award of the American Council of Learned Societies for which the author wishes to express his thanks. Gratefully acknowledged is also a supplementary grant of the Austrian Ministry of Education. The friendly criticism of Professors Peter F. Sugar, of the University of Washington, Seattle, and Theodore R. Crane, of the University of Denver, has helped eliminate some of the shortcomings of the paper. For the remaining ones as well as for the views expressed, the author alone bears full responsibility.

[1] For the formation of the theory of the Crown of St. Stephen, cf. Charles d'Eszlary, *Histoire des institutions publiques hongroises*, II (Paris: Librairie Marcel Rivière et Cie, 1963), 7–15.

[2] Recent Marxian approaches to this "feudal" or "estates nationalism" are Ágnes R. Várkonyi's "A nemzet, a haza fogalma a török harcok és a Habsburg-ellenes

ever, the essentially multiracial character of the Hungarian state.

The concept of a feudal "class-nation," however, was not entirely free from a feeling of xenophobia that the privileges granted by the crown to immigrants tended to keep alive. Also, the idea that Hungary had a mission to fulfill as a "bastion of Christianity," defending Europe against the infidel, first the Mongol and later the Turk, can be followed from the thirteenth century to the baroque vision of the poet-statesman Zrinyi in the seventeenth. Xenophobia and a sense of a mission were frequently mixed in a rather peculiar way in such periods of decline as the sixteenth century when the major part of Hungary was under the Turk and the rest of the country was divided between competing Habsburgs and semi-independent Transylvanian princes.[3]

The imperial armies that liberated Hungary from the Ottoman yoke at the end of the seventeenth century did not bring much relief to the devastated country, as shown by the mass support given to the anti-Habsburg uprisings led by István Bocskay, Imre Thököly, and Ferencz II Rákóczi in the seventeenth and eighteenth centuries. These movements, fomented by social unrest, turned temporarily into nationwide upheavals in which Magyar and non-Magyar nationalities fought shoulder to shoulder under the leadership of the Hungarian feudal nobility.

Protestantism, too, tended to burst class-bound Hungarian feudal "nationalism." As elsewhere, it promoted use of the vernacular and aroused the interest in education. It also strengthened the country's spiritual ties with the Protestant West, turning Hungarian minds into receptive vehicles for the ideas of freedom of conscience, religious liberty, and toleration. All pre-nineteenth century Hungarian anti-Habsburg "national" struggles were fought *cum deo pro patria et libertate,* as suggested by Rákóczi's standards, the term *libertas* meaning not only ancient liberties and feudal privileges but also

küzdelmek idején, 1526–1711," in A *magyar nacionalizmus kialakulása és története* (Budapest: Kossuth kiadó, 1964). Introd. by Erzsébet Andics, pp. 27–78. Cited hereafter as *Magyar Nationalism.* Erik Molnár, "Ideológiai kérdések a feudalizmusban. A nemzeti kérdéshez," *Történelmi Szemle,* IV, No. 3 (1961), 261–78; Pál Zsigmond Pach, "A 'haza' fogalma az osztálytársadalmakban (Hozzászólás Molnár Erik: Ideológiai kérdések a feudalizmusban c. tanulmányához)," *Századok,* XCVI, Nos. 1–2 (1962), 393–99.

[3] Dominic G. Kosáry, A *History of Hungary* (Cleveland: Benjamin Franklin Bibliophile Society, 1941), p. 117.

the free exercise of religion. Calvinism was frequently referred to as the "Magyar creed," and "Protestant," "Magyar," and "rebel" were synonyms during the Catholic counterreformation and the strengthening of Habsburg absolutism in the seventeenth and eighteenth centuries.[4]

Remainders of a sense of Christian mission rooted in the medieval Hungarian kingdom and confirmed by centuries of warfare against the Turk, anti-Habsburg traditions, and Protestant dissent have to be considered along with Verbőczi's class-conscious constitutional concept of *una eademque nobilitas* if one intends to examine the transformation of Hungarian feudal, or "estates" nationalism into modern Magyar national consciousness, a change that occurred approximately between the mid-eighteenth and mid-nineteenth century. In the initial phase of this process, Hungarian feudal nationalism was still primarily a political-legal, i.e., premodern and *a*-national, concept, in spite of its predominantly Magyar character[5] and Protestant outlook. But the twin stimuli of Enlightenment and Romanticism brought about a literary-cultural revival that resulted in an identification of language and national character, a phenomenon not completely unknown before but generally accepted only at the end of the eighteenth and the beginning of the nineteenth century.[6]

The romantic notion that each people has to fulfill its peculiar destiny in its own vernacular coupled with the enlightened ideas

[4] For the role of Protestantism in Hungarian national life, see C. A. Macartney, *Hungary* (London: E. Benn, 1934), pp. 149 ff. and Mihály Bucsay, *Geschichte des Protestantismus in Ungarn* (Stuttgart: Evangelisches Verlagswerk, 1959).

[5] Although the overwhelming majority of the Hungarian nobility was Magyar, the line between Magyar and non-Magyar was not sharply drawn. The powerful Hunyadi family in the fifteenth century was of Romanian origin, the Zrinyis in the sixteenth were Croats, and half of Kossuth's kinship was Slovak. According to the calculation of Elek Fényes, *Magyarország statistikája* (3 vols.; Pest: Trattner-Károlyi, 1842), I, 64 and 118, out of Hungary's population of 11,187,288 in 1840 (without Transylvania), 544,372 persons belonged to the nobility. The latter figure included "about 58,000 Slavs, 21,666 Germans and Romanians, thus leaving 464,705 Magyar-speaking nobles."

[6] For occasional examples of the ethnic-linguistic identification of Magyardom with the *Hungarica natio* or *gens Hungarica* dating back to the thirteenth and fourteenth centuries, see Erik Molnár, "Ideológiai kérdések a feudalizmusban," pp. 273–77. These examples suggest that the ambiguity inherent in the term Magyar—Hungarian can be traced back to the very beginnings of the organized Hungarian state. Cf. Elemér Mályusz, "Haza és nemzet a magyarországi feudalizmus első századaiban" and Antal Bartha, "Hozzászólás Mályusz Elemér előadásához," *Történelmi Szemle*, VI, No. 1 (1963), 4–10 and 56–68, respectively.

that the vernacular is the key to the dissemination of knowledge and that progress is a patriotic duty led to a sharp clash of different linguistic nationalisms. Given the Magyar nobility's legal-constitutional supremacy and its jealous efforts to assert ancient privileges against the centralizing and Germanizing trends emanating from Vienna, Magyar cultural nationalism as reflected in a trend toward Magyarization soon acquired[7] much-resented political overtones. This resentment was not diminished by the fact that some Hungarian political leaders tried to defend feudal institutions and national and social oppression by using arguments produced in the libertarian spirit of western parliaments.

In fact, the resistance of the ruling nobility frustrated many progressive reforms of eighteenth century benevolent and enlightened absolutism. The nobility's refusal to give up its tax exemption was interrelated with an imperial tariff system that hurt Hungary's economic development but also strengthened the trends for economic separatism. This ultimately helped Kossuth in his agitation for a politically motivated Industrial Protective Union, which was but a manifestation of modern economic nationalism on Hungarian soil.[8] The ramifications of this economic nationalism came increasingly to the fore after 1867, to reach their culminating point around the turn of the century in the demand for a completely independent Hungarian customs territory.

Joseph II's policy of centralization and Germanization contributed to the rise of both Magyar and non-Magyar nationalisms by generating an atmosphere of mutual suspicion. The death of Joseph II gave a chance to the Hungarian Estates to have their ancient liberties confirmed by the dynasty. The Diet of 1790–91 stressed that Hungary was an independent and free kingdom with a constitution of its own and had to be governed in accordance with its own laws and customs and not according to the norms applied to other provinces. The Estates, incidentally, based some of their arguments on

---

[7] János Varga, "A nemzeti nyelv szerepe a polgári fejlődésben Magyarországon," *Történelmi Szemle*, IV, No. 3 (1961), 284–301.

[8] For details and bibliography, see Julius Miskolczy, *Ungarn in der Habsburger-Monarchie* (Vienna-Munich: Vlg. Herold, 1959), pp. 20–33, 63 ff., 71–79. For Kossuth, see Domokos Kosáry, *Kossuth és a védegylet. A magyar nacionalizmus történetéhez* (Budapest: Athenaeum, 1942). Cf. R. W. Seton-Watson, "Metternich and Internal Austrian Policy—II," *The Slavonic and East European Review*, XVIII, No. 52 (July, 1939), 137 ff.

the social contract and the political theories of the Enlightenment.[9] True, the French revolution and the discovery of the Martinovics plot, which was partially a reaction against the re-establishment of Estates supremacy[10] served Vienna well in keeping revived Hungarian feudal nationalism under control. But from the third decade of the nineteenth century, the nobility began to play the role of the "third estate" since a western-type bourgeoisie either was entirely absent or was lacking in social prestige and too weak numerically and economically to give leadership to the modernization of national life. To be sure, the most progressive elements of the nobility endeavored to strengthen the middle classes, and the latter contributed to the westernization of Hungarian society and political life. Yet the dominant role of the nobility, unchallenged before 1848 and voluntarily accepted after 1867, left a lasting imprint upon the development of a Magyar intelligentsia and the evolution of modern nationalism in Hungary.[11]

It was the nobility that, as a reaction against the Germanization under Joseph II, took up the fight in 1790 and thereafter, first for equal standing, and then for the supremacy, of the Magyar idiom.[12] Similarly, the pioneers of the eighteenth-century Magyar literary and cultural revival were mostly members of Maria Theresa's noble guard. Inspired by the French and German enlightenment, these "westernizers" set out to create a literature for Hungarians with the

---

[9] Bálint Hóman and Gyula Szekfü, *Magyar Történet* (2d. ed.; Budapest: Kir Magy. Egyetemi Ny., 1936), V, 56 f., 73 f. Cited hereafter as *Hungarian History*. Cf. Peter F. Sugar, "The Influence of the Enlightenment and the French Revolution in Eighteenth Century Hungary," *Journal of Central European Affairs*, XVII, No. 4 (1958), 331–55.

[10] For the Martinovics conspiracy, see Kálmán Benda (ed.), *A magyar jakobinus mozgalom iratai* (3 vols.; Budapest: Akadémiai kiadó, 1952–57), in *Fontes Historiae Hungaricae Aevi Recentioris*, cited hereafter as *Fontes;* also, Ernest Wangermann, *From Joseph II to the Jacobin Trials* (Oxford, 1959), especially pp. 71, 77, 86 ff., 103, 138 f., 153, 156, 173 ff., 179–83; for the rejection of the traditional concept of the Magyar "political nation" by Martinovics, see Endre Arató, *A nemzetiségi kérdés története Magyarországon—1790–1848* (2 vols.; Budapest: Akadémiai Kiadó, 1960), I, 63–67. Cited hereafter as *The Nationality Question*.

[11] Hugh Seton Watson, " 'Intelligentsia' und Nationalismus in Osteuropa 1848–1918," *Historische Zeitschrift*, CXCV, No. 2 (Oct., 1962), 335 f., 339 f.

[12] The pertinent documentation is available in Gyula Szekfü (ed.), *Iratok a magyar államnyelv kérdésének történetéhez 1790–1848* (Budapest: Magyar Történelmi Társulat, 1926), in *Fontes*, cited hereafter as *Documents*. For a critique of the shortcomings of Szekfü's collection, see Arató, *The Nationality Question*, I, 310 f.

intention of elevating them to the cultural level of Europe and of promoting the cause of the fatherland. Political, linguistic, and cultural issues continued to interpenetrate each other even after the emergence of Count István Széchenyi.[13]

Characteristically, the "father of Hungarian reform" began his political career with the foundation of the National Academy at the Diet of 1825. Considered as the opening of the "age of reforms" in Hungary, this gesture coincided with the publication of Vörösmarty's epic *Zalán's Flight* (*Zalán futása*), which, in turn, marked the beginning of an era of "national romanticism" in literature. Vörösmarty and most of his friends were also noblemen, but their writings were destined for an entire nation, not only for the feudal classes. "National romanticism," then, was a unifying spiritual force that tended to eliminate sectional and religious differences from cultural life and prepared the road for the generation of Petőfi and Arany with whom the "people" triumphantly entered the literary scene.[14]

In the wake of European romanticism, Hungarians, too, were looking for their "historical roots." But Herder's prediction concerning the absorption of Magyars by surrounding Slavs, Germans, Romanians, and other peoples[15] had a traumatic effect and may serve as partial explanation, if not as justification, for subsequent efforts to make Magyar the universally accepted language in multinational Hungary and to press Magyarization on the non-Magyar inhabitants of the kingdom. Also, the misinterpretation of Herder may have

---

[13] For literary trends of the late eighteenth and early nineteenth century, see G. F. Cushing, "The Birth of National Literature in Hungary," *The Slavonic and East European Review*, XXXVIII, No. 91 (June, 1960), 459–75. For the Magyar cultural renascence in general, see the introductory chapter of Mihály Horváth, *Huszonöt év Magyarország történelméből* (3d ed.; 3 vols.; Budapest: Ráth M., 1886), still the most informative interpretation, in a liberal nationalist spirit, of the period.

[14] Gyula Farkas, A "*Fiatal Magyarország*" *kora* (Budapest: Magyar Szemle, 1932), pp. 8–11; also Farkas, *A magyar romantika* (Budapest: Akadémiai kiadó, 1930).

[15] "Da sind sie [i.e. the Magyars] jetzt unter Slawen, Deutschen, Wlachen und andern Völkern der geringere Theil der Landeseinwohner, und nach Jahrhunderten wird man vielleicht ihre Sprache kaum finden." Johann Gottfried Herder, *Ideen zur Philosophie der Geschichte der Menschheit*. Pt. IV, Book XVI, chap. 2, pp. 660 f. in *Herders Werke*, ed. Eugen Kuhnsmann, Vol. LXXVII of the series *Deutsche National-Literatur, Historisch-kritische Ausgabe,* ed. Joseph Kurschner (Stuttgart, n.d. [First ed., 1791]). Herder's subsequent more optimistic remarks regrading the development of Magyar language and literature went unheeded in Hungary. Tibor Joó, *A magyar nemzeteszme* (Budapest: Franklin, n.d. [1939]), p. 106.

contributed to the fact that the dominating trend in Hungarian literary and art criticism has always been to regard literature and art as a service to the nation whose task it is to promote patriotism, and to fight against cosmopolitanism and "foreign" decadence.[16]

The appearance of modern Magyar national consciousness coincided with the awakening of non-Magyar peoples in Hungary. But the aristocratic superiority complex of, first, the Magyar nobility and then the rising intelligentsia and middle classes refused to apply the same standards to "historic" Magyar nationalism defying "despotic" Vienna and to Croatian, Romanian, or Slovak petitions asking for their idioms' equal rights and complaining about Magyar oppression. Actually, increasing awareness of national differences suggested to Magyar leaders that perhaps something ought to be done to repair the numerical inferiority of the ruling race.

Magyarization, however, was deeply resented by non-Magyars. True, the noblest representatives of early nineteenth century Magyar nationalism—Kölcsey, Széchenyi, and Wesselényi—were imbued with the enlightened ideas of western liberalism. This and their Christian principles prevented them from supporting forcible Magyarization even when it was being pushed, from the eighteen thirties, with increasing urgency. Yet the leaders of early Magyar liberalism did not always reflect the mood of the majority of the nobility, although one should perhaps make a distinction at this point between the more cosmopolitan and *Habsburgtreu* aristocracy and higher clergy and the more Magyar-minded masses of common noblemen. Furthermore, the letter and spirit of laws enacted by the Diet and sanctioned by the monarch were frequently "adjusted" on the local level by the semiautonomous county administrations that took the interpretation of the law in their own hands.

The patriotic endeavors aimed at embellishing the Magyar idiom and at promoting its use in public life instead of German or Latin were paralleled, as early as the last decade of the eighteenth century, by a forceful Magyarization campaign in the contemporary press, in numerous pamphlets, and in the correspondence circulated among the counties. This agitation extolled the alleged virtues of Magyardom and ridiculed the "scandalous" dreams of non-

[16] See the excellent article of G. F. Cushing, "Problems of Hungarian Literary Criticism," *The Slavonic and East European Review,* XI, No. 95 (June, 1962), 341–55.

Magyars of having separate national entities; it also suggested that Croats, Germans, and so on, become Magyars since only Magyars are capable of forming a nation.[17]

The attempt at Magyarization could not but fail; yet it was made as soon as a younger generation of Magyar nationalists were strong enough to force the hands of Vienna and its supporters. Thus, old-fashioned Hungarian estates nationalism was rapidly turning into linguistic and political Magyar nationalism without, however, abandoning completely its feudal basis. The difference in western languages between the meanings of the words "Hungarian" and "Magyar," is unknown in Hungarian and was but one of the manifold signs indicative of the birthpangs of modern Magyar and central European nationalisms.

Széchenyi's activities gave new direction to awakening Magyar nationalism.[18] His idea of the "ennoblement" of his nation created a new Magyar nation concept that embraced all Hungarians regardless of social class, a vision far above the restricted "political nation" idea of feudal Hungary. Based on conservative gradualism but radical compared to the outlook of an older generation, his proposals would have transformed the feudal constitution and would have prepared the way for the complete emancipation of the serf.[19] Actually, the liberation of the serf in Hungary was due to the agitation of Kossuth rather than Széchenyi. Under the pressure of a progressive noble elite led by Kossuth, and in a revolutionary climate generated by external events, the nobility was willing to give up its constitutional and social privileges in the spring of 1848, a major step toward the real national unity of which Széchenyi dreamed. But the social precondition of this national unity of Magyars, brought about by the enlightened liberalism and the democratic spirit of the West that penetrated Hungary, was sanctioned

---

[17] E. Arató, "Die verschiedenen Formen der nationalen Unterdrückung in Osteuropa und die Madjarisierung in der ersten Hälfte des 19. Jahrhunderts," *Studien zur Geschichte der Österreichisch-Ungarischen Monarchie* (Budapest: Akadémiai kiadó, 1961), pp. 423 ff.

[18] For Széchenyi, see the bibliographical references in my study, *Stephen Széchenyi and the Awakening of Hungarian Nationalism, 1791–1841* (Princeton: Princeton University Press, 1968).

[19] István Barta (ed.), *Széchenyi István válogatott írásai* (Budapest: Gondolat, 1959), p. 183.

by the reactionary Bach regime after 1849 with the opposite aim of weakening that same national unity.[20]

Széchenyi's nationalism took into account the realities of Hungary's international position. Instead of frustrating legalistic opposition to the other half of the empire, he suggested an economically sound patriotism and the elimination of "Hungarocentric" thinking.[21]

To Széchenyi, nationality was a moral category, inseparably interrelated with his ideas on education and Christianity. His aristocratic background and loyalty to the dynasty were additional moderating factors. But he, too, intended to Magyarize, though only through "spiritual supremacy." This is why Széchenyi's thinking was much abused both during the latter half of the nineteenth century and under the neoconservative regime between the two world wars. Similarly exaggerated and distorted were the racial overtones undoubtedly present in his writings, and his obsession with oriental Magyar "uniqueness" and "national sins."[22] But it is true that in the more conservative phase of his career, Széchenyi became increasingly concerned with the intimate connection between social reform and the nationality problem.

This apprehension was not without foundation. The peasants participating in the cholera uprising of 1831 were mostly Slovak, Ruthenian, and Romanian serfs who revolted against their Magyar lords; henceforth, there was a certain association of the peasant and nationality questions in the minds of many a noble landowner.[23] By the eighteen forties, Széchenyi, too, was afraid lest an excessively liberal reform of the constitution weaken the leading role of the numerically inferior Magyar element. Yet he emphatically cautioned against forced Magyarization. His courageous stand, taken especially in his book *People of the Orient* (*Kelet Népe*, 1841) and in

[20] Gyula Szekfü (ed.), *Mi a magyar?* (Budapest: Magyar Szemle Társaság, 1939), pp. 550 f.

[21] Iványi-Grünwald (ed.), *Hitel* (Budapest: Magyar Történelmi Társulat, 1930), pp. 279 f., 328, 351, 360–63, 430, 465, 490 f.

[22] See e.g., Szekfü's Széchenyi interpretation in Hóman and Szekfü, *Hungarian History*, V, 260 f. and 272 f. For a Marxist critique of Szekfü's extremely influential and in many ways misleading Széchenyi portrait, cf. Gyula Mérei, "Szekü Gyula történetszemléletének birálatához," *Századok*, XCIV, Nos. 1–3 (1960), 216–20.

[23] Arató, *The Nationality Question*, I, 27 f., 190, 245 f., 252.

his Academy address of 1842, made him extremely popular among the non-Magyars of Hungary but alienated from him most of his former liberal admirers.[24]

But Széchenyi, too, saw the salvation of his nation in "giving preference to the rescuing of our [Magyar] nationality even over the immaculate purity of our constitution."[25] Aristocratic and moderate nationalist that he was, he visualized the possibility or perhaps necessity of having to choose between ethnic rights and constitutional liberty, like the Romanian patriot Bălcescu in 1848, who went by the assumption that "Until a people can exist as a nation, it cannot make use of liberty."[26] Thus in Hungary the change of central European nationalism described by Hans Kohn as one giving precedence to national rights over human liberty[27] can be traced back to the Age of Reforms. True, Széchenyi always condemned the violation of human rights; but there was an ambiguity even in his romantic nationalism, suggesting that it was extremely difficult to draw the line in a sober and consistent way once the idea of nationality had been accepted as guiding principle. Indeed, humanitarian and moderate nationalists like Eötvös or Deák frequently failed to realize before 1848 that there was a line at all. This is why they, too, supported Kossuth in the polemics between *Pesti Hirlap* and the *People of the Orient;* and this is also why Aurel Dessewffy, leader of the young conservatives who agreed with Széchenyi on the issue of the dangers inherent in Kossuth's agitation, reproached the former of having started the agitation with the publication of his works *Credit* (*Hitel,* 1830) and *Light* (*Világ,* 1831).[28]

Throughout his public career, Széchenyi tried to coordinate Hun-

[24] For details and further references, see the substantial article by Francis S. Wagner, "Széchenyi and the Nationality Problem in the Habsburg Empire," *Journal of Central European Affairs,* XX, No. 3 (Oct., 1960), pp. 289–311. For Széchenyi's popularity among non-Magyars, see Palacký's opinion cited by Saint-René Taillandier, "Hommes d'Etat de la Hongrie. Le comte Stephan Széchenyi," *Revue des deux mondes,* LXX (Aug. 1, 1867), 653 f.; also, Arató, *The Nationality Question,* II, 51 f. and 236 f.

[25] Zoltán Ferenczi (ed.), *Gr. Széchenyi István, A kelet népe* (Budapest: Magyar Történelmi Társulat, 1925), in *Fontes,* p. 215. Cited hereafter as *People of the Orient.*

[26] Cited in Hans Kohn, *The Twentieth Century* (New York: Macmillan, 1957), p. 15.

[27] *Ibid.,* pp. 14 f.

[28] X. Y. Z. (Aurel Dessewffy), "Pesti Hirlap és Kelet Népe közti vitály" in Ferenczi, *People of the Orient,* pp. 590 ff.; also, *ibid.,* Introduction, pp. 90 f.

garian national aims with the over-all interests of the *Gesamtmonarchie.* But Lajos Kossuth's paper, *Pesti Hirlap,* from its beginning (1841), touched upon Hungary's international position and relationship with Austria, and upon its industrialization and trade connections with foreign countries. These issues could not be solved unilaterally and were bound to bring about a clash with the other half of the empire and possibly even with the non-Magyar parts of the kingdom if pursued consistently on a narrowly nationalistic basis. Also, Kossuth's nationalism points from the initial demand for Magyar national unity through unification with Transylvania[29] with increasing clarity toward the goal of an independent nation-state between the German and Russian colossi.[30] Resuming Wesselényi's agitation of the early thirties for Hungary's unification with Transylvania and for the emancipation of serfs, Kossuth failed to inherit Wesselényi's sensitivity to the claims of non-Magyars.[31] Actually, Kossuth openly reversed St. Stephen's admonition of the inherent weakness of a unilingual nation as being "in contradiction with the changed circumstances and with the more recent teachings of political science."[32] While recognizing the municipal rights of Croatia, he denied separate nationhood to that country since "there is but one *nation* here" (Kossuth's italics) and "I shall never but never recognize, under the Holy Crown of Hungary, more than one nation and nationality, the Magyar."[33] This reinterpretation of "Hungary's integrity"[34] on the basis of the exclusive national rights of the Magyar nation came to be regarded as the official creed of all

[29] See his leader "Transylvania and the Union—Unity for the Magyar," in No. 30 (Apr. 14, 1841) of *Pesti Hirlap,* reprinted in Ferenczi, *People of the Orient,* pp. 183 ff.

[30] Reply to an article of the *Augsburger Allgemeine Zeitung* in *Pesti Hirlap,* 1842, No. 179, as cited in Domokos Kosáry, "A Pesti Hirlap nacionalizmusa," *Századok,* LXXVII (1943), 375.

[31] Miklós Asztalos, *Wesselényi Miklós, az első nemzetiségi politikus* (Pécs, 1927), pp. 6, 19.

[32] Speech in the Diet, Dec. 10, 1847, republished in István Barta (ed.), *Kossuth Lajos az utolsó rendi országgyűlésen, 1847–48* (Budapest: Akadémiai kiadó, 1951), *Wesselényi Miklós . . . ,* pp. 19, 47 f.

[33] Speech in the Diet, Dec. 11, 1847, *ibid.,* p. 382; also, Jan. 7, 1848, *ibid.,* p. 435. For similar views held by Deák at the Diet of 1839–40, see Oscar Jászi, *The Dissolution of the Habsburg Monarchy* (Chicago: University of Chicago Press, 1929), p. 305.

[34] Speech in a circular session of the Diet, Jan. 8, 1848, Barta, *Kossuth at the Diet,* p. 439.

Magyar politicians for almost a century, although Kossuth himself had to repent his blunder in the long years of exile.

Thus the national awakening initiated by Széchenyi, which followed the feudal nationalism of the late eighteenth century, was in turn transformed, during the pre-March period, into a dynamic force unable to assert itself without reaching for political power as embodied in a modern nation-state. The younger liberal generation, inspired by the literary and national renaissance of the thirties and forties when even Vienna saw fit to make serious concessions to the Magyar idiom, had few qualms concerning the correctness of its stand. In fact, it even failed to heed Wesselényi's *Admonition in the Matter of Magyar and Slav Nationality* (*Szózat a magyar és szláv nemzetiség ügyében*, 1843), which was hardly reviewed by the contemporary press.[35] But Wesselényi's *Admonition* too, reflected that liberal Russophobia that, on the Hungarian scene, exaggerated the dangers of *Slavismus* and thus contributed to the aggressiveness of Magyar nationalism. Liberals, including Wesselényi, Kossuth, and Deák, and the majority of Magyar public opinion tended to overestimate the political potentials of Russian Pan-Slavism; underestimating, at the time, the dynamism of the autochthonous nation-forming processes among the non-Magyars in the Habsburg domains. The double error, paid for so dearly by Hungary in 1848–49, was aggravated by their illusion that an independent, strong Hungary in alliance with Austria was preferable from the standpoint of Vienna to her traditional allies, Russia and Prussia.

Yet Hungary's relationship with Vienna began to obtain a new political meaning during the pre-March, thanks to the organizational abilities and the skillful maneuvering of Kossuth. True, Kossuth's agitation for an Industrial Protective Union brought but meager economic results. Yet it succeeded in focusing the public's attention on the alleged economic exploitation of Hungary by Austria. This assisted the opposition in winning over the impoverished gentry and the pauperized masses of the "sandal nobility," forces that had originally been mobilized by Vienna and its young conservative supporters against the liberal party in the early forties.[36]

Behind the different spheres of Kossuth's activities there is the

---

[35] Asztalos, *Wesselényi Miklós* . . . , pp. 21, 34–40.
[36] Kosáry, *Kossuth és a védegylet,* pp. 4 *passim.*

driving force of nationalism, which, in a suppressed article written at the end of 1845, he identified with the love for the fatherland, "in which I know no exaggeration and in which, in my opinion, even the rise to fanaticism is only moderation."[37] But it is easy to overstress Kossuth's role in discussing modern Magyar nationalism before 1848.[38] Hungary's greatest poet in the nineteenth century, Sándor Petőfi, leader of the radical intelligentsia, was far from tolerant toward his non-Magyar compatriots although he dreamed of a world revolution. Mihály Táncsics, champion of the embryonic Hungarian proletariat, was a rabid nationalist who suggested the linking of the emancipation of the serf with a Magyarization program designed for the peasantry. Also favoring the unification of the historic lands of old Hungary under Magyar leadership, the radical democrats, more progressive in their social demands than the liberals, differed but little from the latter regarding their national program.[39]

This incipient Magyar imperialism to which even conservatives had to make concessions became a widely held popular creed. It was strengthened by the mistaken belief that no human or national rights were violated by relegating the non-Magyar idioms to the sphere of private life, and that by extending the privileges of the constitution and granting civil rights on an individual basis to non-Magyars, the latter would be eternally obliged to liberal Magyardom.[40] True, with the experience of twentieth-century totalitarian nationalisms, the granting of civil liberty to the individual must not be taken too lightly. Yet, founded on a twofold misconception, the hopes of liberal Magyar imperialism brought only bitter fruits in both 1848 and the "Era of Dualism" after 1867.

The process of both natural and forcible Magyarization has brought its most tangible results in the Hungarian towns; in the

---

[37] Cited, after an article by Viszota, in Kosáry, *Kossuth és a védegylet*, p. 5.

[38] For the limitations of Kossuth's radicalism in the pre-March, so frequently misunderstood in the West, see chaps. iii-iv in Ervin Szabó, *Társadalmi és pártharcok az 1848–49–es magyar forradalomban* (Budapest: Népszava, n.d.), pp. 46–101. He and Széchenyi, to be sure, were the most important representatives of the two main trends of Magyar nationalism before 1848. Those, however, who stood farther left than Kossuth were no less nationalistically minded.

[39] Arató, *The Nationality Question*, II, 58–68.

[40] Jászi, *The Dissolution of the Habsburg Monarchy*, pp. 307 f.; Asztalos, *Wesselényi Miklós . . .* , pp. 19, 47 f.

smaller villages with mixed population the opposite trend prevailed. Jászi attributed this phenomenon to the concentration of government and expanding capital in the cities, the German and Jewish elements of which were willing to accept, especially after the Compromise of 1867, "the standard of life, the customs, and the political ideology of the gentry."[41] This assimilating force of Magyardom in the urban areas can actually be traced back to earlier periods.[42] In the opinion of Kosáry, the Magyarization program of Kossuth and the liberals was aimed chiefly at the creation of a new Magyar middle class. In his view, nationalism inspired the progressive nobility of the Age of Reforms to "complete" the social structure of the Magyar nation yet to be forged with an up-to-then missing "third estate,"[43] a reversal of the nation-forming process in western Europe.

Communication and exchange of ideas between the nobility and the emerging urban middle classes of Hungary, however, was not a one-way road. Kossuth himself was not only a representative and defender of the interests of the lesser nobility but also a member of the poor intelligentsia on the periphery of the middle classes.[44] True, the fight for the enfranchisement of the urban middle classes failed to bring any results in the Diet prior to 1848. But it is also true that as early as 1841, Pest County granted the right to vote in the county assembly to an increasingly important segment of the nonnoble intelligentsia called the *honoratior class*. The *honoratiors* were mostly professional people, lawyers, physicians, teachers, choirmasters, and it was largely due to their votes that Kossuth was elected deputy of Pest County to the Diet of 1847.[45] Thus the appeal to and mood of this nonnoble element or emerging middle-class intelligentsia began to be rather significant even before 1848 and its further analysis may contribute to our understanding of prevolutionary Magyar nationalism.

[41] Jászi, *The Dissolution of the Habsburg Monarchy*, 274–77, 303 f.

[42] For medieval examples (fourteenth to sixteenth centuries) see Zoltán I. Tóth, "Quelques problèmes de l'état multinational dans la Hongrie d'avant 1848," *Acta Historica*, IV, Nos. 1–3 (1955), 131.

[43] Kosáry, "A Pesti Hirlap nacionalizmusa," pp. 407–12.

[44] Domokos Kosáry, *Kossuth Lajos a reformkorban* (Budapest, 1946), p. 369.

[45] For an evaluation of Kossuth's election, see Barta, *Kossuth at the Diet*, pp. 31 ff., 220 ff. For Kossuth's effort to appeal to the patriotic sentiments of the "poorer electorate of Pest County," see his speech held on the eve of the election, Oct. 17, 1847, *ibid.*, p. 211.

One may say, then, that Magyar nationalism in the first half of the nineteenth century was part of a broad modernization process that emanated from the West. The spiritual and economic factors involved could not help affecting all parts of Hungary and, indeed, all of the entire East Central European area. Like other national movements of the region, it was a sign of the advancement of civilization in spite of its many shortcomings and its clashes with similar trends among other peoples. In spite of the feudal remnants surviving in it, Magyar nationalism became, from the eighteen thirties, increasingly antifeudal, i.e., socially progressive and liberal in outlook. In spite of its blindness to the collective national claims of non-Magyars, Magyar nationalism was directly and indirectly interrelated with other branches of central European nationalism in many subtle ways and sometimes even *malgré lui*. Even Kossuth, addressing a delegation of the radical youth in March, 1848, cautioned against the exaggerated claims of Budapest, which he regarded as "the heart but not the master" of revolutionary Hungary, saying

This nation has its liberty, and every member of it wishes to be free. But the term "nation" cannot be arrogated by any one caste or any one city; fatherland and nation consist of fifteen million Hungarians.

To Kossuth, of course, there was but one, indivisible Magyar nation. This "Magyar" nation visualized by him was made up, in its majority, of non-Magyars who could not but benefit, in one way or another, as he put it, from the "constitutional liberty which can unify the races speaking different languages in one common civil nation."[46]

Unfortunately, Kossuth and the leaders of Magyar liberal nationalism, who realized in time that absolute government in the Austrian provinces had an unfortunate impact upon Hungarian affairs, failed to understand, with some rare exceptions, either in 1848 or after 1867 the intimate connections between Magyar and non-Magyar national dynamics in old Hungary.[47]

[46] Barta, *Kossuth at the Diet*, pp. 675, 743. Report on the work of the Diet, Apr. 14, 1848.

[47] For a more detailed analysis and references, see George Barany, "The Awakening of Magyar Nationalism before 1848," *Austrian History Yearbook*, II (1966), 19–50, 52 ff.

II

The revolutionary fight for national independence has been considered by Hungarians as one of the few high points in their nation's modern history. But to contemporaries, the glory of 1848 was adumbrated if not outweighed by the traumatic experience of Russian intervention and the civil war fought against the non-Magyar nationalities. To be sure, the liberal legislation of 1848 did emancipate the peasant and bring about equality before the law and far-reaching civil rights for the individual citizen, yet Batthyány's and Kossuth's governments refused to recognize, with the possible exception of the Croats, the political-national rights of non-Magyars. Although Hungarians managed to achieve complete independence from the Habsburgs for a rather ephemeral period, it was only on the eve of the collapse, on July 28, 1849, that a frightened Parliament in Szeged enacted a nationality law based on the principle of the equality of all nations of Hungary.[48] On the same day, Jews, too, were emancipated; but while Jewish emancipation was to be confirmed by the Compromise of 1867,[49] the latter, with the concomitant legislation affecting the nationalities, was actually a retreat compared to the stillborn Act of July, 1849.

The "platform of 1848" as restored by Deák, Andrássy, and Eötvös in the Compromise of 1867 was also less than the exiled Kossuth and some of his emissaries like Count László Teleki or General Klapka were willing to offer in connection with Kossuth's different plans

[48] For the text of this last-minute effort to reconcile the non-Magyars of Hungary, cf. Gábor G. Kemény, A magyar nemzetiségi kérdés története I. rész. A nemzetiségi kérdés a törvények tükrében, 1790–1918 (Budapest: Gergely, 1946, quoted henceforth as The Nationality Question), I, 36 ff. Ignored largely by nationalist Magyar historiography before the end of World War II, this law remained on the books but was never given a chance. It was intended to grant far-reaching linguistic, cultural, ecclesiastic, and municipal rights to the nationalities, keeping Magyar only as the "diplomatic language" of the administrative, legislative, and military affairs of Hungary. Most importantly, it was not based on the ideology of the one unitary Magyar political nation. Cf. Endre Arató, "A Magyar nacionalizmus kettős arculata a feudalizmusból a kapitalizmusba való átmenet és a polgári forradalom időszakában," in Magyar Nationalism, pp. 102–42; also, the same author's chapters written for György Spira, A magyar forradalom 1848–1849–ben (Budapest: Gondolat, 1959), pp. 146–74; 201–4; 346–58; 556–67; and Zoltán I. Tóth, "The Nationality Problem in Hungary in 1848–1849," Acta Historica, IV, Nos. 1–3 (1955), 235–77.

[49] For the favorable situation of Jews in Hungary's "liberal era," cf. Robert A. Kann, "Hungarian Jewry during Austria-Hungary's Constitutional Period (1867–1918)," Jewish Social Studies, VII, No. 4 (Oct., 1945), 357–86.

for a Danubian-Balkan confederation of small nations. Yet Magyar public opinion, unaware of Kossuth's belated and not quite consistent change of heart, repudiated his socially progressive but constitutionally limited conciliatory gestures in the nationality question. At the same time, Magyar politicians failed to take advantage of the valuable opportunities of the fifties and sixties when, as the saying went, those loyal to the dynasty received as reward what the rebellious Magyars got as punishment.[50] Thus the blunders of the neoabsolutist regime, such as its contempt for the non-Magyar nationalities' demands for political rights or its decision to abolish the self government of cities whose burghers were still mostly German,[51] strengthened Magyar resistance and furthered the assimilation of non-Magyars, including the foreigners in the administration, a process glorified by Mór Jókai in his romantic novel *The New Landlord* (*Az új földesúr*), which became a required reading in all high schools.

In reality, Magyar nationalism under the Bach regime was a mixture of expectation of a miracle, of stubborn resistence to Austrian arbitrariness, and of disillusionment with the spellbinder, Kossuth. Kossuth was still revered in many a peasant hut but he was now blamed for the catastrophe of 1849 by scores of publicists, foremost of whom was the talented novelist, Baron Zsigmond Kemény. This ambivalent attitude is perhaps one of the reasons why there have been historians, both in Hungary and elsewhere, who were inclined to regard Kossuth's plans as unrealistic dreams of an exile divorced from reality.[52] Recognizing the shortcomings of these plans (e.g., insistence on the principle of Hungary's territorial in-

[50] For a survey of the texts of Kossuth's plans for an anti-Habsburg federation of Danubian nations and for a solution of the nationality question of Hungary, on the basis of the law enacted in July, 1849, put forward between mid-1859 and late 1868, cf. Kemény, *The Nationality Question*, I, 42–50. For the reception of Kossuth's —and Count László Teleki's—program in Hungary and its ultimate rejection, cf. György Szabad, "Nacionalizmus és patriotizmus konfliktusa az abszolutizmus korában," in *Magyar Nationalism*, pp. 151–64. For some of the international ramifications of Kossuth's plans cf. the same author's "Kossuth and the British 'Balance of Power' Policy (1859–1861)" in *Études historiques*, publiées par la Commission Nationale des Historiens Hongrois (2 vols.; Budapest: Akadémiai kiadó, 1960), II, 89–135.

[51] Kemény, *The Nationality Question*, I, 38 f. Béla Pukánszky, *Német polgárság magyar földön* (Budapest: Franklin, n.d.), p. 87.

[52] Rudolf Wierer, *Der Föderalismus im Donauraum* (Graz-Köln: Vlg. H. Böhlaus Nachf., 1960), pp. 60 ff.; Lajos Lukács, "Kossuth emigrációs politikájának idealizálásáról," *Századok*, XCVII, No. 4 (1963), 854 f.

tegrity, with the possible exception of Croatia but without regard for Slovaks and Ruthenians), and also the fact that Kossuth failed to repudiate explicitly the mistakes committed in the forties (this, however, was implied in his warnings and in his programs proposing far-reaching legal, linguistic, educational, and municipal rights for *all* the nationalities), it is still fair to point out that in the fifties and early sixties the outcome of the tug-of-war between the dynasty and the Magyars was far from obvious. It was not even sure that Deák's policy of "passive resistance" was going to help the middle nobility and the gentry to the victory achieved in 1867, thanks to external circumstances rather than to domestic conditions. After all, the aristocratic Magyar nationalism of the "Old Conservatives," who alone had access to those in power in the period of neoabsolutism, contributed greatly to the changes that ultimately led to the acceptance of Hungary's home rule.[53] That conservative nationalism *could* become a rallying force for national unity was shown by the solemn manifestations with which people all over Hungary showed their respect to Széchenyi after his suicide in 1860. Eventually, it was under Deák's moderate leadership that conservative and liberal Magyar nationalism united, on the basis of the laws sanctioned by the Crown in April, 1848, and the Pragmatic Sanction, for the restoration of the historic continuity interrupted by the revolutionary events.

The agreement reached with the dynasty and with the Austrian half of the monarchy came to be known as the Compromise of 1867. There is no need to describe it here in any detail; let it be said only that it placed Hungary, in the words of Professor C. A. Macartney,

in a position which in many ways was more favourable than she had enjoyed since Mohács; in some respects, the nation had never before in its history been so truly master of its own destinies.[54]

In addition to receiving complete independence in internal affairs and economic advantages, Hungary also obtained a considerable degree of influence in the direction of the monarchy's foreign rela-

[53] Miskolczy, *Ungarn in der Habsburger-Monarchy*, pp. 119–31.

[54] C. A. Macartney, *Hungary: A Short History* (Chicago: Aldine Publishing Co., 1962), p. 171. Cf. the recent comprehensive study, *Der österreichisch-ungarische Ausgleich von 1867. Vorgeschichte und Wirkungen*, published by the Forschungsinstitut für den Donauraum (Vienna-Munich: Vlg. Herold, 1967).

tions and a free hand in her dealings with the non-Magyars of the kingdom. In the next fifty years, Magyar leaders who would sarcastically brush aside any "interference" by "distinguished foreigners" in Hungarian "domestic" affairs (i.e., nationality problems), to quote István Tisza's reference to his colleague, the prime minister of the Cisleithanian part of the monarchy, would not refrain from raising objections to Austrian domestic measures on the basis of their expected impact upon the dualistic system as interpreted by the Magyar side. The last such act was the declaration of Hungary's separation from Austria on the eve of the collapse of 1918 under the constitutional pretext that the federal transformation of Cisleithania invalidated the Compromise.

All this is well known. It is also known that in Hungary, dualism meant an effort to ossify the existing semifeudal socioeconomic structure *and* to keep the non-Magyar nationalities "in their place." Social injustice, as Oscar Jászi suggested, affected both the Magyar and non-Magyar masses, and was not the result of national or ethnic discrimination. But Robert A. Kann was right in pointing out that the suppression of Magyar and non-Magyar under-privileged classes was markedly different. While the Magyar peasant suffered from social discrimination, the non-Magyar peasant, in addition, suffered from national discrimination.[55]

This circumstance, acknowledged recently also in Hungary, was reexamined in a discussion of "The Nature of the Non-Germanic Societies under Habsburg Rule," published in the *Slavic Review*. In that discussion, Peter F. Sugar stated that the Magyar ruling classes were the "most privileged non-Germans in the Habsburg realm" and Hans Kohn, who stressed international rather than domestic considerations, added that "The really dominant element in the Dual Monarchy, the pressure group most successful in increasing

[55] Robert A. Kann, *The Multinational Empire* (2 vols.; New York: Columbia University Press, 1950), II, 112. The almost complete identification of social oppression with national suppression, criticized by non-Romanian Marxists, can be observed in recent Romanian literature. Cf. "Einige Fragen der landwirtschaftlichen Entwicklung in der Österreichisch-Ungarischen Monarchie (1900–1918)," Report of the National Committee of Historians in Romania (Bucharest, 1964), prepared by Stepan Pascu, Constantin G. Giurescu, Iosif Kovács, and Ludovic Vajda. Presented to the May, 1964, Conference on Austria-Hungary held in Budapest. I am indebted to Professor Charles Jelavich of Indiana University for kindly permitting me to use his material pertinent to the conference.

its share in the communality, was then [i.e. after 1867] no longer the Germans but the Magyars."[56] The appearance of a more flexible trend in new Hungarian historical writings[57] could lead to a reinterpretation of the complex problem of the Compromise.

Among the more hopeful signs of the reformulation of the attitude of Magyardom toward its non-Magyar environment in the era of dualism there were the *Nagodba* concluded with the Croats, the Nationality Law, the recognition of the autonomous status of the Serbian and Romanian Orthodox churches, and the progressive linguistic clauses in the Law for Elementary Education, all enacted in 1868. They were the maximum concessions responsible Hungarian politicians were prepared to make. Although these laws, if honestly executed, would have represented improvement over the pre-1848 situation and would have been comparatively advanced by contemporary standards, taken together they were less than the minimum required by the duly elected representatives of the nationalities. The latter rejected the reassertion of the "politically unitary and indivisibly united Magyar nation of which all citizens of the fatherland, regardless of their nationality, are equal members," insisting on the complete political equality of all nations of Hungary, not on the basis of full-fledged individual rights but in their capacity as recognized and historically legitimate corporate national communities entitled to territorial self-government.[58]

[56] Peter F. Sugar, "The Nature of the Non-Germanic Societies under Habsburg Rule," *Slavic Review*, XXII, No. 1 (1963), 5 *passim* and in the same issue, Hans Kohn, "The Viability of the Habsburg Monarchy," p. 39.

[57] Ede Tóth, "A Kossuth emigrációs politikájáról folytatott vita eredményeiről," *Századok*, XCVIII, No. 4 (1964), 770 f.; also, "A Történettudományi Bizottság vitája a dualizmus kora történetének egyes kérdéseiről," *Századok*, XCVI, Nos. 1–2 (1962), 206–39. Held under the auspices of the Hungarian Academy in December, 1960, the report given by Péter Hanák was discussed by Gy. Szabad, Gy. Ránki, P.Zs. Pach, and E. Molnár. Cf. P. Hanák, "Probleme der Krise des Dualismus am Ende des 19. Jahrhunderts," *Studia Historica*, No. 51 (1961), pp. 337–82, and the discussion in the same journal on pp. 382–87.

[58] For a detailed analysis of the legislation just mentioned, cf. Kemény, *The Nationality Question*, I, 51–112; also Gábor Kemény, *Iratok a nemzetiségi kérdés történetéhez Magyarországon a dualizmus korában*, I (Budapest: Tankönyvkiadó, 1952), 5–170 (this collection of documents, four volumes of which, covering the period 1867–1903, have been published so far, will be cited hereafter as *Documents*). Cf. Branko M. Pešelj, "Der ungarisch-kroatische Ausgleich vom Jahre 1868— Verfassungsrechtlicher Überblick," and C. A. Macartney, "Das ungarische Nationalitätengesetz vom Jahre 1868," both in *Der österreichisch-ungarische Ausgleich von 1867*, pp. 169–85 and 219–30, respectively.

Since the demands of non-Magyar deputies were almost completely ignored in the final formulation of the Nationality Law of 1868 and since the reincorporation of Transylvania in the same year and subsequent Hungarian pressure for the dissolution and partial reincorporation of the Southern Military Border District[59] added to the grievances of the non-Magyars, there began to develop a political impasse the result of which was to appear in its full significance only after the disappearance of Eötvös and Deák from the political scene. By the seventies, both Eötvös and Deák, whose personal integrity was unquestioned even by their political opponents, found it increasingly difficult to restrain their "liberal" followers, who regarded the legislation of 1868 as a magnanimous gesture of the noble Magyar nation. They felt it quite undeserved by the non-Magyars who looked for help to their brethren beyond the borders.

From the seventies, the respect of Hungarian politicians for the linguistic, educational, and cultural rights of non-Magyars vanished rather rapidly, as shown by the new laws aimed at the reorganization of elementary and high school education, the kindergartens, the training of teachers, the administration of counties, townships, and municipalities at all levels. Legislation and ordinances promoting the Magyarization of names of villages and persons, restrictions in the press laws, instructions to village notaries concerning the usage of Magyar in their official correspondence were supplemented by a combination of social and administrative pressure manifest in the dissolution of non-Magyar cultural societies, closing of schools, establishment of clubs in defense of Magyardom, trumped-up charges against the leaders of nationalities and efforts to prevent them from being elected to Parliament or elective offices. Although religious freedom was unrestricted in Hungary in the era of dualism, some of the Catholic and Protestant church leaders participated rather vigorously in the Magyarization campaigns in their dioceses. But it is fair to point out that the only major party around the turn of the century tolerant toward the nationalities, was Count

---

[59] Kemény, *Documents*, I, 277–80; Gunther E. Rothenberg, "The Croatian Military Border and the Rise of Yugoslav Nationalism," *The Slavonic and East European Review*, XLIII, No. 100 (1964), 43 f.; J. Perényi, "Partii i politicheskaia borba sredi serbov v Vengrii (1867–1900 gg.)," *Etudes historiques*, II, 173; 179.

Zichy's Catholic People's Party that was, however, anti-Semitic in its outlook.[60]

Maltreatment could not but arouse the indignation of the rather weak non-Magyar intelligentsia in Hungary. While receiving considerable support in Austria from such different quarters as the Social Democratic Party and the entourage of the Archduke Franz Ferdinand, the non-Magyars of Hungary also managed to appeal, through the works of T. G. Masaryk, R. W. Seton-Watson, and Wickham Steed, to public opinion in the West.

The oppression of the non-Magyars' national life in Hungary—and in this respect, there was not much difference between the policies of the "liberal" governments and of their "independent" opposition before 1914—was part of the general deterioration and corruption of Magyar political life that set in around 1870. Unfortunately, this trend coincided with the increase in Hungary's influence in the monarchy's "common" affairs and international relations. Examples of this were Andrássy's role in thwarting the Bohemian-Austrian Compromise and his success in reorienting Austria-Hungary's foreign policy toward an anti-Russian and pro-German course. It is worth mentioning that a handful of independents at the extreme left of the Hungarian Parliament came out for France and against Prussia in 1870–71; about the same time, this group tried to work out a *modus vivendi* with Romanian and Serb representatives in the form of a bill based on the minority report submitted in the debate on the Nationality Law of 1869. The efforts of the group failed but their leader, Lajos Mocsáry, continued his lonesome fight for the rights of non-Magyars for decades to come. Similarly unsuccessful was the initiative to reverse Andrássy's foreign policy.[61] The

[60] From the more recent literature on Magyar nationalism and the nationality question, cf. Ferenc Pölöskei, "Nacionalizmus a dualizmus korában," in *Magyar Nationalism*, pp. 165–86; Éva V. Windisch, "A magyarországi német nemzetiségi mozgalom előtörténete (1867–1900)," Pts. I–II, *Századok*, XCVIII, Nos. 4 and 5–6 (1964), 635–59 and 1104–27, resp.; Zoltán Horváth, "A nacionalizmus kifejlődése és a nemzetiségi kérdés alakulása a dualista Magyarország utolsó évtizedeiben" (The Development of Nationalism and the Evolution of the Nationality Question in the Last Decades of Hungary's Dualistic Period), *Századok*, XCV, Nos. 2–3 (1961), 300–336; English version in *Acta Historica*, IX, Nos. 1–2 (1963), 1–37; Zoltán I. Tóth, "A nemzetiségi kérdés a dualizmus korában (1867–1900)," *Századok*, XC, No. 3 (1956), 368–93.

[61] Kemény, *The Nationality Question*, I, 118–24; Gusztáv Gratz, *A Dualizmus kora; Magyarország története, 1867–1918*, (2 vols.; Budapest: Magyar Szemle Tár-

latter's Slavophobia and Germanophilism set the pattern, with few exceptions, for most Hungarian politicians. In fact, both features can be regarded as an organic part of pre-World War I Hungarian official nationalism, which thus bears a responsibility comparable only to that of the Habsburg dynasty for the breakup of Austria-Hungary. The same attitude prevailed among the leaders of first generation Hungarian-Americans[62] and among those responsible for Hungary's fate between the two world wars.

One may say that Andrássy's—and the monarchy's—pro-German foreign policy, essentially unchallenged after 1871, took shape after the defeat of France and the unification of Germany by Bismarck. Both events were harsh facts of international life and so was the reassertion of Russian strength in eastern Europe. Austria-Hungary had to adjust to them despite Austrian mistrust and resentment of Prussia, shared by many Hungarian leaders, including Andrássy, prior to the Franco-Prussian war.[63] This policy, as suggested by Hans Kohn,[64] could have been modified later; but it was difficult for Austria-Hungary, with its entrenched authoritarian traditions and interest in the Balkans, to abstain from aggressive attitudes.

Be that as it may, pro-German sentiment seemed to be quite compatible with anti-Habsburg spirit rather characteristic for one brand of Magyar nationalism represented by the Independent Kossuth Party after 1867. This trend, more popular perhaps than the *schwarz-gelb* loyalty of those supporting the dual system in order to secure Magyar supremacy in the Danubian Basin, was no more

saság, 1934), I, 103–9. For the close connection between the Hungarian ruling classes' attitude toward the non-Magyars of Hungary, and their effort to strengthen the monarchy's influence in the Balkans, see Domokos Kosáry, "Kemény és Széchenyi 1849 után," *Irodalomtörténeti Közlemények*, LXVII, No. 2 (1963), 166–70. For the interrelationship of Magyar supremacy and the monarchy's German alliance, cf. Robert A. Kann, *The Habsburg Empire* (New York: Praeger, 1957), pp. 5 ff.; also Henry C. Meyer, *Mitteleuropa in German Thought and Action, 1815–1945* (The Hague: M. Nijhoff, 1955), pp. 37 f. For an unsuccessful attempt to weaken Hungary's association with the German-led Triple Alliance and to revise the traditional Hungarian stand *re* Russia, see István Dolmányos, "Károlyi Mihály és a 'szentpétervári út,' " *Történelmi Szemle*, VI, No. 2 (1963), 167–93.

[62] George Barany, "The Magyars," *The Immigrants' Influence on Wilson's Peace Policy*, ed. Joseph O'Grady (Louisville: University of Kentucky Press, 1967), 143–146.

[63] István Diószegi, *Ausztria-Magyarország és a Francia-Porosz háború, 1870–1871* (Budapest: Akadémiai kiadó, 1965).

[64] Kohn, *The Twentieth Century*, p. 41.

inclined to meet halfway the just aspirations of Hungary's non-Magyar populace, as shown during the tenure of the coalition of the parties of the opposition after the turn of the century. But if the era of dualism witnessed, *mutatis mutandis*, a revival and triumph of the extreme Magyar nationalism of the forties, it also saw a reassertion and a gradual extension of its social basis. In the first half of the nineteenth century the nobility assumed the role played by the third estate in France in its endeavor to create a Magyar nation-state; its progressive elements also encouraged the development of a Magyar bourgeoisie. Having lost its constitutional privileges in 1848, the same nobility's descendants, the landed and landless gentry, continued to dominate the political scene after the Compromise. They took over the civil service, the army, and practically all positions official Hungary could offer, having thus a vested interest in keeping—and spreading—Magyar as the language of all government agencies, including the wireless service and the railroads.[65]

The gentry also set the tone for the upcoming middle classes whose ambitious members, frequently of German, Jewish, or Slavic background, began to imitate the outlook and way of life of the gentry. Dreaming the gentry's dreams included the dream of a Hungarian national army commanded in Magyar, when half of Hungary's population was non-Magyar; a separate Hungarian National Bank and customs territory when the two halves of the monarchy grew increasingly interdependent; the maintenance of the political and social *status quo*, based on the disfranchisement of the masses when hundreds of thousands of Hungarian citizens had to go overseas to eke out a living; and a Hungarian Empire of thirty million Magyars, a slogan first launched in the late nineties by Jenö Rákosi, a Hungarian-German representative of the jingoistic press but subsequently also propagated by journalists of Hungarian-Jewish extraction. Academicians and university professors like Zsolt Beöthy, Mihály Réz and others taught the *Weltanschauung*-shaping subjects of literature, history, and philosophy in this spirit of Magyar imperialism. Yet even in its most aggressive form Magyar na-

[65] For the gentry and its influence, see C. A. Macartney, *Hungary*, with a Foreword by H. A. L. Fisher (London: E. Benn, Ltd., 1934), pp. 180–98; A. J. P. Taylor, *The Habsburg Monarchy, 1809–1918* (new ed.; London: H. Hamilton, 1951), pp. 185–95; Péter Hanák, "Skizzen über die ungarische Gessellschaft am Anfang des 20. Jahrhunderts," *Acta Historica*, X, Nos. 1–2 (1963), 16–25. Also, Pukánszky, *Német polgárság magyar földön*, pp. 93–101; 133 f., 189 f.

tionalism reflected, in its formative period in the early nineteenth century, anxiety and fear of expansive German superiority. This inferiority complex was to a considerable extent the motivating force behind the rather primitive linguistic nationalism revived by Jenö Rákosi in the last decades of the century. Indeed it was he, of all people, who in an analysis of the German unification movement suggested, in 1870, that, should the Germans win against the French, German unity would

further develop under the impact of its natural weight, and its next station would be the reincorporation of Austria in some form. And thus Hungary would be where she was before Königgrätz i.e., in the immediate neighborhood of the whole of Germandom and in a much graver danger than at the time of the old Austrian [danger since she would be] exposed to the Germanizing effect and aspiration of the great and youthful German unity.[66]

Magyarization, then, continued to be at least partially a defensive reaction to the imagined threat of Pan-Slavism and to the potential menace of Pan-Germanism. Unfortunate and inefficient as this response turned out to be in the long run, only a few dared to dissent. Those who ventured to oppose this chauvinistic trend in Magyar nationalism were either isolated politically like Deputy Mocsáry in the late nineteenth century or were prevented *a priori* from participating in parliamentary life like the Social Democrats or the members of Oscar Jászi's radical circle around the periodical *Huszadik Század* (Twentieth Century). Furthermore, the Hungarian Social Democratic Party, that favored, in theory, the equality of all nationalities, underestimated the impact of nationalism on the working classes before World War I. It supported, in practice, Hungary's territorial integrity. Vacillating between the desirability of keeping Hungary within the economically advantageous dualistic system and the popular yearning for "complete" independence from Austria, the official party line was ambiguous, to say the least. As to Jászi, his ideas were shared at best by a small group of intellectuals.[67]

[66] Cited in Pukánszky, *Német polgárság magyar földön,* p. 109.

[67] Tibor Erényi, "Az 1918 előtti magyarországi munkásmozgalom és a nemzeti kérdés," in *Magyar Nationalism,* pp. 189–208; Erényi, "Die sozialdemokratische Partei Ungarns und der Dualismus," paper presented at the May, 1964, Conference

Jászi and his journal, the *Twentieth Century,* were one of the two main centers of intellectual protest against official Hungary. The other was the literary periodical *Nyugat* (The West) and its greatest representative, the poet-publicist Endre Ady. Ady, of impoverished nobility, attacked the hard core of reactionary Hungary. Predicting the "sunset of nationalism," he proclaimed:

> He who is an enemy of progress, of betterment, of the unconditional freedom of the human spirit, is a traitor to the fatherland, even though he may go on singing the national anthem forever . . . . There has never been a bigger lie on the battleground than nationalism. Nationalism has a thousand faces. It blurs the vision of the man with the sharpest eye. It invades every human weakness. It deals in tradition, piety, pride in race, professional jealousy, in all virtues and vices . . . . In Hungary, it is a patriotic thing to hate Germans, Serbs, Romanians, Slovaks, isn't it? If so, I solemnly declare that I am no patriot. I respect every race, tongue, religion, conviction and right, extra et intra Hungariam. What is more, I am not in favor of forcible Magyarization either.

Suggesting that "a civilized man is beyond the disease of nationalism" defined by him as "the *international* conspiracy of darkness, stupidity, and evil authorities' selfishness," Ady warned:

> The country is on the verge of bankruptcy, yet the Magyar nationalists proclaim the whims of *Magyar imperialism.* This ought to be sort of a special Magyar gloire oblivious to hunger but more likely, it is the slogan of an old idea, that of *Regnum Marianum.*

---

on Austria-Hungary (Budapest), especially pp. 2, 5 f.; 22; György Fukász, "A polgári radikálisok nacionalizmusa (Jászi Oszkár és a nemzetiségi kérdés)," in *Magyar Nationalism,* pp. 209–31, and, *A magyarországi polgári radikalizmus történetéhez 1900–1918. Jászi Oszkár ideológiájának bírálata* (Budapest: Gondolat, 1960). Also Zoltán Horváth, *Magyar századforduló. A második reformnemzedék története (1896–1914)* (Budapest: Gondolat, 1961). For a sociological analysis of the whole Era of Dualism, Oscar Jászi's *The Dissolution of the Habsburg Monarchy,* especially the section dealing with Hungary (pp. 271–383) is still indispensable. Cf. Béla K. Király, "The Danubian Problem in Oscar Jászi's Political Thought," *The Hungarian Quarterly,* V, No. 1–2 (1965), 120–34. For the *Nyugat,* see Miksa Fenyő, "The Nyugat Literary Magazine and the Modern Hungarian Literature," *The Hungarian Quarterly,* III, No. 3–4 (1962), 7–19.

Bitter and sarcastic, Ady suggested:

Hungarian history, Hungarian question, Hungarian fate is this: a few hundred violent families ruled and committed perfidy, cruelties, and barbarisms all over Hungary. They proclaimed themselves Hungary, did business in the name of holy Magyardom and were ready to overthrow everything if their pockets suffered a little injury.

No wonder that he was hoping for a "revision of patriotism": "How little shall we speak of the fatherland. How boldly we shall stand comparisons. How unprejudiced, civilized, widely travelled, industrious and Magyar we shall be, shan't we? Woe if we could not believe in this . . . ."[68] In a poem published in 1908, Ady suggested that "Magyar, Romanian, and Slav sorrow/Remains forever one sorrow . . . ," adding,

> Danube and Olt have but one voice,
> A rumbling, muffled, deadly voice.
> Woe to him in Árpád's land
> Who is no lord or no villain.
>
> Are we to take a joint stand yet?
> Are we to say a great big thing,
> We, the crushed ones, the oppressed
> Magyar people and non-Magyars.[69]

It is no surprise that Ady was no favorite of Tisza's iron-fisted regime. And no wonder that the other Magyar genius of this century, Béla Bartók, who set out to discover the true Magyar folksong and soon found himself exploring the folklore of neighboring peoples, sent a volume of Ady's poems to a Romanian friend.[70] But the protests of Ady and Bartók remained cries in the wilderness.

[68] The citations are taken from articles written by Ady after the turn of the century. They were collected and published by Sándor Koczkás and Erzsébet Vezér in Endre Ady, *A nacionalizmus alkonya* (Budapest: Kossuth, 1959), pp. 30, 32, 45, 91, 98, 192, 204.

[69] "Magyar jakobinus dala" (Song of a Magyar Jacobin—author's translation).

[70] Horváth, *Magyar századforduló*, p. 490. Bartók's respect for other peoples, however, did not prevent him from expressing a deeply felt Magyar nationalism in his works.

It was only on the eve of World War I that Count Mihály Károlyi and a few members of Parliament began to demand a reorientation of Hungarian, and by implication Austro-Hungarian, foreign policy. This anti-German and subsequently pacifist trend, however, failed to stem the patriotic fervor of the overwhelming majority of Parliament led by Tisza,[71] which supported both the declaration of war on the Serbian "dogs" and on the Entente. Károlyi, courageous and pro-Entente, nevertheless stood on the ground of Hungarian territorial integrity even at the time of the dissolution of the Habsburg Empire, as did Jászi. This, however, prevented both Károlyi and Jászi from going far enough and fast enough in their negotiations during the war with either the representatives of the Entente or of the properly suspicious nationalities of Hungary. In addition, the fiction of a thousand-year-old Hungary even in the form of a democratic state, based on far-reaching national and municipal autonomy, tended to support the wishful thinking of Magyars. The brusque treatment suffered by Károlyi at the hand of the victors, and the popular disillusionment that followed, undermined whatever chances a democratic republic may have had in Hungary after the war. It was at the crest of national indignation that Béla Kun rode into power and achieved his initial military successes. On the other hand, it was lack of respect for genuine Hungarian national sentiment that helped undo the Hungarian Soviet Republic of 1919 and assisted the establishment of Admiral Miklós Horthy's counter-revolutionary regime.[72]

[71] For some new details concerning the problem of Tisza's initial hesitation during the critical period of the preparation of the ultimatum to Serbia in the summer of 1914, cf. József Galántai, "Tisza és a világháború," Századok, XCVIII, No. 4 (1964), 687–709. A German version appeared in Annales Universitatis Scientiarum Budapestiensis de Rolando Eötvös Nominatae, Sectio Historica, V (Budapest, 1963), 185–205. According to Valiani, it was due to Tisza's opposition that the monarchy failed to make concessions to Italy in the negotiations of February, 1915. Tisza was afraid that concessions to Italy would imply concessions to Romania, something he was totally unprepared to do. Indirectly, Valiani's argument supports Galántai's thesis. Cf. Leo Valiani, "Die internationale Lage Oesterreich-Ungarns, 1900–1918," paper given at the May, 1964, Conference on Austria-Hungary in Budapest.

[72] Alfred D. Low, The Soviet Hungarian Republic and the Paris Peace Conference, LIII, Part 10, of the Transactions of the American Philosophical Society (Philadelphia, 1963), especially pp. 22; 28–33; 37; 40–46; 49–57; 63; 66 f.; 77–83; 87 ff. Cf. Tibor Hajdu, "A nemzeti kérdés és az 1918–1919-es forradalmak. A dualizmus nemzeti politikájának csődje és a monarchia felbomlása," in Magyar Nationalism, pp. 232–79.

III

The regime that was to dominate the Hungarian scene for a quarter of a century referred to itself as "Christian" and "national." Yet the white terror that followed its inauguration was neither more discriminating nor more charitable than was its red predecessor, to which it was supposed to be the "answer." As to its "national" features, they did not include either the enfranchisement of the masses or the satisfaction of their land hunger. Nor did the regime respect the rights granted to minorities in the revolutionary period of 1918–19. Narrowly conservative and aristocratic in outlook, the new "Christian and national" regime organized in Szeged belied its appearance by introducing officially, for the first time in Hungarian history, political anti-Semitism as an organic part of the "Szeged idea."

Besides official anti-Semitism, which was manifest in a 1920 law establishing a *numerus clausus* for Jews at the universities, but which did not keep the regime from consolidating itself with the help of "Jewish" capital, Magyar nationalism acquired yet another new feature in the form of revisionism aimed at resurrecting prewar Greater Hungary and at the destruction of the Little Entente. The source of this revisionist nationalism[73] was Hungarian national pride, which had been deeply hurt by the Treaty of Trianon where large segments of Magyar-inhabited territories had been assigned to Hungary's neighbors. The victors' reluctance to consider at least some of Hungary's complaints served as a pretext for the governments in the interwar period to blame the treaty for all socioeconomic difficulties, to pose as the defender of the rights of Magyar minorities, and to join the camp of the forces dissatisfied with the Versailles system. Indeed no responsible Hungarian politician between the two world wars, Social Democrats included, could bring himself to ignore an opportunity for territorial revision whenever it arose. Revisionism not only blurred the vision of Hungarian leaders, making them vulnerable to their own propaganda, it also implied the insincerity of their pledges to cooperate with neighboring countries in order to avoid some of the disastrous consequences

[73] For a discussion of the social basis of Horthy's regime, cf. the first chapter in C. A. Macartney, *October Fifteenth. A History of Modern Hungary, 1929–1945* (2 vols.; Edinburgh, 1956), I, 3–24.

of the depression. Later it prevented the Hungarians and their neighbors from establishing a common front against Hitler. Those who visited Hungary of the twenties and thirties, will remember the "No! No! Never!" signs and the four "detached" black pieces of Greater Hungary grouped around the white body of the "truncated motherland" that were visible in such public places as parks, offices, and schools, all over the country. Those who lived there will recall that twice a day millions of children were required to recite, along with their prayer before and after school, the "Magyar Creed":

> I believe in one God,
> I believe in one Fatherland,
> I believe in one divine eternal Truth,
> I believe in the resurrection of Hungary. Amen.[74]

This kind of systematic indoctrination, whatever its political justification may have been, was the more dangerous since the authoritarian aspects of first Fascist Italy and then Nazi Germany began to appeal to a new generation of Magyar gentry and middle-class elements in the army, in different paramilitary organizations (MOVE, Levente, etc.),[75] in the civil service, and in the student associations at a time when intellectual unemployment was constantly on the increase; initially, because of the invasion of Magyar refugees who lost their jobs in the areas that went to the successor states, and afterwards because of the overproduction of people with university diplomas in a country that had suddenly shrunk and was unable to provide them with acceptable jobs. Even if younger members of this intelligentsia had been prepared to reorient quickly their interest toward the private sector of the economy (not an easy

[74] Authored by Mrs. Elemér Papp-Váry, the "Magyar Creed" was usually followed by the lines: "Truncated Hungary is no country,/Whole Hungary is heaven."

[75] In order to coordinate and supervise the activities of dozens of legal and illegal, social and paramilitary revisionist associations, Bethlen proposed the creation of an organization under the auspices of the Office of the Chairman of the Council of Ministers. The first leader of the new organization established in 1921 was Count Pál Teleki. See *Docs. 25/a-c* in Dezső Nemes (ed.), *A fasiszta rendszer kiépitése és a népnyomor Magyarországon 1921–1924*, Vol. II of *Iratok az ellenforradalom történetéhez, 1919–1945* (Budapest: Szikra, 1956), pp. 177–81. For a brief survey of secret and legal right-wing organizations, see also Macartney, *October Fifteenth*, I, 29–33.

task psychologically), the world-wide depression would have nipped their chances in the bud. Frustrated as they were, many were inclined to blame the Jews, to look for radical solutions of such things as the land question, and to accept extra-parliamentary methods recommended by a leader like Gömbös or, later, Imrédy.

Thus antiliberal and antiparliamentary trends, too, became gradually integrated, especially in the thirties, into this "reformed" brand of post-World War I Magyar nationalism. One of its most permanent components was a sincerely felt abhorrence of anything related to bolshevism and the Soviet Union. This abhorrence derived from the unfortunate experiment of 1919 and was an additional ideological tie binding the regime to the Axis powers and limiting the freedom of action of its potential opponents who otherwise would have preferred a different political course. Revisionism and antibolshevism constituted the two main factors of interwar Magyar nationalism that united the overwhelming majority of the politically articulate public opinion.

But despite her archconservative leaders' fear of social reform, despite the manipulation of elections that always gave a comfortable majority to the government party, and despite the unrestrained admiration of the Fascist corporate system and of German power by many high ranking officials, Hungary was not transformed into a totalitarian one-party dictatorship before the Nazi occupation of the country in 1944. The social basis of the "white" regime was consolidated by Prime Minister Bethlen in the early twenties in such a way that it included, in addition to representatives of the aristocracy, the great landowners (among whom the churches loomed rather large), the gentry of the army and bureaucracy, and representatives of business and financial circles as well as the upper strata of the peasantry. While Count István Bethlen was at the helm (1921–31), the real power lay in the hands of the landed and financial oligarchy. Yet as time went on, especially during the Depression, shifts and conflicts on questions of both foreign and domestic policy began to develop in this far from monolithic power structure. The appointment of Gyula Gömbös as Minister President in the fall of 1932 contributed to the fascistization of Hungary and to the strengthening of her ties with Italy and Germany, but the midthirties saw some serious efforts to control, if not eliminate altogether, the Fascist trends and to make Hungarian foreign policy less dependent on the Axis powers. Since Hungary had to rely economically, too, on Germany, this was no simple task.

There were, nevertheless, some people who began their careers on the political right who did not make the sharp turn toward totalitarianism. Bethlen and deputies like Tibor Eckhardt and Endre Bajcsy-Zsilinszky were close friends of Gömbös in the twenties and yet, by the late thirties, were in *de facto* alliance with the outnumbered representatives of the liberal bourgeoisie and the Social Democrats. No less anxious to assert Hungarian supremacy in the Danubian area than before, these men grew increasingly fearful of the threat posed by Nazi Germany to Hungarian independence. Their fears, shared by many around Regent Horthy, were not strong enough to curb traditional Magyar nationalism; after some initial hesitation and reluctance, rising largely from anxiety about adverse western reaction, subsequent Hungarian governments took an aggressive part in the "reorganization" of central Europe under Nazi and Fascist auspices. The rather ephemeral successes of tradition-bound Magyar revisionism, however, revealed that the ruling castes had neither learned nor forgotten: the non-Magyars living in the areas returned to Hungary in 1938–41 were treated as second-class citizens and had to suffer, along with the Jews, from some of the most horrible excesses committed against a civilian population.[76]

Revisionist Magyar nationalism was, to a large extent, a revival

[76] For the revisionist aspects of Hungarian foreign policy see, in addition to Macartney's *October Fifteenth*, József Galántai, "Trianon és a revíziós propaganda"; Aladár Kis, "Az ellenforradalmi rendszer külpolitikájának kialakulása (1920–1933)"; Magda Ádám, "Az ellenforradalmi rendszer revíziós külpolitikájához (1933–1941)"; Mihály Korom, "A nácibarát és revíziós külpolitika végső következményei: Magyarország részvétele a második világháborúban," all in *Magyar Nationalism*, pp. 280–301; 302–15; 356–95 and 426–62, respectively. Also, Magda Ádám, "Magyarország és a kisantant a második világháború előtti években (1936–1937)," *Századok*, XCVI (1962), 502–51; Gyula Juhász, *A Teleki-kormány külpolitikája 1939–1941;* (Budapest: Akadémiai kiadó, 1964). For the massacres among the Serbian and Jewish populace of the Bačka, see Macartney, *October Fifteenth*, II, 69–74; 107 f.; 145 f.; 201 f.; for the treatment of the Slovaks, cf. Lóránt Tilkovszky, "Magyar-szlovák viszony és szlovák nemzetiségi mozgalom Magyarországon a bécsi döntés után," *Századok*, XCVIII, No. 3 (1964), 383–416. For a pertinent collection of documents, see *Magyarország és a második világháború: Titkos diplomáciai okmányok a háború elözményeihez és történetéhez,* Magda Ádám et al. (eds., commentators) (Budapest: Kossuth, 1959). On problems related to recent Hungarian literature on the subject, cf. Peter F. Sugar's review in *Slavic Review,* XXI, No. 2 (June, 1962), 358 f.

of the old myth about "historic" Hungary's mission in defense of Christianity. This time the mission was against the Bolshevik danger, with which the other successor states, so the argument went, were either unable or unwilling to cope. This new justification of Magyar supremacy in the Carpathian basin continued to rely on the "doctrine of the Holy Crown" and to stress spiritual-historical rather than ethnic rights, since Hungarian territorial claims went far beyond areas inhabited by the Magyar minorities. This "peculiar Hungarian nation-concept" was a return to the old idea of the Hungarian political nation; it implied, in Tibor Joó's words, that the nation itself was a moral-cultural category indifferent to and independent of the ethnic affiliation of its members, many of whom might belong to different peoples.[77] With its emphasis on the Hungarian nation's multiracial and multilingual character, Joó's book tried to show that the Hungarian nation concept was broad enough to embrace the non-Magyar populace of the former kingdom of Hungary. Writing in mid-1939, he, like Gyula Szekfü and others,[78] attempted to make the Hungarian nation concept more palatable to both Magyars and non-Magyars by rejecting the Nazi *völkisch* ideology and by stressing the significance of spiritual factors in the process of shaping a national community. This endeavor, supported by the Roman Catholic and Protestant churches in Hungary and by the more conservative and moderate leaders of the government, did have some positive aspects at the time, since it implied strong reservations concerning the increasing fascistization of the minds. Yet the limitations of this refined Magyar imperialism were rather considerable. First, Hungarian claims for spiritual leadership assumed that there was something peculiar and unique about Magyardom, qualifying it to resume its idealized historical role in East Central Europe. Furthermore, and this was less in line with Széchenyi's romantic nationalism so popular among the supporters of this school of thought, this spiritualized brand of Magyar nationalism reflected a feeling of Hungarian cultural supremacy. But to a subtle observer,

[77] Tibor Joó, *A magyar nemzeteszme* (Budapest: Franklin, n.d.), pp. 192; 208; 211. In the Epilogue of his study, Joó gives a brief survey of similar ideas of other twentieth-century Hungarian historians, including Gyula Szekfü and József Deér.

[78] Szekfü, *Mi a magyar?* Szekfü, in a note appended to the introductory, approvingly mentions Joó's study.

the myth of Magyar uniqueness was dangerously close to Magyar racism, whereas Hungarian cultural supremacy was anathema to all non-Magyars.[79]

The idea that Magyardom was an historical and ethical quality to be realized through "constructive" cultural development was an essential part of the "neonationalism" of Count Kuno Klebelsberg in the twenties. Klebelsberg was the reorganizer of the educational system of Hungary after World War I. As Minister of Religious Affairs and Public Education, he intended to rearm Hungary ideologically with a new nationalism focused on independent Magyar statehood. He turned against revolutionary and defeatist views, and aimed at enabling a new generation of Magyar leaders to fulfill the historical task of resurrecting thousand-year-old Hungary.[80] The training of a new educated Magyar élite and a larger intelligentsia that were loyal to the national regime were the political goals of Klebelsberg's ambitious, conservative-minded educational reforms. Recognition of Klebelsberg's aims is important in the understanding of the new middle class that developed between the two world wars. This middle class was under the tutelage of the déclassé elements of the old aristocracy, the gentry, and the government bureaucracy, but it was also in competition with them.

Qualitative improvement and democratization of the Hungarian educational system were both intentional and unintentional aspects of Klebelsberg's reforms. Numerous scholarships and the education of the country's best young minds, irrespective of social origin, in such elite institutions as the Eötvös College in Budapest and the *Collegium Hungaricum* with branches in Vienna, Berlin, Rome, and Paris were intended to provide the brain power capable of understanding the West and of presenting to it Hungary's cause on an acceptable intellectual level. The continuous "production" of college graduates comparable to that of Greater Hungary meant, as C. A. Macartney suggested, preparation for a revision of the Treaty of Trianon and "for a Magyarisation of the areas to be recovered which would be far more intensive than anything which the old

[79] For a Marxian interpretation of this ambiguity see József Szigeti, "A szellemtörténeti nacionalizmus" in *Magyar Nationalism*, pp. 340–55.

[80] Sándor Balogh, "A bethleni konszolidáció és a magyar 'neonacionalizmus,'" in *Magyar Nationalism*, pp. 316–39.

days had known." Along with the spread of elementary education in the countryside and with the opening of the high schools to children of lower income groups, the reorganization of the educational system under the guidance of the state was bound to bring about a social change beyond the control of the regime. Developing Szekfü's suggestion made in 1934 that the younger generation of intellectuals had refused to identify itself with the old gentry, Macartney recognized that any radicalization of political or social life was likely to appear in the form of right-wing extremism. It was perhaps inevitable in a country where western democracy was blamed for a harsh peace treaty, where the political left was discredited and subdued as a result of a lost war and subsequent revolutionary and counter-revolutionary trends, and where political propaganda associated all shades of liberalism, socialism, and communism—one may add capitalism, too—with the sinister influence of the Jews.[81]

The ambivalence of an unfortunate historical situation was also reflected in the impact Szekfü's *Three Generations* (*Három nemzedék*) had on the Hungarian mind. This pamphlet, first published in 1920 by Hungary's foremost historian of the post-World War I era, became the ideological handbook of right-wing nationalism. Written by a scholar who began his career as a *Habsburgtreu* and a devout Catholic with a study on the exiled Ferenc II Rákóczi, which was denounced as an insult to national honor by the chauvinistic press on the eve of World War I, *Three Generations* was full of half-truths that indicated, however, the existence of serious socio-economic problems. The work was meant to be a critique of the era of dualism and contributed greatly to the respectability of the anti-liberal attitude and official anti-Semitism of the counterrevolutionary regime. Yet by the mid-thirties, its author became a leader of Magyar moral resistance to the Third Reich. He exposed in numerous studies and in the newspaper *Magyar Nemzet* the fallacy of modern *völkisch* barbarism and opposed it with what he still regarded as the ennobling idea of St. Stephen's Hungary. While his willingness to support the rather weak and disorganized Hungarian resistance movement during the war and to come to the defense even of the Communists participating in it showed a considerable

---

[81] Macartney, *October Fifteenth,* I, 77 ff.

amount of courage, Szekfü's radical revision of his previous views after World War II was an indication of the tremendous pressures Hungarian intellectuals had to face in our century.[82]

Although Szekfü was well aware of the urgent need for social reform in Hungary, it was a writer, Dezső Szabó who, disgusted with the shallowness of the "white" regime, announced in 1925: "Since the end of the world war, there is but one historical class—the Magyar peasantry."[83] Self-righteous and flamboyant, Szabó, like Szekfü, became a propagandist of the counterrevolution with his famous novel, *The Lost Village* (*Az elsodort falu*), in 1919. In a few years, however, he turned against official Hungary, which he felt had restored the old feudal order disguised as "Christian and national," and accused it of having betrayed the aspirations of the Magyar masses. An uncompromising Magyar nationalist, he violently attacked the aristocracy, the clergy, the gentry, the bourgeoisie, the "international" working class and the assimilated "aliens." He defended his classless and racially centered "Magyar socialism" first against the Hungarian revolution, allegedly contaminated by "Jewish imperialism," and then, in the thirties, against the Nazi myth, which he regarded as the vanguard of hated German imperialism.[84] Perhaps the single most important characteristic of this far-from-consistent, yet highly educated and gifted man was his unqualified identification of the cause of true Magyardom with the cause of the Magyar peasantry. Because of this, he may be considered as the most powerful precursor of Hungarian Populism, which began to come into prominence as a literary and political movement in the thirties, and has continued to influence Hungarian thinking to the present.

The movement of the Hungarian Populists or "Village Explorers," like the corresponding trends in eastern Europe, can be traced to that brand of romantic nationalism that regarded folk culture as the

[82] For a Marxist evaluation, see Gyula Mérei, "Szekfü Gyula történetszemléletének bírálatához," *Századok*, XCIV, Nos. 1–3 (1960), 180–255.

[83] Cited in László Péter, "Szabó Dezső Szegeden," *Irodalomtörténeti Közlemények*, LXVII, No. 1 (1963), 76. For Dezső Szabó, see Joseph Reményi, *Hungarian Writers and Literature* (ed., introduction by August J. Molnár) (New Brunswick, N.J.: Rutgers Press, 1964), pp. 341–47, first published in the *Slavonic and East European Review*, Vol. XXIV, No. 63 (1946).

[84] Péter Nagy, "Szabó Dezső ideológiájának forrásai," *Irodalomtörténeti Közlemények*, LXVIII, No. 6 (1963), 710 f.

vehicle of a people's real identity. In the accepted political-philosophical sense of the term, there was no strong Populist movement in nineteenth-century Hungary, perhaps due to the dominating role the nobility and gentry had in both political and cultural life, and to the circumstance that the period of literary romanticism in Hungary preceded rather than followed the "popular-national" classicism represented by the poets Petőfi and Arany. Thus Hungarian Populism was a continuation of the *oeuvre* of the second rather than of the first reform generation, to use Zoltán Horváth's term, the binding links being, in addition to Dezső Szabó, the poet Ady and the novelist Zsigmond Móricz, the composers Béla Bartók and Zoltán Kodály, and the sociologists of Jászi's circle.

Journalists and historians, sociologists and economists, writers and poets, the village explorers did not belong to any single political party.[85] While not all of them were of peasant background, they all had two things in common. They were convinced that the Hungarian peasant, if left alone, was capable of taking care of himself and therefore had to be given a major role in shaping the nation's life; they also firmly believed that, in accordance with Hungarian tradition, the writer had a moral duty to speak up and lead, once the politicians had failed.

Disillusioned with the social demagoguery of Gömbös, in whose sincerity some of them initially believed, in 1937 the Populists organized a broad political-ideological platform that demanded meaningful reforms. Its name, March Front, alluded to the March Revolution of 1848 and the role that writers like Petőfi and Jókai played in it. As an opposition to totalitarian practices, the March Front suggested the strengthening of parliamentary democracy in Hungary by a new emphasis on the individual citizen's rights, by social legislation, and by a land reform aimed at the liquidation of latifundia. The program stressed the need for an independent Hungarian foreign policy as her international relations were threatened by both German and Russian imperialism. Although most Populists and their sympathizers agreed that Hungary must not get involved in the

---

[85] For a general background, see "Hungary's Populist Writers," *East Europe*, VIII, No. 2 (Feb., 1959), 32–41; 57. Also, the series of articles written by William Juhász, *East Europe*, XI, No. 12 (Dec., 1962), 12–17; XII, No. 1 (Jan., 1963), 8–15; XII, No. 3 (March, 1963), pp. 2–5; XII, No. 7 (July, 1963), pp. 6–14; XII, No. 12 (Dec., 1963), 18–22.

disputes of the great powers, this policy of the "third road" proved to be extremely difficult to follow. In subsequent years, some Populists like the poets József Erdélyi and István Sinka supported the most extreme form of Hungarian fascism, the Arrow Cross movement. Others, like the sociologists Imre Kovács and Ferenc Erdei or the writers József Darvas, Pál Szabó and Péter Veres, turned to the left and founded a National Peasant Party, which opposed the Nazis during the war but was "expropriated" by the Communists after Imre Kovács had been forced into emigration in 1947.

Influenced by the ideas of Magyar uniqueness and Magyardom's "manifest destiny" in the Danubian area, the most significant Populist contribution to Magyar nationalism was the concept of the "third road" first formulated by the writer László Németh and supported by Imre Kovács, the poet Gyula Illyés and some other luminaries of Hungarian intellectual life. The "third road" implied that Hungary must resist both German and Russian expansionism; it also implied, as Németh suggested, that Hungary and her neighbors had some common interests that had to be explored and strengthened. Although this idea was not widely accepted by the nationalistic public, its very emergence was important at a time when no Slavic languages were taught in the high schools, when only one of the four Hungarian state universities had a chair for Slavic studies,[86] and when many of those familiar with the history and culture of neighboring peoples succumbed to fashionable trends and were quite willing to translate their patriotism into Hungarian cultural imperialism.[87]

Another aspect of Populist nationalism that could be regarded as the domestic side of the "third road" was its vision of "Garden Hungary," a Hungary without *fidei commissa* and huge estates, consisting of small and medium-size landholdings and voluntary cooperatives, and led by the people's intelligentsia, i.e., highly educated peasants. This democratic agrarian socialism, reflecting the impact both of Scandinavian and of socialistic practices in agriculture, was perhaps somewhat utopian, somewhat anti-urban, anti-intellectual,

[86] István Gál (ed.), *Magyarország és a Balkán; a magyar tudomány feladatai Délkeleteurópában* (Budapest: A Magyar Külügyi Társaság Balkán-Bizottsága, 1942), pp. 7–9.

[87] A characteristic example is a memorandum written by a certain Lajos Terbe and quoted at some length by István Gál, *ibid.*, pp. 18 *passim*.

and anti-Semitic, as was the nationalism of most Populists. But it was a far cry, and a sincere one, from old-fashioned gentry nationalism.

So was the "national radicalism" initiated by Endre Bajcsy-Zsilinszky, the greatest fighter of the anti-Nazi resistance movement. A political opponent of the radical peasant leader András Achim in the early years of the century, he participated, along with Gömbös, in the rightist organization of Awakening Magyars in the twenties. By the end of that decade, however, this Magyar nobleman, truly repentent and driven by his social conscience and by his worries about meaningful Hungarian independence, began to build his own "third road." It was going to bring him into sharp conflict first with his former cronies, then with his own class and the regime, and ultimately with his fatherland's Teutonic occupants, who executed him. Well before that, however, he decided that the only road to independent Magyar statehood and real national unity would be through the cooperation and social elevation of the Magyar peasant. Whereas this view brought him into close contact with the Populists, his courageous stand against German pressure in Parliament and in the press made him a natural leader of the embryonic "Popular Front" that included anti-Fascist intellectuals as well as representatives of the Smallholders Party, the Social Democrats, and the illegal Communists. But this twentieth-century follower of Rákóczi and Kossuth was still thinking in terms of Magyar leadership in the Carpathian Basin; humanitarian and progressive as it was (it was Bajcsy-Zsilinszky who insisted on a thorough investigation of the Ujvidék massacres), his nationalism was a true reflection of the virtues and shortcomings of Hungary's fight in 1848, since it never questioned Hungary's right to the territories lost after World War I.[88]

Thus both the Populist intellectual and the national radical versions of a Magyar "third road" were inherently ambivalent. Furthermore, they were held in check by a suspicious regime that frowned upon all those who were in favor of radical social change. When Horthy's governments began to introduce moderate social legislation in the late thirties, it was done chiefly in order to take the wind

[88] Rózsa Varga, "Bajcsy-Zsilinszky Endre és a népi irók," *Irodalomtörténeti Közlemények*, LXVII, No. 5 (1963), 566–80; Pintér István and Ágnes Rozsnyói, "Bajcsy-Zsilinszky dokumentumok," *Századok*, XCIX, No. 1–2 (1965), 172–205.

out of the sails of the Arrow Cross movement, which showed its strength at the elections of 1939.[89] It is a sad commentary on Hungarian conditions that social "demagoguery" like the demand for a long-overdue radical land reform was, along with anti-Semitic and anticapitalistic slogans, one of the most effective weapons of the extreme right on the eve of World War II.

Whatever efforts decent patriots like Premiers Count Pál Teleki and later Miklós Kállay may have made to detach Hungary from the Third Reich, their revisionist policies made them increasingly dependent on Germany at a time when neither domestic nor international factors seemed to favor Magyar independence. Regent Horthy may have hated the Nazis and their Hungarian stooges, the Arrow Cross men, more than he disliked the Jews[90] but this kind of nationalism, restricted to a handful of leaders,[91] aloof from other, more radical, forces of opposition, had very severe limitations in a country where even anti-German popular moods were fomented mainly by indignant Magyar neoimperialists. It was able to postpone but not to forestall the German occupation of the country.

In a cycle of poems called "My Fatherland," the great proletarian poet Attila József issued a solemn plea, praying:

> To the human, give humaneness!
> To the Magyar, give Magyardom,
>
> Not to be the prey of Teuton.[92]

But the poet was denied his "happier song"; despondent, he committed suicide in 1937. In the years following, humaneness became a rare commodity and "Magyardom" an empty political slogan. Hungary was not spared the fate of a German colony, and the factions of the extreme right helped into power by the Nazis in March,

[89] Macartney, *October Fifteenth*, I, 133; 179; 191; 349–51; Miklós Lackó, "A margyarországi nyilas mozgalom történetéhez (1935–1937)," *Századok*, XCVII, No. 4 (1963), 782–807. For the developing political and social tensions of the thirties, see also László Márkus, "A bethleni kormányzati rendszer bukása," *Századok*, XCVIII, Nos. 1–2 and 3 (1964), 42–71 and 419–54, respectively.

[90] Horthy to Teleki, Oct. 14, 1940. *Doc. 36* in Miklós Szinai and László Szücs (eds.), *The Confidential Papers of Admiral Horthy* (Budapest: Corvina, 1965), pp. 149–54.

[91] Macartney, *October Fifteenth*, I, 379 ff.

[92] From the cycle "Hazám" (author's translation).

1944, were rather successful in outdoing their sponsors. The year separating the Nazi invasion from the end of the war is comparable only to the period of the Mongol occupation in Hungary's history.

IV

Any attempt to assess the role of Magyar nationalism in the post-World War II era must by necessity suffer from a lack of perspective, but a few major trends can be mentioned. The most important appears to be the total transformation of Hungary's socioeconomic structure in the last twenty years. This presumably eliminates that remarkably tenacious and stubborn brand of Hungarian "feudal" nationalism whose remnants managed to survive the critical years of 1848 and 1918.

The forced disappearance of the tradition-bound form of Magyar nationalism as a result of the Allied victory did not annihilate, however, the more positive nation-building forces of that determined patriotism that defies precise definition but which lives among a hard-working and nationally conscious people. Once the hostilities were over, the Magyars, guilt-ridden and destitute, began the work of reconstruction in a land devastated during the last phase of the bitter war and Soviet occupation. The initial successes of their efforts seemed to encourage those Populists and intellectuals who wished to see a democratic Hungary serve as a "bridge" between East and West. Yet by 1947, these dreams all but vanished under the increasing pressure of a new kind of colonial rule that would tolerate no "third road" either in domestic or international affairs.

Indeed, the *Gleichschaltung* of Hungarian political life by the Communist Party coincided with the closing of the "People's Colleges" sponsored by the Populists, the first drive for the collectivization of agriculture, the expropriation of medium-size enterprises by the state, and the physical isolation of Hungary from the outside world.

While fighting all older forms of Magyar nationalism that previously had read them out of the national community, the Communists tried to utilize both the patriotic instincts and frustrations of the masses that had never had the experience of a working democracy. Thus they promoted a dichotomous approach to a rather intricate world situation, part of which was familiar from Hitler's propaganda, in order to build up an "international" frame of reference for what was to be the basis of official patriotism to the present. Linking the idea of social progress to the long-hoped-for national independence in the spirit of class struggle, and tying both to the alleged need for Soviet guardianship, the criteria of patriotism were described as follows:

[As a result of] the imperialistic and anti-Soviet policy of the Western powers and the incipient intensification of the conflicts among the former allies, there emerged, gradually, a new situation from the point of view of domestic struggles. The question was whether Hungary should become an organic part of the camp of socialism and people's democracy that began to take shape; the fate of the toiling people had been inseparably attached to the fate of this camp. The big capitalists, former landlords, all the enemies of the new [popular] power, however, have sought and received support from the Anglo-American imperialists.[93]

Loyalty to the Soviet Union and to the Communist Party were thus incorporated into the Magyar nation-concept in accordance with the general trend imposed on the rest of East Central Europe. This trend, however, did not prevail in the whole area at once. In Hungary where its victory was assured, so it seems in retrospect, by the presence of the Red Army, Stalin did not lay all his cards on the table at the beginning of the game. As late as the summer of 1944, Soviet propaganda held out the hope that a victory of the anti-Axis coalition would redress some of the injustices (e.g. the loss of Transylvania) committed against Hungary at the end of World War I.[94] During the visit of a Hungarian official delegation to Moscow, Stalin and Molotov appeared to have encouraged such hopes, and they were further encouraged by the leaders of the Hungarian Communist Party after the delegation returned to Hungary. Yet at the peace negotiations of 1947 the Soviet Union brushed aside all efforts to obtain slightly more favorable terms for Hungary, imposing on her, in fact, harsher conditions than those of Trianon.[95]

This, of course, hardly supports the theory that a "proletarian" victory would have prevented a "Trianon-like solution" of the na-

[93] Erik Molnár, Ervin Pamlényi, and György Székely (eds.), *Magyarország története* (2 vols.; Budapest: Gondolat, 1964), II, 486 f.

[94] Speeches given by Zoltán Vas, Béla Illés, and others in the summer of 1944 to a group of Hungarian officers and prisoners of war. Author's own observation.

[95] For details and further references, cf. Stephen D. Kertész, *Diplomacy in a Whirlpool, Hungary Between Nazi Germany and Soviet Russia* (Notre Dame, Ind.: University of Notre Dame, 1953), pp. 180–87.

tionality question in the Danubian area in 1919.[96] Even a quarter of a century later the Soviet Union, following the age-old practice of divide and rule, supported the punitive measures taken by Czechoslovakia against its Magyar minority. In putting into practice these measures based on the assumption of the collective guilt of the entire Magyar ethnic community in pre-war Czechoslovakia, the actions of Slovak Communists did not lag far behind the excesses committed by the Hlinka Guard in the era of "independent" Slovakia. The situation improved only after the complete takeover of the governments of both Czechoslovakia and Hungary by the Communists in 1948.[97] In the question of the Hungarian minority in Czechoslovakia as in the question of returning the Hungarian prisoners of war and innocent civilians held in the Soviet Union years after the ending of hostilities, Hungarian Communists tried to capitalize on their alleged good connections with Moscow. They used, in reality, both "questions" as part of their maneuver to undermine the authority of their political rivals.

On the domestic scene, the Communists posed as the only true heirs of "the ideas of 1848."[98] Since they had no mass support whatsoever and were represented as villains without a fatherland before 1945, they frequently pandered to mob instincts and donned the tricolor whenever possible. In their propaganda, they overemphasized the importance of the fight for national independence, and de-emphasized the significance of class struggle and the Hungarian Soviet Republic of 1919 in the first years after the war. This attitude, which followed the Nationalist-Populist rather than the Marxist pattern, has recently been condemned as a reflection of "bourgeois nationalism" that allegedly contributed to the "counter-

[96] Galántai, "Trianon és a reviziós propaganda," in *Magyar Nationalism*, p. 288. For a Communist peace program for the Danubian area proposed at the Fifth Congress of the Comintern in 1924, cf. Stephen Borsody, "Division and Reunion: Problems of Peace and Federalism in Central Europe," *The Central European Federalist*, XII, No. 2 (Dec., 1964), 7.

[97] Francis S. Wagner, "Hungarians in Czechoslovakia, 1945–1949," in *Hungarians in Czechoslovakia* (New York: Research Institute for Minority Studies on Hungarians Attached to Czechoslovakia and Carpatho-Ruthenia, 1959), pp. 11–37; also Kertész, *Diplomacy in a Whirlpool*, p. 186.

[98] Cf. József Révai in *Emlékkönyv Kossuth Lajos születésének 150. évfordulójára* (2 vols.; Budapest: Akadémiai kiadó, 1952), I, VII f.; Erzsébet G. Fazekas, "Sravnenie vengerskikh zakonov o natsionalnostiakh 1849 i 1868 gg. s tochki zreniia progressivnikh sil istorii," *Acta Historica*, I, No. 1 (1952), 93; more recently, Erzsébet Andics, in *Magyar Nationalism*, p. XXXVIII.

revolution of 1956." The same party, which reduced Hungarian history to a series of freedom fights culminating in the establishment of the Communist regime, and which now refers to the previous official line as a "dogmatic distortion" of Marxism-Leninism,[99] initiated, within less than ten years of the Ujvidék massacres, a new series of violence against southern Slavs in Hungary, suggesting today that

the crimes committed against the Southern Slav nationalities in the years 1949–1953 were the direct consequences of Stalin's and Rákosi's cult of personality.[100]

But during the same period textbooks were purged of "nationalistic prejudices" so efficiently that in early 1954, a Resolution of the Central Committee of the party dealing with "the state and tasks of public education" decided to reverse the process and strengthen the patriotic feelings of Hungarians. In order to improve the teaching of the mother tongue, Hungarian literature, history, and geography, the Resolution emphasized, besides revolutionary traditions, "all the important progressive factors of our history (e.g., Széchenyi in addition to Kossuth)"[101] in the curriculum. But ten years after the resolution, the teaching of history continued to pose some serious problems and those interested appear to believe that "textbooks ought to be written chiefly by educators excelling in the teaching profession."[102]

Whatever gaps there may have been in the education of the younger generation, the past decade also revealed that patriotism was not entirely lacking in Hungary. Without ignoring the manifold international and domestic factors that contributed to the revolutionary events of 1956, genuine nationalism seems to have served as the chief connecting matrix for the moral indignation, the widespread social dissatisfaction, and ultimately the determination to fight for a change in the popular upheaval.[103] The discussions in the

[99] Pál Zsigmond Pach, "A nacionalizmus elleni harc történettudományunkban," *Történelmi Szemle*, VII, No. 2 (1964), 303–12, especially.

[100] Péter Simon, "A marxizmus-leninizmus klasszikusai a nemzeti kérdésről," in *Magyar Nationalism*, p. 20.

[101] "A Központi Vezetőség határozata a közoktatás helyzetéről és feladatairól," *Társadalmi Szemle*, IX (1954), 96–103.

[102] Géza Eperjessy "A gimnáziumi tantervi vita és a történelmi műveltség" *Századok*, XCVIII, Nos. 1–2 (1964), 218–25.

[103] Cf. Ferenc A. Váli's *Rift and Revolt in Hungary* (Cambridge, Mass.: Harvard Press, 1961), the subtitle of which is "Nationalism versus Communism."

club of young intellectuals, the Petőfi Circle, demanded the readoption of the Kossuth coat of arms, and the insistence on the restoration of the nation's sovereignty in its relations with the Soviet Union, along with the call for legal and social justice for all, represented a comprehensive effort to achieve that national unity that was incipient but failed to develop in 1848. More significantly, the revival of the idea of the "third road" in the form of a declaration of neutrality, issued only after much soul searching but subsequently defended with admirable firmness by Imre Nagy's revolutionary government even at the cost of the supreme sacrifice, was a most impressive return to the best thinking of previous generations.

Encouraged also by the Austrian example, this open and unexpected public declaration and the appeal to the United Nations suggested that, perhaps for the first time in Hungary's modern history, the politically articulate popular masses and the leaders of the government have realized where the true interest of the whole nation lay. Whereas there were some signs of anti-Semitism among parts of the populace and among some of the leaders of fighting units, conspicuously absent from the Revolution of 1956 was the taint of revisionist irredentism, the hard core and panacea of pre-World War II Magyar nationalism. Characteristically, the Soviet-inspired propaganda of both the Czechoslovak and Romanian regimes endeavored to stress precisely this nonexisting irredentism during and after the revolution, with the double aim of intimidating their own population and discrediting Imre Nagy's government.[104] And although the latter enjoyed the sympathy of Yugoslavia, the Yugoslav attitude was less than unequivocal as revealed by their relief after the second Soviet invasion in November, 1956.[105]

The Hungarian Revolution of 1956 thus again demonstrated the ambivalent attitude of the Soviet government and of the East European Communist regimes toward the issue of nationalism. Using

[104] Coloman Brogyányi, "Hungary's Fight for Freedom and the Hungarian Minorities," in *Hungarians in Czechoslovakia*, pp. 85–106; Introductory to *Magyar Nationalism*, by Andics, p. XXXIX. Cf. Béla Kovrig, "National Communism and Hungary," No. 15 of papers of the Slavic Institute at Marquette University (delivered on Nov. 2, 1958), pp. 103 f.

[105] Cf. Tito's address in Pula, on November 11, 1956, in Paul E. Zinner (ed.), *National Communism and Popular Revolt in Eastern Europe* (New York: Columbia University Press, 1956), pp. 516–41.

the revolution as a pretext, Romania decided to curb the rights of the Magyar minority in Transylvania. Since, however, she began to act rather independently of Moscow both within and outside the Communist orbit in recent years, her high-handed action was interpreted as a revival of old-fashioned "bourgeois nationalism." This came to the fore at a conference on Austria-Hungary held in Budapest in May, 1964; at this meeting of historians, Romanians were reminded by their Hungarian and Soviet colleagues that Romania, too, was a multinational state.[106] Or, to put it bluntly, she was given to understand that there was no reason why Romanian national claims to Bessarabia and northern Bukovina could not be countered with Magyar claims to parts of Transylvania. But the very emergence of Romanian "Titoism" is yet another warning that the Soviet Union, which has tried to play the game Nazi Germany played in the past, may herself get caught on the horns of a dilemma: how to fight revisionism and encourage peaceful coexistence, which implies greater independence for all concerned at the same time.

The Hungarian regime, too, has to come to grips with some thorny problems. Ever since they came into power, the Communists have shown utmost caution regarding the Magyar minorities in neighboring countries, which by now include the Soviet Union. The same prudence has prevailed in the evaluation of past disputes with the surrounding nations as suggested by a number of significant works published recently. It is "truly tragic"—to quote Robert A. Kann—"that only the entrenchment of Communist tyranny has put an end to the frequent smug self-satisfaction of official Magyar historiography in the treatment of the nationality question in royal Hungary."[107]

[106] George Bailey, "Trouble Over Transylvania," *The Reporter*, XXXI, No. 9 (Nov. 19, 1964), 25–30; *East Europe*, XIII, No. 8 (Aug., 1964), 44 f. For a rather subtle Romanian move aimed at "answering" the critics of her Transylvanian policy by veiled references to Bessarabia, cf. *East Europe*, XIV, No. 5 (May, 1965), 53. Also Wayne S. Vucinich, "Whither Rumania?" *Current History*, XLVIII, No. 283 (March, 1965), 165; 167. Also, Ghiță Ionescu, "Communist Rumania and Nonalignment (April, 1964–March, 1965)," *Slavic Review*, XXIV, No. 2 (1965), 252 f. For a Hungarian summary of the Budapest Conference, cf. "Az Osztrák-Magyar Monarchia történeti problémái, 1900–1918," *Századok*, XCIX, No. 2 (1965), 206–28.

[107] Review of *Studien zur Geschichte der Österreichisch-Ungarischen Monarchie* (Budapest: Akadémiai kiadó, 1961) in *The American Historical Review*, LXVII, No. 2 (1962), 409.

Relatively "fair" treatment of the nationality question has been part of the Communist regimes' common fight against the remnants of "bourgeois nationalism" in the whole area. Apart from some serious disagreements, as for example the dating and extent of non-Magyar settlements in medieval Hungary, central European historians have cooperated in research and writing, and this previously unthinkable friendly collaboration is bound to bring significant results both in the study of history and in mutual understanding.

Still, the recent re-emergence of the problem of the largest single Magyar minority under foreign domination in Transylvania makes one wonder about the optimism of a new study on Magyar nationalism, according to which, "Our task is to fight against the remnants of Magyar nationalism. Let us trust that our comrades in other countries will also do their best."[108]

Whatever its Marxist justification, such wishful thinking is less than convincing, although the reluctance of Hungarian officials to concern themselves openly with the plight of the Magyars in neighboring countries is understandable. After all there was not too much the Hungarian government could do to alleviate the situation of the hard-pressed Magyar minorities in either Yugoslavia or Czechoslovakia, let alone the Soviet Union in the first years after the war. And yet it is difficult to overlook completely the Magyars in Transylvania as shown recently when Gyula Illyés, Hungary's leading poet and a former Village Explorer, protested against the suppression of Transylvanian Magyars in an interview given to a French newspaper during his visit to Paris.[109] Although no such protests can be published in Hungary now, Illyés's outspoken stand warns of the existence of powerful forces hidden under the surface.

Indeed, Transylvania has been linked with many subtle ties to the rise of modern Magyar nationalism. In the sixteenth and seven-

---

[108] Simon, "A marxizmus-leninizmus klasszikusai . . . ," p. 21.

[109] *Irodalmi Ujság* (Paris), XVI, No. 3 (Feb. 1, 1965), 6. See also the doubts expressed by Péter Hanák, with the general approval of "those present," in the summary of an informal discussion "On the Nationalistic Remnants of Our Views on History" (Történetszemléletünk nacionalista maradványairól"), in *Történelmi Szemle*, VI, No. 1 (1963), 107. Furthermore, see the reference to the May, 1964, Conference on the History of the Austro-Hungarian Monarchy in Pál Zsigmond Pach, "Marxista történettudományunk fejlődésének problémái," *Századok*, XCVIII, Nos. 5–6 (1964), 1037.

teenth centuries, at the time of the precarious balance between the Habsburg and Ottoman empires, Hungarian patriots thought of the Principality of Transylvania as the only surviving symbol of Magyar independence. In the nineteenth century, Transylvanian politicians like Wesselényi and others infused a spirit of urgency but also a certain amount of self-conscious sectionalism into the main stream of Magyar nationalism. People like István Tisza, Bethlen, and Teleki had special antennae, so to speak, tuned to the wave length of Transylvania, whose writers in particular added a special flavor to modern Hungarian literature. There may well be an element of truth in the "accusation" brought against László Németh that "the idealization of the Transylvanian State had . . . a peculiar function in László Németh's system of thought: it served as a historical fore-runner to the formation of the 'third-road' conception."[110]

The vehement attack on Németh, on his close friend Gyula Illyés, on Péter Veres, and other Populist writers, and the linking of their ideas to "revisionism" and the Revolution of 1956 by the party in-dicates that these ideas may not have been "excluded entirely from the way of people's thinking."[111]

Hence, the issue of the Magyar minorities may be more deeply interwoven with the larger question of Magyar nationalism than is generally assumed. In this respect, too, one is reminded of the last paragraph in Paul E. Zinner's fine book on the Hungarian Revolu-tion of 1956.

. . . the Communist system of government causes tensions despite the propensity for adjustment and accommodation it has recently demon-strated. The dialogue in the Party continues. Revisionism is as old as the Communist movement.[112]

According to a party resolution "On Bourgeois Nationalism and So-cialist Patriotism" issued in 1959 and repeatedly confirmed in sub-sequent years, "nationalism has played a prominent role among the hostile ideologies; derived from different sources and displaying dif-ferent aspects it represents the main threat in our cultural-ideologi-

---

[110] Cited in "Hungary's Populist Writers," p. 40.
[111] *Ibid.*
[112] Paul E. Zinner, *Revolution in Hungary* (New York: Columbia University Press, 1962), p. 364.

cal life."[113] If one is to believe the Resolution of 1959 and subsequent discussions, then there must be a very strong undercurrent of nationalism in present-day Hungary, indeed.

The party, still under the impact of the shock suffered in 1956[114] and aware of the role played by intellectuals and students in awakening the social, national, and moral conscience of Hungarians in the post-Stalin era, attempts to discredit the claims of an intellectual elite to give leadership to the nation.

During the counterrevolution of 1956 we have learned at great cost, at the cost of much blood and material losses where the demand and practical application of the intelligentsia's leadership lead us. Bitter experience has taught us that such a theory is utterly reactionary because it means the liquidation of the power of the proletariat and because it paves the road toward the restoration of the bourgeoisie.[115]

Mistrusting both the people and the intelligentsia, the regime endeavors to be pragmatic by making economic concessions, encouraging contacts with the free world, and avoiding harsh police measures, at least up to a certain point. This neuralgic point is of great

[113] Pál Zsigmond Pach, "A nacionalizmus elleni harc," *Történelmi Szemle,* VII, No. 2 (1964), 312; "A 'haza' fogalma az osztálytársadalmakban," *Századok,* XCVI (1962), 393; "Nad chem rabotaiut vengerskie istoriki," *Voprosi istorii,* XXXVIII, No. 5 (1963), 196.

[114] Cf. the admission by Pál Zsigmond Pach, "Marxista történettudományunk fejlődésének problémái," p. 1032. See also the remarks of Péter Simon in the discussion of "The Patriotic-National Ideology." ("A hazafias-nemzeti ideológiáról. Molnár Erik előadásának vitája az Akadémia 1963. évi nagygyülésén," *A Magyar Tudományos Akadémia Társadalmi-Történeti Tudományok Osztályának Közleményei,* XIII, No. 3 [1963], 323.) Held in April, 1963, the discussion centered around the report and previous views of Erik Molnár, Director of the Historical Institute of the Academy, based on the assumption that "the ideology of patriotism or nationalism is the spiritual expression of the material interests of the bourgeoisie." The thesis itself and especially its implication, that the patriotic fervor of the toiling masses had been self-deception at best in the centuries preceding the establishment of the "People's Democracy," has come under sharp attack and this is reflected in the material of the session which was part of the Annual Meeting of the Academy. Although the session was attended by "several hundred historians," only six participants seem to have taken a stand, and this figure included Dezső Nemes, a member of the Politbureau, who presided over the discussion. The only historian by training who spoke (István Barta) preferred to say nothing about Molnár's views, refuting instead some of the suggestions made by Academic-Sociologist Ferenc Erdei.

[115] Mérei, "Szekfü Gyula," p. 241.

interest since, in the words of a survey conducted at Pécs University,

Nationalism still haunts the colleges and universities. And there are still many, even if not the majority, who state plainly, "I do not engage in politics," and believe that this is a good enough answer . . . . There is even a group which maintains that "politics is a private matter, and not the business of anyone else."[116]

Political apathy, however, *even if* it were the attitude of only a sizable minority, is ideologically unacceptable to Marxists, who view a noncommittal policy as leading inevitably "to the path of Imre Nagy," which, in turn,

would have led from the so-called neutralist foreign policy and from the desertion of the Warsaw Pact to the country's adherence to the imperialist bloc, to the abandonment of our national independence and to the restoration of capitalism . . . .[117]

Thus the policy of "liberalization" must by definition stop short of a policy of the "third road" or genuine neutrality between the overlapping Soviet and non-Soviet orbits in East Central Europe. Here the dreams of men like István Bibó must end[118] because the

[116] *Dunántúli Napló,* May 20, 1964, as quoted in *East Europe,* XIII, No. 7 (July, 1964), 42. For the alienation and political indifference of the masses in Hungary, see the interesting article by Péter Veres, one of the foremost Populist writers of the thirties and a former Chairman of the post-World War II National Peasant Party, in the December, 1964 issue of the Hungarian literary magazine *Kortárs* translated in *East Europe,* XIV, No. 3 (March, 1965), 23–26. Also Imre Kovács, "The Establishment in Hungary" and William Juhász, "Freedom under the Snow: New Trends in Hungarian Writings," *East Europe,* XIV, No. 5 (May, 1965), 2–7 and 8–10, respectively.

[117] From Gyula Kállai's address given at the Party Political Academy, *Népszabadság,* June 25, 1964, as cited in *East Europe,* XIII, No. 8 (Aug., 1964), 36.

[118] Gyula Borbándi, "István Bibó: Hungary's Political Philosopher," *East Europe,* XIII, No. 10 (1964), 2–7. For a recent attack on the concept of the "third road" see Aladár Mód, "A harmadik úttól a márciusi frontig," *Irodalomtörténeti Közlemények,* LXVIII, No. 1, 40–53. Turning an ideological somersault, the article condemns the "sectarian dogmatism" unable to tolerate the humanitarian views of even the proletarian poet Attila József in the thirties, the Populists' "socialism of quality" suggesting the salvation of the nation through the cooperation of the intelligentsia and the peasantry, and the urban writers' "glorification of western culture" all of which, allegedly, "melt into thin air on the bumper of contradictions in 1956." The solution recommended by the author is the well-known recipe for a higher synthesis of Magyardom with humanity: national unity under the leadership of the working class.

regime feels threatened in its very existence by any ideological compromise.

Unfortunate as this impasse may be, there seems to be no solution for it in the immediate future on the ideological level. Considering, however, the apparently growing discrepancy between the regime's more relaxed attitude toward some vitally important aspects of life,[119] and its attempt to close the Hungarian mind to the surrounding world with an ideological steel helmet, one wonders whether such a dichotomy may not be subject to change as time goes on. It is perhaps not altogether unreasonable to assume that if the present trend toward the fragmentation of all empires continues, and if the Soviet Union decides to accept, at some point, true coexistence with the West then, along with some *modus vivendi* in the German problem, some "third road" will have to be found that will be broad enough to accommodate the Soviet Union and a free Europe, and that will eventually be compatible with the genuine national feelings of the Magyar and non-Magyar peoples in eastern Europe.

[119] See Ernst C. Helmreich, "Kádár's Hungary," *Current History*, XLVIII, No. 283 (March, 1965), 142–48; also, J. F. Brown, "Eastern Europe," *Survey*, No. 54 (Jan., 1965), pp. 74 ff. For the limitations of the trend toward liberalization, cf. Imre Kovács, "The Establishment in Hungary," *East Europe*, XIV, No. 5 (May, 1965), 2–7, and Sándor Kiss, "Hungary's Economic Situation," *East Europe*, XIV, No. 5 (May, 1965), 21–27.

PETER BROCK

Polish Nationalism

I

Finis Poloniae, the apochryphal words that have been placed in the mouth of Tadeusz Kościuszko as he lay severely wounded on the battlefield of Maciejowice in 1794, certainly expressed the bewilderment and despair of many educated Poles after the third and final partition of their country, which took place in the following year. The ancient Polish commonwealth (*Rzeczpospolita*) had been wiped from the map; its inhabitants had become subjects of the Russian, Prussian, or Austrian monarchs. That Poland should again rise phoenixlike from these ashes appeared highly improbable even to many patriots. In fact, however, it was during the era when the country lay divided between the partitioning powers that modern Polish nationalism was securely forged.

The old commonwealth, which came into being in 1569 when the Union of Lublin completed the previous dynastic tie, dating back to 1386, between the Kingdom of Poland and the Grand Duchy of Lithuania, was ethnically heterogeneous. But the ruling class, the *szlachta* or gentry, had in the course of the centuries become largely Polonized where its origins were Lithuanian, Belorussian, or Ukrainian. Since the peasantry was still enserfed, the middle class weak and sometimes unassimilated, only the gentry enjoyed the full privileges of a citizen.

The *Rzeczpospolita* provided the original matrix of Polish nationalism: the state's dissolution acted as a powerful stimulus in developing the form this nationalism was finally to take in our own day. The upper class had been knit together by a feeling of "belonging," of membership of the gentry nation. True, its boasted republicanism was based on the exclusion from all participation in affairs of state of not only the non-Polish, but also the Polish masses (for it was not ethnic affinity but shared privilege that provided the bond uniting members of the "nation"). Yet for all its class egotism, as well as its readiness to call for foreign intervention in the interests of faction or personal gain or at the bidding of the great magnates that reached its apogee in the notorious Confederation of Targowica of 1792, this gentry had long been infused with a sense of territorial patriotism, a loyalty to the commonwealth that safeguarded its "golden liberty."

That great movement of reform, the "democratic revolution" of the late eighteenth century, which sprang out of the intellectual Enlightenment, affected Poland as it did the countries of western Europe and colonial America. The French Revolution, rightly regarded as the starting point of modern nationalism, awoke a deep response in Poland, where a group of indigenous reformers succeeded during the sessions of the famous Four Years' Diet of 1788–92 in pushing through a program of modernization of the antiquated state machine. Although the Constitution of the Third of May, 1791, did not go so far as to establish full equality for all citizens, the group of reformers led by two enlightened abbés, Hugo Kołłataj and Stanisław Staszic, time and again in their writings called for a broadening of the concept of the nation to include all social classes. In 1791 one of their most radical protagonists, Father Jezierski, defined a nation in the following terms: "It is a collection of people having in common language, habits and customs framed within one general code of laws for all citizens." The third estate was the most important element in the nation, not the gentry with its cosmopolitan culture, for it was the common people who differentiated one nation from another.[1]

With these writers, as was indeed everywhere common up to this period, the emphasis is on the state as the cement that binds the citizen body making up the nation into one. They are territorial patriots but not yet nationalists in the modern sense of the term. The destruction of the state, therefore, faced all Polish patriots with the agonizing question: did this event inevitably entail the eventual

---

[1] Franciszek Salezy Jezierski, *Wybór pism*, ed. Zdzisław Skwarczyński (Warsaw, 1952), pp. 217, 244. See also A. P. Coleman, "Language as a Factor in Polish Nationalism," *Slavonic and East European Review* (London), XIII, No. 37 (July, 1934), 155, 156; Franciszek Pepłowski, *Słownictwo i frazeologia polskiej publicystyki okresu oświecenia i romantyzmu* (Warsaw, 1961), pp. 106, 107.

dissolution of the nation? Could indeed a nation exist for any length of time without incarnation in a state?

At first many members of the political nation, especially of the magnate class, accepted as an irreversible fact that the loss of statehood signified the end of the nation. For not a few the foreign states under whose rule they had been rudely forced became "our Fatherland"[2]; their loyalty was transferred to St. Petersburg, Berlin, or Vienna. No serious attempt was made by the partitioning powers at this period to impose forcible denationalization on their new subjects; Russia and Austria, at least, courted the upper ranks of the Polish nobility through various concessions. True, the overwhelming mass of the gentry continued to consider themselves Poles; yet in the decades to come the majority made their peace, at least outwardly, with the foreign regime under which they must live. "In a certain sense we are now better off than in Polish times," a Polish gentleman from Ukraine confided to his diary, "although without Poland, we are, nevertheless, in Poland, and are Poles."[3]

The "crisis of national consciousness,"[4] to which even men of the stature of Kościuszko or Kołłataj had briefly succumbed, was, however, overcome within a couple of decades after the loss of political independence. The *émigrés* who had taken refuge in revolutionary Paris after the failure of Kościuszko's uprising in 1794 continued to work for the resurrection of the Polish state. This, in their view, would be achieved by military action and with French support. Thus we get the formation of Polish Legions in 1797 under the command of Jan Henryk Dąbrowski to fight alongside Napoleon's armies in Italy. At home measures began to be taken to preserve the Polish cultural heritage from withering away under foreign rule and to form underground organizations to prepare for another uprising. The most important of these was the Society of Polish Republicans, which represented the radical strand that was present from the beginning in the Polish insurrectionary tradition. Its members were Jacobins; they called for peasant emancipation as an essential condition for the development of the nation. While the res-

[2] Henryk Mościcki (ed.), *Dzieje porozbiorowe Polski w aktach i dokumentach* (Warsaw, n.d.), I, 21.

[3] Quoted in Hans Koch, "Slavdom and Slavism in the Polish National Consciousness 1794–1848," *Eastern Germany* (Würzburg,1963), II, 226.

[4] Marian Kukiel, "Zagadnienie niepodległości w latach 1795–1815," *Pamietnik V powszechnego zjazdu historyków polskich w Warszawie,* I (Lwów, 1930), 505.

toration of the historic state formed the kernel of their program, its establishment on a republican basis was deemed equally important. The Society enjoyed the support of Kościuszko after his release from a Russian prison.

In a pamphlet with the challenging title *Can Poles Regain Independence?*, which appeared anonymously in 1800, Kościuszko told his fellow countrymen: "You cannot be really free unless you win independence by your own effort."[5] However, this warning against overreliance on foreign help was scarcely heeded. Despite repeated disappointments and temporary disillusionment, Polish patriots continued to give their allegiance to Napoleon's France as the instrument that would liberate their country. The setting up in 1806 of the Duchy of Warsaw with its own army (the idea of a national army was always immensely important in the schemes of the independence movement) appeared to foreshadow the reconstitution of the old Polish state as part of a new European order under French leadership. In his Moscow campaign of 1812, Napoleon had no more reliable troops in his *Grande Armée* than the Polish divisions, which remained with him until he went down in final defeat. The Napoleonic legend lived on as part of the "myth" of Polish nationalism. Bonaparte's creation, the Duchy of Warsaw, disappeared: the modernization of its administrative machinery, including the abolition in 1807 of the peasantry's servile status, marked, however, a further stage towards the creation of a modern nation.

In place of the Duchy of Warsaw, the Vienna peacemakers in 1815 established a Kingdom of Poland, the so-called Congress Kingdom, less extensive in territory than the duchy, and with the three partitioning powers still in complete control (if we disregard, as did these powers, certain paper safeguards guaranteeing the unity of the former Polish lands) of the greater part of the area covered by the old commonwealth. The crown of this miniature kingdom was bestowed on Tsar Alexander I of Russia and an indissoluble union proclaimed between his two realms.

A pro-Russian trend, a prominent feature of eighteenth-century Polish history, had revived among the Poles since Alexander I ascended the Russian throne in 1801. Liberal in his outlook and aspirations, the young tsar had taken as his closest adviser and coun-

[5] Henryk Mościcki (ed.), *Pisma Tadeusza Kościuszki* (Warsaw, 1947), p. 172. The pamphlet was dictated to his secretary.

sellor a Polish friend, Prince Adam Czartoryski. For a time Czartoryski acted as his foreign minister: hopes rose that a united Polish state would again arise under the aegis of the liberal tsar. In 1803, Czartoryski was placed in charge of education and cultural life in the whole borderland area that had formed part of the Polish state. Largely as a result of Czartoryski's work here, which continued until 1823, Polish cultural ascendancy was secured for several generations ahead in an area where only the upper crust of society was ethnically and linguistically Polish.

Politically the Russian orientation represented by Czartoryski was conservative, finding its main supporters among the "Lithuanian" magnates and gentry. Intellectually, it formed part of a wider current of thought, Slavophilism, that gained a powerful hold over the minds of many Poles of the left as well as of the right towards the end of the eighteenth and during the first half of the nineteenth century. Slavophile sentiments were manifested to some degree by all the Slav peoples at this time, but the movement was by no means uniform, even within a single nation. Among the Poles there were two major variants.[6] Most widespread was the version in which Poland, with its long tradition of political liberty and its close links with western civilization, was cast in the role of leader of a Slav world laboring under the burden of internal or external despotism. But in the early decades after 1795 a second variation dominated, in which the Poles were summoned to throw in their lot with the rest of Slavdom under the leadership of the mighty Russian Empire in an effort to stem the advance of a decadent and materialist West.

Views like this reflected the pessimism of a generation that had witnessed the disappearance of their country from the map. By association with the one great Slav power, by fusing Poland's efforts with the enormous collectivity of the Slav peoples, compensation was sought for their own nation's weakness. With some Polish Slavophiles of this period, identification with the larger whole reached as far as a denial of the existence of a separate Polish language and culture, but more usual were the various plans to link a future reunited Polish state in some kind of organic union with Russia. This

[6] Zofia Klarnerówna, *Słowianofilstwo w literaturze polskiej lat 1800 do 1848* (Warsaw, 1926), pp. 6, 7. See also Georges Luciani, *La Société des Slaves unis (1823–1825)* (Bordeaux, 1963), Book II, "Les origines polonaises de l'idéologie des Slaves unis."

was partially realized in 1815. As Staszic told the Russians in that year: "Poles are incapable of being your slaves, but are ready to become your brothers. Unite this nation, with a constitution suitable to its own national law and government, into one great realm of the tsardom under one emperor and king."[7] Two further concepts frequently occur in the writings of the Polish Slavophiles: the mission of the peace-loving Slav peoples to regenerate European culture, an idea that owed much to the German, Herder, and the Teutonic menace that necessitated Poland's seeking support from her fellow Slavs.

Language, as the main factor differentiating Slavs from their neighbors, and the Poles from their fellow Slavs, became a matter of increasing concern after the loss of independence both for apolitical Slavophiles and for those who favored insurrectionary politics. If the language disappeared, what was left on which to build? A leading figure in the Society of Polish Republicans wrote as early as 1799 of "the decisive . . . influence of language" in prolonging the existence of the nation.[8] Kołłątaj continually stressed the prime importance for national culture of maintaining the purity of the Polish tongue, going so far as to advocate the exclusion from all but private use of the non-Polish languages spoken within the territories of the former commonwealth.[9] Samuel Bogumił Linde produced his monumental dictionary of the Polish language between 1807 and 1814, an important factor in preserving the literary language. The growing influence of romanticism on Polish intellectual life, and of German romantic nationalism in particular,[10] led a host of scholars —historians, linguists, literary critics, and ethnographers—to deepen their studies of the native culture both by going back to its roots in the distant pre-Christian past, a past that in compensation for the uncertain present was described in idealized and often fan-

[7] Stanisław Staszic, *Pisma filozoficzne i społeczne*, ed. Bogdan Suchodolski (Warsaw), II (1954), 318, 319. For similar views expressed by Czartoryski in 1806, see *Dzieje porozbiorowe Polski*, I, 99–102.

[8] Quoted in Marceli Handelsman, *Rozwój narodowości nowoczesnej*, I, Warsaw [1923], 240.

[9] Hugo Kołłątaj, *Stan oświęcenia w Polsce w ostatnich latach panowania Augusta III* (1750–1764), ed. Jan Hulewicz (Wrocław, 1953), pp. 11–13.

[10] See Walter Kühne, "Von der Entwicklung des polnischen Nationalgefühls," *Volk und Reich* (Berlin), IX, No. 7 (July, 1933), 623–37; IX, No. 12 (Dec., 1933), 998–1007.

tastic terms, and by investigating the stratum of the population
that still, it was believed, preserved this culture intact in the present:
the peasantry, the "people," the *Volk*.

With conservative writers (for a conservative nationalism made
its appearance earlier among the Poles than, for instance, either
in Germany or in Spain), it was a patriarchal system that marked
Polish rural society. More often village democracy appeared to these
scholars as the truly Slav way of life. All saw the Slavs in general as
a simple, peaceful, hard-working race of agriculturalists. A typical
figure among these Slavophiles was Adam Czarnocki, writing under
the pseudonym of Zorian Dołęga Chodakowski, who traveled around
the countryside collecting folk songs and village lore. For Chodakowski, the pure spirit of nationality was to be found only in the
Polish peasantry; the coming of Christianity had corrupted the upper classes by introducing alien ways.

Thus a linguistic and cultural nationalism slowly took shape
alongside the older concept of the nation, identifying it with the
territorial state, actual or potential, and the classes that were admitted to citizenship within the state. These new notions, especially
at first, rarely differentiated clearly between Polish and Slav, and
the language enthusiasts were sometimes active also in political efforts directed towards a revival of the old Polish state. But by centering nationality primarily on community of language (often the
creation of a common Slavic tongue was held up as the ideal),
rather than on a shared history and political life, a development
was initiated that was fraught with the utmost consequence for the
future.

The decade and a half between the establishment of the Congress
Kingdom and the outbreak of the November Revolution of 1830
marked the transition of romantic nationalism from a largely literary to a political movement. It was an era in which among the educated youth, students, journalists, junior army officers, and the lower
ranks of the bureaucracy—for the most part young men of gentry
background—we find a kaleidoscope of secret societies. Many, like
the Wilno Society of Philomaths, were organized at first purely for
the cultivation of the citizen virtues, and then, after attempts at
suppression by the authorities, passed over into political and military conspiracy aimed at the restoration of full independence

throughout all the former Polish lands. The most important of these groups, the National Patriotic Society, even succeeded in establishing contact with the Russian Decembrists. For this first generation of romantic nationalists, part of the European revolutionary movement of the decade following 1820, the fatherland was more than a mere territory; it had now become an individuality, an idea." As the poet Brodziński, a disciple of Herder and Hegel, wrote in his address "Concerning the Nationality of the Poles": "The nation is an inborn idea, which its members, fused into one, strive to realize."[12] And liberty was essential if the nation was to flourish.

For these young nationalists, therefore, the parliamentary opposition that centered around the Niemojowski brothers appeared hopelessly inadequate. The Niemojowski brothers were working to establish constitutional liberties within the context of the Congress Kingdom on the pattern of contemporary French liberalism; they looked to purely legal action in defense of national rights. The parliamentarians thus not only ran into opposition from Polish obscurantists, like the Viceroy Zajączek, and Russian reactionaries of the type of Novosiltsev, they were also hampered by the activities of youthful and often rash conspirators.

The constitutional experiment of the Congress Kingdom, with its promising economic development promoted by the finance minister Lubecki, was in fact brought to an end, not by Russian intervention, but by the precipitate action of the young cadets of the kingdom's army, when the authorities became aware of their underground organization. Their attack on the viceroy's Warsaw residence on November 29, 1830, soon escalated into a full-scale war against Russia, in which the more conservative elements of society were drawn reluctantly to take the lead.

"Independence within the framework of the present Kingdom is a political chimera: we did not rise for such independence," declared Mochnacki, one of the ablest of the romantic nationalist writers.[13] The incorporation (on paper) of the eastern borderlands, "the seized territories (ziemie zabrane)" so dear to the hearts of

---

[11] Jerzy Szacki, *Ojczyzna, Naród, Rewolucja* (Warsaw, 1962), p. 87.

[12] Kazimierz Brodziński, *Mowy i pisma patrjotyczne*, ed. Ignacy Chrzanowski (Cracow, 1926), p. 76. The address was composed in 1831 during the insurrection.

[13] *Dzieła Maurycego Mochnackiego*, IV: *Pisma rozmaite* (Poznań, 1863), p. 3.

successive generations of Poles and so tenaciously upheld as Russian by Russian public opinion,[14] was proclaimed, and a not-too successful effort begun to extend the uprising into these lands. However, not merely did the Polish cause make little appeal to the non-Polish masses in this area, but the patriots failed, too, to enlist the Polish-speaking peasantry as a whole in the fight against the Russians. The left wing was not able to persuade the insurrectionary diet either to abolish labor services or to endow the peasants with the land they worked for themselves—the two measures that might have gained their widespread support. "The Polish nationality is excluded today from the ranks of the nations, but Polish peasants have lost nothing by this," was the bitter comment of an insurrectionary veteran of peasant origin.[15]

For nearly two decades after the insurrection's defeat the center of Polish political life was transferred to the emigration. Among the exiles in western Europe heated and often bitter controversy arose about the reasons for the failure of the uprising, the ways and means to restore Polish independence, and the possible structure of a revived Polish state. The idea of Poland's mission inspired the activities of the émigrés, cutting across political divisions and assuming a variety of different guises.

Brodziński in 1831 in his address on Polish nationality had asserted the necessity of a Poland within the divine harmony of the nations. Its sacrifice, like Christ's, would not be in vain if it remained loyal to its mission of defending "freedom and brotherhood,"[16] which form the basis of the moral order of the universe. Polish messianism did not begin with Brodziński, but his ideas were especially influential on the Polish poets and thinkers who were active during the next three decades. The influence is clear in the work of Adam Mickiewicz, who set forth a messianic view of Poland's past and future at the very outset of his career as an exile. In his *Books of the Polish Nation and of the Polish Pilgrims* (1832) he depicts the martyrdom of his country and its burial. "But on the third day," he declares, "the soul shall return to the body, and the

[14] For schemes to reunite these territories with the Congress Kingdom before 1830, see Henryk Mościcki, *Pod berłem carów* (Warsaw, 1924), chap. iv.

[15] Kazimierz Deczyński, *Pamietnik chłopa-nauczyciela* (Warsaw, 1949), pp. 41–45. The memoirs were written in exile in the 1830's.

[16] Brodziński, *Mowy* . . . , p. 78.

Nation shall arise and free all the peoples of Europe from slavery."
Thus, "the nations shall be saved . . . through the merits of a
martyred nation." Peace between them would be established for
ever. And in this divine scheme it was to be his fellow exiles (unless they were to prove unfaithful to their calling), who must act
as the apostles of their crucified nation.[17] Mickiewicz's hopes that
the *Books* would put an end to political schisms and fuse the
émigrés together in a united effort to achieve the national mission
remained unrealized. But the role he assigned the seer in the spiritual leadership of the nation was taken up by his fellow poets, Juliusz Słowacki and the politically conservative Zygmunt Krasiński,
and by philosophers like Józef Hoene-Wroński, August Cieszkowski,
and Karol Libelt. They proclaimed the approaching advent of a new
era of world history—"the third era" according to Trentowski[18]—
which would be inaugurated by the re-establishment of the Polish
state. For this "our death was needed as will be our resurrection."[19]
In the early eighteen forties this theme was developed by Mickiewicz (then coming under the influence of the mystical fantasies of
Andrzej Towiański) in his lectures at the Collège de France. "Cette
nation," the poet wrote of Poland in 1844, "montant de souffrance
en souffrance vers son Dieu, qui a été sur la terre l'homme de dou-
leur, cette nation . . . s'unit à lui, et lui prépara dans son sein le
sanctuaire."[20] All these writers indeed stressed the redemptive effi-
cacy of Poland's sufferings: the fact of political annihilation became
the cornerstone of the Polish national idea.

Poland had a mission to humanity, but it was a mission that expressed itself through Slavdom. The earlier Slavophilism, with its
predominantly apolitical antiquarianism, lack of emphasis on the
individuality of the separate Slav nations, and vaguely pro-Russian
tendencies, was transformed under the impact of national defeat
into a political philosophy, which sought to justify Poland's right
to independence by its civilizing role in the Slav world. Throughout history, until it finally succumbed to the attacks of freedom's

---

[17] George Rapall Noyes (ed.), *Poems by Adam Mickiewicz* (New York: Polish
Institute of Arts and Sciences, 1944), pp. 379, 380, 407.

[18] Quoted in Hans Kohn, *Pan-Slavism, Its History and Ideology* (New York: Vintage Books, 1960), p. 35.

[19] Zygmunt Krasiński, *Przedświt*, ed. Juliusz Kleiner (Cracow, n.d.), p. 53.

[20] Adam Mickiewicz, *L'Église et le Messie*, II (Paris, 1845), 268, 269.

enemies, Poland had defended the West against the hordes of Asia (in the works of Mickiewicz, for instance, we find Poland pictured as the quite innocent victim, the lamb sacrificed for the sins of others, that was but one example of a widespread idealization of the country's past). Its future role was no less lofty. "In our renascence," wrote a democratic publicist in 1833, "is contained at once the idea of the renascence and enlightenment of all Slavdom and of carrying the light of civilization to the ignorant and backward East."[21] For the left-wing émigrés, Poland's task was not only to civilize the Slavic East but to transplant there the social gospel, the new democratic ideas that had developed out of the French Revolution. According to the researches of Joachim Lelewel and his historical school, liberty, equality, and fraternity were discovered also to have been the principles of the primitive democracy of the early Slav communes, which Polish-gentry democracy had succeeded in preserving throughout the centuries, albeit in a corrupted form. Establish full political democracy, emancipate the peasantry and endow them with land, said the democrats, and the new Poland will lead the Slav peoples, including the Russians (and eventually the whole world), into a federation of free nations.

If the left wing continued to hope for the regeneration of Russia —witness the manifestoes addressed to the Russian people by Lelewel's National Committee at the outset, and the collaboration between Polish democrats and Russian revolutionaries of Herzen's circle at the conclusion of the period of the "Great Emigration"— voices were raised from the right denying the Russians a place within the community of Slav nations. Krasiński, for instance, saw an antithesis between Poland and Russia as deep as that between Ormazd and Ahriman. For Trentowski this dualism of incarnated good and evil was ineradicable: therefore, in Russia's case, talk of unity between peoples or of Slavic brotherhood was highly dangerous.

A few individuals were to be found, on the other hand, who continued to preach amalgamation with Russia as the only way to escape eventual Germanization. What before 1830 had not been deemed inconsistent with some kind of cultural nationalism, now

---

[21] Witold Łukaszewicz and Władysław Lewandowski (eds.), *Postępowa publicystyka emigracyjna 1831–1846* (Wrocław, 1961), p. 218.

took on the form of "national apostasy." Writers like Count Gurowski (erstwhile Polish democrat and future American radical republican) advised the substitution in the schools of Polish by Russian and ultimately its replacing in daily use all the other Slav
tongues.[22] The legal historian, W. A. Maciejowski, portrayed the
west Slavs in his works as corrupted and the source of light and
regeneration as flowing from the east, while the archconservative
novelist, Count Henryk Rzewuski, denied any possibility of prolonging even the cultural separateness of his nation, which should
assimilate as speedily as possible with a Russian-dominated Slavdom. The pessimism that inspired views of this kind, common in the
period following the final partition and becoming widespread again
after the failure of the 1863 insurrection, accorded ill with the
boundless hopes and almost chiliastic enthusiasm of the romantic
generation of the thirties and forties.

Concerning the territorial extent of a revived Polish state and its
ethnic composition, there was near unanimity between the views of
left and right.[23] True, the conservative party that gathered in exile
around Prince Czartoryski was active in trying to persuade the
western powers to intervene in favor of a restoration of the *status
quo* in the Congress Kingdom, on the basis of their rights as guar-
antors of the Vienna settlement. The policy met with stern disap-
proval from the democratic camp, both those in exile and those in
the home country. "Cabinet treaties will never restore Poland, and
monarchical wars will never render justice to her people," they
claimed in the famous manifesto of 1836,[24] urging instead mobiliza-
tion of the masses in a revolutionary war against the occupiers,
which would be fought in alliance with the other peoples of Europe. (A "Young Poland," for instance, worked within Mazzini's
"Young Europe" movement). Some democrats urged the use of
"terror" against members of the indigenous ruling class who opposed social revolution.[25] The long series of conspiracies that un-

[22] See LeRoy H. Fischer, *Lincoln's Gadfly, Adam Gurowski* (Norman, Okla.: University of Oklahoma Press, 1964), chap. ii.

[23] Stanisław Pigoń, *Zręby nowej Polski w publicystyce Wielkiej Emigracji* (Warsaw, 1938), chap. ii.

[24] *Manifesto of the Polish Democratical Society* (London, 1837), p. 14. The translation was published by the Chartist Henry Hetherington.

[25] This idea was set forth in the mid-forties in the influential works of Henryk
Kamieński.

folded in Poland in the thirties and forties were largely, though by no means exclusively, inspired by the *émigré* center and left. But the exile conservatives, too, included among their long-term objectives preparation under the auspices of the landowning class for another armed uprising, which would restore the old commonwealth in the form of a constitutional monarchy.[26]

In the opinion of both left and right, the new Poland, "whole and independent," should embrace all territories forming part of the state at the time of the first partition of 1772. They spoke even of a Poland "from Baltic to Black Sea." Anything less would have seemed to imply approval of the crime committed by the partitioning powers. For many democrats, this was merely a minimum program. From early in the nineteenth century, for the first time for centuries, there were periodic demands for the eventual recovery of territories like East Prussia and Silesia, which had ceased to be part of the Polish state towards the end of the Middle Ages. These lands, Lelewel wrote, were lost by the aristocracy; they would be regained "through the people, through . . . democracy."[27] For if nationality were defined by the language of the masses and not by historic frontiers or the existing level of national consciousness, then the deciding factor in these areas was that their inhabitants still spoke the Polish language.

What then of the vast eastern territories where the people were ethnically and linguistically non-Polish? On what principle did the democrats claim the old frontiers of a prenational era for their people's state of the future? The answer is simple. Whether moderate republicans, radical democrats, or extreme socialists, they all failed to detect any fundamental difference among the submerged peasantries of these lands. However much there might be variations in dialect or local custom, all formed but one nationality; all were Poles. "Already for centuries," Lelewel stated in 1836, "the Ruthenian, Polish and Lithuanian languages have been brothers; they constitute no national division among themselves." Eight years later we find him writing: "The people of former Poland, our beloved Fatherland, are very numerous. Lithuanian, Cracovian, Mazurian, Samogitian, Kashub, 'Prussian,' Ukrainian, Great Polander, all are

[26] Marceli Handelsman, *Francja-Polska 1795–1845* (Warsaw, 1926), pp. 292–94.
[27] Joachim Lelewel, *Polska, dzieje i rzeczy jej,* VIII (Poznan, 1855), 3–6.

Poles."[28] Similar statements can be found without difficulty in other contemporary political literature.

The example of revolutionary France, which had welded the French nation into one, destroying in the process the remnants of feudal separatism and outmoded regionalisms, was a powerful influence in shaping left-wing opinion. The Polish democrats, like their French exemplars, were centralizers (as indeed, for different reasons, were the monarchists of Czartoryski's party). Advocacy of a federal structure was identified with inclination to restore the old hierarchical social order.

Thus Krępowiecki, reddest of the reds, an ardent Socialist who repeatedly expressed admiration for the leaders of Ukrainian peasant revolts against the former Polish state, declared in an article with the significant title "Nationality (Centralization)"[29]: "In face of [social] revolution the spirit of provincialism is a standard of revolt and schism." While mildly separatist tendencies were expressed here and there among the Polish (or Polonized) gentry of Lithuania and Ukraine, the left, despite the cleavages that existed within it on other questions, stood solidly in favor of a unitary nation-state. For them the nationality problem in these areas merely concealed what was basically a social problem. Abolish labor services and satisfy the peasants' land hunger—and then the peoples of the old commonwealth, left free to use their provincial dialects in daily use until these withered away quite naturally, could be fused without trouble into one Polish nation.[30] That neither the *émigré* democrats nor the "apostles" of democracy, like Szymon Konarski, for instance, who worked in the home country often at great personal risk, showed any sympathy with the potential political separateness of Ukrainians or Belorussians, Lithuanians, or Latvians, need not surprise us, however, if we remember that at this period even indigenous cultural movements among these peoples had barely begun. The alternatives presented themselves as either ac-

---

[28] *Ibid.,* XX (1864), 223, 225, 456.

[29] Printed in W. Łukaszewicz, *Tadeusz Krępowiecki: Żołnierz rewolucjonista* (Warsaw, 1954), pp. 163–72.

[30] One Populist radical, however, the youthful Piotr A. Semenenko (soon to become a Catholic priest), called for the establishment of a united Slavdom under Polish leadership indeed, but "based on its most powerful element, on the Ruthenian people." See *Postęp* (Paris, 1834), No. 5, Part I, p. 73. Semenenko was of Belorussian origin.

ceptance of Great Russian statehood in this area or eventual absorption into the Polish nation, with whom over so many centuries the population had shared a common territory and, at least in its politically conscious stratum, a common political tradition. The tragic mistake came later with the failure to recognize the existence of the emergent nationalisms of Poland's eastern borderlands.

The radicals of the period between the 1830 and the 1863 uprisings were indeed essentially Populist nationalists. Penitent gentry for the most part, they shaped a new concept of nationality[31] that, more firmly than earlier attempts, identified nationality with the "people," meaning the peasantry together possibly with the "peasant" gentry (*szlachta zagrodowa*). Conservatives, if they did not still see the nation as an exclusively upper-class affair, regarded it as resulting from a harmony of interests between gentry and peasants. The radicals either excluded the gentry from a place in the nation or assigned them a very subordinate and temporary role. Some saw "a sea of blood" dividing "the country of the Polish people" that must be established from the class—nation of the gentry.[32] Others took a more benevolent view of the latter's contribution in the past, only wishing now to transfer the accrued benefits of the historic culture to all. The citizen body—the nation—would include Jews alongside peasantry and townsfolk and liberal gentry. The idea of the "Pole of Mosaic faith" makes its appearance: Lelewel was one of the most eloquent advocates of equality for the Jews. Some hesitation existed about the advisability of granting full citizen rights to the unassimilated mass of Jews; wealthy Jews came in for attack in the left-wing *émigré* press for their association with industrial capital in the West. But many argued that the granting of equality would in fact act as an effective instrument of assimilation, which was generally regarded on the left as the proper object of an enlightened policy towards the Jews.

The year 1848 proved a bitter disappointment to the Polish nationalists, who had hoped to see all three partitioning powers

---

[31] Pepłowski, *Słownictwo i frazeologia*, pp. 109, 110. The description "penitent gentry" was used by Mierosławski of the Polish *émigré* revolutionaries (see L. B. Namier, *1848: The Revolution of the Intellectuals* [London: Oxford University Press, 1944], p. 14). This usage seems to precede Mikhailovsky's application of the term to the Russian *narodniki* of gentry origin.

[32] Hanna Temkinowa (ed.), *Lud Polski: Wybór dokumentów* (Warsaw, 1957), p. 58.

ejected from Polish territory. Their failure was due in large part to the weakness of the revolutionary impulse, which had been adversely affected by the debacle of 1846 when the long-planned uprising scarcely spread beyond the frontiers of the miniature Free City of Cracow, in comparison with the strength that the partitioning powers could muster once the initial shock of revolution had been overcome. Russian Poland indeed was scarcely touched by the unrest.

The Springtime of the Peoples laid bare three defects in the armor of Polish nationalism. First, we find in Poznania, before the spring ended, fierce national antagonism between the two peoples of the province rapidly replacing the exalted *Polenschwärmerei* of the early moments. The Germans demanded partition; the Poles replied by proposing a plebiscite in West Prussia and Upper Silesia. In the end, superior Prussian government forces brought military defeat to the Poles. And meanwhile almost the whole liberal camp throughout Germany, now that the likelihood of war with Russia seemed remote and the need to cultivate the Poles as allies less pressing, turned its face against serious concessions to Polish demands in the name of "a healthy German egotism."[33] The alliance of the peoples appeared shattered.

In the second place events showed clearly that over wide areas the Polish-speaking peasantry—the "people"—took the side of the partitioning powers against a national movement that they regarded as solely the cause of their social superiors and economic oppressors. The fearful *jacquerie* that took place in central Galicia in 1846 had indeed proved this. In 1848 the sight of the peasant deputies voting obediently in the Austrian *Reichsrat* on the orders of Count Franz Stadion brought the point home to conservative and liberal nationalists alike as they sought from the opposition benches to bring into being some form of autonomy for the Poles of the Habsburg Empire —a version of Austro-Slavism—as a first step towards ultimate reunity.

The Ukrainian (or Ruthenian) question in east Galicia was the third issue that arose to plague the Polish patriots in their endeavors. The influence of Polish romantic nationalism had been one of the factors in the birth of Ukrainian cultural nationalism in the

[33] Wilhelm Jordan, quoted in Namier, *1848*, p. 88.

thirties and forties (there was even a Polish regional school of "Ukrainian" poets). But the spokesmen of the Galician Ukrainians, a peasant people with an intelligentsia still only in the making, who had formed a Chief Ruthenian Council in Lwów, were militantly anti-Polish and solidly pro-Habsburg. Their platform included a variety of political, social, cultural, and religious demands: above all, they insisted on the division of the province into a Polish and Ukrainian half. Their conservative clericalism (the leadership was drawn from the upper ranks of the Uniate clergy) made them anathema to the Polish democrats, whose efforts to organize a rival pro-Polish group among the Ruthenians (*gente Rutheni, natione Poloni*) were not very successful. The Ukrainians appeared to many Poles (as the Poles themselves had appeared for a while to the Germans) as confederates in the fight against tsardom. "The easiest way to disarm the Ruthenians in their struggle against the Poles . . . is to recognize their independence," wrote a follower of Czartoryski in 1850;[34] an independence, of course, that would entail close links with a Polish state. Few, however, among either conservatives or democrats were prepared at this period to go beyond a vague recognition of a "Ruthenian" linguistic "nationality." A leftwinger like Podolecki preaching social revolution to his fellow countrymen could detect no genuine national consciousness among the Galician Ukrainians, whom "only the centuries [to come] can perhaps shape into a true nation": today, he felt, only the Poles had "a national mission."[35] It is not surprising, therefore, that the agreement reached at the Slav Congress in Prague on June 7, whereby in exchange for postponement of a decision on the question of partition, the Polish delegates agreed to "a most liberal programme securing real equality of rights for the Ruthenes in Galicia,"[36] was rejected by the Polish National Council in Lwów.

The defeat of revolution in 1848 and the ensuing reaction caused a re-evaluation in some quarters of Polish national aims. In Poz-

[34] Quoted in Marceli Handelsman, *Ukraińska polityka ks. Adama Czartoryskiego przed wojną krymską* (Warsaw, 1937), p. 149.

[35] Jan Kanty Podolecki, *Wybór pism z lat 1846–1851*, ed. Andrzej Grodek (Warsaw, 1955), pp. LVII, LVIII. Cf. Wiktor Heltman, *Demokracya polska na emigracyi* (Leipzig, 1866), pp. 288, 301.

[36] Namier, *1848*, p. 113. The agreement is printed in Václav Žáček (ed.), *Slovanský sjezd v Praze roku 1848: Sbírka dokumentů* (Prague, 1958), pp. 314, 315. It was also rejected by the Chief Ruthenian Council.

nania, even earlier, a movement had set in among more conservative elements to replace insurrectionary hopes and *émigré* leadership by action directed solely at strengthening the social and economic foundations of the Polish community within the limits of the
province. The experiences of 1848 strengthened this trend; it began
to take root, too, in Galicia and the Congress Kingdom. Harking
back to the climate of opinion during the first years of the century,
this movement marked the beginnings of the "organic work" and
"triple loyalty" that dominated the decades following the 1863 insurrection.

The insurrection was sparked by the hasty action taken against
the revolutionary movement by the head of government in the Congress Kingdom, the Marquis Wielopolski. Wielopolski is one of the
most controversial figures in Polish history. "La noblesse polonaise,"
he had told Metternich just after the Galician Massacre of 1846,

préféra sans doute marcher avec les Russes à la tête de la civilisation slave,
jeune, vigoureuse et pleine d'avenir, que de se traîner . . . à la queue de
votre civilisation décrépite, tracassière et présomptueuse. En compensation de tout ce que nous apporterions à la Russie, elle fournirait à notre
race une vaste carrière de travail social, et d'intérêts positifs et majeurs,
qui rempliraient le vide désespérant de notre situation actuelle.[37]

In 1861 his chance came to carry through, with the support of the
"Tsar-Liberator" Alexander II, a conservative revolution in the Congress Kingdom against the opposition of both "Whites" and "Reds."
The latter sought either by open manifestations or secret conspiracy
to prepare the ground for an anti-Russian uprising. The burgeoning
autonomy that Wielopolski won from the tsar was swept away as a
result of the insurrection's failure. Faulty leadership and the indifference of the western powers, as well as the reluctance of the
peasants in many areas to support the national cause, once again,
as in 1830–31, reinforced the overwhelming military superiority of
the Russians and brought about the defeat of the Poles.

In September, 1862, the "Reds" had reached agreement with Herzen's *émigré* group on the disputed issue of the former commonwealth's eastern territories. Poland, Lithuania, and Ruthenia would

[37] *Lettre d'un gentilhomme polonais sur les massacres de Gallicie adressée au
Prince de Metternich* (Brussels, 1846), pp. 59, 60.

form a tripartite federation of equals—unless the latter wished to opt out. In exchange for this assurance, the Russian revolutionaries acknowledged the Poles' right to organize for an uprising throughout these territories.[38] Yet many democrats regarded this as going too far: it was playing the enemy's game.[39] And later indeed the insurrectionary authorities were to speak with a divided voice on the subject. In ethnic Lithuania and in western Belorussia a number of peasants rallied to the Polish flag; the Roman Catholic clergy, in particular, influenced their parishoners in their attitude. But in central and eastern Belorussia and in Ukraine, despite efforts to popularize the uprising, support was extremely meager, except among the Polish landowning class and a part of the revolutionary student youth. In these areas the cause was associated in the peasant's mind with social oppression by alien Polish "lords" and met with his hostility. Denunciation to the Russian authorities was not uncommon.[40] The fond hopes of Polish nationalists of both left and right of recreating the Polish state within the old boundaries were thus doomed to frustration.

II

The failure of the January Insurrection virtually brought to a close the first period of Polish romantic nationalism. However, renunciation of the insurrectionary tradition, and acceptance of the rule of the three partitioning powers as the framework in which the Polish nation would have to develop for an indefinite period of time, did not come abruptly. The practice of "organic work," as we have seen, had already begun among the Polish community in Poznania; it had one of its most brillant—and ill-fated—exponents in Wielopolski; finally the limited political autonomy granted the historic provinces of the Habsburg monarchy by the October Diploma of 1860, though severely curtailed in the February Patent of 1861, provided the basis for an eventual reconciliation between Austria and the Polish landowning class in Galicia. "Triple Loyalty" as a na-

[38] Stefan Kieniewicz, Tadeusz Mencel, Władysław Rostocki (eds.), *Wybór tekstów żrodłowych z historii Polski w latach 1795–1864* (Warsaw, 1956), pp. 734–36.

[39] Wilhelm Feldman, *Dzieje polskiej myśli politycznej w okresie porozbiorowym* (*Próba zarysu*), I (Cracow, 1913), 419–21, 425, 426.

[40] See Piotr Lossowski and Zygmunt Młynarski, *Rosjanie, Białorusini i Ukraińcy w powstaniu styczniowym* (Warsaw, 1959), chaps. v, vi. Cf. Wacław Lipiński, *Szlachta na Ukrainie*, Part I (Cracow, 1909), pp. 65–68.

tional program, however, only gained full-fledged expression after the Franco-Prussian War and the Eastern Crisis in the seventies finally removed the Polish question from the agenda of European diplomacy. Even after this, a handful of political radicals nurtured the seeds of the independence idea through the winter of political realism.

Austrian Galicia soon became the showpiece of the new political current among the Poles. Here the Polish gentry, seizing the opportunity presented by the reorganization of the Habsburg Empire under the impact of Magyar discontent and successive military defeat by Piedmont and Prussia, succeeded in the sixties and early seventies in winning the Polonization of administration and educational system and eventually complete internal control over the province. As early as 1865, Paweł Popiel, one of the founders of Galician conservatism, had condemned all thought of insurrection in the foreseeable future and called for the concentration of national effort on provincial affairs. In the following year the representatives of the Galician gentry seconded Popiel's thesis in the famous diet address of December 10, 1866. Reminding the Emperor of the constitutional changes promised, that were the implicit condition of the Polish gentry's gesture of conciliation, they concluded with the words: "Without fear . . . of deserting our national idea, with faith in Austria's mission, . . . we proclaim from the depth of our hearts that we stand—and wish to stand—by you, most illustrious sire."[41] The eventual settlement fell short of the more far-reaching autonomy that the Galician diet was to call for in its Resolution of September 24, 1868. But the unsuccessful political struggle to implement the resolution was somewhat half hearted. The Galician gentlemen who held political and economic sway over the province until 1918 remained "good Poles," but many of them in the course of time became better Austrians.

The younger Conservative leaders like the historian Józef Szujski (known as stańczycy) were at first unwilling to break with romantic nationalism. However, they had finally swung over to Popiel's views by the end of the decade, and thereafter, if anything, outdid Popiel in the vehemence with which they attacked what Szujski called the liberum conspiro. This was the standing conspiracy, the

[41] Michał Bobrzynski et al. (eds.), Z dziejów odrodzenia politycznego Galicji 1859–1873 (Warsaw, 1905), pp. 121, 122.

continuous insurrectionary stance of the Polish revolutionaries of previous decades that had proved, in Szujski's opinion, as disastrous to the modern nation as the *liberum veto* had been to the old commonwealth. National politics must be confined henceforth within the bounds of legality and loyalty to the existing state. Another historian of the same "Cracow School," Michał Bobrzyński, reinforced such views with a searing analysis of Poland's past: anarchic tendencies uncurbed by strong government, and not any divine call to the role of the world's suffering servant, had brought about the partitions and the country's subsequent misery.

While anti-Russian sentiment was one of the factors in maintaining the Cracow conservatives' alliance with the dynasty, they sternly abjured the idea of making a Polish Piedmont out of Galicia. Their rule was grounded on the political and economic exploitation of the peasantry, both Polish and Ukrainian, and became increasingly marked by clerical obscurantism. Yet the conservatives left the nation in their debt, not only for their sponsorship of Polish culture and learning, but also because their administration of Galicia proved a school where successive generations of Poles could gain the political experience denied them in most other parts of their divided homeland.

In Prussian Poznania (and also to some extent in West Prussia where Polish national consciousness evolved more slowly, especially among the Kashubs) the policy of "organic work" was exemplified by the same alliance of gentry and church as in Galicia. But there was an essential difference in that the well-to-do Polish farming class that was created by the Prussian emancipation beginning in 1823 was taken into junior partnership. Under the patronage of squire and parish priest an impressive network of agricultural circles, credit associations, and rural banks was built up among the Polish population. Illiteracy was greatly reduced; a popular press found eager readers in the countryside. Bismarck's attack on the Catholic church in the 1870s gave a tremendous impetus to ending the alienation of the rural masses from the gentry nation, on which the chancellor and his successors reckoned in their anti-Polish policy.

With his religion under attack and his right to use his mother tongue impeded, the Polish peasant may still have remained *kaisertreue* to the end, but he began increasingly to feel himself a Pole. The *Kulturkampf* was followed in 1886 by Bismarck's Colonization

Decree, which inaugurated a fierce struggle between the Poles and the German government and influential sections of the German community for possession of the soil.

As in Galicia, Polish policy in Poznania had been opposed to irredentist ideas and had worked within the existing political framework. Maksymilian Jackowski for instance, the famous promoter of agricultural circles, urged his fellow Poznanians to dismiss all thought of national revolution or international action on Poland's behalf. They were only appropriate, he felt, in exceptionally favorable circumstances. In their place he urged the merits of "continuous and quiet development of the domestic and civil virtues, careful guarding of the faith of the fathers as well as the preservation of language and customs, economic improvement, maintenance on the land, and finally unceasing progress in education and custodianship of national dignity."[42]

Every opportunity was seized upon, as during the chancellorship of the conciliatory Caprivi between 1890 and 1894, to attempt to establish an acceptable *modus vivendi* with the state. The proponents of organic work, however, were faced by an increasingly menacing attack on the economic and political status of the Polish community. The activities of the *Ostmarkenverein* from 1894 onwards and the renewed assault of the German government on Polish land and culture after Caprivi's fall met with firm, and to some extent successful, opposition from a united Polish community. Yet the new German Empire was still a *Rechtstaat*, where the government had to function within the limits laid down by the constitution.

At least until the revolution of 1905, Polish national life remained much more exposed in the area under Russian control. The second half of the sixties and the early seventies saw the systematic destruction of the autonomous institutions of the Congress Kingdom, which emerged with a status not differing essentially from that of other parts of the empire. The whole school system was Russified; while in Lithuania, under Muraviev and his successors, Polish cultural life was driven underground and Polish participation in public life ruthlessly curtailed. At the same time, with access to the potentially vast Russian market and a ready labor force in the peasantry emancipated by the *ukaz* of 1864, Polish industrial development began to

[42] Quoted in W. Feldman, *Dzieje polskiej myśli politycznej 1864–1914* (ed.) Józef Feldman (Warsaw, 1933), p. 183.

hold out promise of undreamed of prosperity for this section of the nation.

Polish positivism was the child of political frustration combined with socioeconomic expansionism that was the dominant mood among the educated classes in the decades following the January Insurrection. From the positivist philosophers of western Europe, the Warsaw positivists took over the empirical method and their sceptical outlook, but they were more publicists and literati than professional philosophers. In 1873 their leading representative, Aleksander Świętochowski, outlined a new program for the nation in a series of articles entitled "Work at the Foundations." Salvation by self-improvement was Świętochowski's message. He called upon the influential classes in the countryside, landowners and clergy, to collaborate in raising the deplorably low educational and economic standards of the village. The modernization of the Polish community was to be completed by the steady development of industry and commerce, the setting up of factories, workshops, and mines, construction of railways and roads, the assimilation of the Jews recently emancipated by Wielopolski, who had previously remained outside the nation, and the freedom of women. In this way the old harmful dominance of the landowning class would be broken forever: a new nation with its tone set by a progressive middle class and an enlightened peasantry would replace the pseudo democracy of the gentry. As insistently as the Cracow conservatives, Świętochowski and his fellow liberals, who included several of the most talented Poles of that generation, demanded "a decided break with the tradition of armed risings." Loss of political independence was not necessarily a misfortune. "For the happiness of the people," wrote Świętochowski in his "Political Directions" of 1882, "is not strictly dependent on their power and independence but on their participation in universal civilization as well as on their advancement of their own civilization."[43] Świętochowski felt that incorporation in an alien state need not mean extinction but instead might ultimately prove a blessing to a people, for it could free them from military ambitions and overinvolvement in politics, and it could permit them to concentrate on social and cultural betterment. The economic and cul-

[43] Manfred Kridl, Władysław Malinowski, Józef Wittlin (eds.), *For Your Freedom and Ours: Polish Progressive Spirit Through the Centuries* (New York: Frederick Ungar Publ. Co., 1943), pp. 132, 133.

tural expansionism of a stateless but highly civilized nation could provide, he said, a superior substitute for the military imperialism of the great contemporary nation-states.

Alongside Warsaw positivism, which continued to hold the allegiance of wide circles among the bourgeoisie and intelligentsia of the Congress Kingdom into the nineties, there grew up a second variant of the creed of triple loyalty. Its chief apostle was Włodzimierz Spasowicz, whose paper *The Country* (*Kraj*) in St. Petersburg became from its founding in 1882 the center of efforts to promote conciliation (*ugoda*) between the Poles and the Russian government. Its spokesman at home was Wielopolski's son Zygmunt. Spasowicz's early liberalism gradually became overcast by the conservativism of the great magnates, for the party of conciliation drew its support from the wealthier landowners and the emerging plutocracy. It differed from the Warsaw positivists not so much in tactics or aims but rather in the arguments used by its apologists. The latter depicted the Poles as an essentially conservative element, which tsardom should nurture as an ally in the struggle against socialism and revolution. They played, too, on the theme of Slavic unity, though not to the point of abandoning Polish cultural and ethnic individuality. And, like their Poznanian counterparts, though with even less success, they grasped at every indication of a less repressive policy on the part of the government to underline their loyalty and readiness to collaborate in return for recognition of their right to exist as a cultural entity.

In fact these advocates of organic work and triple loyalty, whether under Russia, Prussia, or Austria, and whatever the differences in detail among them, were essentially cultural nationalists. They all sought to preserve the existence of the nation under adverse circumstances. Survival, in their view (and it was neither ignoble nor lacking in good sense), was possible only by discarding all thought of the restoration of unity and independence in the foreseeable future and by separate accommodation on the most advantageous terms possible with each partitioning power. Calls to merge the national identity, such as that of a former high official in Wielopolski's administration, Kazimierz Krzywicki, who in 1872 urged this policy upon his fellow countrymen in regard to Russia, were rare. Even Spasowicz condemned Krzywicki's views as national suicide. Indeed organic work itself began to lose ground among the new generation that grew to manhood at the end of the century. Something more seemed necessary if the Poles were to retain their national identity in the age of imperialism and *Realpolitik*.

The tradition of romantic nationalism was not entirely extinguished in the course of the decades immediately succeeding the January Insurrection of 1863. In the first place, the old ideas undoubtedly survived in the minds of countless thousands, especially in the manor houses of the eastern borderlands where oppression was most ruthless and the outlook for conciliation bleakest, and even when habit and the demands of day-to-day living brought increasing adjustment to the *status quo*. Above all, throughout the Polish lands the works of the great poets of the preceding generation, with their messianic message, continued to hold men's imaginations; their successors of the positivist era failed to loosen their hold on wide sections of the educated public.

Secondly, we find several small groups that doggedly opposed the new trends despite obloquy and ridicule and political isolation. In Galicia the democrats, even after the failure of the schemes of their leader, Franciszek Smolka, to transform Austria into a federation of nations and Galicia into a focus of Polish irredentism, continued—in theory—to cherish the insurrectionary tradition. After the fizzling out of the comic-opera conspiratorial movement of 1876–78, however, they confined their activities within the bounds of the law, soon allowing this national custodianship to degenerate into empty displays of patriotic fervor on national anniversaries. They failed to make any impact on the peasantry and lacked adherents among the governing gentry; with their influence limited to the vegetating Galician bourgeoisie, their inspiration slowly withered.

More lively and more interesting, though numerically negligible, were the young radicals, many of them holding vaguely socialist views, who took refuge abroad after the failure of the January Insurrection. The post-1863 emigration was not as important as the earlier "Great Emigration," and its links with opinion in the home country were more tenuous. But some of the debates that took place within its narrow circle foreshadowed those that began to divide the nation a quarter of a century later. On the national question, all were agreed on the goal of independence, but there was no unanimity as to the nature of the future state. Most of the veteran *émigrés,* like General Mierosławski, and some of the younger generation, continued to advocate a unitary state within the boundaries of 1772. Among those who reacted most strongly against such opinions was Jarosław Dąbrowski, who was to die during the Paris Commune. He and his friends condemned the traditional reliance on the historic claims of the Polish state and upheld the right of any province after liberation to secede if its inhabitants so desired. The resulting cohesion would compensate for reborn Poland's loss in territory.[44]

The ideas of these *émigré* radicals were nebulous, half thought through and unclear. But the decisive break that they made with the concept of historic rights is significant for the development of Polish nationalism. It was the emergence of an emancipated peasantry and a rapidly growing urban proletariat, especially in the Congress Kingdom, that led a new generation at home, reacting against what they considered the sterility of organic work and triple loyalty, to base a renewed struggle for independence and unification on the broad masses of the nation, who had previously stood aside from the national movement. Thus the second phase of romantic nationalism, at least in its early years, was either Populist or Socialist and sometimes both.

Bolesław Limanowski and the little group of intellectuals he gathered together in the early eighties under the significant name of "The Polish People" (*Lud Polski*) represented the early nationalist trend in Polish socialism. For them social democracy was important primarily because it promised to liberate the classes whose help was essential to regain independence. "I saw in socialism," wrote Limanowski of his youth, "the political force which was capable of raising us from that hellish abyss into which the Muraviev's and the Bergs had pushed us."[45] Therefore national independence, with the exact nature of the tie that would link the former lands of the old commonwealth left undefined (Limanowski himself always favored a restoration of the sixteenth-century Union of Lublin).

[44] Felicja Romaniukowa (ed.), *Radykalni demokraci polscy: Wybór pism i dokumentów 1863–1875* (Warsaw, 1960), pp. liv–lvi, 12–20, 36–39, 360, 530–45. Dąbrowski hoped for some federal tie between Poland and a separate "Ruthenia" (a sort of revival of the abortive Agreement of Hadiach of 1658). See Marja Złotorzycka, "Jarosław Dąbrowski o sprawie ruskiej," *Niepodległość* (Warsaw), IX. No. 3 (1934), 455–63.

[45] Quoted in Feliks Perl, *Dzieje ruchu socjalistycznego w zaborze rosyjskim* (*do powstania PPS*) ([1910], Warsaw, 1958 ed.), p. 38.

figured prominently in the programs of a succession of short-lived organizations sponsored by Limanowski.

At first, however, in the late seventies and during the eighties, this nativist variety of socialism made little headway against cosmopolitan trends, which rejected the old insurrectionary tradition and the goal of an independent state as passionately as did the Cracow conservatives or Warsaw positivists—although for quite different reasons. The object of the cosmopolitans was the overthrow of capitalism by world revolution and its replacement by socialism, which would make national states and frontiers superfluous. "Our fatherland is the whole world," declared their leading exponent, Ludwik Waryński, at a meeting in 1881 to commemorate the fiftieth anniversary of the Insurrection of 1830, "we are compatriots, members of one great nationality 'more unhappy than Poland—the nation of the proletarians.' "[46] Although they considered themselves Marxists, their views clashed with those of Marx and Engels, who continued to advocate a return to the pre-1772 frontiers. The underground *Proletariat* party, which Waryński founded in Warsaw in 1882, carried on—for the first time since the late uprising—an active and vigorous struggle against tsarist rule until mass arrests ended it. But while resistance to national oppression—"the national-political dependence of our country on the invaders"[47]—was regarded as one element in the revolutionary struggle, it was subordinated in the *Proletariat's* program to the fight for economic liberation of the working class from exploitation, domestic as much as foreign. In 1884, agreement was reached with the Russian revolutionary organization *Narodnaya Volya* for coordinated action, but by now both organizations were on the decline.

The mid-eighties saw a renewed attempt on the part of younger Poles to infuse new life into the decaying national tradition by drawing upon the vast potential strength of the peasant masses. While attacks on his faith and his land in Poznania were slowly awakening the national consciousness of the Polish-speaking peasantry, in the Congress Kingdom[48] and in Galicia the peasants' loy-

[46] Alina Molska (ed.), *Pierwsze pokolenie marksistów polskich: Wybór pism i materiałów źródłowych z lat 1878–1886* (Warsaw, 1962), I, 423.

[47] *Ibid.*, II, 9, 10.

[48] However, a revisionist view on this subject based on rather fragmentary evidence has recently been presented by Helena Brodowska, "Ze studiów nad kształto-

alty to the government and often fierce hostility to the Polish landowning class and the national tradition were characteristic of the
early post-emancipation era. Their interests were mainly confined
to the village. "As for national consciousness," writes the peasant
Słomka in his *Memoirs,* "the older peasants called themselves Ma-
surians, and their speech Masurian. They lived their own life, forming a wholly separate group, and caring nothing for the nation."[49]

It was Russian *narodnichestvo* that gave a young Polish engineer,
Bolesław Wysłouch, the impetus to found an independent political
movement among the peasants in Galicia. His work, along with that
of his rival, Father Stanisław Stojałowski, who had started a little
earlier to rally the peasantry on a religious platform, was very important in helping to bring the country folk at last to feel like participants in the historical heritage of the nation and co-builders of its
future. Wysłouch used newspapers, pamphlets, books, and adult
education circles; he made use of public lectures in the villages and
political meetings and demonstrations with peasant participation.
By the establishment of rural reading rooms and a whole array of
economic self-help organizations, he and his wife Maria, and a host
of fellow workers, many of them villagers themselves, reached out
beyond the ranks of adherents of the Peasant Party, which they
finally set up in 1895, to bring about a peasant renaissance that was
at the same time a national reawakening. As suited the Austrian
constitutional régime, the movement was not a revolutionary one:
it was a form of organic work directed towards the earlier national
goals. The "Masurian" peasant was on the way to becoming a Polish
citizen.

However, despite the fact that the movement's main object was
to "nationalize" the peasantry, it was fiercely denounced at the beginning by the Roman Catholic church. Although a major component of Poland's historic and folk cultures, and subtly intertwined
at many points in the national tradition, Catholicism only became an active factor in shaping modern Polish nationalism in areas
where it was under strong pressure from outside. Pressure came, for

waniem się poczucia społeczno-narodowego chłopów w Królestwie Polskim w drugiej
połowie XIX w. (w świetle relacji żandarmerii carskiej z lat 1864–1880)," *Zeszyty
naukowe uniwersytetu łódzkiego,* Series I, No. 34 (1964), pp. 81–98.

[49] Jan Słomka, *From Serfdom to Self-Government.* Translated by William John
Rose (London, 1941), pp. 171.

instance, from Germany during the *Kulturkampf*. And when Orthodox Russia persecuted the Uniates in the districts of Chełm and
Podlasie, the result was that many of these peasants, who were not
ethnically or linguistically Polish, were brought into the Polish national community. On the other hand, in much of the eastern borderlands the Catholicism of the ruling class acted as a dissolvent of
the old territorial nationalism because it made little appeal to the
non-Catholic masses.[50] But within the Polish community the nationalist impulse during most of the nineteenth century came from
sources that stood aloof from or opposed orthodox Catholicism. The
Poles of course remained a Catholic people, but the fact that they
became a modern nation was not closely related to their Catholicism.

Wysłouch was one of the earliest ideologists of modern Polish
nationalism as well as the founder of the Polish peasant movement.
In articles published in the short-lived *Social Review,* he gave expression to a new national creed: that of "ethnographical" Poland.
Poland was its people, not a territory confined within the frontiers
of a bygone state. "If we had created no state organism," he wrote,
"if we had possessed no history of our own, even if no Polish art
or literature or learning had ever existed, nevertheless simply because we live, we need to have the opportunity of creating our
own . . . forms of existence." His principle called for the recovery
of territories like Upper Silesia or Mazuria in the west, which,
though Polish (for language was to be the primary test of nationality), had lain for centuries outside the old commonwealth. It required, too, the abandonment of claims to vast areas in the east
peopled by ethnically non-Polish groups. Wysłouch fully backed the
standpoint of Ukrainian radical nationalists like Dragomanov, who
described the pre-1772 frontiers as constituting a partition of
Ukraine as unjust as that perpetrated subsequently on Poland by
her neighbors. Wysłouch wrote:

Democrats in Ruthenia must be Ruthenians, in Latvia Latvians, etc.,
they must take into consideration the language of the people for whom
they work; they must take on the local color of the nationality. . . . A
Polish democratic party possesses a *raison d'être* only on purely Polish

[50] This outcome was feared, for instance, by Trentowski in the 1840's. See Pigoń,
Zręby, p. 28.

territory . . . . Basing ourselves on the principle of nationality, and rising up against the violation of our own national rights, we equally condemn a similar violation committed against neighboring nationalities by our Polish gentry.[51]

Narodnik influence was also at the root of similar views being expressed simultaneously in a Warsaw paper, *The Voice (Głos)*. Its leading publicist, Jan L. Popławski, went to greater extremes than Wysłouch in underlining the "two nations"—the "two civilizations," as Popławski phrased it, "the folk and the privileged"[52]—that existed among the Poles, in his assertion that the peasantry formed a separate cultural entity from their social superiors, in stressing their total alienation from the historical nation. For Popławski at this period it was the peasantry, the folk, that had preserved the essential core of Polishness, constituting a more virile racial element than the decaying gentry or the *déraciné* middle class. Like Wysłouch, therefore, the *Głos* group looked to the awakening of the peasantry for a renewal of Polish nationalism; like him, they sought to reverse the tide of history by turning the attention of their fellow countrymen to the potential strength for the nation that lay half forgotten in the western territories. The nation, in Popławski's view, was the product of ethnic differentiation rather than of the state and of historical development. From the *Głos* group, which had disintegrated by the mid-nineties, there evolved, after some ideological permutations, the Polish variety of integral nationalism that, beginning in 1897, crystallized around the National Democratic Party (*endecja*). Organizationally, however, the National Democrats stemmed from the Polish League that had been founded in Switzerland in 1887 by veterans of the January Insurrection. The leading figure among them was the aged writer and politician, Zygmunt Miłkowski (T. T. Jeż), who had been prominent in the Polish Democratic Society of the "Great Emigration" period. The League's program called for the restoration of Poland as a federal state within the pre-1772 borders.[53] Earlier in the same year Miłkowski, in a pamphlet that made a deep impression on his younger contemporaries, had chal-

---

[51] Krzysztof Dunin-Wąsowicz (ed.), *Przegląd Społeczny 1886–1887* (Wrocław, 1955), pp. 47–64. The *Social Review* was edited by Wystouch in Lwów.

[52] Jan Ludwik Popławski, *Pisma polityczne* (Cracow-Warsaw, 1910), I, 133.

[53] Stanisław Kozicki, *Historia Ligi Narodowej (Okres 1887–1907)* (London, 1964), p. 487.

lenged the educated classes to abandon their passivity and their obsequiousness towards the partitioning powers and to take the lead once again in "active defense" of the standard of independence. This did not imply direct preparation for another uprising; it did mean keeping the idea of active resistance in the national conscious-ness, gathering funds until the hour should arrive, and enlisting the masses of the people in the national cause. This indeed was not an entirely new program, for it was modeled on that of the "Great Emi-gration" democrats: what was novel was the vigor with which its romantic nationalism was presented in an era of political realism.

The Polish League remained a secret, semiconspiratorial, organi-zation in the home country. It drew support from persons, particu-larly the young, of varying political coloring: liberal Democrats, Populists, and nationally minded Socialists. It included among its most influential members a sprinkling of assimilated Jewish intellec-tuals (if one adopted the vocabulary of the integral nationalism that grew out of the League, he might say that its origins were "Judaeo-masonic"). The transformation in 1893 of the Polish into the Na-tional League was far more than a change of name: it symbolized the reorientation of the movement from a Mazzinian liberal nation-alism to an intense chauvinism based on *Realpolitik* and ethnic ex-clusiveness. The movement now came under the control of the later *endek* triumvirate: Roman Dmowski, a dynamic young man, highly talented intellectually, and with an almost charismatic gift for lead-ership; Popławski, the oldest, who had already made a name for himself on the staff of *Głos;* and Zygmunt Balicki, a former Socialist who became the philosopher of the movement. For a decade these three men and a number of associates used the *All-Polish Review* (*Przegląd Wszechpolski*), which they started up in Lwów in 1895, as a mouthpiece of the new nationalism. Although the National League remained an elitist group, it gained large numbers of ad-herents for national democracy among educated Poles who were attracted by the *endek* leaders' seriousness of purpose, genuine patriotism and youthful vitality. This contrasted favorably with the apathy and indifference that enveloped wide sections of the Polish community at this period.

Part of the *endek* inheritance from the movement's earlier Popu-list stage was its desire to awaken the national consciousness of the peasantry. "Today," stated its paper *Polak* in 1897, "the country

people carry [Poland] on their shoulders alone."[54] Therefore the
endeks produced a special popular press and developed an adult
educational movement in the countryside. It was slowest going at
first in the Congress Kingdom with its oppressive régime; under
Prussia special attention was paid to the Polish-speaking population
of Upper Silesia; in Galicia, where the work was centered because of
the greater liberty enjoyed under Austria, the *endeks* emphasized
the struggle against the Ukrainians in the province's eastern section.
They converted the flourishing People's School Society into an instrument for saving the scattered Polish peasant settlements from
eventual absorption into the Ukrainian community.[55] Finally they
even concluded an alliance with the reactionary Polish landowners
of the area—the "Podolians"—who, surrounded by alien peasantry and threatened by a growing, militant Ukrainianism, had moved
into opposition against the ruling Cracow conservative party, which
favored a *modus vivendi* with moderate Ukrainian nationalism.

Until early in the next century the National Democrats, who continued to stress their democratic and even mildly social radical inclinations, still saw their country's chief enemy in Russian autocracy.
Their efforts, while only potentially insurrectionary, were all directed towards strengthening the national spirit and working for
the restoration of a united Poland. The Russo-Japanese War, from
which Dmowski—in contrast to the Socialist Piłsudski—saw no
chance of enlisting international assistance for Poland, and the subsequent Russian Revolution of 1905 bringing a semiconstitutional
régime throughout the empire worked a change in the political
strategy of the *endeks*.[56] Inside the Duma and without, the party
now strove for mere autonomy for the Congress Kingdom within the
Russian state[57] and for an accommodation, on the basis of anti-
Germanism, with the Russian government (on terms that were not
far from the organic work that the party had recently denounced in

---

[54] Władysław Pobóg-Malinowski, *Narodowa Demokracja 1887–1918* (Warsaw,
1933), p. 208.

[55] Aleksander Świętochowski, *Historja chłopów polskich w zarysie* (Lwów-Poznań,
1928), II, 407–9.

[56] Accounts (both hostile) of this transition are to be found in Adam Próchnik,
Studia i szkice (1864–1918) (Warsaw, 1962), pp. 117–58; Stanisław Kalabiński,
Antynarodowa polityka endecji w rewolucji 1905–1907 (Warsaw, 1955).

[57] See, for instance, the bill of April, 1907, printed in A. L. Pogodin, *Glavnaia
techenia polskoi politicheskoi mysli (1863–1907)* (St. Petersburg, n.d.) pp. 641–62.

its opponents, but were yet more acceptable to the national dignity than those the conservative conciliationists of the Realist Party were offering). The old program of a united, independent Poland was put aside temporarily and elections under all three partitioning powers witnessed to the party's growing support, especially from the new middle class. The *endeks* had ceased to be a revolutionary force; in everyday politics the heady wine of their uncompromising nationalism was rapidly being watered down.

At least in its early years, national democracy was as much a political philosophy as a party program. Its outlook on national affairs came to be shared by countless Poles who were never formal members of one or another of the political organizations under its control. This gives it its great significance in the development of Polish nationalism. We find the philosophy most completely expressed in the writings of Dmowski and Balicki during the first decade or so of this century. These works were the result of more than a decade of intellectual fermentation and at the beginning, it would seem, they were independent of similar programs of integral nationalism being developed by such writers as Barrès and Maurras in France.

At the roots of the national democrats' political philosophy was the concept of the nation as "a living social organism"[58] existing above the individual human beings of whom it might be composed at any given moment of time. Unlike the Warsaw positivists, who also tended to take an organic view of the nation, the *endeks* regarded the nation's embodiment in a nation-state as essential for assuring its permanent existence. Nationalities that failed to reach statehood were doomed to cultural as well as political absorption, by either force or peaceful assimilation, into the national organisms in whose state forms they had been incorporated. Therefore it was essential for Poles to liberate and reunite their territories within a new Polish state if they were to survive. Resignation from this goal, as in the case of the generation succeeding the January Insurrection, was an invitation to national suicide. "The nation," Dmowski wrote in 1905, "is the product of the state's existence."[59]

The *endeks* stressed language as a major component of national

[58] Roman Dmowski, *Myśli nowoczesnego Polaka* (7th ed.; London, 1953), p. 74; Zygmunt Balicki, *Egoizm narodowy wobec etyki* (1914 ed.; Lwow), p. 82. The original versions of both books appeared in 1902.

[59] Dmowski, *Myśli,* pp. 98, 101.

culture alongside common history and racial identity. Roman Catholicism was valued primarily as an essential element of Polish culture. The gentry had preserved the nation's historical tradition through the dark period of national servitude; the peasantry, still possessing the virility of a primitive people, had the power to reinvigorate the ageing culture of the upper classes, and were the unconscious transmitters of its racial characteristics. In the future the two disparate elements must be harnessed in the service of a united national state. Dmowski bitterly attacked the Cracow conservatives, in particular, for neglecting to tap the unexploited resources for the nation that lay in the Polish peasantry.

Liberal nationalism in its various Polish manifestations came under even stronger attack for what Dmowski called its "false humanitarianism."[60] Dmowski and Balicki derided not only Polish messianism, which they regarded as a symptom of sickness in the nation, but all talk of international morality, which they equated with sentimentality. Altruism had been the Poles' downfall; it was merely proof of incapacity for statehood. However distasteful this might be to humanitarians who confused a personal Christian ethic with national policy, where an uninhibited "national egoism" must be the sole criterion of action, strength was the only factor that counted in the struggle natural to international relations, a state of war ameliorated only by an expedient reciprocity of benefits—by the principle *do ut des*. Balicki held up the "soldier-citizen" with his virtues of sacrifice, discipline, obedience, efficiency, and group solidarity, as the type that should be most valued in Polish national life, which had degenerated through the influence of Jewish cosmopolitanism and a pseudo-Tolstoyan passivity. "Military education of the coming generations must begin from childhood," he concludes.[61]

Balicki, somewhat inconsequentially, parried the argument that such conduct would bring civilized man down to the level of the jungle with the assertion that a nation's self respect should prevent it from harming other peoples.[62] The thinking of the *endek* triumvirate was remote from a vulgar, uncultured jingoism; they displayed a discriminating appreciation of the contribution of other nations to world civilization and did not hesitate to point out shortcomings in

[60] *Ibid.*, p. 14.
[61] Balicki, *Egoizm narodowy*, pp. 86, 87, 91, 94.
[62] *Ibid.*, pp. 78 ff.

their own people. Yet their attitude toward the submerged nationalities that shared Poland's historic territories and much of the nation's past—Ukrainians, Belorussians, Lithuanians, and Jews—displayed a chauvinistic ruthlessness that led critics from both right and left to dub them Polish "Hakatists" (the nickname for members of the *Ostmarkenverein*). For the peaceful competition of national cultures that the Warsaw positivists envisaged, they substituted an expansive policy of assimilation in regard to culturally less advanced peoples, with no pity expended on the vanquished.

The Ukrainians (in *endek* publications the older term "Ruthenians" is employed almost invariably) received special attention since their emerging nationalism in east Galicia was already threatening the dominant position of the Poles. In the writings of Dmowski and his colleagues, Ukrainian nationalism often figures as a purely artificial creation either of Franz Stadion, the Austrian viceroy of 1848, or of the Berlin government. At other times they were prepared to give it a somewhat grudging recognition. "If they wish to separate themselves completely from us politically and culturally, let them," wrote Popławski of the Galician Ukrainians, "we however will neither assist them nor make concessions."[63] Dmowski urged that Poles should present the Ukrainians with the choice between Polonization and proving their claim to nationhood "in the fire of struggle, which is still more necessary for them than for us, since they are by nature much more passive and lazy than ourselves." This test Czechs, for example, had passed at the hands of the Germans: "courageous nations fitted for struggle only grow in struggle."[64] In the age of the Prussian expropriation laws and the battle for the soil in Germany's eastern marches, the analogy between the role of the Germans here vis-à-vis the Poles and that of the latter in regard to the Ukrainians and other peoples of Poland's eastern borderlands was not lost on the nationalists of this area.

If the *endek's* Ukrainian policy brought them the support of the "Podolian" gentry, their increasing anti-Semitism found approval among the Polish intelligentsia, *petite bourgeoisie*, and artisan class, who felt themselves increasingly threatened by Jewish competition, especially after Russia's discriminatory policies had caused an influx of Russian Jews from the east. It drew support, too, from some of

[63] Popławski, *Pisma polityczne*, II, 307.
[64] Dmowski, *Myśli*, pp. 56, 57.

the Catholic clergy. Literate anti-Semitism had grown since the foundation in 1883 of Jan Jeleński's *The Soil* (*Rola*) on an anti-Jewish platform; it received a more intellectually respectable form in the writings of the *endek* ideologists. Dmowski struck what was later to become familiar propaganda of the nationalist camp when he attacked sinister Jewish influences in the country's intellectual life (it appeared somehow that *all*, whose political views deviated from national democracy, had been subtly, perhaps unconsciously, impregnated with the Israelite spirit). Equally menacing, in Dmowski's view, was the hold Jews had obtained over Polish economic life. He saw an unbridgeable gulf yawning between the Polish and Jewish culture that made it possible, if racial contamination was to be stemmed, to assimilate only an infinitesimal number of Jews. What was the solution to the problem of these unwelcome guests in the country's midst? For the present, answered Dmowski, "the spiritual isolation of Polish life from Jewish influences," combined with nationwide backing (which in 1912 had already included the economic boycott)[65] of Polish business, industry, and handicrafts against their Jewish competitors. For the future, a wholesale emigration of the Polish Jews appeared more and more to the *endeks* as the only final solution.

While the Jews were seen as the chief danger on the domestic front, after 1905 German imperialism took the place of tsarist Russia as the enemy without. "La Pologne de nos jours," wrote Dmowski, "reprend le rôle historique que joua autrefois la monarchie des Piasts."[66] The Poles were the main obstacle in Germany's *Drang nach Osten*. Not that Dmowski and his colleagues did not display a certain admiration for the virility with which the Germans were acting in Poland's western territories—"the mutual extermination of two races," Dmowski rather colorfully calls the struggle.[67] They also admired the vigor with which the contemporary British and Japanese pursued their imperialist destiny. But they were determined to see to it that it was the Poles who assimilated their neighbors and not the other way round. Indeed, "the need to adapt oneself to

[65] Roman Dmowski, *Upadek myśli konserwatywnej w Polsce* (Warsaw, 1914), pp. 72–74. See also his *Myśli*, p. 91.

[66] Roman Dmowski, *La question polonaise* (Paris, 1909), p. 309. The Polish version appeared in Lwów in the previous year with the title *Niemcy, Rosya i kwestya polska*.

[67] Dmowski, *Myśli*, p. 76.

life in Bismarckian Europe" was rightly claimed by Dmowski as the source of his party's nationalist program.[68]

From 1905 on there is a certain ambiguity in *endek* writing on Poland's role in the east. Although Dmowski's flirtation with neo-Slavism was short-lived, a desire not to offend the susceptibilities of the new Russian ally against the Teutonic menace led him to play down disputes in the Russo-Polish borderlands.[69] His party now placed its trust in a gradual abandonment of Russification and in the superior power of the Poles to hold their own against Russian culture.

Their reliance on Russia and shelving of the direct struggle for unity and independence served to intensify the fierce antagonism about social issues between the National Democrats and those Polish Socialists who continued to cherish the insurrectionary tradition. A Polish Socialist Party (*PPS*) had come into existence in the Congress Kingdom in 1893 as a result of a union formed in Paris in the previous year by four small Socialist groups. The new party, which represented a fusion of more or less orthodox Marxists, anarchosyndicalists, and nationalist socialists, accepted the program drawn up at the Paris congress. This called for the gradual socialization of the means of production and distribution and for the establishment of "an independent democratic commonwealth" in Poland, where all nationalities would enjoy "complete equality on the basis of a voluntary federation."[70] Although separate organizations were soon created for the Austrian and Prussian areas, the new Socialist movement was conceived (in striking opposition to existing liberal or conservative parties) as embracing, in theory, all the lands of the former Polish state as well as the Polish-speaking districts in the west that had lain outside it. Where the non-Polish nationalities of the eastern provinces set up their own Socialist organizations, the *PPS* somewhat optimistically envisaged harmonious collaboration in a common effort to overthrow the existing political and social

[68] Roman Dmowski, *Kościół, Naród i Państwo* (Warsaw, 1927), p. 16.

[69] A good example of this is to be found in the map appended to the French (but not the Polish) version of Dmowski's book on the Polish question, where the ethnographic borders of Polish territory are given maximum extension in the west and minimum in the east. The French edition was of course intended for circulation in a country that was Russia's ally and Germany's potential adversary.

[70] Perl, *Dzieje*, p. 474.

order. Cooperation with the Russian revolutionary movement was acceptable only on condition that in the Russo-Polish borderlands it function under *PPS* control; in fact, among Russian Socialist parties the *PPS* was able to reach an understanding only with the Socialist Revolutionaries, because of the latter's advocacy of federalism and willingness to recognize the border areas in the present as the exclusive terrain of the Polish Socialists and their allies.

These aims and tactics in regard to the national question very soon came under blistering criticism from the group led by Roza Luxemburg, which in 1893 formed a separate Social Democratic Party of the Kingdom of Poland (*SDKP*). The Social Democrats argued that the winning of Polish independence before the achievement of a proletarian revolution would, apart from the one small source of misery that would be removed by the ending of national suppression, leave the workers in exactly the same position of poverty and capitalist oppression as in the present. On the other hand, as a result of a genuinely socialist revolution, all national oppression would automatically disappear; separate states and frontiers dividing them would be of no concern to the liberated proletariat. Since the development of industrial capitalism was rapidly fusing the whole Russian empire into one economic unit, the struggle to overthrow tsarist autocracy by the bourgeois revolution must come first, and then the rule of capitalism itself must be broken by the united effort of the Russian and Polish working classes. A similar "organic incorporation" of the Polish lands into the economies of the Austrian and German monarchies required from Socialists a like renunciation of separate political action there, too. Luxemburg was careful to explain that this did not mean that tsarist oppression should not be combated: the struggle against it, however, must be subordinated to the joint struggle against capitalism—Polish and Russian.[71] Some measure of autonomy for the Congress Kingdom always figured indeed in the Social Democrats' platform.

While Luxemburg quarreled with Lenin over the right of Russia's nationalities to secede after the revolution, her disagreement with the Polish "social patriots," to use one of her favorite epithets, was more basic. Piłsudski wrote in 1903: "A Polish socialist must strive

---

[71] Róża Luksemburg, *Wybór pism* (Warsaw, 1959), I, 406, 407.

for the homeland's independence—independence is a condition characteristic of socialism's victory in Poland."[72] This identification of social and national aims was typical of large numbers who now threw in their lot with the Socialist Party, regarding it primarily— as Piłsudski himself did—as the most effective instrument for bringing a united Poland into being again. For many Polish Socialists, subordination to Russian comrades such as Luxemburg was urging, appeared highly distasteful.

Marxists like Kelles-Krauz argued that "the considerable superiority of Poland's social level in comparison to Russia's," as evidenced by a more progressive historical tradition and a larger and more developed proletariat, made it essential for the *PPS* to work for complete Polish independence as its final goal.[73]

The relationship between socialism and nationality was a particularly acute problem in Poland's eastern borderlands. While the *PPS* rejected the concept of a strictly ethnographic Poland, it acknowledged the right of the non-Polish peoples to a voice in determining the area's future. Russification was directed toward non-Poles as well as against the Poles and discontent among Russia's subject peoples figured prominently in the Polish Socialists' schemes for bringing down tsarist absolutism. Polish Socialists played an important role in organizing the first Socialist groups among Lithuanians, Latvians, and Belorussians,[74] as they had done earlier among the Ukrainians of Austrian Galicia. Yet even while lip service was paid to the right of self-determination, the underlying assumption remained, that after liberation these lands would retain some kind of tie with Poland. While the link with Russia must be broken, a development completely independent of Poland would not be practical politics in view of the area's cultural backwardness. This led to controversy, in particular, with the Jewish *Bund* founded in Wilno in 1897, which the *PPS* saw as a Russifying factor because of its close tie with Russian Social Democracy and its ambivalent attitude towards Polish independence. The Austro-Marxist nationality

[72] Jósef Piłsudski, *Pisma zbiorowe*, ed. Leon Wasilewski (Warsaw, 1937), II, 52.

[73] Kazmierz Kelles-Krauz, *Pisma wybrane* (Warsaw, 1962), II, 33, 147, 148.

[74] See Jerzy Iwanowski, "Dialog polsko-litewski," *Kultura* (Paris), No. 1/99 (January, 1956), p. 83, for the story of the three Iwanowski brothers from a Polish borderland gentry family who, converted to socialism in their youth, worked in the early years of the century in the Polish, Belorussian, and Lithuanian movements, respectively, each adopting the particular nationality among whom he was active.

policy of cultural and linguistic autonomy found many supporters among Polish Socialists,[75] not least because it appeared to provide a workable solution to the problem of the Yiddish-speaking Jews inhabiting the lands of the former commonwealth who, it seemed evident, did not desire assimilation into the Polish community.

The revolution of 1905 not only brought bloodshed between *endeks* and Socialists; in the following year it split the Polish Socialist Party itself. "Around [the] dilemma of insurrection and independence, or mass strike action and autonomy, revolved the endless debates that went on in revolutionary circles," writes Dziewanowski.[76] A left wing in the party, which had adopted a position on the independence issue not far removed from that of Luxemburg's Social Democrats, had expanded rapidly during the revolutionary excitement, and with strong support from younger members, obtained control of the party organization. This *PPS* Left, which took an antiwar line in 1914, eventually fused in December, 1918, with the Social Democrats to form what became the Polish Communist Party. The older activists led by Piłsudski formed a separate "revolutionary fraction," which for several years employed widespread terrorism as a weapon against the Russian authorities. The campaign failed, for the upper classes wished to avoid anything that might imperil even the very limited measure of freedom that still remained after the revolutionary ferment had subsided.

In 1908 Piłsudski transferred his activities to Galicia where, under the benevolent eye of the Austrian authorities, he broadened his plan to achieve military preparedness at the decisive moment for seizing Poland's independence from that of an armed proletariat to the nation in arms. Other political parties now rallied behind him. However, apart from a few splinter groups, the National Democrats remained opposed to his policy of reliance on Austria. They pointed to Germany's growing influence within the Triple Alliance, arguing that in case of victory in a future war (which most Polish leaders believed was imminent) the harsh anti-Polish measures now being enforced in Germany would be intensified and extended to Polish

[75] See for example Kelles-Krauz, *Pisma wybrane*, II, 318–41; Władysław Gumplowicz, *Kwestya polska a socyalizm* (Cracow, 1908), chap. v. Gumplowicz was among the few leading members of the PPS, who advocated the reestablishment of Poland within strictly ethnographic frontiers.

[76] M. K. Dziewanowski, *The Communist Party of Poland: An Outline of History* (Cambridge, Mass.: Harvard University Press, 1959), p. 41.

territory conquered from Russia. It was from a victorious constitutional Russia in the east, they reiterated, that the light of Polish independence would arise.

III

The outbreak of a European war in August, 1914, was welcomed by many Poles as a prelude to the final act of Poland's struggle to regain her freedom. After over a century of partition and alien rule, Polish national consciousness had gradually percolated down to the Polish-speaking masses. During this period, whenever one or another of the partitioning powers had eased the political situation, nationally minded Poles had seized the opportunity to develop at least the cultural life of their compatriots. In literature such works as the historical novels of Henryk Sienkiewicz or the writings of Stefan Zeromski, and—in art—for instance—the historical canvases of Jan Matejko, had served to awaken patriotic feeling in the prewar generations.

In the early stages of the war it was not so easy to foresee the reappearance of a fully independent Polish state. Piłsudski and his associates, who on August 16, 1914, had formed a Supreme National Committee in Cracow, as the mouthpiece of their aims had inscribed the slogan of "Independence" on their banners. But what, in fact, would such independence mean in the event of a victory of the central powers, on which the realization of the program rested? Austrian Galicia would probably be reunited with the former Congress Kingdom, and at least a part of the vast eastern territories of the former Polish commonwealth under Russian rule would be added to form a Polish state under a Habsburg archduke. There was little likelihood, however, of Prussian-ruled Poznania being relinquished by a victorious German Empire—not to speak of West Prussia or Upper Silesia.

A victory of the allied powers, on which Dmowski's National Democrats and their associates reckoned, was scarcely more promising for Polish plans. The watchword of the Polish National Committee set up by Dmowski's followers in Warsaw in November, 1914—"Unification" of all the Polish lands under the tsar—was considerably more modest than Piłsudski's call to independence. For Dmowski, the war was just one more incident in the age-old struggle between Teuton and Slav, a phase in which it was essential for the Slavs' protagonist, tsarist Russia, to emerge victorious if the Poles were to have any future. Therefore he opposed, at least at the moment, any talk of trying to force Russia to define the vague promises of self government given by a magnanimous tsar to his Polish subjects.

The restoration of the Polish state, when it came in November, 1918, was due to three factors: the unexpected collapse of all three partitioning empires, the support of the victorious western allies, and the innate strength of Polish national consciousness. If the outlook for Poland had appeared unpromising in the early war years, the Russian Revolution of March, 1917, opened up for the first time the possibility of a genuine restoration of a Polish state in the event of allied victory. More and more the overriding problem before the Poles became that of the structure and extent of the new state that would emerge at the end of the war. Once again they were faced by opposing solutions, backed by the two political camps that held the allegiance of the most active elements in the nation.

Dmowski, Pilsudski's chief antagonist, had left Russia in November, 1915, frustrated by the unwillingness of the Russian government to commit itself to more than empty declarations where Polish aspirations were concerned. After arriving in the West, Dmowski and the other members of the Polish National Committee he set up in August, 1917, soon established themselves as spokesmen for the Polish cause in the eyes of the western allies; it was they who eventually acted as official representatives of the reborn Polish state at the postwar peace conference. Thus their views became of crucial importance for their country's future. From March, 1917, to March, 1919, Dmowski was responsible for drawing up a series of declarations intended for French, British, and American statesmen and later for the delegates assembled in Paris.[77] Changes in emphasis may be discerned in the argument from one document to another; variations, in particular, in the territorial demands occurred. But on the whole they express a coherent and rounded national program based on a well-defined political philosophy.

The new Polish state, in Dmowski's view, was to have three essential characteristics. In the first place it was to possess "an ex-

---

[77] Polish versions of the relevant documents are printed as appendices in Roman Dmowski, *Polityka polska i odbudowanie państwa* (1925). I have used the third edition (2 vols.; Hanover, 1947).

tensive territory" and "a numerous population." Secondly, this population should be sufficiently cohesive to make it a genuinely national state. And thirdly, its geographical boundaries must be so drawn as to guarantee its political independence against possible aggression.[78] Language alone must not be the criterion. The new Poland was to be a big power able to hold its own against its German and Russian neighbors, but it would not be able to play such a role if the ethnically Polish element within its borders were overwhelmed by the non-Poles. A decision to exclude ethnographically non-Polish areas must result, however, from a weighing of the political and strategic advantages and disadvantages. Geopolitics and not ethnography was the relevant science here. "A strictly ethnographic Poland," wrote Stanisław Kozicki, Dmowski's chief lieutenant at the Peace Conference, "is political nonsense."[79]

Such premises as these reflected a decided ambivalence in the attitude of the representatives of the Polish cause in the West. Poland's very existence derived from the claim of nationalities to self-determination; it was on this foundation that Polish nationalists had eventually come to rest their case. Yet Dmowski and his colleagues appeared to set more store by the maintenance of the old framework of the balance of power and upon anti-German or anti-Communist sentiments in the creation of the new state. Kozicki has frankly stated that he and his colleagues at Versailles used ethnographical arguments as a basis for their claims in the west, while urging *raison d'état* as the criterion for drawing the boundaries to the east.[80]

As a means to create a strong modern state based on a clear predominance of the Polish ethnic group, Dmowski placed great importance on the incorporation of western areas with Polish-speaking populations that had lain outside the old Polish state. Possession of these areas, along with the port of Danzig to give access to the Baltic and the creation of a satellite German state out of the rump of East Prussia, appeared essential to him on both strategic and economic grounds. The possibility that a majority of the Polish-speaking population in some districts (e.g. Mazuria) might be unwilling to break the centuries-long tie with Germany does not ap-

---

[78] Memorial to Wilson, 8 X 1918, in *ibid.*, II, 146, 147, 160.
[79] Stanisław Kozicki, *Sprawa granic Polski na konferencji pokojowej w Paryżu* (Warsaw, 1921), pp. 6, 20, 21, 29–32.
[80] *Ibid.*, p. 31.

pear to have been considered by Dmowski. If he considered it, he apparently felt that the maturing of their as-yet-undeveloped Polishness would only be a matter of time—the decisive factor was the need to weaken Germany and to strengthen the new Poland economically, strategically, and demographically.

The framing of the eastern frontiers was a considerably more complicated and delicate task. Past centuries in some areas had hopelessly mixed up the various ethnic groups. In the west it was desirable, because of the highly developed national consciousness and the cultural and economic strength of the Germans, to reduce their number within the new state to a minimum, but in the east the retarded national development of a large part of the borderland peoples, and the cultural and economic superiority of the Polish element made it essential, in Dmowski's opinion, to incorporate a much larger non-Polish-speaking population. In this area, in fact, lay the key to the question of whether Poland would be a great or an insignificant state.

A restoration of the eastern frontier as it had existed at the time of the first partition was, however, impossible. Talk of a resuscitation of a Jagellonian union was hopelessly unrealistic, an anachronism in the conditions of the twentieth century. This point Dmowski stressed on more than one occasion. Where, then, should the line be drawn in this vast rolling plain, where neither the landscape nor the human element provided clear-cut boundaries? In so far as former Russian territory was concerned, it should include, Dmowski answered, "those provinces where Western (Polish) civilization is ineradicable, where the percentage of Poles is very considerable, or where the majority of the inhabitants are Catholic."[81] This would mean a line slightly to the east of the second partition of 1793. As for east Galicia, its possession by Poland was essential on economic grounds alone (not to speak of historical and cultural claims).

If the new Polish state were established within the western frontiers proposed by the Polish representatives, at least a third of its citizens would be ethnically non-Polish. While there could be little hope of assimilating the German minority, they constituted only a comparatively small percentage of the population. For the much larger Jewish minority, which in the mass did "not form part of the

[81] Citation from the privately printed English edition of Dmowski's *Problems of Central and Eastern Europe* (London, July, 1917), p. 65.

Polish nation," assimilation was undesirable; in Dmowski's view, gradual yet steady emigration would prove the remedy. It was the peoples of the eastern borderlands that constituted the hardest problem with which the national democratic statesmen had to deal.

In connection with Dmowski's attitude toward the Ukrainian, Belorussian, and Lithuanian populations who would find themselves within the frontiers drawn up by himself and his colleagues, two points need to be kept in mind. In the first place, Dmowski was always extremely reluctant to grant that these populations did in fact constitute genuine national entities. He liked to refer to them as peoples "without a history," lacking any sort of cultural background, in contrast to "historic nations" like the Poles. They were still at a lower stage of political evolution, forming an amorphous mass that, if not present within the new state in too great numbers, could be brought within the compass of the Polish national community in due course.[82]

Secondly, even when he appears implicitly to concede that these ethnic groups form nations of the same political genus as the Poles, as in the case of the Lithuanians, he makes clear his belief in their inability to create viable state forms within the foreseeable future. It is here, in his disbelief in the possibility of the peoples bordering on the Poles in the east to create independent national states able to withstand incorporation into Russia or transformation into German satellites, that we find a key to his eastern policy. Application of Wilsonian self-determination to these territories meant, for him, handing them over to Poland's traditional rivals. Partition with Russia was the only effective policy in the existing circumstances, and the presence of these ethnically uncertain elements within the new Polish state provided further justification for the inclusion of the maximum number of Polish speakers in the German-Polish borderlands of the west.

Dmowski's national program undoubtedly enjoyed very considerable support, at this period as well as later, among both the landed gentry and the Polish bourgeoisie and intelligentsia. Its anti-German point made it widely popular in Poznania and among the nationally conscious sections of the Polish community of the other provinces

---

[82] Dmowski, *Problems* . . . , pp. 20, 45, 46, 57, 78. See also his *Polityka polska* . . . , II, 154, 155, 158.

of the former German empire. In the east it was seen as a defense of Polish *raison d'être* in those borderland territories. Not without justification, Kozicki claimed that, despite the unfavorable results of plebiscites in Upper Silesia and Mazuria, the actual frontiers of Versailles and Riga incorporated substantially the same territories as those for which the *endek*-dominated Polish delegation had fought at the conference table.[83] The borders of interwar Poland represented a triumph for the national democrats that was spoiled, in their view, only by the machinations of Lloyd George and the Jews, the selfishness of the French, and the short-sightedness of the Americans. They provided the matrix within which the Polish nation and the non-Polish minorities developed up to the debacle of 1939.

A second program emerged, however, during these years as an alternative to Dmowski's policy. This was the "federalist" idea propounded by the center and left and associated with the name of Piłsudski, a concept that was never elaborated in the same detail as the *endek* solution. The federalist program, centering around the disposition of the borderlands between Poland and Russia, evolved more slowly than the policies of Dmowski's camp. In the latter part of the war, the outlook for the Piłsudski group remained uncertain. The declaration of November 5, 1916, inaugurating a Polish state under the auspices of the central powers, was soon counterbalanced by German patronage of the strongly anti-Polish Lithuanian nationalist movement and by German designs for the political and economic domination of the Ukraine. The collapse of the central powers combined with the chaos in the former Russian Empire, however, opened up immense vistas for the establishment of a federation of nations in these areas under Polish auspices. The immense prestige enjoyed by Piłsudski after his return home from incarceration by the Germans in the fortress of Magdeburg to take up the headship of the new state appeared to offer the possibility of realizing such plans.

Postwar Polish federalism did not stand for a simple revival of the old Polish-Lithuanian union, although memories of its past glories were one of the sources from which it drew inspiration. It represented an attempt to prevent the threatened fragmentation of

[83] Kozicki, *Sprawa granic* . . . , pp. 3, 128. Cf. Ellinor von Puttkamer, *Die polnische Nationaldemokratie* (Cracow, 1944), pp. 109–12.

the area covered by the old Polish commonwealth and the adjacent lands, while at the same time to give recognition to the separate national consciousnesses of the peoples, which had begun to emerge during the preceding half century. Several variant versions were produced by its protagonists. Central to the whole idea, of course, was a Polish-Lithuanian federation. A Ukrainian state, and perhaps also a Belorussian one, was to be attached by a federal link to Poland-Lithuania; Piłsudski also tried to persuade Latvia, Estonia, and Finland to join a federation of this kind.

Many arguments were put forward by the federalists in support of their schemes. They pointed out that large borderland areas were ethnically mixed and that some form of federation was the only practical alternative to placing numbers of people under alien rule. An extensive federation backed by the military strength of Poland would serve as a protection against bolshevist Russia or, in the event of its collapse, against a revival of "white" Russian imperialism. Above all, the federalists appeared profoundly convinced that the non-Polish peoples of these lands would welcome this kind of association with the revived Polish state, which had respected their rights in the past and would protect their freedom in the future. The argument that Dmowski's camp used as a main support of its program of partition with Russia and integral incorporation of the area relegated to Poland, that the new national groups of the borderlands were incapable of maintaining independent states and would soon fall victims of aggression, was regarded by the federalists as the most compelling reason for establishing a Polish-led federation in these lands. Under Polish leadership and protection the national development of the border peoples would be permitted to ripen naturally and gradually, giving adequate time for the forging of unbreakable links between the component nations.

Were federalist schemes merely an ideological cloak to cover sinister imperialist plans for Polish aggrandizement at the expense of the peoples of Soviet Russia? That they had an anti-Russian point seems undoubted, for they were designed to cut Russia off, not merely from the Baltic, but from the riches of the Ukraine and access to the Black Sea. Again, even in the thinking of its advocates among the Polish left (e.g. the Socialist Leon Wasilewski), Poland was cast for the role of an elder brother who would guide the faltering footsteps of the culturally retarded and politically unenlightened border peoples. A "Great Poland," it was argued, would be created in the area[84] that would be a stronger and more stable power than the "Little Poland" of the *endeks,* just because it was ready to take into consideration the national aspirations of its non-Polish peoples. This seems a long step from the restoration of Polish landlordism and national oppression, which an array of Marxists, borderland nationalists, and western critics have seen as the main (often the sole) object of the federalist program of Piłsudski and his associates and its only possible outcome if it had been realized.

The nearest approach that Piłsudski made to an official pronouncement on the subject was in his "Proclamation to the Inhabitants of the Former Grand Duchy of Lithuania," issued on April 22, 1919, after his forces had temporarily regained the city of Wilno from the Communists. Promising free elections to decide the fate of the country, Piłsudski, who was himself a "Lithuanian" Pole, told the people of the area that his object was to bring them "the possibility of developing internal, nationality and religious matters in the manner that you yourselves wish, without any kind of violence or pressure from the side of Poland." He promised to establish an administration to which he would "summon local people, the sons of this land."[85]

The implementation of a federalist program encountered a number of obstacles, which even Piłsudski's military talent and political prestige failed to overcome. First, there was the stubborn resistance of the Lithuanian nationalists, despite a common religious allegiance to Rome, to any talk of a federal tie with Poland. They demanded a separate state centered around their historical capital Vilnius, the Wilno of the Poles. Piłsudski hoped that negotiations to bring in Latvia might make the Lithuanians more amenable. His occupation of Wilno was also in part an attempt to bring the Lithuanians to terms. "I do not imagine," he wrote to Wasilewski on April 8, 1919, "that the Lithuanians would be in a condition to resist this twofold pressure."[86] Wilno, in his thinking, could act not merely as a source

---

[84] Leon Wasilewski, *Józef Piłsudski jakim go znałem* (Warsaw, 1935), p. 172.

[85] Józef Piłsudski, *Pisma zbiorowe,* ed. Kazimierz Świtalski (Warsaw, 1937), V, 75.

[86] *Ibid.,* p. 73.

of discord between the two peoples, but as a link forging them together. He expressed his willingness to see the city allotted to a Lithuania federated with Poland. But if Lithuania remained outside, Poland would retain Wilno by force of arms.[87] Hence his unofficial backing of the shabby conduct of General Żeligowski in seizing Wilno in the autumn of 1920.

Second, Piłsudski had to face not only the tepid response of his western allies, but opposition to his plans from influential sections of his own people almost as stubborn as from the Lithuanians. The Polish diet at this period was dominated by the National Democrats, in alliance with the right wing of the peasant movement, and it came out in April, 1919, in favor of incorporating the territories east of the Bug directly into the Polish state. Such a solution was supported by the overwhelming majority of Poles in these territories; it was from the local Polish landowners and intelligentsia that, despite the fine phrases of the Wilno Proclamation, the local administration was mainly recruited. As a leading Pilsudskiite, Marian Zyndram Kościałkowski, remarked: "Locally a picture is very often created of the times of serfdom, when the lord was . . . the final court of appeal."[88] The crying need for at least some measure of land reform among one of the most depressed peasantries in the whole of Europe was completely neglected: a dangerous inactivity in view of the example of Communist Russia just across the lines.

Third, Polish federalism did overestimate the strength of nationalism among Belorussians and among Ukrainians outside Galicia. Piłsudski gained some support from Belorussian nationalists after his Wilno Proclamation, but the movement was extremely weak at this period. A year later his agreement with Ukrainian hetman Petlura of April 21, 1920, and the ensuing expedition to Kiev, opened up the prospect of establishing some sort of federation in this area. But ironically it was really only in the territory of east Galicia, claim to which had been renounced by Petlura in the agreement, that Ukrainian nationalism was securely rooted. True, some federalists like the Socialist disciple of Piłsudski, Tadeusz Hołówko, had been prepared to forfeit portions of east Galicia to a Ukrainian state, but

---

[87] *Ibid.*, p. 80. See also Władysław Pobóg-Malinowski, *Najnowsza historia polityczna Polski 1864–1945*, II, Part I (London, 1956), 182–92.

[88] Quoted in Józef Lewandowski, *Federalizm—Litwa i Białoruś w polityce obozu belwederskiego* (*XI 1918–IV 1920*) (Warsaw, 1962), p. 214.

even he remained adamant on retaining Lwów for Poland.[89] Indeed Lwów—*Leopolis semper fidelis*, Polish in culture and population and tradition—even more than Wilno aroused the deepest feeling among almost the whole Polish population.

Piłsudski's expedition to Kiev was followed by Communist Russia's invasion of Poland in July, 1920. The repulse of the Soviet armies on the Vistula is a well-known story. Poland had strength enough to drive the invaders back, but it—and Russia too—urgently needed peace to build up resources after years of war. The Soviet-Polish borders that resulted from the subsequent negotiations were the result of compromise. While it brought the country the long-sought peace, "the Treaty of Riga sealed the fate of Piłsudski's federal scheme of 1919–1920."[90] The "grand design" of the pre-national era had proved insufficient in the twentieth century.

While linguistic nationalism thus led ultimately to large-scale curtailment of Polish territory in the east, the same factor resulted in some expansion to the west where, as already mentioned, Polish continued to be spoken in Upper and "Teschen" Silesia and in East Prussia, parts of which had never been integrated into the Polish state. In these areas the Poles formed a submerged nationality—peasants, craftsmen, or industrial workers—whose educated members were constantly being skimmed off by the dominant German culture. If in Poland proper the gentry remained the bearers of the national idea, in these western borderlands Polish speakers occupied the position of nationalities like the Belorussians, or Slovaks, or Transylvanian Romanians. In Upper Silesia national consciousness had begun to awaken even before 1848. The movement, provincial in character, centered at first on maintenance of the language and the defense of Roman Catholicism, with social issues increasing in importance with the rapid industrialization during the second half of the century. At the outset of the twentieth century the old alliance between Poles and the German Catholic Center Party was broken, and now, under the lay leadership of Wojciech Korfanty, a

[89] Quoted in *ibid.*, from *Robotnik*, 24 IV 1919. For his later views on this problem, see Stanisław J. Paprocki, "Ś. p. Tadeusz Hołówko wobec problemów narodowościowych," *Sprawy narodowościowe* (Warsaw), V, No. 4/5 (August–October. 1931), 385, 386, 396, 397.

[90] M. K. Dziewanowski, "Piłsudski's Federal Policy, 1919–1921," Part II, *Journal of Central European Affairs* (Boulder, Colo.), X, No. 3 (October, 1950), 287.

common front with the other Poles of the German Empire came into being. Considerable success was achieved in stemming the advancing tide of Germanization, especially among the industrial proletariat. Nevertheless a "social and cultural lag"[91] between Polish national consciousness there and in Poland proper still existed at the time of the Upper Silesian plebiscite held under the auspices of the League of Nations in March, 1921. And this was even more the case in East Prussia, especially among the Protestant Mazurians, where the plebiscite of the previous year had gone overwhelmingly against the Polish connection. In these areas, Polish speech did not necessarily coincide with consciousness of being Polish. On the other hand, failure to vote for union with Poland did not automatically signify identification with German nationality. Indeterminate nationality was a phenomenon not only of Poland's eastern but also of her western borderlands.

The final establishment of the eastern frontiers in April, and the settlement imposed in Upper Silesia in October, 1921, ended the century-and-a-quarter-long struggle for Polish independence. Energies that had formerly been concentrated on this goal might now be diverted into more directly creative channels. An enormous task faced the nation in building up the new state's economy, establishing an efficient administrative and political machine and setting up a modern educational system. In literature and art a reaction set in against patriotic themes. "In spring let me see the spring—and not Poland," cried the poet Jan Lechoń in his poem "Herostates." A new positivism, a reaction against romantic nationalism, was in the air. It was a positivism, however, that was firmly encased within the framework of a Polish state.

In the interwar period, Polish nationalism found political expression chiefly in differing views on the structure of the new state. Was it to be a Polish national state in which the ethnic minorities would either be gradually assimilated or, where this proved impossible, presented with the alternatives of emigration or permanent acquiescence in a second-class status? Or should the state, while preserving its over-all Polish character, take the minority groups into partnership, respecting their separate cultures and political individuality, and eschewing all thought of Polonization? The debate was

[91] W. J. Rose, *The Drama of Upper Silesia* (Brattleboro, Vermont: Stephen Daye Press, 1935), p. 179.

really a variation of a controversy reaching back into the nineteenth century under the new conditions of national independence. Its protagonists were at first the same, too: the right wing led by Dmowski and his *endeks* and the political left, of which the Polish Socialist Party was the most important representative.[92] Piłsudski's *coup d'état* of May, 1926, added a complicating element, for the authoritarian governments that he dominated until his death in 1935 (and thereafter, one might say, directed from his grave) contained elements that were drawn from both camps. Official policy towards the minorities often appeared to zigzag uncertainly between the two extremes of reconciliation and repression.

For the National Democrats, then, the Polish state was conceived as an instrument to subserve purely Polish interests. Jews were to be excluded from the national community as a first step towards eventual emigration, the German minority was to be kept severely in check, but opinion varied as to the best means to deal with the Ukrainians and Belorussians of the eastern provinces. One school advocated complete cultural assimilation, which might be expedited by extensive colonization of these territories with Polish settlers. Another school regarded these peoples as subgroups of the Polish nation whose demands, like those of the Tatra mountaineers or the Kashubs of the "corridor" area, could be appeased by judicious recognition of their regional peculiarities of dialect and custom. All wings united in urging that the nationalism of these peoples represented no more than the doctrinaire views of a small minority of disgruntled intellectuals, movements without roots in the masses, the artificial creation in the case of the Ukrainians of the anti-Polish policy of the Austrian bureaucracy. "One can speak of the existence of a Ukrainian nation only with great license," wrote Dmowski as late as 1930.[93] Isolated from the intelligentsia, the peasant masses might be gradually won over for the Polish nation. Soviet Russia, so Dmowski believed, was likely to be involved in its internal affairs for many years ahead: with careful treatment on Poland's part, it would not present a serious obstacle to a Polish policy of assimilation. In the mid-1930's a greater awareness of the true strength of

[92] See Konstantin Symmons-Symonolewicz, "Polish Political Thought and the Problem of the Eastern Borderlands of Poland (1918–1939)," *The Polish Review* (New York), IV, No. 1/2 (1959), 65–81.

[93] Roman Dmowski, *Świat powojenny i Polska* (3rd ed.; Warsaw, 1932), p. 238.

Ukrainian national aspirations appeared to be growing among the National Democrats; it was not yet clear, however, how widespread were such views.

The *endek* view of the state, which became increasingly permeated by totalitarian tendencies deriving in part from Fascist Italy, was vigorously challenged by all who believed that the state should serve the welfare of all its citizens, regardless of ethnic affiliation, and that any attempt to block genuine strivings of the national minorities towards political and cultural development was inadmissable, provided these did not jeopardize the security of the state. They urged that conciliation with the peoples of the eastern provinces, in particular, was pressing in view of the danger that the example of the Soviet experiment, as well as German intrigues, presented as centrifugal forces that might eventually succeed in disintegrating the Polish state.

A small but influential section among Piłsudski's supporters produced a new version of the old federalist policy, to which they gave the name "Prometheanism" (*prometeizm*). The movement flourished particularly in the 1930's. While the earlier federalism put emphasis on the liberation of the subject peoples of the Polish-Russian borderlands, the Promethean movement stressed the need to smash Soviet Russia as a necessary prelude to emancipating her enslaved nationalities from the Arctic Ocean to the Caspian Sea and the steppes of Siberia. Protagonists of this school found allies in various non-Russian right-wing *émigré* groups. And if a distinct pro-Russian coloring still lingered on under the anti-bolshevism of the *endeks*, the Promethean movement, for all its belief in Polish military strength, always kept one ear cocked in the direction of Berlin.

The *endeks* were out of office for almost all the interwar period; the political left was entirely excluded from power after 1926. Neither before nor after Piłsudski's *coup d'état* did the actual policies pursued by successive governments clearly reflect either the assimilationist or the conciliationist schools of thought. Interwar Poland's treatment of her minorities is a subject of great complexity on which an immense amount has been written of varying quality.[94] This falls

[94] The most recent survey is Stephan Horak, *Poland and Her National Minorities, 1919–39* (New York: Vantage Press, 1961). A scholarly and reasonably impartial study of the subject still remains to be written.

outside the scope of the present essay, but a few comments of a general nature may be in order.

It should be pointed out that Poland faced minority problems of a magnitude that even old, established states might have found it hard to solve. After the unsuccessful attempt of the Ukrainians to wrest east Galicia from the Poles in 1918 and 1919, the Ukrainian minority throughout the 1920's remained irreconcilably opposed to inclusion within the Polish state. Acts of sabotage were answered by repressive measures on the part of the government, climaxing in the notorious "pacification" in the autumn of 1930. A leading Promethean wrote of this decade that government policy "faced every Ukrainian with the alternative of either becoming a Pole or hating Poland."[95] With the inauguration of a policy of "normalization" in the mid-thirties it looked as though, but for the war, a *modus vivendi* might ultimately have been worked out, whereby the Ukrainian minority could have collaborated in political life without being required to renounce its long-range national aspirations.

With roughly a third of its citizens members of national minorities and thereby, at least during the period of parliamentary rule, often holding the political balance, Poland was peculiarly susceptible to the dangers of both Russian and, especially after the rise of nazism, of German support of irredentism. Every manifestation of nationalist aspirations easily became identical in the eyes of Polish officialdom with subversion, which must be suppressed before it could bring about the disintegration of the state. In the Belorussian areas, for instance, as a result of this kind of policy, "the political life of the area was virtually stifled" from the late 1920's on.[96] The poverty-stricken Belorussian borderlands also presented the new state with an immense economic challenge, which only a radical and consistent policy could have adequately met. The increasing influence of the borderland landowners on government policy meant that in fact nothing really effective was done. Again, the Jewish community of well over three million posed a serious problem, especially with its big imbalance in economic distribution between town and country and its concentration in certain professions and trades, a problem

[95] Aleksander Bocheński, "Problem polityczny ziemi czerwienskiej," in *Problem polsko-ukraiński w ziemi czerwieńskiej* (2d ed.; Warsaw, 1938), p. 18.

[96] Symmons-Symonolewicz, "Polish Political Thought . . . ," p. 73.

that bemusement with anti-Semitic notions on the part of large sections of the governing class made only harder of solution.

Poland, both government and people, resented the Minority Treaty that it was required to sign on June 28, 1919, as an appendage to the Treaty of Versailles.[97] There were just grounds for complaint in the fact that Germany, which still retained a Polish-speaking minority of nearly one-and-a-half millions, was not required to adhere to any general treaty of this nature. Against attempts at Germanization, Poland had no court of appeal except in the special case of German Upper Silesia; at the same time it was held accountable for its own minority policies before the League of Nations.

Nevertheless, after taking into consideration the real disabilities under which it had to act and the relatively short period of independence, interwar Poland's minority policies must still be accounted a failure. The promised autonomy in east Galicia and other measures of conciliation that might have won the more moderate Ukrainians were never implemented. Communism, though illegal, made deep inroads among the Belorussian peasantry. The introduction of "ghetto" benches and the *numerus clausus* in the universities and the economic boycott, backed by the authorities in church and state, showed the bankruptcy of government policy towards the Jews in the thirties. Minority participation in government was virtually nonexistent; the running of the state was almost entirely in Polish hands. Poland's old power of peacefully assimilating foreign elements began to dry up: half-hearted and ineffective attempts to impose Polonization in the cultural and educational fields only aroused even stronger animosity in the minority groups. For one reason or another (it must be emphasized that the minority nationalists sometimes bore part of the responsibility), and over the protests of many liberal-minded Polish patriots, by 1939 a third of Poland's citizens had been made to feel outsiders in the land of their birth. This was a sorry epilogue to a struggle that had been waged for so long with the watchword: "For Our Freedom and Yours."

This study has attempted to outline the history of the idea of modern Polish nationalism from the patriotism of a nonnational

[97] The text is reprinted in C. A. Macartney, *National States and National Minorities* (London: Oxford University Press, 1934), Appendix I. See also chap. vii, sec. 3. Poland abrogated the treaty in 1934.

gentry in the old Polish commonwealth to its outcome during the interwar years in a nation-state centered on the linguistic community.[98] Its evolution was completed, at least for the time being, in the course of the last war and its immediate aftermath.

The struggle against the Germans—and against the Russians until the outbreak of the Soviet-German war in 1941, which brought an agreement between Russians and Poles—had united almost the entire Polish population in patriotic fervor against the occupiers. A reconstructed government in exile based on a coalition of political parties from moderate right to moderate left was soon set up in France, and this in 1940 became located in London. Towards the end of the war, however, as a result of deteriorating Polish-Soviet relations, a second Polish power center came into being under the auspices of the Soviet authorities. Thus not only did two rival governments eventually emerge; the underground movement in the home country also split into two sections. The overwhelming majority of patriots continued to look to "London": a small but vigorous minority with leadership provided by the remnant of Polish Communists who had somehow managed to survive Stalin's purges of the previous decade saw the dawning light of renewed independence in the east. The fact that the liberation from German rule was achieved by the Red Army guaranteed the ascendancy in postwar Poland of the Moscow-oriented political groups controlled to a greater or less degree by the Communists.

In no area was the new Poland's changed position in the world more marked than in the boundaries that were assigned it by its eastern neighbor with the backing eventually of Great Britain and the United States. An ethnic Poland located within (supposedly) strategic frontiers—Dmowski's dream—emerged with the ending of German occupation in 1945. While the ethnically non-Polish territories in the east were incorporated in the Soviet Union, in the

[98] No comprehensive history of Polish nationalism *stricto sensu* exists. Olgierd Górka, *Naród a państwo jako zagadnienie Polski* (Warsaw, 1937), combines adulation for Piłsudski with, however, a sensitive approach to the problem of Polish nationalism within a multinational state. See Konstanty Symonolewicz, *The Studies in Nationality and Nationalism in Poland between the Two Wars (1918–1939): A Bibliographical Survey* (reprinted from *Bulletin of the Polish Institute of Arts and Sciences in America*, II, No. 1 [October, 1943], 57–125) (New York, 1944), for the extensive interwar literature on the subject in various academic disciplines.

west the boundaries of early medieval Poland were restored—somewhat ironically—under the auspices of a government dominated by the Communists, whose internationalism during the interwar period had led them to denounce the chauvinism of the state's rulers. The new frontiers, backed by mass transfers of population, represented indeed a geopolitical shift in Poland's position that roughly corresponded with the evolution of its nationalist ideology in this century.

The concept of Polish nationalism has not substantially changed during the two decades of the post-1945 era, although it has undergone some alteration in its forms. Except among the *émigrés*, who, for all their numerical strength, have been singularly uncreative in the realm of political thought if compared with the "Great Emigration" of the previous century, Polish nationalism for most of this period has only found expression indirectly or in roundabout and undercover ways. Yet in the atomic age, when generally there has been an ever increasing awareness of the common fate of mankind, nationalist sentiment has far from vanished in Poland. Erupting with sudden and narrowly suppressed violence in 1956, it has been a force that the ruling Communist party has had to reckon with both before and after that date.

The Poland that emerged at the end of the second World War, in contrast to interwar Poland, was virtually a uninational state; the overwhelming majority of its inhabitants now shared the same language and historic tradition. True, there were minute residual minorities scattered mainly along the eastern borderlands (just as there were Poles left on the other side of the frontier even after the population exchanges and the return of the Soviet deportees were completed). These groups came to enjoy a modest measure of cultural rights only after the end of the Stalinist period.

A curious—and in some ways tragic—phenomenon was the imposition of Polish national identity on the "autochthonous" inhabitants of the former German territories of Silesia and East Prussia who, though in part Germanized, either still spoke a Polish dialect or were proved to be of Polish descent: a policy that resembled in reverse the notorious *Volksliste* of the German occupation and one that was, however, largely abandoned with the overthrow of Stalinism. Some fifty thousand Jews in Poland had survived the wartime holocaust; like the pain in an amputated leg anti-Semitism has lingered on in the Polish community. Intense hatred of the Germans, widespread among all social strata and continuing little abated up to the present, has been a bitter legacy of the atrocities committed under the Nazi occupation that followed over a century of Polish-German antagonism. Anti-Russian feeling, which was strong before 1939 and, especially among the intelligentsia, blended in with anti-Communist sentiments, had been heightened during the war by the experiences of the Polish population in areas under Soviet rule. Katyn and the deportations to Siberia were remembered alongside Auschwitz and Nazi terror, even if only the latter could be publicly denounced in the years after 1945. In this period the interference of the Soviet Union in the internal affairs of a nominally independent Polish state, symbolized by the appointment in November, 1949, of the Russian marshal Rokossovsky as Polish defense minister and commander-in-chief of the army, was especially galling to Polish national pride. Satellite status vis-à-vis the country's powerful neighbor, anti-communism, the loss at the end of the war of previously Polish territory in the east, especially painful for its former inhabitants, and memories of past antagonisms, all combine to give the nationalist sentiments of many Poles a sharp anti-Russian tinge.

Yet the new political régime, in which the Communist party (now rechristened the Polish Workers' Party) played a dominant role from the beginning and an almost exclusive part from the end of 1948 on, did achieve some success in harnessing nationalism to its own policies. There were two issues in particular where the Communists and their political allies enjoyed a distinct advantage in this respect.

In the first place, with the country in ruins the primary need appeared to many patriotic non-Communists to be domestic peace and concentration of all energies on building up the depleted human and material resources of the war-devastated land. "Reconstruction" became a slogan as attractive to large sections of the population as "organic work" had been to the bourgeoisie in the Russian-occupied Congress Kingdom three quarters of a century before. Henceforward, any thought of even passive resistance seemed to many as unrealistic as conspiratorial action had appeared to their predecessors. In a land that justly boasted under the Nazis of being "a country without Quislings," collaboration with the Russian-dominated state was frequently undertaken, if not without reservation, at least with a feeling that this was the best means of contributing to the nation's welfare. This was shown, for instance, in the emergence of a group of "progressive Catholics," whose qualified support of government policies cannot be explained away merely by the presence among them of some undoubted political careerists. (Even the strange case of Bolesław Piasecki, the pre-war Fascist turned post-war Communist agent with the task of infiltrating the Roman Catholic church, does not appear solely as the outcome of undiluted time-serving.)

Secondly, the régime was perhaps fortunate in having at its disposal a sentiment rising out of the widespread fears of Germany that were intensified during the last war. Over the last two decades there has been continued apprehension concerning the rapid revival of West German political stability and economic prosperity and the plans of the western powers for rearming the Federal German Republic. There has been, as well, anxiety concerning the fate of the "regained territories" that Poland had acquired from Germany at the conclusion of the war without gaining at the same time full international recognition of the new boundaries. This has led, if somewhat grudgingly, to widespread acquiescence in the close diplomatic and military ties with the Soviet Union, which alone have seemed to give assurance against the possibility of revived German expansion in the east. At the scent of danger to the Oder-Neisse line, Communist, non-Communist and even anti-Communist tend to rally behind the government's foreign policy.

Only for one brief but highly significant moment in Poland's post-war history has there been likelihood of a serious clash with the Soviet Union. This came in October, 1956. The bloodless revolution of that month originated in three sources: widespread reaction against the political and cultural repression and economic hardships of the Stalinist era that had become only slightly relaxed by that date; an upsurge of nationalist feeling among the populace that was directed primarily against the domination exercised by the Soviet Union over most aspects of the country's life; and national communism of varying degrees of intensity within the ranks of the ruling party. The catalyst acting in this case was the "thaw" that had begun in Russia after Stalin's death and then spread to the satellites.

Much of the pent-up discontent that now found momentary release was of course directed against internal maladministration over the previous decade. The accompanying nationalistic excitement that swept the country in the late summer and early autumn of 1956 was of a traditional character; it represented long-delayed protest against the alien mold in which the country's institutions and culture were being reshaped, against political satellitehood, and economic exploitation. If the worker actively and the peasant passively demonstrated their distate for such subordination, the intelligentsia, with writers and students the most vocal element, demanded the re-establishment of Poland's cultural independence and the renewal of contacts with the West. During the October days, the Soviet authorities complained, not even "bourgeois" Finland went so far in attacking the Soviet Union as did the Polish press in its newfound freedom.[99]

More novel in recent Polish history was the phenomenon of "national communism" that now came to the surface and found clear expression for the first time. In prewar days it had needed a Stalin to scent out nationalist deviation in the ranks of the rigidly Marxist and internationalist Communist Party of Poland; his suspicions, however, cost almost all of its leaders, who had fled to the Soviet Union from repression at home, either their lives or long years in Soviet labor camps. In the reborn Communist party three developments were chiefly responsible for implanting the seeds of a genuine nationalism in a body that in theory professed strict internationalism and in practice adhered to unquestioning subordination to the leading nation in the "socialist" camp. In the first place we must reckon the patriotic line of the war and immediately postwar years. The Polish Workers' Party, first through the People's Army (*Armia Ludowa*) and then through control of a "People's Democracy," sought to utilize patriotic slogans and nationalistic policies to win support from sections of the population that could not otherwise be won over. As a result the rapidly expanding party, as well as its auxiliary organizations, came to include many tens of thousands of members who had not abandoned their patriotic feelings of the past in a newly found allegiance to Marxism-Leninism in its Stalinist variation. While this was especially true on the lower rungs of the party ladder, it also held for the upper echelons, especially where a functionary had served his party apprenticeship in the home country

[99] *Nowe drogi* (Warsaw), X, No. 88 (October, 1956), 114.

rather than in Moscow. In addition, the enforced fusion of the Socialists with the Polish Worker's Party in 1948 brought into the latter's ranks an element that still possessed something of the strong nationalist feeling of the prewar *PPS*, even though the leadership had been largely purged of its right-wing members. Just before the merger the leader of the PPS, Prime Minister Józef Cyrankiewicz, had spoken reprovingly of "the fatal seed of nationalism" in his party.[100]

Finally the impact of the Yugoslav breakaway from the Soviet camp in 1948 was immense, although delayed in Poland first by the removal from power and then by the arrest and imprisonment of Władysław Gomułka and those like him who wished to take into consideration peculiarly Polish circumstances—including the long tradition of patriotism—in creating a Communist system in the country. Yugoslavia provided for Polish Communists a successful model of a Communist state pursuing an independent domestic and foreign policy; it showed the possibility of a genuine alliance between nationalism and communism. Repression did not eradicate the seeds of nationalism in the ranks of the Polish party. In the course of a speech on October 21, 1956, at the epoch-making Eighth Plenum of the Central Committee of the United Polish Workers' Party, Edward Ochab, the retiring first secretary of the party, spoke of the strong anti-Russian sentiments then being voiced even among convinced party members, "people ardently wishing for the victory of the Communist cause" and for friendly—but equal—relations with the Soviet Union.[101]

The outcome of "October" meant much wider freedom for Poland, both domestically and in its external relations, within the framework of the Soviet bloc and a revival of the concept of "a Polish way to socialism aiming at the consolidation of socialist democracy and Polish sovereignty."[102] It is improbable that the Russians would have tolerated the new leader if he had not been a Communist; while if he had not at the same time become identified

---

[100] *Obrady rady naczelnej Polskiej Partii Socjalistycznej 18–22 września 1948r,* supplement to *Przegląd socjalistyczny* (Warsaw), IV, No. 9–12 (35–38) (October–December, 1948), 10.

[101] *Nowe drogi,* X, No. 88, 113.

[102] Quoted from a speech by Władysław Gomułka, 4 XI 1956, in *National Communism and Popular Revolt in Eastern Europe,* ed. Paul E. Zinner (New York: Columbia University Press, 1956), p. 306.

with the nation's cause as a victim of the Stalinist régime, it is equally unlikely that the Polish people would have given him their confidence at the moment of national crisis. For all the tensions and frustrations that have accumulated over the decade following "October," the revolution of 1956 left a form of national communism the uneasy heir of the centuries-old tradition of Polish independence.

Only one institution still remains to challenge the authority of the all-powerful state—the Roman Catholic church. The alliance of church and state that came into being under the sponsorship of Gomułka and Cardinal Wyszyński in 1956, after several years of fierce antagonism, broke apart in the subsequent period. And in this year of the millenium of Poland as a Christian country (1966), the two forces face each other with a mutual suspicion that is mingled with hostility. Each side represents a coalescence of nationalism and internationalism; each side has valid claims to represent the nationalist aspirations of the Polish people and each side can represent the other as an element dependent on an outside center. This polarity in nationalist allegiance is, however, a situation that has repeated itself several times in the course of the last century and a half of Polish history.

Polish nationalism, as we have seen, has evolved a long way from its roots in the old pre-partition commonwealth.[103] From the third decade of the twentieth century, whether the reconstituted state has been ruled by bourgeois liberals, semiauthoritarian military elite, or Communists, the concept of Polish nationality has been broadened to include the whole Polish-speaking citizenry that has been reared through the public school system in the same Polish historic and cultural tradition. Only after 1945 did citizenship and nationality coincide, but this occurred through the exclusion from the new state of territories inhabited by a majority of non-Polish speakers or of the non-Polish speakers inhabiting old or newly incorporated areas. It did not really represent the creation of a nationality based on supranational citizenship, on allegiance to a common state rather than on linguistic affinity, such as can be found in countries of western Europe like Switzerland, Belgium, or Great

---

[103] See Tadeusz Łepkowski, *Polska-Narodziny nowoczesnego narodu 1764–1870* (Warsaw, 1967) for a perceptive account of the earlier stages of this evolution. The volume reached me, however, too late for consideration in the present study.

Britain, or in many of the newly independent states of Asia and Africa. For this to have happened in Poland would have been to reverse the trend of nearly two centuries.

The search for political independence, democracy as represented by the successive influences of Enlightenment, French Revolution, liberalism, and later of Socialist and especially Populist ideas, and cultivation of the language were the three forces that have shaped Polish nationalism since the end of the eighteenth century. On the other hand, the development of separate literary languages, the gradual spreading of democratic ideals, and the desire for independent statehood on the part of the non-Polish ethnic groups that formerly shared a common state and territory with the Poles have been responsible, along with the expansionist ambitions of Poland's neighbors, for the extensive shifts that have periodically occurred in this period in the geographical location of the Polish state. But whether it is a question, as it was until this century, of a proposed Poland from Baltic to Black Sea or of a contemporary Poland that stretches merely from the river Bug to the Oder, Polish nationalism provides one of the keys to understanding the recent history of this area.

STEPHEN FISCHER-GALATI

Romanian Nationalism

We are summoned, comrade deputies, to adopt the fundamental law of
Socialist Romania embodying the most daring dreams of our people, the
dreams for which our best sons have fought, worked and died. Unlimited
opportunities loom on the horizon; no previous generation has been fortunate enough to participate in such grandiose social changes, to be on
the threshhold of national glory. What greater wish could anyone have
than to take part in the struggle and work for the attainment of his country's glorious future, for the progress and prosperity of his Fatherland.

We are convinced that, under the leadership of the Romanian Communist Party, the working people will spare no effort to develop the socialist
economy and culture, to pave the way for the triumphant march toward
the society in which all our people's activities will flourish and in which all
who work will lead a life of plenty and happiness—the Communist
society.[1]

With these words, strongly reminiscent of similar statements by
nationalist political leaders of yore, Nicolae Ceauşescu concluded
his address to the Constituent Assembly called in August, 1965, to
immortalize the attainment of his party's and the Romanian people's penultimate historic goals—the national socialist society. To
what extent is the Communist claim to the national historic legacy
justified and necessary?[2]

The establishment of a greater Romanian state has been the
dream of poets and patriots and the slogan of ambitious politicians

[1] Nicolae Ceauşescu, *Raport cu privire la proiectul de Constituţie a Republicii
Socialiste România* (Bucharest, 1965), pp. 31–32.

[2] On this point consult the basic study on Romanian nationalism by John C.
Campbell, "French Influence and the Rise of Roumanian Nationalism" (Ph.D.
dissertation, Harvard University, 1940) and the controversial, but stimulating, work
by Pamfil Şeicaru, *Unirea Naţională* (Madrid, 1959).

demagogues for over one hundred years.[3] From Bălcescu to
tianu, from Alexandri to Antonescu, from Eminescu to Ceau-
șescu, Romanians have been urged to fight all oppressors and find
glory in a resuscitated modern Daco-Roman state. The enemy was
usually the foreign, rarely the domestic. The Turk, Greek, Hungarian, Russian, and Jew was blamed for the sufferings of the Romanian masses far more than the native landlord or industrial en-
trepreneur. Few were those who could find in the obscure records
of the historic past a mandate for both national and social reconstruction. In fact, before 1848, Romanian nationalism was generally
devoid of reformist connotations, and even during the last century
it provided a shield against meaningful socioeconomic and political
reform.

The rediscovery of the national past in the eighteenth century
was not politically inspired. Bishop Inocenţiu Micu-Klain, the Latin
scholar, and his disciples in the Transylvanian Latinist School were
slow to develop political doctrines based on their philological studies.[4] The thrill of tracing the spoken language of the Romanians of
Transylvania to the inhabitants of ancient Rome arrested whatever
thoughts of social and political justice they might have entertained.
The translation into political idiom of their philological findings,
when it occurred toward the middle of the eighteenth century, was
characterized by extreme conservatism. Latinity meant chronological primacy for the Romanian nation in Transylvania and, by implication, usurpation of the Romanians' rights by latecomers. In concrete terms, first formulated in the celebrated petition to Emperor
Leopold, the *Supplex libellus Valachorum*, the Transylvanian Ro-

---

[3] An interesting anthology of Romanian nationalist literature is in effect con-
tained in Nicolae Iorga, *Istoria literaturii românești* (Bucharest, 1925–26), Vol. II.
The "nationalist psychosis" is also illustrated in the same author's *Războiul pentru
Independenţa României; acţiuni diplomatice și stări de spirit* (Bucharest, 1927).

[4] The political implications of the work of Inocenţiu Micu-Klain have been
grossly exaggerated by both nationalist and neonationalist, socialist, historians both
seeking to demonstrate his Romanianism and unionism. See, for instance, Constantin
Daicoviciu *et al.*, *Din Istoria Transilvaniei* (2nd ed.; Bucharest, 1965), I, 249–53
and particularly p. 250, n. 1. R. W. Seton-Watson provides a more moderate account of Micu's views and aspirations in *History of the Roumanians* (Cambridge,
England: Cambridge University Press, 1934), pp. 174–81. However, the most
balanced discussion of the activities and ideas of the Latinist School is by Keith
Hitchins, "Samuel Clain and the Rumanian Enlightenment in Transylvania," *Slavic
Review*, XXIII, No. 4 (Dec., 1964), pp. 660–75.

manians asked the Habsburg ruler to grant the Romanian *natio* the same rights as those enjoyed by the privileged nations of the province, the Magyars, Szeklers, and Saxons.[5] Such *national* rights included gradual incorporation of Romanians into the Magyar-dominated oligarchy, political representation in Transylvania's political institutions and cessation of discriminatory practices. They were to be extended only to the *natio* in the most restrictive medieval sense —the Romanian bourgeoisie, higher clergy, and "bourgeois intellectuals." The peasantry did not belong to the nation nor did the inhabitants of other Romanian provinces within or without the confines of the Habsburg Empire. A smaller Romania would be difficult to conceive.

Elsewhere in the Greater Romania of the future, in Wallachia and Moldavia, an even narrower concept of the Romanian nation prevailed.[6] The incipient Romanian "nationalism" could be traced neither to the "natio" nor to philological arguments of the Transylvanian Latinist School. Rather it should be linked with reaction against political domination by Phanariote Greeks. Paradoxically, the Romanian boyars, the earliest exponents of what may be called Romanian nationalism in Wallachia and Moldavia, borrowed an anti-Turkish philosophy superficially based on the theories of the French Enlightenment, as expounded by the Greek intelligentsia, to seek liberation from their own masters.[7] The new ideology was not rooted in early Romanian history. It made no mention of the patriotic deeds of men who later became celebrated as national heroes, or "unifiers," like Mircea the Old, Stephen the Great, or Michael the Brave. It was hardly concerned with the common Latin origin of all Romanians nor advocated close ties with the Romanians elsewhere. But it did invoke vague principles of natural rights and

[5] The text of the document may be found in D. Prodan, *Supplex libellus Valachorum* (Cluj, 1948), pp. 243–73. Its significance is discussed in Marxist terms in Academia Republicii Populare Romîne, *Istoria Romîniei* (Bucharest, 1964), III, 492–513 and in a broader context by Hitchins, "Samuel Clain and the Rumanian Enlightenment. . . ."

[6] See Stephen Fischer-Galati, "The Origins of Modern Rumanian Nationalism," *Jahrbücher für Geschichte Osteuropas,* XII (1964), 49–50.

[7] The most comprehensive discussion of these aspects is contained in Campbell, "French Influence and the Rise of Roumanian Nationalism," pp. 25 ff. See also P. Eliade, *De l'influence française sur l'esprit public en Roumanie* (Paris: Leroux, 1898), pp. 229 ff.

nationality borrowed directly from Greek ideology and the *Supplex libellus Valachorum* to express narrow class views in the name of the "Romanian nation." The spokesmen for the Romanians of Moldavia and Wallachia, unlike those of Transylvania, requested privileges and rights only for the upper aristocracy to the exclusion of all other groups.[8] The demands voiced in 1791 did not recall the principles of the French Revolution, made no pretense at extension of liberty, equality, and fraternity to other classes of Moldavian and Wallachian society; they merely sought freedom from foreign domination for the Romanian nation represented by the "democratic-national" upper aristocracy. Nor were these concepts substantially modified after direct contacts with French consular officials in the Romanian provinces were established and the first "National Party" was created in the Danubian provinces during the early years of the Revolution.[9] The Moldavian and Wallachian branches of the National Party neither advocated the union of the two Romanian provinces nor envisaged a greater Romania. In fact there was little liaison between Moldavians and Wallachians and none between the Transylvanian leaders and those of the Danubian provinces.

The extension of such contacts and the formulation of somewhat broader concepts of nationalism occurred only in the second and third decades of the nineteenth century during which years the characteristic features of nascent Romanian nationalism are revealed. The first manifestation is that of greater emphasis on Latinism in Wallachia and Moldavia subsequent to direct contacts with Romanian refugees from Metternich's empire. Yet the influence of the savant Gheorghe Lazăr—perhaps the leading exponent of Tran-

---

[8] In recent years historians of eighteenth-century Romania have singled out the "class interests" of the feudal aristocracy as best expressed in the boyars' proposals to Russia on the eve of the peace treaty of Şiştova in 1791. Correct as this interpretation of the plans and motivations of the upper Romanian aristocracy may be, it has been blurred by even more recent attempts to stress the nationalist elements inherent in the petition itself. The boyars' proposals were actually devoid of any but the most rudimentary nationalist concepts, rooted in a narrow class frame of reference. The removal of Graeco-Turkish domination was clearly their immediate (and sole) goal, even at the cost of Russian suzerainty or even outright incorporation of their lands into Russia. See Fischer-Galati, "The Origins of Modern Rumanian Nationalism," p. 49.

[9] Eliade, *De l'influence française* . . . , pp. 229 ff.

sylvanian Latinism—led the Wallachian and Moldavian boyars along different paths than those of the early Transylvanian scholars and nationalists. Latinism in the Danubian Principalities was associated with France—the leading Latin nation in the world—and with elements borrowed from French political philosophy, particularly constitutionalism. Thus, in Moldavia and especially in Wallachia, nationalism took a Francophile form to the extent of striving for national independence under French protection and for constitutionalism based on the French prototype. It also expressed itself in rejection of non-French (or Latinist) influence, whether ideological or political. In short, Wallachian and Moldavian nationalism gradually assumed the character of a movement for national independence from the political and cultural influence of the Greek Phanariotes, Slavic Russia, and, of course, the Ottoman Empire.[10] The rejection by Romanian nationalists of the appeal by the *Philike Hetairia* in 1821 and the pursuance of a generally anti-Russian course during the following years, can be explained in these terms.[11] It is for this reason, too, that the nationalist poets of the 1820's sing the glory of Romanian Latinity and affinity with France. But the choice of France rather than Rome and Italy, its heir, as the true source of Latinity stems also from political considerations.[12] The early exponents of nationalist views and theories in the Danubian provinces could find in French constitutionalism the bases of a national political philosophy and institutions that would satisfy their class interests. It is indeed noteworthy that the Romanian *Carbonari*, whose membership was derived primarily from the second-class boyars, never adopted the political views of its Italian progenitors. Rather they advanced the political theories of the third estate with the normal substitution of the lower boyardom as the

[10] Campbell, "French Influence . . . ," **pp. 25 ff.**

[11] The fundamental work on the *Philike Hetairia* and its influence in Romania is by A. Oțetea, *Tudor Vladimirescu și mișcarea eteristă in Țările Românești, 1821–1822* (Bucharest, 1945), pp. 9 ff. Important collections of documents related to these problems have been published under Oțetea's supervision in A. Oțetea *et al.*, *Documente privind istoria Rominiei. Răscoala din 1821* (5 vols., Bucharest, 1959–62). Several important addenda are contained in Dimitrije Djordjević, *Révolutions nationales des peuples balkaniques 1804–1914* (Belgrade, 1965), pp. 39–45 and in Notis Botzaris, *Visions balkaniques dans la préparation de la Révolution Grècque 1789–1821* (Geneva, 1962), pp. 143–54; 225–35.

[12] Campbell, "French Influence. . . ."

leading political force in the Romanian provinces. Even the first-rank boyar oligarchy chose to adapt French constitutionalism as the model for the Russian-imposed "Organic Statutes" in the 1830's. The class-oriented nationalism in the early decades of the nineteenth century thus remained relatively unchanged from the primitive prototype of the late eighteenth. As an original movement it developed only in the late thirties and early forties, primarily as a political reaction to specific conditions prevailing in the Danubian Principalities on the one hand and independently in Transylvania.[13]

It was during the period of the *Réglements Organiques*, when the social problems of the Romanian masses in Moldavia and Wallachia were viewed from a reformist point of view by the Russian governor-general General Kisseleff (Kiselev), that the anti-Russian groups—the second-class boyars and on occasion sons of the upper aristocracy—decided that an independent social reform program was essential for making a "nationalist" program appealing to the peasant masses.[14] The fresh memories of Tudor Vladimirescu's revolution of 1821, which brought out so clearly the cleavage between the nationalist leadership and the peasant masses, was a determining factor in the reformulation of nationalist doctrine. The changing nature of nationalist philosophy was also, and primarily, a reaction against the domination of Russia and the upper boyar-oligarchy (which was paying lip service to Kisseleff's programs); this is evidenced by the adherence of such Wallachian and Moldavian nationalist leaders as Câmpineanu, Rosetti, Bolliac to the anti-Russian views of Czartoryski and other refugees from post-1830 Poland.[15] Russia's imperialist policies, according to the Poles and their Romanian supporters, were designed to bring about incorporation of Moldavia and Wallachia into Russia, and her championing of social and economic reform was merely an attempt to win the support of the masses. Thus, to prevent Russia from attaining these aims, the nationalists had

[13] Consult *Acte și documente relative la istoria renașcerei României, 1391–1859* (Bucharest, 1889–1909), Vol. I. An interesting and comprehensive review of these problems is contained in Seton-Watson, *History of the Roumanians*, pp. 192–215.

[14] A penetrating analysis of the process of change may be found in *Istoria Rominiei*, III, 987–94.

[15] *Ibid.*, pp. 937 ff.

to alter their doctrine.[16] The Philharmonic Society, their principal organization in the thirties, began to voice the philosophy of social reform stressing improvement of the lot of the masses and the need to enroll them in the cause of national liberation. At the same time it advocated the union of Moldavia and Wallachia as a bulwark against Russian seizure.

Equally significantly, the Moldavian and Wallachian nationalists turned away from the France of Louis Philippe, which had refused to support their anti-Russian plans. The Philharmonic Society and its literary mouthpiece, *Curierul Românesc*, thus shifted to an imitation of the Transylvanian Latinist position emphasizing the Roman (pre-French) ancestry of the Romanian nation and language and chanting the glories of "national heroes" like Stephen the Great, Michael the Brave, and Tudor Vladimirescu as fighters for Romanian and peasant freedom. Moreover, closer alignment with the "bourgeois" reformist and Latinist views of the Transylvanians was sought, although the two nationalist movements of the Danubian Principalities and Transylvania remained essentially independent.[17] Neither side advocated the creation of a greater Romanian state; however, in the later thirties and early forties social reform became the common link of the two movements and Romanian nationalism assumed a growing socialist character. These trends were further developed in the mid-forties when the nationalists driven out of Wallachia and Moldavia as elements subversive to the attainment of Russian aims fell more and more under the influence of early French social thinkers and the revolutionary emigrés from Italy and Poland who also converged in Paris.

It was in Paris, then, that early Wallachian and Moldavian nationalist philosophy, as ultimately expressed in the revolutions of 1848, took its final form. The Brătianu brothers, C. A. Rosetti, and Bălcescu, in the ranks of the Wallachian contingent, now assumed the ideological leadership of the movement. The social-reform theme became an integral component of their nationalistic program,

---

[16] The best discussion of these problems is contained in P. P. Panaitescu, *Emigraţia polonă şi Revoluţia Română de la 1848* (Bucharest, 1929), pp. 3 ff.

[17] An excellent critical discussion of these problems is by John C. Campbell, "The Influence of Western Political Thought in the Rumanian Principalities, 1821–1848: The Generation of 1848," *Journal of Central European Affairs*, IV (Oct., 1944), 262–73. See also Campbell, "French Influence," pp. 126 ff.

dly influenced by Saint-Simon and Fourier and attendance
let's and Michelet's lectures.[18] An atmosphere of radicalism
gency emanated from secret societies (to which Mazzini's
ion ers, several Romanians and perennial Polish nationalist emigrés belonged) and this unquestionably intensified the revolutionary ardor of the Romanian aristocracy in their comfortable quarters
in the French capital.

Wallachian nationalism was expressly directed toward liberation
of the Danubian provinces from Russian domination. Broad but
superficial social reform centering on the emancipation of the peasantry and promotion of the rising bourgeoisie was, however, at the
very core of the Wallachian nationalist program. The generation of
1848 indeed emphasized social revolution and political independence more than union with Moldavia and Transylvania into a
greater Romanian state.[19] In this respect the Wallachian movement
differed from the Moldavian, which was much more concerned with
the reestablishment of the historic tradition than with social revolution. This deviation from the earlier common trends can be attributed largely to Moldavia's proximity to Russia and the pragmatic
lessons derived from the peasant revolt in Galicia in 1846 that
threatened destruction of the very class to whom the members of
the Moldavian nationalist party belonged. Moreover, Kogălniceanu
and other Moldavian leaders had been exposed more to the conservative German university life and German political and social
thought of the forties than to the radical Parisian intellectual climate. The Moldavians' political views of 1848 emphasized union of
Moldavia and Wallachia into a liberal state in which the conditions
of the several social classes would be improved and the ruling boyar
oligarchy would be replaced by themselves, the liberal younger
members of the aristocracy.[20]

[18] Consult S. Stoian, "Teodor Diamant și socialismul utopic în Principatele
Dunărene," Analele Universității C. I. Parhon. Seria Științe Sociale, Vol. VIII (1957);
G. Mladenatz, "Influența socialismului mic-burghez în publicistica Tărilor Române
din secolul XIX," Probleme Economice, Vol. X, No. 8 (1957).

[19] Consult documents contained in Anul 1848 în Principatele Române (Bucharest,
1898–1910), Vols. I–V. A stimulating analysis of these problems in Șeicaru, Unirea
Națională, pp. 90 ff.

[20] See in particular V. Popovici, "Dezvoltarea mișcării revoluționare din Moldova
după evenimentele din martie 1848," Studii și cercetări științifice (Iași), 5 vols.
(1954), Vols. I, II.

Noteworthy also is the independence of the Transylvanian movement. Throughout the thirties and forties it adhered closely to the Latinist inheritance of Inocenţiu Micu and his disciples. And even though later leaders like Bariţiu, for instance, maintained contacts with their Wallachian and Moldavian counterparts, they were not concerned with union or liberation from Russia. The basic aim of the Transylvanian nationalists in the thirties and forties was social reform within the Habsburg Empire, strengthening of the political rights of the Romanian intellectuals and middle class and, as a necessary extension of their philosophy, the emancipation of the peasantry. In short, their ideology was derived from the Latinist tradition, the *Supplex libellus Valachorum* and the several plans for sociopolitical reform circulating in the Habsburg monarchy. Significantly enough, the Romanian leaders in Transylvania sought cooperation with "progressive" (primarily Magyar) elements of the empire at least as much as with the leaders of the Moldavian and Wallachian nationalist movements, both before and even during 1848. The possibility and even desirability of national union was not excluded by Bariţiu, Sever, Laurian, and others, but to them, and particularly to Avram Iancu—the leader of 1848—social reform and the gaining of political rights in Transylvania itself were foremost goals. In this respect the Transylvanians were much closer to the Wallachians than to the Moldavians but, at all times, they had reservations as to the depth of the reformist convictions of their Wallachian and Moldavian "brethren"—suspicions based in no small measure on the social origin of the leadership of the Danubian Principalities and the superficiality of their views.[21] Historic developments in 1848 and shortly thereafter confirmed the basic differences between the Transylvanian movement and that in the Danubian provinces.

Moldavian and Wallachian nationalism assumed an entirely different form after 1848 when the experience of that year showed the dangers of social reform platforms and independent political action against Russian domination. Whereas Transylvanian nationalism insisted on social reform and the gaining of full "nation" status long after 1848, that of Wallachia and Moldavia found that the achieve-

---

[21] Daicoviciu *et al., Din Istoria Transilvaniei*, II, 1 ff.; R. Pantazi, "Ideile social-politice ale lui G. Bariţiu," *Din istoria filozofiei în Romînia* (5 vols.; Bucharest, 1957), Vol. II.

the historic tradition of Latinism through mere unification
everal Romanian provinces into a greater Romanian state
h a safer and more realizable goal than the adaptation of
European constitutionalism and socialism to the Danubian
provinces. And this divergence became a crucial issue in the development of modern Romanian nationalism after 1848.[22]

The principal victim of 1848 was the social-reform element in
the nationalist movement. Whereas it may be exaggerated to claim
that the "bourgeois" revolutionaries of Transylvania and the "aristocratic" revolutionaries of Moldavia and Wallachia sold out the
peasantry in the process of reconciliation with their rulers, it is clear
that reformist nationalism was buried in the fifties throughout the
Romanian provinces. This change cannot be ascribed to the Bach
System or Russo-Turkish oppression alone. Nor can it be justified
in terms of *Realpolitik*. A relatively simple explanation may be offered for the Transylvanian movement: disenchantment with the
Hungarians and hopes that the emperor would undertake reform
from above and provide equal rights, within the well-defined class
structure, to all inhabitants of the empire. But there was no *Kaisertreue* in Wallachia and Moldavia, only conservatism and opportunism.

The prevailing view that the Russian occupation of the Romanian
provinces after the debacle of 1848 cooled the nationalist fever
ignores the fact that conservative nationalism was not arrested or
discouraged by the occupying forces.[23] The Romanian princes themselves, particularly Bibescu, championed national self-identity as
energetically as the aristocratic oligarchy.[24] It is true that this was
the nationalism of a power elite banked on continuing Russian
hegemony and was sympathetic to Russian socioeconomic views.

[22] Consult the fundamental bibliographical articles by Dan Berindei and
V. Curticăpeanu, "Revoluția de la 1848–1849," *Studii*, XV, No. 6 (1962), 1579–95;
Cornelia C. Bodea and G. Chiriță, "Formarea Statului Național," *Studii*, XV, No. 6
(1962), 1597–1611.

[23] Academia Republicii Populare Romine, *Istoria Romîniei* (Bucharest, 1964), IV,
224 ff., agrees somewhat reluctantly with this interpretation. Compare the contemporary nationalist Marxist interpretation with Nicolae Iorga, *Viața și domnia
lui Barbu Știrbei, domn al Tării Românești, 1849–1856* (Vălenii de Munte, 1910)
in which the celebrated Romanian historian defends Știrbei's nationalist record.

[24] Particularly revealing are the sources contained in Nicolae Iorga, *Corespondența
lui Știrbei Vodă* (Bucharest, 1904) and I. Nistor, *Corespondența lui Coronini din
Principate. Acte și rapoarte din iunie 1854–martie 1857* (Cernăuți, 1938).

It is also true that these men regarded the Austrian occupiers of the provinces during the Crimean War as interchangeable with the Russian forces they replaced. And it is a matter of record that the anti-Romanian policies pursued by the Habsburg in their own empire did not impede collaboration between the "imperialists" and the "nationalists" in Moldavia and Wallachia. The most charitable interpretation of these post-1848 nationalist manifestations would be to account for fraternization with Russia and Austria in terms of a common effort against the archenemy of the Romanian nation, the Turk. However, such an explanation would not be entirely accurate because many of the forty-eighters who had not fled to Paris were, in the early fifties, cautiously exploring the possibility of a compromise within the framework of Ottoman suzerainty. The fact is that only the fugitives in Paris were contemplating a "total" national solution: outright independence, for the attainment of which they were prepared to sacrifice the reformist principles of 1848.

The principal arguments presented by the main protagonists of the Romanian national cause—by Ion Brătianu, Golescu, and even Bălcescu—to the entourage and friends of Napoleon III and the emperor himself dealt with the advantages that would be reaped by France as the champion of the national liberation movement of oppressed sister Latin states. Brătianu's "Mémoire sur l'Autriche dans la question d'Orient" is perhaps the most outspoken expression of this point of view; but in no way except stylistic sophistication do his words differ from those contained in the rudimentary *feuilletons* "România Viitoare" or "Republica Română" published by his ambitious and occasionally idealistic fellow émigrés. Certain social-reformist ideas crept into the writings of the "Parisians," but in general their plans and programs for the French-protected independent Romania of the future were fully patterned on Napoleon's. Thus they were progressive only in terms of Austrian, Russian, and Turkish political antedeluvianism.[25] Nevertheless, the uncompromising advocacy of a national Romanian state, including Moldavia and Wallachia, and the lip service paid to western political institutionalism placed the emigrants in the forefront of the architects of the national Romanian state set up after the Crimean War. The union

[25] An excellent discussion of these problems, with complete bibliographic references, is contained in Seton-Watson, *History of the Roumanians*, pp. 220 ff. See also *Istoria Rominiei*, IV, 222–60.

of the Romanian provinces represented the attainment of the goal
of political independence ultimately favored by all nationalists, but
regardless of their immediate tactics, it did not provide solutions to
the socioeconomic and political problems, internal or external, of
Moldavia and Wallachia. But now these could be discussed *en famille* with no obligation to consult foreign relatives other than those
who could further the interests of one or another competing Romanian faction in the struggle for political power.

The extent to which internecine conflict transcended the common
bond of nationalism was dramatically revealed in the initial elections for a ruling prince both in Moldavia and Wallachia.[26] Fraudu-
lent as the anti-unionist majority reported by the Turks may have
been, the negative vote cast by the conservative landowners nevertheless reflected fear of transferring power to the "liberals," Francophiles, and nonpropertied classes. And the same fears were also reflected in the election of 1859, which resulted in the choice of
Alexandru Ion Cuza and the eventual unification of the two provinces. In fact, the strength of the conservatives was such that it
blocked the election of anyone but the compromise candidate and
would-be figurehead Alexandru Ion Cuza. The price exacted by the
conservative aristocracy from the "forty-eighters" was the acceptance of the union as the sole political goal and abandonment of any
plans for socioeconomic reform in the United Principalities. This
was hardly too high a price for the "liberals" who were fully prepared to commit themselves and accept any compromise that would
facilitate the attainment of the supreme national goal of union and
the corollary furtherance of their own political careers—even the
abandonment of all principles enumerated in 1848.[27] Their expediency was most clearly exposed after the union had been achieved
when the majority of the "forty-eighters" together with the conservative nationalists repudiated Cuza's socioeconomic reforms as
incompatible with the attainment of the next installment of their

[26] Consult the documentary materials contained in *Acte şi documente relative la
istoria renaşcerei României*, Vols. I–X; Dan Berindei et al., *Documente privind
Unirea Principatelor* (Bucharest, 1959–1961), Vols. I, II.

[27] In addition to references given in n. 26, above see also A. Oţetea et al., *Studii
privind Unirea Principatelor* (Bucharest, 1960) and R. V. Bossy, *Agenţia diplomatică
a României în Paris şi legăturile politice franco-române sub Cuza Vodă* (Bucharest,
1931).

program—total independence from Istanbul. The gentlemen's agreement to remove the self-styled social reformer from power following the emancipation of the peasantry and to accept the arch-conservative Carol of Hohenzollern as his successor speaks more eloquently for the true values of the Romanian nationalists than their theoretical discourses on popular sovereignty and political democracy. Carol's accession thus marked the attainment of the basic goal of primitive political nationalism—the Romanian national state.[28] If disenchantment soon set in among the surviving "forty-eighters" it was on account of Carol's Germanophile tendencies and pro-"conservative" policies, which were regarded as incompatible with the "liberals'" political ambitions. For these reasons alone did the political malcontents brand him and the "Whites" as betrayers of the country's nationalist tradition conveniently equated with French political ideas and practices. The misinterpretation of the French political legacy (which, had it been indeed transplanted to the Romanian political soil, would have resulted in bona fide constitutionalism and social reform) imparted after 1870 a distinct anti-German color to the Romanian national movement. It did not, however, alter the basic economic conservatism of the Francophiles who readily reconciled the continuation of the feudal order and the rigid class restrictions incorporated in the Romanian Constitution of 1866 with the principles of the Third Republic.[29]

In the late sixties, but particularly in the seventies, Ion Brătianu and his coterie argued that the establishment of the truly independent Romania for the Romanians had priority over social and economic reform. To most the frontiers of this Romania were not to encompass Austro-Hungarian territories; but the eventual union of the United Principalities with Transylvania was by no means alien to extremists. Chauvinism with particularly strong anti-Semitic overtones, however, became an integral part of the nationalist creed. As non-Romanian, the German prince and his foreign entourage

---

[28] A penetrating analysis of these developments may be found in *Istoria Romîniei,* IV, 518–33. Consult also the basic works on the subject: Paul Henry, *L'abdication du Prince Couza et l'avènement de la dynastie de Hohenzollern au trône de Roumanie; documents diplomatiques* (Paris: Alcan, 1930) and Nicolae Iorga, *Cuza Vodă și dușmanii săi a doua zi după detronare* (Vălenii de Munte, 1909).

[29] On these points consult *Istoria Romîniei,* IV, 535–60; 583–85.

were suspect; but the Jews, whom Carol supported, were branded as *the enemies* of the Romanian people and of Romania's politically ambitious. In fact, nationalism became synonymous with anti-Semitism for Romanian politicians, ironically more so for the liberals than the conservatives.[30]

The anti-Semitic character of the new nationalism was, in the liberals' case, justified through their seeking the political support of the peasantry, the clergy, and the rural and urban intelligentsia, who all united in blaming the Jews and their protectors, the Germans and Germanophile boyars, for the wretched status of the village and general poverty of the masses. The liberals' appeal to xenophobic prejudices and vague promises of a Romania for the Romanians gained momentum in the early seventies and reached its climax after the War of Independence and the formal establishment of independent Romania in 1878. As leading nationalists they took credit for shedding the Turkish suzerainty and blamed the conservatives and the monarchy for the loss of Romanian territory to Russia at Berlin.[31]

It is now generally recognized that the loss of southern Bessarabia to Russia in 1878 unleashed nationalist sentiments transcending the mere recouping of that province. However, the thought of a Greater Romania through dismemberment of the Austro-Hungarian Empire became indeed difficult after Brătianu and the liberals engineered and supported the secret alliance with Germany and Austro-Hungary in 1883. But this impasse was short-lived.

In the eighties and nineties, the urban intellectuals of Bucureşti and Iaşi and their political sponsors added the Magyars to their list of bêtes noires headed by the Jews and Russians and including all oppressors of Romaniandom—Bulgarians "with fat necks," Greeks "with thin noses," Turks of all descriptions. No mention was made of social reform, which could await the Romanization of society in a Romanian Romania, and in this omission lay the weakness of the

---

[30] Illuminating discussions of these aspects of nationalism are contained in Seton-Watson, *History of the Roumanians*, pp. 318 ff.; Anasatase Hâciu, *Evreii în Tările Româneşti*. (Bucharest, 1943); Wilhelm Filderman, *Adevărul asupra problemei evreeşti în România*. (Bucharest, 1925).

[31] Seton-Watson, *History of the Roumanians*, 331 ff.; Nicoale Iorga, *Correspondance diplomatique roumaine sous le roi Charles Ier (1866–1880)*. (Bucharest, 1938). Invaluable for the entire period are the parliamentary debates contained in *Monitorul oficial al României* (Bucharest, 1876–   ).

nationalist message trumpeted by the politicians of the Old Kingdom.[32]

Whether the views of the Wallachians and Moldavians were shared by the Transylvanians is still a matter of dispute among historians and politicians. Similar sentiments were shared and even voiced by a few extremist nationalist intellectuals, but the vast majority of the Romanian inhabitants of Transylvania as well as of the sister regions of the Banat, Crişana, and Maramureş were at best lukewarm toward the nationalist propaganda emanating from the Old Kingdom. Their primary concern was the establishment of a satisfactory *modus vivendi* with the Hungarians within the framework of the Habsburg monarchy rather than the attainment of foolhardy and unrealizable ventures and their attitude reflected the difference separating the nationalist movement in the Hungarian-dominated regions from the Moldavian and Wallachian.[33]

After the fiasco of 1848, the Romanians sought an accommodation with the Habsburg emperor. Before the Austro-Hungarian Compromise of 1867, they aspired to equality with all nations in the monarchy. Extension of privileges to the propertied classes and emancipation of the peasantry were to be the bases for national reconciliation within the Empire and consolidation of the Romanians' traditional loyalty to the "benevolent emperor," the proverbial *Kaisertreue*. Even after the *Ausgleich*, so unfavorable to Romanian interests, only a handful of intellectuals and merchants—men like Ioan Maiorescu, A. T. Laurian, G. Bariţiu—became advocators of civil insubordination and closer relations with the "brethren" of Moldavia and Wallachia. The majority of the "bourgeois-nationalists," grouped in such political parties as the National Party of Transylvania or the National Party of the Romanians of Banat and Hungary, demanded only cessation of discriminatory economic policies and cultural Magyarization. A compromise comparable to the Austro-Hungarian rather than political union with the Old Kingdom was their avowed goal in the closing decades of the nineteenth

[32] On the activities of the intelligentsia consult Nicolae Iorga, *Istoria literaturii româneşti*. (2d ed., Bucharest, 1925–1926), Vol. II. In general politico-literary terms these activities are also discussed in some detail in *Istoria Rominiei*, IV, 685 ff.

[33] A review of these problems, with ample bibliographical references, is contained in Dan Berindei and V. Curticăpeanu, "Revoluţia de la 1848–1849," *Studii*, XV, No. 6 (1962), 1587 ff.

century. Loyalty to the imperial order, suspicion of the politicians of the Old Kingdom, and a basic "bourgeois" commitment to socio-economic reform were the determining factors in their "cowardly" attitude.[34]

It was precisely because the national movement in Transylvania, Banat, Crişana, and Maramureş was led by members of the bourgeoisie and bourgeois intellectuals that its values and goals differed from the aristocracy-dominated Moldavian and Wallachian. The "Românii de dincolo" were not landowners in conflict with the peasant masses; their conservatism was a function of commercial considerations, as were their socioeconomic and political desiderata. The peasant's lot had to be improved, his socioeconomic status raised so that he might become a respectable member of society, a customer of Romanian commercial and banking interests. Anti-Semitism and anti-Russianism had no place in their doctrine. In turn the peasants endorsed these aspirations. Their political platform favored "bourgeois democracy" whether they agreed, like the "activists" to seek representation and political action in the Hungarian-dominated political institutions or like the "passivists" withdrawal until such time as the Romanians would be allowed equitable representation in parliament. Most significantly, the celebrated *Memorandum* of 1892, submitting political demands to the crown, was a dispassionate petition not dissimilar to the *Supplex libellus Valachorum* and similar "bourgeois" demands of eighteenth century western and central Europe. Thus the "bourgeois nationalism" of the Romanians of Transylvania was basically incompatible with the "aristocratic-feudal" nationalism of the Old Kingdom. And these incompatibilities were major obstacles to the realization of the supreme national goal advocated by the "independent" Romanians— the Greater Romania for all Romanians.[35]

By contrast, the propaganda emanating from Bucureşti in the eighties and nineties found a receptive audience among nationalists in the Bukovina. In that province, the intellectuals had been the mainstay of anti-Ruthenian, anti-Polish, anti-Austrian, and anti-Semitic manifestations since wresting cultural concessions from the

---

[34] A summary statement and critical review of these issues is contained in Stephen Fischer-Galati, "The Rumanians and the Habsburg Monarchy," *Austrian History Yearbook* (1967), III, Part II, 430–49.

[35] Details will be found in Daicoviciu *et al.*, *Din Istoria Transilvaniei*, II, 187–264.

Habsburgs in 1848. In the absence of a Romanian middle class or aristocracy but in the presence of a peasantry fleeced by Jewish moneylenders and a non-Romanian bureaucracy, the intellectuals shared the anti-Semitic, anti-Slavic, and anti-Habsburg prejudices of the politicians and intelligentsia of the Old Kingdom. With little to lose or to conserve, the politically active Romanians in Bukovina in the late nineteenth century favored the creation of a Greater Romania in which they could play some ill-defined role. But even their enthusiasm was dampened early in the twentieth century when the possibilities for national unification was severely jolted by the peasant revolt that occurred in the Old Kingdom in 1907.[36] Paradoxically, this bloody uprising, which resulted from ruthless exploitation of the masses by the landed aristocracy and, in Moldavia, from exploitation by the Jewish locum tenens, was interpreted by those responsible for these basic socioeconomic abuses as a victory for the cause of nationalism, as a patriotic manifestation by a Romanian peasantry directed against oppression by foreigners—the Jews. This misleading reading of the events of 1907 contributed to the radicalization of the nationalist movement in the Old Kingdom that assumed an increasingly more pronounced anti-Semitic character in years immediately preceding World War I. The liberals excelled in demagogic oratory and factual distortion, accusing the conservatives, then in power, of social injustice and pursuit of policies, domestic and foreign, contrary to the national interest. Brătianu's views, particularly influential among Romanian politicians and intellectuals opposed to the Romanian monarchy and its pro-German proclivities, became the credo of all nationalists: unification at all cost—even over Carol's dead body.[37]

It is doubtful that their assumption of leadership of the unionist movement exonerated the liberals from complicity with the conservatives in the eyes of the peasantry. The masses did not regard a Greater Romania as a substitute for agrarian reform. Nor were they deceived by the nationalists' attempt to blame the evils of the

[36] An intelligent and comprehensive discussion of Romanian nationalism in Bukovina will be found in Erich Prokopowitsch, *Die rumänische Nationalbewegung in der Bukowina und der Dako-Romanismus* (Graz, 1965), pp. 35 ff.

[37] On the events of 1907 and their impact, consult M. Roller, (ed.), *Răscoala țăranilor din 1907* (Bucharest, 1948–49), Vols. I–III; M. Ionescu, "Despre însemnătatea și urmarile răscoalei din 1907," *Studii*, X, No. 2 (1957), 7 ff.; Lucretiu D. Pătrașcanu, *Un veac de frământări sociale, 1821–1907* (Bucharest, 1945), pp. 197 ff

countryside on Jews and Socialists. However, the slogan "a Greater Romania for the Romanians" was effective in appeasing the peasants' land hunger, pending the attainment of the nationalists' goal. A similar attitude was displayed also by the Romanians in Transylvania, who, after the peasant revolts, pursued their efforts to seek an accommodation with Vienna or Budapest, or merely straddled the fence between the Austro-Hungarian monarchy and the Old Kingdom. By 1913, however, the nationalists' stock went up throughout the Romanian-inhabited territories. The acquisition of southern Dobrudja after the second Balkan War was regarded as a prelude to the incorporation of Bukovina, Transylvania, the Banat, Crişana, Maramureş, and Bessarabia into a United Romania by all opponents of the intransigent Austro-Hungarian ruling group. And the drive to enroll all the Romanians in the national cause assumed dynamic proportions as World War I neared.

It is to the credit of the nationalists of the Old Kingdom that they assumed a militantly antiroyal position even before the outcome of the war could be predicted. But it is also to the credit of the monarchy and the conservatives in the Old Kingdom and the Habsburg provinces inhabited by Romanians that they resisted the nationalists' demands to betray their allies and their monarchs respectively. Only after Carol's death was the die cast in the Old Kingdom; only as the war's outcome became clear did the Romanian leaders of Transylvania, the Banat, Maramureş, and Crişana decide to abandon the dying Habsburg empire and seek union with the Old Kingdom. Most significantly, however, the Romanians of Transylvania, as well as those of the Bukovina and Bessarabia, made ratification of their own rights and execution of the land reform promised in the Old Kingdom in 1917 a prerequisite for union into a Greater Romania. Sterile nationalist slogans were rejected in the moment of truth under the impact of the Bolshevik Revolution and the reality of a Greater Romania.[38]

The significance of the Bolshevik Revolution on the history of the Romanian nationalist movement exceeded in importance the tsarist

---

[38] The best general discussion of these problems in Seton-Watson, *History of the Roumanians*, pp. 346 ff. Valuable bibliographical information on this period will be found in Tr. Lungu and An. Iordache, "Romînia la începutul secolului al XX-lea (1900–1917)," *Studii*, XV, No. 6 (1962), 1639–51.

seizure of Bessarabia in 1878. The spreading of bolshevism into Bessarabia and Moldavia and the favorable reception of at least its agrarian program by the Romanian peasantry forced the monarchy, in the fall of 1917, to issue, to the despair of conservatives and liberals alike, the celebrated promise of drastic land reform. The proposed social revolution was equally unwelcome to Brătianu and Ferdinand. However, the same Russian pressures provided Brătianu with the necessary trump cards in 1918: His most extravagant plans for a Greater Romania received endorsement of the victorious allies, who were fearful of bolshevism.[39] As the champion of an anti-Communist crusade, the Romanian nationalist leader received the allies' mandate to rid Bessarabia and Hungary of the enemy at the expense of social reform. The anti-Communist trademark assumed by the creators of Greater Romania, the Bucureşti Liberal Party, thus provided an alibi for delaying the implementation of the promises made at the time of the union. It also provided an essential ingredient to the extreme irredentism that characterized the interwar nationalist movement: the preservation of the gains of 1918 against the Bolshevik irredentism. The complementary "struggle" against Hungarian revisionism was also related, whenever convenient, to the legacy of Béla Kun. Finally, in the promotion of their program of national supremacy for the Romanians in their Greater Romania, Brătianu and his associates made liberal use of the association of bolshevism and Judaism, thus keeping alive the anti-Semitic tradition. This brand of nationalism minimized social reform and stressed anti-Semitism, anti-bolshevism, and irredentism.[40] But this private band of Wallachian bankers and landowners was unrepresentative of the majority of the Romanians, who preferred

[39] Important new data on the impact of the Bolshevik revolution is contained in V. Liveanu, *1918. Din istoria luptelor revoluţionare în Romînia* (Bucharest, 1961). The exploitation of the Bolshevik threat by Brătianu and the Liberal Party is ably discussed by Sherman D. Spector, *Rumania at the Paris Peace Conference. A Study of the Diplomacy of Ioan I.C. Brătianu* (New York: Bookman Associates, 1962), pp. 67 ff.

[40] On these points consult the masterful analysis of Romanian political developments in this period contained in Henry L. Roberts, *Rumania: Political Problems of an Agrarian State* (New Haven: Yale University Press, 1951), pp. 94 ff. See also the brilliant discussion of Romanian politics in this period contained in Hugh Seton-Watson, *Eastern Europe Between the Wars, 1918–1941* (Cambridge, England: Cambridge University Press, 1945), pp. 198 ff.

either the patriotism propounded by the National Peasant Party of postwar years or the outright Romanian Fascist variety propagated by Corneliu Zelea Codreanu and his Iron Guard.

If retention of the territorial gains and political power attained after World War I was the credo of the Liberals, the less fortunate but equally ambitious opposition was quick to expose the Brătianu cynicism. Only through the reconciliation of national and regional differences, only through the creation of a prosperous and united country, could a viable Greater Romania be maintained, argued the National Peasant Party and the extreme right. The National-Peasant views, seeking democratic social reform and justice for all inhabitants of the country, found acceptance among the patriotic and socially progressive intelligentsia and professional people as well as the peasantry. But they were rejected by Liberals, supranationalists, students, anti-Bolsheviks, and anti-Semites.[41] The extremists were contained until both the formulae of the National Peasant Party and the Liberals' panaceas proved worthless in the face of socioeconomic chaos. Irredentism or patriotism alone, even when mixed with hand-to-mouth "bourgeois" reformism, could not solve the crises that affected the Romanian masses in the early thirties. And thus the stronger palliatives proposed by the Iron Guard could be sold more effectively.[42]

The feature distinguishing "guardism" from tamer forms of nationalism was social reformism rather than virulent anti-Semitism. The Jew had been the whipping boy for all but a few nationalists, and the anti-Semitism of men like A. C. Cuza and his followers was far more extreme than Codreanu's. The Iron Guard, however, preached Christian mass regeneration; its fundamental message was purification of the existing political and socioeconomic order infested by Jews and Jew-like politicians. The existing political order —which failed to undertake needed social reform, to provide respectability and prosperity to the masses, to allow true Romanians (imbued with "honest" Romanianism) to reach the top echelons in the state and society—had to be abolished and replaced by one

[41] On the nationalism of the National Peasant Party see Roberts, *Rumania: Political Problems* . . . , 130 ff.

[42] The most authoritative statement on Romanian fascism and the Iron Guard is by Eugen Weber, "Romania," in Hans Rogger and Eugen Weber (eds.), *The European Right. A Historical Profile* (Berkeley, Calif.: University of California Press, 1965), pp. 501–74.

dedicated to these goals. Codreanu and his followers endorsed all nationalist doctrines advocating the maintenance of Greater Romania, and combating Judeo-communism; but they also sought national reconciliation with all minority elements in Greater Romania other than the Jew, and his friends.[43] This brand of nationalism, fiercely combated by the monarchy, Liberals, National Peasants, and most other political organizations, was embraced by the young, much of the peasantry, many intellectuals and discontented bureaucrats, and even by industrial workers, by conviction as much as by the opportunism generated by triumphant European fascism. The most effective opposition and alternative to "guardism" was provided by King Carol II's "monarcho-fascism"—a nationalism of a higher order than the traditional through its entertainment of a modicum of social reform. Even if its main ingredients—patriotic demagoguery, irredentism, and anti-Semitism—were shopworn, the call for moderation and resistance to guardist extremism provided a theoretical alternative to those opposed to German control of the Romanian fascist movement and the Fatherland itself. But Carol's synthesis was doomed to failure after annexation by Russia of Bessarabia and northern Bukovina and the further dismemberment of Greater Romania by the Vienna Diktat which destroyed the *raison d'être* of monarcho-fascism.[44] A reformulation of the Romanian nationalist philosophy was then provided by the triumphant Iron Guard and the Romanian Führer, General Ion Antonescu.

The doctrinal aridity of triumphant fascism, particularly evident in the case of the guardists for whom victory meant desecration and confiscation of Jewish property and assassination of political enemies, was also evident in Antonescu's words and deeds. Romanization at home and territorial compensation abroad at the expense of the Romanians' greatest enemies, the Jews, the Soviet Union, and Russian communism were the essentials of his doctrines. The social-reformism originally inherent in the Iron Guardist philosophy was subordinated to the attainment of the immediate goal of the Greater Romania for Christian Romanians.[45]

[43] Codreanu's own views will be found in Corneliu Zelea Codreanu, *Pentru legionari* (Bucharest, 1937).

[44] On Carol's views and ideas consult Roberts, *Rumania: Political Problems . . . ,* pp. 187 ff.

[45] Antonescu's doctrine is most clearly expressed in Ion Antonescu, *Generalul Antonescu către Țară. 6 Septemvrie 1940–42 Iunie 1941* (Bucharest, 1941).

The failure of Antonescu's crusade and the subsequent destruction of the Fascist regime by the forces of Russian communism was viewed at the end of World War II as the nadir of Romanian nationalism. A new, international, Communist order built on the ashes of an obsolete and primitive nationalist tradition was in the offing as Romania's "liberation from fascism" was celebrated in August, 1944. However, this reading of the history of Romanian nationalism proved to be erroneous. In their determination to maintain political identity in the face of Stalinist and post-Stalinist pressures exerted by the Soviet Union, the new Romanian leaders slowly abandoned internationalism in favor of national communism. Gheorghe Georghiu-Dej and his associates, who initially claimed the historic legacy only as executors of the unfulfilled social revolutionary tradition became, in the mid-fifties, champions of the nation's historic tradition as well. As Khrushchev's internationalism became more persistent, the Romanian Communists stressed more the national than the social revolutionary legacy. By 1965, as Nicolae Ceauşescu succeeded Gheorghiu-Dej, the accent was clearly on nationalism; social revolution was taken for granted. The traditional characteristics of the "bourgeois-landlord" nationalism became incorporated into the Communist version. Chauvinism, anti-Semitism, anti-Russian and anti-Hungarian attitudes, and excessive patriotism were integral parts of the new nationalism; perhaps as important as socioeconomic reform. A Greater Socialist Romania for the Romanians is the Communist adaptation of Brătianu's slogan to the realities of the socioeconomic order of the second half of the twentieth century.[46]

On the other hand, Communist nationalism differs considerably in origin and purpose from the nationalism of former years. Its primary purpose is securing mass acceptance of a revolution contrary to the desiderata of the Romanian people, in the broadest sense, acceptance of the Communist order. Whether the masses will ever regard national communism as the contemporary equivalent of the reformist nationalism advocated by the National Peasant Party or by the National-Socialists of the thirties and accept it in that spirit is uncertain. But it is evident that the rekindling of the

---

[46] A detailed discussion of these problems will be found in Stephen Fischer-Galati, *The New Rumania: From People's Democracy to Socialist Republic* (Cambridge: M.I.T. Press, 1967).

fires of bourgeois nationalism, of traditional national prejudices and sentiments, has helped the cause of the Communists in Romania. In a sense, Ceauşescu's nationalism may be said to represent a synthesis of the aspirations and prejudices (other than anti-communism) of the Romanians. If and when contemporary authoritarian communism were to become more closely identifiable with democratic socialism, that synthesis could indeed be regarded as representative of the Romanian nationalist tradition. Whether socialism in any form, or private capitalism, for that matter, are essential components of Romanian nationalism is still open to question.[47] In the absence of historic evidence the Communists' claim and formulae are as valid or invalid as those of their political predecessors. At the present level of socioeconomic development and under present political conditions, national and international, Ceauşescu's statement of August, 1965, was politically justifiable; it may very well also have been accurate.

[47] A summary statement will be found in Stephen Fischer-Galati, "East Central Europe: Continuity and Change," *Journal of International Affairs*, XX, No. 1 (1966), 1–8.

IVO J. LEDERER

Nationalism
and the Yugoslavs

I

It is a hallmark of eastern Europe in modern times that nationalism
—that blend of *national* consciousness, ethnic passion, and cultural-
economic politics, has long been its way of life. In this respect eastern Europe has not been unique, but for peculiar reasons it has
sometimes seemed to be so. The eastern European "way of life" is
akin to a stream made up of a variety of tributaries of which nationalism is only one, but nationalism has run so deep and strong that
it has appeared to possess an elemental, almost gravitational, quality. Time, location, and circumstances have, of course, altered its
flow, as have war, revolution, social-economic transformation, ideology, perhaps even some of the brave attempts at emancipation from
the bondage of historical fancy. Still, nationalism has been the
fundamental fact of life for nearly two hundred years.

Nowhere has this been so clearly and agonizingly the case as in
the lands of the Yugoslavs.[1] Moreover, nowhere in Europe can a
more complex web of interactions be found. Among the Yugoslavs
specific nationalisms have intertwined with an over-all nationalism,
with regionalism, and (if the word existed) with "ethnocratisms"
of diverse sorts: religious, linguistic, cultural, and economic. Such
multiplicity characterizes a number of eastern European societies
and has been further compounded by conflicting territorial ambi-

[1] The term "Yugoslavs" is used here to denote the peoples of present-day Yugoslavia. In this chapter the term "southern Slavs" will also be used in the same
meaning and will not include the Bulgarians. The term "Yugoslavia," officially in
use only since 1929 will, for the sake of convenience, be applied as of December,
1918.

tions and competing cultural claims. In these respects, the territory of the Yugoslavs has unfolded as a microcosm of the region as a whole.

Unified as a result of the first World War, Yugoslavia combined a number of national groups into a single state whose territory approximated in size that of the United Kingdom (or the state of Wyoming). The three dominant nationalities—Serbs (slightly over four million in 1921), Croats (roughly two and three-fourths million), and Slovenes (slightly over one million)[2]—had distinctly separate histories and, prior to 1918, had never shared a common homeland.[3] Divided by religion (Orthodox, Catholic, Muslim), by alphabet (Cyrillic, Latinic), by cultural tradition (Byzantine, Ottoman, central European), social structure (aristocratic, patriarcho-feudal, agrarian, quasi-industrial), and other characteristics, the Yugoslavs did not constitute a distinct nation or nationality. The very denomination "Yugoslav" represented in 1918 a subterfuge designed to deemphasize the points of division between the component groups.

Yet it remains a fact that the Yugoslav union of 1918 was a logical and even natural consequence of various factors, including the collapse of the Central Powers and the disintegration of the Habsburg Empire. Despite religious, cultural, and other differences, the Serbs, Croats, and Slovenes shared significant political and geostrategic interests, and economic aspirations. By the late nineteenth century they also began to be drawn to each other by a desire for collective security against the great powers.

Echoing the romantic and nationalist impulses of the Risorgimento and the German national movement, the southern Slavs had

[2] For historical population statistics see: Alfred Gurtler, *Die Volkszahlungen Maria Theresias und Josef II, 1753–1790* (Innsbruck, 1909); Paul F. Myers and Arthur A. Campbell, "The Population of Yugoslavia," ("U.S. Bureau of the Census, International Population Statistics Reports, Series P-90," No. 5 [Washington, D.C.: U.S. Government Printing Office, 1954]); V. Goehlert, "Die Entwickelung der Bevölkerung in den Länder der ungarischen Krone seit 100 Jahren," *Statistische Monatschrift*, XII (1886), pp. 336–52; Sava Obradović *et al.*, "Stanovištvo Narodne Republike Srbije od 1834–1953," *Zavod za Statistiku i Evidenciju N. R. Srbije, Serija B.*, sv.1 (June, 1953).

[3] The Napoleonic experiment with the Illyrian Provinces (1809–13) briefly brought Serbs, Croats, and Slovenes into a common political-administrative framework, but the majority of Serbs still remained in Ottoman dominions and in the Kingdom of Hungary.

developed a signal cultural-political movement, *Yugoslavism,* which propounded a theory of common cultural identity, a program of liberation, and the unification of all southern Slavs. By 1914, Yugoslavism had become a magnetic force in all southern Slav lands (in Vienna and Budapest it was viewed as a grave threat to the Dual Monarchy). It is difficult to ascertain how widely Yugoslavism engaged the popular imagination and to what extent it coexisted with or displaced the more particularistic loyalties of Serbism or Croatism.[4] It is equally unclear by what complex process this essentially *international* disposition obtained popular support, for the notion of "Jugoslavenstvo" was of fairly recent origin and not a continuation of traditional feelings. It was by no means comparable to the emotional poignancy of *Italianitá* or *Deutschtum.* (The symbolization of Serbia as the Piedmont of the southern Slavs tended to obfuscate fact and to promote fiction, but the slogan worked!)

In the nineteenth and twentieth centuries, Yugoslavism was closely intertwined with Croatian, Serbian, and Slovene nationalisms. Immediately after the two world wars it overshadowed these particularistic nationalisms, but did not eliminate them. For on both occasions they re-emerged, for different reasons and in different forms, to create problems for the Yugoslav state. Yugoslavism appears to have become a solid, though not unchallenged, force among the south Slavs. But whether it will ever fully displace the particularistic nationalisms will remain an open question for some time.

II

For centuries the southern Slavs manifested little sense of national identity, cultural homogeneity, or political power. Before the later eighteenth century Serbs, Croats, and Slovenes knew little about themselves and even less about each other. There were no significant contacts between them, of the sort that promoted national consciousness. Their worlds and world views were shaped by foreign rulers whose interests led them to keep their subjects isolated, di-

[4] This constitutes an area of investigation to which the techniques of the social sciences might well be applied. Historians of the south Slavs have not thus far undertaken rigorous inquiries into the state of public opinion; nor have they attempted content analyses of the press, literary journals, schoolbooks, etc. It is unlikely that understanding of political emotions, ideas, and loyalties will be advanced until the problem is subjected to new methods of analysis.

vided, and uninformed. The subject territories were meant to be military and economic assets and were utilized as reservoirs of manpower, foodstuffs, raw materials, and other resources. Their social structure, economic development, and political and cultural activities were governed by policies designed first and foremost to advance imperial interests—Habsburg and Ottoman.

As through all of southeast Europe, the protracted struggle between Ottoman and Habsburg dominated regional, and often local, life and development, just as in earlier epochs Byzantium and Rome, Asiatic invaders, and classical Mediterranean empires had held sway. Geostrategy here evolved into something elemental—militarily, culturally, politically—that rendered the Balkans into an insecure foyer between Christian central Europe and the heathen Ottoman east, and later imperial Orthodox Russia as well.[5] In this unstable environment of motley armies and sequent overlords privacy was a function of inaccessibility (e.g., certain redoubts in Montenegro and Albania, some islands, and so on) and illiteracy the common coin. Ethnic and national considerations were on the whole irrelevant—unlike security, taxes, and the church. Where once native states and cultures bore a semblance of ethnic consistency, migration, colonization, and, above all, exigencies of war brought into being new administrative territorial entities, such as the Habsburgs' Military Frontier.[6] Until the late eighteenth century the condition of south Slav life was, in a word, nonnational.[7]

As a result of several trends the picture gradually changed over the course of the eighteenth century. First, in the Habsburg-Ottoman power equation the military scales had distinctly tipped in favor of Austria. Military defeats and territorial losses, furthered now by increasing Russian activities and ambitions, accelerated the process of decay in the Ottoman dominions, much as they para-

[5] A challenging interpretation of this phenomenon may be found in William H. McNeill, *Europe's Steppe Frontier*, 1500–1800 (Chicago: University of Chicago Press, 1964).

[6] See Gunther E. Rothenberg, *The Austrian Military Border in Croatia, 1522–1747* ("Illinois Studies in the Social Sciences," XLVIII [Urbana, Ill.: University of Illinois Press, 1960]), and the same author's *The Military Border in Croatia, 1740–1881* (Chicago: University of Chicago Press, 1966).

[7] This of course does not mean that it was denationalized. The Serbs, in particular, through the oral tradition of epic poetry and through the Serbian church maintained alive a sense of national feeling.

doxically stemmed from it. As Turkish oppression intensified, especially in the spheres of taxation and religious affairs, the once placid Slav subjects increasingly resorted to revolt. Expanding contacts and connections with central Europe and with Russia,[8] operating in both directions, and the economic boom in southern Hungary that vastly strengthened the position and influence of the Austrian-Serbs, goaded the Ottoman Serbs to greater resistance and, before long, developed a sense of community. Conditions of life led to curiosity, then to interest, to contact. Eventually, the sympathy, material help, and intellectual direction of the Austrian Serbs were the catalytic agents that helped convert rebellion into a national movement and, after 1804, the handiwork of insurgency into a *national* state.[9]

Concurrently, in Austrian dominions different forces were at work.[10] With the waning of the Turkish threat the Habsburgs resumed the offensive in the arena of the Holy Roman Empire and in their traditional struggle with France. The loss of Silesia to Prussia dramatized the westward shift of the center of gravity. It also forced the Austrian monarchy to centralize and to modernize. This process set off a chain reaction among all the subjects of the empire and culminated in the national movements and nationalist programs of the nineteenth century. In the hope of making "out of the multi-national empire a unified state," Emperor Joseph II pursued the objectives of "unity, centralization, a German state language, a powerful imperial administration, and the elimination of feudal particularisms."[11] He achieved considerable success, but at the cost (not perceived as such) of stirring up bitter Magyar opposition and setting off a debilitating century-long struggle. The

[8] Contacts with Russia became particularly significant for Montenegro and the Vojvodina. See M. Kostić, *Carski duhovnici, propagatori Unije medju Srbima* (Sremski Karlovci, 1922); and J. Jovanović, *Južna Srbija od XVIII veka do oslobodjenja* (Belgrade, 1941).

[9] See *Gradja iz Zemunskih Arhiva za Istoriju Prvog Srbskog ustanka, I: 1804–1808* (Belgrade: Istorijski Arhiv, 1955); M. Djordević, *Politička Istorija Srbije XIX-XX Vijeka, 1806–1813* (Sarajevo, 1961).

[10] This is not the place to analyze the nature of the Habsburg Empire in the eighteenth and nineteenth centuries. The reader, however, might usefully refer to Chap. I in this volume by Professor Sugar, to Oscar Jászi, *The Dissolution of the Habsburg Monarchy* (Chicago: University of Chicago Press, Phoenix Edition, 1961), particularly pp. 40–85; and Robert A. Kann, *The Habsburg Empire, A Study in Integration and Disintegration* (New York: Praeger, 1957), pp. 25–119.

[11] Jászi, *The Dissolution of the Habsburg Monarchy*, p. 67.

Croats and other Slavic nationalities opposed Josephinist reforms as well, but their opposition was not so crucial in the Habsburg scheme—at least for some time. In the long run, this "subsidiary" opposition became equally significant, for it triggered two cultural movements that turned political and nonarrestable: the Croatian and the Yugoslav.

The crucial period in the development of Serbian and Croatian national awareness and the beginnings of serious political action came between 1790 and 1815. In the same era the Slovenes, too, began to stir and to exhibit a nascent sense of entity. However, the momentum of the Slovene national movement lagged behind that of the Serbs and the Croats by at least a generation. At this time, due to the Napoleonic wars and the Illyrian interlude, the first Yugoslav experiment, though short-lived, established a precedent that would in the 1830s and 1840s provide fuel for the ideologists of Yugoslavism.

Still, the development of national awareness among the southern Slavs at the beginning of the nineteenth century must not be exaggerated. As Sir Lewis Namier once cogently observed, if "anyone had attempted in 1815 to draw a nationality map of Europe he would have treated . . . the Czech and Slovene provinces of Austria as German . . . practically all Hungary as Magyar; the Austrian Littoral as Italian . . . and the Christian populations of Turkey possibly as Greek."[12] To an illiterate and on the whole leaderless population the idea of nationality was as alien as it was irrelevant. In terms of the proposition, advanced by Hans Kohn, that "for the formation of nationalities, the most essential element is a living and active corporate will. Nationality is formed by the decision to form a nationality . . ."[13]—no such state of mind obtained.

The conventional view that the French Revolution, the communications revolution caused by Napoleon's campaigns, and German philosophic teachings combined into a force that occasioned national and nationalist reverberations throughout the continent does not hold in the case of the southern Slavs. In Serbia (the Paşalik of Beograd) there were in 1810 only two elementary schools. In both the language of instruction was Greek. Throughout the Turkish

[12] Sir Lewis Namier, *Vanished Supremacies* (London: H. Hamilton, 1958), p. 168.
[13] Hans Kohn, *The Idea of Nationalism* (2d ed.; New York: Macmillan, 1961), p. 15.

occupation—and that involves half a millennium!—there was not on Yugoslav territory one secondary or advanced school, no university, not even a printing plant.[14] In Montenegro the first elementary school was founded by Vladika Njegoš in 1834.[15] In Croatia-Slavonia the picture was somewhat different as by 1767 there were twenty-four primary schools, seventy-six in 1790, and fifty-five in 1815.[16] For Slovenia figures for the period before 1849 are uncertain, but

[14] Traian Stoianovich, "The Pattern of Serbian Intellectual Evolution 1830–1880," *Comparative Studies in Society and History*, I, No. 3 (March, 1959), 248; Mijo Mirković, *Ekonomska Historija Jugoslavije* (Zagreb, 1958), p. 150. In 1807 of all the Serbian senators only one could read (Tihomir Djordjević, *Iz Srbije Kneza Miloša* [Belgrade, 1922], pp. 74–75). By 1827 the literate population was "conceivably less than half of one percent," (Stoianovich, "The Pattern of Serbian Intellectual Evolution, 1830–1880," p. 250). By 1847 there were 213 elementary schools, by 1868, there were 318, by 1910, 1304 (Slobodan Jovanović, *Ustavobranitelji i Njihova Vlada (1838–1858)*, [Belgrade, 1933], p. 80; V. Karić, *Srbija, Opis Zemlje Naroda i Države* [Belgrade, 1887], p. 247; D. Mishev, *Public Instruction in Switzerland and in the Balkan States* [Lausanne, 1919], p. 65). In 1910 there were also twelve gymnasia, two pedagogical institutes, five trade and professional schools, and one university (*Statistički Godišnjak Kraljevine Srbije*, 1910).

[15] By 1868 the number rose to 31, by 1910 to 143. In the same year there were two secondary schools, one theological seminary, but no university or academy. For a sketch of the development of schools and education in Montenegro see Blažo Savićević, "Crna Gora: Školstvo," *Enciklopedija Jugoslavije*, II (1956), 445–48.

[16] Bogo Grafenauer *et al.* (eds.), *Historija Naroda Jugoslavije* (Zagreb, 1959), II, 1092; Antun Cuvaj (ed.) *Gradja za Povijest Školstva Kraljevine Hrvatske i Slavonije* (Zagreb, 1911), II, 20, 171. The reduction in the number of schools between 1790 and 1890 is accounted for by the fact that many of the schools, opened during the reign of Joseph II, were closed after several years for lack of teachers and other circumstances. As regards secondary schools, there were eight gymnasia in 1767 and one pedagogical institute; six in 1815; nine in 1868 and twenty-two in 1910. The eight gymnasia were founded as follows: Lepoglava (1543), Zagreb (1607), Rijeka (1630), Varaždin (1636), Križevci (1695), Požega (1698), Osijek (1760), Sremski Karlovci (1720). The first seven were run by the Jesuits or Paulis orders. The gymnasium in S. Karlovci was an Orthodox Latin school. In 1786, with the dissolution of the Paulist order, the Lepoglava and Križevci schools were closed. The Zagreb Academy consisted of a Theological Faculty established in 1632 and Philosophy in 1662; and the Lepoglava Academy of Faculties of Philosophy and Theology was established in 1656 and 1687. The Zagreb Academy was run by the Jesuits and Lepoglava by the Paulist order. A Royal Academy was a partial university, offering a two-year course beyond the secondary school. In 1784, the major theological seminaries were closed. The theological faculty of the Zagreb Academy was made a separate institution. The faculties of Law and Philosophy remained within the Zagreb Academy. The Lepoglava Academy was closed in 1786. The University of Zagreb was founded in 1874 with faculties of Theology, Philosophy, and Law. Pharmacy was added in 1882.

it would appear that here the primary school system was most highly developed. By 1849 there were over one thousand elementary schools.[17] Nevertheless, in Slovenia, too, the population was mainly illiterate, uneducated, unrepresented, uninterested, and unresponsive either to "the call of blood" or to "the power of an idea," that is the raw material of which, in Kohn's view, nationalities are formed.[18]

Quite apart from the measures of literacy and education, by 1815 the *people* had not attained a level of political or cultural maturity comparable to western Europe. Moreover, south Slav lands were developing unevenly and there was no one distinct southern Slav environment. Yet in this diversity a common denominator, tenuous at first but increasingly significant, did emerge. In the practical condition of life, more or less an equivalent force enkindled Serb, Croat, and Slovene nationalisms, and Yugoslav as well, namely foreign misrule: Ottoman, Austrian, Magyar, and French in "Illyria." Lord Acton's observation about the nature of alien rule could be applied to all south Slav cases, but especially to Serbia where, in his words, the Turks "were attacked, not as usurpers, but as oppressors—because they misgoverned, not because they were of a different race."[19] The modern Serbian state emerged out of agrarian and social revolts, before and after 1804. In the process of emerging, the Serbian state assumed a discernably *national* configuration. From 1815 on, by its very existence and struggle for survival it generated national and nationalistic impulses within Serbia as among the Serbs of the Habsburg monarchy.

At the beginning of the nineteenth century, the Serbian problem was considerably more complex than that of the Croat or the Slovene. It was at one and the same time "national" and "interna-

[17] Austria; K. u. K., Statistisches Central-Commission, *Detail Conscription der Volksschulen in den im Reichsrathe vertretenen Königreiche und Länder nach dem Stande vom Ende des Schuljahres 1865* (Vienna, 1870); Joseph Alexander Freiherr von Helfert, *Die Gründung der Österreichischen Volksschule durch Maria Theresia* (Prague, 1860); Wilhelm Leitgeb, "Die Hoch-und Mittelschulen der im Reichsrathe vertretenen Königreiche und Länder von 1851 bis 1870," *Mittheilungen aus dem Gebiete der Statistik*, III, 18, 27–107.

[18] Kohn, *The Idea of Nationalism*, p. 16.

[19] Lord Acton, *Essays on Freedom and Power* (Glencoe, Ill.: The Free Press, 1948), p. 167.

tional." Historical circumstances, mainly Turkish pressures and campaigns that began in the fourteenth century, had caused several waves of Serbian migration into the Danubian plains, one as late as the mid-eighteenth century. Thus while the bulk of the Serbian population remained subject to the Ottoman Empire, substantial numbers of Serbs colonized southern Hungary, and others settled in Slavonia, Dalmatia, and various parts of central Croatia.[20] In the military frontier the Serbs came to number about one third of the population and played a vital military role in the Habsburg defense system.[21] In return they received special privileges from Austrian emperors, legal ownership of land, and important economic advantages.[22] They served the Austrian court against feudal magnates and rebelling peasants alike, all in efforts to protect their special privileges. They lent themselves to imperial maneuvers, particularly under Leopold II (1790–92), to weaken Magyar and Croat resistance to Austrian centralization, in return for a semblance of autonomy. But under the Emperor Francis II (1792–1835) the Serbs of the monarchy gradually lost both their military importance and administrative privileges. Moreover, under the stimulus of Catholic zeal and a deep suspicion of Russian influence, which had measurably grown through the eighteenth century, Francis II and Metternich attempted to push the Serbs into the Uniate church. To these efforts, and to the increasingly clamorous manifestations of Magyar nationalism, the Serbs of the monarchy responded at first with protest. Soon, however, they initiated resistance and active involvement in the affairs of the emerging Serbian state to the south. In the first quarter of the nineteenth century the Vojvodina, already an established transmission belt of ideas from central and western Europe

---

[20] On Serbian migrations and colonization see Grafenauer et al., Historija Naroda Jugoslavije, II, 840–53; A. Ivić, Migracije Srba u Hrvatsku (Subotica, 1923); A. Ivić, Migracije Srba u Slavoniju (Subotica, 1923); D. Popović, Srbi u Banatu do kraja XVIII veka (Belgrade, 1952). Zwitter, Šidak, and Bogdanov (in Fran Zwitter et al., Les problèmes Nationaux dans la Monarchie des Habsbourg [Belgrade, 1960], pp. 14–18) calculate that in the mid-nineteenth century the Serbs represented a substantial minority in all southern parts of Hungary. While only 3.7 per cent of Hungary proper, they composed 24 per cent of Slavonia and Croatia and about a third of the Military Frontier.

[21] This figure is for the year 1850–51.

[22] Leonard W. Doob, Patriotism and Nationalism: Their Psychological Foundations (New Haven, Conn.: Yale University Press, 1964), p. 6.

into the Paşalik of Beograd, became an active reservoir of administrative, political, and intellectual leadership for "Serbia."

In sum, by the very distribution of the Serbs their nationalism—once it was so perceived—superimposed a "national" conception onto an international setting. And, just as communality of language stoked the cultural and intellectual cauldrons, so irredentism inexorably fueled the fires of national and international politics. The elemental fact that all through the nineteenth century the frontiers of the Serbian state did not coincide with those of the Serbian nation lent a galvanic quality to the very notion of Serbian nationality while, politically and ideologically, every Serbian national program perforce looked to changes in the international status quo. Serbian nationalism in the nineteenth century was not capable of localization but intruded naturally into the affairs of the Habsburg and Ottoman empires. Seen in this light, and over the span of the whole century, the vagaries of Serbian foreign policies (especially after the Načertanije of 1844) reflected tactical adjustments to shifts in the international environment, while its strategic direction remained largely on a steady course. At the same time, from the vantage points of Vienna, Budapest, and Istanbul, the affairs of Serbia could not be solely viewed as the affairs of a neighboring state for they became in essence also domestic Habsburg and Ottoman affairs.

The struggle for Serbian privileges and autonomy developed in two separate arenas: the Paşalik of Beograd and the Kingdom of Hungary. In both instances it was essentially reactive: in the one reactive to Magyar nationalism and eventually Austrian centralization; in the other to Turkish misrule and oppression. These struggles were rooted in practical exigencies, not in ideology or philosophy. Before long, however, by the turn of the 1830s at the latest, a process of *national* rationalization enveloped Serbian political action. By the mid-1840s the fusion of politics with notions of Serbian patriotism and nationality appeared complete, and from then on indissoluble.

The emergence and gradual intensification of Serbian "nationalism"—in the sense of a "set of more or less uniform demands. (1) which people in a society share, (2) which arise from their patriotism, (3) for which justifications exist and can be readily expressed, (4) which incline them to make personal sacrifices in behalf of their government's aims . . ."[23] was most evident in the conduct of foreign policy from Ilija Garašanin (1840s) to Prince Michael (1860s). In the era of Nikola Pašić (1903–18) it became supreme.[24] The quest for international recognition of Serbian autonomy (1815–32), sovereignty (1832–56), Balkan leadership (1860–68), the assertion of cultural proprietary interests in Macedonia (1870–76), the efforts at territorial expansion (1877–1918) were all carried on in the name of a Serbian nationality (*Srpstvo*). Its dynamic quality derived from a combination of irredentism, the need for strategic security and a romantic proclivity (by no means unique to the Serbs) to recapture the lost grandeur of Serbia's ancient tsardom.[25]

Foreign policy was closely connected with internal developments, though in the first half of the nineteenth century the connection was less dramatic. During this period the main problems at home pertained to the establishment of state organs and a national economy and the struggle to delimit the arbitrary rule of the prince. Nationalism as such cannot be said to have intruded into the political life of the various coteries, though the nascent educational system and Serbian cultural life at large were exhibiting a firm and conscious sense of Serbian entity and "destiny." With the development of

[23] It would seem that the periods of retrenchment in foreign policy (under Milan and Alexander Obrenović in particular) in which nationalism appeared to be relatively subdued, represent not its abandonment but a shifting emphasis to dynastic politics.

[24] See L. S. Stavrianos, *Balkan Federation: A History of the Movement Toward Balkan Unity in Modern Times* (Northampton, Mass.: Smith College, 1944); W. S. Vucinich, *Serbia Between East and West, 1903–1908* (Palo Alto, Calif.: Stanford University Press, 1955); H. W. V. Temperley, *A History of Serbia* (London: G. Bell & Sons, Ltd., 1917); B. H. Sumner, *Russia and the Balkans, 1870–1880* (Oxford: Oxford University Press, 1937); D. Djordjević, *Révolutions Nationales des Peuples Balkaniques, 1804–1917* (Belgrade, 1965); and the works on nineteenth-century Serbia, too numerous to list here, by Slobodan Jovanović.

[25] For the development of "national" programs in political parties see Andrija Radenić, *Svetoandrejska Skupština* (Belgrade, 1964), and "Iz Stranačkih Programa Posle Majskog Prevrata 1903 godine," *Istorijski Glasnik*, 1–2 (Belgrade, 1960), pp. 95–110; Čedomil Mitrinović and Miloš N. Brašić, *Jugoslavenske Narodne Skupštine i Sabori* (Belgrade, 1937); V. Čubrilović, *Istorija Političke Misli u Srbiji XIX Veka* (Belgrade, 1958); Vaso Bogdanov, *Historija Političkih Stranaka u Hrvatskoj* (Zagreb, 1958); Mirjana Gross, "Socijalna Demokracija Prema Nacionalnom Pitanju u Hrvatskoj, 1890–1902," *Historijski Zbornik*, IX (Zagreb, 1956), 1–29; M. Gross, "Osnovni Problemi Pravaške Politike, 1878–87," *Historijski Zbornik*, XV (1962), 61–120; M. Gross, "Geneza Frankove Stranke," *Historijski Zbornik*, XVII (1964), 1–83.

modern popular political parties (after 1878) and such newspapers
as *Srpska Nezavisnost* (1887) and *Srpska Zastava* (1891), internal
political life exuded nationalist overtones. The slogans of constitutionalism, parliamentarianism, and individual liberties became consciously articulated in terms of Serbian national objectives and
rights. From 1882 on Serbian political parties—ranging the full spectrum from socialist to conservative—gradually ceased to distinguish
between issues of political and economic democratization and modernization on the one hand and the national "mission" of all-Serbian
unity, involving liberation from foreign rule, on the other. In short,
Serbian affairs at home and abroad were perceived essentially as a
whole. In terms of the "national mission" it might even be argued
that the dynastic struggle between the houses of Obrenović and
Karadjordjević symbolized alternative means to the same end
abroad.[26]

While nineteenth-century Serbian "nationalism" received impetus
from foreign misrule and gained momentum from the internal and
external situations of the young Serbian state and the geographic
distribution of the Serbs, the development of Serbian "national
consciousness" began before the uprising of 1804. The precondition
of community consciousness—a common language—existed, although it was on the whole a passive factor. A more direct contribution to national consciousness came from the Serbian church that—
despite the high incidence of illiteracy among the clergy—over the
ages succeeded in keeping alive a sense of Serbian entity. This was
especially true while the Ottoman millet system functioned uncor-
rupted. Orthodoxy, surrounded by Catholic and Muslim peripheries,
and rooted in a population whose life under the Turks was increasingly forlorn, became a national elixir. As the church produced vigorous leadership in the eighteenth century it assumed a dominant
role in Serbian religious and secular affairs. In the Vojvodina it set

[26] The Serbo-Bulgarian War of 1885 represents an attempt—that failed—to solve
the Serbian national problem in the east within an Austro-Hungarian diplomatic
framework. The very alliance with Austria-Hungary, beginning with 1881, signified
Milan Obrenović's calculation that the patronage of Austria would simultaneously
strengthen his unpopular rule at home and allow Serbian expansion—eastward only—
abroad. When in 1878 Russia opted to sponsor the new Bulgarian state and to
maintain it as Russia's principal base in the Balkans, thereby "abandoning" Serbia,
turning to Austria appeared to King Milan as the only logical alternative course.

up printing presses, reading rooms and schools, and maintained regular communication with Serbian communities to the south.[27]

In the formation of Serbian consciousness one important strand emanated from Russia. Russian monasteries had maintained contact with the Orthodox world of the Balkans all through the Turkish era. In the eighteenth century, however, Montenegro and even more so the Vojvodina became points of special attention. As Russian political interest in southeast Europe grew, the successors of Peter the Great expanded the scope of ecclesiastic channels and began to pursue secular interests as well. A growing stream of Russian funds, books, scholarships, and schoolteachers reached the Serbs, and the Vojvodina became something of a center of Russian influence. The spread of Russophilism among the Serbs irked and troubled the Austrian government to the point of taking countermeasures through the Uniate movement. The Russian connection, however, served to bolster the position of the Serbian church, provided the educated Serbs with an awareness of a potential—no matter how remote—patron, and altogether helped assert the Serbian identity.[28]

The effectiveness of language, church, and religion as cornerstones of national consciousness would doubtless have remained limited but for another major factor: the transformation of the Serbian social and economic base in Habsburg lands. By the end of the eighteenth century, while the economy of the paşalik remained pastoral, the Serbs of Hungary experienced a boom. The new Serbian merchant class—on the whole prosperous, confident, and conversant with both central Europe and the Balkans—had developed a market and money economy and dominated interregional commerce.[29] From its ranks came the leadership in the struggle for Serbian privileges within the monarchy and a helping hand in the formation of the Serbian state after 1804. And through its ranks the political philosophy of Europe was filtered to the south. It gave substance to political life and cultural activity and considerable intellectual vigor to Serbian nationalism.

---

[27] See D. Popović, *Srbi u Banatu do Kraja XVIII Veka* (Belgrade, 1952).

[28] See M. Kostić, *Carski Duhovnici, Propagatori Unije Medju Srbima* (Sremski Karlovci, 1922).

[29] See Mijo Mirković, *Ekonomska Historija Jugoslavje* (Zagreb, 1958), pp. 161–210, and Jozo Tomasevich, *Peasants, Politics and Economic Change in Yugoslavia* (Palo Alto, Calif.: Stanford University Press, 1955), pp. 32–38.

III

Among the Croats as among the Serbs nationalism developed in response to external forces and pressures. However, there the parallel ends.

Reacting to the centralizing policies of Joseph II, the Croat nobility, supported by the Catholic church, struggled to defend its privileges and to resist Germanization and secularization. Since the same battle was being waged with greater effect by the more powerful Magyar nobility, the Croats in the 1780s lent the Magyars their support. In so doing they fell into a singular trap.

Bound to the Hungarian crown by vague dynastic ties since 1102 and to the Habsburg monarchy since 1526, Croatia had gradually lost its national identity. In pursuit of their own privileges, the church and the nobility continued to propound the constitutional fiction of a Croatian state. When in 1779 Maria Theresa transferred to Magyars the principal administrative responsibility for Croatia, the *de facto* inequality between Pozsony and Zagreb was officially sanctioned. Still, in the 1780s Croat nobles saw in their Magyar counterparts a lesser evil than the Emperor. When Joseph died in 1790 the Magyar nobility launched a counteroffensive against Austria and in the following year—with the specter of the French Revolution haunting central (and Roman) Europe—extracted a significant concession from the frightened Croats—acceptance of the Magyar language.

The Magyar national movement had been striving to establish the primacy of Hungarian over Latin, the official language of both Hungary and Croatia, in response to Austrian absolutism and centralism which had sought to establish the primacy of German. In 1791 the *Sabor* in Zagreb admitted Hungarian as the optional language of Croatia, and thereby set in motion a reaction to establish the primacy of Croatian over Hungarian. The war of the languages never really came to an end; in 1827 the Diet forced Magyar through as the compulsory school language in Croatia. By the time the Hungarian linguistic "threat" subsided (after 1849) a new foe emerged in the guise of Serbian. (The eruption of the Croatian-Serbian language issue in the 1960s testifies to its intensity and tenacity, and to the fact that "language" serves as the living symbol of a nation's franchise.) Hungarian nationalism gradually turned into political-cultural imperialism, seeking complete dominance over the nationalities inhabiting the crownlands of St. Stephen. For the Croats, Budapest soon became more a formidable and dangerous foe than Vienna. Yet in significant ways Croatian nationalism of the nineteenth century was a by-product of Magyar initiatives.

In 1832 Count Janko Drašković published what might be called the founding document of the Croat national movement.[30] Written in the *štokavski* dialect, soon to be put forward both as the Croatian and Yugoslav literary language, Drašković elaborated a program that called for: 1) the assertion of Croatian over Latin as the language of Croatian public life; 2) the administrative-political union of Croatia, Slavonia, and Dalmatia (the Triune Croatian Kingdom); 3) Croatian control over the Military Frontier and the district of Fiume (Rijeka); 4) the eventual absorption of Slovenia and Bosnia; 5) the formation of a greater Illyria, actually a Greater Croatian kingdom, that 6) must be modernized economically and become educationally developed in order to stand on its own within the Habsburg framework.

In this scheme the Magyars played a three-fold role. They were simultaneously the foe who threatened to engulf the Croats, the model to be emulated (at least in their strategies regarding Austria and in internal Magyar affairs), and a needed partner in view of the Croatian dependence on Hungarian talents and material resources. Drašković's program epitomized the Croatian political and psychological dilemma all through the nineteenth century, namely to reconcile differences with and hostility toward the Magyars with the practical need to collaborate with them. Since "independence" for Croatia, in the sense of breaking the Habsburg or Crown of St. Stephen ties, was neither contemplated nor practicable, especially in the eras of Metternich and Bach, Croat nationalist thought pursued the elusive line between self-assertion and accommodation. The result, in broad terms, was political frustration that, in turn, rendered inevitable the splintering after 1860, of Croatian nationalist thought into channels of Greater Croatian extremism, opportunist collaboration with Budapest and Vienna, and—into a seeming contradiction of Croatianism—Yugoslavism.

In this trichotomy the Serbian factor inevitably came to loom as

[30] See K. Georgijević, "Grof Janko Drajković, 1770–1856," *Pitanja Književnosti i Jezika,* IV (1958), 27–54.

large as the Magyar; after 1878 even larger. In the first place, the formation of an adjacent independent Serbian state captivated the imagination of a significant segment of Croat intellectuals. As the Serbian state and its ambitions matured and as its position came to preoccupy all Europe, the Croats could hardly feel indifference. The Serbian success—diplomatic and military reverses notwithstanding—was at once admired, envied, or resented, regarded as a possible model, a potential instrumentality (through alliance or Yugoslavism) for gaining Croat goals, or a threat to Croatian cultural and religious claims and ambitions of political leadership in the south Slav world. In many instances Croat attitudes toward Serbia combined elements of all, especially since Croat perceptions were also affected—positively or negatively—by the current state of Serbian relations with Budapest and Vienna. Numerous paradoxes were at work, though on the whole the Serbian factor produced one distinct and lasting effect: it compounded Croatian frustrations, to this very day.

The Yugoslav movement—based on the notion of a Serb-Croat-Slovene ethnic community and the desire for its unification—developed in Croatia in the 1830s and 1840s. Its intellectual antecedents, however, reach back to the sixteenth century and to the fertile cultural-political environment of Dubrovnik (Ragusa), the only independent southern Slav republic at the time.[31] In the seventeenth century, the Croatian monk Juraj Križanić became something of an apostle of Yugoslavism by searching for a reconciliation between Slavic Orthodoxy and Catholicism. But his was as yet a voice in the wilderness. At the beginning of the eighteenth century another Croat, Pavao Ritter Vitezović, made another, albeit oblique, contribution to the Yugoslav idea. More a precursor of Pan-Croatianism than of Yugoslavism, Vitezović propounded the view that all south Slavs were originally Croats. Thereby he helped lay the foundations for the thesis of a single south Slav ethnic community with its own historical unity and identity.

Actually, in the eighteenth century such ideas were seldom expressed. There was little contact between Serbs, Croats, and Slovenes. To the Orthodox world of Ottoman Serbia and Montenegro,

[31] The literature on the history of the Yugoslav idea and movement is by now enormous. The interested reader may usefully consult the works of Ferdo Šišić, Jaroslav Šidak, Viktor Novak, Vaso Bogdanov, and Jorjo Tadić.

Croatia seemed more distant than Russia. Here and there signals of common concern appeared, as in the Croatian poem of 1745 "Lamentacije zgubljenoga Beograda" (Lamentations of Lost Beograd). But toward the end of the century both the rate and the scope of contact and interest increased. Soldiers, churchmen, and especially Serbian tradesmen from the Vojvodina became carriers of information and helped bridge the abyss of ignorance that separated the adjacent worlds of the southern Slavs.

At the beginning of the eighteenth century neither the Serbs nor the Croats had a written national history of their own, set down in the national language. Vitezović wrote in Latin and was, in any case, more a polemicist than a historian. The Serbs of the Ottoman empire had a rich tradition of epic folk poetry that, however, did not directly stimulate an intellectual or political renaissance. The folk poets were many, but they were mostly illiterate and unschooled. They dealt in legend, not in questions of economic progress, political programs, or in the science of history.

Those tasks were left to others, mainly to the Serbs living north of the Danube and later on to Serbs from the Paşalik who had studied, traveled, or lived abroad. One of the first attempts at a national history of the Serbs came from the quill of Djordje Branković, a native of Jenopolj in the Banat. Written shortly before his death in 1711, it was little more than a clumsy chronicle, much of it devoted to the Branković family history. Also, unlike Vitezović, Branković was not concerned with the other southern Slavs.

By midcentury the picture began to change. A Croatian Franciscan monk, Andrija Kačić-Miošić, set a new course by publishing (in 1756) a general account of all the southern Slavs—*Razgovor ugodni naroda slovinskoga*—in whose ranks he even included the Albanians. By dealing with all the Yugoslavs, not merely the Croats, he set an important precedent. Shortly after, though not as a result of Miošić's work, Anton Linhart, a Slovene layman, wrote the first national history of the Slovenes, with some reference to all the southern Slavs of Austria. Written in German and published in Ljubljana in 1788, Linhart's work marked the prologue to the national awakening of the westernmost Yugoslavs whose life had so long been overwhelmed by German and Italian influences.

By the end of the eighteenth century, the southern Slavs still had not produced national histories as such, though they had embarked on that road. In 1790, for example, the Royal Academy of Sciences in Zagreb (founded in 1766) petitioned Emperor Leopold II to convert the Academy into a university by adding a medical branch to the existing theological, juridical, and philosophical faculties. According to the petition, the Croatian academicians sought to establish a "national" university that would attract the youth of Bosnia and Serbia that, they hoped, would soon be liberated from the Turks.

A Serbian example, on the other hand, can be seen in the works of the archimandrite Jovan Rajić, a native of Karlowitz (Sremski Karlovci), who counts as Serbia's first modern historian. As an Orthodox monk, Rajić was at first concerned only with theology. But extensive travels, including two trips to Russia, turned his attention to more mundane matters. Rajić's masterwork, published in 1794, was "History of the Several Slavic Peoples, Particularly the Bulgarians, Croats and Serbs." That Rajić was mainly interested in the Serbs is reflected in his work. But he also believed in the kinship of all southern Slavs—Orthodox as well as Catholic—and set out to demonstrate it in what has been called "the first patriotic history of the South Slavs, written in the national language."[32] His work circulated widely, both among Serbs and Croats, and appears to have been read by several leaders of the Serbian uprising of 1804.

Rajić's handiwork was continued and enlarged by Dositej Obradović, also a native of the Vojvodina. At the age of seventeen (in 1760) Obradović left home to become an Orthodox monk, and spent years of study and travel abroad. He lived in Germany and traveled extensively in England, France, Russia, and throughout the Balkans. The influence of western Europe led him to question the confining horizons of Orthodoxy and the Byzantine world and to write on secular subjects. It inspired him to develop a modern Serbian literary language and the foundations, in Serbia after 1804, of a modern educational system. The example of what he called the "enlightened nations of Europe" filled him with ambitions for Serbia and drove him, in his own words, "to communicate my thoughts to my fellow men and to tell them whatever good and sensible things I have heard and learned from others."[33]

[32] See Ferdo Šišić, *Jugoslovenska Misao* (Belgrade, 1937), p. 40.
[33] G. R. Noyes (tr. and ed.), *The Life and Adventures of Dimitrije Obradović* (Berkeley: University of California Press, 1953), p. 107.

Obradović died a year before Napoleon's march on Russia, leaving behind a legacy that nourished generations of Serbian intellectuals, statesmen, and patriots. He did not contribute directly to Yugoslavism. But without his impact on the Serbian consciousness, Yugoslavism would not likely have found an early response in Serbia. By promoting secularism, education, and a literary language, Obradović broke the ground for the edifice that Vuk Karadžić was soon to complete. And Karadžić, the literary titan of nineteenth-century Serbia, revolutionized the Serbian and, indirectly, the Yugoslav cultural environment. His editions of Serbian folk poetry linked the southern Slavs with the mainstream of European romanticism. His phonetic reform of old Cyrillic, his Serbian grammar, and dictionary became the cornerstones of Serbian cultural nationalism but at the same time, ironically, his work as a whole eventually made possible a *Yugoslav* cultural interaction.

Just as the Serbian revival was rooted in political and social realities, so was the Croatian. So indeed, on the Croatian side, was the Yugoslav movement—which in the 1830s and 1840s took the name of Illyrianism. The Illyrian-Yugoslav conception, unlike the pure Serbian or Croatian ones, was greatly influenced by central European romantic philosophy. The works of J. Dobrowský, J. Kollár, F. Palacký and P. J. Šafařík—representing variations on the theme of Slavonic unity—provided a number of young Croat intellectuals with a rationale for the idea of southern Slav unity, based on a common literary language. Ljudevit Gaj, who in 1835 started the newspaper *Danicza Horvatska, Slavonzka i Dalmatinzka* around which rallied the best young Croat literati of the day, used the concept of Illyrianism as a symbol of political and cultural unity of the southern Slavs.

"Illyrianism" proved to be an illusion, for it rested on two basic fallacies. The first involved the "incorrect assumption that the old Illyrians were of Slav descent and the autochthons of the Southern Slavs,"[34] and that Napoleon's brief experiment of uniting Slovene and Croat territories into an "Illyrian" administrative unit (1809–13) represented a viable political precedent. The second involved an unrealistic disregard of Serbian state independence, historical separateness, and Orthodox uniqueness (vis-à-vis the Catholic Croats and

[34] Jaroslav Šidak, "The Jugoslav Concept of Nationalism," *Papers of the Fifth American-Jugoslav Seminar* (Novi Sad, 1965), p. 5.

Slovenes). As Jaroslav Šidak, the foremost historian of the subject, put it, the

Yugoslav national idea in its Illyrian form . . . came into being from resistance to the danger of Magyarization—which threatened neither the Slovene people as a whole nor the Principality of Serbia—in a philologically not fully balanced environment marked by strong regional particularism which was based on century-old [sic] political dissidence in the Croat lands.[35]

Equally important, Illyrianism was *au fond* neither consonant with Austro-Slavism nor palatable to Budapest and Vienna. Hence, it was foredoomed to failure in the era of Metternich.

The Illyrian movement, officially suppressed by the monarchy in 1843, nevertheless marked an epochal development and left an enduring imprint on Yugoslav affairs. Gaj's handiwork ennobled the idea of Croatian self-abnegation by renouncing the Croatian *kajkavian* dialect in favor of the *štokavian*, which was spoken by the Serbs as well, and which alone could serve as a common and genuine Serbo-Croatian or Croato-Serb language. Moreover, the Illyrians succeeded in firmly placing the issue of unity on the southern Slav agenda, in evoking Serbian and Slovene echoes—though they also provoked a hardening of Croat and Serb nationalist thought[36]—

---

[35] *Ibid.,* p. 7.

[36] Thus the emergence in 1841 of political parties in Hungary prompted the formation of the Croato-Hungarian party as the first modern Croatian party. Its adherents, the so-called *Madjaroni,* called for the suppression of Illyrianism, the abandonment of Štokavian and a return to the purely Croatian Kajkavian dialect. The *Madjaroni* received considerable support and, though their fortunes waned, they remained a political factor until 1918. Among the Serbs, meantime, there developed a reaction around 1839–41 against Illyrianism. Under the influence of Karadžić numerous Serbs came to regard Štokavian as purely Serbian. This view soon led to the extreme view that anyone who spoke Štokavian, *no matter of what religion,* was a Serb. There developed an inevitable polemic in regard to Bosnia and Hercegovina where Štokavian prevailed and where Catholic, Orthodox, and Muslim were intermingled (see Leo von Südland [Ivo Pilar], *Die Südslawische Frage* [Vienna, 1918]). By 1841 the Vojvodina Serbs had on the whole become disassociated from Illyrianism, having clearly opted for Serbianism. As for the Principality of Serbia, there developed—especially after the 1844 *Načertanije* of Garašanin—the almost mystical idea that modern Serbia should seek to reconstitute the ancient Serbian empire of Tsar Dušan as an alternative to Illyrianism or Yugoslavism. As the latter drew Serbia to the west so the former drew Serbia to the south and east. In short, Illyrianism as a Yugoslav idea, in the words of Šidak, "retained its

and, not least, in alerting the cultural circles and the political rulers of central Europe to the potentiality of a larger southern Slav design.

IV

Croatian and Serbian policies received their first practical test in the upheavals of 1848–49.[37] Responding to multiple stimuli—the anti-Slavism of Magyar nationalism, Palacký's Austro-Slav movement, the agitation for a federative rearrangement of the Empire, King Ferdinand's grudging pledge (March, 1848) of a constitutional parliamentary system—the Croatian political scene exploded into action. First, the former Illyrians became a dominant influence. Second, the *Sabor* in Zagreb on March 25 elected Colonel Josip Baron Jelačić, the man appointed by King Ferdinand two days earlier as Ban of Croatia, to leadership. Next, it called for the union of all the Triune Kingdom lands, the abolition of serfdom and feudal relationships, the establishment of a regular Croatian parliament and government and emancipation from Hungarian control. Budapest retaliated by "deposing" the Ban. This gesture, however, had no practical effect. Croatia's purpose was self-assertive and anti-Magyar—but it was not anti-Habsburg.

In May, 1848, the Serbs of Hungary convened a national assembly in Karlowitz and there proclaimed their separation from the Magyars and their union with Croatia. In June, Serbia's Prince Miloš Obrenović suddenly appeared in Zagreb. Thus fleetingly, south Slav unity and national-revolutionary solidarity appeared to have been forged. They proved a Fata Morgana, no less so than the Austro-Slav

---

importance only within the Croat environment in which it had come into being" ("The Jugoslav Concept of Nationalism," p. 9). As for Slovenia, where for a time literary circles showed an inclination toward Illyrianism and considered the adoption of Štokavian as an advanced and common south Slav literary language, a negative reaction set in as well. Under the leadership of the Slovene literary giants of the age, F. Prešeren and B. Kopitar, Slovenian—a distinctly separate south Slav language, became the *national* Slovene intellectual coin.

[37] See Slobodan Jovanović, *Ustavobranitelji i Njihova Vlada* (Belgrade, 1933); A. Lebl, *Revolucionarni Pokret u Vojvodini, 1848–1849* (Novi Sad, 1960); S. L. Gavrilović, *Srem u Revoluciji 1848–49* (Belgrade, 1963); D. Pavlović, *Srbija i Srpski Pokret u Južnoj Ugarskoj, 1848–1849* (Belgrade, 1904); Herman Wendel, *Aus dem Südslawischen Risorgimento* (Gotha, 1921), pp. 63–71.

dream of unity that permeated the Slavonic Congress in Prague (June) in which Croat and Serb delegates took part.

In the multilateral maneuvers between the Habsburg government, Kossuth, the provincial centers of the monarchy, and the principal powers of Europe, local and universal issues became blurred. Social revolution and the "national" cause blended into one. The Croats, under Jelačić, were aroused by Magyar hegomonic proclamations and responded to calls of help from the Vojvodina Serbs. At the same time they also responded to entreaties and pressures from Vienna, taking to the field against the Magyars in defense of the Habsburg cause. Serbs from the Vojvodina and Croats expressed practical solidarity on the battlefield as they joined forces against the Magyars in the autumn of 1848. Their solidarity had been sanctified by the dramatic ceremony in which the Patriarch of the Vojvodina Serbs, Josip Rajačić, conferred public blessings on Colonel Jelačić when he became Croatia's Ban. At the same time from the Principality of Serbia, whose government remained officially uninvolved, eight thousand volunteers crossed over into the Vojvodina. This Serbian volunteer movement was particularly important in cementing community feelings between Serbs on the two sides of the Sava and the Danube.[38]

In Slovene territory, meantime, the 1848 revolution produced the first tangible national Slovene program. Generated from within liberal, intellectual, student, and liberal clergy ranks, it called for the primacy of the Slovene language and the territorial union of all Slovenes into one autonomous province within a Habsburg framework. It was on the whole a modest program, not merely as ferocious in tone as the proclamations issued in Croatia and the Vojvodina. Slovene political ambitions at this time gave first priority to the acceptance by Austria of the Slovene language and its introduction into schools. Second priority was assigned to the admission of Slovene personnel into responsible administrative ranks. The rest was considered desirable but not cardinal. The extent of popular support in Slovenia for these aims remains uncertain.

[38] In 1849 substantial numbers of Vojvodina Serbs took refuge in the Principality of Serbia and there fanned feelings of Serbian solidarity. See V. Krestić, "Vojvodjanske izbeglice u Srbiji 1849 godine," *Zbornik Matice Srpske za Društvene Nauke* (Novi Sad, 1961), No. 29.

Clearly, however, the Slovene elite hoped for a Habsburg monarchy reformed along federalistic lines.[39]

In 1848 a number of Slovene intellectuals pressed for the union of Slovenia and Croatia, and in some cases the Vojvodina as well, into a south Slav or Yugoslav entity within the Habsburg monarchy. While this sentiment did not prevail, neither was it fiercely opposed; it presaged future directions of Slovene political thought. In 1848–49 the immediate problem revolved around social emancipation and the awakening of a sense of Slovene national community. Still, the incipient voices of Slovene Yugoslavism were noted and welcomed in the adjacent east.

Jelačić's failure to win political or military victory against Budapest and to earn concessions or gratitude from Vienna brought to an end the Yugoslavism of the day. When through Russia's intervention the Magyar revolution collapsed and Habsburg order was restored throughout the monarchy, the southern Slav scene fragmented back into its component settings: Montenegrin, independent Serbian, Ottoman, Vojvodina Serbian, Croatian, and Slovene. 1848–49 remained remembered, but everywhere other forces now came into their own.

Nowhere was this more clear than in Croatia. Bach's absolutist system abolished the *Sabor* and all significant Croat self-administering bodies. Once again Vienna became the nerve center of Croat affairs. Dealing with Vienna was for most Croats preferable to dealing with Budapest, and in the years after 1849 the Croats gained some tangible advantages. In 1852, for example, the church was detached from Budapest and an archbishopric was established in Zagreb. Local patriots hailed this event, as for them, in the apt words of one historian, "religion and nationalism were in effect synonymous."[40]

Another consequence of 1848–49 was the disappearance of Illyrianism. Just as Austro-Slavism was buried in the rubble of the revolutionary edifice so Illyrianism—and Gaj—became scorned.

[39] See F. Zwitter, J. Šidak, and V. Bogdanov, *Les problèmes nationaux dans la monarchie des Habsbourg* (Belgrade, 1960); I. Prijatelj, *Slovenska Kulturnopolitična in Slovstvena Zgodovina, 1848–1895* (4 vols.; Ljubljana, 1945–1961); F. Zwitter, "Slovenski politični preporod XIX Stoletja v okiru europske nacionalne problematike," *Zgodovinski Časopis*, XVIII (Ljubljana, 1964).

[40] Charles Jelavich, "The Croatian Problem in the Habsburg Empire in the Nineteenth Century," *Austrian Yearbook*, III, Part 2 (1967), 96.

During the Bach era, which ended with the October Diploma in 1860, the Croatian political scene responded to various internal and external developments. The response produced three distinct political currents between 1860 and 1867, that is, the years of maneuverings throughout the empire over the issue of its reorganization. Their common denominator was hostility to Austria; beyond that their main consequence was to fragment Croatian political unity.

The first current was represented by the Unionist party of the old *Madjarons,* loyal to the ancient bonds with Hungary, and now once again bent on making common cause with Budapest against Vienna. Cooperation with the Magyars was not of itself unsound, but it involved overlooking past Magyar behavior and, in effect, accepting for Croatia a secondary role. The Unionists were never insignificant, but always in the minority.

The second current, following a decade of inertness, revived the ideas and ideals of Illyrianism, but now (after 1860) specifically in the guise of *Yugoslavism.* The handiwork of Bishop Josip Juraj Strossmayer, leader of the popular People's Party, and Canon Franjo Rački, its main theorist and the leading Croat historian, Yugoslavism in the 1860s developed into an earnest political force.[41] Gaj and the Illyrians had focused on establishing a common literary Croato-Serbian language. They had paid little heed to the problem of religious differences between the two peoples. Their perspectives were Austro-Slav, loyalties pro-Habsburg, and politics unrealistic; they never quite rose above romantic sentimentalism. The Yugoslavists, on the other hand, while not entirely emancipated from a romantic view of south Slavdom, had more advanced practical instincts and were better politicians.

Strossmayer conceived of the Croatian future—cultural as well as political—as being realizable only in the wider context of unity with the Serbs and Slovenes. *E pluribus unum,* while not so phrased, was his fundamental aim; the only promising response to the ancient and successful Habsburg policy of *divide et impera.* Sensitive to the spirit and directions of the Risorgimento and the German national movement, Strossmayer systematically kindled national consciousness within Croatia proper and, deliberately, in Dalmatia and

[41] See F. Šišić, *Jugoslavenska Misao* (Belgrade, 1937); F. Šišić, *Strossmayer i Jugoslavenska Ideja* (Belgrade, 1922); *Korespondencija Rački-Strossmayer* (5 vols.; Zagreb, 1928–33); V. Novak, *Franjo Rački (1828-1894)* (Belgrade, 1958).

Bosnia. He became patron of the University in Zagreb where also, in 1864, he founded the *Yugoslav* Academy of Arts and Sciences. The term Yugoslav henceforth served a dual purpose. It alerted Vienna and Budapest, no less than the Croat public, to the proposition that if Croatian interests were disregarded within the Habsburg mansion, the issue would be played out in a Balkan, international context. At the same time, mindful of the dynamic Serbian policy of Prince Michael (1860–68) which aimed at Balkan unity at the expense of the Ottoman world, and by extension the Habsburg empire. Yugoslavism served as a bridge to the Serbs. Hopefully, it would draw them westward; it also placed the Serbs on notice that Yugoslavism was a Croatian initiative, a point that did not escape the Serbs.

In opposition to Yugoslavism there developed a countermovement of chauvinism and a program of Pan-Croatianism. Its initiators were Ante Starčević and Eugen Kvaternik, both embittered former Illyrians and implacable foes of Austria.[42] Recoiling at Croatian failures, Starčević in particular pushed his views to extremes through his Party of Right (*Prava*). His ultimate dream was Croatian independence, although for the time being, in grudging concession to reality, he accepted dynastic union with the Habsburgs. Starčević demanded the unification of all Croats, whom he considered to inhabit all the southern Slav lands. He denied the historical or ethnic validity of any national denomination other than "Croat," and rejected the existence of a Serbian race for which he coined the epithet *Slavoserb,* meaning by that Orthodox slaves to other Slavs.

Such extremism derived in part from reaction to Croato-Yugoslavism, in part to excesses of Serbian nationalism—Karadžić, for example, had reached the point of claiming that all the southern Slavs were Serbs—in part from fury at Austria (Bach, Schmerling), in part from disgust at Croatian political impotence. The idea of *Pravaštvo* was twofold: to sanctify the Croat cause and imbue the "nation" with self-confidence by harping on the glories of its past

---

[42] Kvaternik, while an emigré in France in 1859, actually worked out its theoretical basis. Starčević, however, became its leading oracle and political strategist. See J. Horvat, *Ante Starčević* (Zagreb, 1940); M. Gross, "Die nationale Idee der Kroatischen Rechtspartei und ihr Zusammenbruch," *Österreichische Osthefte,* VI (Vienna, 1964), 373–88.

and a great future destiny, and at the same time to poison the well-springs of Croato-Serbo-Slovene cooperation and reciprocity. The prospect of separatism and eventually independence was heady tonic for a nation that had felt victimized for seven hundred years; hence *Pravaštvo* elicited considerable popular support. Its rhetoric exuded political virility. It also laid the groundwork for the Ustaša movement and its creation: Ante Pavelić's Croatian quasi-state of World War II.

In the final third of the nineteenth century the Croatian political scene was thus fragmented. The dualism established in 1867 only exacerbated this division, for by the terms of the *Ausgleich,* Vienna left the Croats to their own devices and, in effect, made them once again wards of Budapest.[43] In 1868, mainly as a palliative, Budapest allowed Zagreb (represented by the Unionists) to conclude the *Nagodba,* a "settlement" that on paper established equality between the Kingdom of Hungary and Croatia-Slavonia. In theory, the *Nagodba* created a common state for purposes of foreign policy and defense, while in their internal affairs Hungary and Croatia were to be separate. On paper, thus, Croatian statehood—and from the Magyar and Unionist viewpoints Croatian national dreams—had become fulfilled. In practice, however, the *Nagodba* did little of the sort as Croat representation in the Hungarian Parliament turned into a political formality, financial dependence on Budapest a reality, and the powers and the person of the Ban subject to controls by the prime minister of Hungary. The *Nagodba* quickly became equated with betrayal by most Croatian patriots—from Strossmayer to Starčević. After nearly three years of unsuccessful Croatian maneuvers within the new dualistic framework of the monarchy, an embittered Kvaternik attempted an armed rebellion in late 1871 in the name of total independence. The effort misfired and its principal result—except for Kvaternik's death on the altar of this solitary outburst—was to demoralize the Croats further and to expose them to more rigorous repressions.

---

[43] In the early 1860's Ivan Mažuranić's Independent Party had propounded the view that Zagreb should make its peace with Vienna, lest Budapest do so first, inevitably at the expense of the Croats. The argument was prophetic but the party went to decisive electoral defeat in 1865. After the *Ausgleich* the People's Party and the Yugoslavists, indeed all foes of an understanding with the Magyars, were officially repressed.

The basic division among the Croats and the conflict of the three main national conceptions did not significantly change until the first decade of the twentieth century. Even the incorporation of the Military Frontier into Croatia in 1881, an old national desideratum, did not assuage internal political hostilities. Nor did the fact that in 1878 Bosnia-Hercegovina came under Habsburg administration. This event removed Bosnia-Hercegovina from the Serbian orbit, much to the chagrin of the Serbs, and for that and other reasons catered to Croat nationalist sentiments. Even the twenty-year stern rule of Count Khuen-Héderváry (1883–1903), appointed by Budapest as Ban in order to "pacify" and wherever possible Magyarize Croatia, did not cause the local adversaries to rally together. Khuen-Héderváry's excesses aroused the nation and helped spawn three additional political constellations: a more radical-nationalist offshoot of Starčević's movement, the Party of Pure Right under Josip Frank; the Social-Democratic Party of Croatia-Slavonia, supported by various student and youth groups; and an active grouping of the Serbs of Croatia, who were soon to be led by Svetozar Pribičević in the Independent Party.

When viewed against the background of the successful Italian, Romanian, and German national movements, Croatian nationalism and Croato-Yugoslavism in the nineteenth century failed to achieve notable results. By 1900 the Croats felt frustrated and disoriented, and showed symptoms both of admiration and resentment for Serbia which, despite numerous reverses in foreign policy, had made impressive gains and was becoming the political epicenter of the south Slav world.

The Slovenes, in the last third of the nineteenth century, were also politically divided, though they made great strides forward in the cultural and economic spheres. Threatened on the one hand by Italian irredentism along the Littoral and throughout Istria, and on the other, by Austrian administrative repressions, the Slovene national movement split over problems of priorities and tactics, on whether to support Vienna in order to counter Italian encroachments or to concentrate on resisting Austria. One consequence of this dilemma was the development of a Slovene-Yugoslavism—calling for concerted south Slav political-cultural action within the Habsburg framework—which gained momentum after 1870. Also, Slovene intellectuals became increasingly interested in liaisons with

Serbia, the ideas of Pan-Slavism, and in Russia which to many seemed to offer the only promise of "final national liberation."[44]

Clerical circles, the strongest political influence in Slovenia, concluded by the late 1890s that the struggle for the internal primacy of the Slovene language and for Slovene political rights was leading nowhere. Tactical alliances with German Austrian liberals, then with conservatives and clericals, and after 1897 even with Christian Socialists had proven unproductive. From 1898 on, therefore, the Clericals lent their support to the essentially Croatian conception of trialism, propounded by the Party of Right as an indispensable alternative to the dualism established by the *Ausgleich* of 1867. Trialism was not a latter-day version of the 1848–49 conception of a Yugoslav bloc within the monarchy; nor was it so conceived in Zagreb and in Ljubljana. In Fran Zwitter's succinct words:

> The Croatian Party of Right demanded first of all the union of Croatia, Dalmatia and Bosnia, considering all three as Croatian provinces, joining to this also the demand for the incorporation of the Slovene provinces; for the Great-Croatian tradition of this party proclaimed the Serbs in these provinces for "Orthodox Croats" and the Slovenes for "Mountain Croats." With the Slovene Clerical Party the point of religion was decisive; it wanted to paralyze the German pressure by uniting the Slovenes with the Catholic Croats; . . . yet, they were not in favour of the union with the Orthodox Serbs [of the Monarchy].[45]

In the end the program of trialism did no more to advance the Croat and Slovene national causes than did other schemes. For it to work would have required the concurrence of Budapest and Vienna, and neither had reason to abandon the dualist arrangement that had functioned effectively since 1867. Moreover, a major change in the position of the southern Slavs would lead to crises with other nationalities, particularly with the Czechs. Equally important, the Croats and the Slovenes did not share the same view of trialism, nor were their political parties united in its favor. Finally, while a trialist solution, in theory at least, might have satiated some Croat and Slovene yearnings for autonomy or responsibility

---

[44] See Fran Zwitter, "The Slovenes and the Habsburg Monarchy," *Austrian Yearbook*, III, Part 2 (1967), 175.

[45] *Ibid.*, p. 178.

within the monarchy, it would not have resolved the issue that became fundamental in the decade before World War I: the relationship between the Habsburg southern Slavs and Serbia.

In the half century before 1914 this relationship had grown more complex and problematical. In the spirit of the *Načertanije* and influenced by the examples of Cavour and Bismarck, Serbian statesmen in the 1860s and 1870s undertook major activities in Bosnia-Hercegovina to the west and in Macedonia to the east. Irredentism became a central feature of Serbian nationalism and the disintegration of the Ottoman Empire its concrete goal. At the same time, intimate links were developed with the Serbs of Dalmatia and the Vojvodina, and closer contact with Montenegro. In the Vojvodina, meanwhile, the Popular Liberal Party of Svetozar Miletić had worked for the federalization of the monarchy prior to the *Ausgleich;* after 1870 Miletić—whose influence was enormous—propounded the dissolution of Austria-Hungary. At another level, the Serbian United Youth Movement, originating in the Vojvodina in the 1860s, drew into its orbit young Serbian intellectuals and radicals in Serbia, Dalmatia, Croatia, Bosnia, and Montenegro. The youth movement gave practical expression to the idea of "a community of fate" and the feasibility of concerted nationalist action.[46] The picture was completed by Svetozar Marković, founder of Serbian socialism, who with revolutionary directness called for the break-up of the Ottoman and Habsburg empires, the union of all Serbs and the transformation of Serbian state and society.

Gradually but tangibly Serbian nationalism—and state policy—thus came to assume as basic premises: a) the unification of all Serbs, b) the consequent necessity for the territorial acquisition of Bosnia-Hercegovina and "Serbian" Macedonia, c) the principle of "the Balkans for the Balkan peoples," thereby calling for noninterference by the European powers, d) the eventual destruction of the Ottoman and Habsburg empires, and as the logical culmination, e) the liberation of all southern Slavs and their unification under the

---

[46] An interesting British observation on south Slav affairs is contained in a report to the Foreign Secretary, Earl Russel, from the British Consul in Dubrovnik, dated February 24, 1865: ". . . to me it appears that the leaven of national life in Belgrade, Agram [and elsewhere] is much too small. . . . I think it not unprobable that at some future time the shock of European Revolutions may create a comprehensive Jugo-Slavic Monarchy . . . ." Cited in H. V. Temperley, "The Jugoslav Movement in British Eyes, 1860–1871," in Šišićev Zbornik (Zagreb, 1929), p. 31.

scepter of Serbia. This outlook was widely shared throughout the Serbian political spectrum, from the Liberal Party of Jovan Ristić to the Radical Party of Nikola Pašić, and from conservatives to Socialists alike. A thirty-year chain of discouraging developments— the collapse of Prince Michael's Balkan alliance in 1868; Russian abandonment of Serbia and patronage of the Bulgarian national movement, culminating in the treaty of San Stefano (1878); the "loss" of Bosnia-Hercegovina to the Habsburg Empire by the Treaty of Berlin (1878); the humiliating acceptance by King Milan of Austro-Hungarian tutelage in 1882; the military debacle in the Serbo-Bulgarian war of 1885; the general stalemate of the 1890s; and the growing all-Serbian dynastic ambitions of King Nicholas of Montenegro—all these developments only fortified Serbian nationalist determinations to make of Serbia the "Piedmont" of the southern Slavs.

In Serbian nationalist eyes, Yugoslavism became one particular aspect of Serbia's "destiny," and the liberation of the Habsburg southern Slavs (non-Serbs as well as Serbs) a national responsibility. But to Croat and Slovene nationalists—whose zealous Catholicism was at once anti-Orthodox and hypersensitive to the clamorous anti-Catholicism of the Serbs[47]—Serbian interest in Yugoslavism seemed a cloak for territorial expansion.[48] Inevitably, the issue of Bosnia-Hercegovina became the neuralgic point in south Slav affairs. Which national viewpoint would in the end prevail? The Croat view of Bosnians as Croats and the Serb view of Bosnians as Serbs produced diatribes on both sides and an avalanche of "scientific" treatises on the historical, linguistic, ethnic, religious, anthropological "facts" involved. The problem, however, was insoluble for the generation before World War I, as it became insoluble for the generation that preceded World War II.

[47] "Sloga Srbo-Hrvata" (MS in Nikola Pašić Collection, Archive of the Serbian Academy of Sciences, Belgrade [Document No. 11857]). While undated, this document was most probably penned in the 1890's and reveals profound distrust and dislike of Croatian Catholicism and clerical Croatianism. It reflects widespread Serbian feelings of the day.

[48] The territory of Serbia doubled between 1817 and 1905, in which year it encompassed 48,000 square kilometers. For details see I Ginić, "Teritorija i Naseljenost Ustaničke Srbije," *Prikazi i Studije: Prilozi Statističkom Izučavanju Prvog Srpskog Ustanka*, XIV (June, 1955), 27–36. But the most dramatic Serbian territorial gains were achieved in the Balkan wars of 1912–13, a period in which official policy was replete with "Yugoslav" overtones.

The real problem of Bosnia-Hercegovina in the Yugoslav equation was one of cultural geopolitics rather than of establishing a "truth" that, by the very nature of the region, could not (and cannot) be established. By the time Austria-Hungary formally annexed Bosnia-Hercegovina in 1908—to the delight of most Croats and the mortification of all Serbs—it was evident that a profound psychological rift obtained. Serb and Croat passions reflected a contest between Orthodoxy and Catholicism, between Balkan and central European values and ways of life. They also involved recognition of an elemental fact of life, namely that the party that could legitimize or secure its proprietary claim to the Bosnian middle zone would likely become dominant in any future Yugoslav state.

Paradoxically, such predispositions testified not only to the tensions between Serbia and the Habsburg south Slavs before World War I, but also to the wide acceptance on both sides of the inevitability of eventual Yugoslav unification, in one form or another. This does not mean that in Croatia and Slovenia the fibers of *Kaisertreue* had worn out; it was an anomaly of the age that Serbo-Croat-Slovene unity in a Habsburg context and the vague expectation of an all-Yugoslav union in the future were not thought to be inconsistent. In the absence of immediate necessity and opportunity the issue was not pressing. When the war erupted and when, in 1917–18, the opportunity arose, it disappeared.

The decade before 1914 set the course which in the end demolished the frontiers that had separated Serbia and the Habsburg southern Slavs. In 1903 the accession of King Petar Karadjordjević removed Serbia from the Habsburg orbit and restored Serbian initiative in Yugoslav affairs, both in the international diplomatic arena and in internal Habsburg and Ottoman affairs.[49] The efforts of Budapest and Vienna in 1904–6 to strangle the Serbian economy failed. The customs war only intensified Serbian anti-Habsburg feelings, as did the annexation of Bosnia-Hercegovina in 1908, and aroused new sympathies for Serbia among Croats and Slovenes and in Europe at large. The development of effective constitutional-parliamentary life in Serbia after 1903 also stimulated Serbophile sentiments.

In Croatia, partly in response to Serbian developments and, more significantly, in response to the departure of the hated Khuen-

[49] Vucinich, *Serbia Between East and West, 1903–1908*, pp. 75–121.

Héderváry a new political party was formed in 1905, foreshadowing a "Yugoslav" solution to the national problem. Under the leadership of two prominent Dalmatian *pravaši*, Frano Supilo and Ante Trumbić, a meeting of principal Croat and Serb political figures of the monarchy in October, 1905, in Rijeka (Fiume), produced a resolution and a common plan of action. The Croato-Serb Coalition, founded in the same year, quickly became the majority party and retained that position until the collapse of the Habsburg empire.[50] Despite its frequently opportunistic tactics, the Coalition managed to attune public opinion to the notion that the only practical way of advancing Croat interests was in a Yugoslav framework, through cooperation with the Slovenes, the Habsburg Serbs, and with Serbia: in other words, through fundamental changes in the international sphere. In the system of limited suffrage and Magyar political preponderance the likelihood of reorganizing the Habsburg monarchy was almost nil, especially so in the face of the Germanic *Drang nach Osten* that, among other things, aimed at perpetuating the subjugation of all Slavs. By 1908 this view also prevailed among the Slovenes who were perhaps the principal south Slav victims of Germanization. It was shared by the Croatian Peasant Party, founded by Stjepan Radić in 1904.

While the political scenes in Croatia and Slovenia still remained fragmented, the educated and active public thought increasingly in international terms. Considerable interest developed in Russia—especially on the part of Radić—in the teachings of Masaryk, in Neo-Slavism, and in the affairs of Serbia. Congresses, meetings, public manifestations, and a spate of new journals, reviews, and newspapers championed the Yugoslav cause and, by direction or indirection, propagated anti-Habsburg views. The youth in particular—some inclined to socialism, some not—turned into an activist force of impatient revolutionary slogans and, in numerous localities, one that resorted to terroristic actions against Habsburg officials and local pro-Habsburg leaders.

After the Bosnian crisis and the Zagreb High Treason trials of 1909, Serbia became the nerve center and exchequer of various societies, revolutionary or ultranationalist, some open, some secret

[50] See Mirjana Gross, *Vladavina Hrvatsko-Srpske Koalicije, 1906–1907* (Belgrade, 1960); F. Čulinović, *Zadarska Rezolucija* (Zadar, 1964); J. Horvat, *Frano Supilo* (Belgrade, 1961); Ante Trumbić, *Suton Austro-Ugarske* (Zagreb, 1936).

and paramilitary. They all—*Slovenski Jug, Narodna Odbrana, Mlada Bosna, Ujedinjenje ili Smrt*—shared two points in common: hatred of Austria-Hungary and the vision of an eventually united Yugoslav state. After the crisis of 1908, official Serbian policy searched for a basis of coexistence with the Habsburg monarchy. But that prospect proved chimeric. By 1911, spurred by pro-Yugoslav currents in Croatia, Slovenia, Montenegro, and particularly in Dalmatia, Beograd, with the blessings of St. Petersburg, set out to revive earlier Serbian dreams of a Balkan concert. The new alliance produced dramatic results and the triumph of Serbian arms in 1912–13 lent credence to Serbia's mission as the Piedmont of the south Slav world. Following the conquest, or rather liberation, of Macedonia in 1913, Bosnia came onto center stage. With Yugoslavism now a fanatical, revolutionary, nationalist creed—at least for significant sectors of the youth, the Serbian officer corps and numerous intellectuals and politicians on both sides of the Habsburg-Serbian frontier—the momentum of nationalist violence grew. This circumstance was aggravated by the political myopia and the martial language of Vienna. The assassination of Archduke Francis Ferdinand represented both a continuation and the culmination of a process that fed on political and social grievances and nationalist passions. The deed of Sarajevo set loose the larger European tensions and, through the conflict that ensued, made possible the formation of an independent and unified Yugoslav state.

The Kingdom of Serbs, Croats, and Slovenes[51] was proclaimed in Beograd on December 1, 1918; significantly, six weeks before the Paris Peace Conference convened. It was not a creation of Versailles, especially as a revolutionary Croato-Serbo-Slovene government had already been established in Zagreb on October 29, nearly a week before the Austrian surrender at Padova on November 3.

Though not created by the peacemakers—who were faced with a political *fait accompli* for which they had to determine national frontiers—the new Yugoslav state owed its existence to three basic

---

[51] This cumbersome name was adopted at the insistence of Nikola Pašić who viewed the name "Yugoslavia" as symbolizing the demise of Serbia. It is worth noting, in this connection, that Serbia and Montenegro set a historic precedent in 1918 by voluntarily relinquishing their sovereignty in favor of establishing a larger and different national entity. Critics of Serbian nationalism are prone to disregard this rather significant point.

circumstances: 1) military victory of the Entente, 2) the unwilling-ness or inability of Vienna to conclude a separate peace in the spring of 1918, and, 3) the wartime activities of Yugoslav leaders exiled in the West, and to some extent those who had remained at home.

If victory had gone to the Central Powers it is safe to assume that no independent Yugoslavia would have been allowed to emerge. Similarly, if in the spring of 1918 Austria-Hungary had concluded separate peace—and this was the prime objective of Al-lied policy at the time—an independent Yugoslav state would again not have come about. Woodrow Wilson's Fourteen Points specifi-cally envisaged the continued existence of a Habsburg monarchy, reformed and so reconstituted as to grant wider autonomies to its constituent nationalities. The gambit was to lure Vienna into sepa-rate peace and Allied grand strategy had clear priority over the desiderata of Habsburg subject nationalities. Only when Vienna declined to accept the proferred hand did Allied leaders, late in May, 1918, decide upon the dissolution of the Habsburg empire. This decision, too, was seen pre-eminently in terms of strategic ne-cessity, though it was sanctified in a political litany that stressed the principles of nationality, self-determination, and historic jus-tice.[52]

Without this Allied disposition the Yugoslavs could not have im-posed their will; with it they could and did take the initiative that produced the *fait accompli* of the new state. But during the four long years of the war Yugoslav opinion and political strategy were far from single minded. With the opening of hostilities, a host of Croat and Slovene leaders fled to the West where, under the guid-ance of Supilo and Trumbić, they established the Yugoslav Com-mittee, which in 1915 moved its seat from Rome to London.[53] Is-

[52] On the evolution of Allied views and strategic plans see Victor Mamatey, *The United States and East Central Europe, 1914–1918* (Princeton, N.J.: Princeton University Press, 1957).

[53] For a detailed analysis of its activities see Milada Paulova, *Jugoslavenski Odbor* (Zagreb, 1923). Also, the very valuable special studies of Bogdan Krizman, too numerous to be listed here. In addition, a useful compendium of documents is to be found in Dragoslav Janković and Bogdan Krizman (eds.), *Gradja o stvaranju Jugoslo-venske Države* (2 vols.; Belgrade, 1965). For the role of Supilo—whose death in 1917 placed the leadership of the Yugoslav Committee in the hands of Trumbić—see Dragovan Šepić, *Memoari Frane Supila, 1914–1917* (Belgrade, 1967).

suing a dramatic manifesto in 1915 calling for the dissolution of the Habsburg monarchy and the union of all Yugoslavs into a sovereign state, the committee gradually prepared British, French, American, and tsarist Russian opinion for this cause. Working through sympathetic Allied academic and journalistic circles, it also elicited first the private and ultimately the public support of Entente leaders, including Woodrow Wilson, Lloyd George, French Foreign Minister Pichon, and, somewhat more ambiguously, Vittorio Emanuele Orlando. Trumbić and his associates in exile, in short, had mounted such a widespread, vigorous, and articulate campaign that the union of all Yugoslavs was psychologically accepted in Entente circles, even before the tide of military fortunes made it a practicable and desirable objective of Allied grand strategy.

The cause of Yugoslav unification was also advanced by the Serbian government of Pašić, albeit its position on the matter was less clear and pushed with lesser vigor or enthusiasm. Pašić, first and foremost a Serbian patriot and nationalist—and in World War I a septuagenarian of unbending persuasions—contemplated the "liberation" of the Habsburg Yugoslavs under the aegis of Serbia, modeled on the recent liberation of Macedonia. His great Serbian conception did not allow for a Serbo-Croatian-Slovene-Montenegrin partnership, or federative arrangement in the tradition of Miletić, or as envisaged by Supilo, Trumbić, and the Yugoslav Committee. For such an outcome would spell the end of Serbian sovereignty (and national pride), a dilution of Orthodox culture and a potential surrender to Croatian Catholic central European values and influences. However, wartime exigency and widespread Serbian support of Yugoslavism—particularly in the ranks of his political opposition —as well as the pressure of western opinion, prompted Pašić to pay lip service to the Yugoslav formula. His view of Serbia's national interest and destiny led him, however, to work for a Serbian liberation of the Habsburg Yugoslavs. Two calamities removed the initiative from his hands: the Bulgarian invasion of Serbia in 1915 that forced his government into exile on Corfu, and two years later, the downfall of tsarism in Russia, which eliminated Serbia's principal and solitary international champion and patron. Alone, resentful, frustrated and distraught, Pašić, in the summer of 1917, joined with the Yugoslav Committee in the Declaration of Corfu that, on paper at least, established a concerted Yugoslav national plan for liberation, unification, and independence.

From mid-1917 on, the Entente powers thus had to consider a Yugoslav solution as an integral part of any reorganization of southeast Europe. Much uncertainty, though, was caused by the ceaseless bickering between the Serbian government and the Yugoslav Committee on the future character of the Yugoslav union. Additional uncertainty in Entente ranks was caused by the determination of Italy's foreign minister, Baron Sidney Sonnino, to forestall the formation of a viable Yugoslav state. In fact, however, Italian diplomacy, beginning with the Treaty of London of April, 1915—whereby the Entente secured Italy's entry into the war by promising Rome substantial Yugoslav territories, including much of the Dalmatian coast—caused the Entente discomfort in two ways. By its opposition to Yugoslav ambitions it was clearly solidifying Yugoslav ranks. In the face of the Italian threat, Pašić had no choice but to defend the "fraternal" interests of the Croats and Slovenes. Hence the Allies had to cope with ever more sanguine protestations by the Yugoslavs and their many friends in western Europe and America. At the same time, Italy's thrust in inter-Allied councils tested Entente unity, which few were willing to jeopardize on account of the south Slavs, especially as Habsburg armies naturally contained large Croat and Slovene contingents. But the territorial deal of 1915 stood in defiance of Wilson's pronouncements on the rights of nations and the evils of secret diplomacy. By their public adherence to Wilsonian principles, the Entente in effect legitimized Yugoslav aspirations. In the end what diplomacy was unable to resolve, military contingency rendered possible. In deciding to destroy the Habsburg imperial framework, the Allies invited a revolution from within. In September–October, 1918, the Croat and Slovene components evaporated from the Habsburg armies, while their political leaders prepared to cut the ties that for centuries had bound Serbs, Croats, and Slovenes with Budapest and Vienna.[54]

---

[54] Already in May, 1917, Croat and Slovene deputies in the Parliament in Vienna issued a declaration favoring a Yugoslav union within a Habsburg framework. This act has often been cited as proof of Croat and Slovene loyalty to the Habsburg empire. Such a view, however, is not supportable by the logic of the situation of 1917, nor by the clearly understood, though unarticulated, motives of the signatory deputies. The manifesto was meant to weaken the monarchy and officially to rally the Croat and Slovene parties behind a program of Yugoslavism. An open call for

World War I, in sum, created the first real opportunity for a unified Yugoslav state. Had Serbs, Croats, and Slovenes not willed it, no doubt the Entente would not have imposed it. But given Entente victory, most Yugoslavs assumed it and that premise involved relegating, at least temporarily, pure Croatianism and Serbianism to an uncertain second place. It was not long, however, before these currents re-emerged.

V

It would not serve much purpose in this brief survey to attempt a detailed account of the national and regional problems, developments, and ideological currents since 1918. In terms of nationalism the central question of the past half century is whether Yugoslav statehood has produced a sense of Yugoslav nationhood that runs sufficiently deep to withstand the strains and stresses of Serbian, Croatian, Slovene, and—more recently—Macedonian particularistic nationalisms. Evidently, there is no simple or single answer to the question.

Yugoslav citizenship has not become coequal with Yugoslav nationality. Similarly, Yugoslav nationalism—which has essentially meant political support for the Yugoslav state as an alternative to independence for its constituent parts—has not obliterated emotional loyalties to "Serbia" or "Croatia" or other "national" cradles. In the course of its short existence, Yugoslavia, as most multinational states, has been a mosaic, not a melting pot. By virtue of his separate language and other characteristics, the Slovene has felt himself to be first a Slovene. By virtue of his religion, as well as script and culture and history, the Serb has remained and remains a Serb. And so forth. Yet for all the intensity and immediacy of the separate—and in extremist circles blatantly separatist—nationalisms and regionalist loyalties, Yugoslavia has endured most severe tests, on occasion flourished, and over the half century proven itself a vibrant force.

---

a Yugoslav union *outside* a Habsburg framework would have been an overt act of treason, punishable by customary wartime standards. The real meaning of the manifesto was clear to one and all in Zagreb, Ljubljana, Budapest, and Vienna. The Yugoslav Committee in London received it with clear approval, especially as it was intended (a) to counteract Italian charges that the Croat and Slovene parties were, by conviction, on the Habsburg side, and (b) to gain the favor of England, France, and America.

It might of course be argued that its strength has been rooted not so much in a general allegiance to a *Yugoslav* community or a psychological kinship between its several peoples—whose individual needs and aspirations have not been truly fulfilled by the union—as in political and international realities. Yugoslavia has led an embattled existence since its inception and the precarious, even hostile, international environment—whether in the guise of the revisionist encirclement by Italy, Hungary, Bulgaria, and Italian-dominated Albania between the two wars or the wrathful Stalinist encirclement of the late 1940s—has dictated unity rather than fragmentation. In this context the national issue, particularly between the two wars, was compounded by the fact that the external vulnerability of the state could be exploited for purposes of domestic politics. But—except for lunatic fringes, singularly the Ustašas who were maintained in exile and manipulated by Mussolini—there were limits beyond which even the aggrieved and disgruntled Croatian Peasant Party would not venture in exploiting the international vulnerability of the state. In fact, when the Yugoslav state as such faced dire crisis, its bitterest critics, among them the Croatian Peasant Party leader Vladko Maček, elected to save the state rather than to destroy it.[55] Emergency-induced unity or solidarity had little to do with real internal harmony; still, it did testify, in the 1930s as in 1948, salutary and constructive political realism.

While the fierce and often venomous conflict between Serbs and Croats in the interwar years and their economic-cultural-political contest in the 1960s weakened the position of the state, internal discord by itself neither sufficed nor sought to bring about the dismemberment of Yugoslavia. In this context, the nationalist abandon of World War II with its genocidal hysteria (mainly among the Croatian Ustaši) and reciprocal slaughter (pursued more ferociously by the Croatian side) was by no means the logical outcome of twenty years of internal disillusionment and discord. Rather, the unspeakable excesses of 1941–45 were triggered by war and invasion, fanned by Nazi example, and carried by the momentum of a simultaneous civil war, ideological and revolutionary conflict, and patriotic resistance to foreign occupation. Marxist Yugoslav historiography,

[55] It would not be unreasonable to argue that Maček's final ambivalence in the wake of the German invasion of April, 1941, is in no way inconsistent with this view, for by this time the Yugoslav state was, temporarily at least, beyond salvation.

carried away by pride of Communist performance during the war, has magnified not only the brutality of its opposition—whether foreign or collaborationist, or royalist, or just anti-Communist—but also the intensity of the prewar malaise, for that places the C.P.Y. squarely in the role of savior. It should be remembered, however, that animalistic behavior during World War II was not a monopoly of Croatian and Serbian chauvinists and that in other parts of Europe the day, at first, belonged to political psychopaths who fashioned themselves in the Nazi mirror.[56] The wounds of World War II —on the condition, once again, of Allied victory—did not prove fatal; if anything, they proved regenerative and from the early stages of the war inspired renewed fervor for Yugoslavism, from which the partisan movement drew considerable capital.

As in the nineteenth century, so in the twentieth, Yugoslavism has proven a refuge in adversity, particularly when adversity took the form of foreign domination or, as in 1948, the threat of it. War and a common foe pull individuals and kindred nationalities together. Not unnaturally 1918 and 1945 thus denoted zenith years in the history of Yugoslavism, each followed by periods of gradual erosion as regional differences and nationalisms, perhaps inevitably, came to the fore. There are, however, paramount differences in the situations that evolved after the two world wars.

In 1918–20 the new state faced the problem of integrating diverse regions and peoples who were in effect strangers into a single administrative entity. Inebriated by "victory" and the ostensible panacea of Wilsonianism and democracy, the Serbs, Croats, and Slovenes had neither the resources nor the experience to cope with the legion of problems at hand, or to develop at once effective and constructive multiparty parliamentary government. The high illiteracy rate, the unfavorable industrial-agricultural ratio, the sudden emergence of a large Communist Party and the disgruntled holdovers of the *ancien regimes* did not augur an easy or stable future.

To make matters worse, the new state existed for two years un-

---

[56] Communist portrayals of Draža Mihajlović as deriving from the same mold that produced Ante Pavelić and his European counterparts are nonsense. In this connection it should be noted that the extent and real strength of Serb and Croat chauvinism during World War II cannot as yet be fully assessed. The day has not yet come when comprehensive research can be undertaken with regard to the "losers" of World War II in Yugoslav lands, though it is clear that the population everywhere, Croatia's included, recoiled from official nationalist excesses.

certain of its final frontiers, which had a demoralizing effect on internal conditions. The protracted negotiations at the peace conference, relative to Yugoslav frontiers with all neighboring states, in the end left almost half a million Yugoslavs in foreign, mainly Italian, hands. That in itself proved a bitter pill. Equally significant, however, Yugoslav diplomatic tribulations over frontier questions led to serious differences within the Yugoslav peace delegation as well as political circles at home. Mutual suspicions and recriminations between the Serbs (led by Pašić) and the Croats (led by foreign minister Trumbić) were emblematic of chasm within the family.

The course of subsequent political life was rendered inexorable by the first Yugoslav constitution, the Vidovdan constitution of 1921, which created a centralized unitary system—as opposed to Croatian federative schemes—and gave Beograd and the Serbs effective control of the state apparatus and national finances. Increasingly, party activities and parliamentary life revolved around the "national question," at the expense of the pressing social and economic issues of the day. The murder, in 1928, of Stjepan Radić, by a Montenegrin deputy gone berserk on the floor of parliament, brought about the end of parliamentary life and the assumption of dictatorial powers by King Alexander. In turn, the assassination of Alexander in Marseilles in 1934 set in motion a cycle of political in-fighting at home in which opponents were again ranged along ethnic lines.

In these adverse political circumstances it is perhaps remarkable that the Yugoslav union not only endured but in many ways prospered. Social and economic gains—curbed by the world depression that also deprived Yugoslavia of western support and opened the way to German penetration—were tangible. So was the development of a *Yugoslav* countercurrent to Serbian and Croatian nationalist zeal. Enkindled from the top, directly by Alexander, but also from the ranks of the wartime political partisans of the union, interwar Yugoslavism was a constructive force and showed signs of strength and growing acceptance. By constitutional terms, the government was officially committed to the thesis that the Serbs, Croats, and Slovenes were one nationality known by three names (Macedonians and Montenegrins were considered Serbs) and the government became the fountainhead of a formal Yugoslav nationalism. The "single nationality" thesis, though it flew in the face of contemporary and historical fact, nevertheless obtained much support, especially among the center blocs in all parts of the country as the only hope for long-run stability.[57] As such it attracted youth and elder statesmen who, unwilling to bend to the winds of cynicism, did not find the patience, idealism, and realism to be inconsistent.

On balance, before World War II, Yugoslavism and Croatian/Serbian chauvinism evolved in a complicated pattern of counterpoint and dissonance. The national union did not fulfill the all-too-high expectations of 1918. Whether it could have in so short a time and in the unstable international environment of the 1920s and 1930s is an issue that, perforce, will continue to produce controversy. Despite its shortcomings, however, the Yugoslav framework appears to have gained decisive acceptance. It is doubtful that it would have fallen apart had it not been for war and invasion in 1941.

In the wake of the war and the holocaust it had brought on, 1945 —quite apart from the revolutionary terror of the day—witnessed a reconsecration of Yugoslavism. The partisan movement had drawn strength during the war and had attracted non-Communists into its ranks by equating patriotism with Yugoslavism. Moreover, the intelligent wartime (1943) decision to restructure the Yugoslav state into a federal system with constitutional autonomy and equality of nationalities was designed to counteract volatile regional particularisms. The Communist monopoly of the means of power—along with party discipline, the suppression of all opposition, and the imposed social-economic transformation—created a new equation in Yugoslav affairs: the interlocking of centralized rule and decentralized nationality development. In this scheme, the assignment of nationality franchise to Macedonia and Montenegro—the one sig-

---

[57] The fifteen years before the onslaught of 1941 witnessed a "war" between publicists and scholars in favor or against Yugoslavism. A characteristic of the era was the fact that pro-Yugoslav writings were more serious and judicious in tone. One of the most serious and interesting products of the time is to be found in Vladimir Dvorniković's *Karakterologija Jugoslavena* (Belgrade, 1939), an ambitious anthropological-sociological treatise that sought to establish the existence of a common Yugoslav-Dynaric type. Bitterly criticized, exorcised by the Ustašas, the work remains controversial (though mostly unread) to this day. It continues to testify, however, to constructive possibilities that have, save for Dvorniković's enormous effort, not been pushed very far.

nificantly induced by considerations affecting Bulgaria and Greece; the other by considerations of historical tradition and the numerical relation between Croats and Serbs—played a strategic role. But perhaps the cardinal element in the scheme has been the establishment of Bosnia-Hercegovina as a constituent republic of the federation. This resolved by circumvention the thorny issue of whether Bosnians are Serbs or Croats.

For a decade and a half after the war the general formula operated fairly smoothly, particularly as larger internal and external problems relegated the "national question" to the shadows. Several other circumstances contributed to this result. Least important though not altogether insignificant was the fact of Tito being a Croat, a point vaguely reassuring to non-Serbs. More important was the post-war achievement of almost complete south Slav ethnic frontiers, especially the "liberation" of Istria and the Zadar region from Italian hands, thereby eliminating Slovene and Croat irredentism and healing their respective "national" wounds. Most important, the crisis with Stalin in 1948 had the effect of drawing the nation together and arousing a *Yugoslav* pride in that feat of defiance and survival. It may be the irony of that grim crisis that it was a blessing in disguise.

Since the early 1950s, however, the "national" scene has undergone perceptible erosion, which in the mid-1960s reached disquieting proportions. The process of decentralization in agriculture and industry, and altogether the general trend of political and cultural liberalization, appear to have created special problems among the nationalities. The effort to uplift the undeveloped southern parts of the country—Macedonia, Montenegro, Bosnia-Hercegovina—while maintaining the momentum of industrial development in the north has strained the nation's limited resources. Rapid development of the south could only be achieved by sacrifices for the north that, essentially, the average Serb, Croat, and Slovene has been reticent to bear. This situation was further compounded by Tito's determination to pursue an expensive global foreign policy and at home to experiment in combining political planning with the natural interplay of a market economy. The resulting uncertainties, even in the face of relative prosperity, has produced manifestations of economic nationalism, particularly in Croatia and Serbia. The polemic between Zagreb and Beograd—and, to a lesser extent, Skopje and Beograd—concerning capital allocation and long-range economic plans spread from technical and academic circles to the highest councils of the Communist party, and to the public at large.

In this society of undying memories and emotions it is not surprising that in the sixties symbols of economics have been translated into the terminology of cultural rivalry. But this terminology has not assumed the vituperative, almost racialistic, tones of times past. The basic problem has continued to revolve around the issue of the uneven economic development of the country. Regional tensions between Serbs and Croats or Macedonians and Serbs (or other combinations) have on occasion been acute, certainly judging by Tito's frequent exhortations for unity and restraint. Strains and stresses, "national" frustrations and attempts at self-assertion, have thus not passed from the scene. In a mosaic state, however, that may be an inescapable fact of life. The real question is whether the mosaic's outer frame and inner design are fundamentally secure. On this score the prevailing evidence points to the fact that they are. The perspectives and the ambitions of the present generation exceed the constricting and essentially futile nationalist imbroglios of the past. Nationalism remains a dynamic force, but Yugoslavism and regional-ethnic loyalties may by now have reached the point of symbiosis.*

* Part of the research for this study was made possible by a grant from the American Council of Learned Societies, for which I wish to express my appreciation.

Index

CONTRIBUTORS

GEORGE BARANY is professor of history at the University of Denver. His published work includes a book, *Stephen Széchenyi and the Awakening of Hungarian Nationalism, 1791–1841* (1968), and articles in numerous periodicals, including *East European Quarterly, Journal of Central European Affairs, Papers of the Michigan Academy of Science, Arts and Letters,* and *Slavic Review.*

PETER BROCK is professor of history at the University of Toronto. In addition to three books of Polish history written in Polish and published abroad between 1956 and 1962, he is the author of *The Political and Social Doctrines of the Unity of Czech Brethren in the Fifteenth and Early Sixteenth Centuries* (1957) and *Pacifism in the United States: From the Colonial Era to the First World War* (1968). His articles have appeared in *Slavonic and East European Review, Polish Review,* and *English Historical Review,* among others.

STEPHEN FISCHER-GALATI is professor of history at the University of Colorado and editor of the *East European Quarterly.* His published books include *Ottoman Imperialism and German Protestantism, 1521–1555* (1959), *Rumania, A Bibliographic Guide* (1963), *The New Rumania: From People's Democracy to Social Republic* (1967), *Twentieth Century Europe: A Documentary History* (1967), and *The Socialist Republic of Rumania* (1969). His articles have appeared in many periodicals.

IVO J. LEDERER is professor of history and chairman of the Committee on Russian and East European Studies at Stanford University. He is editor of *Russian Foreign Policy: Essays in Historical Perspective* (1962), and author of *Yugoslavia at the Paris Peace Conference: A Study in Frontier-making* (1963).

MARIN PUNDEFF is professor of history at San Fernando Valley State College. His books are *Bulgaria: A Bibliographic Guide* (1965) and *History in the USSR: Selected Readings* (1967). In addition to chapters in several volumes dealing with Eastern Europe, he has published articles and book reviews in *American Historical Review, Harvard Educational Review, Saeculum, Südost-Forschungen, Revue des Etudes Slaves,* and other journals.

PETER F. SUGAR is professor of history at the University of Washington. He is the author of *The Industrialization of Bosnia-Hercegovina, 1878–1918* (1963), as well as many articles in *Slavic Review, Journal of Central European Affairs, Austrian History Yearbook,* and several European publications.

STEPHEN G. XYDIS teaches International Politics at Hunter College, the City University of New York. His books include *Greece and the Great Powers, 1944–1947: Prelude to the "Truman Doctrine"* (1963) and *Cyprus: Conflict and Conciliation, 1954–1958* (1967). In addition, he has published numerous articles and book reviews in various scholarly periodicals, such as the *Middle East Journal, American Slavic and East European Review,* and *Balkan Studies.*

JOSEPH F. ZACEK is associate professor of history and chairman of the Committee on East European Area Studies at the State University of New York at Albany. He is the author of *Palacký: The Historian as Scholar and Nationalist* (1969) and numerous scholarly articles and chapters in multi-authored books.

TAJAR ZAVALANI was head of the Assembly of Captive European Nations delegation in England until his death in August of 1966. His books include *Albania under Nazi Oppression* (1943), *How Strong Is Russia?* (1952), *Albania, 1912–1952* (1953), and *Histori e Shqipnis* (History of Albania) (1957).